Program Authors

Dr. Douglas Fisher
San Diego State University
San Diego, California

Dr. Jan Hasbrouck
Educational Consultant and Researcher
J.H. Consulting
Vancouver, Washington
Gibson Hasbrouck and Associates
Wellesley, Massachusetts

Dr. Timothy Shanahan
University of Illinois at Chicago
Chicago, Illinois

McGraw Hill Education

Bothell, WA • Chicago, IL • Columbus, OH • New York, NY

 TextEvaluator.

Cover and Title pages: Nathan Love

www.mheonline.com/readingwonderworks

Copyright © 2014 McGraw-Hill Education

Send all inquiries to:
McGraw-Hill Education
Two Penn Plaza
New York, New York 10121

ISBN: 978-0-02-129882-2
MHID: 0-02-129882-3

Printed in the United States of America.

3 4 5 6 7 8 9 RMN 18 17 16 15 14   B

Program Authors

Dr. Douglas Fisher

San Diego State University

Co-Director, Center for the Advancement of Reading, California State University

Author of *Language Arts Workshop: Purposeful Reading and Writing Instruction* and *Reading for Information in Elementary School*

Dr. Jan Hasbrouck

J. H. Consulting

Gibson Hasbrouck and Associates

Developed Oral Reading Fluency Norms for Grades 1–8

Author of *The Reading Coach: A How-to Manual for Success* and *Educators as Physicians: Using RTI Assessments for Effective Decision-Making*

Dr. Timothy Shanahan

University of Illinois at Chicago

Professor, Urban Education

Director, UIC Center for Literacy Chair, Department of Curriculum & Instruction

Member, English Language Arts Work Team and Writer of the Common Core State Standards

President, International Reading Association, 2006

Program Reviewers

Kelly Aeppli-Campbell

Escambia County School District
Pensacola, FL

Whitney Augustine

Brevard Public Schools
Melbourne, FL

Shanalee Cannon

Southern Nevada Regional Professional Development Program
Las Vegas, NV

Fran Clay

Howard County School District
Ellicott City, MD

Fran Gregory

Metro Nashville Public Schools
Nashville, TN

Elaine M. Grohol, NBCT, Ed.S.

Osceola County School District
Kissimmee, Florida

Randall B. Kincaid

Sevier County Schools
Sevierville, TN

Angela Reese

Bay District Schools
Panama City, FL

Program Components

Interactive Worktext

Apprentice Leveled Readers

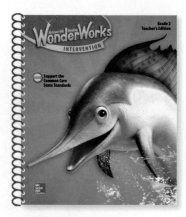

Teacher's Edition

Assessment

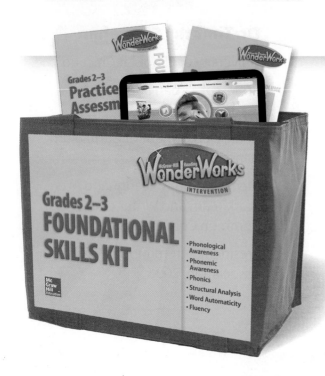

Grades 2–3 FOUNDATIONAL SKILLS KIT
• Phonological Awareness
• Phonemic Awareness
• Phonics
• Structural Analysis
• Word Automaticity
• Fluency

ADAPTIVE LEARNING

ck th

Decodable Reader VOLUME 1

they

are

P p piano

Foundational Skills Kit

 Go Digital

For the Teacher

For the Students

 Plan
Customizable Lesson Plans

 Manage and Assign
Student Grouping and Assignments

Professional Development
Lesson and CCSS Videos

 My To Do List
Assignments Assessments

 Words to Know
Build Vocabulary

 Teach
Instructional Lessons

 Assess
Online Assessments Reports and Scoring

Additional Online Resources
Graphic Organizers

Read
e Books Interactive Texts

Reading Wonders **Adaptive Learning**

www.connected.mcgraw-hill.com

Teach and Model

Interactive Worktext

Interactive Worktext

- Write-in worktext
- Same weekly content and vocabulary as *Reading Wonders*
- Interactive activities to help students develop close reading skills

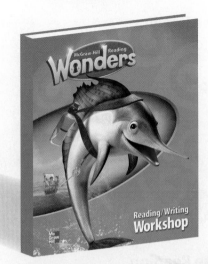

Reading/Writing Workshop

Practice and Apply

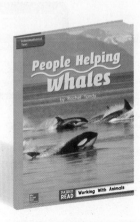

Apprentice Level

Apprentice Leveled Reader

- Same weekly content and vocabulary as *Reading Wonders*
- Two selections in each reader that allow students to apply close reading skills
- Acceleration plan that allows students to level up to the leveled readers in *Reading Wonders*

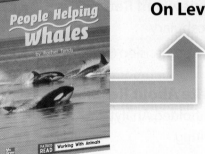

On Level

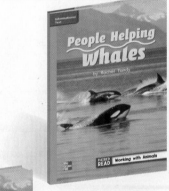

Approaching Level

Scaffold Weekly Concept
Grade-Appropriate Topics, including Science and Social Studies

Close Reading
Scaffolded Complex Texts

Respond to Reading

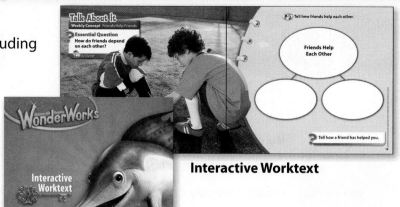

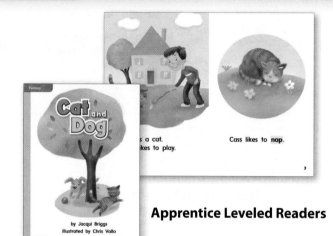

Interactive Worktext

- **Visual Vocabulary Cards**
- **Interactive Graphic Organizers**
- **Interactive Minilessons**
- **e Books**

PRACTICE AND APPLY

Close Reading
Scaffolded Complex Texts

Respond to Reading

- **Interactive Graphic Organizers**
- **Interactive Minilessons**
- **e Books**

Apprentice Leveled Readers

WRITE AND ASSESS

Review and Reteach
Vocabulary

Comprehension Skills

Write About Reading
Scaffolded Analytical Writing

Assess
Weekly Assessment

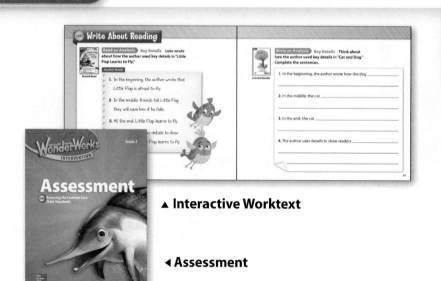

▲ Interactive Worktext

◀ Assessment

- **e Books**
- **Online Assessment and Reports**

Support the Common Core State Standards!

DIFFERENTIATE Foundational Skills

Foundational Skills Kit

- Flexible, explicit instruction for the following strands:
  - Phonological Awareness
  - Phonemic Awareness
  - Phonics
  - Structural Analysis
  - Word Recognition
  - Fluency
- Ample practice for achieving accuracy and fluency
- Assessment to monitor progress and mastery

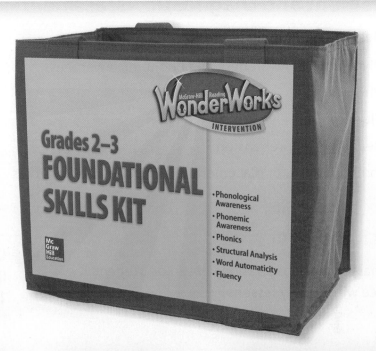

Foundational Skills Lesson Cards

Foundational Skills Practice and Assessment

Decodable Readers

Digital Support
- e Books
- Online Assessments and Reporting

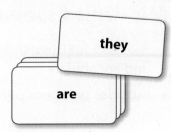

High-Frequency Word Cards

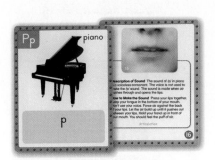

Sound-Spelling Cards

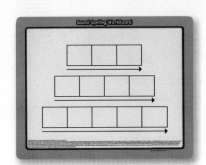

Sound-Spelling WorkBoards

ADAPTIVE LEARNING

Letter and Word-Building Cards

Photo Cards

Assessment in *WonderWorks*

Placement and Diagnostic Assessment

Includes diagnostic assessments for

- Phonological Awareness and Phonemic Awareness
- Phonics
- Fluency
- Reading Comprehension

Recommendations for placement into *Reading WonderWorks*

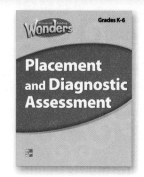

Wonders Placement and Diagnostic Assessment

Quick Checks

Informal teacher observations based on student practice within daily lessons

 Quick Check **Can children identify key details? If not, review and reteach using the instruction on page 16 and assign the Unit 1 Week 1 digital mini-lesson.**

Weekly Assessment

- Assesses comprehension and vocabulary
- Focused on finding and citing text evidence
- Includes written short responses
- One text per test
- 50% Literature and 50% Informational Text

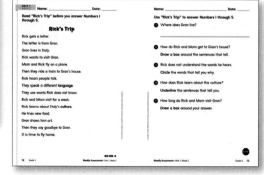

WonderWorks Assessment

Mid-Unit Assessment

- Assesses text-dependent comprehension and vocabulary
- Includes two texts per test with text-dependent questions
- 50% Literature and 50% Informational Text

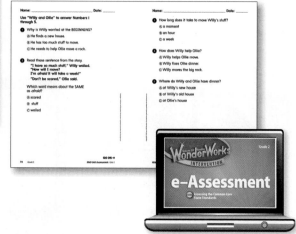

WonderWorks Assessment

Unit Assessment

Every 6 weeks

- Assesses text-dependent comprehension and vocabulary
- Includes two texts per test with text-dependent questions
- 50% Literature and 50% Informational Text

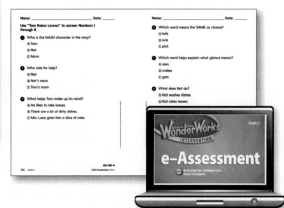

WonderWorks Assessment

Foundational Skills Assessment

Every 6 weeks

- Phonological Awareness
- Phonemic Awareness
- Letter Naming Fluency
- Sight Word Fluency
- Phonics and Structural Analysis Survey
- Oral Reading Fluency Assessment

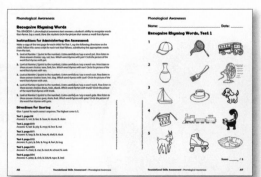

WonderWorks Foundational Skills Practice and Assessment

Exit Test

- Assesses text-dependent comprehension and vocabulary
- Includes two texts per test with text-dependent questions
- 50% Literature and 50% Informational Text

Exiting Out of *WonderWorks*

Students who score 85% or higher on the *Reading WonderWorks* Unit Assessment participate in "Level Up" instruction during Week 6 of the unit and take the Exit Test.

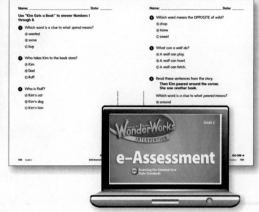

WonderWorks Assessment

If students

- score 85% or higher on the *Reading WonderWorks* Exit Test
- achieve Fluency Assessment goals for the unit
- successfully apply close reading skills with the Approaching Leveled Reader
- score mostly 3–4 on the Level Up Write About Reading prompt
- reach grade-level benchmarks in the Foundational Skills Assessments and *Reading Wonders* Adaptive Learning

Then consider moving students out of *Reading WonderWorks*.

Contents

Unit 1

(t to b) Tim Beaumont; Janet Broxon

x

Unit 2

(t to b) Greg Newbold; Accent Alaska.com/Alamy

Contents

Unit 3

Unit 4

Contents

Unit 5

 Week 1 **Being a Good Citizen** 246

Shared Read: "A Difficult Decision"

Apprentice Leveled Reader: "Fixing the Playground"

Week 2 **Cooperation Works!** 256

Shared Read: "Soccer Friends"

Apprentice Leveled Reader: "Rainy Day"

Week 3 **Our Heroes** 266

Shared Read: "César Chávez"

Apprentice Leveled Reader: "Rudy Garcia-Tolson"

Mid-Unit Assess and Monitor Progress 276

Week 4 **Preserving Our Earth** 278

Shared Read: "The Art Project"

Apprentice Leveled Reader: "Let's Carpool"

Week 5 **Rights and Rules** 288

Shared Read: "Visiting the Past"

Apprentice Leveled Reader: "Government Rules"

Week 6 **Assess and Differentiate** 298

Unit 6

(t to b) Xiao Xin; ©Jeremy Woodhouse/Blend Images/Corbis

UNIT 1 PLANNER
Friends and Family

Week 1 Friends Help Friends	Week 2 Families Around the World	Week 3 Pets Are Our Friends

ESSENTIAL QUESTION

How do friends depend on each other?

Build Background

CCSS Vocabulary

L.2.4a *actions, afraid, depend, nervously, peered, perfectly, rescue, secret*

Access Complex Text A C T

Connection of Ideas

CCSS Comprehension

RL.2.1 Skill: Key Details
Respond to Reading

CCSS Write About Reading *Analytical Writing*

W.4.9 Inform/Explain: Key Details

ESSENTIAL QUESTION

How are families around the world the same and different?

Build Background

CCSS Vocabulary

L.2.4a *aside, culture, fair, invited, language, plead, scurries, share*

Access Complex Text A C T

Connection of Ideas

CCSS Comprehension

RL.2.3 Skill: Character, Setting, Events
Respond to Reading

CCSS Write About Reading *Analytical Writing*

W.4.9 Inform/Explain: Genre

ESSENTIAL QUESTION

How can a pet be an important friend?

Build Background

CCSS Vocabulary

L.2.4a *decide, different, friendship, glance, proper, relationship, stares, trade*

Access Complex Text A C T

Organization

CCSS Comprehension

RL.2.3 Skill: Character, Setting, Events
Respond to Reading

CCSS Write About Reading *Analytical Writing*

W.4.9 Inform/Explain: Character, Setting, Events

A S S E S S M E N T

✔ *Quick Check*

Vocabulary, Comprehension

✔ **Weekly Assessment**
Assessment Book, pp. 10–11

✔ *Quick Check*

Vocabulary, Comprehension

✔ **Weekly Assessment**
Assessment Book, pp. 12–13

✔ *Quick Check*

Vocabulary, Comprehension

✔ **Weekly Assessment**
Assessment Book, pp. 14–15

✔ **MID-UNIT ASSESSMENT**
Assessment Book, pp. 72–119

Fluency Assessment
Assessment Book, pp. 234–249

Use the Foundational Skills Kit for explicit instruction of phonics, structural analysis, fluency, and word recognition. Includes *Reading Wonders* Adaptive Learning.

Week 4
Animals Need Our Care

ESSENTIAL QUESTION
How do we care for animals?

Build Background

 **Vocabulary**
L.2.4a *allowed, care, excited, needs, roam, safe, wandered, wild*

Access Complex Text
Organization

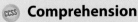 **Comprehension**
RI.2.1 Skill: Key Details
Respond to Reading

 **Write About Reading** *Analytical Writing*
W.4.9 Opinion: Key Details

Week 5
Families Working Together

ESSENTIAL QUESTION
What happens when families work together?

Build Background

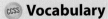 **Vocabulary**
L.2.4a *check, choose, chores, cost, customers, jobs, spend, tools*

Access Complex Text
Connection of Ideas

 Comprehension
RI.2.1 Skill: Key Details
Respond to Reading

Write About Reading *Analytical Writing*
W.4.9 Inform/Explain: Key Details

Week 6
ASSESS

RETEACH   LEVEL UP

Reteach
Comprehension Skills
Vocabulary
Write About Reading

Level Up
Read Approaching Leveled Reader

Write About Reading:
Compare Texts

A S S E S S M E N T

✓ **Quick Check**
Vocabulary, Comprehension

✓ **Weekly Assessment**
Assessment Book, pp. 16–17

✓ **Quick Check**
Vocabulary, Comprehension

✓ **Weekly Assessment**
Assessment Book, pp. 18–19

✓ **Unit Assessment**
Assessment Book, pp. 122–130

✓ **Fluency Assessment**
Assessment Book, pp. 234–239

EXIT TEST
Assessment Book, pp. 178–186

UNIT 1 OPENER,
pp. 16–17

The Big Idea

How do families and friends learn, grow, and help one another?

Talk About It

Read aloud the Big Idea on page 16 of the **Interactive Worktext:** *How do families and friends learn, grow, and help one another?* Say: *Let's think about times we have helped a family member or friend, or a time when a family member or friend has helped us.* Model telling about a time someone helped you in your own life. Then ask volunteers to provide examples of a time someone helped them. Encourage children to listen carefully as volunteers share their stories.

Discuss the photo on pages 16–17. Ask: *What is happening in this picture?* (A family and some friends are fishing.) *Is someone helping someone else?* (Yes, the parents are teaching the children how to fish.) *How do you know?* (The dad and son are both holding the fishing rod. The mom is helping to untangle the fishing line.)

Ask: *Have any of you been fishing or know someone that has?* Encourage children to describe their experiences. Then ask them to talk about what they learned and if they helped someone or if someone helped them.

Then say: *Let's look back at our Big Idea. Why might families and friends help one another?* Have children discuss and then share their ideas with the group. Explain that they will be discussing the Big Idea throughout the unit.

Build Fluency

Each week, use the **Interactive Worktext** Shared Reads and **Apprentice Leveled Readers** for fluency instruction and practice. Keep in mind that reading rates vary with the type of text that children are reading as well as the purpose for reading. For example, comprehension of complex informational texts generally requires slower reading.

Explain/Model Use the Fluency lessons on pages 378–382 to explain the skill. Then model the skill by reading the first page of the week's Shared Read or Leveled Reader.

Practice/Apply Choose a page from the Shared Read or Leveled Reader. Have one group read the top half of the page one sentence at a time. Remind children to apply the skill. Have the second group echo-read the passage. Then have the groups switch roles for the second half of the page. Discuss how each group applied the skill.

> **Weekly Fluency Focus**
>
> **Week 1** Expression
> **Week 2** Expression
> **Week 3** Intonation
> **Week 4** Intonation
> **Week 5** Phrasing

Foundational Skills Kit You can also use the **Lesson Cards** and **Practice** pages from the **Foundational Skills Kit** for targeted Fluency instruction and practice.

Interactive Worktext

	Week 1	Week 2	Week 3	Week 4	Week 5
	"Little Flap Learns to Fly"	"Maria Celebrates Brazil"	"Finding Cal"	"Taking Care of Pepper"	"Families Work!"
Quantitative	Lexile 170 TextEvaluator™ 6	Lexile 220 TextEvaluator™ 6	Lexile 170 TextEvaluator™ 6	Lexile 310 TextEvaluator™ 6	Lexile 280 TextEvaluator™ 6
Qualitative	• Connection of Ideas • Vocabulary	• Connection of Ideas • Prior Knowledge • Vocabulary	• Organization • Connection of Ideas • Vocabulary	• Organization • Prior Knowledge • Vocabulary	• Connection of Ideas • Genre
Reader and Task	The Weekly Concept lessons will help determine the reader's knowledge and engagement in the weekly concept.				
	Weekly Concept: p. 6 Questions and tasks: pp. 8–9	Weekly Concept: p. 16 Questions and tasks: pp. 18–19	Weekly Concept: p. 26 Questions and tasks: pp. 28–29	Weekly Concept: p. 38 Questions and tasks: pp. 40–41	Weekly Concept: p. 48 Questions and tasks: pp. 50–51

Apprentice Leveled Reader

	Week 1	Week 2	Week 3	Week 4	Week 5
	"Cat and Dog"	"Music in My Family"	"Too Many Pets?"	"People Helping Whales"	"Families at Work"
Quantitative	Lexile 70 TextEvaluator™ 6	Lexile BR TextEvaluator™ 6	Lexile 30 TextEvaluator™ 6	Lexile 120 TextEvaluator™ 6	Lexile 180 TextEvaluator™ 6
Qualitative	• Connection of Ideas • Vocabulary	• Connection of Ideas • Genre • Organization • Vocabulary	• Organization • Connection of Ideas • Vocabulary	• Organization • Prior Knowledge • Genre • Connection of Ideas • Vocabulary	• Connection of Ideas • Genre • Organization • Vocabulary
Reader and Task	The Weekly Concept lessons will help determine the reader's knowledge and engagement in the weekly concept.				
	Weekly Concept: p. 6 Questions and tasks: pp. 10–13	Weekly Concept: p. 16 Questions and tasks: pp. 20–23	Weekly Concept: p. 26 Questions and tasks: pp. 30–33	Weekly Concept: p. 38 Questions and tasks: pp. 42–45	Weekly Concept: p. 48 Questions and tasks: pp. 52–55

See page 383 for details about Text Complexity measures.

WEEKLY
LESSON
1

Objectives
• Develop oral language
• Build background about friendship
• Understand and use weekly vocabulary
• Read a fantasy story

Materials
• Interactive Worktext, pp. 18–27
• Visual Vocabulary Cards: 1–8
• High-Frequency Word Cards

☞ Go Digital
• Interactive eWorktext,
• Visual Vocabulary Cards

Scaffolding for **Wonders** Reading/Writing Workshop

WEEKLY CONCEPT

5–10 Minutes   SL.2.1b   SL.2.4   CCSS

Talk About It

Essential Question Read aloud the Essential Question on page 18 of the **Interactive Worktext**: *How do friends depend on each other?* Explain that when you depend on a friends you need a friend's help. Provide examples of how friends depend on each other, such as to play a game, to help learn something new, or to complete a class activity. Say: *We depend on, or need, our friends because friends help us in many ways. Our friends depend on us, too.*

• Discuss the photograph on page 18. Ask: *What is happening in the picture?* (A boy is helping another boy tie his shoe.) Have children look at the picture for clues as to what game the boys are playing. (Clues: cleats, goalie gloves; Game: soccer)

I Do Say: *I am going to look at the photo and think about how one friend helps the other friend.* (One boy is helping another boy tie his shoe.) *I will write on the web on page 19 how they are helping each other.*

We Do Say: *Let's think about other ways friends help each other. They say nice things to make us feel better. Friends are kind. They help us do school work and chores. Friends are thoughtful, or caring.* Guide children to think of times when their friends were kind and thoughtful. Then have children choose one way friends help each other to add to their web.

You Do Guide partners to work together to talk about how friends help each other. Have children use the words from the web to start their sentences: *Friends help each other _____.*

REVIEW VOCABULARY

10–15 Minutes   L.2.5a   L.2.6   RF.2.3   CCSS

Review Weekly Vocabulary Words

• Use the **Visual Vocabulary Cards** to review the weekly vocabulary.

• Read together the directions on page 20 of the **Interactive Worktext**. Then complete the activity.

1 **actions** Tell children you will show some *actions* you do in your kitchen. Demonstrate *actions* such as cutting, mixing, and pouring. Ask a volunteer to guess each action and say: *That action shows _____.* Guide children to show *actions* they do to get ready for school. (Possible answers: brush teeth, comb hair)

2 **afraid** Describe a time you were *afraid* of something. Use movements or gestures to show how you felt. Have a volunteer share something they are *afraid* of. Then guide children to write two things a child might be *afraid* of. Have them complete this sentence starter: *A child could be afraid of _____.* (Possible answers: thunder, scary rides)

3 **secret** Explain to children that a *secret* is something that is only known by you and whomever you share it with. Say: *Someone might tell a friend a* secret *that they don't want others to know, such as being afraid of something.* Ask a volunteer to share something that could be a *secret*.

4 **nervously** Write the word *nervously* and have children read it aloud. Explain that some people get *nervous* when they speak in front of others. Demonstrate speaking *nervously* with gestures. Help children name things they might do *nervously*. (Possible answers: perform at a show, hold a ladybug)

5 **peered** Demonstrate *peering* through a window for children. Say: *I peered through the window to see if my friend was outside.* Then have partners share their ideas with each other using the sentence starter: *I peered through _____.* (Possible answers: a doorway, a hole, a magnifying glass)

6 **perfectly** Model using *perfectly* in a sentence: *She can play the song on the piano* perfectly *without making a mistake.* Guide children to identify the root word, or "smaller word," in *perfectly.* (perfect) Have a volunteer name something they can do *perfectly.*

7 **rescue** Display pictures of lifeguards. Describe how they use special equipment, such as tubes and rings, to *rescue* people in a pool or ocean. Ask: *Why might a person need to be* rescued *in the ocean?* (They might not be able to swim.) Then help children identify who might *rescue* someone from a fire. (firefighter)

8 **depend** Explain that in some schools children *depend* on a cook to make their lunch. Then assist children as they draw a picture of someone they *depend* on to get to school. (Possible answers: parent, older family member, crossing guard) Have children complete the sentence: *I depend on _____.*

High-Frequency Words

Have children look at page 21 in the **Interactive Worktext**. Help them to read, spell, and write each high-frequency word. Guide partners to use each word in a sentence. Then read the story aloud with children. Guide partners to work together to reread the story and circle the high-frequency words. (likes, they, wants, too, now, are) Listen in and provide assistance reading the high-frequency words, as necessary.

ELL ENGLISH LANGUAGE LEARNERS

Display the **High-Frequency Word Cards** for: *they, now, are, too, likes, wants.* Write a sentence with each word. Have children echo-read each sentence, and point out the high-frequency word. Then ask them to use the word in a new sentence.

READ COMPLEX TEXT
15–20 Minutes RL.2.1 RL.2.7 SL.2.1b

Read "Little Flap Learns to Fly"

- Have children turn to page 22 in the **Interactive Worktext** and read aloud the Essential Question. Point to the birds in the picture. Say: *What kind of animals do you see in this picture?* (birds) *Let's read to find out how these birds depend on each other.* Have children echo-read the title.

- Read the story together. Note that the weekly vocabulary words are highlighted in yellow. Expand Vocabulary words are highlighted in blue.

- As children read, have them use the "My Notes" section on page 22 to write questions they have. Children can also write words they don't understand or things they want to remember. Model how to use the "My Notes" section. *When I read the last sentence on page 23, I find out that the birds will have to learn to fly. I wonder if learning to fly will be hard for them. I will write a question about learning to fly in the "My Notes" section.*

ELL ENGLISH LANGUAGE LEARNERS

As you read together, have children highlight parts of the text they have questions about. After reading, review the questions children have. Then help them locate the answers to their questions in the text.

 Quick Check Can children understand the weekly vocabulary in context? If not, review vocabulary using the **Visual Vocabulary Cards** before teaching Lesson 2.

Can children read high-frequency words in context? If not, review using the Read/Spell/Write routine and the High-Frequency Word Cards.

Objectives
- Read a fantasy story
- Understand complex text through close reading
- Recognize and understand key details
- Respond to the story using text evidence to support ideas

Materials
Interactive Worktext, pp. 22–29

☞ **Go** Digital
- Interactive eWorktext
- Key Details Mini-Lesson

Scaffolding for **Wonders** Reading/Writing Workshop

REREAD COMPLEX TEXT

20–25 Minutes   RL.2.1   RL.2.7   L.2.5a   **CCSS**

Close Reading: "Little Flap Learns to Fly"

Reread "Little Flap Learns to Fly" from **Interactive Worktext** pages 22–27 with children. As you read together, discuss important passages in the text. Guide children to respond to questions using evidence from the text.

🔍 Pages 22–23

Key Details Explain that key details help readers learn important information in a story. Point to the picture of Little Flap in his nest. Then read aloud the first sentence on page 23 and guide children to underline the words that tells *where* Little Flap lives. (in a nest) Ask: *Where is Little Flap's nest?* (in a tree)

Expand Vocabulary Have children reread the last paragraph. Explain that the word *learn* means to study or practice something until you know it well. Say: *What do the birds need to* learn *to do? I read that the birds must learn to fly.* Guide children to circle the words. (to fly)

Connection of Ideas Ⓐ Ⓒ Ⓣ Say: *I read that Little Flap and his friends must learn to fly.* Have children reread the page to answer the question: *Why do Little Flap and his friends need to learn how to fly?* Guide children to draw a box around the answer. (They want worms.)

🔍 Page 24

Expand Vocabulary Read aloud the first two sentences. Guide children to underline the sentence that tells what *flapping* means. (Her wings go up and down.) Demonstrate the action using your arms.

Connection of Ideas Ⓐ Ⓒ Ⓣ Reread the page again with children. Explain that many of the sentences tell about Little Flap, but one sentence tells Little Flap's secret. Ask: *What is Little Flap's secret? I will reread the third paragraph to find out. Guide children to draw a box around the answer.* (He is afraid to fly.)

Key Details Point to the illustration. Say: *I see Little Flap looking down. How does he feel when he looks down?* I will reread the page to see how he feels. Guide children to circle the word *nervously* and chorally read the sentence aloud. Ask: *Why might Little Flap feel nervous when he looks down?* (Possible answer: He might be afraid to fall.)

🔍 Page 25

Key Details Point to Little Flap and ask: *Why is Little Flap afraid to fly?* Have children reread the first sentence. Have a volunteer answer the question in their own words. (Possible answer: He is afraid to fall.) Guide children to write their answer.

Expand Vocabulary Reread the last paragraph with children. Write the word *save* and explain that it means to help someone or to rescue someone. Guide children to circle the word *save*. Ask: *Who will* save *Little Flap?* (His friends, Tuff and Fluff) Guide children to circle the picture of Tuff and Fluff.

Connection of Ideas Ⓐ Ⓒ Ⓣ Read aloud the last paragraph. Ask: *Why does Little Flap feel better now?* (He knows his friends will save him.) Guide children to underline the answer in the text.

🔍 Page 26

Expand Vocabulary Draw a picture of a tree with branches. Point to the *branch*. Write *branch* on the board. Say the word aloud and have children repeat it. Explain that it is the smaller part that grows out of the tree trunk. Guide children to circle the *branch* in their worktext.

Key Details Guide children to look at the picture and point to Little Flap. Ask: *Is Little Flap flapping his wings?* (yes) *What do Little Flap and his friends do when they start flapping?* (They fly.) Guide children to underline the words in the story that tell the answer. (They all fly perfectly.)

Connection of Ideas Have children think about the beginning of the story. Say: *Little Flap decided to fly. Why did Little Flap want to learn to fly?* (He wanted to get worms.) If children have difficulty answering this question, have them return to pages 22–23 and reread the text.

🔍 Page 27

Expand Vocabulary Point to the word *land*. Explain that the word *land* is a multiple-meaning word. Ask: *What meanings of the word* land *do you know?* If children have difficulty, say: Land *can mean an area of the earth or it can mean to come down after flying.* Then guide children to look for clues in the sentence to identify the correct meaning of the word. Ask: *What do the birds land on?* (the ground) *What is the meaning of the word* land *in this sentence?* (to come down after flying)

Key Details Help children circle the words that tell who finds a big worm. (Little Flap.) Ask: *Why does Little Flap like to fly now?* (He found food.)

Connection of Ideas Have children reread what happens after Little Flap finds the worm. Ask: *How is Little Flap a good friend to Fluff and Tuff?* (He found a worm and shared it with his friends.) Have children draw a box around the words in the story. (Little Flap finds a big worm. He shares it with Fluff and Tuff.) Help children understand that Little Flap is happy to have friends that he can depend on.

RESPOND TO READING
10–20 Minutes   RL.2.1   RL.2.7   SL.2.1a

Respond to "Little Flap Learns to Fly"

Read aloud the questions about "Little Flap Learns to Fly" on page 28 of the **Interactive Worktext**. Guide children to read the questions. Then read aloud the "Discussion Starter" for each of the questions. Guide children to work with a partner to answer the questions orally using the "Discussion Starters." Have children find text evidence to support their answers. Ask children to write the page number(s) on which they found the text evidence for each question.

1. *What does Little Flap need to learn to do?* (Possible answer: Little Flap must learn to fly. He must do this to get worms. Text Evidence: p. 23)

2. *How does Little Flap feel?* (Possible answer: Little Flap feels afraid to fly. I read that he thinks he will fall. Text Evidence: pp. 24–25)

3. *How do friends help Little Flap?* (Possible answer: Fluff and Tuff tell Little Flap they will save him. Then Little Flap decides to try. Text Evidence: p. 25)

After children discuss the questions, have them use the sentence starters to answer the question on page 29. Circulate and provide guidance.

✓ *Quick Check* **Do children understand vocabulary in context? If not, review and reteach using the instruction on page 14.**

Can children identify key details? If not, review and reteach using the instruction on page 14 and assign the Unit 1 Week 1 digital mini-lesson.

Can children write a response to "Little Flap Learns to Fly"? If not, review the sentence starters and prompt children to respond orally. Help them write their responses.

Objectives
• Access prior knowledge
• Understand and use new vocabulary words
• Read high-frequency words
• Read a fantasy story

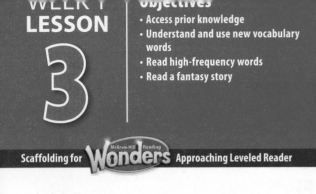

Materials
"Cat and Dog" Apprentice Leveled Reader
• High-Frequency Word Cards

☞ **Go** Digital
• Apprentice Leveled Reader eBook
• Downloadable High-Frequency Word Cards

BEFORE READING

10–15 Minutes   SL. 2.1a   SL.2.6   L.2.6   RF.2.3f

Introduce "Cat and Dog"

• Read the Essential Question on the title page of "Cat and Dog" **Apprentice Leveled Reader**: *How do friends depend on each other?*

• Read the title of the main read. Point to the cover. *What characters are in this story?* (a cat and a dog) *What are they doing?* (playing) *Is this the way cats and dogs usually act with each other?* (Children may point out that they often don't like each other.) *Let's read about a cat and a dog who play together.*

High-Frequency Words

Display the **High-Frequency Word Cards** for the words *all, like, now, play, they, to,* and *want.* Use the Read/Spell/Write routine to teach each word. Guide partners to use each word in a sentence. Provide assistance reading the high-frequency words, as necessary.

Expand Vocabulary

Before reading "Cat and Dog," help children read the following words that they will encounter. Display each word below. Use the Define/Example/Ask routine. Tell children to look for the word later on as they read "Cat and Dog."

1 cool (page 13)

Define: Something *cool* is more cold than hot.

Example: The fan helped us to feel *cool.*

Ask: What clothes do you wear when it is *cool* outside?

2 follows (page 12)

Define: to go after something

Example: The player *follows* the ball.

Ask: When do you *follow* someone else?

3 glad (page 11)

Define: to be happy about something.

Example: I am *glad* it is sunny out.

Ask: What makes you feel *glad*?

4 hisses (page 9)

Define: to makes a sound like a long *s,* usually to show dislike

Example: A cat *hisses* if you step on its tail.

Ask: What else might make a cat *hiss*?

5 nap (page 3)

Define: to sleep during the day

Example: I take a *nap* when I'm tired.

Ask: When have you taken a *nap*?

6 wags (page 9)

Define: to move quickly from side to side or up and down

Example: My dog *wags* its tail when I come home.

Ask: What other animals *wag* their tails?

DURING READING

20–30 Minutes   RL. 2.1   RL.2.3   RL.2.7   L.2.4a

Pages 2–3

Shared Reading

Tell children you will now read "Cat and Dog." Tell them to note the vocabulary and high-frequency words you just introduced as you read the story. Stop to model understanding of the story as you go.

Pages 2–3

High-Frequency Words Make sure children can read the high-frequency words *like, to,* and *play.*

Comprehension Check Model beginning to read the story. Say: *The first thing I notice about this story is that it seems to be about a cat named Cass. I'll ask myself what I can learn about Cass. I learn that she lives with a boy. She likes to play and she likes to nap. She seems happy.*

Pages 4–5

High-Frequency Words Make sure children can read the high-frequency word *wants.*

Comprehension Check *I will stop and think about what just happened. A dog named Dibs has moved in. The text says he wants a friend. I see he is running next door to Cass's house. I wonder if he will meet Cass.*

Pages 6–7

Vocabulary *The text says that Ron and Kim meet and that Cass and Dibs* meet. *What can you tell about the word* meet *from the picture? What are Ron and Kim doing?* (They are looking at each other and smiling.) *What are Cass and Dibs doing?* (They are looking at each other too but don't seem friendly.) *What is the same about the two pairs?* (Both are seeing each other for the first time.)

Pages 8–9

Vocabulary On page 8, read the sentence *"Cass peered at Dibs."* Focus on the word *peered.* Ask: *Can you point to Cass peering in the picture? What is another word for peered?* (<u>Possible answers</u>: looked, gazed, stared)

Vocabulary Focus on *hisses* and *wags.* Ask: *What does the text say Cass is doing?* (She hisses.) *What does Cass look like in the picture?* (She looks upset and scared and is making a noise.) *What does the text say Dibs is doing?* (He wags his tail.) *What does Dibs look like in the picture?* (He looks happy and his tail is up.)

Pages 10–11

Comprehension Check Say: *I am going to stop here to make sure I understand what I am reading. I know that Cass did not want to play. She was afraid. But now she is playing with Dibs and having fun. Why did she change? I look back in the text and see that Dibs helps Cass and is kind. I think that helped Cass not to be afraid.*

Pages 12–13

High-Frequency Words Make sure children can read the high-frequency words *now* and *they.*

Vocabulary Point to the picture on page 12. Ask children how the picture helps them to understand the word *follow.* Ask: *Who is going first?* (Cass) *Where is Dibs?* (He is behind Cass.)

Pages 14–15

High-Frequency Words Make sure children can read the high-frequency word *all.*

Comprehension Check *The story says that Cass and Dibs are friends. I am going to think about how that happened. Dibs wanted a friend. Cass was afraid of dogs. Dibs was nice and Cass got to like him. Then Cass helped Dibs find a cool place to nap. They helped each other and are friends.*

 Quick Check **Can children understand vocabulary in context? If not, review and reteach using the instruction on page 14.**

Can children read high-frequency words in context? If not, review using the Read/Spell/Write routine and the High-Frequency-Word Cards.

WEEK 1 LESSON 4

Objectives
- Understand complex text through close-reading
- Read a fantasy story
- Recognize and understand key details
- Respond to the selection using text evidence to support ideas

Scaffolding for **Wonders** McGraw-Hill Reading Approaching Leveled Reader

Materials
"Cat and Dog" Apprentice Leveled Reader
- Key Details Graphic Organizer

☞ **Go** Digital
- Apprentice Leveled Reader eBook
- Downloadable Graphic Organizer
- Key Details Mini-Lesson

DURING READING

20–30 Minutes SL.2.2 RL.2.3 RL. 2.6 RL .2.7 CCSS

Tell children they will now reread the selection, "Cat and Dog." Review the vocabulary and high-frequency words that they will encounter as they read.

Close Reading

Pages 2–3

Key Details Remind children that key details are information in the words and pictures that help us understand a story. Reread page 2. Ask what key details they learned on that page. (Cass is a cat and Cass likes to play.) Model filling in the Key Details Chart.

Pages 4–5

Key Details Reread pages 4 and 5. Point to the picture of Dibs. Say: *This is Dibs. What kind of animal is Dibs?* (a dog) *Why is there a truck in front of his house?* (Dibs just moved in.) Help children record these details on their Key Details charts.

Connection of Ideas ACT Point to the picture on page 5. Ask: *Why does Dibs run next door?* (He wants a friend to play with.)

Pages 6–7

Key Details Reread page 6. Point to Kim and Ron in turn as you read their names. Point to Kim and ask: *Who is Dibs with?* (Kim) *Dibs is Kim's dog.* Point to Ron and ask: *Who is Cass with?* (Ron) *Cass is Ron's cat.*

Key Details Point to the picture of Cass. Ask: *How does she look like she is feeling?* (She looks worried or upset.) Point to the picture of Dibs. Ask: *What do you think Dibs is feeling?* (He looks excited or happy.) Help children fill in these details on their Key Details charts.

Pages 8–9

Key Details Reread page 8. Point to Kim and Ron in the picture. Ask: *Are Kim and Ron playing?* (yes) Point to Dibs. *Is Dibs playing?* (yes) Point to Cass. *Is Cass playing?* (no)

Key Details Point to the picture of Cass on page 9. *Let's look at the picture. Is Cass smiling in the picture?* (no) *Is Cass frowning in the picture?* (yes) *Do you think Cass is happy?* (no) Point to Cass. *What else shows that she is not happy?* Help children point to her tail and flattened ears.

Connection of Ideas ACT Reread page 9. Ask: *Does Dibs want to play?* (yes) *Does Cass want to play?* (no) *Why does Cass not want to play? Read the sentence that tells us.* (Cass is afraid of dogs.)

Pages 10–11

Key Details Before reading, help children review what they wrote on their Key Details charts to recall the story's events so far. *What does Dibs want?* (a friend) *Does Cass want to play with Dibs?* (no) *Why not?* (Cass is afraid of dogs.) *Let's see what happens next.*

Connection of Ideas ACT Reread page 10. *What is Dibs's plan? How does he act?* (He helps Cass and is kind.) *Why do you think he does that?* (He wants Cass to like him and not to be afraid.)

Key Details Reread page 11. Ask: *What is Cass doing now?* (She is playing and having fun.) *How is Dibs feeling about that? Read the sentence that tells us.* (Dibs is glad.) Have children add these details to their Key Details charts.

Pages 12–13

Connection of Ideas **A** **C** **T** Point to Cass in the picture. *Is Cass smiling in the picture?* (yes) Flip back to the picture on page 9. Say: *Cass did not want to play before.* Bring children's attention to visual cues like Cass's tail, ears, and frown. Then flip back to page 11. *Now Cass is playing. She is happy.*

Key Details After reading page 12, ask: *What does Cass show Dibs?* (a bush) *Why does she show Dibs that?* (They are hot and it is a cool place to nap.) Have children add these details to their Key Details charts.

Pages 14–15

Key Details *Think back to the start of the story. Did Cass like Dibs then?* (no) *What happened to make her change her mind?* (Dibs played with Cass and was kind.) *How did Cass help Dibs?* (She brought him to a good place to nap.) *Cass likes Dibs now. They are friends.* Have children record details on their Key Details charts.

Connection of Ideas **A** **C** **T** *How are Ron and Kim like Cass and Dibs?* (They are friends who just met.) *How is their story different from Cass's and Dibs's?* (They wanted to play together right away.) *What do you think Cass learned?* (She learned to be open to someone she didn't think she would like.)

AFTER READING

10–15 Minutes   SL. 2.4a   RL.2.1   RL. 2.5   RF. 2.4b   W.2.8

Respond to Reading

Compare Texts Guide children in comparing the characters in "Cat and Dog" with the characters in "Little Flap Learns to Fly." Help children think about which characters change and how they help each other. Then ask: *How do you help friends?*

Summarize Have children turn to page 16 and guide them in summarizing the selection. (Answers should select important details that demonstrate the story's development.)

Text Evidence

Have partners work together to answer questions on page 16. Remind children to use their Key Details charts.

Key Details (Dibs wants a friend.)

Vocabulary (Dibs helps Cass, which is being kind.)

Write About Reading (Cass and Dibs become friends because Dibs is very nice to Cass.)

Read "Uncle Max"

Encourage children to read the paired selection "Uncle Max" on pages 17–19. Have them summarize the selection and compare it to "Cat and Dog." Have them work with a partner to answer the "Make Connections" questions on page 19.

Independent Reading

Have pairs of children reread "Cat and Dog." Have them talk about how the characters are feeling.

 Quick Check **Can students identify key details? If not, review and teach using the instruction on page 14 and assign the Unit 1 Week 1 digital mini-lesson.**

Can students respond to the selection using text evidence? If not, provide, sentence frames to help them organize their ideas.

Objectives
- Review weekly vocabulary words
- Review key details
- Write an analysis about an author's use of key details

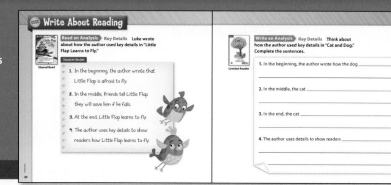

Materials
- Visual Vocabulary Cards, 1–8
- Interactive Worktext, pp. 30–31
- Assessment Book, pp. 10-11

☞ **Go** Digital
- Visual Vocabulary Cards
- Key Details Mini-Lesson
- Interactive eWorktext
- eAssessment

Scaffolding for **Wonders** Reading/Writing Workshop

REVIEW AND RETEACH

5–10 Minutes   L.2.5a   RL.2.1 · RL.2.7   CCSS

Weekly Vocabulary

Display one **Visual Vocabulary Card** at a time and guide children to use the vocabulary word in a sentence. If children have difficulty creating a sentence, have them find the word in "Little Flap Learns to Fly" or "Cat and Dog" and use the context clues in the passage to define the vocabulary word.

Comprehension: Key Details

I Do Write and say: *Tim wants to play soccer. It rains outside. He decides to stay inside. He reads a book.* Ask: *Why doesn't Tim play soccer? I can look for key details to learn the answer.* Circle "It rains outside," and write *key detail.* Say: *Tim can't play soccer because it's raining outside. I can tell that this is a key detail because it gives me important information that helps me answer other questions.*

We Do Display: *Maria is at home. She is cleaning her room. She is happy. Her cousin visits today.* Ask: *What key detail tells us why Maria is happy?* (Her cousin visits today.) *How can you tell?* (I read it in the last sentence.)

You Do Display: *Tim goes to the store with his Mom. They buy food. They take the food home. Then they cook dinner together. They make tacos.* Guide one partner to ask a question and the other partner to find a key detail that helps answer it. Have partners switch and discuss their answers.

WRITE ABOUT READING

25–35 Minutes   W.2.3   W.2.8   W.4.9   CCSS

Read an Analysis

- Guide children to look back at "Little Flap Learns to Fly" in the **Interactive Worktext**. Have volunteers review the key detail they marked on page 23. Repeat with pages 24–27. *Say: Today we will think about how the author used key details to help readers understand the text.*

- Read aloud the directions on page 30. Read aloud the student model. *This student's writing is not a summary. It is an analysis, or description, of how the author used key details in "Little Flap Learns to Fly."*

- *When you write an analysis, you should include key details from the text that tell about the story. Read Luke's first sentence. Circle the details.* (Little Flap is afraid to fly.) *What part of the story do the details come from?* (the beginning)

- *Read the second sentence. Draw a box around the details from the story you see in Luke's writing.* (Friends tell Little Flap they will save him if he falls.) *What part of the story Is he writing about?* (the middle)

- Guide children to point to the third sentence. *This sentence explains what happened at the end of the story. What details does Luke include?* (Little Flap learns to fly.)

- Model analyzing how the author used details to write the story. Read the last sentence that Luke wrote. *Why is this sentence a good ending?* (Luke explained how the author used key details to support the story.)

Analytical Writing | Write an Analysis

Guided Writing Read the prompt on page 31 together. Guide children to review their Key Details charts for "Cat and Dog." Have children use their charts to complete the sentence starters. Children can also write the analysis using another selection previously read this week.

Peer Conference Guide children to read their analysis to a partner. Listeners should summarize the details that support the beginning, middle, and ending sentences. They should discuss any parts that are unclear.

Teacher Conference Check children's writing for complete sentences and whether they included details from the story. Review the last sentence and ask: *Did the author use details to support the story?* If necessary, guide children to revise their sentences by adding more details.

Level Up

▲ Approaching Leveled Reader

▲ Reading/Writing Workshop

▲ Apprentice Leveled Reader

▲ Interactive Worktext

IF children read the Apprentice Level Reader and the **Interactive Worktext** Shared Read fluently and answer the Respond to Reading questions

THEN read together the Approaching Level Reader main selection and the **Reading/Writing Workshop** Shared Read from *Reading Wonders*. Have children take notes as they read, using self-stick notes. Then ask and answer questions about their notes.

Writing Rubric

	4	3	2	1
Text Evidence	Includes three or more details from the text	Includes two or more details from the text	Includes only one detail from the text	No text evidence is cited.
Writing Style	Writes in complete sentences. Uses correct spelling and grammar.	Uses complete sentences. Writing has spelling and grammar errors.	Few complete sentences. There are many spelling and grammar errors.	Writing is not accurate or in complete sentences.

ASSESSMENT

Weekly Assessment

Have children complete the Weekly Assessment using **Assessment** book pages 10–11.

WEEK 2 LESSON 1

Objectives
- Develop oral language
- Build background about families
- Understand and use weekly vocabulary
- Read a realistic fiction story

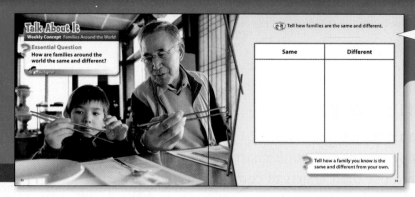

Materials
- Interactive Worktext, pp. 32–41
- Visual Vocabulary Cards: 9–16
- High-Frequency Word Cards

☞ **Go** Digital
- Interactive eWorktext
- Visual Vocabulary Cards

Scaffolding for **Wonders** Reading/Writing Workshop

WEEKLY CONCEPT

5–10 Minutes   SL.2.1b   SL.2.4   CCSS

Talk About It

Essential Question Read aloud the Essential Question on page 32 of the **Interactive Worktext**: *How are families around the world the same and different?* Explain that families in different parts of the world are alike and different in many ways. Provide examples of how families are alike, such as families eat together, they play together, they work together, and so on.

- Discuss the photograph on page 32. Ask: *What is happening in this picture?* (A boy and his grandpa are sitting at a table.) Ask: Why are they sitting at the table? (They are going to eat a meal together.)

 I Do Say: *I am going to look at the photograph and think about how this family is the same or different from my family. This family eats meals together and my family eats meals together. I will write "eats meals together" on the chart on page 33 under the heading "Same."*

We Do Say: *Let's think of other ways this family is the same or different from our families.* Guide children to look for clues in the photograph and ask a volunteer to name one way this family is the same or different from his or her own. Then have children each write an idea on their own chart. Have children share their ideas with the class.

You Do Guide partners to talk together about ways this family is the same or different from their own. Have children use the headings from the chart to complete this sentence starters: *Families are the same because they all _____. Families can be different because they _____.* Then have partners write their ideas on the chart.

REVIEW VOCABULARY

10–15 Minutes   L.2.4a   L.2.6   RF.2.3   CCSS

Review Weekly Vocabulary Words

- Use the **Visual Vocabulary Cards** to review the weekly vocabulary.

- Read together the directions on page 34 of the **Interactive Worktext**. Then complete the activity.

❶ plead Clasp your hands together and model for children how to *plead* to stay up late. Have them repeat the action with a partner. Describe some situations in which the children might *plead* for something. Then guide them to think of another word for *plead*. (Possible answer: beg)

❷ culture Discuss some aspects of American *culture*. List a few examples, such as an American flag, apple pie. Then have children name objects from their *culture* using this sentence starter: *In my culture we have _____.* (Possible answers: a toy, item of food or clothing, an object)

❸ share Ask children why it is important to *share* items. Guide them to list items they *share* at home. Then have them look around the classroom at the things they *share*. Tell children to use the following sentence frame: *_____ is something I share with the other kids in school.* (Possible answers: pencils, books, art supplies)

❹ language Say: *In the United States many people speak English, but there are other languages that people speak, such as Spanish or Cantonese.* Have children think of someone they know of who speaks another *language*. Use this sentence starter: *_____ speaks _____.* (Possible answers: name of a language)

5 **invited** Ha... *invited* some... Did they sen... person? Give... starter: *I would...* answers: the b...

6 **scurries** Displ... Read the senten... how to *scurry*. Th... in the sentence w... meaning. (Possible...

7 **aside** Model movi... ...on a shelf as you explain what *aside* means. Invite a volunteer to walk toward you and move *aside* to let the child pass. Then guide children to move *aside* with a partner. Have a few volunteers use this sentence starter: *I moved* aside *so _____ could pass by.* (name of a classmate.)

8 **fair** Ask children to think of a *fair* way to share an orange with a friend. Discuss what makes the division *fair*, and how it could not be *fair*. Then have children use the following sentence frame: *A _____ is an easy food to split in a* fair *way.* (Possible answers: pizza, sandwich, or fruit cut in equal halves)

High-Frequency Words

Have children look at page 35 in the **Interactive Worktext**. Help them read, spell, and write each high-frequency word. Guide partners to use each word in a sentence. Then read the story aloud with children. Guide partners to work together to reread the story and circle the high-frequency words. (is, of, not, go, can, see) Listen in and provide assistance reading the high-frequency words, as necessary.

(handwritten note) Week 2 Vocab WW 2
- plead
- culture
- share
- language
- invited
- scurries
- aside
- fair

READ COMPLEX TEXT

15–20 Minutes   RL.2.3   RL.2.7   SL.2.1b

Read "Maria Celebrates Brazil"

- Have children turn to page 36 in the **Interactive Worktext** and read aloud the Essential Question. Point to the picture. Say: *What is the girl in the picture wearing?* (a costume) *Let's read to find out why the girl is wearing a costume.* Have children echo-read the title.

- Read the story together. Note that the weekly vocabulary words are highlighted in yellow. Expand Vocabulary words are highlighted in blue.

- As children read, have them use the "My Notes" section on page 36 to write questions they have. Children can also write words they don't understand or things they want to remember. Model how to use the "My Notes" section. Say: *When I read the second sentence on page 37, I find out that Maria is going to be in a parade. I wonder what kind of parade it will be. I will write a question about the parade in the "My Notes" section.*

✓ *Quick Check* Can children understand the weekly vocabulary in context? If not, review vocabulary using the **Visual Vocabulary Cards** before teaching Lesson 2.

Can children read high-frequency words in context? If not, review using the Read/Spell/Write routine and the High-Frequency Word Cards.

WEEK 2
LESSON
2

Objectives
• Read realistic fiction.
• Understand complex text through close reading
• Recognize and understand Character, Setting, Events
• Respond to the story using text evidence to support ideas

Materials
Interactive Worktext, pp. 36–43

☞ Go Digital
• Interactive eWorktext
• Character, Setting, Events Mini-Lesson

Scaffolding for **Wonders** Reading/Writing Workshop

REREAD COMPLEX TEXT

20–25 Minutes   RL.2.3 RL.2.7 L.2.5a

Close Reading: "Maria Celebrates Brazil"

Reread "Maria Celebrates Brazil" from **Interactive Worktext** pages 36–41 with children. As you read together, discuss important passages in the text. Guide children to respond to questions using evidence from the text.

🔍 Pages 36–37

Prior Knowledge A C T Have children reread the title of the story. Explain that Brazil is a country in South America. Point out Brazil on a map. Say: *People in Brazil have a parade to celebrate their beliefs and traditions.*

Character, Setting, Events Tell children that characters, settings, and events are all parts of a story. A character can be a person or an animal. The setting of a story is where or when it takes place. Have children reread the page. Ask: *What are the names of two characters in the story?* Guide children to draw a box around the names of two characters. (Maria, Mãe)

Connection of Ideas A C T Have children reread the first paragraph. Say: *The text says Maria is going to be in a parade. Then it says she does not want to go to practice. Maria must be practicing for the parade.* Guide children to underline the word that tells what Maria is practicing for. (parade)

Expand Vocabulary Have children read the second paragraph. Explain that the word *Mãe* means *mother* in Portuguese. Ask: *What does Mãe want Maria to do?* Guide children to circle the words that tell. (go to practice)

🔍 Page 38

Expand Vocabulary Read the second paragraph aloud. Explain that *Pai* means *father* in Portuguese. Point to the picture. Ask: *Which of these characters is Pai?* Guide children to circle the picture of Maria's father.

Character, Setting, Events Explain to children that events are the main things that happen in a story. Say: *The setting and events of a story affect what the characters do and say.* Reread the first paragraph. Ask: *What does Maria want to do?* (She wants to go to Ana's house.) Guide children to draw a box around the answer.

Connection of Ideas A C T Say: *I read that Pai thinks the parade is important.* Have children reread the second paragraph. Ask: *Why is the parade important?* Guide children to underline the sentences that tell. (Many people will come see it. They will learn about our culture.)

🔍 Page 39

Connection of Ideas A C T Have children reread the page. Guide children to the sentence "He is right." Ask: *This sentence means that Pai is right that Maria can see Ana another time. It means she should go to practice.* Guide children to underline one reason that tells why she should go to practice. (Possible answers: The children have worked hard. They have practiced their dance steps. They have made their own costumes.)

Character, Setting, Events Show children the picture of Maria wearing her costume. Then, read the last paragraph aloud. Ask: *What did the children make for the parade?* Guide children to draw a box around the sentence that tells. (They have made their own costumes.)

Page 40

Character, Setting, Events Remind children that sometimes events in a story can affect what a character says and does. Read the first sentence aloud. Ask: *What decision does Maria make about going to practice?* Guide children to draw a box around the words that tell. (she will go to practice)

Expand Vocabulary Have children reread the second paragraph of the story. Explain that *passes* means to go by. Ask: *How much time* passes *between practice and the parade?* Guide children to circle the words that tell. (one week)

Connection of Ideas   Review the meaning of the word *culture*. Explain that culture can include the arts, beliefs or traditions of a group of people. Point to the picture of Maria and read the second paragraph aloud. Ask: *What is something in this picture that tells about Maria's culture?* Guide children to underline an item in the picture that shows something about Maria's culture. (Possible answers: Maria's dress, Maria's headdress, the maracas)

Page 41

Connection of Ideas   Have children reread the first paragraph. Ask: *Why does the crowd move aside?* Guide children to underline the sentence that tells the answer. (The children come down the street.)

Character, Setting, Events Reread the last paragraph. Ask: *How does Maria feel at the end of the parade?* Guide children to write the word that tells. (proud)

RESPOND TO READING

10–20 Minutes   RL.2.3   RL.2.7   SL.2.1b

Respond to "Maria Celebrates Brazil"

Read aloud the questions about "Maria Celebrates Brazil" on page 42 of the **Interactive Worktext**. Then read aloud the "Discussion Starter" for each of the questions. Guide children to work with a partner to answer the questions orally using the "Discussion Starters." Have children find text evidence to support their answers. Ask children to write the page number(s) on which they found the text evidence for each question.

1. *What do we learn about Maria's culture?* (Possible answers: I read that Maria's family comes from Brazil. In Maria's country, they have parades. Text Evidence: p. 37)

2. *How is Maria's family the same as yours?* (Answers will vary. Text Evidence: pp. 38–41)

3. *How is Maria's family different than yours?* (Answers will vary. Text Evidence: pp. 38–41)

After children discuss the questions on page 42, have them use the sentence starters to answer the question on page 43. Circulate and provide guidance.

✓ *Quick Check* **Do children understand vocabulary in context? If not, review and reteach using the instruction on page 24.**

Can children identify character, setting, and events? If not, review and reteach using the instruction on page 24 and assign the Unit 1 Week 2 digital mini-lesson.

Can children write a response to "Maria Celebrates Brazil"? If not, review the sentence starters and prompt children to respond orally. Help them write their responses.

WEEK 2
LESSON
3

- Access prior knowledge
- Understand and use new vocabulary words
- Read high-frequency words
- Read a fiction story

are going out.
re are we going?

We are going to a music **festival**.
Lots of **bands** are **invited**.

Materials
- "Music in My Family" Apprentice Leveled Reader
- High-Frequency Word Cards

Go Digital
- Apprentice Leveled Reader eBook
- Downloadable High-Frequency Word Cards

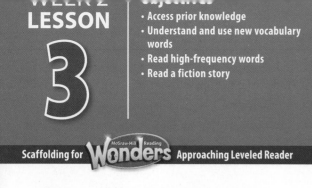
Scaffolding for **Wonders** Approaching Leveled Reader

BEFORE READING
10–15 Minutes   SL.2.1a   SL.2.6   L.2.6   L.2.5a   RF.2.3f   **CCSS**

Introduce "Music in My Family"

- Read the Essential Question on the title page of "Music in My Family" **Apprentice Leveled Reader:** *How are families around the world the same and different?*

- Read the title of the main read. Point to the cover. *What characters are in this story?* (a man and two girls) *What musical instrument do you see?* (a guitar) *What are some other musical instruments you know about? Let's read about a family who likes music.*

High-Frequency Words

Display the **High-Frequency Word Cards** for the words *have, look, my, see, out,* and *there.* Use the Read/Spell/Write routine to teach each word. Guide partners to use each word in a sentence. Provide assistance reading the high-frequency words, as necessary.

Expand Vocabulary

Before reading "Music in My Family," help children read the following words that they will encounter. Display each word below. Use the Define/Example/Ask routine. Tell children to look for the word later on as they read "Music in My Family."

① **bands** (page 3)

Define: a group of musicians playing together

Example: I like *bands* with guitars, drums, and singers.

Ask: What are things that *bands* use?

② **festival** (page 3)

Define: a special celebration, usually with lots of people and events

Example: Lots of people came to the park for the music *festival.*

Ask: What *festivals* have you been to?

③ **proud** (page 15)

Define: to feel very good about something you or someone else did

Example: Mom was *proud* of me for helping my little brother.

Ask: What makes you feel *proud*?

④ **stage** (page 13)

Define: a place where people sing, dance, or act

Example: The singer stepped onto the *stage.*

Ask: What have you seen on a *stage*?

⑤ **surprise** (page 5)

Define: something you don't know about before it happens

Example: My grandmother's visit was a great *surprise.*

Ask: What is a *surprise* you would like?

⑥ **wait** (page 5)

Define: to stay in place until something happens

Example: We had to *wait* an hour for the bus.

Ask: What don't you like to *wait* for?

DURING READING

20–30 Minutes   SL.2.2   RL. 2.1   RL.2.7   L.2.4a

Shared Reading

Tell children you will now read "Music in My Family." Tell them to note the vocabulary and high-frequency words you just introduced as you read the story. Stop to model understanding of the story as you go.

Pages 2–3

High-Frequency Words Make sure children can read the high-frequency word *out*.

Expand Vocabulary Read page 3. Focus on the word *festival*. Ask: *Where does the text say that the girls are going?* (They are going to a music festival.) *Who will be at the music festival?* (lots of bands) *What do you think the bands will do at the festival?* (play music)

Comprehension Check Model beginning to read. Say: *The first thing I notice is that two girls are getting ready to go out. They are putting on coats. Next, I find out they are going to a music festival. I think that is what the story will be about. I wonder what will happen at the festival.*

Pages 4–5

High-Frequency Words Make sure children can read the high-frequency words *my, have,* and *see*.

Vocabulary Read page 5. Focus on the word *beg*. Ask: *Which word in the third sentence tells you that the girls really want to know the surprise right away?* (beg) Invite children to say "Tell us!" in a begging way. Ask: *Why do you think Dad wants the girls to wait?* (He thinks it will be fun to be surprised.)

Comprehension Check *On page 5 I read that Dad has a surprise. I wonder what the surprise will be. As I read I will look for clues to help me figure it out.*

Pages 6–7

Comprehension Check *I will stop and think about what is happening at the festival. The story says that it is fun. People are sharing food and a band is playing. The pictures show that everyone is having a good time.*

Pages 8–9

High-Frequency Words Make sure children can read the high-frequency word *look*.

Pages 10–11

Comprehension Check *I am going to stop here to make sure I understand what I am reading. The story tells me that the children are asking if each new band is the surprise. I wonder if a band will be the surprise.*

Pages 12–13

High-Frequency Words Make sure children can read the high-frequency word *there*.

Expand Vocabulary On page 13 read *"A singer comes on stage."* Ask: *Which word in the sentence tells where the singer is?* (stage) Have children point to the stage in the picture.

Comprehension Check *I read on page 12 that Dad tells the children it is time for the surprise. On page 13 I find out that the singer on stage. It is Mom! Is that the surprise?*

Pages 14–15

Expand Vocabulary On page 15 read *"We feel so proud."* Ask which word in the sentence tells how the family is feeling. (proud) Ask: *Why does the family feel proud?* (Mom is singing and playing on stage for lots of people. It is an honor to be asked to play.)

Comprehension Check *I am going to think about what happened in this story. Dad's surprise for the children is that Mom will play and sing on stage at the festival. I read that they feel very proud of her. That lets me know that the surprise was a very happy one for the whole family.*

 Quick Check **Can children understand vocabulary in context? If not, review and reteach using the instruction on page 24.**

Can children read the high-frequency words in context? If not, review using the Read/Spell/Write routine and the High-Frequency Word Cards.

Objectives
- Understand complex text through close-reading
- Read a fiction story
- Recognize and understand character, setting, events
- Respond to the selection using text evidence to support ideas

Materials
- "Music in My Family" Apprentice Leveled Reader
- Graphic Organizer: Character, Setting, Events

☞ **Go** Digital
- Apprentice Leveled Reader eBook
- Downloadable Graphic Organizer
- Character, Setting, Events Mini-Lesson

DURING READING

20–30 Minutes   SL.2.1a   RL.2.3   RL.2.6   RL.2.7   (CCSS)

Tell children they will now reread the selection, "Music in My Family." Review the vocabulary and high-frequency words that they will encounter as they read.

Close Reading

Pages 2–3

Genre (A C T) Have children reread the first two pages of "Music in My Family." Remind them that realistic fiction tells a made-up story about made-up characters and events, but that the events could happen in real life. Ask: *Could a family really be acting this way?* (Yes, a family could really be going out to a music festival.) *Does anything happen that could not happen in real life?* (no)

Character, Setting, Events Remind children that events tell what happens in a story. Ask: *What has happened in the story so far?* (Two girls are getting ready to go out to a music festival.) Help children record this story event on their Character, Setting, Events charts.

Pages 4–5

Character, Setting, Events Point out that characters are the people or animals in a story. Ask: *Who are the characters?* (Mom, Dad, and two girls) Help children record this on their Character, Setting, Events charts.

Connection of Ideas (A C T) Reread page 5. Ask: *What happens when Dad tells the girls he has a surprise?* (They really want to know what it is.) *What does Dad say when they beg him?* (He tells them to wait.) *How do you think knowing about the surprise will change the way the girls act?* (The girls will be looking for the surprise.)

Pages 6–7

Character, Setting, Events Tell children that the setting is when and where a story takes place. Say: *The family is at the music festival. Let's read to find out more about the setting of this story.* Reread page 6. Point to the people eating food. Ask: *What is something that people do at a music festival?* (They share food.) *What are the bands doing?* (They are playing music.) Help children record the setting on their Character, Setting, Events charts.

Pages 8–9

Connection of Ideas (A C T) Reread page 8 and then point to the picture. Ask: *Is the man playing the instrument the surprise?* (no) *Why did the girl ask that?* (Dad told them there was a surprise, and now they think everything might be the surprise.)

Pages 10–11

Character, Setting, Events Before reading, help children review what they wrote on their Character, Setting, Events charts. Ask: *What are the girls doing now?* (They are seeing different bands.)

Organization (A C T) Reread pages 10–11. Ask: *What happens on these two pages that is the same?* (The girls see musicians playing interesting instruments. They are enjoying the instruments.) *What do the girls ask on each page?* (They ask if the band is the surprise.) *What does Dad say on each page?* (He tells them that the band is not the surprise.) Have children find other pages in the story that follow this pattern.

Pages 12–13

Character, Setting, Events After rereading page 12, ask: *Who comes out on stage?* (a new band) *What does Dad tell the children it is time for?* (the surprise) *Let's keep reading to find out what happens next.*

Character, Setting, Events Reread page 13, ask: *Who comes on stage next?* (Mom) Help children record the event on their Character, Setting, Events charts.

Pages 14–15

Connection of Ideas *Think back to the beginning of the story. What did we learn about how Mom feels about music?* (Mom loves music and can play music.) *Did Mom go with them to the festival?* (no) *What is Dad's big surprise?* (Mom went on stage to play and sing with a band.)

Character, Setting, Events Reread page 15, ask: *How did this surprise make the family feel?* (They felt proud of Mom.) Help children record this final event on their Character, Setting, Events charts.

AFTER READING

10–15 Minutes   SL.2.4a   RL.2.1   RL.2.5   RF.2.4b   W.2.8

Respond to Reading

Compare Texts Guide children in comparing the characters in "Music in My Family" with the characters in "Maria Celebrates Brazil." Help children think about ways the two families are the same and ways they are different. Then ask: *How is your family like the two families in the stories? Does your family like to listen to or play music? Does anyone in your family like to dance?*

Summarize Have children turn to page 16 and guide them in summarizing the selection. (Answers should include details that show how the family got a big surprise at the music festival when Mom went on stage.)

Text Evidence

Have partners work together to answer questions on page 16. Remind children to use their Character, Setting, Events charts.

Character, Setting, Events (The story takes place at a music festival.)

Vocabulary (Children should point to the sitar in the picture and describe it as having a long neck and strings.)

Write About Reading (The girls see a big stage with bands playing. They see people sharing food and listening to music.)

Read "Making Music"

Encourage children to read the paired selection "Making Music" on pages 17–19. Have them summarize the selection and compare it to "Music in My Family." Have them work with a partner to answer the "Make Connections" questions on page 19.

Independent Reading

Have pairs of children reread "Music in My Family." Have them talk about what the family saw and did at the music festival.

✔ *Quick Check* **Can students identify character, setting, and events? If not, review and reteach using the instruction on page 24 and assign the Unit 1 Week 2 digital mini-lesson.**

Can students respond to the selection using text evidence? If not, provide sentence frames to help them organize their ideas.

WEEK 2
LESSON

5

Objectives
• Review weekly vocabulary words
• Review character, setting, events
• Write an analysis about an author's use of character, setting, events

Scaffolding for **Wonders** Reading/Writing Workshop

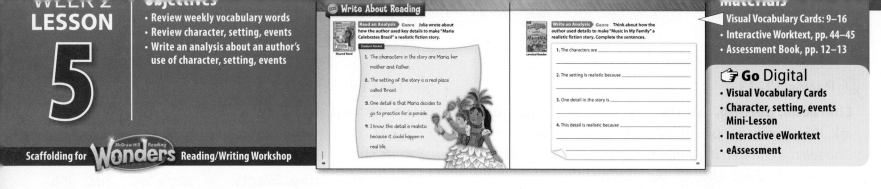

Materials
• Visual Vocabulary Cards: 9–16
• Interactive Worktext, pp. 44–45
• Assessment Book, pp. 12–13

☞ **Go** Digital
• Visual Vocabulary Cards
• Character, setting, events Mini-Lesson
• Interactive eWorktext
• eAssessment

REVIEW AND RETEACH

5–10 Minutes   L.2.4a   RL.2.3   RL.2.7

Weekly Vocabulary

Display one **Visual Vocabulary Card** at a time and guide children to use the vocabulary word in a sentence. If children have difficulty creating a sentence, have them find the word in "Maria Celebrates Brazil" or "Music in My Family" and use context clues in the passage to define the vocabulary word.

Comprehension: Character, Setting, Events

I Do Write and say: *Chris goes to an animal shelter. He sees a brown dog. The dog barks and jumps in the yard. Chris thinks the dog is cute. Chris takes the dog home.* Say: *Who are the characters? I can find the answers in the first two sentences.* Circle "Chris" and "dog." Ask: *Where does the story take place?* Circle "animal shelter." Say: *What is the main event in this story?* Circle: "Chris takes the dog home."

We Do Display: *Grace and Rob go to a concert in the park. Grace likes the music. The music is too loud for Rob. He leaves the concert and goes home.* Ask: *Who are the characters?* (Grace and Rob) *Where are they?* (a concert in the park) *What happens to Rob at the concert?* (The music is too loud. Rob leaves the concert.)

You Do Display: *The snow fell all night. The next day school was closed. The children all went sledding. They made snowmen. They had snowball fights. They had a great time together.* Guide partners to ask questions about the characters, setting, and events of the story.

WRITE ABOUT READING

25–35 Minutes   W.2.3   W.2.8   W.4.9

Read an Analysis

• Guide children to look back at "Maria Celebrates Brazil" in the **Interactive Worktext**. Have volunteers review the details about character, setting, and events they marked on page 37. Repeat with pages 38–41. *How did the author use events to make this story realistic?*

• Read aloud the directions on page 44. Read aloud the student model. *This student's work is not a summary. It is an analysis, or description, of how the author used details to make "Maria Celebrates Brazil" a realistic story.*

• *When you write an analysis, you should include key details from the story that tell about the story. Read Julia's first sentence. Circle the details.* (The characters in the story are Maria, her mother, and her father.) *In what part of the story do you learn these details?* (the beginning)

• *Read the second sentence. Draw a box around the details from the story you see in Julia's writing.* (a real place called Brazil.) *What part of the story does this detail come from?* (the beginning)

• Guide children to point to the third sentence. *What detail do you see in this sentence?* (Maria decides to go to practice for a parade.) *Tell the part of the story where this detail comes from.* (the middle)

• Model analyzing how the author made the story realistic. Read the last sentence that Julia wrote. *Why is this sentence a good ending?* (Julia explained that the detail is realistic because it could happen in real life.)

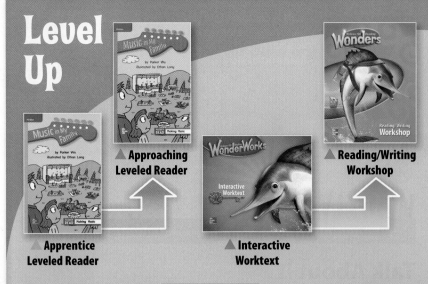

▲ Approaching Leveled Reader

▲ Reading/Writing Workshop

▲ Apprentice Leveled Reader

▲ Interactive Worktext

✏️ *Analytical Writing* Write an Analysis

Guided Writing Read the writing prompt on page 45 together. Guide children to review their Character, Setting, and Events charts for "Music in My Family." Have children use their charts to complete the sentence starters. Children can also write an analysis using another selection previously read this week.

Peer Conference Guide children to read their analysis to a partner. Listeners should summarize the strongest details that the author used to make this a realistic fiction story. They should discuss any parts that are unclear.

Teacher Conference Check children's writing for complete sentences and whether they included details from the story. Review the ending sentence and ask: *Did the author use details to support the story?* If necessary, guide children to revise their sentence by adding more details.

IF children read the `Apprentice Level` Reader and the **Interactive Worktext** Shared Read fluently and answer the Respond to Reading questions

THEN read together the `Approaching Level` Reader main selection and the **Reading/Writing Workshop** Shared Read from *Reading Wonders*.

Writing Rubric

	4	3	2	1
Text Evidence	Includes three or more details from the text.	Includes two or more details from the text.	Includes only one detail from the text.	No text evidence is cited.
Writing Style	Writes in complete sentences. Uses correct spelling and grammar.	Uses complete sentences. Writing has spelling and grammar errors.	Few complete sentences. There are many spelling and grammar errors.	Writing is not accurate or in complete sentences.

ASSESSMENT

Weekly Assessment

Have children complete the Weekly Assessment using **Assessment** book pages 12–13.

WEEK'S
LESSON

1

Objectives
• Develop oral language
• Build background about pets
• Understand and use weekly vocabulary
• Read a fiction story

Scaffolding for **WONDERS** Reading/Writing Workshop

Materials
Interactive Worktext, pp. 46–55
• Visual Vocabulary Cards: 17–24
• High-Frequency Word Cards

☞ **Go** Digital
• Interactive eWorktext
• Visual Vocabulary Cards

WEEKLY CONCEPT

5–10 Minutes   SL.2.1b SL.2.4 CCSS

Talk About It

Essential Question Read aloud the Essential Question on page 46 of the **Interactive Worktext:** *How can a pet be an important friend?* Explain that pets can be friends to their owners. Say: *There are all kinds of pets and they can be our friends in different ways. Let's think of some things you do with your pets.* Have children name activities they do with their pets. Provide examples, such as cuddling with a cat, playing fetch with a dog, or petting a hamster.

• Discuss the photograph on page 46. Ask: *What is happening in the picture?* (A girl and a cat are hugging.) How are they feeling? (They both look happy.)

I Do Say: *I am going to look at the photo and think about how the girl and the cat are important friends to each other. I think this photo tells me that they are important friends because they care about each other. I will write on the web on page 47 how they are friends.*

We Do Say: *Let's think about other ways we know that people and their pets are friends. One way a pet can be a friend is that a pet can make us laugh. For example, a playful kitten can make us laugh when it gets tangled up in a ball of yarn.* Guide children to think of other ways pets are friends and then choose one way to add to their web.

You Do Guide partners to work together to talk about other ways pets can be important friends. Have children use the following sentence starter in their discussion: *A pet can _____.* Have children add their ideas to the web.

REVIEW VOCABULARY

10–15 Minutes   L.2.5a L.2.6 RF.2.3 CCSS

Review Weekly Vocabulary Words

• Use the **Visual Vocabulary Cards** to review the weekly vocabulary.

• Read together the directions on page 48 of the **Interactive Worktext**. Then complete the activity.

1 **glance** Demonstrate *glancing* outside to see what the weather is. Say: *I glance outside to see what the weather is.* Then have partners each *glance* at the clock. Then partners can share their ideas with each other using this sentence starter: *I glance at _____.* (Possible answers: a calendar, a book, my friend)

2 **stares** Tell children that people sometimes *stare* at something they find surprising. Explain that if there was a blizzard outside, you might *stare* out the window. Demonstrate *staring.* Then ask: *What is something that you might stare at?* (Possible answers: stars at night, a lightning storm)

3 **decide** Explain that when you *decide* on something, such as what to eat, you think of the choices and then choose one. Ask children to act out how they look when they try to *decide* what to wear to school. Guide them to think of another word for *decide.* (Possible answers: choose, make up your mind)

4 **trade** Explain to children that a *trade* is when two people each exchange something they have with the other person. Have children name something that they would *trade* for an apple. Guide children to pick items that would make a fair *trade.* (Answers will vary.)

5 **different** Say the following sentence starter on the board: An *apple is* different *from a banana because* _____. Have volunteers complete the sentence orally. Then have them discuss how a pen and pencil are *different*. (Possible answers: pens have ink; pencils are made of wood)

6 **relationship** Have children look around the room at each other. Ask: *What is the* relationship *between you and the other children in this class?* (Possible answers: we are classmates; we learn together) Suggest other similar *relationships*, if necessary. Then have children name a person they have a good *relationship* with. (Answers will vary.)

7 **proper** Explain that there are *proper* ways to do certain things. Model the *proper* way to greet someone new.(Possible answers: Hello, How are you?, My name is _____.) Then discuss the proper way to dress for a wedding. (wear clean, formal clothing)

8 **friendship** Invite children to think about a friend. Discuss the qualities of a friend by having children fill in this sentence orally: *A friendship happens when* _____. Then assist them as they draw a picture of the person they have a *friendship* with.

High-Frequency Words

Have children look at page 49 in the **Interactive Worktext**. Help them read, spell, and write each high-frequency word. Guide partners to use each word in a sentence. Then read the story aloud with children. Guide partners to work together to reread the story and circle the high-frequency words. (little, two, look, could, play, said) Listen in and provide assistance reading the high-frequency words, as necessary.

> **ELL** **ENGLISH LANGUAGE LEARNERS**
>
> Display the **High-Frequency Word Cards** for: *little, play, said, could, two, look*. Write a sentence with each word on the board. Have children echo-read each sentence, and point out the high-frequency word. Then ask them to use the word in a new sentence.

READ COMPLEX TEXT

15–20 Minutes   RL.2.3   RL.2.7   SL.2.1b

Read "Finding Cal"

- Have children turn to page 50 in the **Interactive Worktext** and read aloud the Essential Question. Point at the dog in the picture. Say: *What kind of pet do you see in this picture?* (a dog) *Let's read about how the boy and the dog become special friends.* Have children echo-read the title.

- Read the story together. Note that the weekly vocabulary words are highlighted in yellow. Expand Vocabulary words are highlighted in blue.

- As children read, have them use the "My Notes" section on page 50 to write questions they have. Children can also write words they don't understand or things they want to remember. Model how to use the "My Notes" section. *When I read the fourth sentence, I learn that the boy will get a dog. I wonder where the boy will find a dog. I will write a question about where the boy will get a dog in the "My Notes" section.*

> **ELL** **ENGLISH LANGUAGE LEARNERS**
>
> As you read together, have children highlight parts of the text they have questions about. After reading, review the questions children have. Then help them locate the answers to their questions in the text.

 Quick Check Can children understand the weekly vocabulary in context? If not, review vocabulary using the **Visual Vocabulary Cards** before teaching Lesson 2.

Can children read high-frequency words in context? If not, review using the Read/Spell/Write routine and the High-Frequency Word Cards.

WEEK 3 LESSON 2

Objectives
- Read a fiction story
- Understand complex text through close reading
- Recognize and understand character, setting, events
- Respond to the selection using text evidence to support ideas

Materials
Interactive Worktext, pp. 50–57

☞ **Go** Digital
- Interactive eWorktext
- Character, Setting, Events Mini-Lesson

Scaffolding for **Wonders** Reading/Writing Workshop

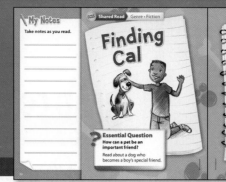

REREAD COMPLEX TEXT

20–25 Minutes   RL.2.3   RL.2.7   L.2.5a   CCSS

Close Reading: "Finding Cal"

Reread "Finding Cal" from **Interactive Worktext** pages 50–55 with children. As you read together, discuss important passages in the text. Guide children to respond to questions using evidence from the text.

 Page 50–51

Expand Vocabulary Have children read the first line. Explain that a *diary* is a book a person writes in to record what happens each day. Say: *When a person begins an entry in a* diary, *they write* Dear Diary. Guide children to circle the words that tell this is a diary entry. (Dear Diary)

Organization A C T Explain that when a person writes a new entry in a diary, they write the date. Say: They do this so they will be able to remember when they were writing about. Say: *I see that this boy wrote his diary entry on September 25.* Guide children to underline the date. (September 25)

Character, Setting, Events Explain that children can reread to find details about character, setting, and events in the story. Have children reread the page. Guide children to draw a box around the name of the character who said the boy could get a dog. (Dad)

Page 52

Organization A C T Explain that the story is organized by showing a boy's diary over time. Point to the date on the page. Ask: *How much time has passed since the boy's last diary entry?* (one day) Guide children to reference the date on the previous page if necessary. Then have them write their answer.

Expand Vocabulary Remind children that a *shelter* is a home for animals that do not have owners. Have children reread the first paragraph. Say: *When I reread the first paragraph, I read that there were many different dogs at the shelter.* Have children circle the word that tells what kind of animals are at the shelter. (dogs)

Connection of Ideas A C T Have children reread the first paragraph. Point to the word "Some" in the third, fourth, and fifth sentences. Explain to children that sometimes writers use the word *some* instead of the actual name of a group of people, animals, or objects. Ask: *What does the word* some *refer to here?* (dogs)

Character, Setting, Events Reread the second paragraph. Say: *This text tells about Jake seeing Cal for the first time. How does Jake feel about Cal? Let's find the sentence that tells us.* Guide children to identify the second sentence and draw a box around it. (I knew I liked him.)

Page 53

Expand Vocabulary Reread the first sentence with children. Write the word *leash* on the board and guide children to circle the *leash* in the picture. Ask: *What is Jake using the* leash *for?* (to walk Cal)

Character, Setting, Events Remind children that the setting is where and when the story takes place. Say: *Look at the picture. Where does Jake take Cal?* (outside) Guide children to find text evidence for their answer and draw a box around the word *outside* in the text.

Character, Setting, Events Tell children that important events often happen in the middle of a story. Reread the last two sentences. Ask: *How do we know that Cal likes Jake?* (Cal licks Jake's hand) Have children underline the answer. Ask: *Why is this an important event?* (Possible answer: It shows that Jake and Cal will be great friends.)

Page 54

Character, Setting, Events Reread the first paragraph with children. Ask: *What do Jake and his dad decide to do with Cal?* Have children draw a box around the sentence. (Soon we took Cal home.) Say: *Can you point to the text that tells why Jake wanted to take Cal home?* (We already have a good relationship). Explain that Jake and the dog are already friends.

Organization Ⓐ Ⓒ Ⓣ Point to the date on the page. Ask: *When did Jake write this diary entry?* (October 10) Have children write the answer. Then have them reread the second paragraph. Ask: *How much time has passed since Jake took Cal home from the shelter?* (two weeks)

Expand Vocabulary Reread aloud the second paragraph. Write the word *tricks* on the board. Explain that people often train their dogs to do *tricks*. Ask: *What trick does Jake say Cal has learned to do?* (roll over) Have children circle the answer. Point to the picture. Ask: *What other trick has Cal learned?* (Possible answer: stand up)

Page 55

Character, Setting, Events Reread the first two sentences with children. Ask: *Who are the characters in this part of the story?* (Dad, Jake, and Cal) *What is the setting?* (outside, on the way to school) *What does Cal do when Jake and his dad walk to school?* (He goes with them.) Guide children to draw a box around the words that tell. (Cal comes with us.)

Expand Vocabulary Explain that *lies* is a multiple meaning word. Ask: *What meanings of the word* lies *do you know?* If children have difficulty, say: Lies *can mean does not tell the truth or it can mean to rest on your back or belly*. Have children find clues in the illustration to identify the correct meaning. Ask: *What is the meaning of the word* lies *in this sentence?* (to rest on your back or belly) Have children circle where Cal *lies* in the picture.

Character, Setting, Events Have children reread the page and think about how Jake feels about Cal at the end of the story. Then have children underline the two sentences that tell how the boy feels. (We have a great friendship. I love Cal.)

RESPOND TO READING

10–20 Minutes RL.2.3 RL.2.7 SL.2.1b

Respond to "Finding Cal"

Read aloud the questions about "Finding Cal" on page 56 of the **Interactive Worktext**. Then read aloud the "Discussion Starter" for each of the questions. Guide children to work with a partner to answer the questions orally using the "Discussion Starters." Have children find text evidence to support their answers. Ask children to write the page number(s) on which they found the answer for each question.

1. *How does Jake meet Cal?* (Possible answers: Jake's dad says he can get a dog. I read that Jake goes to a shelter. Text Evidence: pp. 51, 52)

2. *How do Jake and Cal get along?* (Possible answers: After they meet, Jake and Cal go outside. I can tell that Jake and Cal get along because Jake pets Cal and Cal licks Jake's hand. Text Evidence: p. 53)

3. *How does Jake feel about Cal at the end of the story?* (Possible answers: At the end of the story, I read that Jake feels that he and Cal have a good friendship. I know Jake cares for Cal because he wrote "I love Cal!" Text Evidence: p. 55)

After children discuss the questions on page 56, have them use the sentence starters to answer the question on page 57. Circulate and provide guidance.

 Quick Check **Do children understand vocabulary in context? If not, review and reteach using the instruction on page 34.**

Can children identify the characters, setting, and events? If not, review and reteach using the instruction on page 34 and assign the Unit 1 Week 3 digital mini-lesson.

Can children write a response to "Finding Cal"? If not, review the sentence starters and prompt children to respond orally. Help them write their responses.

Objectives
- Access prior knowledge
- Understand and use new vocabulary words
- Read high-frequency words
- Read a fiction story

Materials
- "Too Many Pets?" Apprentice Leveled Reader
- High-Frequency Word Cards

☞ **Go** Digital
- Apprentice Leveled Reader eBook
- Downloadable High-Frequency Word Cards

 Scaffolding for **Wonders** Approaching Leveled Reader

...is my **family**.
...are five of us.

Here are my pets.
There are ten of them.

BEFORE READING

10–15 Minutes   SL.2.1a   SL.2.6   L.2.5a   L.2.6   RF.2.3f   CCSS

Introduce "Too Many Pets?"

- Read the Essential Question on the title page of "Too Many Pets?" **Apprentice Leveled Reader:** *How can a pet be an important friend?*

- Read the title of the main read. Point to the title page. *What story characters do we see on the page?* (a girl and two cats) *What can you tell about the girl and the cats from the picture?* (Children may point out that they look happy.) *What are some pets you have had or would like to have? Let's read about a family with a lot of pets.*

High-Frequency Words

Display the **High-Frequency Word Cards** for the words *five, four, ten, their, two,* and *very.* Use the Read/Spell/Write routine to teach each word. Guide partners to use each word in a sentence. Provide assistance reading the high-frequency words, as necessary.

Expand Vocabulary

Before reading "Too Many Pets?" help children read the following words that they will encounter. Display each word below. Use the Define/Example/Ask routine. Tell children to look for the word later on as they read "Too Many Pets?"

1 **cuddly** (page 7)

Define: soft and warm and nice to hold

Example: The small kitten was *cuddly* and cute.

Ask: What else is *cuddly*?

2 **family** (page 2)

Define: people who are related or connected

Example: My mother, father, and little sister are part of my *family.*

Ask: Who are other members of a *family*?

3 **gift** (page 6)

Define: something special that you give to someone

Example: I gave my mom a *gift* I made in art class.

Ask: What is a *gift* have you given?

4 **stay** (page 5)

Define: to not leave

Example: I had to *stay in* the house because it rained

Ask: When do you *stay* with someone else?

DURING READING

20–25 Minutes   RL.2.1   RL. 2.3   RL2.7   L.2.4a   CCSS

Shared Reading

Tell children you will now read "Too Many Pets?" Tell them to note the vocabulary and high-frequency words you just introduced as you read the story. Stop to model understanding of the story as you go.

Pages 2–3

High-Frequency Words Make sure children can read the high-frequency words *five* and *ten.*

Comprehension Check Model beginning to read the story. Say: *At first I learn that this is a story about a family. Then I learn that the family has ten pets. That's a lot of pets! The title is "Too Many Pets?" There is a question mark at the end. I think I may learn how the family got so many pets. I may also learn if ten is really too many pets.*

Vocabulary Read page 2. Focus on the word *family*. Ask: *How many people are part of the family?* (five) *What are some words that name the different family members?* (mom, dad, brother, sister)

Pages 4–5

High-Frequency Words Make sure children can read the high-frequency word *two*.

Point to the picture on page 4. Read the second sentence. Ask: *How does the picture help you to understand the expression "moved in"?* (Mom and Dad are carrying boxes; they are moving in to a new home.)

Vocabulary On page 5, read *"We decided they can stay."* Ask: *Which word in the sentence means that the cats did not have to leave when the family moved in?* (stay)

Pages 6–7

High-Frequency Words Make sure children can read the high-frequency word *very*.

Vocabulary Read page 7 and focus on the word *cuddly*. Ask: *What makes the rabbits* cuddly? (The rabbits' fur makes them cuddly.) *Can you think of other words that mean* cuddly? (warm and soft, furry)

Comprehension Check *So far I am learning how the family got ten pets. I know the cats were there when the family moved in. I know that the rabbits were a gift. The family seems to like these pets. I think the next pages will tell me how they got more pets.*

Pages 8–9

Vocabulary On page 8, read the sentence, *"Next we got a dog."* Focus on the word *next*. Say: *The word* next *helps us to understand the order in which things happen.* Turn back to page 4 and ask, *Which pets did the family get when they moved in?* (two cats) Turn to page 6, point to the word *then*, and say: *Then they got two rabbits.* Turn to page 8, point to the word *next*, and say: *Next the family got a dog.*

Pages 10–11

High-Frequency Words Make sure children can read the high-frequency words *four* and *their*.

Vocabulary *The text on page 11 says that the family can trade their eggs? What does it mean to trade something?* (To trade means to give something and then get something in return.) Ask children to turn to a partner and discuss what it means to *trade*. Ask them to talk about things that can be traded.

Pages 12–13

Vocabulary On page 12, read *"Next, a duck showed up."* Ask: *Which word in the sentence tells what showed up next?* (duck) Have children point to the duck in the picture.

Comprehension Check *I'm going to stop here and make sure I understand what I am reading. I read on page 13 that now the family has ten pets. I can read to find out how Mom feels about having so many pets. She says that ten is too many pets.*

Vocabulary Reread page 13 and focus on the word *too*. Ask: *What number word sounds the same as* too? (two) Have children use each word in a sentence.

Pages 14–15

Vocabulary Read page 14 and point to the words, *Oh, no!* Ask: *Why might someone say these words?* (We might say "Oh, no!" when we are surprised by something we see or hear.) *Would you say it about something we think is good or bad?* (bad)

Comprehension Check *The story says that now the family has four new pets. The picture shows me that the cat has four babies, or kittens. I know that the family had ten pets before. Now they have four more pets. This means that the family now has 14 pets in all!*

 Quick Check Can children understand vocabulary in context? If not, review and reteach using the instruction on page 34.

Can children read the high-frequency words in context? If not, review using the Read/Spell/Write routine and the High-Frequency Word Cards.

WEEK 3 LESSON 4

Objectives
- Understand complex text through close-reading
- Read a fiction story
- Recognize and understand character, setting, events.
- Respond to the selection using text evidence to support ideas

Scaffolding for McGraw-Hill Reading **Wonders** Approaching Leveled Reader

Materials
"Too Many Pets?" Apprentice Leveled Reader
- Graphic Organizer: Character, Setting, Events

👉 **Go Digital**
- Apprentice Leveled Reader eBook
- Downloadable Graphic Organizer
- Character, Setting, Events Mini-Lesson

Too Many Pets?
by Michael McDade
illustrated by Viviana Garofoli

PAIRED READ Poetry

...is my family.
...are five of us.

Here are my pets.
There are ten of them.

3

DURING READING

20–30 Minutes   RL. 2.1   RL.2.3   RL 2.7 CCSS

Tell children they will now reread the selection, "Too Many Pets?" Review the vocabulary and high-frequency words that they will encounter as they read.

Close Reading

🔍 Pages 2–3

Character, Setting, Events Reread pages 3 and 4. Point out that characters are the people or animals in a story. Ask: *Who are the characters in this story?* (The characters are a family and ten pets.) Model filling in the Character, Setting, Events Chart.

Connection of Ideas **ACT** Ask: *Who is telling this story.* (Someone in the family.) *How can you tell it is someone in the family?* (They say "my family.") Point out that you don't yet know who is speaking.

🔍 Pages 4–5

Character, Setting, Events Remind children that the setting is where a story takes place. Say: *What can we learn about the setting from the picture?* (The setting is a new home for the family.) Say: *Events are the things that happen in the story. What do we see waiting for the family on the steps?* (two cats) Help children record these details on their Character, Setting, Events charts.

Organization **ACT** Point out that the narrator is now going to explain how the family got so many pets. Ask: *What question does the narrator ask in the beginning.* (How did we get ten pets?) *What does he tell us next?* (How the family got their very first pets.) Invite children to notice that most of the rest of the book will answer this question.

Connection of Ideas **ACT** Point to the picture of the cats on page 4 and then point to the picture on page 5. Ask: *Have the cats found a new home? How do you think they like the family who moved in?* (The cats are sleeping happily on the girl's lap. They seem happy.) *What does the text tell us?* (The sister loves them.)

🔍 Pages 6–7

Character, Setting, Events Reread page 6. Ask: *What event happened on these pages?* (The family got a gift of two rabbits) *Are they happy to get the rabbits? How can you tell?* (They seem happy. They think the rabbits are cuddly.) Help children record the details on their Character, Setting, Events charts.

Organization **ACT** Focus on the way the book is organized by drawing attention to the similarities between these pages and the two previous pages. Ask: *How are these two pages like the last two pages?* (Both sets of pages tell how the family got one of their pets.) Ask: *Who likes the rabbits best?* (the older boy) *Who liked the cats best?* (the sister) Point out that so far the big brother and the sister each have a favorite pet. Ask: *Who do you think the next pet might go with?*

🔍 Pages 8–9

Character, Setting, Events Reread page 8 and then point to the picture. Ask: *What pet do we learn about next?* (a new dog) Reread and point to page 9. *Ask: Who likes the dog?* (the boy) *Who is talking on this page?* (the boy) Point out that on this the page, we finally know who the narrator is.

Organization **ACT** Ask: *How are these two pages like the last two pages?* (It tells how the family got one of their pets.) *Who likes this new pet best?* (the smaller boy)

Pages 10–11

Character, Setting, Events Help children review what they wrote on their Character, Setting, Events charts. Ask: *What have we learned about the characters?* (The characters are a family who keep getting more pets.) *What is the setting for this story?* (the family's home) *How has the family gotten so many pets?* (The cats were there when they moved in. Their neighbors gave them two rabbits. A friend gave them a dog. Then four chickens came.) *Let's keep reading to find out what happens next.*

Pages 12–13

Organization Ⓐ Ⓒ Ⓣ Invite children to notice how the pattern changes. Ask: *What does the first page tell about?* (how a duck became a pet) *What does the second page tell about?* (It tells they have ten pets, and Mom isn't happy.) Ask: *How is this different from the other second pages?* (Usually the second page tells why they liked the new pet or how they let it stay.)

Character, Setting, Events Ask: *How many pets are there now?* (ten) *How does Mom feel about the pets?* (She think there are too many.) Add this to the Character, Setting, Events Chart.

Pages 14–15

Character, Setting, Events Reread page 15. Ask: What happens on this page? (Four new kittens are born.) *Is the narrator surprised? How can you tell?* (He seems to be surprised. He says: "Oh no!" and he looks surprised.) Help children add this information to the Character, Setting, Events Chart.

Organization Ⓐ Ⓒ Ⓣ Focus on how the book is now telling about brand new pets and not the pets that were there in the beginning. Ask: *Were these kittens there in the beginning of the book?* (no) *Were the animals on the other pages there in the beginning?* (yes) *How many pets does the family have now?* (the family has 14 pets) *Do you think they will keep these pets? Why or why not?* (Probably they will keep these because they kept all of the others.)

AFTER READING

10–15 Minutes   SL.2.4a   RL.2.1   RL.2.5   RF.2.4b   W.2.8

Respond to Reading

Compare Texts Guide children in comparing the family in "Too Many Pets?" with the family in "Finding Cal." Ask: *What are some ways that pets and people show they are friends to each other?*

Summarize Have children turn to page 16 and guide them in summarizing the selection. (Answers should include details about how the family got the pets.)

Text Evidence

Have partners work together to answer questions on page 16. Remind children to use their Character, Setting, Events charts.

Character, Setting, Events (They were there when the family moved in.)

Vocabulary (Show up means to come or arrive.)

Write About Reading (Answers should focus on a pet.)

Read "My Dog Loves Me"

Encourage children to read the paired selection "My Dog Loves Me" on pages 17–19. Have them summarize the selection and compare it to "Too Many Pets?" Have them work with a partner to answer the "Make Connections" questions on page 19.

Independent Reading

Have pairs of children reread "Too Many Pets?" Have them talk about how the family felt about the pets.

✓ *Quick Check* Can students identify the characters, setting, and events in the story? If not, review and reteach using the instruction on page 34 and assign the Unit 1 Week 3 digital mini-lesson.

Can students respond to the selection using text evidence? If not, provide sentence frames to help them organize their ideas.

WEEK 3
LESSON
5

Objectives
• Review weekly vocabulary words
• Review character, setting, events
• Write an analysis about an author's use of character, setting, and events

Scaffolding for **Wonders** Reading/Writing Workshop

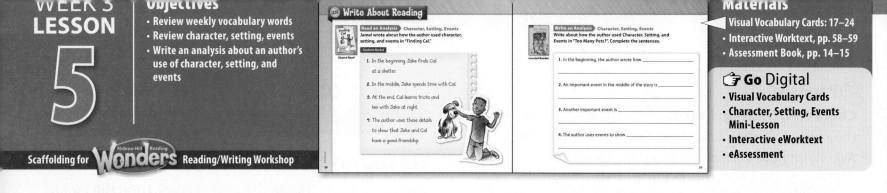

Materials
• Visual Vocabulary Cards: 17–24
• Interactive Worktext, pp. 58–59
• Assessment Book, pp. 14–15

☞ **Go** Digital
• Visual Vocabulary Cards
• Character, Setting, Events Mini-Lesson
• Interactive eWorktext
• eAssessment

REVIEW AND RETEACH

5–10 Minutes   RL.2.3 RL.2.7 L.2.4a

Weekly Vocabulary

Display one **Visual Vocabulary Card** at a time and guide children to use the vocabulary word in a sentence. If children have difficulty creating a sentence, have them find the word in "Finding Cal" or "Too Many Pets?" and use context clues in the passage to define the vocabulary word.

Comprehension: Character, Setting, Events

I Do Write and say: *Jenna and Nick walk down the beach. The sun is going down. Jenna finds a pretty white shell.* Ask: *Who are the characters?* Circle "Jenna and Nick," and write *characters*. Say: *These are the people the story is about.* Ask: *What is the setting? I know the setting is the place and time of the story, so I will look for details about place and time.* Circle "the beach" and "The sun is going down," and write *setting*. Say: *These details tell me that the setting is the beach at sunset.*

We Do Continue by guiding children to understand the events of a story. Ask: *What event takes place? I will look for something that happens.* Circle "Jenna finds a pretty white shell," and write *event. I can see that this is the important thing that happens.*

You Do *Rosa ran down the sidewalk. She was late for the school bus. She ran right into Mr. Stanley. They both fell down!* Ask: *Who are the characters?* (Rosa and Mr. Stanley) *What is the setting?* (the sidewalk) *What is the important event?* (Rosa runs into Mr. Stanley and they both fall down.)

WRITE ABOUT READING

25–35 Minutes   W.2.3 W.2.8 W.4.9

Read an Analysis

• Guide children to look back at "Finding Cal" in the **Interactive Worktext**. Have volunteers review the details about the characters, setting and events they marked on page 51 and summarize the text. Repeat with pages 52–55. *How did the author use character, setting, events in "Finding Cal"?*

• Read aloud the directions on page 58. Read aloud the student model. *This student's work is not a summary. It is an analysis, or description, of how the author used character, setting, events in "Finding Cal."*

• *When you write an analysis, you should include key details from the story that tell about the story. Read Jamal's first sentence. Circle the characters and the setting.* (Jake, Cal)

• *Read the second sentence. Draw a box around the event from the story you see in Jamal's writing.* (Jake spends time with Cal.) *What part of the story is he writing about?* (the middle)

• Guide children to point to the third sentence. *This sentence explains the events, or what happened, at the end of the story. What events does Jamal include?* (Cal learns tricks and lies next to Jake at night.)

• Guide children to point to the fourth sentence. *Why is Jamal's last sentence a good ending?* (Jamal explained how the author used characters and events to support the story.)

Analytical Writing — Write an Analysis

Guided Writing Read the writing prompt on page 59 together. Guide children to review their Character, Setting, Events charts for "Too Many Pets." Have children use their charts to complete the sentence starters. Children can also write an analysis using another selection previously read this week.

Peer Conference Guide children to read their analysis to a partner. Listeners should summarize the events, or what the characters say and do in the story. They should discuss any parts that are unclear.

Teacher Conference Check children's writing for complete sentences and whether they included details from the story. Review the ending sentence and ask: *Did the author use events to support the story?* If necessary, guide children to revise their sentence by adding events.

Level Up

▲ Apprentice Leveled Reader

▲ Approaching Leveled Reader

▲ Interactive Worktext

▲ Reading/Writing Workshop

IF children read the Apprentice Level Reader and the **Interactive Worktext** Shared Read fluently and answer the Respond to Reading questions

THEN read together the Approaching Level Reader main selection and the **Reading/Writing Workshop** Shared Read from *Reading Wonders*.

Writing Rubric

	4	3	2	1
Text Evidence	Includes three or more details from the text.	Includes two or more details from the text.	Includes only one detail from the text.	No text evidence is cited.
Writing Style	Writes in complete sentences. Uses correct spelling and grammar.	Uses complete sentences. Writing has spelling and grammar errors.	Few complete sentences. There are many spelling and grammar errors.	Writing is not accurate or in complete sentences.

ASSESSMENT

Weekly Assessment

Have children complete the Weekly Assessment using **Assessment** book pages 14–15.

WEEK 3

▶ **Mid-Unit Assessment,** pages 72 – 79

▶ **Fluency Assessment,** pages 234 – 249

Unit 1 Mid-Unit Assessment

CCSS TESTED SKILLS

✔ COMPREHENSION	✔ VOCABULARY:
• Key Details RL.2.1	• Context Clues L.2.4
• Character, Setting, Events RL.2.3	
• Character, Setting, Events RL.2.3	

Using Assessment and Writing Scores

↻ RETEACH	IF ...	THEN ...
COMPREHENSION	Students answer 0–5 multiple-choice items correctly ...	... reteach tested skills using instruction on pages 364–375.
VOCABULARY	Students answer 0–2 multiple-choice items correctly ...	... reteach tested skills using instruction on page 364.
WRITING	Students score mostly 1–2 on weekly writing rubrics throughout the unit ...	... reteach writing using instruction on pages 376–377.

Fluency Assessment

Conduct assessments individually using the differentiated fluency passages in Assessment. Students' expected fluency goal for this Unit is 41–61 WCPM with an accuracy rate of 95% or higher.

Weeks 4 and 5

Monitor students progress on the following to inform how to adjust instruction for the remainder of the unit.

ADJUST INSTRUCTION	
ACCESS COMPLEX TEXT	If students need more support for accessing complex text, provide additional modeling of prompts in Lesson 2 of Week 4, pages 40–41, and Week 5, pages 50–51. After you model how to identify the text evidence, guide students to find text evidence in Lessons 3 and 4 of Week 4, pages 42–45, and Week 5, pages 52–55.
FLUENCY	For those students who need more support with Fluency, focus on the Fluency lessons in the Foundational Skills Kit.
WRITING	If students need more support incorporating text evidence in their writing, conduct the Write About Reading activities in Lesson 4 and 5 as group writing activities.
FOUNDATIONAL SKILLS	Review students' individualized progress in *Reading Wonders* Adaptive Learning to determine which foundational skills to incorporate into your lessons for the remainder of the unit.

WEEK 4 LESSON 1

Objectives
- Develop oral language
- Build background about caring for animals
- Understand and use weekly vocabulary
- Read narrative nonfiction

Scaffolding for **McGraw-Hill Reading Wonders** Reading/Writing Workshop

Talk About It
Weekly Concept Animals Need Care
Essential Question How do we care for animals?

Tell what an animal's needs are.

Animal Needs

Tell how you or a friend has cared for an animal.

Materials
Interactive Worktext, pp. 60–69
- Visual Vocabulary Cards: 25–32
- High-Frequency Word Cards

☞ Go Digital
- Interactive eWorktext
- Visual Vocabulary Cards

WEEKLY CONCEPT

5–10 Minutes   SL.2.1b   SL.2.4

Talk About It

Essential Question Read aloud the Essential Question on page 60 of the **Interactive Worktext:** *How do we care for animals?* Explain that when you care for animals, you provide food, water, and shelter. Provide examples of how different people care for animals, such as owners of pets, veterinarians, and so on. Say: *We care for animals in many ways. Animals depend on us for their care.*

- Discuss the photograph on page 60. Ask: *What do you see in this picture?* (I see a boy and a girl with a dog in a tub.) *How are the boy and girl caring for the dog?* (The boy and girl are giving the dog a bath.) Say: *I know dogs need baths because they are outside a lot and they get dirty.*

I Do Say: *I am going to look at the photo and think about how people care for animals.* (These children are caring for the dog by keeping it clean.) *I will write on the web on page 61 that some animals need to be kept clean.*

We Do Say: *Let's think of other ways people care for their pets. I know that pets have many needs. I know they need fresh food and water each day.* Guide children to think about how pet owners feed their pets each day. Then have children add this idea to their web.

You Do Guide partners to work together to talk about other ways that people care for animals. Have children use the following sentence starter to share their ideas with their partner: *Animals need _____.*

REVIEW VOCABULARY

10–15 Minutes   L.2.5a   L.2.6   RF.2.3

Review Weekly Vocabulary Words

- Use the **Visual Vocabulary Cards** to review the weekly vocabulary.

- Read together the directions on page 62 of the **Interactive Worktext**. Then complete the activity.

1 **excited** Describe a time you were *excited* about something. Say: *Feeling* excited *happens when you are looking forward to something or enjoying something special.* Then have partners take turns using this sentence starter before they act out being *excited*: I feel *excited* when _____. (Answers will vary.)

2 **needs** Explain that in order to grow, plants have *needs*. Ask children why a plant *needs* dirt. (Possible answers: for roots to grow, to get nutrients) Then ask: *Why do plants* need *sunlight?* (to grow) Then have children think of something else a plant *needs*. (water, air) If necessary, help children by describing some of the things people *need* to live.

3 **safe** Explain what it means to stay *safe*. Discuss when children might need to stay *safe*. (Possible answers: when riding a bike, when there's a thunderstorm or other bad weather) Ask: *Who helps people stay safe in a swimming pool?* (Possible answers: life guard, a parent)

4 **wild** Explain that some animals live where people take care of them, such as pets in homes or animals in the zoo. Tell children that other animals live in the *wild*. Review the meaning of the word *wild*. Then ask children: *Which of these animals lives in the* wild? (elephant) If necessary, describe some other animals that live in the *wild*.

5 **allowed** Explain that there are different rules at home than at school. Have volunteers share some things they are *allowed* to do at home that they are not *allowed* to do at school. (Answers will vary.)

6 **wandered** Write the word *wandered* and read it aloud. Point out the ending *-ed*. Have a volunteer underline the base word. Prompt children with the sentence frame: *The girl* wandered *around the _____ looking at the pictures.* (<u>Possible answers</u>: museum, house) Then have children think of a time they *wandered* somewhere. (Answers will vary.)

7 **roam** Explain that you might *roam* around the room because you are looking for something or you feel like stretching your legs. Help children think about why an animal might *roam* around a field. (<u>Possible answers</u>: to find food, to stalk prey)

8 **care** Invite children to think about something in their home that they have to take *care* of. Say: *It can be a pet you have to feed or walk or a chore like doing the dishes.* Then have children draw a picture of something at home they have to take *care* of. (Answers will vary.)

High-Frequency Words

Have children look at page 63 in the **Interactive Worktext**. Help them read, spell, and write each high-frequency word. Guide partners to use each word in a sentence. Then read the story aloud with children. Guide partners to work together to reread the story and circle the high-frequency words. (every, day, more, after, then, goes) Listen in and provide assistance reading the high-frequency words, as necessary.

ELL ENGLISH LANGUAGE LEARNERS

Display the **High-Frequency Word Cards** for: *more, after, day, then, goes, every.* Write a sentence with each word on the board. Have children echo-read each sentence, and point out the high-frequency word. Then ask them to use the word in a new sentence.

READ COMPLEX TEXT

15–20 Minutes RI.2.1 RI. 2.5

Read "Taking Care of Pepper"

- Have children turn to page 64 in the **Interactive Worktext** and read aloud the Essential Question. Point to the picture. Say: *What kind of animal do you see in this picture?* (horse) *Let's read to find out how this horse is cared for.* Have children echo-read the title.

- Read the story together. Note that the weekly vocabulary words are highlighted in yellow. Expand Vocabulary words are highlighted in blue.

- As children read, have them use the "My Notes" section on page 64 to write questions they have. Children can also write words they don't understand or things they want to remember. Model how to use the "My Notes" section. *When I read the last sentence on page 65, I find out that looking after a horse is a big job. I wonder if it takes a lot of time to look after a horse. I will write a question about looking after a horse in the "My Notes" section.*

ELL ENGLISH LANGUAGE LEARNERS

As you read together, have children highlight parts of the text they have questions about. After reading, review the questions children have. Then help them locate the answers to their questions in the text.

 Quick Check Can children understand the weekly vocabulary in context? If not, review vocabulary using the **Visual Vocabulary Cards** before teaching Lesson 2.

Can children read high-frequency words in context? If not, review using the Read/Spell/Write routine and the High-Frequency Word Cards.

Objectives

- Read narrative nonfiction
- Understand complex text through close reading
- Recognize and understand key details
- Respond to the selection using text evidence to support ideas

Scaffolding for **WONDERS** Reading/Writing Workshop

Materials

Interactive Worktext, pp. 64–71

☞ **Go** Digital
- Interactive eWorktext
- Key Details Mini-Lesson

4071500129737

REREAD COMPLEX TEXT

20–25 Minutes   RI.2.1   RI.2.5   L.2.5a   CCSS

Close Reading: "Taking Care of Pepper"

Reread "Taking Care of Pepper" with children from **Interactive Worktext** pages 64–69. As you read together, discuss important passages in the text. Guide children to respond to questions using evidence from the text.

Pages 64–65

Key Details Tell children that they can find important details in the photos and text of a nonfiction selection. Point to the photo of Jack and Pepper. Say: *I see Jack has a carrot for Pepper and is patting him. Let's reread the page and draw a box around the sentence that tells who takes care of Pepper.* Guide children to draw a box around the answer. (Jack takes care of him.)

Key Details Point to the photo of Jack and Pepper and ask: *Is taking care of a horse an easy or hard job?* Guide children to reread the page and draw a box around the answer in the text. (Looking after a horse is a big job.)

Page 66

Key Details Have children reread the first paragraph. Explain that the text has stated that taking care of a horse is a big job. Ask: *Where does Jack go early in the morning?* Guide children to draw a box around the words that tell. (He and his father go to Pepper's stall.)

Expand Vocabulary Read aloud the first paragraph. Explain that a *stall* is a space in a building that horses sleep in at night. Guide children to look at the photo and circle the *stalls*. Ask: *How many* stalls *do you see in this photo?* (five)

Prior Knowledge Ⓐ Ⓒ Ⓣ Explain to children that *hay* is a type of grass that is cut and dried to feed some farm animals, including horses. Ask: *Who will eat the* hay? (Pepper)

Organization Ⓐ Ⓒ Ⓣ Explain to children that this selection is organized to show how Jack spends his day. Say: *The author uses sequence words such as* first, next, then, *and* finally *to show the sequence.* Reread the third paragraph with children. Ask: *What is the first thing Jack does in the morning?* Guide children to underline the words that tell. (First, Jack feeds him hay.) Next, have children point to the word *Then*. Ask: *What does Jack do next?* Guide children to place two lines under the words that tell. (Then he cleans the stall.)

Page 67

Expand Vocabulary Point to Pepper's coat in the photos on pages 66 and 67. Explain that a horse's *coat* is the hair that covers its body. Have children reread the first two sentences. Ask: *What word describes Pepper's* coat? Guide children to circle the word that tells. (brown)

Organization Ⓐ Ⓒ Ⓣ Have children reread the first paragraph. Ask: *What does Jack do after he takes care of Pepper in the morning?* Guide children to underline the text that tells. (Then Jack goes to school) Have children point to the sequence word *Then* and remind them that sequence words help tell the order of events in a selection.

Key Details Have children look at the photo and reread the caption. Remind children that they can get important details from a photo and caption in a nonfiction selection. Ask: *What does Jack feed Pepper in the afternoon?* Guide children to draw a box around the words that tell what Jack feeds Pepper. (more hay and water)

Page 68

Expand Vocabulary Have children reread the last paragraph. Explain that when you *exercise*, you move around to keep yourself healthy. Names some different forms of *exercise*. Ask: *Who helps Pepper get exercise?* Guide children to circle the word that tells. (Jack)

Key Details Have children look at the photo on page 68 and reread the caption. Ask: *What is Pepper doing in the photo?* Guide children to draw a box around the words that tells. (runs for exercise)

Page 69

Expand Vocabulary Explain to children that in order to ride a horse, you need to have a *saddle*. A *saddle* is a seat that keeps you from falling off the horse. Have children reread the first paragraph. Ask: *Who rides on a saddle?* (Jack, Mom)

Organization (A)(C)(T) Remind children to look for sequence words to help them undersand how the author organized the text. Read aloud the last paragraph. Ask: *What does Jack do at the end of the day to take care of Pepper?* Guide them to underline the words that tell. (gives Pepper more hay, more water) Ask: *What sequence word tells you this is what happens last?* (Finally)

Key Details Have children look at the photo on page 69 and reread the caption. Ask: *What does Pepper wear on his feet to keep them safe?* Guide children to draw a box around the word that tells. (horseshoes)

RESPOND TO READING

10–20 Minutes   RI.2.1   RI.2.5   SL2.1b   CCSS

Respond to "Taking Care of Pepper"

Read aloud the questions about "Taking Care of Pepper" on page 70 of the **Interactive Worktext**. Then read aloud the "Discussion Starter" for each of the questions. Guide children to work with a partner to answer the questions orally using the "Discussion Starters." Have children find text evidence to support their answers. Ask children to write the page number(s) on which they found the text evidence for each question.

1. *What does Jack do after he gets up early each day?* (Possible answers: I read that Jack takes care of Pepper by feeding him hay and water. Another way Jack takes care of Pepper is by cleaning his stall. Text Evidence: p. 66)

2. *How does Jack help Pepper get exercise during the day?* (Possible answers: I read that Pepper first gets exercise by walking around the field. Then Jack rides Pepper. Text Evidence: pp. 68, 69)

3. *What does Jack do after Pepper's ride?* (Possible answers: After the ride, Jack grooms Pepper with a brush. At the end of the day, Jack gives Pepper more hay and water. Text Evidence: p. 69)

After children discuss the questions on page 70, have them use the sentence starters to answer the question on page 71. Circulate and provide guidance.

 Quick Check Do children understand vocabulary in context? If not, review and reteach using the instruction on page 46.

Can children identify key details? If not, review and reteach using the instruction on page 46 and assign the Unit 1 Week 4 Key Details digital mini-lesson.

Can children write a response to "Taking Care of Pepper"? If not, first help children review their answers on page 70 and then use this information to help them fill in the sentence frames on page 71.

WEEK 4 LESSON 3

Objectives
- Access prior knowledge
- Understand and use new vocabulary words
- Read high-frequency words
- Read informational text

Materials
"People Helping Whales" Apprentice Leveled Reader
- High-Frequency Word Cards

☞ **Go Digital**
- Apprentice Level Reader eBook
- Downloadable High-Frequency Word Cards

Scaffolding for **Wonders** Approaching Leveled Reader

BEFORE READING

10–15 Minutes   SL. 2. 1a   SL. 2.6   L.2.6   RF.2.3f   CCSS

Introduce "People Helping Whales"

- Read the Essential Question on the title page of "People Helping Whales" **Apprentice Leveled Reader:** *How do we care for animals?*

- Read the title of the main read. Point to the cover. *What animal do we see on the cover?* (a whale) *Why do you think the whale is on the beach?* (It may be sick. It came too close to the shore.) *Let's read to learn more about whales and how people can care for them.*

High-Frequency Words

Display the **High-Frequency Word Cards** for the words *away, live, people, through, together,* and *water.* Use the Read/Spell/Write routine to teach each word. Guide partners to use each word in a sentence. Provide assistance reading the high-frequency words, as necessary.

Expand Vocabulary

Before reading "People Helping Whales," help children read the following words that they will encounter. Display each word below. Use the Define/Example/Ask routine. Tell children to look for the word later on as they read "People Helping Whales."

1 **crane** (page 13)

Define: a large machine used to lift heavy things

Example: The big *crane* lifts the heavy boxes onto the ship.

Ask: Where might you see a *crane?*

2 **groups** (page 6)

Define: a number of persons or things that belong together

Example: A *group* of kindergarten children is using the swing set.

Ask: What are some animals that live or travel in *groups?*

3 **pour** (page 10)

Define: to make liquid go from one thing to another

Example: I will *pour* milk into my cup.

Ask: What are some things that you *pour?*

4 **raft** (page 13)

Define: a kind of flat boat

Example: My dad helped me build a *raft* with logs.

Ask: How is a *raft* different from a sailboat?

5 **stranded** (page 8)

Define: to be left in a helpless position

Example: When our car broke down, we were *stranded* in another city.

Ask: How could a *stranded* person get off an island.

DURING READING

20–30 Minutes SL.2.2 RI.2.4 L.2.4a

Shared Reading

Tell children you will now read "People Helping Whales." Tell them to note the vocabulary and high-frequency words you just introduced as you read the story. Stop to model understanding of the story as you go.

Pages 2–3

High-Frequency Words Make sure children can read the high-frequency words *live* and *water*.

Comprehension Check Model beginning to read the book. Say: *The first thing I notice about this book is that it it has photographs of whales. When I begin to read, I see it tells facts about whales. I learn that whales are the biggest animals. I think this book will tell me more facts about whales. I will keep track of what I learn as I read.*

Vocabulary Read page 2. Focus on the word *biggest*. Say: *The text says that whales are the biggest animals. Which word tells us about the size of whales?* (biggest)

Pages 4–5

High-Frequency Words Make sure children can read the high-frequency word *through*.

Vocabulary On page 4 read "Whales have fat called blubber." Ask: *Which word in the sentence helps us understand the meaning of* blubber? (fat)

Comprehension Check *I will stop and think about what I've learned about whales. I know that whale's blubber helps keep them warm. I know that whales breathe air so that means they have to come up to the surface of the water.*

Pages 6–7

High-Frequency Words Make sure children can read the high-frequency word *together*.

Comprehension Check *The text says that most whales live in groups. I wonder how they are like other groups of animals that stay together. I wonder if they help each other find food.*

Pages 8–9

High-Frequency Words Make sure children can read the high-frequency word *people*.

Vocabulary Focus on the word *stranded*. Say: *The sentence before this one may give us clues about the meaning of the word* stranded. *Read the sentence* "Whales may swim too close to land." *Ask: What happens when a whale is stranded?* (The water is too shallow, and the whale can't swim back so it gets stuck on the sand.)

Pages 10–11

High-Frequency Words Make sure children can read the high-frequency word *away*.

Comprehension Check *I see now that the book is telling how to help whales that are stranded. These pages tell me that whales need to be kept wet and cool.*

Pages 12–13

Comprehension Check *I read on page 12 that people will move the whale. I know that whales need to live in the water so I think that the people will move the whale out to sea.*

Vocabulary On page 13 read "A crane lifts the whale." Ask children to point to the picture that shows the crane. Read *"It puts it on a raft."* Ask: *Which word tells the kind of boat the whale is put on?* (raft)

Pages 14–15

Comprehension Check *The story says that the whale is safe. I am going to think about what caused the whale to get stranded. I know that the whale swam too close to land and it got stuck. Then people came to help the whale by keeping it cool and wet. Other people used a crane and raft to lift the whale off the sand and take it out to sea. They cared for the whale and worked to get it back to its home.*

 Quick Check Can children understand vocabulary in context? If not, review and reteach using the instruction on page 46.

Can children read the high-frequency words in context? If not, review using the Read/Spell/Write

WEEK 4
LESSON

4

Objectives
- Understand complex text through close-reading
- Read informational text
- Recognize and understand key details
- Respond to the selection using text evidence to support ideas

Scaffolding for **Wonders** McGraw-Hill Reading Approaching Leveled Reader

Materials
- "People Helping Whales" Apprentice Leveled Reader
- Graphic Organizer: Key Details

☞ **Go** Digital
- **Apprentice Leveled Reader eBook**
- **Downloadable Graphic Organizer**
- **Key Details Mini-Lesson**

DURING READING

20–25 Minutes   SL.2.2   RI. 2.1   RI. 2.3   RI.2.4   CCSS

Tell children they will now reread the selection, "People Helping Whales." Review the vocabulary and high-frequency words they will encounter as they read.

Close Reading

Pages 2–3

Key Details Remind children that key details are information in the words and pictures that help us understand what we read. Reread pages 2 and 3. Ask what key details they learned on these pages. (Whales are the biggest animals and they live in the water.) Model filling in the Key Details Chart.

Genre **A C T** Point to the photo of the whale. Say: *In a nonfiction book, a lot of information can be found in the pictures.* Ask: *What does this photo tell you about whales?* (They are big with a tail and two fins. They have big mouths and eyes near the top of their heads.)

Pages 4–5

Key Details Reread pages 4 and 5. Ask: *What key detail on page 4 tells us how whales stay warm?* (They have fat called blubber that keeps them warm.) *What key detail on page 5 tells us how whales breathe?* (through a blowhole) Add this to the Key Details Chart.

Prior Knowledge **A C T** Help children use their prior knowledge of animals that live in the water to understand what they are reading. Ask: *Do fish need to come up out of the water to breathe air?* (no) *Do fish have blowholes?* (no) Point out that one of the things that makes a whale special is that it is a mammal that lives in the water, and mammals need to breathe air.

Genre **A C T** Focus on the way the text and photographs work together. Ask: *What are you learning about whales on page 5*? (A whale has blowholes to breathe.) *How does the picture help you understand the words?* (It shows a whale with a blowhole. You can see where the blowhole is and that water is coming out.)

Pages 6–7

Key Details Reread pages 6 and 7. Point to the whales and ask: *Do these whales live alone or in a group?* (a group) *What do the groups do together?* (swim) Help children record the details on their Key Details charts.

Organization **A C T** Point out that different kinds of whales appear on each page. Ask children to describe the whales in the photographs on pages 6 and 7. Have them turn back to pages 4 and 5. Say: *Which whales are most like the whales shown on pages 6 and 7. How are they alike?* (The whales on page 4 are most like the whales on pages 6 and 7. They are black and white. The whale on page 5 is different because it is gray.)

Pages 8–9

Key Details Reread page 8 and then point to the picture. Ask: *What happens if whales swim too close to land?* (They may get stranded.) Help children record these key details on their Key Details charts.

Pages 10–11

Key Details Before reading page 10, help children review what they wrote on their Key Details charts. Ask: *What do you know about the size of whales?* (They are the biggest animals.) *Where do whales live?* (in the water) *How do whales stay warm?* (They have fat called blubber.) *How do whales breathe?* (They breathe air through a blowhole.) *Let's keep reading to find out if the people can help the stranded whale.*

Pages 12–13

Key Details After reading page 12, ask: *Why will the people move the whale?* (It needs to be in the water to be safe.) *How do people use a crane to help the whale?* (The crane lifts the whale and puts it on the raft.)

Organization **ACT** Help children recognize that the focus of the book has changed. Instead of learning about what whales are like, they are learning how we can rescue whales. Ask: *What did you learn about whales in the beginning of this book?* (how big they are, how they stay warm, how they breath) *What are you learning about whales now?* (what happens to them when they get stranded and how to help them) *Find the page where the book changes.* (on page 8, when a whale got stranded)

Connection of Ideas **ACT** Point to the picture on page 13. *What does this picture show us about how the whale is being helped?* (The whale is lifted off the sand and put on the raft.) *Do you think the people could have helped the whale get back into the water without the crane? Why or why not?* (No, the whale is too big to be moved by the people without the help of the crane.)

Pages 14–15

Key Details Reread page 15. Ask: *Were the people successful in helping the whale?* (yes) *What key detail lets you know this?* (The whale was able to swim away.) Have children record this key detail on their Key Details charts.

AFTER READING

10–15 Minutes   RI.2.1   L2.4d   RF. 2.4b   W.2.8   CCSS

Respond to Reading

Compare Texts Guide children in comparing the way people cared for the stranded whale in "People Helping Whales" with the way Jack cared for his horse in "Taking Care of Pepper." Help children think about the needs of both animals. Then ask: *How do you care for animals?*

Text Evidence

Have partners work together to answer questions on page 16. Remind children to use their Key Details charts.

Key Details (People can help keep the whales wet and cool.)

Vocabulary (The words "blow" and "hole" are in the word "blowhole.")

Write About Reading (People help stranded whales by keeping them wet and cool until a crane can help lift them onto a raft and get them back into the sea.)

Read "Working With Animals"

Encourage children to read the paired selection "Working With Animals" on pages 17–19. Have them summarize the selection and compare it to "People Helping Whales." Have them work with a partner to answer the "Make Connections" questions on page 19.

Independent Reading

Have pairs of children reread "People Helping Whales." Have them talk about how the people helped the stranded whales.

✓ *Quick Check* Can students identify Key Details? If not, review and reteach using the instruction on page 46 and assign the Unit 1 Week 4 Key Details digital mini-lesson.

Can students respond to the selection using text evidence? If not, provide sentence frames to help them organize their ideas.

Objectives
- Review weekly vocabulary words
- Review key details
- Write an opinion about an author's use of key details

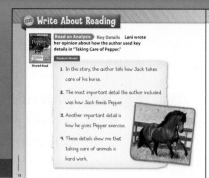

Materials
- Visual Vocabulary Cards: 25–32
- Interactive Worktext, pp. 72–73
- Assessment Book, pp. 16–17

☞ **Go** Digital
- Visual Vocabulary Cards
- Key Details Mini-Lesson
- Interactive eWorktext
- eAssessment

REVIEW AND RETEACH

5–10 Minutes   L.2.4a   RI.2.1   RI.2.5   CCSS

Weekly Vocabulary

Display one **Visual Vocabulary Card** at a time and guide children to use the vocabulary word in a sentence. If children have difficulty creating a sentence, have them find the word in "Taking Care of Pepper" or "People Helping Whales" and use context clues to define the vocabulary word.

Comprehension: Key Details

 I Do   Write and say: *Jill wants to ride her new bike. She got this bike for her birthday. The bike has a flat tire. She will ride her skateboard.* Ask: *Why can't Jill ride her bike? I can look for key details to learn the answer.* Circle "The bike has a flat tire," and write *key detail.* Say: *Jill can't ride her bike because it has a flat tire. I can tell that this is a key detail because it gives me important information that can help me answer other questions.*

We Do   Display: *Sam just got home from school. He unpacks his backpack. He is hungry. Sam's mom will fix him a snack.* Ask: *What key detail tells us why Sam's mom will fix him a snack?* (He is hungry.) *How can you tell?* (I read it in the second sentence.)

You Do   Display: *Carlos wakes up early. He does not feel well. His mother takes his temperature. He has a fever. His mother calls the doctor. Later that day, they visit the doctor. The doctor says James will be fine after a few days of rest.* Have partners take turns asking questions and having each other find key details in the story.

WRITE ABOUT READING

25–35 Minutes   W.2.2   W.2.8   W.4.9   CCSS

Read an Analysis

- Guide children to look back at "Taking Care of Pepper" in the **Interactive Worktext**. Have volunteers review the key details they marked on page 65 and summarize the text. Repeat with pages 66–69. *How did the author use key details in "Taking Care of Pepper"?*

- Read aloud the directions on page 72. Read aloud the student model. *This student's work is not a summary. It is her opinion of how the author used key details in "Taking Care of Pepper."*

- *When you write an opinion, you should include key details that support your beliefs about the text. Read Lani's first sentence. What does Lani say this story is about?* (Jack takes care of his horse, Pepper.)

- *Read the second sentence. What does Lani think is the most important detail from the story?* (how Jack feeds Pepper) Review with children that this is Lani's opinion. Ask: *What do you think is the most important detail from the story?* (Answers will vary.)

- Guide children to point to the third sentence. *What other detail does Lani think is important?* (how Jake gives Pepper exercise) *Point to the place in the story where this detail comes from.*

- Model analyzing how the author used details to make a summary. Read the last sentence that Lani wrote. *Why is this sentence a good ending?* (Lani explained what the details showed her.)

Write an Analysis

Guided Writing Read the writing prompt on page 73 together. Guide children to review their Key Details charts for "People Helping Whales." Have children use their charts to complete the sentence starters. Children can also write an opinion using another selection previously read this week.

Peer Conference Guide children to read their opinions to a partner. Listeners should summarize the strongest details that support the beginning, middle, and ending sentences. They should discuss any parts that are unclear.

Teacher Conference Check children's writing for complete sentences and whether they included details from the story. Review the ending sentence by asking, *Did the author use details to support her opinion?* If necessary, guide children to revise their sentence by adding more details.

Level Up

Apprentice Leveled Reader → **Approaching Leveled Reader**

Interactive Worktext → **Reading/Writing Workshop**

IF children read the Apprentice Level Reader and the **Interactive Worktext** Shared Read fluently and answer the Respond to Reading questions

THEN read together the Approaching Level Reader main selection and the **Reading/Writing Workshop** Shared Read from *Reading Wonders*.

Writing Rubric

	4	3	2	1
Text Evidence	Includes three or more details from the text.	Includes two or more details from the text.	Includes only one detail from the text.	No text evidence is cited.
Writing Style	Writes in complete sentences. Uses correct spelling and grammar.	Uses complete sentences. Writing has spelling and grammar errors.	Few complete sentences. There are many spelling and grammar errors.	Writing is not accurate or in complete sentences.

ASSESSMENT

Weekly Assessment

Have children complete the Weekly Assessment using **Assessment** book pages 16–17.

Objectives
• Develop oral language
• Build background about families working together
• Understand and use weekly vocabulary
• Read an expository text

Materials
Interactive Worktext, pp. 74–81
• Visual Vocabulary Cards: 33–40
• High-Frequency Word Cards

☞ **Go** Digital
• Interactive eWorktext
• Visual Vocabulary Cards

Scaffolding for **Wonders** Reading/Writing Workshop

WEEKLY CONCEPT

5-10 Minutes   SL.2.1b SL.2.4

Talk About It

Essential Question Read aloud the Essential Question on page 74 of the **Interactive Worktext:** *What happens when families work together?* Explain that families often work together. Say: *Families work together to get things done. They work together to cook, clean, shop, do laundry, and other tasks at home. There are many different ways families work together.*

• Discuss the photograph on page 74. Ask: *What is happening in the picture?* (A girl and her mom are planting flowers in their garden.) Have children look at the picture to see if there are any tools they are using. (watering can, trowel, gardening gloves)

I Do Say: *I am going to look at the photo and think about how families work together. The girl is working with her mom to plant flowers. I will write on the web on page 75 that helping each other in the garden is one way families can work together.*

We Do Say: *Let's think about other ways families work together. In some families, members of the family cook together. They help each other prepare meals.* Guide children to think of other ways families work together. Then have children choose one way families work together to add to their web.

You Do Guide partners to work together to talk about how their families work together. Have children use words from the web to start their sentences: *Families work together to _____.*

REVIEW VOCABULARY

10–15 Minutes   L.2.5a L.2.6 RF.2.3f

Review Weekly Vocabulary Words

• Use the **Visual Vocabulary Cards** to review the weekly vocabulary.

• Read together the directions on page 76 of the **Interactive Worktext**. Then complete the activity.

❶ **choose** Display a variety of writing utensils. Invite children to come up one at a time and *choose* a writing utensil. Have children use the following oral sentence starter: *I choose a _____.* (pencil, pen) Then have children suggest synonyms for *choose* as you list them on the board. (Possible answers: pick, select)

❷ **customers** Have volunteers act out being a sales clerk at a store while other children stand in line as *customers*. Invite the sales clerk to call out, *"May I please help the next* customer?" Then guide children to complete the activity. (Possible answers: have a sale, create an advertisement, make a commercial)

❸ **chores** Invite volunteers to suggest *chores* that children sometimes do at school. Have children use this sentence frame: *_____ and _____ are* chores *someone might have to do at school.* (hand out supplies, feed a class pet) Then have children use this oral sentence frame to complete the activity: *_____ and _____ are chores someone might have to do at home.* (wash dishes, clean bedroom)

❹ **jobs** Write the word *jobs*. Ask: *What is my job?* (teacher) Write *teacher* under *jobs*. Invite volunteers to suggest other *jobs* as you list them. Have children use the following sentence frame: *_____ and _____ are two jobs I would like to have when I grow up.* (Possible answers: firefighter, lawyer, writer)

5 **tools** Write the word *tools*. Invite volunteers to name different *tools* their families have at home as you list them. Then guide children to discuss what *tools* firefighters use. Help children write their answers. (<u>Possible answers</u>: ax, hoses, fire extinguisher)

6 **check** Discuss with children some of the other meanings of the word *check*, including a restaurant bill, a type of payment, a pattern of squares, and so on. Then have children use this oral sentence frame: *I check my backpack for _____ when I leave school.* (<u>Possible answers</u>: homework, books, lunchbox)

7 **spend** Write the word *spend* on the board. Have volunteers suggest things that people *spend* money on. Then have children do the activity using this oral sentence starter: *I might* spend *my money on a _____.* (<u>Possible answers</u>: game, snack, toy)

8 **cost** Have children suggest items that do not *cost* a lot of money. Assist children as they draw their picture. Then have them tell about their picture, using the following sentence frame: *A _____ does not* cost *a lot of money.* (Answers will vary.)

High-Frequency Words

Have children look at page 77 in the **Interactive Worktext**. Help them read, spell, and write each high-frequency word. Guide partners to use each word in a sentence. Then read the story aloud with children. Guide partners to work together to reread the story and circle the high-frequency words. (buy, things, at, had, only, Each) Listen in and provide assistance reading the high-frequency words, as necessary.

ELL ENGLISH LANGUAGE LEARNERS

Display the **High-Frequency Word Cards** for: *had, only, each, at, buy, things*. Write a sentence with each word on the board. Have children echo-read each sentence, and point out the high-frequency word. Then ask them to use the word in a new sentence.

Read "Families Work!"

- Have children turn to page 78 in the **Interactive Worktext** and read aloud the Essential Question. Point to the photos. Say: *What jobs do you think the adults in these pictures have?* (The women is a doctor. The man is a firefighter.) *Let's read to find out about the jobs these family members have and how the family works together.* Have children echo-read the title.

- Read the story together. Note that the weekly vocabulary words are highlighted in yellow. Expand Vocabulary words are highlighted in blue.

- As children read, have them use the "My Notes" section on page 78 to write questions they have. Children can also write words they don't understand or things they want to remember. Model how to use the "My Notes" section. *When I read the first paragraph on page 78, I find out Ellen Yung is a doctor and works long hours. I wonder why a person would work so much. I will write a question about this in the "My Notes" section and then look for the answer as I read.*

ELL ENGLISH LANGUAGE LEARNERS

As you read together, have children highlight parts of the text they have questions about. After reading, review the questions children have. Then help them locate the answers to their questions in the text.

 Quick Check Can children understand the weekly vocabulary in context? If not, review vocabulary using the **Visual Vocabulary Cards** before teaching Lesson 2.

Can children read high-frequency words in context? If not, review using the Read/Spell/Write routine and the High-Frequency Word Cards.

LESSON 2

- Read an expository text
- Understand complex text through close reading
- Recognize and understand key details
- Respond to the selection using text evidence to support ideas

Scaffolding for **Wonders** Reading/Writing Workshop

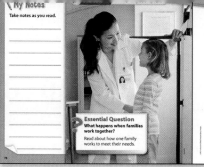
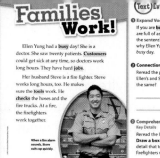

Interactive Worktext, pp. 78–83

☞ **Go Digital**
- Interactive eWorktext
- Key Details Mini-Lesson

REREAD COMPLEX TEXT

20–25 Minutes   L.2.4a   RI.2.1   RI.2.5   **CCSS**

Close Reading: "Families Work!"

Reread "Families Work!" from **Interactive Worktext** pages 78–81 with children. As you read together, discuss important passages in the text. Guide children to respond to questions using evidence from the text.

Pages 78–79

Expand Vocabulary Explain to children that if you are *busy,* you are full of activity. Say: *On a* busy *day, you may have many different things you need to get done.* Reread the first paragraph and ask: *Why did Ellen Yung have a* busy *day?* Guide children to circle the sentence that tells. (She saw twenty patients.)

Connection of Ideas **ACT** Have children echo-read the page with you. Say: *We read about Ellen's job. She works long hours because she has so many patients. We also read about Steve's job. He works long hours, too.* Say: *I think Ellen's and Steve's jobs are the same because they both work long hours.* Guide children to write the answer. (Possible answer: They both work long hours.)

Key Details Explain to children that key details are the most important details of a selection. Say: *In an informational text, key details may be facts or explanations that help readers understand the topic. We can often find key details in the text of a selection. We can also use a selection's illustrations or photos to find key details that tell us more about a topic.* Read the last paragraph aloud and ask: *Where do firefighters all work together?* Guide children to draw a box around the text that tells. (at a fire)

Page 80

Key Details Remind children that key details are important pieces of information that tell us more about a topic. Reread the first paragraph aloud. Ask: *What does the family do at home?* Guide children to draw a box around the words that tell. (the family works together)

Connection of Ideas **ACT** Say: *We know that Zac wanted a laptop. We also know that the family needs a new washing machine so they can have clean clothes.* Have children reread the last paragraph and ask: *Why did the family have to choose between a washing machine and a laptop?* Guide children to underline the sentence that tells. (They could only spend money on one item.)

Expand Vocabulary Explain to children that the word *bought* is the past tense of the word *buy.* Tell children that if you *bought* something, you paid money to own it. Have children reread the last paragraph and guide children to circle the words that tell what the family bought. (a washing machine)

Page 81

Genre **ACT** Explain to children that expository texts often use text features such as photos, captions, graphs, and charts that give more information so readers can better understand a topic. Point to the chart at the top of the page and say: *This chart lists some needs and wants. Needs are things we must have to survive. Wants are things that would be nice to have, but that we don't need to survive. What is the first thing listed under "Needs"?* (water) *What is the first think listed under "Wants"?* (skateboard)

Key Details Have children reread the chart. Ask: *Is clothing something you need or something you want?* Remind children to read the heading of each column of the chart before they read the items listed under the headings. Guide children to write their answer. (need)

Connection of Ideas Say: *We read that when Zac's parents work hard, they bring home money.* Have children reread the paragraph and ask: *What does the money that Zac's parents bring home pay for?* Guide children to underline the words that tell. (their needs and wants)

Expand Vocabulary Explain to children that if something happens in the *future,* it happens at a time after the present. Read the paragraph on the page aloud. Ask: *What will the family buy in the* future? (a laptop)

RESPOND TO READING

15–20 Minutes   SL.2.1a   RI.2.1   RI.2.5

Respond to "Families Work!"

Guide children read the questions about "Families Work!" on page 82 of the **Interactive Worktext**. Then read aloud the "Discussion Starter" for each of the questions. Guide children to work with a partner to answer the questions orally using the "Discussion Starters." Have children find text evidence to support their answers. Ask children to write the page number(s) on which they found the text evidence for each question.

1. *How do Ellen and Steve help the family?* (<u>Possible answers</u>: I read that Ellen is a doctor. Steve is a firefighter. They work hard to bring home money. <u>Text Evidence</u>: p. 79, 81)

2. *How does the family work together at home?* (<u>Possible answers</u>: The family does chores such as mopping and laundry. Mom makes a list of needs and wants. <u>Text Evidence</u>: p. 80)

3. *How does the family work together to decide what to buy?* (<u>Possible answers</u>: Zac wanted a laptop. The family also needed a washing machine. The family decided to buy what they needed most. <u>Text Evidence</u>: p. 81)

After children discuss the questions on page 82, have them use the sentence starters to answer the question on page 83. Circulate and provide guidance.

✓ *Quick Check* Do children understand vocabulary in context? If not, review and reteach using the instruction on page 56.

Can children identify key details? If not, review and reteach using the instruction on page 56 and assign the Unit 1 Week 5 digital mini-lesson.

Can children write a response to "Families Work!" If not, review the sentence starters and prompt children to respond orally. Help them write their responses.

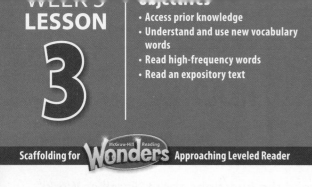

• Access prior knowledge
• Understand and use new vocabulary words
• Read high-frequency words
• Read an expository text

Materials
• "Families at Work" Apprentice Leveled Reader
• High-Frequency Word Cards

☞ **Go** Digital
• Apprentice Leveled Reader eBook
• Downloadable High-Frequency Word Cards

Scaffolding for **Wonders** Approaching Leveled Reader

BEFORE READING

10–15 Minutes   SL.2.1a   SL. 2.6   L.2.6   L.2.5a   RF.2.3f CCSS

Introduce "Families at Work"

• Read the Essential Question on the title page of "Families at Work" **Apprentice Leveled Reader:** *What happens when families work together?*

• Read the title of the main read. Point to the cover. *What do you think this family is doing?* (making cookies) *How is the family working together?* (The mother adds milk to a mixture while one daughter holds the bowl and another daughter stirs the milk in.) *Let's read more about how families work together.*

High-Frequency Words

Display the **High-Frequency Word Cards** for the words *buy, do, help, little, they,* and *work.* Use the Read/Spell/Write routine to teach each word. Guide partners to use each word in a sentence. Provide assistance reading the high-frequency words, as necessary.

Expand Vocabulary

Before reading "Families at Work," help children read the following words that they will encounter. Display each word below. Use the Define/Example/Ask routine. Tell children to look for the word later on as they read "Families at Work."

❶ deliver (page 3)

   Define: to bring something to a place or person

   Example: I have to *deliver* these art supplies to Ms. Herman's classroom.

   Ask: What might you *deliver* to a home?

❷ owners (page 9)

   Define: the people who own something

   Example: Mrs. and Mr. Willis are *owners* of a store.

   Ask: Who here is a pet *owner*?

❸ special (page 4)

   Define: different from others in a certain way

   Example: Mom made a *special* dinner for my birthday.

   Ask: What is a *special* day for you?

❹ stand (page 7)

   Define: a small place where things are sold

   Example: We buy apples from a farmer's *stand*.

   Ask: What would you like to sell from a *stand*?

DURING READING

20–30 Minutes   SL.2.2   RI.2.1   RI.2.2   RI.2.4   L.2.4a CCSS

Shared Reading

Tell children you will now read "Families at Work." Tell them to note the vocabulary and high-frequency words you just introduced as you read the story. Stop to model understanding of the story as you go.

 Pages 2–3

High-Frequency Words Make sure children can read the high-frequency words *do, help, they,* and *work.*

Comprehension Check Model beginning to read the story. Say: *The first thing I notice is that kids do different jobs. Some do chores done around the house. Some do jobs for money. As I read, I'll look for different kinds of jobs that kids and families do.*

Vocabulary Focus on the difference between a *job* and a *chore*. *Ask: Why are the kids taking out the trash ?* (to help out at home or school) *Why is the boy delivering news papers?* (It is a job he has so that he can make money.)

Vocabulary Ask if children know what a newspaper is. (something you read that tells what is happening in the world or your town) Explain that in some places, people get newspapers delivered to their homes rather than buying them at a store or reading them online.

Pages 4–5

High-Frequency Words Make sure children can read the high-frequency word *little*.

Vocabulary After reading page 4, ask: *What is special about the clothes these people have on?* (They are clothes that show people you work at the store and should only be worn at work.)

Comprehension Check *On page 4, I learn that big kids can work in stores. That is different sort of work from delivering papers and doing chores. It's a job where you go to a certain place to work.*

Pages 6–7

High-Frequency Words Make sure children can read the high-frequency word *buy*.

Vocabulary After reading page 6, ask: *What are the kids going to do with the stand?* (sell lemonade) *What is something else kids could sell at a stand?* (<u>Possible answers</u>: iced tea, cookies or other baked goods)

Comprehension Check *On page 7, I learn that adults in a family can help kids do some jobs, such as building something with tools. As I read, I am going to notice what jobs people of different ages do.*

Pages 8–9

Comprehension Check *I read on page 8 about how moms and dads can help kids cook. The picture shows the family working together. On page 9, I see that the girl is helping out the owners of the house by feeding their pet cat when they are away. I can also think about ways I can help other people do things around their house to help them.*

Pages 10–11

Comprehension Check *I read on page 10 and 11 about different kinds of work that big kids can do. These kids can do work that little kids cannot do. It would be hard for little kids to walk five dogs at one time. It would also be hard for a little kid to push another kid on a tire swing.*

Pages 12–13

Comprehension Check *I will stop here to think about what I have read so far. I read that there are chores kids do around the house to help out their families. I have also read that both little kids and big kids can do different kinds of jobs to help make extra money. Sometimes the moms and dads help. On pages 12 and 13, the pictures show me that big kids can babysit. The text tells me that they can feed babies or read to little kids.*

Pages 14–15

Vocabulary Focus on the word *teamwork*. Ask: What is teamwork? (working together). *How is the family doing on in this picture showing teamwork?* (They are wrapping gifts together. The boy is holding the paper while the girl tapes.)

Comprehension Check *The story tells me that there are big jobs and little jobs that families can do. Sometimes kids will need the help of parents and sometimes we can work on our own. Kids can do a lot, no matter how old they are. There is always a way for someone to help out. I just read about what teamwork is. One thing I like about teamwork is that everybody in a family gets to work together. I can think of different chores around the house that I can do alone or with others to help out my family.*

 Quick Check Can children understand vocabulary in context? If not, review and reteach using the instruction on page 56 and assign the Unit 1 Week 5 digital mini lesson.

Can children read the high-frequency words in context? If not, review using the Read/Spell/Write routine and the High-Frequency Word Cards.

WEEK 5
LESSON
4

Objectives
• Understand complex text through close-reading
• Read an expository text
• Recognize and understand key details
• Respond to the selection using text evidence to support ideas

Materials
"Families at Work" Apprenteice Leveled Reader
• Graphic Organizer: Key Details

☞ **Go** Digital
• Approaching Leveled Reader eBook
• Downloadable Graphic Organizer
• Key Details Mini-Lesson

Scaffolding for **Wonders** Approaching Leveled Reader

DURING READING

20–30 Minutes   RI. 2.1   RI. 2.2   RI. 2.7   CCSS

Tell children they will now reread the selection, *Families at Work*. Review the vocabulary and high-frequency words that they will encounter as they read.

Close Reading

Pages 2–3

Key Details Remind children that key details are the most important details of a selection. Explain that key details give more information about the selection. Say: *key details may be facts or information that help readers understand the topic. When we read, we can find key details in the text and photos.* Reread page 2 with children and ask: *How can kids work to help out at home and at school?* (Kids can do chores.) Reread page 3 with children and ask: *How can kids make money?* (Kids can have jobs.) Model recording these answers on the Key Details chart.

Genre Ⓐ Ⓒ Ⓣ Remind children that in expository text additional information can be found in the pictures or other features. Ask: *How does this photograph help you understand how this boy delivers newspapers?* (The boy delivers newspapers on his bike by steering the bike with one hand and throwing the papers with the other hand.) *Why do you think the boy uses a bicycle to deliver the papers rather delivering them on foot?* (Possible answers: It is faster and he can go farther.)

Pages 4–5

Key Details Reread page 4 with children and ask: *What can big kids do for work that little kids cannot do?* (Big kids can work in stores.) *What kind of store is this big kid working in?* (He is working in a store that sells tools, such as hammers.)

Connection of Ideas Ⓐ Ⓒ Ⓣ Have children look at the picture and say: *We know that people who work in a store sometimes wear special clothes. What special clothing are the people in this picture wearing?* (They are wearing red vests with name tags on them. They are also wearing matching shirts and pants.) *Why do you think these people wear special clothes in the store?* (so people who come into the store will know who the workers are) *Who do you think the man standing next to the boy is?* (He is another worker at the store. He might be the boy's boss.)

Key Details Reread page 5 with children and ask: *What is one thing kids can sell?* (lemonade)

Genre Ⓐ Ⓒ Ⓣ Ask: *How does the photo help you understand more about how the kids will sell lemonade?* (One girl is pouring lemonade. There are lemons on the table. There is a sign telling the price of the lemonade.) *How much will the kids sell the lemonade for?* (50 cents)

Pages 6–7

Key Details Reread pages 6 and 7 with children. Ask: *How can moms and dads help kids who want to sell lemonade?* (They can help make the stand.) Help children record this information on their Key Details charts.

Connection of Ideas Ⓐ Ⓒ Ⓣ Ask: *How is having a lemonade stand the same as working in a store?* (In both jobs, you are selling things to people.) *How is it different from working in a store?* (Kids and their families do everything on their own. They make their own stand and their own things to sell.)

Pages 8–9

Key Details Reread page 8 with children and ask: *How else can moms and dads help kids with a lemonade stand?* (They can help make cookies to sell at the stand.) Help children record this in their Key Details charts.

Pages 10–11

Connection of Ideas **A** **C** **T** Reread pages 10 and 11 with children. Point to the photo on page 10. Ask: *Why is it a good idea for only big kids to walk dogs?* (You need to be strong to be able to handle that many dogs.)

Organization **A** **C** **T** Point out that the text is partly organized according to jobs that big kids can do and jobs that little kids can do. Ask: *What are the jobs on these pages?* (walking dogs and babysitting) Ask: *What kinds of kids can do these?* (big kids) *What else could big kids do?* (work in a store) *What are good jobs for little kids?* (taking out trash, lemonade stand, feeding pets)

Pages 12–13

Key Details Reread pages 12 and 13 with children. Ask: *What types of things do babysitters do?* (feed babies and read to kids) Add this to the Key Details charts.

Pages 14–15

Key Details Reread pages 14 and 15 with children and ask: *What kinds of jobs can families do?* (Families can do big jobs and little jobs.) *How is this family working together?* (They are wrapping presents together.) *Is everyone in the photo helping?* (yes) Invite children to add this last detail to their Key Details charts.

AFTER READING

10–15 Minutes   RI.2.1   L.2.4d   RF. 2.4a   W.2.8   **CCSS**

Respond to Reading

Compare Texts Guide children in comparing the information in "Families at Work" with the information in "Families Work!" Help children think about different jobs and chores people in a family do. Then ask: *What happens when people in a family work together?*

Summarize Have children turn to page 16 and guide them in summarizing the selection. (Answers should include key details about families at work.)

Text Evidence

Have partners work together to answer questions on page 16. Remind children to use their Key Details charts.

Key Details (Moms and dads can help make the stand and bake cookies.)

Vocabulary (The text reads, "Big kids can babysit. They can feed a baby." The picture shows a kid feeding a baby its bottle. These clues tell us that *babysit* means to take care of a child or baby.)

Write About Reading (Answers will vary but should tell about how some of the families in the book work together.)

Read "A Family Sawmill"

Encourage children to read the paired selection "A Family Sawmill" on pages 17–19. Have them summarize the selection and compare it to "Families at Work." Have them work with a partner to answer the "Make Connections" questions on page 19.

Independent Reading

Have pairs of children reread "Families at Work." Have them talk about different ways that families work together.

 Quick Check **Can students identify key details? If not, review and reteach using the instruction on page 56 and assign the Unit 1 Week 5 digital mini-lesson.**

Can students respond to the selection using text evidence? If not, provide sentence frames to help them organize their ideas.

Objectives
- Review weekly vocabulary words
- Review key details
- Write an analysis about an author's use of key details in a selection

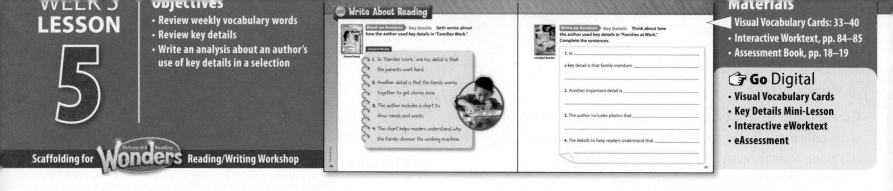

Materials
- Visual Vocabulary Cards: 33–40
- Interactive Worktext, pp. 84–85
- Assessment Book, pp. 18–19

☞ **Go** Digital
- Visual Vocabulary Cards
- Key Details Mini-Lesson
- Interactive eWorktext
- eAssessment

Scaffolding for **Wonders** Reading/Writing Workshop

REVIEW AND RETEACH

5–10 Minutes   RI.2.1   RI.2.5   L.2.4a

Weekly Vocabulary

Display one **Visual Vocabulary Card** at a time and guide children to use the vocabulary word in a sentence. If children have difficulty creating a sentence, have them find the word in "Families Work!" or "Families at Work" and use context clues in the passage to define the vocabulary word.

Comprehension: Key Details

I Do   Write and say: *Ben's family is going on a picnic. Ben is getting some games to take with them. They will have a picnic at the lake. They will go for a hike.* Ask: *Where is Ben's family going? I can look for key details to find the answer.* Circle: "on a picnic" Write: *key detail.* Say: *Ben's family is going on a picnic. I can tell this is a key detail because it gives me important information about the story.*

We Do   Display: *Anna and Kate will camp in Anna's back yard. Anna's mom will help set up the tent. Anna and Kate like to sleep in a tent. Anna has two flashlights to help them read at night.* Ask: *What key detail tells us who will help set up the tent?* (Anna's mom) *How can you tell?* (I read it in the second sentence.)

You Do   Display: *Ben and his brother Ethan like to collect rocks. They find rocks at the park. They dig up rocks in their backyard. They have many kinds of rocks. They keep their rocks in a special display case.* Guide one partner to ask a question and the other partner to find a key detail that helps answer it. Have partners switch and discuss their answers.

WRITE ABOUT READING

25–35 Minutes   W.2.2   W.2.8   W.4.9

Read an Analysis

- Guide children to look back at "Families Work!" in the **Interactive Worktext**. Have volunteers review the key details they marked on page 79. Repeat with pages 80–81. *How did the author use key details in the selection?*

- Read aloud the directions on page 84. Read aloud the student model. *This student's work is not a summary. It is an analysis, or description, of how the author used key details in "Families Work!"*

- *When you write an analysis, you should include key details from the text. Read Beth's first sentence. Circle the details.* (the parents work hard) In what part of the story do you learn this detail? (the beginning)

- *Read the second sentence. Draw a box around the details from the story you see in Beth's writing.* (the family works together to get chores done) *What part of the story is she writing about?* (the middle)

- *Guide children to point to the third sentence. What information does Beth include in this sentence?* (The author included a chart to show needs and wants.)

- Model analyzing how the author used key details. Read the last sentence that Beth wrote. *Why is this sentence a good ending?* (Beth writes how the chart helps readers understand that needs are more important than wants.)

Write an Analysis

Guided Writing Read the writing prompt on page 85 together. Guide children to review their Key Details charts for "Families at Work." Have children use their charts to complete the sentence starters. Children can also write an analysis using another selection previously read this week.

Peer Conference Guide children to read their analysis to a partner. Listeners should summarize the strongest details that support the beginning, middle and ending sentences. They should discuss any parts that are unclear.

Teacher Conference Check children's writing for complete sentences and whether they included details from the story. Review the ending sentence and ask: *Did the author use details to support the story?* If necessary, guide children to revise their sentence by adding more details.

▲ Approaching Leveled Reader

▲ Reading/Writing Workshop

Apprentice Leveled Reader

▲ Interactive Worktext

IF children read the Apprentice Level Reader and the **Interactive Worktext** Shared Read fluently and answer the Respond to Reading questions

THEN read together the Approaching Level Reader main selection and the **Reading/Writing Workshop** Shared Read from *Reading Wonders*. Have children take notes as they read, using self-stick notes. Then ask and answer questions about their notes.

Writing Rubric

	4	3	2	1
Text Evidence	Includes three or more details from the text.	Includes two or more details from the text.	Includes only one detail from the text.	No text evidence is cited.
Writing Style	Writes in complete sentences. Uses correct spelling and grammar.	Uses complete sentences. Writing has spelling and grammar errors.	Few complete sentences. There are many spelling and grammar errors.	Writing is not accurate or in complete sentences.

ASSESSMENT

Weekly Assessment

Have children complete the Weekly Assessment using **Assessment** book pages 18–19.

▶ **Unit Assessment,**
pages 122 –130

▶ **Fluency Assessment,**
pages 234 – 239

▶ **Exit Test,**
pages 178 – 186

Unit 1 Assessment

✔ COMPREHENSION	✔ VOCABULARY:
• Key Details RL.2.1	• Context Clues L.2.4a
• Character, Setting, Events RL.2.3, RL.2.5	
• Character, Setting, Events RL.2.3, RL.2.5	
• Key Details RI.2.1	
• Key Details RI.2.1	

Using Assessment and Writing Scores

⟳ RETEACH	IF ...	THEN ...
COMPREHENSION	Students answer 0–7 multiple-choice items correctly ...	... reteach tested skills using instruction on pages 364–375.
VOCABULARY	Students answer 0–3 multiple-choice items correctly ...	... reteach tested skills using instruction on page 364.
WRITING	Students score mostly 1–2 on weekly Write About Reading rubrics throughout the unit ...	... reteach writing using instruction on pages 376–377.

⬆ LEVEL UP	IF ...	THEN ...
COMPREHENSION	Students answer 8–10 multiple-choice items correctly ...	... have students read the *People Saving Whales* Approaching Leveled Reader. Use the Level Up lesson on page 58.
WRITING	Students score mostly 3–4 on weekly Write About Reading rubrics throughout the unit ...	... use the Level Up Write About Reading lesson on page 59 to have students compare two selections from the unit.

Fluency Assessment

Conduct assessments individually using the differentiated fluency passages in **Assessment**. Students' expected fluency goal for this Unit is 41–61 WCPM with an accuracy rate of 95% or higher.

Exit Test

If a student answers 13–15 multiple choice items correctly on the Unit Assessment, administer the Unit 1 Exit Test at the end of Week 6.

Time to Exit

Exit Text

If...

Students answer 13–15 multiple choice items correctly...

Fluency Assessment

If...

Students achieve their Fluency Assessment goal for the unit...

Level Up Lessons

If...

Students are successful applying close reading skills with the Approaching Leveled Reader in Week 6...

If...

Students score mostly 4–5 on the Level Up Write About Reading assignment...

Foundational Skills Kit

If...

Students have mastered the Unit 1 benchmark skills in the Foundational Skills Kit and *Reading Wonders* Adaptive Learning...

Then...

... consider exiting the student from *Reading WonderWorks* materials into the Approaching Level of *Reading Wonders*.

WEEK 6

▶ **Read Approaching Leveled Reader**

Approaching Leveled Reader

Apprentice Leveled Reader

▶ **Write About Reading**

Interactive Worktext Shared Read

Apprentice Leveled Reader

Apprentice to Approaching Level

L.2.5   RI.2.10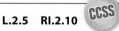

People Helping Whales

Before Reading

Preview Discuss what children remember about whales and how people help care for them. Tell them they will be reading a more challenging version of "People Helping Whales."

Vocabulary Use the routines on the **Visual Vocabulary Cards** to review the Weekly Vocabulary words. Use pages 44 to review the Expand Vocabulary words.

A C T During Reading

▶ **Specific Vocabulary** Review with children the following science words that are new to this level: *tons* (page 2), *orcas* (page 3), *pods* (page 6), *shore* (page 8), *beach* (page 8). Provide the meaning of each word for children. Model how to use available context clues to determine each word's meaning, and use photos when possible.

▶ **Genre** Remind children that informational texts, such as "People Helping Whales", often have photographs with captions that provide additional information that is not in the text. Point out the inset photo on page 3 and read the caption. Ask: *What is another name for orcas?* (killer whales) *How do you know?* (I read it in the caption.) Now point out the photo on page 8 and have children read the caption. Ask: *Why is it dangerous for a whale to be stuck on the beach?* (Whales cannot live on the beach for long.)

▶ **Connection of Ideas** Children may be confused by the text on page 10 that says people must be careful to not get water in a whale's blowhole when the photo on page 3 shows a whale shooting water out of its blowhole. Explain that a whale's blowhole is similar to a person's nose. Ask: *Can you breathe water in through your nose?* (no) *What could happen if you did?* (I could cough and choke.) *Just like people need to not bring water in through their noses, whales need to not bring water in through their blowholes. It can be dangerous.*

After Reading

Ask children to complete the Respond to Reading on page 16 after they have finished reading. Children may need additional support with the vocabulary strategy question. Provide help, as needed.

Write About Reading

RI.3.9   W.4.9

Read an Analysis

- Distribute the Unit 1 Downloadable Model and Practice. Point out that the model compares two related texts, the **Interactive Worktext** Shared Read "Taking Care of Pepper" and the **Apprentice Leveled Reader** "People Helping Whales." Read the sentences aloud to children.

- Point out the key details in each sentence that come from the texts. Point out the signal word *both*. Explain to children that this word shows readers that the sentence is comparing two different texts.

- Ask: *What details show that the two texts are alike?* (Both texts tell about ways people care for animals. Both texts give facts and information about an animal. Both texts tell about where an animal lives.) *How is "People Helping Whales" different?* ("People Helping Whales" talks about how people help whales that get stranded on land, not about how people care for them every day.)

- Model analyzing how the student used details to make a summary. Read the last sentence. *Why is this sentence a good ending?* (The student explained what the details had in common.)

Write an Analysis

Guided Writing Explain to children that they will be comparing the **Interactive Worktext** Shared Read "Families Working Together" and the **Apprentice Leveled Reader** "Families at Work."

- Guide children to compare the two texts as they complete the sentences on the Unit 1 Downloadable Model and Practice.

- Point out the signal words, such as *also, both*, and *different,* to children and discuss how these words are used to compare the texts.

- Alternatively, let children select two texts to compare.

Teacher Conference Check children's writing for complete sentences. Did they use key details to tell how the texts are the same and different? Did they use text evidence? Did they write in complete sentences?

Writing Rubric

	4	3	2	1
Text Evidence	Includes three or more details from the text.	Includes two or more details from the text.	Includes only one detail from the text.	No text evidence is cited.
Writing Style	Writes in complete sentences. Uses correct spelling and grammar.	Uses complete sentences. Writing has spelling and grammar errors.	Few complete sentences. There are many spelling and grammar errors.	Writing is not accurate or in complete sentences.

UNIT 2 PLANNER
Animal Discoveries

Week 1
Animals and Nature

ESSENTIAL QUESTION
How do animals survive?

Build Background

CCSS Vocabulary
L.2.4a *adapt, climate, eager, freedom, fresh, sense, shadows, silence*

Access Complex Text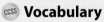
Sentence Structure

CCSS Comprehension
RL.2.5 Skill: Plot
Respond to Reading

CCSS Write About Reading *Analytical Writing*
W.4.9 Inform/Explain: Genre

Week 2
Animals in Stories

ESSENTIAL QUESTION
What can animals in stories teach us?

Build Background

CCSS Vocabulary
L.2.4a *believe, delicious, feast, fond, lessons, remarkable, snatch, stories*

Access Complex Text
Connection of Ideas

CCSS Comprehension
RL.2.3 Skill: Problem and Solution
Respond to Reading

CCSS Write About Reading *Analytical Writing*
W.4.9 Inform/Explain: Problem and Solution

Week 3
Animal Habitats

ESSENTIAL QUESTION
What are features of different animal habitats?

Build Background

CCSS Vocabulary
L.2.4a *buried, escape, habitat, journey, nature, peeks, restless, spies*

Access Complex Text
Connection of Ideas

CCSS Comprehension
RI.2.2 Skill: Main Topic and Key Details
Respond to Reading

CCSS Write About Reading *Analytical Writing*
W.4.9 Inform/Explain: Main Topic and Key Details

ASSESSMENT

 Quick Check
Vocabulary, Comprehension
Weekly Assessment
Assessment Book, pp. 20–21

 Quick Check
Vocabulary, Comprehension
Weekly Assessment
Assessment Book, pp. 22–23

 Quick Check
Vocabulary, Comprehension
Weekly Assessment
Assessment Book, pp. 24–25

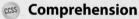 **MID-UNIT ASSESSMENT**
Assessment Book, pp. 80–87

Fluency Assessment
Assessment Book, pp. 234–239

Use the Foundational Skills Kit for explicit instruction of phonics, structural analysis, fluency, and word recognition. Includes *Reading Wonders* Adaptive Learning.

Week 4
Baby Animals

ESSENTIAL QUESTION
How are offspring like their parents?

Build Background

CCSS Vocabulary
L.2.4a *adult, alive, covered, fur, giant, groom, mammal, offspring*

Access Complex Text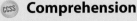
Genre

CCSS Comprehension
RI.2.2 Skill: Main Topic and Key Details
Respond to Reading

CCSS Write About Reading *Analytical Writing*
W.4.9 Opinion: Main Topic and Key Details

Week 5
Animals in Poems

ESSENTIAL QUESTION
What do we love about animals?

Build Background

CCSS Vocabulary
L.2.4a *behave, express, feathers, flapping,*

Poetry Words
poem, rhyme, rhythm, word choice

Access Complex Text
Connection of Ideas

CCSS Comprehension
RL.2.1 Skill: Key Details
Respond to Reading

CCSS Write About Reading *Analytical Writing*
W.4.9 Inform/Explain: Word Choice

Week 6
ASSESS

RETEACH   LEVEL UP

Reteach
Comprehension Skills

Vocabulary

Write About Reading

Level Up
Read Approaching Leveled Reader

Write About Reading:
Compare Texts

A S S E S S M E N T

✓ *Quick Check*
Vocabulary, Comprehension

✓ **Weekly Assessment**
Assessment Book, pp. 26–27

✓ *Quick Check*
Vocabulary, Comprehension

✓ **Weekly Assessment**
Assessment Book, pp. 28–29

✓ **Unit Assessment**
Assessment Book, pp. 131–139

✓ **Fluency Assessment**
Assessment Book, pp. 234–249

EXIT TEST
Assessment Book, pp. 187–195

UNIT 2 OPENER,
pp. 86–87

The Big Idea

How do animals play a part in the world around us?

Talk About It

Read aloud the Big Idea on page 86 of the **Interactive Worktext:** *How do animals play a part in the world around us?* Ask children to name different animals they have seen or interacted with. List them on the board. Then have children name places where these animals live. (At the zoo, in people's homes, at shelters, in the wild, and so on.)

Discuss the photo on pages 86–87. Ask: *What is happening in the picture?* (A frog is leaping out of the water to catch a fly.) *What will the frog do with the fly?* (The frog will eat it.) *What else do you know about frogs?* (Answers will vary.)

Then ask: *How can animals help people in everyday life?* Have children discuss and share their ideas. If children have difficulty, provide an example, such as a cat giving an owner comfort or a seeing-eye dog helping a blind person. Encourage children to think about different kinds of animals.

Then say: *Let's look back at our Big Idea. How do animals play a part in the world around us?* Have children discuss and share their ideas with the group. Explain to children that they will be discussing the Big Idea throughout the unit. Each week they will talk, read and write about animals and how they play a part in the world around us.

Build Fluency

Each week, use the **Interactive Worktext** Shared Reads and **Apprentice Leveled Readers** for fluency instruction and practice. Keep in mind that reading rates vary with the type of text that children are reading as well as the purpose for reading. For example, comprehension of complex informational texts generally requires slower reading.

Explain/Model Use the Fluency lessons on pages 378–382 to explain the skill. Then model the skill by reading the first page of the week's Shared Read or Leveled Reader.

Practice/Apply Choose a page from the Shared Read or Leveled Reader. Have one group read the top half of the page one sentence at a time. Remind children to apply the skill. Have the second group echo-read the passage. Then have the groups switch roles for the second half of the page. Discuss how each group applied the skill.

> **Weekly Fluency Focus**
>
> **Week 1** Phrasing
> **Week 2** Expression
> **Week 3** Phrasing
> **Week 4** Pronunciation
> **Week 5** Phrasing

Foundational Skills Kit You can also use the **Lesson Cards** and **Practice** pages from the **Foundational Skills Kit** for targeted Fluency instruction and practice.

Interactive Worktext

	Week 1	Week 2	Week 3	Week 4	Week 5
	"A Visit to the Desert"	"The Boy Who Cried Wolf"	"A Prairie Guard Dog"	"Eagles and Eaglets"	"Cats and Kittens"
Quantitative	Lexile 270 TextEvaluator™ 6	Lexile 240 TextEvaluator™ 6	Lexile 310 TextEvaluator™ 14	Lexile 320 TextEvaluator™ 6	Lexile NP TextEvaluator™ NP
Qualitative	• Sentence Structure • Vocabulary	• Connection of Ideas • Vocabulary	• Connection of Ideas • Genre • Organization • Vocabulary	• Genre • Connection of Ideas • Vocabulary	• Connection of Ideas • Vocabulary
Reader and Task	The Weekly Concept lessons will help determine the reader's knowledge and engagement in the weekly concept.				
	Weekly Concept: p. 66 Questions and tasks: pp. 68–69	Weekly Concept: p. 76 Questions and tasks: pp. 78–79	Weekly Concept: p. 86 Questions and tasks: pp. 88–89	Weekly Concept: p. 98 Questions and tasks: pp. 100–101	Weekly Concept: p. 108 Questions and tasks: pp. 110–111

Apprentice Leveled Reader

	Week 1	Week 2	Week 3	Week 4	Week 5
	"Hippos at the Zoo"	"The Cat and the Mice"	"A Tree Full of Life"	"Animal Families"	"Amira's Petting Zoo"
Quantitative	Lexile 180 TextEvaluator™ 6	Lexile 180 TextEvaluator™ 6	Lexile 130 TextEvaluator™ 6	Lexile 310 TextEvaluator™ 6	Lexile 130 TextEvaluator™ 6
Qualitative	• Sentence Structure • Genre • Connection of Ideas • Vocabulary	• Connection of Ideas • Organization • Genre • Vocabulary	• Connection of Ideas • Prior Knowledge • Genre • Vocabulary	• Genre • Organization • Vocabulary	• Connection of Ideas • Sentence Structure • Organization • Vocabulary
Reader and Task	The Weekly Concept lessons will help determine the reader's knowledge and engagement in the weekly concept.				
	Weekly Concept: p. 66 Questions and tasks: pp. 70–73	Weekly Concept: p. 76 Questions and tasks: pp. 80–83	Weekly Concept: p. 86 Questions and tasks: pp. 90–93	Weekly Concept: p. 98 Questions and tasks: pp. 102–105	Weekly Concept: p. 108 Questions and tasks: pp. 112–115

See page 383 for details about Text Complexity measures.

WEEK 1
LESSON 1

Objectives
• Develop oral language
• Build background about how animals survive
• Understand and use weekly Vocabulary
• Read a realistic fiction story

Scaffolding for **Wonders** Reading/Writing Workshop

Materials
Interactive Worktext, pp. 88–97
• Visual Vocabulary Cards: 41–48
• High-Frequency Word Cards

☞ **Go** Digital
• Interactive eWorktext
• Visual Vocabulary Cards

WEEKLY CONCEPT

5–10 Minutes   SL.2.1a SL.2.4

Talk About It

Essential Question Read aloud the Essential Question on page 88 of the **Interactive Worktext:** *How do animals survive?* Say: *Some animals in the wild need to adapt to very hot and cold climates. Animals adapt to these climates in different ways.* Provide examples of animals adapting such as a walrus storing an extra layer of blubber to stay warm in the freezing waters or arctic birds growing an extra layer of feathers to keep warm. Say: *Animals adapt in many ways.*

• Discuss the photograph on page 88. Ask: *What is happening in this picture?* (An adult polar bear is huddling with two polar bear cubs in the snow.) Ask: *Why are the animals huddling together?* (Possible answer: They may be trying to stay warm.)

I Do Say: *I am going to look at the photo and think about how these animals survive in the cold weather. I will look closely at the animals to see what helps them survive. They have fur to keep them warm.* Say: *I will write on the web on page 89 what helps them survive.*

We Do Say: *Let's think about other ways these animals adapt to the cold weather. I see they are huddling in the snow to keep them out of the cold wind.* Guide children to think of other ways these polar bears have adapted to the weather. Discuss and have children choose one way animals survive to add to their webs.

You Do Guide partners to work together to talk about other ways animals adapt to cold weather. Have children use the words from the web to complete their sentences: *Animals survive by _____.*

REVIEW VOCABULARY

10–15 Minutes   L.2.5a L.2.6 L.2.4c RF.2.3f

Review Weekly Vocabulary Words

• Use the **Visual Vocabulary Cards** to review the weekly vocabulary.

• Read together the directions on page 90 of the **Interactive Worktext**. Then complete the activity.

1 **climate** Explain to children that the *climate* of a place is the kind of weather there. Discuss the local *climate*. Then provide the names of a few places that have very cold weather. (Possible answers: Alaska, Antarctica) Help children brainstorm animals that live in cold *climates*. (Possible answers: penguin, polar bear)

2 **adapt** Review the photograph and discuss how certain animals *adapt* to the weather. Ask *Why is a polar bear not cold in the arctic?* Ask children what they can do to *adapt* to changes in weather. Use *When it is hot outside, _____ to stay cool.* (Possible answers: drink water, sit in the shade)

3 **fresh** Ask children to name some of their favorite foods. Explain that most foods will go bad if they are not stored properly or used quickly. Ask: *What happens to fruit when it goes bad?* (Possible answers: it turns brown, it will stink)

4 **eager** Have children think of a time they were *eager* or excited to do something. Have them use this sentence starter: *I was* eager *to _____.* Then have them act out how a child who is *eager* to answer a question acts. (Possible answer: raises their hand and waves it.)

5 **sense** Explain that sometimes you can get a *sense* about a change in the weather before it happens. Ask them what made Henry *sense* there would be a change in the weather. (the dark clouds) Then help children to think of another word for *sense*. (feeling)

6 **freedom** Model using *freedom* in a sentence: *Gabby used the* freedom *of her summer vacation to learn how to ride a bike.* Guide children to identify the base word, or "smaller word," in *freedom*. (free) Ask children to write down what *freedom* means to them. (Possible answer: I can do what I want.)

7 **silence** Demonstrate for children what a moment of *silence* is like. Ask them how *silence* can be important. Have children use the sentence frame: *I go to _____ to find silence.* (Possible answers: my room, the family room)

8 **shadows** Display a picture of people where their *shadows* are showing. Explain that there must be a source of light for these *shadows* to exist. Then assist children as they draw a picture of two people with *shadows*. Have children complete the sentence: *The* shadows *are caused by the _____.*

High-Frequency Words

Have children look at page 91 in the **Interactive Worktext**. Help them read, spell, and write each high-frequency word. Guide partners to use each word in a sentence. Then read the story aloud with children. Guide partners to work together to reread the story and circle the high-frequency words. (to, How, live, The, This, helps) Listen in and provide assistance reading the high-frequency words, as necessary.

ELL ENGLISH LANGUAGE LEARNERS

Display the **High-Frequency Word Cards** for: *how, the, helps, live, this, to.* Write a sentence with each word on the board. Have children echo-read each sentence, and point out the high-frequency word. Then ask them to use the word in a new sentence.

READ COMPLEX TEXT

15–20 Minutes   RL.2.3   RL.2.1   SL.2.1b

Read "A Visit to the Desert"

- Have children turn to page 92 in the **Interactive Worktext** and read aloud the Essential Question. Point to the illustration of the rabbit in the desert. Say: *What kind of animals do you see in this picture of the desert?* (jack rabbit, lizard) *Let's read to find out how animals survive in the desert.* Have children echo-read the title.

- Read the story together. Note that the weekly vocabulary words are highlighted in yellow. Expand Vocabulary words are highlighted in blue.

- As children read, have them use the "My Notes" section on page 92 to write questions they have. Children can also write words they don't understand or things they want to remember. Model how to use the "My Notes" section. *When I read the last sentence on page 93, I find out that Grandma will take Tim on a desert hike. I wonder if they will see any animals on their hike. I will write a question asking what kinds of animals live in the desert in the "My Notes" section.*

ELL ENGLISH LANGUAGE LEARNERS

As you read together, have children highlight parts of the text they have questions about. After reading, review the questions children have. Then help them locate the answers to their questions in the text.

 Quick Check Can children understand the weekly vocabulary in context? If not, review vocabulary using the **Visual Vocabulary Cards** before teaching Lesson 2.

Can children read high-frequency words in context? If not, review using the Read/Spell/Write routine and the High-Frequency Word Cards.

Objectives
- Read realistic fiction
- Understand complex text through close reading
- Recognize and understand plot
- Respond to the selection using text evidence to support ideas

Materials
Interactive Worktext, pp. 92–99

☞ **Go Digital**
- Interactive eWorktext
- Plot Mini-Lesson

REREAD COMPLEX TEXT

20–25 Minutes   RL.2.3 RL.2.1 L.2.4a CCSS

Close Reading: "A Visit to the Desert"

Reread "A Visit to the Desert" with children from **Interactive Worktext** pages 92–97. As you read together, discuss important passages. Guide children to respond to questions using evidence from the text.

Pages 92–93

Expand Vocabulary Show children the picture of Tim with his mother. Tell them that Tim is getting ready for *vacation*. Explain that a *vacation* is a time of rest from school or work. Have children reread the first paragraph. Ask: *What will Tim do on his* vacation? Guide children to write the answer. (Tim will visit Grandma.)

Expand Vocabulary Explain that a *desert* is an area that is very hot, dry, and sandy. Tell children a *desert* has few plants and animals. Ask: *What animals do you see that live in the* desert? Guide children to circle the animals in the picture. (rabbit, lizard)

Plot Explain to children that the plot is the key events that happen in the story. Have children reread the first paragraph. Ask: *Why is Tim unhappy at the beginning of the story?* Guide children to draw a box around the text that tells. (He wanted to see his friends.)

Page 94

Plot Point out that children can identify the plot by thinking about the key events in the beginning, middle, and end of the story. Read aloud the first paragraph. Ask: *Where did Tim and his family go with Grandma?* Have children draw a box around the text that tells. (Then they drove to the desert.)

Expand Vocabulary Show children the picture. Point out the picture of Tim's mom and dad hiking in the desert. Explain that if you *hiked* somewhere, you took a long walk. Ask: *Where did Tim and his family* hike? Guide children to circle the answer. (through the desert) Demonstrate hiking by walking in place.

Sentence Structure Ⓐ Ⓒ Ⓣ Point out the quotation marks and the sentences Grandma says. Explain that quotation marks show someone in the story is speaking. Point to *she said* and explain that these words show who the speaker is. Have children reread the second paragraph. Ask: *What sentence tells what Grandma said first?* Guide them to underline the text that tells. (They have freedom to move around.)

Page 95

Plot Remind children how Tim was feeling at the beginning of the story. (unhappy) Have children reread the second paragraph. Ask: *How does Tim feel in the middle of the story?* Guide children to write the word that tells. (excited) Discuss why Tim's feelings about his trip to the desert have changed.

Vocabulary Point to the word *burrow*. Explain that a *burrow* is a hole dug in the ground by an animal. Have children reread the third and fourth paragraphs. Then ask: *Why does the tortoise go into a* burrow? (It likes the silence. It likes the sense of safety.)

Expand Vocabulary Point to the picture of the *tortoise*. Explain that a *tortoise* is a turtle that lives on land. Read aloud the second paragraph on page 95 Ask: *What is the* tortoise *looking for?* Guide children to circle the word that tells. (shade) Review that the desert is hot and animals must find ways to stay cool.

Sentence Structure (ACT) Write the sentences: *The dog sat down. It was tired.* Explain to children that authors will sometimes use a pronoun such as *it* to replace the name of an animal or thing that has already been mentioned once in a paragraph. Ask: *What does the word* it *refer to in this sentence?* (the dog) Read the third paragraph aloud. Ask children to find the word *It* in the last sentence. Ask: *What does the word* It *refer to?* Guide children to underline the words that tell. (the tortoise)

Page 96

Plot Have children reread the first paragraph. Ask: *What does Grandma teach Tim about jack rabbits?* Guide children to draw a box around this character's name. (Its large ears help it stay cool.)

Sentence Structure (ACT) Have children reread the second paragraph. Ask: *What words let you know that Tim is the speaker?* Guide children to underline the words that tell. (Tim said)

Expand Vocabulary Explain to children that the word *during* means "at the time of." Have them reread the last paragraph. Ask: *Why does the owl sleep* during *the day?* Guide children to circle the words that tell. (This is how it keeps cool.)

Page 97

Plot Read the first two paragraphs aloud. Ask: *Does Tim seem happier at the end of the story than he is at the beginning of the story?* (yes) Ask: *What does Tim think about the vacation?* Guide children to draw a box around the text that tells. (This vacation is going too fast.)

Sentence Structure (ACT) Remind children that when a question mark appears with quotation marks, a character has asked a question. Have children reread the last paragraph. Ask: *What question did Tim ask?* Guide them to underline the question. (What heat?)

Plot Reread the last paragraph of the story aloud. Ask: *How does Tim feel at the end of the story?* Guide children to draw a box around the words that tell. (fresh and cool) Discuss how Tim's feelings changed about the desert over the course of the story.

RESPOND TO READING

10–20 Minutes RL.2.3 RL.2.7 SL.2.1a

Respond to "A Visit to the Desert"

Read aloud the questions about "A Visit to the Desert" on page 98 of the **Interactive Worktext**. Then read aloud the "Discussion Starter" for each of the questions. Guide children to work with a partner to answer the questions orally using the "Discussion Starters." Have children find text evidence to support their answers. Ask children to write the page number(s) on which they found the text evidence.

1. *What is it like for animals to live in the desert?* (Possible answers: Animals like the desert because they have the freedom to move around. Animals adapt to the desert by learning to live in the heat. Text Evidence: p. 94)

2. *How does a tortoise survive in the desert?* (Possible answers: Tortoises stay cool by resting in the shadows of rocks. Tortoises go in underground burrows to stay safe. Text Evidence: p. 95)

3. *How do other animals survive in the desert?* (Possible answers: A jack rabbit's long ears help it stay cool when it is hot. I see that an owl sleeps during the day. Text Evidence: p. 96)

After children discuss the questions, have them use the sentence starters to answer the question on page 99. Circulate and provide guidance.

 Quick Check **Do children understand vocabulary in context? If not, review and reteach using the instruction on page 74.**

Can children identify the plot? If not, review and reteach using the instruction on page 74 and assign the Unit 2 Week 1 digital mini-lesson.

Can children write a response to "A Visit to the Desert"? If not, review the sentence starters and prompt children to respond orally. Help them write their responses.

WEEK 1 LESSON 3

Objectives
- Access prior knowledge
- Understand and use new vocabulary words
- Read high-frequency words
- Read a realistic fiction story

Materials
- "Hippos at the Zoo" Apprentice Leveled Reader
- High-Frequency Word Cards

☞ **Go** Digital
- Apprentice Leveled Reader eBook
- Downloadable High-Frequency Word Cards

Scaffolding for **Wonders** Approaching Leveled Reader

BEFORE READING

10–15 Minutes   SL.2.1a   SL. 2.6   L.2.6   L.2.5a   RF.2.3f   CCSS

Introduce "Hippos at the Zoo"

- Read the Essential Question on the title page of "Hippos at the Zoo" **Apprentice Leveled Reader:** *How do animals survive?*

- Read the title of the main read. Point to the cover. *Who or what is this realistic fiction story about?* (hippos) *What do hippos look like?* (big, gray, small ears) *What else do you know about hippos? Let's read to learn more about hippos.*

High-Frequency Words

Display the **High-Frequency Word Cards** for the words *about, know, walk, who, why,* and *write.* Use the Read/Spell/Write routine to teach each word. Guide partners to use each word in a sentence. Provide assistance reading the high-frequency words, as necessary.

Expand Vocabulary

Before reading "Hippos at the Zoo," help children read the following words that they will encounter. Display each word below. Use the Define/Example/Ask routine. Tell children to look for the word as they read "Hippos at the Zoo."

1 facts (page 3)

Define: something known to be true or real

Example: A book about sea life can help you learn *facts* about whales.

Ask: What are some *facts* you know about animals?

2 float (page 11)

Define: to rest on top of water or other liquid and not sink

Example: I learned to *float* before I could swim.

Ask: What are some things that can *float?*

3 hippo (page 6)

Define: short for hippopotamus; a large, heavy animal that lives near rivers and lakes

Example: A *hippo* eats plants growing near the river.

Ask: What are some animals that are smaller than a *hippo?*

4 huge (page 6)

Define: very big in size

Example: A mouse is small, but an elephant is *huge.*

Ask: What are some other animals you could describe as *huge?*

5 zoo (page 2)

Define: a park where wild animals are kept for people to see

Example: I visited the *zoo* with my grandpa and saw a big tiger.

Ask: What are some other animals you might see in a *zoo?*

DURING READING

20–30 Minutes   SL.2.2   RL. 2.1   RL.2.7   L.2.4a

Shared Reading

Tell children you will now read "Hippos at the Zoo." Tell them to note the vocabulary and high-frequency words you just introduced as you read the story. Stop to model understanding of the story as you go.

Pages 2–3

High-Frequency Words Make sure children can read the high-frequency word *about*.

Comprehension Check Model beginning to read the story. Say: *The first thing I notice about this story is that Val and Mom are at the zoo. They are going because Val needs to learn facts about an animal. I will look out for facts that Val is learning as I read.*

Vocabulary Read page 3. Focus on the word *facts*. Ask: *What kind of facts does Val have to learn?* (facts about an animal) *What are some facts she could learn?* (what an animal eats, where it lives)

Pages 4–5

High-Frequency Words Make sure children can read the high-frequency word *who*.

Comprehension Check *On page 5, I read that Val wants to know who lives in this part of the zoo. I can use clues in the picture to figure it out. I see water so I know it must be an animal that lives in or near the water. I also see hay so I think this animal eats plants. I'll keep reading to find out.*

Pages 6–7

High-Frequency Words Make sure children can read the high-frequency word *why*.

Vocabulary On page 6, read *"A huge head pops up."* Focus on the phrase *"pops up."* Ask: *Where is the hippo's head now?* (out of the water) *Where was it on the last page?* (in the water) *What do you think "pops up" means?* (comes out suddenly)

Pages 8–9

High-Frequency Words Make sure children can read the high-frequency word *know*.

Vocabulary On page 9, read the sentence *"Hippos live in a hot climate."* Focus on the word *climate*. Say: *When I am not sure what a word means, I look at the words close by to see if there is a clue. I want to know what the word* climate *means. I think the word* hot *is a clue. I can also keep reading to see if there is a clue in the next sentence. Read the next sentence. Ask: How do these clues help me understand the word* climate? (The *word climate* tells about the weather where the hippos live. They live where it is hot, so they have to keep cool in the mud.)

Pages 10–11

Comprehension Check *I see that a man who works at the zoo is helping Val learn facts about the hippo. What facts has Val learned ?* (Hippos live in a hot climate. They use mud to keep cool. They can't swim.)

Pages 12–13

High-Frequency Words Make sure children can read the high-frequency word *walk*.

Pages 14–15

High-Frequency Words Make sure children can read the high-frequency word *write*.

Comprehension Check *The story says that Val and Mom had a good day at the zoo. I am going to think about how that happened. Val had homework. She had to learn facts about an animal. She saw where the hippos live and a man who works at the zoo told her all about them. She learned many facts about the hippos to write about. She did what she came to do and had fun doing it.*

 Quick Check Can children understand vocabulary in context? If not, review and reteach using the instruction on page 74.

Can children read the high-frequency words in context? If not, review using the Read/Spell/Write routine and the High-Frequency Word Cards.

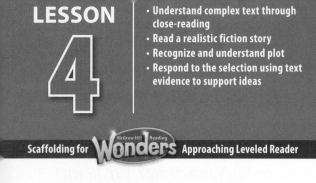

LESSON 4

• Understand complex text through close-reading
• Read a realistic fiction story
• Recognize and understand plot
• Respond to the selection using text evidence to support ideas

McGraw-Hill Reading
WONDERS Approaching Leveled Reader
Scaffolding for

"Hippos at the Zoo" Apprentice Leveled Reader
• Graphic Organizer: Beginning, Middle, End

👉 **Go Digital**
• Apprentice Leveled Reader eBook
• Downloadable Graphic Organizer
• Plot Mini-lesson

DURING READING

20–30 Minutes　　RL.2.1　RL. 2.5　RL.2.7　SL.2.2　CCSS

Tell children they will now reread the selection, "Hippos at the Zoo." Review the vocabulary and high-frequency words that they will encounter as they read.

Close Reading

Pages 2–3

Plot Remind children that we can identify the plot by thinking about the key events in the beginning, middle, and end of the story. Reread pages 2 and 3. Ask: *What happened at the beginning?* (Val and Mom went to the zoo.) *Why did they go?* (Val needs to learn about an animal for school.) Model filling in the Beginning, Middle, End Chart.

Pages 4–5

Genre (A C T) Remind children that realistic fiction tells a made-up story about something that could really happen. Ask: *Does anything happen that could not happen in real life?* (No, people go to zoos in real life and the animals in this zoo act like real animals.)

Pages 6–7

Sentence Structure (A C T) Reread the first sentence on page 6. Ask: *What is the punctuation at the end of this sentence?* (exclamation mark) Ask children why an exclamation mark might belong at the end of this sentence. (The girl is surprised, and the head is huge.) On page 7, point to the quotation marks. Ask: *What do these marks tell us?* (that someone is speaking)

Plot Ask children what important event has just happened. (Val sees a hippo and asks why it is in the mud.) Help children record the event on their Beginning, Middle, End charts.

Pages 8–9

Plot Reread pages 8 and 9. Ask: *What facts did Val learn from the man?* (She learned that hippos live in a hot climate and that the mud keeps them cool.) *Why are these facts important?* (They help you understand what hippos need to survive.) Help children record this information on their Beginning, Middle, End charts.

Connection of Ideas (A C T) Ask: *Who tells Val and Mom that he knows the answer to Val's question?* (a man who works at the zoo) *Think back to the beginning. Why is this an important event in the story?* (Because Val needs to learn facts about an animal for her homework.)

Pages 10–11

Plot Reread pages 10 and 11. Remind children that it is important think about the events taking place. Explain that using pictures, along with the text, is a good way to better understand what is happening in a story. Ask: *How does the picture help you understand what is happening?* (The man is talking and Val is writing. She is probably writing down the facts that the man is telling her about hippos.) Guide children to record this event on their Beginning, Middle, End charts.

Sentence Structure (A C T) On page 11, read "Hippos like water but can't swim or float." Point out that this sentence has two different parts. Ask: *What do you learn in the first part of this sentence?* (Hippos like water.) *What do you learn in the second part of this sentence?* (They can't swim or float.) *What word connects the two parts of the sentence?* (but)

Genre (A C T) Children may be confused about the presence of the real information in a fiction story. Explain that while fiction tells a made-up story, it may also contain real information. Ask: *What real information about hippos did you learn?* (Hippos stay cool in the mud and can't swim or float.)

Pages 12–13

Connection of Ideas **A C T** Say: *On page 12, we read that hippos walk in water. Think back to the last page. we read. What did we learn there?* (Hippos can't swim or float.) Explain that before we learned what hippos couldn't do in water so now we learn what they can do.

Plot After reading pages 12 and 13, ask: *Who has to go?* (the man who works at the zoo) *How do you think Val felt about having the man help her?* (She was happy that he answered her questions so she could do her homework.) *What shows this in the text?* (Val thanks him.)

Pages 14–15

Sentence Structure **A C T** Reread the second sentence on page 14. Point out that this sentence has two parts. Ask. *What do we learn in the first part of this sentence?* (Val is eager) Point out that the second part will tell us what she is eager to do. Ask: *What is Val eager to do?* (to write about hippos)

Plot Reread pages 14 and 15. Point to the picture on page 14 and ask: *What is Val doing now?* (She is writing about hippos.) Point to the picture on page 15 and ask children what is happening. (Val and Mom are leaving the zoo.) Ask: *Did Val do what she set out to do?* (Yes, she got facts about an animal.) Help children record this final event on their Beginning, Middle, End charts.

AFTER READING

10–15 Minutes   RL.2.2   RL.2.7   L. 2.4d   W.2.8   **CCSS**

Respond to Reading

Compare Texts Guide children in comparing the animals in "Hippos at the Zoo" with the animals in "A Visit to the Desert." Help children think about ways the animals adapt and survive. Then ask: *What new facts did you learn about animals and how they survive?*

Summarize Have children turn to page 16 and guide them in summarizing the selection. (Answers should include details from the beginning, middle, and end of the story.)

Text Evidence

Have partners work together to answer questions on page 16. Remind children to use their Beginning, Middle, End charts.

Plot (Val and Mom visit the zoo. Val has homework to learn facts about a zoo animal. They see a lion and a hippo.)

Vocabulary (It is a compound word: home + work. It means work that you have to do at home.)

Write About Reading (Answers will vary, but children should explain what Val learns about hippos from the man who works at the zoo.)

Read "Hippos"

Encourage children to read the paired selection "Hippos" on pages 17–19. Have them summarize the selection and compare it to "Hippos at the Zoo." Have them work with a partner to answer the "Make Connections" questions on page 19.

Independent Reading

Have pairs of children reread "Hippos at the Zoo." Have them talk about what Val learned about hippos.

✔ *Quick Check* Can students identify Plot? If not, review and reteach using the instruction on page 74 and assign the Unit 2 Week 1 digital mini-lesson.

Can students respond to the selection using text evidence? If not, provide sentence frames to help them organize their ideas.

Objectives
- Review weekly vocabulary words
- Review plot
- Write an analysis about how the author used key details

Materials
- Visual Vocabulary Cards: 41–48
- Interactive Worktext, pp. 100–101
- Assessment Book, pp. 20–21

☞ **Go** Digital
- Visual Vocabulary Cards
- Plot Mini-Lesson
- Interactive eWorktext
- eAssessment

REVIEW AND RETEACH

5–10 Minutes   L.2.4a   RL.2.3   RL.2.7   **CCSS**

Weekly Vocabulary

Display one **Visual Vocabulary Card** at a time and guide children to use the vocabulary word in a sentence. If children have difficulty creating a sentence, have them find the word in "A Visit to the Desert" or "Hippos at the Zoo" and use context clues in the passage to define the vocabulary word.

Comprehension: Plot

I Do Write and say: *Rosa is at the park. She can't find her friend Dan. They were going to meet. Rosa looks around. She sees Dan on the swings!* Ask: *What happens to Rosa at the beginning of the story?* Circle "She can't find her friend Dan." Say: *At the beginning of the story Rosa is at the park and can't find her friend Dan. I can tell that this is a key event because they were going to meet. This gives me important information that I can use to look for what happens in the middle.*

We Do Display: *Ben knocked on Matt's door. Matt did not answer. Ben heard Matt in the backyard. Ben found Matt playing with his new puppy.* Ask: *What key event happens at the end of the story?* (Ben found Matt playing with his new puppy.) *How can you tell?* (I read it in the last sentence.)

You Do Display: *When Bill wakes up, he eats breakfast. He wants to go to the park with his friend Lisa but it is too early. He reads a book. Finally, it is time for him to go to the park.* Guide one partner to ask a question and the other partner to answer it. Have partners focus on the events that happen in the beginning, middle, and end of the story.

WRITE ABOUT READING

25–35 Minutes   W.2.3   W.2.8   W.4.9   **CCSS**

Read an Analysis

- Guide children to look back at "A Visit to the Desert" in the **Interactive Worktext**. Have volunteers review the details about the plot they marked on page 93 and summarize the text. Repeat with pages 94–97. *How did the author use details to make this story realistic?*

- Read aloud the directions on page 100. Read aloud the student model. *This student's work is not a summary. It is an analysis, or description, of how the author used details to make "A Visit to the Desert" a realistic story.*

- *When you write an analysis, you should include key details from the story that tell about the story. Read Chen's first sentence. Circle the details.* (the characters do real things like go hiking) *In what part of the story do you learn these details?* (the beginning)

- *Read the second sentence. Draw a box around the details from the story you see in Chen's writing.* (It takes place at the desert, a real place.) Provide a sentence frame and guide children to fill it in for each detail they found: *I think this detail is realistic because _____.*

- Model analyzing how the author made the story realistic. Read the last sentence that Chen wrote. *Why is this sentence a good ending?* (It tells how the author made the story realistic.)

Write an Analysis

Analytical Writing

Guided Writing Read the writing prompt on page 101 together. Guide children to review their Plot charts for "Hippos at the Zoo." Have children use their charts to complete the sentence starters. Children can also write an analysis using another selection previously read this week.

Peer Conference Guide children to read their analysis to a partner. Listeners should summarize the strongest details that support the beginning, middle, and ending sentences. They should discuss any parts that are unclear.

Teacher Conference Check children's writing for complete sentences and whether they included details from the story. Review the ending sentence and ask: *Did the author use details to support the genre of the story?* If necessary, guide children to revise their sentence by adding more details.

Level Up

▲ **Approaching Leveled Reader**

▲ **Reading/Writing Workshop**

▲ **Apprentice Leveled Reader**

▲ **Interactive Worktext**

IF children read the Apprentice Level Reader and the **Interactive Worktext** Shared Read fluently and answer the Respond to Reading questions

THEN read together the Approaching Level Reader main selection and the **Reading/Writing Workshop** Shared Read from *Reading Wonders*. Have children take notes as they read, using self-stick notes. Then ask and answer questions about their notes.

Writing Rubric

	4	3	2	1
Text Evidence	Includes three or more details from the text.	Includes two or more details from the text.	Includes only one detail from the text.	No text evidence is cited.
Writing Style	Writes in complete sentences. Uses correct spelling and grammar.	Uses complete sentences. Writing has spelling and grammar errors.	Few complete sentences. There are many spelling and grammar errors.	Writing is not accurate or in complete sentences.

ASSESSMENT

Weekly Assessment

Have children complete the Weekly Assessment using **Assessment** book pages 20–21.

Objectives
- Develop oral language
- Build background about fables
- Understand and use weekly vocabulary
- Read a fable

Materials
- Interactive Worktext, pp. 102–111
- Visual Vocabulary Cards: 49–56
- High-Frequency Word Cards

☞ **Go** Digital
- Interactive eWorktext
- Visual Vocabulary Cards

Scaffolding for **Wonders** McGraw-Hill Reading Reading/Writing Workshop

WEEKLY CONCEPT

5–10 Minutes   SL.2.1b   SL.2.4   CCSS

Talk About It

Essential Question Read aloud the Essential Question on page 102 of the **Interactive Worktext:** *What can animals in stories teach us?* Explain that fables are stories that teach you a lesson. The characters in fables are usually animals.

- Discuss the illustration on page 102. Ask: *What is the mouse doing?* (The mouse is chewing through a rope.) Ask: *Why does the Lion have a rope around him?* (The rope is tying the lion down.)

I Do Say: *I am going to think about what the animals in this picture can teach me. This looks like the story "The Lion and the Mouse." I see the mouse is helping to free the lion. That is pretty unusual that such a small animal could help such a large and powerful animal. I think the lesson learned is that no matter what your size, you can always help someone.* Have children add this to their web on page 103.

We Do Say: *Let's think about other animal stories that teach us lessons. In the well-known fable "The Tortoise and the Hare," the slow Tortoise challenges the fast Hare to a race. The Hare laughs because he knows he is faster. He is so confident that he will win that he takes a nap during the race. The Tortoise ends up winning the race.* Ask: *What is the lesson learned?* (The lesson learned is that sometimes, if you are slow but steady, you can win a race.) Have children add this to their web.

You Do Guide partners to think of another lesson that could be learned from "The Tortoise and the Hare." Have children use the words from the web to end their sentences: *The lesson learned is that _____.*

REVIEW VOCABULARY

10–15 Minutes   L.2.5a   L.2.6   RF.2.3   CCSS

Review Weekly Vocabulary Words

- Use the **Visual Vocabulary Cards** to review the weekly vocabulary.
- Read together the directions on page 104 of the **Interactive Worktext**. Then complete the activity.

1 **stories** Guide children to brainstorm some of their favorite *stories*. Tell them that *stories* can be told in many different ways. Ask volunteers to name where they can find *stories* to read. (Possible answers: in a book, in a magazine, on a tablet)

2 **believe** Tell children that when you *believe* something, you feel sure that something is true. Have a volunteer read the sentence in the Worktext. Ask a volunteer to give another word for *believe* that would fit in the sentence. (think)

3 **remarkable** Act out for children how you look when you see something *remarkable*. Have children imitate your expression. Ask them what kinds of things they say when they see something *remarkable* (Possible answers: Wow! That's amazing!). Then ask children what is another word for *remarkable*. (Possible answers: amazing, incredible)

4 **fond** Explain to children that if you are *fond* of something, you really like it. Name something you are *fond* of and explain why. Then have volunteers complete the following sentence frame: *I am* fond *of _____. I am most* fond *of _____.* (Possible answers: my desk, the class pet)

5 **delicious** Have children use their hands and faces to show how it looks when they are eating something that tastes *delicious*. Say: *When I eat something delicious, I say, _____.* (Possible answers: Yum! That's tasty!) Then have children think of a word that means the opposite of *delicious*. (Possible answers: unpleasant, disgusting)

6 **lessons** Explain to children that they can learn things from *lessons*. Tell them that learning to ride a bike and learning to play guitar are all *lessons*. Have children complete the sentence frame: *A teacher might give me lessons on _____.* (Possible answers: music, reading)

7 **snatch** Act out for children what it looks like to *snatch* something quickly. Have the children imitate your actions. Then have them name things that a cat might *snatch* quickly with its paw. (Possible answers: mouse, toy, ball of yarn)

8 **feast** Explain to children that when you *feast* on something, you eat a large meal of food. Have children draw a picture of something they might *feast* on at Thanksgiving. (Drawings may include turkey, stuffing, mashed potatoes, and pie.)

High-Frequency Words

Have children look at page 105 in the **Interactive Worktext**. Help them read, spell, and write each high-frequency word. Guide partners to use each word in a sentence. Then read the story aloud with children. Guide partners to work together to reread the story and circle the high-frequency words. (find, away, found, with, would, better) Listen in and provide assistance reading the high-frequency words, as necessary.

ELL ENGLISH LANGUAGE LEARNERS

Display the **High-Frequency Word Cards** for: *find, found, with, better, away, would.* Write a sentence with each word on the board. Have children echo-read each sentence, and point out the high-frequency word. Then ask them to use the word in a new sentence.

Read "The Boy Who Cried Wolf"

- Have children turn to page 106 in the **Interactive Worktext** and read aloud the Essential Question. Point to the picture. Say: *What is the boy in the picture doing?* (sitting on a hill with some sheep) *Let's read to find out what the shepherd boy learns.* Have children echo-read the title.

- Read the story together. Note that the weekly vocabulary words are highlighted in yellow. Expand Vocabulary words are highlighted in blue.

- As children read, have them use the "My Notes" section on page 106 to write questions they have. Children can also write words they don't understand or things they want to remember. Model how to use the "My Notes" section. *When I read the first paragraph on page 107, I find out that the shepherd boy does not like his job. I wonder what remarkable thing the boy would like to have happen. I will write a question about this in the "My Notes" section.*

ELL ENGLISH LANGUAGE LEARNERS

As you read together, have children highlight parts of the text they have questions about. After reading, review the questions children have. Then help them locate the answers to their questions in the text.

 Quick Check Can children understand the weekly vocabulary in context? If not, review vocabulary using the **Visual Vocabulary Cards** before teaching Lesson 2.

Can children read high-frequency words in context? If not, review using the Read/Spell/Write routine and the High-Frequency Word Cards.

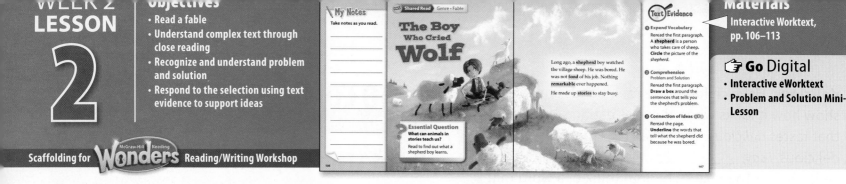

WEEK 2
LESSON 2

Objectives
- Read a fable
- Understand complex text through close reading
- Recognize and understand problem and solution
- Respond to the selection using text evidence to support ideas

Materials
Interactive Worktext, pp. 106–113

☞ **Go** Digital
- Interactive eWorktext
- Problem and Solution Mini-Lesson

Scaffolding for **Wonders** Reading/Writing Workshop

REREAD COMPLEX TEXT

20–25 Minutes   RL.2.3   RL.2.5   L.2.4a   CCSS

Close Reading: "The Boy Who Cried Wolf"

Reread "The Boy Who Cried Wolf" from **Interactive Worktext** pages 106–111 with children. As you read together, discuss important passages in the text. Guide children to respond to questions using evidence from the text.

Pages 106–107

Expand Vocabulary Have children reread the first paragraph. Explain that a *shepherd* is someone whose job it is to take care of sheep. Say: *I see a picture of a person who is surrounded by sheep. This must be the* shepherd. Guide children to circle the *shepherd* in the picture.

Problem and Solution Tell children that the plot of a story may include a problem the character needs to solve. Say: *To find the problem, look closely at the beginning of the story. What is wrong?* Read the first paragraph aloud. Ask: *What is the shepherd boy's problem?* Guide children to draw a box around the sentences that tell. (He was bored. He was not fond of his job.)

Connection of Ideas Ⓐ Ⓒ Ⓣ Say: *I read that the boy was bored and was not fond of his job.* Ask: *What did the shepherd do because he was bored?* Have children reread the page to answer the question. Guide children to underline the words that tell. (He made up stories to stay busy.)

Page 108

Problem and Solution Explain to children that a character may try to solve a problem in a story. Say: *The shepherd boy's problem is that he is bored.* Reread the first paragraph aloud. Ask: *What words tell you the shepherd boy's idea for solving his problem?* (He cried out, "Wolf! Wolf! The wolf is chasing the sheep!")

Expand Vocabulary Read the second paragraph aloud. Say: *A villager is someone who lives in a village. A village is a small town.* Ask: *Why do the villagers run up the hill when the shepherd boy cries out?* Guide children to circle the words that tell. (to help him)

Connection of Ideas Ⓐ Ⓒ Ⓣ Say: *The shepherd boy was bored but then he cried "Wolf, Wolf!"* Ask: *How do you know the boy is no longer bored?* Have children reread the second paragraph to answer the question. Guide children to underline the words that tell. (The boy laughed.)

Page 109

Expand Vocabulary Have children locate the word *angry*. Explain that the word *angry* means a strong feeling of unhappiness. Guide children to reread the paragraph and to circle the words that tell who is *angry*. (the villagers) If children still have difficulty, point to the word *They* in the sentence *They were angry*. Explain to children that the word *they* is a pronoun that takes the place of the words *the villagers*.

Problem and Solution Explain to children that the shepherd boy came up with a solution to his problem, but his solution caused another problem. Then, read the page aloud. Ask: *Why has the shepherd boy made the villagers angry?* Guide children to write their answer. (There was no wolf.)

Connection of Ideas Have children think about what happened after the shepherd cried "Wolf!" the first time. (The villagers were angry and told him not to cry "Wolf!") Then reread the page aloud. Guide children to underline the sentence that shows that the boy is still having fun. (The boy smiled.)

🔍 Page 110

Connection of Ideas Say: *I read that the shepherd boy saw a real wolf.* Reread the first paragraph aloud. Ask: *What is the shepherd worried the wolf will do?* Guide children to underline the words that tell. (eat the sheep) *Why does he call "Wolf! Wolf!"* (He wants the villagers to come as they did before.)

Expand Vocabulary Have children locate the word *tricking* in the first paragraph. Explain that the word *tricking* means lying to someone or cheating someone out of something. Say: *Circle the picture of who tricked the villagers.* (the shepherd boy)

🔍 Page 111

Connection of Ideas Show children the picture of the man talking to the shepherd boy. Reread the paragraph aloud. Ask: *How do you know the villagers are no longer angry at the shepherd boy?* Guide children to underline the words that tell. (He said the villagers would help the boy find the sheep.)

Problem and Solution Explain to children that the ending of a story usually tells how a character solved or tried to solve a problem. Have children reread the paragraph. Ask: *What should the shepherd boy do in the future?* Guide children to draw a box around the words that tell the solution to his problem. (tell the truth)

RESPOND TO READING

10–20 Minutes   RL.2.3   RL.2.5   SL.2.1b

Respond to "The Boy Who Cried Wolf"

Read aloud the questions on page 112 of the **Interactive Worktext** about "The Boy Who Cried Wolf." Then read aloud the "Discussion Starters" for each of the questions. Guide children to work with a partner to answer the questions orally using the "Discussion Starters." Have children find text evidence to support their answers. Ask children to write the page number(s) on which they found the text evidence for each question.

1. *What happens in the beginning of the story?* (Possible answers: In the beginning, the boy is bored and cries "Wolf!" When the villagers come to help, there is no wolf. Text Evidence: pp. 107, 108)

2. *What happens when the boy really sees a wolf?* (Possible answers: When the boy sees a real wolf, he cries "Wolf!" This time the villagers do not come because they think the boy is tricking them. Text Evidence: p. 110)

3. *What lesson does the boy learn at the end of the story?* (Possible answers: The boy learns that nobody believes a person who lies. He learns that it is better to tell the truth. Text Evidence: p. 111)

After children discuss the questions on page 112, have them use the sentence starters to answer the question on page 113. Circulate and provide guidance.

✔️ *Quick Check* Do children understand vocabulary in context? If not, review and reteach using the instruction on page 84.

Can children identify problem and solution? If not, review and reteach using the instruction on page 84 and assign the Unit 2 Week 2 digital mini-lesson.

Can children write a response to "The Boy Who Cried Wolf"? If not, review the sentence starters and prompt children to respond orally. Help them write their responses.

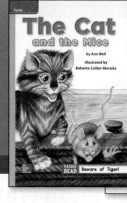

Objectives
- Access prior knowledge
- Understand and use new vocabulary words
- Read high-frequency words
- Read a fable

Materials
- "The Cat and the Mice" Apprentice Leveled Reader
- High-Frequency Word Cards

☞ **Go** Digital
- Apprentice Leveled Reader eBook
- Downloadable High-Frequency Word Cards

Scaffolding for **Wonders** Approaching Leveled Reader

BEFORE READING

10–15 Minutes · SL.2.1a · SL 2.6 · L.2.6 · RF.2.3f · CCSS

Introduce "The Cat and the Mice"

- Read the Essential Question on the title page of "The Cat and the Mice" **Apprentice Leveled Reader:** *What can animals in stories teach us?*

- Read the title of the main read. Point to the title page. *What characters are in this fable?* (mice) *What are they doing?* (holding hands in a circle) *Do mice in real life look like these mice?* (Children may point out that real mice don't wear clothing.) *Let's read about some mice who have a problem with a cat.*

High-Frequency Words

Display the **High-Frequency Word Cards** for the words *could, make, put, said, then,* and *they.* Use the Read/Spell/Write routine to teach each word. Guide partners to use each word in a sentence. Provide assistance reading the high-frequency words, as necessary.

Expand Vocabulary

Before reading "The Cat and the Mice," help children read the following words that they will encounter. Display each word below. Use the Define/Example/Ask routine. Tell children to look for the word later on as they read "The Cat and the Mice."

❶ chase (page 2)

Define: to run after and try to catch

Example: I saw two squirrels *chase* each other in the park.

Ask: When do you *chase* someone?

❷ fables (page 15)

Define: stories that teaches a lesson

Example: I read a *fable* about a crow that learned to be kind.

Ask: What are some *fables* that you have heard or read?

❸ meeting (page 4)

Define: when people get together to talk about something

Example: We had a *meeting* at school to talk about the new playground.

Ask: What are some things that happen at a *meeting*?

❹ problem (page 10)

Define: a question to be thought about and answered

Example: Mom says my messy room is a big *problem*.

Ask: What is a *problem* that you have had?

❺ solved (page 10)

Define: to find the answer to a problem

Example: My dad and I *solved* the puzzle in the newspaper.

Ask: What is a problem that you have *solved*?

❻ trap (page 5)

Define: something used to catch an animal

Example: The bear hurt his leg when he stepped into the *trap.*

Ask: What is a reason someone might use a *trap*?

DURING READING

20–30 Minutes   SL.2.2 RL.2.2 RL.2.3 L.2.4a

Shared Reading

Tell children you will now read "The Cat and the Mice." Tell them to note the vocabulary and high-frequency words you just introduced as you read the story. Stop to model understanding of the story as you go.

Pages 2–3

High-Frequency Words Make sure children can read the high-frequency word *then*.

Comprehension Check Model beginning to read the story. Say: *The first thing I notice about this story is that there is a cat who is eating mice. The mice in the picture look very unhappy and are trying to get away from the cat. I will look out for what the mice can do to stop the cat.*

Vocabulary Read page 2. Focus on the word *chase*. Ask: *Which word in the text means that the cat liked to run after the mice?* (chase) Ask children to discuss which animal can probably run faster, a cat or a mouse.

Pages 4–5

High-Frequency Words Make sure children can read the high-frequency words *they* and *make*.

Vocabulary On page 4, read the sentence *"The mice had a meeting."* Ask: *Can you point to the part of the picture that helps you understanding the meaning of meeting? Why did the mice have the meeting?* (to discuss what they can do about Cat)

Pages 6–7

High-Frequency Words Make sure children can read the high-frequency words *said* and *put*.

Vocabulary Read page 6. Focus on the word *old*. Ask: *What is a word that means the opposite of old?* (young) *Why do you think the mice all listened to the old mouse?* (being old can make you wise)

Comprehension Check *I can think about what would happen if a cat had a bell on its neck. I think that it couldn't sneak up on the mice because they would hear the bell.*

Pages 8–9

High-Frequency Words Make sure children can read the high-frequency word *could*.

Pages 10–11

Vocabulary Read the sentence on page 10. Focus first on the word *problem*. Ask: *What problem did the mice have?* (Cat chased the mice and often snatched them up and ate them.) *What does it mean if the problem has been solved?* (that an answer has been found)

Comprehension Check *On page 11, a mouse asks who will put the bell on the cat. I think that is a good question. To put the bell on the cat means that one of the mice will have to get very close to the cat, and this might not be a good idea.*

Pages 12–13

Comprehension Check *No one wants to put the bell on the cat. I think the mice are afraid to get near the cat.*

Pages 14–15

Vocabulary *A lesson is something that we learn. What is the lesson that we can learn from this fable?* (easier said than done) Have children turn to a partner and discuss what they think this lesson means.

Comprehension Check *The end of these story is a little surprising. The mice did not think of a way to stop the cat. It is not a happy ending for the mice. But the last page explains that the story teaches a lesson. That helps to explain the ending.*

 Quick Check Can children understand vocabulary in context? If not, review and reteach using the instruction on page 84.

Can children read the high-frequency words in context? If not, review using the Read/Spell/Write routine and the High-Frequency Word Cards.

Objectives
- Understand complex text through close-reading
- Read a fable
- Recognize and understand problem and solution
- Respond to the selection using text evidence to support ideas

Materials
- "The Cat and the Mice" Apprentice Leveled Reader
- Graphic Organizer: Problem and Solution

☞ **Go Digital**
- Apprentice Leveled Reader ebook
- Downloadable Graphic Organizer
- Problem and Solution Mini-Lesson

Scaffolding for **Wonders** Approaching Leveled Reader

DURING READING

20–30 Minutes   SL.2.2   RL.2.1   RL. 2.2   RL.2.3   CCSS

Tell children they will now reread the selection, "The Cat and the Mice." Review the vocabulary and high-frequency words that they will encounter as they read.

Close Reading

🔍 Pages 2–3

Problem and Solution Remind children that a story often has characters who have a problem. Explain that good readers think about the problem and the steps that characters take to solve the problem to better understand a story. Reread pages 2 and 3. Ask: *What problem does the characters have?* (Cat is eating the mice.) Model filling in the Problem and Solution chart.

🔍 Pages 4–5

Problem and Solution Reread page 4. Ask: *What do the mice decide to do?* (have a meeting) *What do they talk about at the meeting? Point to the sentence that tells.* ("What can we do about Cat?") *How will having a meeting help them?* (It gives the mice a chance to figure out a solution.) Guide children in adding this to their Problem and Solution charts.

Connection of Ideas (A C T) Point to the picture on page 4. Ask: *Why is the mouse holding a trap?* (He offers a suggestion that they could make a trap for the cat.) *What do you think the mice know about traps like this?* (It is the kind of trap that people often set for mice.)

🔍 Pages 6–7

Problem and Solution Reread page 6. Say: *Offering ideas at this meeting is another step to figuring out how to solve their problem.* Ask: *What idea does the old mouse offer?* (to put a bell on the cat) Reread page 7 and ask why putting a bell on the cat would help the mice solve their problem. Have children turn to a partner to discuss their ideas. Guide children to add this step to the Problem and Solution charts.

🔍 Pages 8–9

Problem and Solution Reread pages 8 and 9. *Why do the mice say that they could run and hide?* (If the cat wore a bell, they would hear it ring and that would give them time to run and hide before Cat could catch them.) *Do the mice like this idea?* (yes)

Connection of Ideas (A C T) Reread page 9. Ask: *Do you think the mice feel they have solved their problem? Why or why not?* (They do because they are so happy.)

🔍 Pages 10–11

Connection of Ideas (A C T) Reread page 10. Say: *It says in the text that the mice had solved their problem. Have they really?* (no) *How does the picture help you understand this?* (The picture of the cat is shown inside a cloud. This tells me it is just a thought.)

Organization (A C T) Point out that on page 10 it seems as if the story is almost over. The mice have solved their problem. Reread page 11. Ask: *Why is this an important question to ask?* (The idea won't work unless they can figure out how to put the bell on the cat.) Explain that this is part of solution that the mice had not thought through. Ask: *Do you think the story is almost over now?* (no) Invite children to notice that now a new part of the story will begin. The story was organized by problem and solution, but now there is a new twist.

 **Pages 12–13**

Problem and Solution Reread pages 12 and 13. Ask: *Why are the mice looking at the old mouse?* (Because they want him to put the bell on the cat.)

 **Pages 14–15**

Problem and Solution Ask: *Why do none of the mice want to put the bell on the cat?* (They are too afraid to get near the cat.) *Did the mice solve their problem?* (no) Have children fill in these details on their Problem and Solution charts.

Genre **ACT** Reread page 15. Ask: *How is this ending different than the way stories usually end?* (This page tells a lesson, but most stories just tell what happens.) Ask: *What is the lesson of this story* ("Easier said than done.") *What is "easier said than done" in this story?* (The idea of putting a bell on the cat is easier than doing it.) *Point out that in a fable the most important thing is the lesson the characters learn. That is why the story ends there.*

AFTER READING

10–15 Minutes   RL. 2.1   RL. 2.2   RL.2.7   L . 2.4a   W.2.8   **CCSS**

Respond to Reading

Compare Texts Guide children in comparing the lessons in "The Cat and the Mice" with the lesson in "The Boy Who Cried Wolf." Help children think about what fables can teach us. Then ask: *How do these stories help you know how to act?*

Summarize Have children turn to page 16 and guide them in summarizing the selection. (Answers should include the problem, the steps to solve the problem, and the solution.)

 Text Evidence

Have partners work together to answer questions on page 16. Remind children to use their Problem and Solution charts.

Problem and Solution (The mice have a problem with the cat chasing and eating them.)

Vocabulary (The text reads "The mice were thrilled!" The picture shows five mice dancing with happy expressions on their faces. These clues tell us that *thrilled* means "happy, merry, joyful.")

Write About Reading (Answers will vary but should explain that the mice think of making a trap (page 5) and of putting a bell on the cat.)

Read "Beware of Tiger!"

Encourage children to read the paired selection "Beware of Tiger!" on pages 17–19. Have them summarize the selection and compare it to "The Cat and the Mice." Have them work with a partner to answer the "Make Connections" questions on page 19.

Independent Reading

Have pairs of children reread "The Cat and the Mice". Have them talk about ways the mice tried to solve their problem.

✔ **Quick Check** Can students identify Problem and Solution? If not, review and reteach using the instruction on page 84 and assign the Unit 2 Week 2 digital mini-lesson.

Can students respond to the selection using text evidence? If not, provide sentence frames to help them organize their ideas.

WEEK 2 LESSON 5

Objectives
- Review weekly vocabulary words
- Review problem and solution
- Write an analysis about the author's use of problem and solution

Scaffolding for **McGraw-Hill Reading Wonders** Reading/Writing Workshop

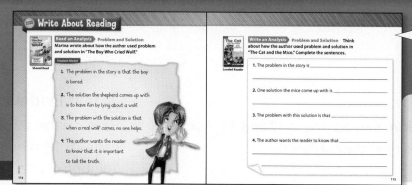

Materials
- Visual Vocabulary Cards: 49–56
- Interactive Worktext, pp. 114–115
- Assessment Book, pp. 22–23

☞ **Go Digital**
- Visual Vocabulary Cards
- Problem/Solution Mini-Lesson
- Interactive eWorktext
- eAssessment

REVIEW AND RETEACH

5–10 Minutes   L.2.4a   RL.2.3   RL.2.5

Weekly Vocabulary

Display one **Visual Vocabulary Card** at a time and guide children to use the vocabulary word in a sentence. If children have difficulty creating a sentence, have them find the word in "The Boy Who Cried Wolf" or "The Cat and the Mice" and use context clues to define the vocabulary word.

Comprehension: Problem/Solution

I Do Write and say: *Will and Meg want to start a comic book club at school. They don't have a place to hold their meetings. Will and Meg ask Mr. Evans to help them find a room. Mr. Evans lets Will and Meg use his classroom for the meetings.* Ask: *What problem do Will and Meg have?* Circle "They don't have a place to hold their meetings." Ask: *What step do Will and Meg take to solve their problem?* Circle "Will and Meg ask Mr. Evans for help finding a room." Say: *How does Mr. Evans help Will and Meg solve their problem?* Circle "Mr. Evans lets Will and Meg use his classroom for the meetings."

We Do Display: *Gwen finds three kittens on the sidewalk. The kittens need food and water. Gwen takes the kittens home and feeds them.* Ask: *What problem does Gwen face in this story?* (The kittens need food and water.) *How does Gwen solve this problem?* (Gwen takes the kittens home and feeds them.)

You Do Display: *For his birthday, Paul got a new bike. Paul is afraid to learn how to ride it. His father tells him he will help him. Paul agrees to try.* Guide one partner to ask a question about the problem or solution and the other partner to respond with details that answer it.

WRITE ABOUT READING

25–35 Minutes   W.2.3   W.2.8   W.4.9

Read an Analysis

- Guide children to look back at "The Boy Who Cried Wolf" in the **Interactive Worktext**. Have volunteers review the notes about the problem and solution they marked on page 107 and summarize the text. Repeat with pages 108–111. *How did the author use problem and solution to help you understand the story?*

- Read aloud the directions on page 114. Read aloud the student model. *This student's work is not a summary. It is an analysis, or description, of how the author used problem and solution in "The Boy Who Cried Wolf."*

- *When you write an analysis, you should include key details from the story that tell about the story. Read Marina's first sentence. Circle the details.* (the boy is bored) *In what part of the story do you learn these details?* (the beginning)

- *Read the second sentence. Draw a box around the details from the story you see in Marina's writing.* (The solution the shepherd comes up with is to lie about a wolf.) *What part of the story is she writing about?* (the middle)

- Guide children to point to the third sentence. This sentence explains the problem with the shepherd's solution. *What does Marina say is the problem with the solution?* (When a real wolf comes, no one helps.)

- Model analyzing how the author used details to write the story. Read the last sentence that Marina wrote. *Why is this sentence a good ending?* (Marina explained how the author use the story to tell a message.)

Write an Analysis
Analytical Writing

Guided Writing Read the writing prompt on page 115 together. Guide children to review their Problem and Solution charts for "The Cat and the Mice." Have children use their charts to complete the sentence starters. Children can also write an analysis using another selection previously read this week.

Peer Conference Guide children to read their analysis to a partner. Listeners should summarize the strongest details that tell the problem, steps to the solution, and the solution. They should discuss any parts that are unclear.

Teacher Conference Check children's writing for complete sentences and whether they included details from the story. Review the ending sentence and ask: *Did the author use details to support the story?* If necessary, guide children to revise their sentence by adding more details.

Level Up

▲ Apprentice Leveled Reader

▲ Approaching Leveled Reader

▲ Interactive Worktext

▲ Reading/Writing Workshop

IF children read the **Apprentice Level** Reader and the **Interactive Worktext** Shared Read fluently and answer the Respond to Reading questions

THEN read together the **Approaching Level** Reader main selection and the **Reading/Writing Workshop** Shared Read from *Reading Wonders*. Have children take notes as they read, using self-stick notes. Then ask and answer questions about their notes.

Writing Rubric

	4	3	2	1
Text Evidence	Includes three or more details from the text.	Includes two or more details from the text.	Includes only one detail from the text.	No text evidence is cited.
Writing Style	Writes in complete sentences. Uses correct spelling and grammar.	Uses complete sentences. Writing has spelling and grammar errors.	Few complete sentences. There are many spelling and grammar errors.	Writing is not accurate or in complete sentences.

ASSESSMENT

Weekly Assessment

Have children complete the Weekly Assessment using **Assessment** book pages 22–23.

WEEK'S LESSON

1

Objectives
• Develop oral language
• Build background about animal habitats
• Understand and use weekly vocabulary
• Read a narrative nonfiction selection

Scaffolding for **Wonders** Reading/Writing Workshop

Materials
Interactive Worktext, pp. 116–125
• Visual Vocabulary Cards: 57–64

☞ **Go** Digital
• Interactive eWorktext
• Visual Vocabulary Cards

WEEKLY CONCEPT

5–10 Minutes　　SL.2.1a　SL.2.4　CCSS

Talk About It

Essential Question Read aloud the Essential Question on page 116 of the **Interactive Worktext**: *What are features of different animal habitats?* Explain that a habitat is the environment where wild animals live, such as a forest or a desert. Provide examples of the features of a habitat, such as the trees and plants that grow in the forest. Say: *Habitats provide food and shelter for animals that live in them.*

• Discuss the photograph on page 116. Ask: *What do you see in the photograph?* (Many fish are swimming around some coral.)

I Do Say: *I am going to look at the photo and think about the features of this habitat.* (I see fish swimming below some coral. The small spaces in the coral provide a place for fish to hide from predators.) *I will write how this ocean habitat provides shelter from predators on the web on page 117.*

We Do Say: *Let's think about other features of this ocean habitat. I see the coral has bright colors, similar to the fish. This could provide camouflage for the fish. The bright colors of the coral confuse predators.* Have children talk with a partner about other features and choose one to add to their web.

You Do Guide partners to work together to continue talking about other features of this ocean habitat. If children have difficulty, prompt them to think about what fish eat. Have them orally complete the sentence starter: *Ocean habitats provide _____ for fish.*

REVIEW VOCABULARY

10–15 Minutes　　L.2.5a　L.2.6　RF.2.3f　CCSS

Review Weekly Vocabulary Words

• Use the **Visual Vocabulary Cards** to review the weekly vocabulary.

• Read together the directions on page 118 of the **Interactive Worktext**. Then complete the activity.

1 **spies** Explain that the word *spies* has more than one meaning. Say: *The word* spies *can mean to watch someone secretly or to catch sight of something. Think about the meaning of* spies *in this sentence: If you are looking for a shooting star, you will spy it in the night sky.* Have children tell the meaning of the word. (To catch sight of.)

2 **buried** Explain that when something is *buried* it is put under things. Model using *buried* in a sentence: *The letter was* buried *in a pile of papers.* Have children use the following sentence starter: *At the beach, I found a _____* buried *in the sand.* (Possible answers: shell, piece of glass, shovel)

3 **journey** Tell children about a *journey* or trip that you or someone you know has taken. Ask them to tell their partners about a *journey* they would like to be on. Have children complete the following sentence: *If I could travel anywhere on a long* journey, *I would travel to _____.* (Answers will vary.)

4 **restless** Tell children that to be *restless* means you cannot be still. Model using *restless* in a sentence. Say: *Bill was* restless *and kept getting up during the show.* Have children tell about a time they were *restless* using this sentence starter: *I was* restless *when _____.* Ask volunteers to demonstrate how people act when they are *restless.*

5 habitat Describe for children a *habitat* nearby. Ask them to contribute to the description. Write the following animals on the board: *pig, bear, frog, cow.* Ask a volunteer to point out which animal lives in a pond *habitat.* (frog) Then ask which animal lives in a forest *habitat.* (bear)

6 peeks Demonstrate for the children how to *peek* from behind a book. Have the children imitate your action and make sure that they are doing it quickly. Read the sentence chorally and then invite children to replace *peeks* with another word with a similar meaning. (Possible answers: looks, glances)

7 escape Explain that when you *escape* from something, you get out of it. Ask children to explain how a tiger might *escape* from its cage at the zoo. Then guide children in thinking of another way to say *escape.* (Possible answers: get out, break free)

8 nature Have a volunteer describe what they might see on a camping trip or in a park. (Possible answers: trees, birds, plants, flowers, rocks and so on.) Then have children draw a picture of something in *nature.* Use the sentence starter: *On a* nature *hike, I might see a _____.*

High-Frequency Words

Have children look at page 119 in the **Interactive Worktext**. Help them read, spell, and write each high-frequency word. Guide partners to use each word in a sentence. Then read the story aloud with children. Guide partners to work together to reread the story and circle the high-frequency words. (I, four, eat, Soon, out, run) Listen in and provide assistance reading the high-frequency words, as necessary.

> ### ELL ENGLISH LANGUAGE LEARNERS
> Display the **High-Frequency Word Cards** for: *I, run, eat, soon, out, four.* Write a sentence with each word. Have children echo-read each sentence, and point out the high-frequency word. Then ask them to use the word in a new sentence.

READ COMPLEX TEXT

15–20 Minutes   RI.2.1   RI.2.2   SL.2.1b CCSS

Read "A Prairie Guard Dog"

- Have children turn to page 120 in the **Interactive Worktext** and read aloud the Essential Question. Point to the picture. Say: *This animal is called a prairie dog.* Have children repeat: *prairie dog. Let's read to find out where this animal lives.* Have children echo-read the title.

- Read the story together. Note that the weekly vocabulary words are highlighted in yellow. Expand Vocabulary words are highlighted in blue.

- As children read, have them use the "My Notes" section on page 120 to write questions they have. Children can also write words they don't understand or things they want to remember. Model how to use the "My Notes" section. *When I read the title, I wonder what a "prairie guard dog" is. I wonder what it does. I will write a question about what a prairie guard dog is in the "My Notes" section.*

> ### ELL ENGLISH LANGUAGE LEARNERS
> As you read together, have children highlight parts of the text they have questions about. After reading, review the questions children have. Then help them locate the answers to their questions in the text.

 Quick Check Can children understand the weekly vocabulary in context? If not, review vocabulary using the **Visual Vocabulary Cards** before teaching Lesson 2.

Can children read high-frequency words in context? If not, review using the Read/Spell/Write routine and the High-Frequency Word Cards.

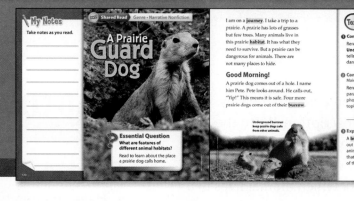

WEEK 3 LESSON 2

Objectives
- Read narrative nonfiction
- Understand complex text through close reading
- Recognize and understand main topic and key details
- Respond to the selection using text evidence to support ideas

Scaffolding for **WONDERS** McGraw-Hill Reading Reading/Writing Workshop

Materials
Interactive Worktext, pp. 120–127

☞ **Go** Digital
- Interactive eWorktext
- Main Topic and Key Details Mini-Lesson

REREAD COMPLEX TEXT

20–25 Minutes   RI.2.1   RI.2.2   RI.2.4   L.2.4a   **CCSS**

Close Reading: "A Prairie Guard Dog"

Reread "A Prairie Guard Dog" from **Interactive Worktext** pages 120–125 with children. As you read together, discuss important passages in the text. Guide children to respond to questions using evidence from the text.

Pages 120–121

Connection of Ideas **A C T** Say: *I read that a prairie has lots of grasses but few trees.* Point out that trees are a good place for animals to hide. Say: *I also read that the prairie can be a dangerous place for animals. There are not many places to hide.* Guide children to reread the first paragraph and underline the words that tell why a prairie can be dangerous. (There are not many places to hide.)

Main Topic and Key Details Point out to children that they can use key details to figure out the main topic of a story. Guide children to look at the photos in the spread. Then, reread the second paragraph aloud. Ask: *What is the main topic of this selection?* Remind children that the main topic is what the selection is mostly about. Guide children to write their answer. (prairie dogs)

Expand Vocabulary Explain that a *burrow* is a home dug out of the ground by an animal. It has a hole in the top where animals enter. Have children look at the photo on page 121 and reread the second paragraph. Ask: *What comes out of the* burrow? Guide children to circle the text that tells. (prairie dogs)

Genre **A C T** Point out the section head "Good Morning!" to children. Explain that narrative nonfiction selections give information in a sequence. Note that this selection begins in the morning of a given day.

Page 122

Expand Vocabulary Have children locate the word *guard* on the page. Explain that a *guard* watches over others to keep them safe. Tell children that Pete is the *guard*. Ask: *Who does* Pete *guard?* Guide children to circle the words that tell. (the other prairie dogs)

Main Topic and Key Details Remind children that key details are important to understanding the main topic of a selection. Have children reread the paragraph. Ask: *What is the key detail that tells what Pete's family does while he looks for danger?* Guide children to draw a box around the words that tell. (eat, groom each other)

Page 123

Organization **A C T** Remind children that sometimes nonfiction selections are divided into sections. The heading of each section gives information about what the author will tell about in the text below the heading. Ask: *What is the title of the section?* ("A Scare") *What do you think will happen in this section?* (The prairie dogs will get scared.)

Expand Vocabulary Point to the photo on page 123. Explain that a *badger* is an animal that also lives on the prairie and hunts prairie dogs. Ask: *What does Pete do when he spies a* badger? Guide children to circle the words that tell. (barks loudly "Yap! Yap!") Discuss why Pete barks. (to warn the other prairie dogs)

Main Topic and Key Details Have children reread the second paragraph. Remind them that key details give more information about the main topic. Ask: *What key detail tells what Pete does when the badger runs toward him?* Guide children to draw a box around the words that tell what Pete does. (Pete runs to escape.)

Connection of Ideas **A C T** Reread the third paragraph. Ask: *Why does Pete peek his head out?* Guide children to write the answer. (To continue guarding the burrow.)

Page 124

Expand Vocabulary Have children reread the first paragraph. Demonstrate with gestures how the sun gets *higher.* Ask: *What happens when the sun gets* higher? Guide children to circle the words that tell. (The prairie gets hot.)

Main Topic and Key Details Read the first paragraph aloud. Ask: *Why do the prairie dogs go inside when the prairie gets hot?* Guide children to draw a box around the words that tell. (It is cool there.)

Connection of Ideas **A C T** Reread the second paragraph. Guide children to think about how prairie dogs use their burrows. Ask: *How do burrows help prairie dogs survive?* (Possible answers: Burrows keep prairie dogs cool and give them a place to sleep and eat.)

Page 125

Expand Vocabulary Explain to children that if Gary is on *duty,* he is doing his job. Ask: *What will Gary do on* duty? Guide children to write the answer to the question. (Possible answers: look for danger, be the guard)

Connection of Ideas **A C T** Have children reread the rest of the page. Ask: *What do the other prairie dogs do when Gary calls "Yip"?* Guide them to underline the words that tell. (come out)

Main Topic and Key Details Have children look at the illustration on page 124 and reread the chart on page 125. Remind children that charts and illustrations often give more information about the main topic. Ask: *What words in the chart give key details about the prairie dogs' shelter?* Guide children to draw a box around the text that tells. (underground burrows with many rooms)

RESPOND TO READING

10–20 Minutes   RI.2.1   RI.2.2   SL.2.1b

Respond to "A Prairie Guard Dog"

Read aloud the questions on page 126 of the **Interactive Worktext**. Guide children read the questions about "A Prairie Guard Dog." Then read aloud the "Discussion Starters" for each of the questions. Guide children to work with a partner to answer the questions orally using the "Discussion Starters." Have children find text evidence to support their answers. Ask children to write the page number(s) on which they found the text evidence for each question.

1. *What is a prairie dog's habitat like?* (Possible answers: A prairie dog's habitat is called a prairie. A prairie has lots of grasses but few trees. Text Evidence: p. 121)

2. *How do prairie dogs stay safe in their habitat?* (Possible answers: A prairie dog lives in a burrow underground. The burrow helps them stay safe from badgers and other dangers. Text Evidence: p. 123)

3. *How else does a prairie dog's habitat help it survive?* (Possible answers: When the sun gets hot, prairie dogs go in their burrows to stay cool. Their burrows give them a safe place to live. Text Evidence: p. 124)

After children discuss the questions on page 126, have them use the sentence starters to answer the question on page 127. Circulate and provide guidance.

 Quick Check Do children understand vocabulary in context? If not, review and reteach using the instruction on page 94.

Can children identify main topic and key details? If not, review and reteach using the instruction on page 94 and assign the Unit 2 Week 3 digital mini-lesson.

Can children write a response to "A Prairie Guard Dog"? If not, review the sentence starters and prompt children to respond orally. Help them write their responses.

WEEK 3 LESSON 3

Objectives
- Access prior knowledge
- Understand and use new vocabulary words
- Read high-frequency words
- Read expository text

Materials
"A Tree Full of Life" Apprentice Leveled Reader
- High-Frequency Word Cards

☞ **Go Digital**
- Apprentice Leveled Reader eBook
- Downloadable High-Frequency Word Cards

Scaffolding for **Wonders** Approaching Leveled Reader

BEFORE READING

10–15 Minutes SL.2.1a SL.2.6 L.2.5a L.2.6 RF.2.3f CCSS

Introduce "A Tree Full of Life"

- Read the Essential Question on the title page of "A Tree Full of Life" **Apprentice Leveled Reader:** *What are features of different animal habitats?*

- Read the title of the main read. Point to the cover. *What do you think this informational text will be about?* (a tree) *What are some things that live in a tree?* (Possible answers: birds, squirrels) *What animal have you seen that lives in a tree? Let's read to learn about life in a tree.*

High-Frequency Words

Display the **High-Frequency Word Cards** for the words *come, full, good, many, other,* and *use.* Use the Read/Spell/Write routine to teach each word. Guide partners to use each word in a sentence. Provide assistance reading the high-frequency words, as necessary.

Expand Vocabulary

Before reading "A Tree Full of Life," help children read the following words that they will encounter. Display each word below. Use the Define/Example/Ask routine. Tell children to look for the word later on as they read "A Tree Full of Life."

 nectar (page 13)

Define: sweet liquid formed in flowers

Example: Bees use *nectar* to make honey.

Ask: What are some other animals that like the *nectar* of flowers?

2 paste (page 7)

Define: a mixture used to stick things together

Example: I used *paste* to stick a paper flower on my art paper.

Ask: What are some other uses for *paste*?

3 roots (page 12)

Define: the part of the plant that grows underground

Example: When the old tree fell we could see its big *roots.*

Ask: Why do plants need *roots*?

4 wood (page 7)

Define: the material that trees are made of

Example: The cabin was made out of *wood.*

Ask: What in the classroom is made from *wood*?

DURING READING

20–30 Minutes SL.2.2 RI.2.2 RI. 2.4 L.2.4a CCSS

Tell children you will now read "A Tree Full of Life." Tell them to note the vocabulary and high-frequency words you just introduced as you read the story. Stop to model understanding of the story as you go.

Pages 2–3

High-Frequency Words Make sure children can read the high-frequency word *good.*

Comprehension Check Model beginning to read the text. Say: *The first thing I notice about this book is that it begins with a picture of a tree. The text says it is a special tree called a eucalyptus tree. It says that this tree is a good home for plants and animals. As I read, I will be on the lookout for plants and animals that live there. I will also look out for what makes this tree such a good home.*

Vocabulary Read page 3. Focus on the word *trunks*. Explain that the word *trunk* is a multiple-meaning word. Ask: *What meanings of the word* trunk *do you know?* (a part of a tree, an elephant's nose, something you put things in) Guide children to look for clues in the text to identify which meaning is correct here. Ask: *What is this text about?* (eucalyptus trees) *What does the sentence tell us that they have?* (big trunks) *What is the meaning of the word* trunks *in this sentence?* (the main stem of a tree)

Pages 4–5

Vocabulary Read the first sentence on page 4. Ask: *What animal does the sentence tells about?* (koalas) Ask children how they can know what a koala is. (look at the picture) Have children describe the koala in the picture.

Comprehension Check *I will stop and think about what I've read. I have been reading about eucalyptus trees. I know that they are big trees and have leaves that smell sweet. I learn that koalas live in the trees and like to eat the leaves. Having sweet leaves is one thing that makes this tree a good home. On page 5, I learn that the tree makes a good bed. So that is another way it is a good home.*

Pages 6–7

High-Frequency Words Make sure children can read the high-frequency words *many* and *come*.

Comprehension Check *I think about the termites eating the wood and making paste. I wonder what they use the paste for. I'll keep reading to find out.*

Pages 8–9

High-Frequency Words Make sure children can read the high-frequency word *use*.

Vocabulary On page 8, focus on the word *nests*. Point out that children know that a bird's nest is something birds make to use for laying eggs. Ask: *How does knowing about a bird nest help you to understand the termite nest?* (It is something termites build where they can lay eggs).

Comprehension Check *When I read page 9, I learn that the bird is in a hole the termites made. I think the termites made this hole when they ate the wood.*

Pages 10–11

High-Frequency Words Make sure children can read the high-frequency word *other*.

Comprehension Check *On page 11, I read that possums eat leaves. I remember reading about another animal that lives in trees and eat leaves. I can turn back to the beginning of this text to recall what I read. On page 4, I read that koalas live in trees and eat eucalyptus leaves.*

Pages 12–13

Vocabulary Read page 12 and focus on the word *roots*. Ask: *Where can the roots of a tree be found?* (Roots are the part of a tree that grows underground.) *What animal likes to eat the roots?* (wombats)

Vocabulary On page 13, read the sentence *"They look for nectar to eat."* Ask: *What clue in this sentence helps us understand the meaning of* nectar? (The words *to eat* let us know that nectar is a kind of food.)

Pages 14–15

High-Frequency Words Make sure children can read the high-frequency word *full*.

Comprehension Check *The text told about many things that live in a tree. I learned about both animals and plants that live in the trees. I learned about the parts of a tree that some plants and animals eat. I think that "A Tree Full of Life" is a good title for this text.*

✓ *Quick Check* **Can children understand vocabulary in context? If not, review and reteach using the instruction on page 94.**

Can children read the high-frequency words in context? If not, review using the Read/Spell/Write routine and the High-Frequency Word Cards.

WEEK 3
LESSON
4

Objectives
• Understand complex text through close-reading
• Read expository text
• Recognize and understand main topic and key details
• Respond to the selection using text evidence to support ideas

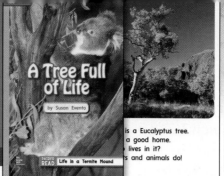

Materials
"A Tree Full of Life" Apprentice Leveled Reader
• Graphic Organizer: Main Topic and Key Details

☞ Go Digital
• Apprentice Leveled Reader ebook
• Downloadable Graphic Organizer
• Main Topic and Key Details Mini-Lesson

Scaffolding for WONDERS Approaching Leveled Reader

DURING READING

20–30 Minutes   RI.2.1   RI.2.2   RI.2.5   **CCSS**

Tell children they will now reread the selection, "A Tree Full of Life." Review the vocabulary and high-frequency words that they will encounter as they read.

Close Reading

Pages 2–3

Main Topic and Key Details Explain that the main topic is what a text is mostly about. Reread page 2. Ask: *What does the text tell us about eucalyptus trees?* (They are good homes for plants and animals.) Point out that this is the main topic of the book. Explain that key details tell more about the main topic. Reread page 3. Ask what they learn about eucalyptus trees here (they have big trunks, their leaves smell sweet) Model recording details on the Main Topic and Key Details charts.

Genre A C T Explain that expository texts often include text features such as photos with labels. Explain that labels can give important information about the photo. Point to the label on page 3. Say: *The label tells us what kind of leaves are shown in the photo.*

Pages 4–5

Main Topic and Key Details Reread pages 4 and 5. Ask: *Where do koalas live?* (in the tree) *What do they eat?* (leaves) *Where do koalas sleep?* (in the branches) Guide children in adding these details to their Main Topic and Key Details charts.

Pages 6–7

Main Topic and Key Details Reread page 7. Ask: *How do termites use the tree?* (They eat the wood and make paste.) Guide children to add these details to their Main Topic and Key Details charts.

Genre A C T Point to the labels on page 7. Say: *The labels tell us what is shown in the photo. What is in the photo?* (termites and wood) *What does the photo tells us that the text does not?* (Many termites eat together.)

Pages 8–9

Genre A C T Point to the label on page 8. Ask: *What does this photo show?* (a termite nest) *What does the photo help us understand about the text on the page?* (It shows how big the termite nest is.)

Main Topic and Key Details Reread pages 8 and 9. Ask: *How do termites use the paste from the wood they eat?* (to make big nests) Ask: *What else can use the nests the termites make?* (birds) Prompt children to include these details on their Main Topic and Key Details charts.

Pages 10–11

Prior Knowledge A C T Point to the label on page 10. Say: *A sugar glider is a type of possum. It likes to eat sweet food and it can glide hundreds of feet. What other animals might live in a hole like this?* (owls, bats)

Main Topic and Key Details Point to the picture on page 10. Ask: *Where are these animals?* (in a hole in a tree made by termites) Read page 11. Ask: *What part of the tree do possums use for food?* (leaves) Help children add these details to their Main Topic and Key Details charts.

Pages 12–13

Main Topic and Key Details After reading page 12, ask: *What part of a tree does a wombat use for food?* (roots) Reread page 13 and ask: *How do bats use trees and other plants?* (They eat the nectar.) *Where would bats need to look to find nectar?* (Nectar is found in a plant's flowers.) Guide children in adding these details to their Main Topic and Key Details charts.

Connection of Ideas A C T Reread page 13. Have children turn to partners to recall what they have learned about ways that animals need plants. Suggest that partners flip back to previous pages and use pictures to talk about the relationships between animals and plants.

Pages 14–15

Genre A C T Reread pages 14 and 15 and point to the labels. Ask: *What do the labels tell you that the text does not tell you?* (The label tells the name of the plant living in the eucalyptus tree: mistletoe.)

Main Topic and Key Details Reread page 15 and ask: *What kind of plant lives in this tree?* (mistletoe) Ask children to point to the part of the picture that shows the mistletoe plant. *How does the mistletoe plant use the tree?* (It eats the sap.) Help children add these details to their Main Topic and Key Details charts.

Main Topic and Key Details Have children review the details recorded on their Main Topic and Key Details charts. Remind them of the main topic they identified in the beginning, that the eucalyptus tree is a good home. Review each detail and discuss how it supports the main topic. Guide children in completing their Main Topic and Key Details charts.

AFTER READING

10–15 Minutes   RI.2.2   RI. 2.4   RI. 2.9   RF.2.4b   W.2.8   CCSS

Respond to Reading

Compare Texts Guide children in comparing the habitats of the animals in "A Tree Full of Life" and "A Prairie Guard Dog." Help children think about the important features of the animals' habitats. Then ask: *What do you think is the most important feature of an animal's habitat?*

Summarize Have children turn to page 16 and guide them in summarizing the selection. (Answers should demonstrate an understanding of relevant details and how they support the main topic.)

Text Evidence

Have partners work together to answer questions on page 16. Remind children to use their Main Topic and Key Details charts.

Main Topic and Key Details (Answers will vary but should explain that koalas eat the tree's leaves and sleep in its branches.)

Vocabulary (The text reads, "This plant lives in the tree. It eats the tree's sap." Sap must mean something that comes from the tree that can be eaten.)

Write About Reading (Answers will vary but should state that the main idea is that many animals—and even a plant—use eucalyptus trees for food and shelter. Look for key details from the story in their answers.)

Read "Life in a Termite Mound"

Encourage children to read the paired selection "Life in a Termite Mound" on pages 17–19. Have them summarize the selection and compare it to "A Tree Full of Life." Have them work with a partner to answer the "Make Connections" questions on page 19.

Independent Reading

Have pairs of children reread "A Tree Full of Life" together. Have them talk about the different animals and plants that use trees.

 Quick Check Can students identify the Main Topic and Key Details? If not, review and reteach using the instruction on page 94 and assign the Unit 2 Week 3 digital mini-lesson.

Can students respond to the selection using text evidence? If not, provide sentence frames to help them organize their ideas.

Objectives
• Review weekly vocabulary words
• Review main topic and key details
• Write an analysis about how the author used main topic and key details.

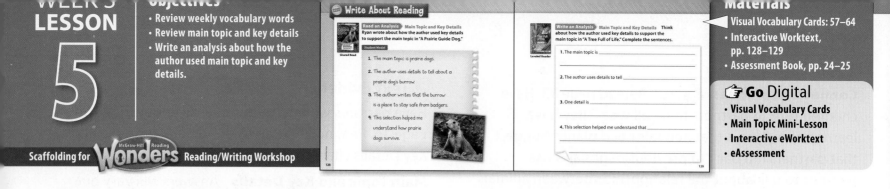

Materials
• **Visual Vocabulary Cards:** 57–64
• **Interactive Worktext,** pp. 128–129
• **Assessment Book,** pp. 24–25

☞ **Go** Digital
• **Visual Vocabulary Cards**
• **Main Topic Mini-Lesson**
• **Interactive eWorktext**
• **eAssessment**

Scaffolding for **Wonders** Reading/Writing Workshop

REVIEW AND RETEACH

5–10 Minutes   L.2.5a   RI.2.1   RI.2.2

Weekly Vocabulary

Display one **Visual Vocabulary Card** at a time and guide children to use the vocabulary word in a sentence. If children have difficulty creating a sentence, have them find the word in "A Prairie Guard Dog" or "A Tree Full of Life" and use context clues to define the vocabulary word.

Comprehension: Main Topic and Key Details

I Do Write and say: *My dog Rex is funny. He likes us to chase him. He jumps around while we eat dinner. Rex sleeps in my room.* Ask: *What is this story about? I can look for the main topic.* Circle the words *Rex* and *He. I notice that each sentence is a detail about Rex. Rex must be the main topic of this story.*

We Do Display and say: *It is fall. The leaves are changing colors. It is getting cooler. I go back to school.* Ask: *What do all of these sentences have in common? What are they all about?* (fall) *How can you tell?* (I reread each sentence and they each tell something about fall.)

You Do Display: *The soccer team won the game today. They played well. The players worked together. They passed the ball to each other. The coach was proud of the team.* Have partners read the sentences out loud to each other. Then guide one partner to tell the main topic. Have partners discuss the answer.

WRITE ABOUT READING

25–35 Minutes   W.2.2   W.2.8   W.4.9

Read an Analysis

• Guide children to look back at "A Prairie Guard Dog" in the **Interactive Worktext**. Have volunteers review the details about the main topic they marked on page 121 and summarize the text. Repeat with pages 122–125. *How did the author use key details to tell about the main topic of the story?*

• Read aloud the directions on page 128. Read aloud the student model. *This student's work is not a summary. It is an analysis, or description, of how the author used details to support the main topic in "A Prairie Guard Dog."*

• *When you write an analysis, you should include key details from the story that tell about the story. Read Ryan's first sentence. What does Ryan say is the main topic of this selection?* (prairie dogs) *In what part of the selection do you learn the main topic?* (the beginning)

• *Read the second sentence. Ryan writes about how the author uses details. What did the author use details to tell about?* (a prairie dog's burrow)

• Guide children to point to the third sentence. *What details does Ryan include?* (a burrow is a safe place) *What other details could Ryan have used?* Provide a sentence frame and guide children to fill it in for each detail they think of: *Another detail about a prairie dog's burrow is _____.*

• Model analyzing how the author used details to write the story. Read the last sentence that Ryan wrote. *Why is this sentence a good ending?* (Ryan explained how details helped him understand the selection.)

✏️ *Analytical Writing* **Write an Analysis**

Guided Writing Read the writing prompt on page 129 together. Guide children to review their Main Topic and Key Details charts for "A Tree Full of Life." Have children use their charts to complete the sentence starters. Children can also write an analysis using another selection previously read this week.

Peer Conference Guide children to read their analysis to a partner. Listeners should summarize the strongest details that support the main topic of the selection. They should discuss any parts that are unclear.

Teacher Conference Check children's writing for complete sentences and whether they included details from the selection. Review the ending sentence and ask: *Did the author use details to support the selection?* If necessary, guide children to revise their sentence by adding more details.

Level Up

▲ **Approaching Leveled Reader**

▲ **Reading/Writing Workshop**

▲ **Apprentice Leveled Reader**

▲ **Interactive Worktext**

IF children read the Apprentice Level Reader and the **Interactive Worktext** Shared Read fluently and answer the Respond to Reading questions

THEN read together the Approaching Level Reader main selection and the **Reading/Writing Workshop** Shared Read from *Reading Wonders*. Have children take notes as they read, using self-stick notes. Then ask and answer questions about their notes.

Writing Rubric

	4	3	2	1
Text Evidence	Includes three or more details from the text.	Includes two or more details from the text.	Includes only one detail from the text.	No text evidence is cited.
Writing Style	Writes in complete sentences. Uses correct spelling and grammar.	Uses complete sentences. Writing has spelling and grammar errors.	Few complete sentences. There are many spelling and grammar errors.	Writing is not accurate or in complete sentences.

ASSESSMENT

Weekly Assessment

Have children complete the Weekly Assessment using **Assessment** book pages 24–25.

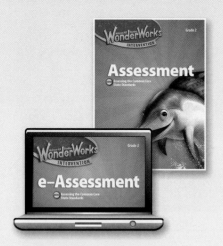

▶ **Mid-Unit Assessment,** pages 80 – 87

▶ **Fluency Assessment,** pages 234 – 239

Unit 2 Mid-Unit Assessment

CCSS TESTED SKILLS

✔ **COMPREHENSION**	✔ **VOCABULARY:**
• Character, Setting, Plot **RL.2.5**	• Context Clues **L.2.4**
• Problem and Solution **RL.2.3, RL.2.5**	
• Main Topic and Key Details **RI.2.1, RI.2.2**	

Using Assessment and Writing Scores

↻ RETEACH	IF ...	THEN ...
COMPREHENSION	Students answer 0–5 multiple-choice items correctly ...	... reteach tested skills using instruction on pages 364–375.
VOCABULARY	Students answer 0–2 multiple-choice items correctly ...	... reteach tested skills using instruction on page 364.
WRITING	Students score mostly 1–2 on weekly writing rubrics throughout the unit ...	... reteach writing using instruction on pages 376–377.

Fluency Assessment

Conduct assessments individually using the differentiated fluency passages in Assessment. Students' expected fluency goal for this Unit is 62–82 WCPM with an accuracy rate of 95% or higher.

Weeks 4 and 5

Monitor students progress on the following to inform how to adjust instruction for the remainder of the unit.

ADJUST INSTRUCTION	
ACCESS COMPLEX TEXT	If students need more support for accessing complex text, provide additional modeling of prompts in Lesson 2 of Week 4, pages 100–101, and Week 5, pages 110–111. After you model how to identify the text evidence, guide students to find text evidence in Lessons 3 and 4, in Week 4, pages 102–105, and Week 5, pages 112–115.
FLUENCY	For those students who need more support with Fluency, focus on the Fluency lessons in the Foundational Skills Kit.
WRITING	If students need more support incorporating text evidence in their writing, conduct the Write About Reading activities in Lesson 4 and 5 as group writing activities.
FOUNDATIONAL SKILLS	Review students' individualized progress in *Reading Wonders* Adaptive Learning to determine which foundational skills to incorporate into your lessons for the remainder of the unit.

Teach and Model WORKTEXT

Objectives
- Develop oral language
- Build background about baby animals and their parents
- Understand and use weekly vocabulary
- Read an expository text

Materials
- Interactive Worktext, pp. 130–139
- Visual Vocabulary Cards: 65–72
- High-Frequency Word Cards

☞ **Go Digital**
- Interactive eWorktext
- Visual Vocabulary Cards

Scaffolding for **Wonders** Reading/Writing Workshop

WEEKLY CONCEPT

5–10 Minutes   SL.2.1b SL.2.4

Talk About It

Essential Question Read aloud the Essential Question on page 130 of the **Interactive Worktext:** *How are offspring like their parents*? Explain that baby animals and their parents are similar in many ways. Provide examples of how some baby animals resemble their parents. Say: *A baby kitten has many similarities to its parents: It has fur, four legs, a tail, two ears, and so on.*

- Discuss the photograph on page 130. Ask: *What is this picture of?* (It shows a baby deer and a grown deer in the woods. The adult deer is probably its parent.) Say: *A baby deer is called a fawn.*

I Do Say: *I am going to look at the photo and think about how these animals are the same.* (I notice both the fawn and its parent have four legs.) *I will write how they are the same on the chart on page 131.* Point out the headings "Same" and "Different" on the chart and add this information to the "Same" column.

We Do Say: *Let's think about other ways the fawn is the same as its parent. I also notice they both have two pointed ears. Their ears are the same shape.* Guide children to discuss other similarities between the fawn and its parent. Then have children choose one similarity to add to their web.

You Do Guide partners to think about ways the fawn and its parent are different. Have children look closely at the photo to come up with ideas. Have them use the words from the web to start their sentences: *The fawn is different from its parent because it _____.* Then have them add these ideas to the "Different" column on the chart.

REVIEW VOCABULARY

10–15 Minutes   L.2.5a L.2.6 RF.2.3

Review Weekly Vocabulary Words

- Use the **Visual Vocabulary Cards** to review the weekly vocabulary.

- Read together the directions on page 132 of the **Interactive Worktext**. Then complete the activity.

1 **offspring** Explain that the *offspring* of an animal is its baby. Model using the word in a sentence. Say: *The mother cow has three* offspring. Write the list of animals on the board. Ask a volunteer to point out the animal whose *offspring* are kittens. (cat)

2 **mammal** Describe for children what a *mammal* is. Say: *A* mammal *is an animal that has fur or hair and breathes air.* Begin naming several animals and asking children if they are *mammals*. Have them complete the sentence frames: *Between a fish and a goat, the animal that is a* mammal *is a _____.* (goat, because it has hair and breathes air)

3 **giant** Describe for children something that is *giant*, like a mountain or the pyramids. Model using *giant* in a sentence. Say: *The* giant *tree is much taller than our house.* Read the sentence chorally and then invite children to replace *giant* with another word with a similar meaning. (Possible answers: huge, very large)

4 **alive** Hold up an inanimate object and point out that it is not a living thing. Remind children that the word *alive* relates to the words *living* and *life*. Have children look around the classroom and name one thing that is *alive* and one thing that is not *alive*. (Possible answers: alive: person, plant, class pet; not alive: desk, chair, book)

5 **groom** Ask children to act out how Ben from the sample sentence might brush his teeth. Remind children to think of how they get ready for school. Then have them name another way that people *groom* themselves. (Possible answers: brushing their hair, washing their face)

6 **covered** Ask: *What sometimes covers the ground during the winter?* (snow) Write the word *covered*. Underline the base word *cover*. Then ask: *What do you get* covered *with when you are in bed?* (Possible answer: blanket, sheet)

7 **adult** Describe one way an *adult* is different from a child. Have volunteers tell other differences. Ask children to name a member of their family who is an *adult* and one who is a child. (Possible answers: mom, dad, grandma; me, sister's name, brother's name)

8 **fur** Ask children to think of an animal that is covered with thick *fur*. Use: *A _____ has a lot of* fur. (Possible answers: bear, dog, bison) Have them draw a picture of the animal in the box while you draw one on the board. Ask volunteers to name the animal and point to the *fur*. Help children label their drawings.

High-Frequency Words

Have children look at page 133 in the **Interactive Worktext**. Help them read, spell, and write each high-frequency word. Guide partners to use each word in a sentence. Then read the story aloud with children. Guide partners to work together to reread the story and circle the high-frequency words. (have, three, do, about, are, grow) Listen in and provide assistance reading the high-frequency words, as necessary.

ELL ENGLISH LANGUAGE LEARNERS

Display the **High-Frequency Word Cards** for: *do, grow, are, three, have, about*. Write a sentence with each word on the board. Have children echo-read each sentence, and point out the high-frequency word. Then ask them to use the word in a new sentence.

READ COMPLEX TEXT

15–20 Minutes   RI.2.1   RI.2.2   SL.2.1b

Read "Eagles and Eaglets"

- Have children turn to page 134 in the **Interactive Worktext** and read aloud the Essential Question. Point to the eagle in the picture. Say: *What kind of animal do you see in this picture?* (a bald eagle) Point to the eaglets in the picture. Say: *An eagle's babies are called "eaglets." Let's read about how young bald eaglets are like their parents.* Have children echo-read the title.

- Read the story together. Note that the weekly vocabulary words are highlighted in yellow. Expand Vocabulary words are highlighted in blue.

- As children read, have them use the "My Notes" section on page 134 to write questions they have. Children can also write words they don't understand or things they want to remember. Model how to use the "My Notes" section. *When I look at the picture I see that the eaglets' feathers look different from their parent's feathers. I wonder what is different about an eaglet's feathers. I will write a question asking about the eaglet's feathers in the "My Notes" section.*

ELL ENGLISH LANGUAGE LEARNERS

As you read together, have children highlight parts of the text they have questions about. After reading, review the questions children have. Then help them locate the answers to their questions in the text.

 Quick Check Can children understand the weekly vocabulary words in context? If not, review vocabulary using the **Visual Vocabulary Cards** before teaching Lesson 2.

Can children read high-frequency words in context? If not, review using the Read/Spell/Write routine and the High-Frequency Word Cards.

WEEK 4 LESSON 2

Objectives
- Read expository text
- Understand complex text through close reading
- Recognize and understand main topic and key details
- Respond to the selection, using text evidence to support ideas

Scaffolding for **WONDERS** Reading/Writing Workshop

Materials

Interactive Worktext, pp. 134–141

☞ **Go** Digital
- Interactive Worktext
- Main Topic and Key Details Mini-Lesson

REREAD COMPLEX TEXT

20–25 Minutes   RI.2.1 RI.2.2 RI.2.7 L.2.5a CCSS

Close Reading: "Eagles and Eaglets"

Reread "Eagles and Eaglets" from **Interactive Worktext** pages 134–139 with children. As you read together, discuss important passages in the text. Guide children to respond to questions using evidence from the text.

Pages 134–135

Genre Ⓐ Ⓒ Ⓣ Point to the heading "It's Nesting Time." Explain to children that expository texts often have headings that tell what the section of text below the heading will be about. Read the heading out loud with children. Ask: *What will the section of text be about?* (nesting) If children have difficulty, point to the picture of the nest on the page. Explain that pictures can also give clues about the text.

Main Topic and Key Details Say: *The main topic of a text is what the text is mainly about.* Have children reread the page, reminding them to pay attention to what is being written about. Ask: *What is the main topic of the selection so far?* (bald eagles) Point out all of the times eagles are mentioned on the page. Have children draw a box around the word *eagle*.

Expand Vocabulary Reread the last four lines on page 135 with children. Explain that to *hatch* means to come out of an egg. Tell children that chicks come out of chicken eggs. Ask: *What comes out of a bald eagle's egg?* Guide children to circle the part of the picture that answers the question. (eaglets) Explain that a baby eagle is called an eaglet.

Connection of Ideas Ⓐ Ⓒ Ⓣ Point out that the text says that the eagles build their nests high in the trees to keep the eggs safe. Have children reread the third paragraph and ask: *What else gives you a clue that the eaglets need to be kept safe?* (The parents watch over the nest.) Explain to children that in nature there are often predators that animals need to watch out for.

Page 136

Expand Vocabulary Read aloud the first paragraph. Write the word *helpless*. Underline the root *help* in the word *helpless*. Explain that something that is *helpless* needs help to live. Ask: *Who is* helpless *in the text?* Guide children to circle the word that tells them. (eaglets)

Main Topic and Key Details Have children reread the first paragraph. Ask: *Who do eaglets depend on to get their food?* Model how to look for the text evidence that answers the question. Have children draw a box around the sentence that gives the answer. (They need their parents for food.)

Genre Ⓐ Ⓒ Ⓣ Point to the second heading and paragraph. Explain that this paragraph tells about what eaglets must learn to do to grow up. Have children reread the second paragraph. Ask: *What is one thing an eaglet must learn to do?* Guide children to write their answer. (Possible answers: to fly fast, to catch fish)

Page 137

Expand Vocabulary Point to the word *down*. Explain that the word *down* is a multiple-meaning word. Say: Down *can mean the opposite of up or it can mean small soft feathers.* Guide children to look for clues in the first two sentences to identify the correct meaning. Ask: *What is the meaning of the word* down *in the second sentence?* (small soft feathers) Guide children to circle the eaglets on page 136.

Main Topic and Key Details Have children reread the paragraph. Tell them to pay attention to key details as they read. Ask: *What happens to an eaglet's wings as it grows?* Guide children to draw a box around the sentence that tells them the answer. (They grow feathers.)

Genre **A C T** Point to the diagram on page 137. Remind children that expository text may include diagrams that explain more about the topic. Point to the labels and say: *The labels show the different parts of an eagle.* Have children reread page 136. Then ask: *What do eagles need claws for?* Guide children to write the answer. (to catch fish)

Page 138

Main Topic and Key Details Tell children to reread the paragraph. Ask: *How long do eagles live?* Guide children to draw a box around the sentence that tells the answer. (Eagles stay alive for up to thirty years.)

Page 139

Expand Vocabulary Reread the first sentence. Write the word *soar* and ask: *What words tell you how long an eagle can* soar? (for hours) Guide children to circle the words.

Main Topic and Key Details Reread the page aloud. Ask: *What does a bald eagle use to clean itself?* Guide children to draw a box around the word that tells. (beak)

Genre **A C T** Point to the caption above the picture on page 139. Explain that captions can give important information that is not mentioned anywhere else in the text. Have children echo read the caption. Ask: *What do you learn about an eagle's wings?* Guide children to underline the words that tell. (they are giant, it spreads out its feathers)

RESPOND TO READING

10–20 Minutes   RI.2.1 RI.2.2 SL.2.1b

Respond to "Eagles and Eaglets

Read aloud the questions on page 140 of the **Interactive Worktext** about "Eagles and Eaglets." Then read aloud the "Discussion Starter" for each of the questions. Guide children to work with a partner to answer the questions orally using the "Discussion Starters." Have children find text evidence to support their answers. Ask children to write the page number(s) on which they found the text evidence for each question.

1. *What are eaglets like when they are first born?* (Possible answers: At first eaglets are helpless because they cannot walk. Eaglets also need their parents for food. Text Evidence: p. 136)

2. *What do eaglets need to learn to become adult eagles?* (Possible answers: Eaglets learn to use their claws to catch fish. Eaglets also need to grow feathers. Then they can learn to fly. Text Evidence: pp. 136, 137)

3. *What do adult eagles do?* (Possible answers: I read that adult eagles use their beaks to clean their feathers. Adult eagles live for up to thirty years. Text Evidence: pp. 138, 139)

After children discuss the questions on page 140, have them use the sentence starters to answer the question on page 141. Circulate and provide guidance.

 Quick Check **Do children understand vocabulary in context? If not, review and reteach using the instruction on page 106.**

Can children identify main topic and key details? If not, review and reteach using the instruction on page 106 and assign the Unit 2 Week 4 digital mini-lesson.

Can children write a response to "Eagles and Eaglets"? If not, review the sentence starters and prompt children to respond orally. Help them write their responses.

Objectives
- Access prior knowledge
- Understand and use new vocabulary words
- Read high-frequency words
- Read expository text

Materials
- "Animal Families" Apprentice Leveled Reader
- High-Frequency Word Cards

☞ **Go Digital**
- Apprentice Leveled Reader eBook
- Downloadable High-Frequency Word Cards

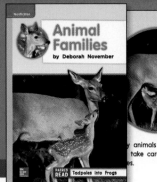

Deer mothers feed their babies. Soon the young deer can eat grass.

Scaffolding for **Wonders** Approaching Leveled Reader

BEFORE READING

10–15 Minutes SL. 2.1 SL.2.5a SL.2.6 L.2.6 RF.2.3f CCSS

Introduce "Animal Families"

- Read the Essential Question on the title page of "Animal Families" **Apprentice Leveled Reader:** *How are offspring like their parents?* Remind children that offspring is another word for children

- Read the title of the main read. Point to the cover. *What animal do you see on the cover?* (a deer) *What do you think this animal is caring for?* (a baby deer) *Which of these do you think is the parent?* (the deer) *Which is the offspring?* (the baby deer) *Let's read to learn about animals and their families.*

High-Frequency Words

Display the **High-Frequency Word Cards** for the words *carry, every, grow, soon, warm,* and *work.* Use the Read/Spell/Write routine to teach each word. Guide partners to use each word in a sentence. Provide assistance reading the high-frequency words, as necessary.

Expand Vocabulary

Before reading "Animal Families," help children read the following words that they will encounter. Display each word below. Use the Define/Example/Ask routine. Tell children to look for these words later on as they read "Animal Families."

1 **foot** (page 14)

   Define: a length of 12 inches

   Example: The piece of wood is one *foot* long.

   Ask: What are some things that are about one *foot* in length?

2 **pouch** (page 7)

   Define: a pocket of skin in some animals' fur

   Example: A baby kangaroo lives in its mother's *pouch.*

   Ask: Why might a baby be safe in a *pouch?*

3 **protects** (page 13)

   Define: to keep from harm

   Example: A parent *protects* it's babies from danger.

   Ask: What are some ways an animal parent *protects* it's offspring?

4 **spots** (page 4)

   Define: marks or areas of color on a background that is a different color

   Example: The black dog had white *spots* all over it.

   Ask: What are some animals that have *spots?*

5 **young** (page 3)

   Define: belonging to the early part of life

   Example: The *young* boy learned to ride his new bike.

   Ask: What are some things you did when you were *young?*

DURING READING

20–30 Minutes   SL.2.2   RI. 2.1   RI.2.2   L.2.4a

Shared Reading

Tell children you will now read "Animal Families." Tell them to note the vocabulary and high-frequency words you just introduced as you read the story. Stop to model understanding of the story as you go.

Pages 2–3

High-Frequency Words Make sure children can read the high-frequency word *soon.*

Comprehension Check Model reading the text. Say: *I notice photos of animals in this text. I see that the baby deer looks a lot like its mother except that it has spots.*

Vocabulary On page 2, point out that the word *babies* tells about the age of the little deer. On page 3, read "Soon the young deer can eat grass." Ask: *Which word tells about the age of the deer?* (young)

Pages 4–5

High-Frequency Words Make sure children can read the high-frequency word *grow.*

Vocabulary Read page 5 and ask: *What word on this page tells us about the age of the deer?* (adult) *What does this sentence tell us about adult deer?* (They grow big.)

Pages 6–7

Vocabulary Read page 7. Ask: *Which word tells where a joey lives?* (pouch) *How does the label help you understand the word?* (The label points to the part of the kangaroo that is the pouch.)

Comprehension Check *I will stop here and think about what I've read. I have been reading about animals and their families. I have learned that adults help take care of the babies that are too young to care for themselves.*

Pages 8–9

Vocabulary *Focus on the word* fur. Ask: *What color is the koala's fur?* (gray) *What do you think the koala's fur feels like?* (Possible answers: soft, warm)

Comprehension Check *I will stop and think about what I've just read. On page 9 I read that a baby koala lives in a pouch. I think about another animal I've just read about that lives in a pouch—the baby kangaroo.*

Pages 10–11

High-Frequency Words Make sure children can read the high-frequency words *work* and *warm.*

Comprehension Check *After I read page 11, I can think about the order in which things happen. First, the baby penguins come out of the eggs. Then the mother keeps them warm.*

Pages 12–13

High-Frequency Words Make sure children can read the high-frequency word *carries.*

Vocabulary On page 13 read the sentence "She protects them." Ask: *What does the mother alligator do to protect her babies?* (She carries them on her back.)

Pages 14–15

High-Frequency Words Make sure children can read the high-frequency word *every.*

Vocabulary Read page 14. Focus on the word *foot.* Say: *The word* foot *is a multiple-meaning word. In this sentence the word means a measurement of 12 inches.* Ask: *What is another meaning for* foot? (The part of the body at the end of a leg.)

Comprehension Check *This informational text helped me learn facts about animals and their families. I learned that animal parents take care of their babies until they are big enough to care for themselves.*

 Quick Check Can children understand vocabulary in context? If not, review and reteach using the instruction on page 106.

Can children read the high-frequency words in context? If not, review using the Read/Spell/Write routine and the High-Frequency Word Cards.

Objectives
- Understand complex text through close-reading
- Read expository text
- Recognize and understand main topic and key details
- Respond to the selection using text evidence to support ideas

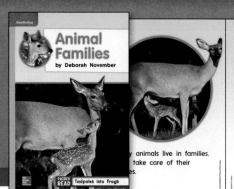

Materials
- "Animal Families" Apprentice Leveled Reader
- Graphic Organizer: Main Topic and Key Details

☞ **Go** Digital
- Apprentice Leveled Reader eBook
- Downloadable Graphic Organizer
- Main Idea and Key Details Mini-Lesson

Scaffolding for **Wonders** Approaching Leveled Reader

DURING READING
20–30 Minutes   RI.2.1   RI.2.2   RI.2.5   CCSS

Close Reading
Tell children they will now reread the selection, "Animal Families." Review the vocabulary and high-frequency words that they will encounter as they read.

 Pages 2–3

Main Topic and Key Details Remind children that the main topic is what a book is mostly about. Reread the first page. Ask: *What is this book about?* (animal families) *What does the text say you will learn about animal families?* (how they care for their babies). Point out that details tell more about the main topic. Reread page 3. Ask: *What details did you learn about deer families?* (Deer mothers feed their babies until they are able to eat on their own.) Model recording the main topic and key details on the Main Topic and Key Details Chart.

Genre ACT Remind children that informational text gives facts and details about a topic. Say: *The words in the text give important information. Text features such as photos can tell us details, too.* Point to the picture of the baby deer on page 2 and then to the young deer on page 3. Ask: *What are some ways the baby deer changes as it begins to grow?* (It loses its spots. It gets bigger.)

Pages 4–5

Main Topic and Key Details Reread pages 4 and 5. Ask: *Why do baby deer have spots?* (to keep safe so they can hide in the grass) *What do boy deer grow as they become adults?* (antlers) Guide children in adding these details to their Main Topic and Key Details charts.

Genre ACT Point to the picture of the adult deer on page 5. Say: *Informational text sometimes has text features such as labels. What does this label tell you?* (It tells which part of the deer is the antlers.)

Pages 6–7

Main Topic and Key Details Reread page 7. Ask: *How does a mother kangaroo keep her joey safe?* (She keeps the joey in her pouch.) Guide children to add these details to their Main Topic and Key Details charts.

Genre ACT Point to the photo on page 7 and read the label aloud. Ask: *How does this photo help us know more about a mother kangaroo's pouch?* (The photo shows how a joey fits and is carried in the pouch.)

Pages 8–9

Main Topic and Key Details Reread page 9. Ask: *How are kangaroos and koalas alike?* (Both have babies that live in a pouch.) Ask: *What is another way that a koala mother cares for her baby?* (She grooms its fur.) Prompt children to add these details to their Main Topic and Key Details charts.

Pages 10–11

Main Topic and Key Details Point to the picture on page 10. Ask: *What is this father penguin doing?* (He is watching the egg.) Remind children that using pictures, along with the text, is a good way to understand key details. Read page 11 and ask: *How does the penguin mother care for the babies?* (She keeps them warm and feeds them.) Help children add these details to their Main Topic and Key Details charts.

Genre ACT On page 11, we learn that the penguin mother keeps the babies warm. Ask: *What does the photo show you about how she keeps the babies warm?* (She sits near them and protects them with her fur and body.)

🔍 Pages 12–13

Main Topic and Key Details Reread page 12. Ask: *Where do alligator eggs hatch?* (the nest) Reread page 13, and ask: *How does an alligator mother protect her babies?* (She carries them on her back.) Guide children in adding these details to their Main Topic and Key Details charts.

🔍 Pages 14–15

Main Topic and Key Details After reading pages 14 and 15, ask children what they learned about animal babies (that they can grow a foot a year) Then reread page 15. Ask: *How does this page help us to understand what we have just learned?* (It points out that in all of the pages that came before, we saw how animals take care of their babies.) Guide children in adding these details to their Main Topic and Key Details charts.

Organization Explain that authors may organize a nonfiction text by giving information about one thing and then giving information about another thing. Point out that each part of this book tells about a new animal family. Ask: *What does the author tell about each animal family?* (how they take care of their young)

AFTER READING

10–15 Minutes   RI.2.2   RI. 2.4   RI.2.9   RF.2.4b   W.2.8

Respond to Reading

Compare Texts Guide children in comparing the way animals care for their young in "Animal Families" and "Eagles and Eaglets." Help children think about ways the animals' offspring are like their parents. Then ask: *Which animals do you think are most alike in the way they care for their offspring? How are they alike? How are they different?*

Summarize Have children turn to page 16 and guide them in summarizing the selection. (Answers should demonstrate an understanding of relevant details and how they support the main topic.)

🔍 Text Evidence

Have partners work together to answer questions on page 16. Remind children to use their Main Topic and Key Details charts.

Main Topic and Key Details (Mother deer give their babies milk. Then the young eat grass.)

Vocabulary (There is a photo of a deer with antlers, and a label pointing to the antlers. Antlers are something that grows out of the head of a boy/male deer.)

Write About Reading (Answers will vary but should include details, such as the mother alligator carrying and protecting her babies.)

Read "Tadpoles Into Frogs"

Encourage children to read the paired selection "Tadpoles into Frogs" on pages 17–19. Have them summarize the selection and compare it to "Animal Families." Have them work with a partner to answer the "Make Connections" questions on page 19.

Independent Reading

Have pairs of children reread "Animal Families." Have them talk about the different animals families and the ways the parents care for their babies.

✅ *Quick Check* Can students identify the Main Topic and Key Details? If not, review and reteach using the instruction on page 106 and assign the Unit 2 Week 4 digital mini-lesson.

Can students respond to the selection using text evidence? If not, provide sentence frames to help them organize their ideas.

Objectives
- Review weekly vocabulary words
- Review main topic and key details
- Write an opinion about an author's use of main topic and key details

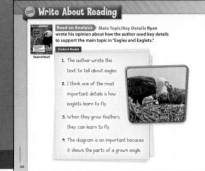

Materials
Visual Vocabulary Cards: 65–72
- Interactive Worktext, pp. 142–143
- Assessment Book, pp. 26–27

☞ **Go** Digital
- Visual Vocabulary Cards
- Main Topic Mini-Lesson
- Interactive eWorktext
- eAssessment

Scaffolding for **Wonders** Reading/Writing Workshop

REVIEW AND RETEACH

5–10 Minutes   RI.2.1   RI.2.2   L.2.4a

Weekly Vocabulary

Display one **Visual Vocabulary Card** at a time and guide children to use the vocabulary word in a sentence. If children have difficulty creating a sentence, have them find the word in "Eagles and Eaglets" or "Animal Families" and use context clues in the passage to define the vocabulary word.

Comprehension: Main Topic and Key Details

I Do   Write and say: *Blue whales are the largest animals on earth. Blue whales are mammals. They feed milk to their young. Young blue whales are called calves.* Ask: *What is the main topic?* Circle "Blue whales," and write *main topic*. Say: This is what the sentences are mainly about. Ask: *What is one key detail?* Circle "Blue whales are mammals" and write *key detail*. Say: I know this is a detail because it gives information about the topic.

We Do   Display and say: *The sun is a star at the center of the solar system. The sun is more than one hundred times bigger than Earth. It is 4.6 billion years old.* Ask: *What is the main topic?* (sun) *What detail can you find that tells us about the size of the sun?* (The sun is more than one hundred times bigger than Earth.)

You Do   Display several groups of short sentences that include a main topic and key details. Guide one partner to ask the other to identify the main topic and the other partner to find key details about the topic in the text. Have partners discuss their answers.

WRITE ABOUT READING

25–35 Minutes   W.2.1   W.2.8   W.4.9

Read an Analysis

- Guide children to look back at "Eagles and Eaglets" in the **Interactive Worktext**. Have volunteers review the key details about the main topic they marked on page 135 and summarize the text. Repeat with pages 136–139. *What is your opinion of how the author use key details to support the main topic of the selection?*

- Read aloud the directions on page 142. Read aloud the student model. *This student's work is not a summary. It is an opinion of how the author used details to support the main topic in "Eagles and Eaglets."*

- *When you write an analysis, you should include key details from the selection that tell about the story. Read Ryan's first sentence. What does Ryan say is the main topic of the story?* (eagles) *In what part of the selection do you learn the main topic?* (the beginning)

- *Read the second sentence. This show Ryan's opinion. Draw a box around the details from the selection.* (how eaglets learn to fly) *What part of the selection is he writing about?* (the middle)

- Guide children to point to the third sentence. *What other detail does Ryan include?* (When they grow feathers, they can learn to fly.) *What other details could Ryan have used?* Provide a sentence frame and guide children to fill it in for each detail they think of: *I think another important detail is _____.*

- Model analyzing how the author used details. Read the last sentence that Ryan wrote. *Why is this sentence a good ending?* (Ryan explained how details in the diagram helped him learn about eagles.)

Write an Analysis

Analytical Writing

Guided Writing Read the writing prompt on page 143 together. Guide children to review their Main Topic and Key Details charts for "Animal Families." Have children use their charts to complete the sentence starters. Children can also write an analysis using another selection previously read this week.

Peer Conference Guide children to read their analysis to a partner. Listeners should summarize the strongest details that support the main topic. They should discuss any parts that are unclear.

Teacher Conference Check children's writing for complete sentences and whether they included details from the story. Review the ending sentence and ask: *Did the author use details to support the story?* If necessary, guide children to revise their sentence by adding more details.

Level Up

▲ Approaching Leveled Reader

▲ Reading/Writing Workshop

Apprentice Leveled Reader

▲ Interactive Worktext

IF children read the Apprentice Level Reader and the **Interactive Worktext** Shared Read fluently and answer the Respond to Reading questions

THEN read together the Approaching Level Reader main selection and the **Reading/Writing Workshop** Shared Read from *Reading Wonders*. Have children take notes as they read, using self-stick notes. Then ask and answer questions about their notes.

Writing Rubric

	4	3	2	1
Text Evidence	Includes three or more details from the text.	Includes two or more details from the text.	Includes only one detail from the text.	No text evidence is cited.
Writing Style	Writes in complete sentences. Uses correct spelling and grammar.	Uses complete sentences. Writing has spelling and grammar errors.	Few complete sentences. There are many spelling and grammar errors.	Writing is not accurate or in complete sentences.

ASSESSMENT

Weekly Assessment

Have children complete the Weekly Assessment using **Assessment** book pages 26–27.

WEEK 5 LESSON 1	**Objectives**	**Materials**

Objectives
- Develop oral language
- Build background about animals
- Understand and use weekly vocabulary
- Read poetry

Materials
- Interactive Worktext, pp. 144–151
- Visual Vocabulary Cards: 73–76
- High-Frequency Word Cards

☞ **Go** Digital
- Interactive eWorktext
- Visual Vocabulary Cards

Scaffolding for **Wonders** Reading/Writing Workshop

WEEKLY CONCEPT

5–10 Minutes   SL.2.1a   SL.2.4

Talk About It

Essential Question Read aloud the Essential Question on page 144 of the **Interactive Worktext:** *What do we love about animals?* Talk to children about what they love about animals. Have volunteers name an animal they like and describe what they like about it. Say: *To describe an animal, you can tell how it behaves and how it expresses itself. You can also describe how an animal looks, feels, and sounds.* Allow time for children to share their ideas. Prompt children to use sensory words as they describe their animals.

- Discuss the photograph on page 144. Ask: *What is happening in the picture?* (A girl is holding onto a horse. The horse has a saddle on it. They are standing in a field.)

I Do Say: *I am going to look at the photo and think about words to describe this horse. The horse has brown hair and a white mane. I will write this description on the web on page 145.*

We Do Say: *Let's think about other words we can use to describe this horse. A horse's hair feels soft to the touch. It also feels smooth.* Guide children to think about other sensory words that describe a horse. Then have children choose words to add to their web.

You Do Guide partners to work together to talk about other ways to describe a horse. They may also describe how a horse behaves or expresses itself. Have children use words from the web to start their sentences: *A word that describes a horse is _____.*

REVIEW VOCABULARY

10–15 Minutes   L.2.4a   L.2.6   RF.2.3

Review Weekly Vocabulary Words

- Use the **Visual Vocabulary Cards** to review the weekly vocabulary.

- Read together the directions on page 146 of the **Interactive Worktext**. Then complete the activity.

1 **express** Tell children that people *express* themselves in different ways. Read the sentence aloud and ask: *What is another word for* express *in this sentence?* (Possible answer: show) If children have difficulty, show pictures of people *expressing* different emotions and use the word *express* to describe the pictures.

2 **behave** Write the word *behave* on the board. Have children talk about how they have *behaved* bravely when they got hurt. Have children use this oral sentence starter: *I behaved bravely when I _____.* (Answers will vary.) Have children think of another word for *behave.* (Possible answers: act, perform, react)

3 **flapping** Demonstrate how a bird flaps its wings with children. Then have children think of things that *flap* in the wind. Have children use this oral sentence frame: *I have seen a _____ flapping in the wind.* (Possible answers: flag, curtain, laundry on a clothesline)

4 **feathers** Ask: *What animals have feathers?* (birds) Then have children draw a bird with colorful *feathers.* Assist children as they draw their picture. You may wish to provide children with pictures of a variety of colorful birds. Have children tell about their bird, using this oral sentence frame: *A _____ has _____ feathers.* (Answers will vary.)

Review Weekly Poetry Words

- Read together the directions for the "Poetry Words" activity on page 147 of the **Interactive Worktext**. Read the poem aloud with children. Then complete the activity.

5 **poem** Remind children that a *poem* is a form of writing that expresses imagination or strong feelings. Ask: *How can you tell that "Fish" is a* poem? (It shows strong feelings.) Discuss the feelings of the narrator towards the fish. Then have children use the following oral sentence starter: *This* poem *is about _____.* (how fish behave and make the poet feel)

6 **rhyme** Invite a volunteer to say a word that *rhymes* with a word you say. Say the word *hot.* (Possible answers: pot, cot, not, spot) Repeat with *dig, lap,* and *cake.* Explain that rhyming helps create a poem's rhythm. Have children use this oral sentence frame: *The words _____ and _____ rhyme in the poem.* (Possible answers: fish/swish; close/nose; food/mood)

7 **rhythm** Explain that *rhythm* helps the words of a poem move along. Write the first two lines of "Fish" on the board. Read the lines out loud. Have children clap along with the *rhythm.* Then have children clap the rhythm again and count the beats. Ask: *How many beats are in the first line?* (4) Ask: *How many beats are in the second line?* (4) If children have difficulty, underline the stressed words to help them count the beats. (love, watch, little, fish; scales, shine, tail, swish)

8 **word choice** Write the words *big* and *enormous* on the board. Ask: *Which of these two words best helps you picture an elephant?* (enormous) Say: *You chose the word* enormous. *You just made a* word choice! Have children use the following oral sentence frames: *A good use of word choice in the poem is _____.* (Answers will vary.) *The poet made this* word choice *because _____.* (Answers will vary.)

READ COMPLEX TEXT

15–20 Minutes   RL.2.1   RL.2.4   SL.2.1b

Read "Cats and Kittens," "Desert Camels," and "A Bat Is Not a Bird"

- Have children turn to page 148 in the **Interactive Worktext** and read the Essential Question aloud. Have children echo-read the poems' titles with you. Point to the image of the cats on page 148 and say: *The author of the first poem loves cats. How would you describe the cats in this picture?* (Possible answers: orange, gray, striped, playful) *Let's read some poems that describe animals.*

- Read the poems together. As children read, have them use the "My Notes" section on page 148 to write questions they have. Children can also write words they don't understand or things they want to remember. Model how to use the "My Notes" section. Say: *When I read the last two lines on page 149, I see the phrase "in one great flash of fur," I wonder what "one great flash of fur" means. I will write a question about it in the "My Notes" section.*

> **ELL ENGLISH LANGUAGE LEARNERS**
>
> As you read together, have children highlight parts of the text they have questions about. After reading, review the questions children have. Then help them locate the answers to their questions in the text.

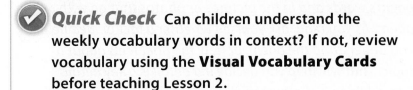 **Quick Check** Can children understand the weekly vocabulary words in context? If not, review vocabulary using the **Visual Vocabulary Cards** before teaching Lesson 2.

WEEK 5
LESSON 2

Objectives
- Read poetry
- Understand complex text through close reading
- Recognize and understand key details
- Respond to the selection using text evidence to support ideas

Scaffolding for **Wonders** Reading/Writing Workshop

Materials
Interactive Worktext, pp. 148–153

☞ **Go** Digital
- Interactive eWorktext
- Key Details Mini-Lesson

REREAD COMPLEX TEXT

20–25 Minutes   RL.2.1   RL.2.4   L.2.6   CCSS

Close Reading: "Cats and Kittens," "Desert Camels," and "A Bat Is Not a Bird"

Reread "Cats and Kittens," "Desert Camels," and "A Bat Is Not a Bird" from **Interactive Worktext** pages 148–151 with children. As you read together, discuss important passages in the text. Guide children to respond to questions using evidence from the text.

 Pages 148–149

Rhyme Point out to children that there are different types of poems. Explain that "Cats and Kittens" is a rhyming poem. Say: *Rhyming poems have words that rhyme, or end with the same sounds.* Give children several examples of words that rhyme and write them on the board (for example, *peach* and *teach*, *how* and *now*, etc.). Reread the first two lines of "Cats and Kittens" aloud to children. Ask: *What two words rhyme in these lines?* Guide children to circle the words. (views *and* mews)

Key Details Remind children that in a poem, key details give important pieces of information that help them understand the poem. Say: *You can find key details in a poem's words and in the pictures or photos that go with a poem. As you read, ask yourself whether a fact or idea helps you understand the poem, or how the poet feels about a topic. That will help you decide if a detail is a key detail.* Reread lines 3–4 aloud to children. Ask: *How do cats clean themselves?* Model drawing a box around the words that tell. (They use their tongues)

Connection of Ideas Ⓐ Ⓒ Ⓣ Say: *A poet may use colorful or expressive language to help the reader picture what the poet is writing about.* Reread lines 7–10 with children. Say: *When something* flashes, *it moves fast. What does the narrator mean by* "one great flash of fur"? Guide children to write their answers. (Possible answer: It means a cat is running fast.)

 Page 150

Key Details Remind children that in a poem, key details give important pieces of information that help them understand the poem. Reread the first two lines of "Desert Camels" with children. Ask: *What are camels humps used for?* Guide children to draw a box around the key detail that tells. (To carry people and their sacks) Ask: *What does this tells us about camels?* (Possible answer: They are very strong, powerful animals.)

Connection of Ideas Ⓐ Ⓒ Ⓣ Have children reread the poem. Then remind children of the essential question: *What do we love about animals?* Say: *Underline the sentence that tells you the author likes camels.* (I'd like a camel for a pet) Then discuss what the author likes about camels. Have children use text evidence to support their answers.

Rhythm Review the concept of *rhythm* with children. Remind them that the rhythm is the pattern of repeating accents in a poem. Say: *You can clap the beats in a poem to identify the rhythm.* Reread "Desert Camels" with children. Say: *Listen to the rhythm. The poet uses this rhythm because it has the bouncy feel of a camel ride.* Clap out the beats of the first two lines with children. Then ask: *How many beats do you hear in the last two lines?* Guide children to write their answers. (four beats) If children have difficulty, have them underline the beats in each sentence: I'd <u>like</u> a <u>camel</u> <u>for</u> a <u>pet</u>,/but <u>haven't</u> <u>asked</u> my <u>mother</u> <u>yet</u>.

🔍 Page 151

Key Details Remind children that the key details of a poem can give more information about the subject to help the reader understand the poem better. Reread the first two lines of "A Bat Is Not a Bird" with children. Ask: *What does a bat do instead of chirp?* Instruct children to draw a box around the answer. (Shriek)

Word Choice Say: *Remember, poets choose their words carefully to help readers create pictures in their minds. In the poem "A Bat Is Not a Bird," the poet chooses certain words so the reader can picture a bat in his or her mind.* Have children reread lines 3–4. Ask: *What words does the poet use to describe a bat's wings?* Instruct children to circle the words. (flapping, leathery)

Connection of Ideas **A C T** Reread the title and the first two lines of the poem with children. Say: *The poem tells us that bats do not have feathers or a beak and that they do not chirp. What animal chirps and has feathers and a beak?* (a bird) *What is the author comparing the bat to?* Instruct children to underline the word on the page that names the animal. (bird)

RESPOND TO READING

10–20 Minutes | RL.2.1 RL.2.7 SL.2.1a |

Respond to "Desert Camels"

Read aloud the questions on page 152 of the **Interactive Worktext**. Guide children to read the question about "Desert Camels." Then read aloud the "Discussion Starter" for each of the questions. Guide children to work with a partner to answer the questions orally using the "Discussion Starters." Have children find text evidence to support their answers. Ask children to write the page number(s) on which they found the text evidence for each question.

1. *What does the narrator think is special about camels?* (Possible answers: I read that camels have humps on their backs. A camel's hump can carry people and their sacks. Text Evidence: p. 150)

2. *What does the narrator love about what camels can do?* (Possible answers: Camels are very strong. They can go for long periods without drinking. They can give people bouncy rides. Text Evidence: p. 150)

3. *What does the narrator want at the end of the poem?* (Possible answers: The narrator wants a camel for a pet. This tells me how much the narrator loves camels. Text Evidence: p. 150)

After children discuss the questions on page 152, have them use the sentence starters to answer the question on page 153. Circulate and provide guidance.

 Quick Check Do children understand vocabulary in context? If not, review and reteach using the instruction on page 116.

Can children identify key details? If not, review and reteach using the instruction on page 116 and assign the Unit 2 Week 5 digital mini-lesson.

Can children write a response to "Desert Camels"? If not, review the sentence starters and prompt children to respond orally. Help them write their responses.

WEEK 5
LESSON

3

Objectives
• Access prior knowledge
• Understand and use new vocabulary words
• Read high-frequency words
• Read fiction

Materials
• "Amira's Petting Zoo" Apprentice Leveled Reader
• High-Frequency Word Cards

☞ **Go** Digital
• Apprentice Leveled Reader eBook
• Downloadable High-Frequency Word Cards

Scaffolding for **Wonders** Approaching Leveled Reader

BEFORE READING

10–15 Minutes   SL. 2.1a   SL.2.6   RF.2.3f   L.2.5   L.2.6   CCSS

Introduce "Amira's Petting Zoo"

• Read the Essential Question on the title page of "Amira's Petting Zoo" **Apprentice Leveled Reader:** *What do we love about animals?*

• Read the title of the main read. Point to the cover. Ask: *What character do you see in the story?* (a girl) *What animal do you see?* (a goat) *Where do you think they are* (petting zoo) *Let's read about a girl who goes to the petting zoo to see some animals.*

High-Frequency Words

Display the **High-Frequency Word Cards** for the words *could, into, many, new, people,* and *water.* Use the Read/Spell/Write routine to teach each word. Guide partners to use each word in a sentence. Provide assistance reading the high-frequency words, as necessary.

Expand Vocabulary

Before reading "Amira's Petting Zoo," help children read the following words that they will encounter. Display each word below. Use the Define/Example/Ask routine. Tell children to look for the word later on as they read "Amira's Petting Zoo."

1 **groaned** (page 8)

Define: made a deep sound when unhappy or when something bad happened

Example: I *groaned* when I bumped my knee on the ground.

Ask: What have you *groaned* about?

2 **pen** (page 5)

Define: a place where animals are kept fenced in

Example: The farmer opened the *pen* to let the pigs out.

Ask: What is something else that is kept in a *pen*?

3 **pressed** (page 13)

Define: pushed or touched hard

Example: John *pressed* his hand into mine when he shook it.

Ask: What have you *pressed* when you have played video games?

4 **splashed** (page 7)

Define: caused liquid to hit something

Example: My brother *splashed* water on me at the pool.

Ask: Where have you *splashed* water?

5 **worry** (page 2)

Define: to be unsure or scared

Example: I sometimes *worry* that the bus will be late.

Ask: What do you *worry* about?

DURING READING

20–30 Minutes   RL.2.1   RL.2.3   L.2.5   L.2.6

Shared Reading

Tell children you will now read "Amira's Petting Zoo." Tell them to note the vocabulary and high-frequency words you just introduced as you read the story. Stop to model understanding of the story as you go.

Pages 2–3

Comprehension Check Model beginning to read. Say: *The first thing I see is that Amira and her grandma are at the petting zoo. Then I read that the petting zoo is crowded. Next, the line for the bunnies was too long. I wonder if Amira will get to pet other animals.*

Vocabulary Read page 2. Focus on the word *worry*. Say: *Amira says the petting zoo is too crowded. Grandma tells her not to* worry. *What do you think Amira is worried about?* (that she will not get to pet the animals)

Pages 4–5

Vocabulary Read page 5. Point to the word *pen*. Say: *It says here that the* pen *is closed. What kind of animal is kept in this* pen? (piglets) *Look at the picture. What keeps the animals closed in?* (a fence) Point out that that is the pen.

Comprehension Check Say: *I read on page 4 that Amira is worried. Then on page 5, she sees the piglets. The exclamation point tells me that Amira is excited to see the piglets. But then I read that the pen is closed. It seems like Amira might not get a chance to pet the piglets.*

Pages 6–7

High-Frequency Words Make sure children can read the high-frequency word *water*.

Comprehension Check Say: *I read that Grandma will show Amira the ducks. On page 7, I read that a duck splashed water on Amira. Amira is having a tough time so far. Maybe things will get better for her soon.*

Pages 8–9

Vocabulary Point to the word *groaned*. Ask: Do you groan when you are happy or unhapppy about something? (unhappy) *Why has Amira* groaned *in the story?* (because she is all wet)

Pages 10–11

High-Frequency Words Make sure children can read the high-frequency words *could, many,* and *people.*

Comprehension Check Say: *I read that there are many people at the petting zoo. On page 11, I read that Amira cannot find any animals to feed. Then, Grandma tells her not to worry. Amira looks worried, but Grandma is trying to make her feel better.*

Pages 12–13

High-Frequency Words Make sure children can read the high-frequency word *new.*

Vocabulary Read pages 12 and 13. Say: *I read that the baby goat pressed its nose against Amira's hand. What is Amira holding in her hand?* (the bag of food) *Why do you think the goat pressed its nose into Amira's hand?* (because it wants the food)

Pages 14–15

High-Frequency Words Make sure children can read the high-frequency word *into.*

Comprehension Check Say: *I read that Amira finally gets to pet an animal. It is a baby goat. On page 15, I read that Amira loves the petting zoo. She is not worried any more. Grandma was right when she told Amira not to worry!*

 Quick Check **Can children understand vocabulary in context? If not, review and reteach using the instruction on page 116 and assign the Unit 2 Week 5 digital mini-lesson.**

Can children read the high-frequency words in context? If not, review using the Read/Spell/Write routine and the High-Frequency Word Cards.

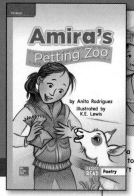

WEEK 5 LESSON

4

Objectives
- Understand complex text through close-reading
- Read fiction
- Recognize and understand key details
- Respond to the selection using text evidence to support ideas

Materials
- "Amira's Petting Zoo" Apprentice Level Reader
- Graphic Organizer: Key Details

☞ **Go Digital**
- Apprentice Level Reader eBook
- Downloadable Graphic Organizer
- Key Details Mini-Lesoon

Scaffolding for **WONDERS** Approaching Leveled Reader

DURING READING

20–30 Minutes   RL.2.1   RL.2.2   RL.2.7   **CCSS**

Tell children they will now reread the selection, "Amira's Petting Zoo." Review the vocabulary words that they will encounter as they read.

Close Reading

🔍 Pages 2–3

Key Details   Explain that key details are details that give important information about the story. Say: *Ask yourself: Does this detail help me understand the important parts of a story?* Reread page 2 with children. Ask: *Who are the characters in the story?* (Amira and Grandma) *Is this a key detail?* (yes) *Why?* (because it tells important information about the characters who are in the story) Ask: *Where are Amira and Grandma?* (at the petting zoo) *Why is this a key detail?* (because it tells the setting of the story)

Key Details   Reread page 3. Ask: *What happens when Amira tries to go see the bunnies?* (The line is too long.) *Why is this a key detail?* (because Amira wants to pet an animal and the zoo is too crowded) Model adding this information to the Key Details Chart.

🔍 Pages 4–5

Key Details   Remind children that key details help us understand the story. Reread page 5 with children. Ask: *What happens when Amira tries to see the piglets?* (The pen is closed.) Add this to the Key Details Chart.

Connection of Ideas **ACT**   Ask: *How is what happens with Amira and the piglets similar to what happened with the rabbits?* (Amira didn't get to see or pet either the rabbits or the piglets.)

🔍 Pages 6–7

Key Details   Reread pages 6 and 7. Point out that key details can be found in both the text and the illustrations. Point to the illustration on page 6. Ask: *What does the illustration tell us about how Amira feels?* (She looks sad in the illustration.) *Why is Amira sad?* (She has not been able to pet any animals yet.) Model adding these details to the Key Details Chart.

Sentence Structure **ACT**   Point to the quotation marks on page 6. Say: *These are quotation marks. They tell us that someone is speaking. To find who is speaking, look at the words before and after the words in quotation marks. Who is speaking on page 6?* (Grandma)

Key Details   Ask: *What is the next thing that happens to Amira?* (A duck splashes her with water.)

🔍 Pages 8–9

Key Details   Say: *Remember, key details tell us about important events in the story. What important event happens on page 9?* (Amira gets some food for the animals.) *What do you think Amira will do with the food?* (She will feed the animals.) *How will this help her?* (She may get to pet one if she gives it food.) Add this information to the Key Details Chart.

🔍 Pages 10–11

Connection of Ideas **ACT**   Reread page 11. Say: *Grandma keeps telling Amira the same thing. What does Grandma tell Amira on pages 4, 6, and 11?* (Don't worry.) *Why does she say that?* (so Amira won't be upset that she isn't petting any animals yet)

🔍 Pages 12–13

Key Details Reread pages 12 and 13. Say: *It looks like Amira finally found an animal to pet! What kind of animal does she meet on page 13?* (a baby goat)

Connection of Ideas **A C T** Point to the picture on page 12. Ask: *How does Amira seem to feel now?* (She looks happy.) *Why is she happy?* (She is getting to be close to an animal.)

🔍 Pages 14–15

Key Details Reread page 15. Say: *It looks like Amira has changed her mind about the petting zoo. She was unhappy with it until she saw the goat. What key detail tells us that Amira is happy with the petting zoo on page 15?* (Amira says "I love the petting zoo!") Add this detail to the Key Details Chart.

Organization **A C T** Focus on the organization of the story. Ask: *What did Amira want when she came to the zoo?* (to pet an animal) *What happened when she tried to get what she wanted?* (She always ran into problems. First, the lines were too long, then the pigpen was closed, and then the ducks splashed her.) *What happened with the goat?* (Amira did get to pet it.) Point out that the book is organized by what Amira wants and how after many failed attempts, she got what she wanted.

AFTER READING

10–15 Minutes   RL.2.1   L2.4d   RF. 2.4b   W.2.8

Respond to Reading

Compare Texts Guide children in comparing the events in "Amira's Petting Zoo" with the poems "Cats and Kittens," "Desert Camels," and "A Bat Is Not a Bird." Help children think about different animals. Then ask: *What are the animals that you love?*

Summarize Have children turn to page 16 and guide them in summarizing the selection. (Answers should include key details from the book that tell about what happened.)

🔍 Text Evidence

Have partners work together to answer questions on page 16. Remind children to use their Key Details charts.

Key Details (Answers will vary but might include the following key details: the petting zoo has bunnies, piglets, and goats available for petting [pages 3, 5, and 13]; it can be crowded with long lines [pages 2, 3]; it is a place where you can feed the animals [page 9].)

Vocabulary (A zoo where you can touch baby animals. Petting means to touch in a nice way.)

Write About Reading (Answers will vary but should explain that Amira was worried because many of the things she wanted to do didn't seem possible. When she first arrived at the park with her grandma, she saw that the zoo was crowded and that the lines were long. She worried that she would not have a chance to pet any of the animals.)

Read "Sheep Season"

Encourage children to read the paired selection "Sheep Season" on pages 17–19. Have children note the rhythm and rhyme as they read it aloud. Have them summarize the selection and compare it to "Amira's Petting Zoo." Have them work with a partner to answer the "Make Connections" questions on page 19.

Independent Reading

Have pairs of children reread "Amira's Petting Zoo." Have them retell the story making sure to include key details.

✅ *Quick Check* **Can students identify key details? If not, review and reteach using the instruction on page 116 and assign the Unit 2 Week 5 digital mini-lesson.**

Can students respond to the selection using text evidence? If not, provide sentence frames to help them organize their ideas.

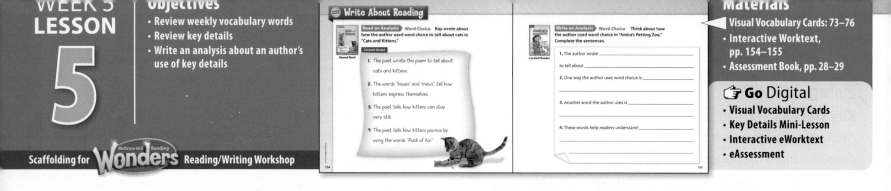

Objectives
• Review weekly vocabulary words
• Review key details
• Write an analysis about an author's use of key details

Materials
• Visual Vocabulary Cards: 73–76
• Interactive Worktext, pp. 154–155
• Assessment Book, pp. 28–29

☞ Go Digital
• Visual Vocabulary Cards
• Key Details Mini-Lesson
• Interactive eWorktext
• eAssessment

Scaffolding for **Wonders** Reading/Writing Workshop
McGraw-Hill Reading

REVIEW AND RETEACH

5–10 Minutes — RL.2.1 L.2.4a L.2.6 CCSS

Weekly Vocabulary

Display one **Visual Vocabulary Card** at a time and guide children to use the vocabulary word in a sentence. If children have difficulty creating a sentence, have them find the word in "Cats and Kittens," "Desert Camels," "A Bat Is Not a Bird," or "Amira's Petting Zoo" and use context clues to define the vocabulary word.

Comprehension: Key Details

I Do Write and say: *Carrie loves her pet hamster! She likes to take care of it by giving it food and water. She also loves to hold the hamster in her lap and pet it. Carrie and the hamster are friends!* Ask: *What does Carrie love about her pet hamster? I read that Carrie likes to give her hamster food and water.* Underline the second sentence and write "key detail." Say: *The third sentence tells me that Carrie likes to hold the hamster and pet her. That is another key detail.*

We Do Display: *The Booker family had a great day. They went to the park for a picnic. After they ate, they went for a nice hike. When they got home, the kids had fun playing a game. Mom and Dad had a nap.* Ask: *What detail tells us what the Bookers did?* (They had a picnic.) *What did the family do after they ate?* (They went on a nice hike.)

You Do Display: *Ian loves to play the drums. He takes drumming lessons. He practices the drums every day. His family likes to listen to him play. Ian is always thinking about drumming. He even taps a beat while he reads!* Guide partners to ask each other to identify the key details.

WRITE ABOUT READING

25–35 Minutes — W.2.5 W.2.8 W.4.9 CCSS

Read an Analysis

• Guide children to look back at "Cats and Kittens" in the **Interactive Worktext**. Have volunteers review the details about how the author used word choice they marked on page 151. *How did the author use word choice in the poem?*

• Read aloud the directions on page 154. Read aloud the student model. *This student's work is not a summary. It is an analysis, or description, of how the author used word choice in "Cats and Kittens."*

• *When you write an analysis, you should include key details from the text that tell how the author used word choice in the poem. Read Ray's first sentence. What important information does he include in this sentence?* (The poet wrote this poem to tell about cats and kittens.) *What part of the poem does this information come from?* (the beginning)

• *Read the second sentence. Ray writes important words from the poem. Draw a circle around the words from the poem.* ("hisses," "mews") *What part of the poem do these words come from?* (the beginning)

• *Guide children to point to the third sentence. This sentence explains what happened in the middle of the poem. What information does Ray include?* (The poet tells how kittens can stay very still.)

• Model analyzing how the poet used word choice. Read the last sentence that Ray wrote. *Why is this sentence a good ending?* (Ray writes how the kitten pounces by using the words "flash of fur.")

✏️ Analytical Writing **Write an Analysis**

Guided Writing Read the writing prompt on page 155 together. Guide children to think about how the author used Word Choice in "Amira's Petting Zoo." Have children complete the sentence starters. Children can also write an analysis using another selection previously read this week.

Peer Conference Guide children to read their analysis to a partner. Listeners should summarize the strongest use of word choice in the beginning, middle, and ending sentences. They should discuss any parts that are unclear.

Teacher Conference Check children's writing for complete sentences and whether they included details from the story. Review the ending sentence and ask: *Did the author make good word choices to support the story?* If necessary, guide children to revise their sentence by adding examples of word choice.

Level Up

▲ Approaching Leveled Reader

▲ Reading/Writing Workshop

▲ Apprentice Leveled Reader

▲ Interactive Worktext

IF children read the Apprentice Level Reader and the **Interactive Worktext** Shared Read fluently and answer the Respond to Reading questions

THEN read together the Approaching Level Reader main selection and the **Reading/Writing Workshop** Shared Read from *Reading Wonders*. Have children take notes as they read, using self-stick notes. Then ask and answer questions about their notes.

Writing Rubric

	4	3	2	1
Text Evidence	Includes three or more details from the text.	Includes two or more details from the text.	Includes only one detail from the text.	No text evidence is cited.
Writing Style	Writes in complete sentences. Uses correct spelling and grammar.	Uses complete sentences. Writing has spelling and grammar errors.	Few complete sentences. There are many spelling and grammar errors.	Writing is not accurate or in complete sentences.

ASSESSMENT

Weekly Assessment

Have children complete the Weekly Assessment using **Assessment** book pages 28–29.

Unit Assessment

✔ **COMPREHENSION**	✔ **VOCABULARY:**
• Plot RL.2.5	• Context Clues L.2.4a
• Problem and Solution RL.2.3, RL.2.5	
• Main Topic and Key Details RI.2.1, RI.2.2	
• Main Topic and Key Details RI.2.1, RI.2.2	
• Key Details RL.2.1	

Using Assessment and Writing Scores

↻ **RETEACH**	**IF ...**	**THEN ...**
COMPREHENSION	Students answer 0–7 multiple-choice items correctly ...	... reteach tested skills using instruction on pages 364–375.
VOCABULARY	Students answer 0–3 multiple-choice items correctly ...	... reteach tested skills using instruction on page 364.
WRITING	Students score mostly 1–2 on weekly Write About Reading rubrics throughout the unit ...	... reteach writing using instruction on pages 376–377.

⬆ **LEVEL UP**	**IF ...**	**THEN ...**
COMPREHENSION	Students answer 8–10 multiple-choice items correctly ...	... have students read the *A Tree Full of Life* Approaching Leveled Reader. Use the Level Up lesson on page on page 118.
WRITING	Students score mostly 3–4 on weekly Write About Reading rubrics throughout the unit ...	... use the Level Up Write About Reading lesson on page 119 to have students compare two selections from the unit.

Fluency Assessment

Conduct assessments individually using the differentiated fluency passages in **Assessment**. Students' expected fluency goal for this Unit is 41–61 WCPM with an accuracy rate of 95% or higher.

Exit Test

If a student answers 13–15 multiple choice items correctly on the Unit Assessment, administer the Unit 2 Exit Test at the end of Week 6.

Time to Exit WonderWorks

Exit Text

If...

Students answer 13–15 multiple choice items correctly...

Fluency Assessment

If...

Students achieve their Fluency Assessment goal for the unit...

Level Up Lessons

If...

Students are successful applying close reading skills with the Approaching Leveled Reader in Week 6...

If...

Students score mostly 4–5 on the Level Up Write About Reading assignment...

Foundational Skills Kit

If...

Students have mastered the Unit 2 benchmark skills in the Foundational Skills Kit and *Reading Wonders* Adaptive Learning...

Then...

... consider exiting the student from *Reading WonderWorks* materials into the Approaching Level of *Reading Wonders*.

Read Approaching Leveled Reader

Approaching Leveled Reader

Apprentice Leveled Reader

Write About Reading

Interactive Worktext Shared Read

Apprentice Leveled Reader

A Tree Full of Life

Before Reading

Preview Discuss what children remember about eucalyptus trees and the different plants and animals that live in this habitat. Tell them they will be reading a more challenging version of "A Tree Full of Life."

Vocabulary Use the routines on the **Visual Vocabulary Cards** to review the Weekly Vocabulary words. Use page 92 to review the Expand Vocabulary words.

A C T During Reading

▶ **Genre** Review that nonfiction text is about real things. Narrative nonfiction tells about living things, people, or events in story form. Point out that narrative nonfiction can include text features such as maps and photographs with captions that can give readers more information about the topic. Point to the caption and photo on page 3 and ask: *What information does the caption give about eucalyptus leaves?* (They are sweet but poisonous.) Have children remember to read the captions on each page.

▶ **Sentence Structure** Write the following sentences from page 2 on the board: *The eucalyptus tree stands tall. It grows in Australia.* Point to the word *It*. Review with children that authors will sometimes use the pronoun *it* to replace the name of a thing or animal that has already been mentioned. Read the sentence aloud and ask: *What thing in the first sentence does the author use the word* it *to replace in the second sentence?* (eucalyptus tree) Follow the same routine with *It* on page 4 (koala bear) and *They* on page 8 (termites).

▶ **Prior Knowledge** Children may not be familiar with the country of Australia. Point out the map of Australia on page 2 and explain that Australia is a country just as the United States is a country. Point out the key to the map and explain that eucalyptus trees can be found all over Australia. Tell children that most of the plants and animals they will be reading about are not found in nature in the United States, because Australia is in a different part of the world.

After Reading

Ask children to complete the Respond to Reading on page 16 after they have finished reading. Provide support with the vocabulary strategy question as needed.

Write About Reading

RI.3.9 W.4.9

Read an Analysis

- Distribute the Unit 2 Downloadable Model and Practice. Point out that the model compares two related texts, the **Interactive Worktext** Shared Read "A Prairie Guard Dog" and the **Apprentice Leveled Reader** "A Tree Full of Life." Read the sentences aloud to children.

- Point out the key details in each sentence that come from the texts. Point out the signal words *also* and *both*. Explain that these words show readers that the sentences are comparing two different texts.

- Ask: *What details show that the two texts are different?* (*A Tree Full of Life* tells about different plants and animals, not just one.) *What details show that the two texts are the same?* (Both texts talk about how animals survive in their habitats. Both texts tell what how the habitats provide food and shelter.) *What opinion did the student give in sentence 3?* (The author did a good job of showing how the animals survive.)

- Model analyzing how the student used details to support her opinion. Read the last sentence. *How does this sentence support the student's opinion?* (The student gave text evidence supporting her opinion.)

Write an Analysis

Guided Writing Tell children that they will be comparing the **Interactive Worktext** Shared Read "Eagles and Eaglets" and the **Apprentice Leveled Reader** "Animal Families." Explain to children that they will write their opinion about how the authors describe different ways animal offspring are like their parents.

- Guide children to compare the two texts as they complete the sentences on the Unit 2 Downloadable Model and Practice.

- Point out the signal words, such as *also, both*, and *different, to children and discuss how these words are used to compare the texts.*

- Alternatively, let children select two texts to compare.

Teacher Conference Check children's writing for complete sentences. Did they use key details to tell how the texts are the same and different? Did they use text evidence? Did they write in complete sentences? Did they use evidence to support their opinion?

Writing Rubric

	4	3	2	1
Text Evidence	Includes three or more details from the text.	Includes two or more details from the text.	Includes only one detail from the text.	No text evidence is cited.
Writing Style	Writes in complete sentences. Uses correct spelling and grammar.	Uses complete sentences. Writing has spelling and grammar errors.	Few complete sentences. There are many spelling and grammar errors.	Writing is not accurate or in complete sentences.

UNIT 3 PLANNER

Live and Learn

Week 1 The Earth's Forces	Week 2 Look at the Sky	Week 3 Ways People Help

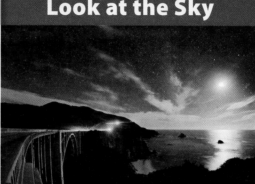

Week 1 — The Earth's Forces

ESSENTIAL QUESTION
How do the Earth's forces affect us?

Build Background

CCSS Vocabulary
L.2.4a *amazing, force, measure, objects, proved, speed, true, weight*

Access Complex Text A C T
Connection of Ideas

CCSS Comprehension
RI.2.6 Skill: Author's Purpose
Respond to Reading

CCSS Write About Reading   *Analytical Writing*
W.4.9 Inform/Explain: Author's Purpose

Week 2 — Look at the Sky

ESSENTIAL QUESTION
What can we see in the sky?

Build Background

CCSS Vocabulary
L.2.4a *adventure, delighted, dreamed, enjoyed, grumbled, moonlight, neighbor, nighttime*

Access Complex Text A C T
Sentence Structure

CCSS Comprehension
RL.2.5 Skill: Sequence
Respond to Reading

CCSS Write About Reading   *Analytical Writing*
W.4.9 Inform/Explain: Sequence & Illustrations

Week 3 — Ways People Help

ESSENTIAL QUESTION
How can people help out their community?

Build Background

CCSS Vocabulary
L.2.4a *across, borrow, countryside, idea, insists, lonely, solution, villages*

Access Complex Text A C T
Connection of Ideas

CCSS Comprehension
RI.2.6 Skill: Author's Purpose
Respond to Reading

CCSS Write About Reading   *Analytical Writing*
W.4.9 Inform/Explain: Author's Purpose

ASSESSMENT

✓ Quick Check
Vocabulary, Comprehension

✓ Weekly Assessment
Assessment Book, pp. 30–31

✓ Quick Check
Vocabulary, Comprehension

✓ Weekly Assessment
Assessment Book, pp. 32–33

✓ Quick Check
Vocabulary, Comprehension

✓ Weekly Assessment
Assessment Book, pp. 34–35

✓ MID-UNIT ASSESSMENT
Assessment Book, pp. 88–95

Fluency Assessment
Assessment Book, pp. 250–265

Use the Foundational Skills Kit for explicit instruction of phonics, structural analysis, fluency, and word recognition. Includes *Reading Wonders* Adaptive Learning.

Week 4
Weather Alert!

ESSENTIAL QUESTION
How does weather affect us?

Build Background

 Vocabulary
L.2.4a *damage, dangerous, destroy, event, harsh, prevent, warning, weather*

Access Complex Text
Genre

Comprehension
RI.2.2 Skill: Main Idea and Key Details
Respond to Reading

Write About Reading *Analytical Writing*
W.4.9 Opinion: Main Idea & Details

Week 5
Express Yourself

ESSENTIAL QUESTION
How do you express yourself?

Build Background

 Vocabulary
L.2.4a *cheered, concert, instrument, movements, music, rhythm, sounds, understand*

Access Complex Text
Sentence Structure

Comprehension
RI.2.2 Skill: Main Idea and Key Details
Respond to Reading

Write About Reading *Analytical Writing*
W.4.9 Inform/Explain: Main Idea & Details

Week 6
ASSESS

RETEACH   LEVEL UP

Reteach
Comprehension Skills

Vocabulary

Write About Reading

Level Up
Read Approaching Leveled Reader

Write About Reading:
Compare Texts

A S S E S S M E N T

✓ **Quick Check**
Vocabulary, Comprehension

✓ **Weekly Assessment**
Assessment Book, pp. 36–37

✓ **Quick Check**
Vocabulary, Comprehension

✓ **Weekly Assessment**
Assessment Book, pp. 38–39

✓ **Unit Assessment**
Assessment Book, pp. 140–148

✓ **Fluency Assessment**
Assessment Book, pp. 250–265

EXIT TEST
Assessment Book, pp. 196–204

UNIT 3 OPENER,
pp. 156–157

The Big Idea

What have you learned about the world that surprises you?

Talk About It

Read aloud the Big Idea on page 156 of the **Interactive Worktext:** *What have you learned about the world that surprises you?* Tell children that there are many things in the natural world that surprise us. Ask children to think of something in nature that surprises them. Have them use details to describe the experience. If children have difficulty, provide an example of something in nature that surprised you, such as seeing lightning, a waterfall or the desert for the first time.

Discuss the photo on pages 156–157. Ask: *What is happening in the picture?* (A boy is looking at a butterfly through a magnifying glass.) *What do you know about butterflies?* (Answers will vary.) *What might surprise the boy?* (Answers will vary.)

Then ask: *Is there something in the natural world that you would you like to learn about?* Have children discuss and share their ideas with the group. Encourage children to think of ways to learn more about their ideas. (books, the internet, interviews, trips and so on.)

Then say: *Let's look back at our Big Idea. What have you learned about the world that surprises you?* Tell children they will be discussing the Big Idea in this unit. Tell them they will be reading and writing about different places and events, some of which may be surprising.

Build Fluency

Each week, use the **Interactive Worktext** Shared Reads and **Apprentice Leveled Readers** for fluency instruction and practice. Keep in mind that reading rates vary with the type of text that children are reading as well as the purpose for reading. For example, comprehension of complex informational texts generally requires slower reading.

Explain/Model Use the Fluency lessons on pages 378–382 to explain the skill. Then model the skill by reading the first page of the week's Shared Read or Leveled Reader.

Practice/Apply Choose a page from the Shared Read or Leveled Reader. Have one group read the top half of the page one sentence at a time. Remind children to apply the skill. Have the second group echo-read the passage. Then have the groups switch roles for the second half of the page. Discuss how each group applied the skill.

> **Weekly Fluency Focus**
>
> **Week 1** Intonation
>
> **Week 2** Intonation
>
> **Week 3** Expression
>
> **Week 4** Phrasing
>
> **Week 5** Pronunciation

Foundational Skills Kit You can also use the **Lesson Cards** and **Practice** pages from the **Foundational Skills Kit** for targeted Fluency instruction and practice.

Access Complex Text

Qualitative · Quantitative

Reader and Task

TEXT COMPLEXITY

Interactive Worktext

	Week 1	Week 2	Week 3	Week 4	Week 5
	"Magnets Work!"	"Starry Night"	"Lightning Lives"	"Tornado!"	"They've Got the Beat!"
Quantitative	Lexile 380 TextEvaluator™ 6	Lexile 310 TextEvaluator™ 6	Lexile 390 TextEvaluator™ 13	Lexile 390 TextEvaluator™ 6	Lexile 420 TextEvaluator™ 14
Qualitative	• Connection of Ideas • Vocabulary	• Sentence Structure • Vocabulary	• Connection of Ideas • Genre • Vocabulary	• Genre • Vocabulary	• Sentence Structure • Genre • Vocabulary
Reader and Task	The Weekly Concept lessons will help determine the reader's knowledge and engagement in the weekly concept.				
	Weekly Concept: p. 126 Questions and tasks: pp. 128–129	Weekly Concept: p. 136 Questions and tasks: pp. 138–139	Weekly Concept: p. 146 Questions and tasks: pp. 148–149	Weekly Concept: p. 158 Questions and tasks: pp. 160–161	Weekly Concept: p. 168 Questions and tasks: pp. 170–171

Apprentice Leveled Reader

	Week 1	Week 2	Week 3	Week 4	Week 5
	"Forces at Work"	"A Special Sunset"	"City Communities"	"Weather All Around"	"The Sounds of Trash"
Quantitative	Lexile 200 TextEvaluator™ 6	Lexile 180 TextEvaluator™ 6	Lexile 240 TextEvaluator™ 6	Lexile 270 TextEvaluator™ 6	Lexile 250 TextEvaluator™ 6
Qualitative	•Connection of Ideas • Sentence Structure • Vocabulary	• Sentence Structure • Connection of Ideas • Vocabulary	• Connection of Ideas • Genre • Organization • Vocabulary	• Genre • Connection of Ideas • Organization • Vocabulary	• Sentence Structure • Genre • Prior Knowledge • Vocabulary
Reader and Task	The Weekly Concept lessons will help determine the reader's knowledge and engagement in the weekly concept.				
	Weekly Concept: p. 126 Questions and tasks: pp. 130–133	Weekly Concept: p. 136 Questions and tasks: pp. 140–143	Weekly Concept: p. 146 Questions and tasks: pp. 150–153	Weekly Concept: p. 158 Questions and tasks: pp. 162–165	Weekly Concept: p. 168 Questions and tasks: pp. 172–175

See page 383 for details about Text Complexity measures.

Teach and Model **WORKTEXT**

Objectives
- Develop oral language
- Build background about the Earth's forces
- Understand and use weekly vocabulary
- Read an expository text

Materials
- Interactive Worktext, pp. 158–167
- Visual Vocabulary Cards: 77–84
- High-Frequency Word Cards

☞ **Go Digital**
- Interactive eWorktext
- Visual Vocabulary Cards

Scaffolding for **Wonders** Reading/Writing Workshop

WEEKLY CONCEPT

5–10 Minutes   SL.2.1b SL.2.4

Talk About It

Essential Question Read aloud the Essential Question on page 158 of the **Interactive Worktext:** *How do the Earth's forces affect us?* Explain that there are many forces on Earth. Tell children that gravity is one force on Earth that pulls things down. Provide examples of some of the ways they can see gravity at work, such as children sliding down a slide or jumping down from a step. Say: *We can see gravity at work all around us.*

- Discuss the photograph on page 158. Ask: What is happening in the picture? (A boy is sliding down a snowy hill on a tube.) Have volunteers describe what it feels like to go sledding or sliding down a slide.

I Do Say: *I am going to look at the photo and think about how Earth's forces affect us.* Have children discuss what makes the tube slide down the hill. (gravity and the snow) *How does the snow help gravity?* (It is wet and slippery.) *I will write on the web on page 159 that gravity can pull tubes down a snowy hill.*

We Do Say: *Let's think about other things gravity pulls down around us.* Ask: *What happens when we throw a ball up in the air?* (It comes back down) Guide children to think of other ways they see gravity at work around them. Have children share their ideas. Then have children choose one way and add it to their web.

You Do Guide partners to work together to talk about gravity at work around them. Have children use the words from the web to start their sentences: *Gravity pulls _____ down.* Have children add these ideas to the web.

REVIEW VOCABULARY

10–15 Minutes   L.2.4a L.2.6 RF.2.3f

Review Weekly Vocabulary Words

- Use the **Visual Vocabulary Cards** to review the weekly vocabulary.

- Read together the directions on page 160 of the **Interactive Worktext**. Then complete the activity.

1 measure Display a ruler and a scale. Ask: What does a ruler *measure*? (Possible answers: length, how long something is) What does a scale *measure*? (Possible answers: weight, how much something weighs) Guide children to name a tool that can *measure* rice. (Possible answers: measuring cup, measuring spoon)

2 force Stand next to your desk and act out pushing it with great *force*. Say: *It would take a lot of* force *to move this desk.* Have children push first a pen and then a book across their desks. Have them use this oral sentence starter: *It would not take a lot of* force *to move a _____.* (book, pen)

3 objects Ask children to tell you how many *objects* are on their desks right now. Have them use the following oral sentence frame: *There are _____ objects on my desk.* (Answers will vary.) Continue by having children write the names of two *objects* in the classroom.

4 true Explain to children that most statements can be either *true* or false. Give an example of a *true* sentence, such as *I am a teacher.* Then give an example of a false sentence: *I am a child.* Have partners ask each other *true* or false questions. (Possible answer: I rode the school bus today: *True* or false?)

5 **proved** Explain to children that when you have *proved* something, you have shown it to be true. Tell children what the weather is today. Then have them look out the window and see how you *proved* it to be so. Have children read the sentence and think of another word for *proved*. (Possible answer: showed)

6 **speed** Guide children to brainstorm animals that can walk or run. Then have children use this oral sentence frame: *A(n) _____ can run at a very fast* speed. (Possible answers: horse, cheetah)

7 **weight** Act out for children what it looks like to lift a very heavy *weight*. Have children imitate your actions. Display pictures of various heavy items. Have children use this oral sentence frame: *A(n) _____ has a very heavy* weight. (Possible answers: computer, television, desk)

8 **amazing** Write the word *amazing* on the board. Have children think of things that are *amazing*. After children have drawn their pictures, have them use this oral sentence frame: *I _____. It was* amazing! (Possible answers: caught a fish, saw an eagle)

High-Frequency Words

Have children look at page 161 in the **Interactive Worktext**. Help them read, spell, and write each high-frequency word. Guide partners to use each word in a sentence. Then read the story aloud with children. Guide partners to work together to reread the story and circle the high-frequency words. (pull, around, know, these, one, other) Listen in and provide assistance reading the high-frequency words, as necessary.

ELL ENGLISH LANGUAGE LEARNERS

Display the **High-Frequency Word Cards** for: *these, one, know, around, other, pull*. Write a sentence with each word on the board. Have children echo-read each sentence, and point out the high-frequency word. Then ask them to use the word in a new sentence.

READ COMPLEX TEXT

15–20 Minutes   RI.2.6   RI. 2.8   SL.2.1b

Read "Magnets Work!"

- Have children turn to page 162 in the **Interactive Worktext** and read aloud the Essential Question. Point to the picture. Say: *This girl is playing with a magnet.* Have children repeat: "magnet." *Let's read to find out how magnets work.* Have children echo-read the title.

- Read the story together. Note that the weekly vocabulary words are highlighted in yellow. Expand Vocabulary words are highlighted in blue.

- As children read, have them use the "My Notes" section on page 162 to write questions they have. Children can also write words they don't understand or things they want to remember. Model how to use the "My Notes" section. *When I read the title, I wonder what makes magnets work. I will keep that question in mind as I read the text.*

ELL ENGLISH LANGUAGE LEARNERS

As you read together, have children highlight parts of the text they have questions about. After reading, review the questions children have. Then help them locate the answers to their questions in the text.

 Quick Check Can children understand the weekly vocabulary in context? If not, review vocabulary using the **Visual Vocabulary Cards** before teaching Lesson 2.

Can children read high-frequency words in context? If not, review using the Read/Spell/Write routine and the High-Frequency Word Cards.

LESSON 2

- Read an expository text
- Understand complex text through close reading
- Recognize and understand author's purpose
- Respond to the selection using text evidence to support ideas

Scaffolding for **WONDERS** Reading/Writing Workshop

Interactive Worktext, pp. 162–169

☞ **Go** Digital
- Interactive eWorktext
- Author's Purpose Mini-Lesson

REREAD COMPLEX TEXT

20–25 Minutes   RI.2.1   RI.2.4   RI.2.5   L.2.5a

Close Reading: "Magnets Work!"

Reread "Magnets Work!" with children from **Interactive Worktext** pages 162–167. As you read together, discuss important passages in the text. Guide children to respond to questions using evidence from the text.

🔍 Page 163

Expand Vocabulary Remind children that *uses* can be a verb and a noun. In this case it is a noun that means the ways that a thing can be used. Guide them to look at the photo on the page. Ask: *What are some of the* uses *of a magnet in the photo?* Have children circle their answers. (holding paper clips, attracting metal filings)

Connection of Ideas **A C T** Help children reread the second paragraph. Explain that one of the ideas of this text is that magnets do many things. Say: *The question is asking me where I can find magnets. As I reread the second paragraph, I see it says there are magnets in a can opener.* Guide children to underline the answer. (can opener)

Author's Purpose Point out to children that the information in a text can help you figure out the author's purpose. Have children reread the page. Note that the opening paragraph talked about finding out about a magnet's uses. Ask: *What is something that a magnet can do?* Guide children to draw a box around their answer. (The magnet can pull off the top of the can.)

🔍 Page 164

Genre Explain to children that informational texts often contain headings, photographs, captions, and diagrams. Say: *These text features give more information to readers. On this page there is a diagram that shows the poles of a magnet. This diagram helps to explain how the poles of magnets work.*

Author's Purpose Remind children that as they read, they can look for clues to figure out the author's purpose for writing. Guide them to reread the first paragraph. Ask: *What is something magnets can do?* Have children draw a box around the answer. (Magnets pull objects made of metal.)

Expand Vocabulary Explain to children that something that is *wooden* is made from the wood of a tree. Ask: *How does a magnet react to* wooden *objects?* Guide children to locate and circle the words that answer. (It will not pull wooden or plastic things.)

Connection of Ideas **A C T** Point out that the text on a page is connected to other features on the page, such as photos or diagrams. Have children look at the diagram and caption on page 164. Ask: *Which poles pull objects together?* Guide children to read both the labels and caption. Have them underline their answers. (unlike poles; north pole, south pole) Explain that "unlike" means not alike, so for magnets to pull together, they need to have different poles, or north and south poles, facing each other.

🔍 Page 165

Expand Vocabulary Point to the diagram on page 165. Explain that when two magnets *repel*, they push away from each other. Explain that this happens when two of the same poles are facing each other. Ask: *What parts of the picture show that the magnets are* repelling? Guide children to circle their answer. (the arrows)

Author's Purpose Have children reread this page. Ask: *Why did the author use a diagram on this page?* Guide children to notice the diagrams on pages 164 and 165. Guide children to write their answers. (To show how the force of magnets work.)

Page 166

Author's Purpose Guide children to read the heading and look at the photograph. Then reread the paragraph. Ask: *What can magnets do that is powerful?* Guide children to draw a box around the text that answers the question. (They can move light or heavy things.)

Connection of Ideas **ACT** Reread the paragraph and guide children to examine the photo. Ask: *What is a heavy object that magnets can help move?* Children should underline their answer. (the train in the photo)

Page 167

Connection of Ideas **ACT** Have children reread the first paragraph. Ask: *What is important about a train that uses magnets?* Guide them to underline the text that answers the question. (It is faster than trains without magnets.)

Author's Purpose Have children look at the sentences they have drawn boxes around throughout this selection. Ask: *What do you think the author's purpose was for writing this text?* Guide children to write their answers. (Possible answer: The author wanted to give information about how we use magnets.)

RESPOND TO READING

15–20 Minutes   RI.2.6   RI.2.8   SL.2.1b

Respond to "Magnets Work!"

Read aloud the questions on page 168 of the **Interactive Worktext**. Guide children read the questions about "Magnets Work!" Then read aloud the "Discussion Starter" for each of the questions. Guide children to work with a partner to answer the questions orally using the "Discussion Starters." Have children find text evidence to support their answers. Ask children to write the page number(s) on which they found the text evidence for each question.

1. *What do magnets do?* (Possible answers: I read that magnets can pull the top off a can. Magnets pull objects that are made of metal. Text Evidence: pp. 163–164)

2. *How do the poles of magnets work?* (Possible answer: When two of the same poles touch, they push each other away. When two opposite poles touch, they snap together. Text Evidence: p. 165)

3. *How can magnets help us?* (Possible answer: I read that magnets can help us by moving light or heavy things. A new train uses magnets to hold it above the track and push it forward. Text Evidence: pp. 166, 167)

After children discuss the questions on page 168, have them use the sentence starters to answer the question on page 169. Circulate and provide guidance.

 Quick Check **Do children understand vocabulary in context? If not, review and reteach using the instruction on page 134.**

Can children identify author's purpose? If not, review and reteach using the instruction on page 134 and assign the Unit 3 Week 1 digital mini-lesson.

Can children write a response to "Magnets Work!" If not, review the sentence starters and prompt children to respond orally. Help them write their responses.

WEEK 1
LESSON

3

Scaffolding for **Wonders** Approaching Leveled Reader

Objectives
- Access prior knowledge
- Understand and use new vocabulary words
- Read high-frequency words
- Read expository text

Materials
"Forces at Work" Apprentice Leveled Reader
- High-Frequency Word Cards

☞ **Go** Digital
- Apprentice Leveled Reader eBook
- Downloadable High-Frequency Word Cards

BEFORE READING

10–15 Minutes   SL.2.1a   SL.2.6   L.2.6   RF.2.3f   **CCSS**

Introduce "Forces at Work"

- Read the Essential Question on the title page of "Forces at Work" **Apprentice Leveled Reader:** *How do Earth's forces affect us?*

- Read the title of the main read. Point to the title page. *What is this boy wearing to help him move fast?* (skates) *What do skates have to help skaters go?* (wheels) *What do you know about how skaters slow down or stop? Let's read to learn more about forces and how they work.*

High-Frequency Words

Display the **High-Frequency Word Cards** for the words *down, fall, her, now, off,* and *pull.* Use the Read/Spell/Write routine to teach each word. Guide partners to use each word in a sentence. Provide assistance reading the high-frequency words, as necessary.

Expand Vocabulary

Before reading "Forces at Work," help children read the following words that they will encounter. Display each word below. Use the Define/Example/Ask routine. Tell children to look for the word later on as they read "Forces at Work."

1 brakes (page 12)

Define: something that stops or slows a bike, car, or other moving vehicle

Example: He used the *brakes* to stop his bike at the stop sign.

Ask: What are some other vehicles that use *brakes*?

2 drags (page 11)

Define: to pull or move along slowly or heavily

Example: Dad *drags* the heavy trunk across the room.

Ask: What sounds might you hear when something *drags*?

3 grab (page 12)

Define: to take hold of suddenly

Example: Nate *grabs* has backpack and runs to the bus.

Ask: What do you *grab* on the playground?

4 less (page 13)

Define: not as much

Example: This balloon has *less* air in it than that one.

Ask: What word is the opposite of *less*?

5 rub (page 5)

Define: to move back and forth against something

Example: This chair leg *rubs* the carpet when I move it.

Ask: What are some things that *rub* against each other?

6 smooth (page 14)

Define: something that does not feel bumpy or rough

Example: The old sidewalk was rough and crumbling, but the new sidewalk is *smooth*.

Ask: What can you name that has a *smooth* surface?

DURING READING

20–30 Minutes   RI. 2.1   RI.2.6   L.2.4a

Shared Reading

Tell children you will now read *Forces at Work*. Tell them to note the vocabulary and high-frequency words you just introduced as you read the story. Stop to model understanding of the story as you go.

Pages 2–3

High-Frequency Words Make sure children can read the high-frequency word *pulls*.

Comprehension Check Model beginning to read the story. Say: *This book begins by telling us that a force pushes or* pulls *things. I see a boy pushing a swing and a girl pulling a wagon. I will be looking for more information about how things are pushed or pulled as I read.*

Pages 4–5

High-Frequency Words Make sure children can read the high-frequency words *down* and *fall*.

Pages 6–7

High-Frequency Words Make sure children can read the high-frequency word *her*.

Vocabulary On page 6, read the sentence "*Friction slows her speed.*" Ask: *What did we learn about friction on the last page?* (that friction happens when you rub two things together) *How is friction slowing her?* (Her body is rubbing against the slides and that slows her down.)

Comprehension Check *I am going to stop here to think about what I am reading. I know that I am learning about different forces such as gravity and friction. On page 6, I see a girl sliding. On page 7, I see two boys playing ball. The text and pictures help me understand ways that I can see forces at work every day—such as on the playground.*

Pages 8–9

High-Frequency Words Make sure children can read the high-frequency word *now*.

Pages 10–11

High-Frequency Words Make sure children can read the high-frequency word *off*.

Comprehension Check *I read on pages 10 and 11 that friction is an important part of skating. I can think about what happens when a skater pushes* off *and also what a skater must do to get the skates to slow down or stop. I think that the force known as friction is an important part of skating. I'll keep reading to see if I can learn about some other important ways that friction works.*

Pages 12–13

Vocabulary Read page 12. Focus on the words *brakes* and *grab*. Ask: *What do the* brakes *on a bike do?* (They *grab* the wheels.) *What happens when the brakes grab the wheels?* (The brakes grab the wheels to make friction, and that causes the bike to stop.)

Vocabulary *I read on page 13 that the* shape *of a football makes less friction, and this helps the football to go faster. How is a football's shape different from other balls?* (It is longer and thinner.) *I can think about the shape of other things that go through the air, such as an airplane. That looks a little like a football.* Talk about why that shape is better than a round shape for moving quickly through the air.

Pages 14–15

Comprehension Check *I read on this page that forces are everywhere. I can look back at what I've read and think about different ways that I see forces at work every day. I can use the examples in the text to give me ideas for looking at ways that forces are at work around me at school and at home.*

 Quick Check **Can children understand vocabulary in context? If not, review and reteach using the instruction on page 134 and assign the Unit 3 Week 1 digital mini-lesson.**

Can children read the high-frequency words in context? If not, review using the Read/Spell/Write routine and the High-Frequency Word Cards.

LESSON 4

- Understand complex text through close-reading
- Read expository text
- Recognize and understand author's purpose
- Respond to the selection using text evidence to support ideas

"Forces at Work" Apprentice Leveled Reader
- Author's Purpose Graphic Organizer

☞ **Go** Digital
- Apprentice Leveled Reader Ebook
- Downloadable Graphic Organizer
- Author's Purpose Mini-Lesson

Scaffolding for **McGraw-Hill Reading WONDERS** Approaching Leveled Reader

DURING READING

20–30 Minutes   RI.2.1 RI.2.3 RI.2.6 **CCSS**

Tell children they will now reread the selection, "Forces at Work." Review the vocabulary and high-frequency words that they will encounter as they read.

Close Reading

 Pages 2–3

Author's Purpose Remind children that good readers think about why an author writes a text. Explain that when reading, it helps to look for clues to figure out an author's purpose. Reread pages 2 and 3. Ask: *What does the author want you to know?* (what a force is) *What does the author tell you about a force here?* (It pushes or pull things.) Model filling in the Author's Purpose Chart.

Sentence Structure **A C T** Reread the first sentence. on page 2. Point out that it has two parts. Ask: *What is the first thing this sentence tells you a force can do?* (push things) *What is the second thing it tells you it can do?* (pull things) Have children point to the word that connects the two parts. (or)

Pages 4–5

Author's Purpose Reread page 4. Ask: *What does the author want you to know about gravity?* (Gravity is a force that pulls things to Earth.) Reread page 5. Ask: *What does the author want you to know about friction?* (Friction is a force that happens when you rub two things together.)

Sentence Structure **A C T** Explain that authors sometimes use the word *it* instead of repeating a word to make the sentence sound smoother. Reread the first two sentences of page 4. Ask: *What does the word* it *mean?* (gravity) Repeat with the second two sentences.

Pages 6–7

Author's Purpose Reread page 6. Ask: *What do you think the author wants us to know about the girl on the slide?* (The author wants us to know that the girl on the slide shows both gravity and friction at work.) Help children record these clues in their Author's Purpose charts.

Connection of Ideas **A C T** Point to the picture on page 7. Ask: *Do you think the soccer ball would roll faster over grass or over the smooth surface of a gym floor? Tell why you think so.* (A soccer ball would roll faster on a gym floor because the grass slows it down due to friction.)

Pages 8–9

Author's Purpose Reread pages 8 and 9. Ask: *Why do you think the author includes this information about the shoe on page 8 and the soccer ball being kicked through the air on page 9?* (The author wants to make sure we understand friction, so she is including these examples of ways that friction works.)

Sentence Structure **A C T** Reread page 8. Ask children what the word *it* in the second and third sentences stands for. (the shoe) Reread the page replacing the word *it* with *the shoe.* Ask children why they think the author chose to use the word *it.* (It sounds smoother.)

Pages 10–11

Author's Purpose Reread pages 10 and 11. Remind children that it is important to stop and think about what an author wants you to know as you read. Ask: *What does the author want you to know about skaters and the force of friction?* (Friction helps skaters push off as they begin to skate, and also to slow down and stop.) Guide children as they include clues in their Author's Purpose charts.

Pages 12–13

Author's Purpose After rereading page 13, ask: *Why is the author including this information about the shape of a football?* (To explain that a football goes fast because of its shape. She wants us to know that its shape means there is less friction with the air.) Help children record these clues in their Author's Purpose charts.

Connection of Ideas **ACT** Reread page 12 and ask: *When the brakes grab the wheels does that make more friction or less friction?* (more) *Does more friction mean more speed or less speed?* (less) Then reread page 13 and ask: *Does the shape of the football make more friction or less friction?* (less) *Does less friction mean more speed or less speed?* (more)

Pages 14–15

Author's Purpose Reread page 14 and ask: *What does the author want us to know about swimmers?* (They wear smooth caps and suits so they can swim faster in the water.) Help children record this final clue in their Author's Purpose charts.

Connection of Ideas **ACT** Focus on the last sentence on page 14, *"Forces are everywhere!"* Say: *Think back to the beginning of the text. What are some examples the author included to help us understand that forces are everywhere?* (She used examples of pushing a swing, pulling a wagon, going down a slide, kicking a soccer ball, wearing soccer shoes, skating, using brakes on a bike, the shape of a football, and the smoothness of swimmers' caps and suits.)

AFTER READING

10–15 Minutes RI.2.6 RI.2.9 L.2.4a RF.2a W.2.8 **CCSS**

Respond to Reading

Compare Texts Guide children in comparing the information in "Forces at Work" with the information in "Magnets at Work." Help children think about ways Earth's forces affect us. Then ask: *What are some ways that you see forces, such as gravity, friction, or the pull of magnets at work in your life?*

Summarize Have children turn to page 16 and guide them in summarizing the selection. (Answers should include details about the author's purpose.)

Text Evidence

Have partners work together to answer questions on page 16. Remind children to use their Author's Purpose charts.

Author's Purpose (Answers will vary but should note that the author wants to explain how various forces like friction and gravity work and encourages readers to see them at work in their lives.)

Vocabulary (The text reads, "Swimmers wear caps and suits." The picture shows a swimmer in a cap and swimsuit. These clues tell us that suits are pieces of specialized clothing worn while swimming.)

Write About Reading (Answers will vary but should explain that players kick the ball around, friction slows the ball and the players down (pages 7–9), and gravity brings the ball to Earth (page 4)

Read "Machines to Push and Pull"

Encourage children to read the paired selection "Machines to Push and Pull" on pages 17–19. Have them summarize the selection and compare it to "Forces at Work." Have them work with a partner to answer the "Make Connections" questions on page 19.

Independent Reading

Have pairs of children reread "Forces at Work." Have them talk about ways they see friction at work.

 Quick Check Can students identify Author's Purpose? If not, review and reteach using the instruction on page 134 and assign the Unit 3 Week 1 digital mini-lesson.

Can students respond to the selection using text evidence? If not, provide sentence frames to help them organize their ideas.

WEEK 1 LESSON 5

Objectives
- Review weekly vocabulary words
- Review author's purpose
- Write an analysis about how the author conveyed his or her purpose

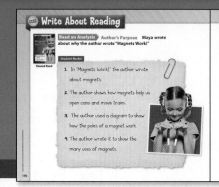

Materials
- Visual Vocabulary Cards: 77–84
- Interactive Worktext, pp. 170–171
- Assessment Book, pp. 30–31

☞ **Go Digital**
- Visual Vocabulary Cards
- Author's Purpose Mini-Lesson
- Interactive eWorktext
- eAssessment

Scaffolding for **Wonders** McGraw-Hill Reading   Reading/Writing Workshop

---

REVIEW AND RETEACH

5–10 Minutes   L.2.4c   RI.2.1   RI.2.5

Weekly Vocabulary

Display one **Visual Vocabulary Card** at a time and guide children to use the vocabulary word in a sentence. If children have difficulty creating a sentence, have them find the word in "Magnets Work!" or "Forces at Work" and use context clues to define the vocabulary word.

Comprehension: Author's Purpose

I Do Write and say: *Soccer is a sport. There are two teams. Players use their feet to try to kick a ball into a goal on either end of the field. Players on the same team pass the ball to each other. The winner is the team with the most points at the end of the game.* Ask: *What is my purpose in telling you these things?* Say: *An author's purpose can be to answer a question, explain something or describe something. My purpose for the soccer story was to explain how soccer is played.*

We Do Display: *Summer is the best season! You can swim and eat popsicles. The sun doesn't go down until very late, so you can play outside for a long time. Most children do not go to school in summer.* Ask: *What is the purpose of these sentences?* (To give an opinion about why summer is the best season.)

You Do Display: *Red-eyed tree frogs live in the rainforest. A red-eyed tree frog has a green body and red eyes and feet. When it closes its eyes, its eyelids are green. Being green helps it hide. During the day, red-eyed tree frogs rest. At night, they are active.* Guide partners to work together to decide on the purpose of the text. (To describe what red-eyed tree frogs are and how they behave.)

WRITE ABOUT READING

25–35 Minutes   W.2.2   W.2.5   W.4.9

Read an Analysis

- Guide children to look back at "Magnets Work!" in the **Interactive Worktext**. Have volunteers review the details about the author's purpose they marked on page 163 and summarize the text. Repeat with pages 164–167. *Why did the author write this selection?*

- Read aloud the directions on page 170. Read aloud the student model. *This student's work is not a summary. It is an analysis, or description, of why the author wrote "Magnets Work!"*

- *When you write an analysis, you should include key details from the story that tell about the story. Read Maya's first sentence. Circle the details.* (The author wrote about magnets.) *In what part of the story do you first learn these details?* (the beginning)

- *Read the second sentence. Maya gives us clues as to what the author's purpose is. What clues does Maya include?* (The author shows how magnets can open cans and make trains move.)

- Guide children to point to the third sentence. This sentence explains how text features show the author's purpose. *What details does Maya include?* (The author used a diagram to show how the poles of a magnet work.) *Guide children to suggest other reasons the author may have included the diagram. The author included the diagram because _____.*

- Read the last sentence that Maya wrote. *Why is this sentence a good ending? Maya tells why the author wrote the selection. Draw a box around the author's purpose.* (to show how magnets work)

---

134   UNIT 3 WEEK 1

Analytical Writing Write an Analysis

Guided Writing Read the writing prompt on page 171 together. Guide children to review their Author's Purpose charts for "Forces at Work." Have children use their charts to complete the sentence starters. Children can also write an analysis using another selection previously read this week.

Peer Conference Guide children to read their analysis to a partner. Listeners should summarize the strongest details that support the author's purpose for writing the selection. They should discuss any parts that are unclear.

Teacher Conference Check children's writing for complete sentences and whether they included details from the story. Review the last sentence and ask: *Why did the author write "Forces at Work"?* If necessary, guide children to revise their sentences.

Level Up

▲ Approaching Leveled Reader

▲ Reading/Writing Workshop

Apprentice Leveled Reader

▲ Interactive Worktext

IF children read the Apprentice Level Reader and the **Interactive Worktext** Shared Read fluently and answer the Respond to Reading questions

THEN read together the Approaching Level Reader main selection and the **Reading/Writing Workshop** Shared Read from *Reading Wonders*. Have children take notes as they read, using self-stick notes. Then ask and answer questions about their notes.

Writing Rubric

	4	3	2	1
Text Evidence	Includes three or more details from the text.	Includes two or more details from the text.	Includes only one detail from the text.	No text evidence is cited.
Writing Style	Writes in complete sentences. Uses correct spelling and grammar.	Uses complete sentences. Writing has spelling and grammar errors.	Few complete sentences. There are many spelling and grammar errors.	Writing is not accurate or in complete sentences.

ASSESSMENT

Weekly Assessment

Have children complete the Weekly Assessment using **Assessment** book pages 30–31.

WEEK 2
LESSON
1

• Objectives
  • Develop oral language
  • Build background about the sky
  • Understand and use weekly vocabulary
  • Read a fiction text

Talk About It
Weekly Concept Look at the Sky
Essential Question
What can we see in the sky?

Tell what you can see in the sky.

Daytime Sky	Nighttime Sky

Talk with a partner about how the sky changes.

Materials
Interactive Worktext, pp. 172–181
• Visual Vocabulary Cards: 85–92
• High-Frequency Word Cards

☞ Go Digital
• Interactive eWorktext
• Visual Vocabulary Cards

Scaffolding for **Wonders** Reading/Writing Workshop

WEEKLY CONCEPT

5–10 Minutes   SL.2.1b   SL.2.4   CCSS

Talk About It

Essential Question Read aloud the Essential Question on page 172 of the **Interactive Worktext:** *What can we see in the sky?* Explain that when you look up in the sky, you can see many things, such as airplanes, clouds, and the sun.

• Discuss the photograph on page 172. Ask: *What is this a picture of?* (This is a picture of a nighttime sky. The picture is of the sky, an ocean, and mountains.)

I Do Say: *I am going to look at this photo and think about what I see in the sky at nighttime. I see that the sky is dark. It looks bluish in color. There are stars in the sky.* Point out the two-column chart on page 173 and read the headings aloud. Explain that the class will begin a list of things they see in the daytime and nighttime skies. Say: *I will write there are stars in the sky in the "Nighttime" column of the chart.*

We Do Say: *Let's think about what else we see in the nighttime sky.* Point to the moon and ask a volunteer to identify it. Discuss the different phases of the moon and how it sometimes looks different at night. Guide children to add the moon to the "Nighttime" column of their chart.

You Do Guide partners to work together to talk about the daytime sky. Have them think of things they have seen in the daytime sky. Have children use the words from the web to start their sentences: *In the daytime sky, I have seen _____.*

REVIEW VOCABULARY

10–15 Minutes   L.2.4a   L.2.4c   L.2.4d   CCSS

Review Weekly Vocabulary Words

• Use the **Visual Vocabulary Cards** to review the weekly vocabulary.

• Read together the directions on page 174 of the **Interactive Worktext**. Then complete the activity.

1 **delighted** Have children think about something that has pleased or *delighted* them. Have them use this oral sentence starter: *I felt* delighted *when _____.* (Possible answers: I heard my favorite song. I got a letter in the mail.)

2 **nighttime** Write the word *daytime* on the board. Underline the words *day* and *time* and explain that *daytime* is a compound word. Guide children to understand that if they know the meanings of the two smaller words in a compound word, they can figure out its meaning. Then have volunteers underline the words in *nighttime* and tell what they do during the *nighttime*. (Possible answers: read, go to sleep)

3 **moonlight** Explain that *moonlight* is actually light that comes from the sun and is reflected off of the moon. Note that *moonlight* is also a compound word. Guide children to underline the two words in *moonlight*. Then ask: *When can you see* moonlight? (nighttime)

4 **grumbled** Make an upset face and *grumble* about something. Then have children think about things that upset them. Ask them to use this oral sentence starter: *I* grumbled *because _____.* (Possible answer: It started to rain.)

5 **adventure** Explain that *adventure* means an exciting or unusual experience. Have children read the choices on the page and identify where they might find *adventure*. (Possible answers: jungle) Then have them use this oral sentence starter to name other places they could find adventure: *I would find adventure _____.*

6 **neighbor** Explain that *neighbors* often do kind things for each other. Have them complete this sentence orally: *My next-door neighbor is _____.* (Answers will vary.) Have them think of ways they could be kind to their *neighbors*. (Answers will vary.)

7 **dreamed** Write the word *dreamed* on the board. Have children think of another word that means the same. (Possible answer: imagined) Then guide children to name something they have *dreamed* about.

8 **enjoyed** Have children think of games they have *enjoyed* playing. Help them write a sentence to go with their picture, using this sentence starter: *I enjoyed playing _____.* Have children share their sentences orally.

High-Frequency Words

Have children look at page 175 in the **Interactive Worktext**. Help them read, spell, and write each high-frequency word. Guide partners to use each word in a sentence. Then read the story aloud with children. Guide partners to work together to reread the story and circle the high-frequency words. (many, were, been, for, up, light) Listen in and provide assistance, as necessary.

ELL ENGLISH LANGUAGE LEARNERS

Display the **High-Frequency Word Cards** for: *many, up, for, been, were, light*. Write a sentence with each word on the board. Have children echo-read each sentence, and point out the high-frequency word. Then ask them to use the word in a new sentence.

READ COMPLEX TEXT

15–20 Minutes RL.2.1 RL. 2.5 SL.2.1b

Read "Starry Night"

- Have children turn to page 176 in the **Interactive Worktext** and read aloud the Essential Question. Point to the picture. Say: *What is the class doing?* (looking at a picture of the sun and the planets) *Let's read to find out what we can see in the sky.* Have children echo-read the title.

- Read the story together. Note that the weekly vocabulary words are highlighted in yellow. Expand Vocabulary words are highlighted in blue.

- As children read, have them use the "My Notes" section on page 176 to write questions they have. Children can also write words they don't understand or things they want to remember. Model how to use the "My Notes" section. *When I read the last paragraph on page 177, I find out that Mr. Cortes thinks the class will have fun learning about the nighttime sky. I will write a question about what they might see in the sky in the "My Notes" section.*

ELL ENGLISH LANGUAGE LEARNERS

As you read together, have children highlight parts of the text they have questions about. After reading, review the questions children have. Then help them locate the answers to their questions in the text.

✓ *Quick Check* Can children understand the weekly vocabulary in context? If not, review vocabulary using the **Visual Vocabulary Cards** before teaching Lesson 2.

Can children read high-frequency words in context? If not, review using the Read/Spell/Write routine and the High-Frequency Word Cards.

WEEK 2
LESSON
2

Objectives
• Read a fiction story
• Understand complex text through close reading
• Recognize and understand sequence
• Respond to the selection using text evidence to support ideas

Materials
Interactive Worktext, pp. 176–183

☞ **Go** Digital
• Interactive eWorktext
• Sequence Mini-Lesson

Scaffolding for **McGraw-Hill Reading Wonders** Reading/Writing Workshop

REREAD COMPLEX TEXT

20–25 Minutes   RL.2.1 RL.2.5 L.2.4a

Close Reading: "Starry Night"

Reread "Starry Night" with children from **Interactive Worktext** pages 176–181. As you read together, discuss important passages in the text. Guide children to respond to questions using evidence from the text.

Page 176–177

Expand Vocabulary Explain to children that when Josie and Ling *planned* to do something, they thought out a way of doing it ahead of time. Reread the second paragraph aloud. Ask: *What had Josie and Ling* planned? *In the story, I see that they* planned *to sleep outside in a tent at Josie's house.* Guide children to circle the words that tell. (to sleep outside in a tent in Josie's backyard)

Sequence Remind children that the plot is the key events that happen in a story. Say: *Sequence is the order in which these events take place.* Have children reread the third paragraph. Ask: *Where does the first event take place in the story? I read that the girls were in class at school and I can see that in the picture.* Guide children to draw a box around the word that tells. (class)

Sentence Structure Ⓐ Ⓒ Ⓣ On the board write: *When he finished his lunch, Jack asked, "Can I go to the park?"* Say: *The words in the quotation marks show what a person says or said. Underline the words in quotations marks. Then point to the remaining words and explain that these words are words the narrator of the story is saying.* Have children reread the third paragraph. Ask: *What are the words Mr. Cortes says in the first sentence?* Guide children to underline the answer. ("Your homework is to look at the nighttime sky.")

Page 178

Sequence Explain to children that clue words such as *first, next, then,* and *last* can help tell the story's sequence. Ask: *After the girls leave school, where do they go next in the story?* Guide children to draw a box around the words that tell. (Josie's house)

Sequence Have them reread the second paragraph. Ask: *What does Josie's dad want the girls to do next?* Guide children to draw a box around the word that tells. (homework)

Sentence Structure Ⓐ Ⓒ Ⓣ Explain to children that after one character speaks, the words another character speaks will often start a new line. Point out that if a speaker has already been named in an earlier sentence on the page, the author may not include the character's name after each time he or she speaks. Reread the last four lines aloud. Ask: *Who is Josie speaking to?* Guide children to write their answers. (Josie's dad)

Page 179

Expand Vocabulary Point to the picture of the Big Dipper on page 179. Tell children that you have *spotted* the Big Dipper on the page. Explain that if you *spotted* something, you saw it. Have children reread the first paragraph. Ask: *Which words tell how Josie* spotted *the moon.* Guide children to circle the words that tell. (looked up)

Sentence Structure Ⓐ Ⓒ Ⓣ Explain to children that more than one character can speak in a paragraph. Read aloud the first paragraph. Ask: *Which two characters are speaking in this paragraph?* (Josie and Ling) Then, ask: *Which words does Josie speak in this paragraph?* Guide children to underline the answer. ("The moon's light comes from the sun, but it's called moonlight.")

Sequence Have children reread the page. Ask: *What did Josie's dad point out to the girls?* Guide children to write the words that tell. (stars, the Big Dipper)

Page 180

Expand Vocabulary Point to the *telescope* on the page and explain that it is used to make objects look closer and larger. Ask: *What does Josie see when she first looks through the* telescope? (stars)

Sentence Structure (ACT) Have children reread the paragraph and look for the quotation marks that signal a character is speaking. Ask: *Which words tell what Josie says in this paragraph?* Guide children to underline the words Josie speaks. ("There are so many stars!")

Sequence Remind children that Ling saw a bright light moving in the sky. Have children reread the page. Ask: *What did Ling see in the telescope after Josie saw the stars?* Guide children to draw a box around the words that tell. (a shooting star)

Page 181

Expand Vocabulary Read the first paragraph aloud. Explain that if you have seen *enough*, you have seen as much as you need to. Ask: *Josie's dad said they had seen* enough *what?* Guide children to circle their answers. (stars)

Sequence Have children reread the first paragraph. Ask: *What does Josie's dad think the girls want to do next?* Guide them to draw a box around the words that tell. (go play)

Sequence Have children reread the page. Ask: *What do Josie and Ling want to do at the end of the story?* Guide them to draw a box around the words that tell. (keep looking)

Author's Purpose Explain to children that authors sometimes have more than one purpose in writing a story. Point out that the author wrote "Starry Night" not only to entertain readers, but also to give facts to help us learn about something. Ask: *What did the author of this story want us to learn about?* (things we can see in the nighttime sky)

RESPOND TO READING

10–20 Minutes   SL.2.1a   RL.2.1   RL.2.5

Respond to "Starry Night"

Read aloud the questions on page 182 of the **Interactive Worktext**. Guide children read the question about "Starry Night." Then read aloud the "Discussion Starter" for each of the questions. Guide children to work with a partner to answer the questions orally using the "Discussion Starters." Have children find text evidence to support their answers. Ask children to write the page number(s) on which they found the text evidence for each question.

1. *Why do Josie and Ling look at the nighttime sky?* (Possible answer: I read that Josie and Ling have planned to have a sleepover. Their homework was to look at the nighttime sky. Text Evidence: p. 177)

2. *What does Josie teach Ling?* (Possible answer: I read that Josie first sees the moon. Josie explains to Ling that moonlight is light from the sun. Text Evidence: p. 179)

3. *What do Josie and Ling learn about stars?* (Possible answer: I read that they learn that the Big Dipper is a group of stars. I also read that they see a shooting star. Text Evidence: pp. 179, 180)

After children discuss the questions on page 182, have them use the sentence starters to answer the question on page 183. Circulate and provide guidance.

 Quick Check Do children understand vocabulary in context? If not, review and reteach using the instruction on page 144.

Can children identify sequence? If not, review and reteach using the instruction on page 144 and assign the Unit 3 Week 2 digital mini-lesson.

Can children write a response to "Starry Night"? If not, review the sentence starters and prompt children to respond orally. Help them write their responses.

Objectives
- Access prior knowledge
- Understand and use new vocabulary words
- Read high-frequency words
- Read fiction

Materials
- "A Special Sunset" Apprentice Leveled Reader
- High-Frequency Word Cards

☞ **Go** Digital
- Apprentice Leveled Reader eBook
- Downloadable High-Frequency Word Cards

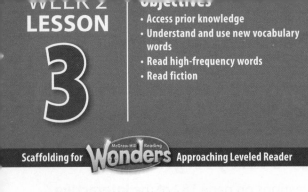

Scaffolding for **Wonders** Approaching Leveled Reader

BEFORE READING

10–15 Minutes   SL.2.1a   SL.2.6   L.2.6   RF.2.3f   CCSS

Introduce "A Special Sunset"

- Read the Essential Question on the title page of "A Special Sunset" **Apprentice Leveled Reader:** *What can we see in the sky?*

- Read the title of the main read. Point to the cover. *What characters are in this story?* (a girl, a man) *What are they doing?* (sitting inside a plane) *What does this tell us about the characters?* (They are going on a trip.) *Let's read to find out more about this special trip.*

High-Frequency Words

Display the **High-Frequency Word Cards** for the words, *be, by, do, light, soon* and *why.* Use the Read/Spell/Write routine to teach each word. Guide partners to use each word in a sentence. Provide assistance reading the high-frequency words, as necessary.

Expand Vocabulary

Before reading "A Special Sunset," help children read the following words that they will encounter. Display each word below. Use the Define/Example/Ask routine. Tell children to look for the word later on as they read "A Special Sunset."

❶ **airport** (page 2)

Define: a place where airplanes take off and land

Example: Mom and I watched my uncle's airplane land at the *airport*.

Ask: What are some things you might see at an *airport*?

❷ **clouds** (page 8)

Define: gray or white mass of tiny drops of water or ice floating high in the sky

Example: I like to look for funny shapes in the *clouds* that float over our house.

Ask: What are some words you can use to describe *clouds*?

❸ **glow** (page 8)

Define: to shine brightly and steadily

Example: The stars began to *glow* in the night sky.

Ask: What are some other things that *glow*?

❹ **late** (page 5)

Define: coming after the usual time

Example: Mom didn't hear the alarm clock, which made her *late* for work.

Ask: What are some things that could make you *late* for school?

❺ **sunset** (page 10)

Define: when the sun goes down at night

Example: After dinner we went outside to watch the *sunset*.

Ask: What are some colors you might see when you watch a *sunset*?

DURING READING

20–30 Minutes   RL.2.1   RL.2.5   L.2.4a

Shared Reading

Tell children you will now read *A Special Sunset*. Tell them to note the vocabulary and high-frequency words you just introduced as you read the story. Stop to model understanding of the story as you go.

Pages 2–3

High-Frequency Words Make sure children can read the high-frequency word *be*.

Comprehension Check Model beginning to read the story. Say: *The first thing I notice about this story is that it seems to be about a girl and her dad at the airport. I see that they have bags with them so I think they are probably there to take a trip. I'll ask myself where they are going to go and what will happen on their adventure.*

Expand Vocabulary Read page 2. Focus on the word *airport*. Ask: *Where are Maria and Dad?* (airport) *What can you tell about an airport from the picture?* (There is plane in the sky and people with luggage.)

Pages 4–5

Comprehension Check *On page 5 , I read that Maria is upset because the plane is late. But Dad is pointing. I think that Dad wants her to know that the plane has arrived.*

Pages 6–7

High-Frequency Words Make sure children can read the high-frequency words *by* and *soon*.

Pages 8–9

High-Frequency Words Make sure children can read the high-frequency word *light*.

Expand Vocabulary On page 8, read the sentence "*Its light makes them glow.*" Ask: *How does the picture on page 8 help us better understand the word* glow? (The picture shows the clouds and they have the reddish purple color of the sun as it begins to set.)

Pages 10–11

High-Frequency Words Make sure children can read the high-frequency words *do* and *why*.

Expand Vocabulary Read the sentence on page 10. Ask: *What two smaller words do you see in the word* sunset? (sun, set) Guide children in a discussion to talk about how the two smaller words, *sun* and *set,* help them understand the meaning of the word *sunset*.

Comprehension Check *I read on pages 10 and 11 that Maria and Dad are flying, but they are not flying past the sunset. Maria wants to know why. I'll keep reading to see if I can learn the answer to Maria's question.*

Pages 12–13

Comprehension Check *I read on pages 12 and 13 that Dad is answering Maria's question. He tells her that they pass things that are closer to Earth much more quickly than things that are far away. Because the sun is far away it takes longer to pass it. I can stop here to think about this answer, and it will help me to understand and remember the information.*

Pages 14–15

Comprehension Check *I can think about what has changed by looking back at pages 8 and 9 and then flipping forward to pages 14 and 15. On pages 8 and 9, the pictures showed the sun as it was beginning to set. It made the clouds glow. On pages 14 and 15, I learn that the sun has now set. I can see how the view out Maria's window has changed. This helps me understand what has taken place in the story.*

 Quick Check Can children understand vocabulary in context? If not, review and reteach using the instruction on page 144 and assign the Unit 3 Week 2 digital mini-lesson.

Can children read the high-frequency words in context? If not, review using the Read/Spell/Write routine and the High-Frequency Word Cards.

Objectives
- Understand complex text through close-reading
- Read fiction
- Recognize and understand sequence
- Respond to the selection using text evidence to support ideas

Materials
- "A Special Sunset" Apprentice Leveled Reader
- Graphic Organizer: Sequence

☞ **Go** Digital
- Apprentice Leveled Reader eBook
- Downloadable Graphic Organizer
- Sequence Mini-Lesson

DURING READING

20–30 Minutes   SL.2.1a   RL.2.1   RL.2.5   RL.2.7   (CCSS)

Tell children they will now reread the selection, "A Special Sunset." Review the vocabulary and high-frequency words that they will encounter as they read.

Close Reading

Pages 2–3

Sequence Tell children that when reading a story it is helpful to think about the order in which things happen. Reread pages 2 and 3. Ask: *What is something that happens at the beginning of this story?* (Maria and Dad go to the airport.) Model filling in the Sequence Chart.

Sentence Structure A C T Read page 3. Say: *The text says "they" will take a plane. Who are "they"?* (Dad and Maria)

Pages 4–5

Sentence Structure A C T Reread the last sentence on page 5. Point out that this sentence has two parts. Ask: *Who is the focus of the first part of the sentence?* (Maria) *What does Maria do?* (feel upset) *Who is the focus of the second part of the sentence?* (Dad) *What does Dad do?* (point to the plane) *How does pointing to the plane change Maria from being upset?* (She was upset that the plane wasn't there, but now it is, so she is not upset.) *Which word connects both parts of the sentence?* (but)

Pages 6–7

Sequence Reread page 6. Say: *The text tells us that Maria sits by the window. Then we read: "Soon, the plane takes off."* Ask: *What does the word* soon *tell you about the order of the events on this page?* (that the plane takes off not long after Maria sits by the window.) Help children record this information in their Sequence charts.

Connection of Ideas A C T Point to the picture on page 7. Ask: *What does Maria see as the plane begins to fly higher? How does her view change?* (She begins to see the land below her. She can see things get smaller as she flies higher.)

Pages 8–9

Sequence Reread pages 8 and 9. Ask: *What do we learn is taking place on pages 8 and 9?* (The sun is beginning to set.) *What can Maria see out the window that is changing?* (She can see the color of the sky change as the sun begins to set. She can see that they are flying past trees, lakes, and houses.) Guide children to include details about what is happening to their Sequence charts.

Pages 10–11

Sequence Reread pages 10 and 11. Remind children that it is helpful to stop and think about the order in which story events happen. Ask: *What is Maria now noticing about the sunset?* (She has noticed that they still have not flown past the sunset even though they have flown past other things, such as trees, lakes, and houses.)

Pages 12–13

Key Details After rereading pages 12 and 13, ask: *What does Dad's explanation tell Maria about why things such as trees, lakes, and houses pass by them so quickly but the sun takes longer to pass?* (The trees, lakes, and houses are closer so they seem to pass by more quickly than something far away, such as the sun.)

Connection of Ideas A C T Point to the picture on page 13 and ask: *What else does Maria see in the sky out her window?* (stars) *Do you think the stars pass by quickly or more slowly? Why do you think so?* (I think the stars pass by more slowly, like the sun, because they are far away.)

Organization (A)(C)(T) Point out that so far the book has been organized by events leading up to Maria's question about the sunset. First, she gets on the plane. Then, she sees everything flying past but the sunset. Then, she asks why. Ask: *What happens now to help you know that the book will no longer be about Maria's question?* (Dad answers her question, then Maria adds her thoughts. It seems that the question is solved.) Point to the picture on page 13 and ask children if it looks darker now. (yes) Explain that this can help them to know that that the main part of the book is over, too.

🔍 Pages 14–15

Sequence Focus on the last sentence on page 14, "At last, the sun sets." Ask: *How does the phrase "at last" help you understand the order of the story events?* (The words tell me that after some time passes, the sun finally sets.) Reread page 15 and say: *The text tells me that Maria will now follow the moon. What did they follow before they began to follow the moon?* (the sun) Help children record these final details in their Sequence charts.

Connection of Ideas (A)(C)(T) *Think back to the start of the story. How has Maria changed?* (She has learned what it's like to fly in an airplane.) *Do you think Maria will now understand why they can see the moon for such a long time? Why do you think so?* (Yes, I think she will understand that, like the sun, the moon is far away so it will seem to take longer for it to pass by.)

AFTER READING
10–15 Minutes RL.2.1 RL.2.5 L. 2.4a RF.2.4a W.2.8 CCSS

Respond to Reading

Compare Texts Guide children in comparing the events in "A Special Sunset" with the events in "Starry Night." Help children think about what can be seen in the night sky. Then ask: *What are some things you have seen in the night sky?*

Summarize Have children turn to page 16 and guide them in summarizing the selection. (Answers should include details about the sequence.)

🔍 Text Evidence

Have partners work together to answer questions on page 16. Remind children to use their Sequence Chart.

Sequence (Maria sees the moon rise and shine on the clouds.)

Vocabulary (The text reads, "Maria is upset. She turns away." The picture shows her looking sad. And to turn away from something is a way of showing that you are not happy with it. These clues tell us that to be upset means to be not happy.)

Write About Reading (Answers will vary but should describe a plausible sight, such as the sunrise or the airport at Maria's destination.)

Read "Shadows and Sundials"

Encourage children to read the paired selection "Shadows and Sun Dials" on pages 17–19. Have them summarize the selection and compare it to "A Special Sunset." Have them work with a partner to answer the "Make Connections" questions on page 19.

Independent Reading

Have pairs of children reread "A Special Sunset." Have them retell the story making sure to tell the events in the correct order.

✓ **Quick Check** Can students identify Sequence? If not, review and reteach using the instruction on page 144 and assign the Unit 3 Week 2 digital mini-lesson.

Can students respond to the selection using text evidence? If not, provide sentence frames to help them organize their ideas.

LESSON
5

- Review weekly vocabulary words
- Review sequence
- Write an analysis about an author's use of sequence

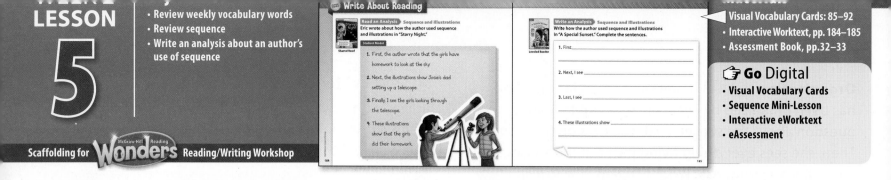

Scaffolding for **Wonders** Reading/Writing Workshop

- Visual Vocabulary Cards: 85–92
- Interactive Worktext, pp. 184–185
- Assessment Book, pp.32–33

☞ **Go** Digital
- **Visual Vocabulary Cards**
- **Sequence Mini-Lesson**
- **Interactive eWorktext**
- **eAssessment**

REVIEW AND RETEACH

5–10 Minutes   RL.2.5   L.2.4a   L.2.4c

Weekly Vocabulary

Display one **Visual Vocabulary Card** at a time and guide children to use the vocabulary word in a sentence. If children have difficulty creating a sentence, have them find the word in "Starry Night" or "A Special Sunset" and use context clues in the passage to define the vocabulary word.

Comprehension: Sequence

I Do   Write and say: *First, Mike and Anna saw the rain outside. Next, they decided to see a movie. Then, they called the theater to see what movies were playing. The last thing they needed to do was ask Mike's dad for a ride.* Ask: *What happens* first *in this story?* Circle "Mike and Anna saw the rain outside" and write *First.* Say: *The sequence is the order of the key events in a story.* Ask: *What event happens* next? *I know that words such as* first, next, then, last, *and* finally *can help tell the order of what happens in a story.* Circle "Next, they decided to see a movie" and write *Next.* Continue with remaining events.

We Do   Display and say: *First, the bear was hungry. Next, the bear looked for food. Then the bear found some berries.* Ask: *What is the first event that happens?* (The bear was hungry.) *What clue word helps tell what the order of this event in the story?* (First) *What clue word tells what happens at the end of the story?* (Then)

You Do   Display: *My friend, Tara, came over. First, we ate dinner together. Next, we played games. Then we read books. Finally, we went to sleep.* Guide one partner to ask the other to identify the story's sequence of events. Have partners discuss the clue words.

WRITE ABOUT READING

25–35 Minutes   W.2.3   W.2.8   W.4.9

Read an Analysis

- Guide children to look back at "Starry Night" in the **Interactive Worktext**. Have volunteers review the details about the sequence in the text they marked on page 177 and summarize the text. Repeat with pages 178–181. *How did the author use sequence in the selection?*

- Read aloud the directions on page 184. Read aloud the student model. *This student's work is not a summary. It is an analysis, or description, of how the author used sequence in "Starry Night."*

- *When you write an analysis, you should include key details from the story. Eric's analysis is about the use of sequence and illustrations in the story. Read Eric's first sentence. Circle the details about what happens first.* (the girls have homework to look at the sky)

- *Read the second sentence. Eric explains how the illustrations support what happens next. Draw a box around what the illustrations show.* (Josie's dad setting up the telescope)

- Guide children to point to the third sentence. This sentence talks about details from the end of the story. *What details does Eric include?* (I see the girls with the telescope) *What sequence word did Eric include to let the reader know the order of this event?* (Finally)

- Read the last sentence that Eric wrote. *What do the illustrations show?* (Eric explained that the illustrations used helped show girls did their homework.)

Write an Analysis

Analytical Writing

Guided Writing Read the writing prompt on page 185 together. Guide children to review their Sequence charts for "A Special Sunset." Have children use their charts to complete the sentence starters. Children can also write an analysis using another selection previously read this week.

Peer Conference Guide children to read their analysis to a partner. Listeners should summarize the strongest details and illustrations that support the sequence of the story. They should discuss any parts that are unclear.

Teacher Conference Check children's writing for complete sentences and whether they included details from the story. Review the sentences and ask: *Did the author use sequence to support the story?* If necessary, guide children to revise their sentence by adding more details.

Level Up

▲ Apprentice Leveled Reader

▲ Approaching Leveled Reader

▲ Interactive Worktext

▲ Reading/Writing Workshop

IF children read the **Apprentice Level** Reader and the **Interactive Worktext** Shared Read fluently and answer the Respond to Reading questions

THEN read together the **Approaching Level** Reader main selection and the **Reading/Writing Workshop** Shared Read from *Reading Wonders*. Have children take notes as they read, using self-stick notes. Then ask and answer questions about their notes.

Writing Rubric

	4	3	2	1
Text Evidence	Includes three or more details from the text.	Includes two or more details from the text.	Includes only one detail from the text.	No text evidence is cited.
Writing Style	Writes in complete sentences. Uses correct spelling and grammar.	Uses complete sentences. Writing has spelling and grammar errors.	Few complete sentences. There are many spelling and grammar errors.	Writing is not accurate or in complete sentences.

ASSESSMENT

Weekly Assessment

Have children complete the Weekly Assessment using **Assessment** book pages 32–33.

WEEK 3
LESSON

1

Objectives
• Develop oral language
• Build background about helping the community
• Understand and use weekly vocabulary
• Read a narrative nonfiction text

Scaffolding for **Wonders** McGraw-Hill Reading • Reading/Writing Workshop

WEEKLY CONCEPT

5-10 Minutes   RI.2.6   RI.2.8   SL.2.1a   CCSS

Talk About It

Essential Question Read aloud the Essential Question on page 186 of the **Interactive Worktext:** *How can people help out their community*? Explain that there are different ways people can help out their community. Provide examples, such as cleaning up a local park. Say: *Our communities often rely on volunteers to help out. Let's think of some ways we can help out.*

• Discuss the photograph on page 186. Ask: *What is happening in the picture?* (A girl and her mom are cleaning up a park.) Have children look at the photograph for clues as to what they are cleaning up. (bottles)

I Do Say: *I am going to look at the photo and think about how these people are helping their community. I see they are keeping the park clean. I will write on the web on page 187 how these people are helping out their community.*

We Do Say: *Let's think about other ways people can help out in their communities. Some people help out by volunteering their time at a local library.* Guide children to think of what jobs volunteers could do at the library. Then have them add their ideas to the web.

You Do Guide partners to work together to talk about other ways people can help out their community. Encourage them to think about how volunteers help out at their school, local park, playground, or town. Have children use words from the web to start their sentences: *One way to help out is _____.*

REVIEW VOCABULARY

10–15 Minutes   L.2.5a   L.2.4d   L.2.6   CCSS

Review Weekly Vocabulary Words

• Use the **Visual Vocabulary Cards** to review the weekly vocabulary.

• Read together the directions on page 188 of the **Interactive Worktext**. Then complete the activity.

1 **across** Tell children that the word *across* can have slightly different meanings. Ask: *What is the name of the person sitting* across *from you?* Then demonstrate walking *across* the room. Have children use this oral sentence starter: *A car could drive* across _____. (Possible answers: the street, a road)

2 **solution** Describe a simple problem to children and have them provide a *solution*, using the oral sentence starter *The* solution *is _____.* For example, say: *The problem is my pencil is dull.* A volunteer can respond: *The* solution *is to sharpen it.* Then guide children to think of another word for *solution*. (answer)

3 **borrow** Model asking to *borrow* a pencil from a child in the room. Have children practice *borrowing* something from a partner. Have children use this sentence frame: *I might* borrow *a _____ from a friend.* (Possible answers: pencil, toy, book)

4 **lonely** Tell children that the word *lonely* can have slightly different meanings. Say: *A lonely place is one that very few people visit. What places feel* lonely? (empty playground, the desert) Then have children think about people feeling *lonely.* Have children use this oral sentence starter: *Kids feel* lonely *when they _____.* (Possible answers: do not have any friends, do not have anyone to play with)

5 **villages** Ask children if they live in a city, a town, or a *village*. Have children discuss what they might find in a *village*. Have children use the following sentence frame: *I might find _____ in villages.* Then guide them to circle the correct answer. (houses, cars)

6 **insists** Write the word *insists* on the board and have children read it chorally. Then help children complete the following sentence frame: *My family* insists *that I _____ before I go to school each morning.* (Possible answers: eat breakfast, brush my teeth)

7 **idea** Guide children to brainstorm *ideas* for a game to play. Then help them complete the following sentence starter orally: *My* idea *for a game to play is _____.* (Possible answers: tag, hide-and-seek, a card game)

8 **countryside** Write the word *countryside* on the board. Underline the words *country* and *side*. Guide children to understand that they can figure out the meaning of a compound word if they know the meanings of the two smaller words. Have children talk about the pictures they drew by using the following sentence frame: *I see _____ in the* countryside. (Possible answers: cows, farms, barns)

High-Frequency Words

Have children look at page 189 in the **Interactive Worktext**. Help them read, spell, and write each high-frequency word. Guide partners to use each word in a sentence. Then read the story aloud with children. Guide partners to work together to reread the story and circle the high-frequency words. (work, people, She, good, about, new) Listen in and provide assistance reading the high-frequency words, as necessary.

ELL ENGLISH LANGUAGE LEARNERS

Display the **High-Frequency Word Cards** for: *she, new, good, about, people, work.* Write a sentence with each word on the board. Have children echo-read each sentence, and point out the high-frequency word. Then ask them to use the word in a new sentence.

READ COMPLEX TEXT

15–20 Minutes   RI.2.6   RI.2.8   SL.2.1b

Read "Lighting Lives"

- Have children turn to page 190 in the **Interactive Worktext** and read aloud the Essential Question. Point to the picture. Say: *What is the woman in the picture wearing?* (goggles) *Let's read to find out how the woman helps people in her community.* Have children echo-read the title.

- Read the selection together. Note that the weekly vocabulary words are highlighted in yellow. Expand Vocabulary words are highlighted in blue.

- As children read, have them use the "My Notes" section on page 190 to write questions they have. Children can also write words they don't understand or things they want to remember. Model how to use the "My Notes" section. *When I read the title, I wondered what it means. I will write a question about the title "Lighting Lives" in the "My Notes" section.*

ELL ENGLISH LANGUAGE LEARNERS

As you read together, have children highlight parts of the text they have questions about. After reading, review the questions children have. Then help them locate the answers to their questions in the text.

 Quick Check Can children understand the weekly vocabulary in context? If not, review vocabulary using the **Visual Vocabulary Cards** before teaching Lesson 2.

Can children read high-frequency words in context? If not, review using the Read/Spell/Write routine and the High-Frequency Word Cards.

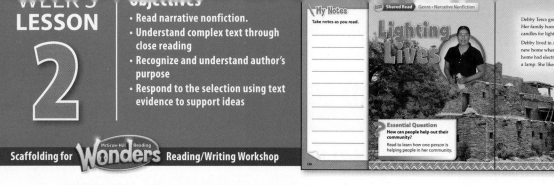

WEEK 3
LESSON
2

• Read narrative nonfiction.
• Understand complex text through close reading
• Recognize and understand author's purpose
• Respond to the selection using text evidence to support ideas

Scaffolding for **Wonders** Reading/Writing Workshop

Interactive Worktext, pp. 190–197

☞ **Go** Digital
• Interactive eWorktext
• Author's Purpose Mini-Lesson

REREAD COMPLEX TEXT

20–25 Minutes   RI.2.6   RI.2.8   L.2.5   CCSS

Close Reading: "Lighting Lives"

Reread "Lighting Lives" from **Interactive Worktext** pages 190–195 with children. As you read together, discuss important passages in the text. Guide children to respond to questions using evidence from the text.

Pages 190–191

Expand Vocabulary Have children reread the first paragraph. Explain that *electricity* is energy that gives power to appliances, such as lights. Tell children that most homes today have electrical outlets, which are used to plug in appliances. Ask: *What did Debby use instead of lights in her home?* Guide children to write the words that tell. (She lit candles.)

Author's Purpose Explain to children that a *purpose* is the reason someone does something. Author's *purpose* is the reason the author writes a selection. Tell children to look for clues to the author's *purpose* as they read. Read the second paragraph aloud. Ask: *What was important to Debby about her new house?* Guide children to draw a box around the sentence that tells. (Her new home had electricity!) Discuss the ways Debby and her family might have used electricity in their new home.

Genre A C T Tell children that narrative nonfiction tells about a real person. It also tells events in order. Ask: *When do the events on page 191 happen in Debby's life?* (They happen when she was a child.) Ask: *How do you know?* (The text says she was ten years old when she moved to her new home.) *I read that the main event on page 191 is that Debby moved to a home with electricity. I think the author wants to show how important having electricity was to Debby.*

Page 192

Connection of Ideas A C T Have children reread the first paragraph. Say: *Debby was excited to have electricity in her new home.* Ask: *As she grew, what did Debby want to learn about?* Guide them to underline the words that tell. (Debby wanted to learn more about solar power.)

Expand Vocabulary Have children locate the word *provided* in the second paragraph. Explain that if something is *provided,* it is given. Say: *The company that Debby worked for* provided *what to people's homes?* Guide children to circle the words that tell. (solar power)

Author's Purpose Remind children to look for clues that tell about the author's purpose as they read. Say: *Think about what the author wants you to know.* Reread the second paragraph aloud. Ask: *What does Debby think about solar power?* Guide children to draw a box around the sentence that tells. (It was a good solution for people that had no electricity.)

Page 193

Author's Purpose Explain to children that they should look for another clue to help them find the author's purpose. Read the first paragraph aloud. Ask: *Who did Debby want to help?* Guide children to draw a box around the words that tell. (people in villages)

Connection of Ideas A C T Read the second paragraph aloud. Say: *I read that Debby helps people in villages. They don't have electricity.* Ask: *How does Debby help families get solar power?* Guide children to underline the sentence that tells. (Debby helps families borrow money from a bank to buy the panels.)

Page 194

Author's Purpose Read the first paragraph aloud. Ask: *Where does Debby travel to help people learn about solar power?* Guide children to draw a box around the sentence that tells. (Debby travels across Arizona and New Mexico.)

Connection of Ideas Have children reread the caption. Ask: *Who does Debby help?* Guide children to underline the words that tell. (Hopi and Navajo people) Explain that these are Native American tribes of people who live in the villages she visited in Arizona and New Mexico.

Expand Vocabulary Have children reread the second paragraph. Explain that the word *demands* means to ask for something with force or to order it. Ask: *Debby demands what from the families she helps?* Guide the children to circle the sentence that tells them. (She insists the families learn how solar power can help them.)

Page 195

Expand Vocabulary Have children reread the first paragraph. Explain that when you *heat* something you make it warm or hot. Ask: *What do families in the story want to* heat? Guide children to circle the words that tell. (their homes)

Author's Purpose Tell children to look back at the clues they drew boxes around on pages 191–194. Ask: *What do you think the author's purpose was in writing this selection?* Guide children to write the answers. (The author explains how Debby helps people get solar power.)

RESPOND TO READING

10–20 Minutes   RI.2.6   RI.2.8

Respond to "Lightning Lives"

Read aloud the questions about "Lightning Lives" on page 196 of the **Interactive Worktext.** Then read aloud the "Discussion Starter" for each of the questions. Guide children to work with a partner to answer the questions orally using the "Discussion Starters." Have children find text evidence to support their answers. Ask children to write the page number(s) on which they found the text evidence for each question.

1. *What was it like for Debby Tewa growing up?* (Possible answers: I read that when Debby was a child, she had no electricity. She moved to a home with electricity when she was ten. Text Evidence: p. 191)

2. *What did Debby do when she grew up?* (Possible answers: Debby learned about solar power. She worked for a company that brought solar power into people's homes. Text Evidence: p. 192)

3. *How did Debby use solar power to help others?* (Possible answers: Debby helped people who did not have electricity. She helped these people borrow money to get solar panels. Text Evidence: pp. 193, 194)

After children discuss the questions, have them use the sentence starters to answer the question on page 197. Circulate and provide guidance.

✓ *Quick Check* Do children understand vocabulary in context? If not, review and reteach using the instruction on page 154.

Can children identify the author's purpose? If not, review and reteach using the instruction on page 154 and assign the Unit 3 Week 3 digital mini-lesson.

Can children write a response to "Lightning Lives"? If not, review the sentence starters and prompt children to respond orally. Help them write their responses.

WEEK 3
LESSON
3

Objectives
• Access prior knowledge
• Understand and use new vocabulary words
• Read high-frequency words
• Read narrative nonfiction

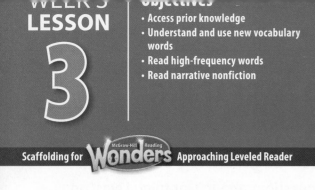

Materials
• "City Communities" Apprentice Leveled Reader
• High-Frequency Word Cards

👉 Go Digital
• Apprentice Leveled Reader eBook
• Downloadable High-Frequency Word Cards

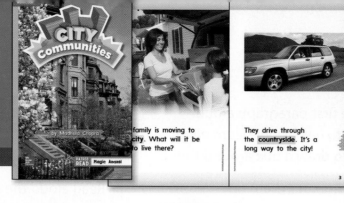

Scaffolding for **Wonders** Approaching Leveled Reader

BEFORE READING

10–15 Minutes   SL.2.1a   SL.2.6   L.2.6   RF.2.3f   CCSS

Introduce "City Communities"

• Read the Essential Question on the title page of "City Communities" **Apprentice Leveled Reader:** *How can people help out their community?*

• Read the title of the main read. Point to the cover. *What are some things you might see in a city?* (tall buildings, lots of traffic, many people) *Let's read to learn more about what it's like to live in a city.*

High-Frequency Words

Display the **High-Frequency Word Cards** for the words *from, here, live, long, through,* and *today.* Use the Read/ Spell/Write routine to teach each word. Guide partners to use each word in a sentence. Provide assistance reading the high-frequency words, as necessary.

Expand Vocabulary

Before reading "City Communites," help children read the following words that they will encounter. Display each word below. Use the Define/Example/Ask routine. Tell children to look for the word later on as they read "City Communities."

1 **apartment** (page 4)

Define: a room or group of rooms used as a place to live

Example: My family lives in an *apartment* on the third floor.

Ask: How is an *apartment* different from a house?

2 **block** (page 11)

Define: the part of a city street that is between other streets.

Example: My best friend and I live on the same *block*.

Ask: What might you see in a neighborhood *block*?

3 **city** (page 2)

Define: an area larger than a town where many people live and work

Example: We live in the country but we like to visit the *city* when we can.

Ask: What are some things you can do in a *city*?

4 **exhibit** (page 10)

Define: something that is shown in a public place

Example: Dad has several paintings in our town's art *exhibit*.

Ask: What are some things you might see in an *exhibit*?

5 **free** (page 13)

Define: something that doesn't cost anything

Example: When you work without getting paid, it means you work for *free*.

Ask: Who are some people who give their help for *free*?

6 **museums** (page 10)

Define: buildings where objects of art, science, or history are kept and displayed for people to see

Example: Our class took a field trip to the space *museum* last week.

Ask: What can you see at a *museum*?

DURING READING

20–30 Minutes RI.2.1 RI.2.4 RI.2.6 L.2.4a

Shared Reading

Tell children you will now read "City Communities." Tell them to note the vocabulary and high-frequency words you just introduced as you read the story. Stop to model understanding of the story as you read.

Pages 2–3

High-Frequency Words Make sure children can read the high-frequency words *live, long,* and *through.*

Comprehension Check Model beginning to read the story. Say: *The first thing I notice about this story is that a family is putting boxes and furniture in their car. They are probably moving from the house they live in to a new place. I'll look for clues as I read to help me figure out where they are moving and what their new home is like.*

Pages 4–5

Comprehension Check *On page 4, I learn that the family will live in an apartment. The picture shows the doorman and the text tells me that he helps the people who live there. I think about how a building is different from a house and about how the doorman is part of their community.*

Pages 6–7

Vocabulary After reading page 6, ask: *What is a garden?* (a place where you grow plants) *How can a garden help a neighborhood?* (People work together to grow food and flowers and make a nice place for all.)

Comprehension Check *On pages 6 and 7, I learn some new things about what life is like in a city. I learn that neighbors help each other by working together in a garden. Page 7 shows me that city children walk to school.*

Pages 8–9

Comprehension Check *I read on pages 8 and 9 about ways people have fun in a city. I'll think about ways that I have fun where I live. Thinking about what I read and also what I know from my own life helps me better understand and remember information.*

Pages 10–11

High-Frequency Words Make sure children can read the high-frequency word *here.*

Vocabulary Read page 10. Focus on the words *museums* and *exhibit.* Ask: *What does the picture show you about* museums? (A museum is a place where you might see a dinosaur exhibit.) Point to the children in the picture and explain that the word *exhibit* means that the dinosaur is on display for people to see.

Pages 12–13

Comprehension Check *I read on pages 12 and 13 that people find ways to help their cities. Some people run races to get money to help the city and other people give their help for free to make their cities better.*

Expand Vocabulary On page 13, focus on the word *free.* Ask: *What does it mean to give something for* free? *How does it help the city for this man to give his help for* free? (To do something for free means not to get paid. It helps because the city can use that money to help out people in other ways.)

Pages 14–15

High-Frequency Words Make sure children can read the high-frequency word *today.*

Comprehension Check *The story says that this family is moving to the city. Now that I know what life is like in a city, I can answer the questions on page 15. I think that they might live in an apartment building and visit the parks. Maybe they will have a doorman to help them out. They may have neighbors who will help them grow a garden, too. I know a lot about living in the city now.*

 Quick Check Can children understand vocabulary in context? If not, review and reteach using the instruction on page 154 and assign the Unit 3 Week 3 digital mini-lesson.

Can children read the high-frequency words in context? If not, review using the Read/Spell/Write routine and the High-Frequency Word Cards.

WEEK 3
LESSON
4

Objectives
- Understand complex text through close-reading
- Read narrative nonfiction
- Recognize and understand author's purpose
- Respond to the selection using text evidence to support ideas

Materials
- "City Communities" Apprentice Leveled Reader
- Graphic Organizer: Author's Purpose

👉 Go Digital
- "Apprentice Leveled Reader eBook
- Downloadable Graphic Organizer
- Author's Purpose Mini-Lesson

Scaffolding for **Wonders** Approaching Leveled Reader

DURING READING

20–30 Minutes   RI.2.1   RI. 2.6   CCSS

Tell children they will now reread the selection, "City Communities." Review the vocabulary and high-frequency words that they will encounter as they read.

Close Reading

🔍 Pages 2–3

Author's Purpose Tell children that good readers think about why the author is writing a story and what the author wants them to know about a story. Reread pages 2 and 3. Ask: *What does the author want you to know about this family?* (They are moving to the city.) Model filling in the Author's Purpose Chart.

Genre (A)(C)(T) Explain that you can better understand an author's purpose by knowing the genre. Ask: *Do you think this book will tell a story with made-up characters or give information about real life? Why or why not?* (It will give information because the photographs show real people and real places. The text is telling real things.)

🔍 Pages 4–5

Author's Purpose Reread page 4. Ask: *How does the author help you understand where the family will be living now?* (The author explains that the family will live in an apartment.) Reread page 5. Ask: *Why does the author give this information about cars and buses in a city?* (This helps show what the city is like and that there is lots of traffic.)

Genre (A)(C)(T) Explain to children that photos in a nonfiction selection can give more information about a topic. Point to the photo on page 5 . Ask: *What can you learn about the city street from this photo?* (You can see all kinds of vehicles, buildings, streetlights, and people.)

Connection of Ideas (A)(C)(T) Ask children to think back to the family on the first two pages. *What kind home did they live in before?* (a house with a driveway, probably on a quiet street) *What is their new home like?* (It is a big building. It is probably on a busy street.)

🔍 Pages 6–7

Author's Purpose Reread page 6. Ask: *What does the author tell readers about the people the family will meet in the city?* (They are neighbors who help each other.) *How do children in a city get to school?* (They walk to school with the help of adults who help them cross the busy streets.) Guide children as they record clues in their Author's Purpose charts.

🔍 Pages 8–9

Author's Purpose Reread pages 8 and 9. Ask: *What do you think is the author's main purpose for including the information on pages 8 and 9?* (The author wants readers to know about ways that people have fun in a city.) Help children to record clues in their Author's Purpose charts.

Organization (A)(C)(T) Ask children what they are learning about living in the city on these pages. (how to have fun) Then ask what they learned about living in the city on the previous pages. (where people live, how they get around, how neighbors help) Point out that most of the pages focus on a new topic about living in the city. That is how the book is organized. Have children suggest new topics that could be part of the book.

🔍 Pages 10–11

Author's Purpose Reread pages 10 and 11. Ask: *Why does the author write about museums and block parties?* (to include many different examples of things that people can do in a city) Guide children as they include this information in their Author's Purpose charts.

🔍 Pages 12–13

Author's Purpose After rereading page 13, ask: *What does the author want us to know about ways people help their cities?* (She wants us to know that there are different ways people can help out. She gives us two examples of people who have helped their cities.) Help children record these clues in their Author's Purpose charts.

Connection of Ideas Ⓐ Ⓒ Ⓣ *Why do you think people participate in activities that help their cities?* (They want to find ways they can make their communities better places to live.) *Who else in this book has helped?* (the doorman, the neighbors who garden, crossing guards)

🔍 Pages 14–15

Author's Purpose Reread pages 14 and 15. Ask: *Why do you think the author included the two questions on page 15?* (She wants us to think about what we have learned. We can use the information we have learned about living in a city to answer questions about what it will be like for this family when they move to the city.)

Organization Ⓐ Ⓒ Ⓣ Ask: *Is this the same family that you saw at the beginning?* (no) *Why do you think the author is including another family?* (to show that many people move to the city)

Connection of Ideas Ⓐ Ⓒ Ⓣ *Use what you've learned about the city to tell what you think it will be like for this family when they move to the city.* (Answers will vary but could include that they will find ways to have fun in the city. They will meet their neighbors and visit parks and museums. They will find ways to help out, too.)

AFTER READING

 10–15 Minutes   RI.2.6   RI.2.9   L.24a   RF.2.4a   W.2.8   CCSS

Respond to Reading

Compare Texts Guide children in comparing the events in "City Communities" with the events in "Lighting Lives." Help children think about ways that people help their communities. Then ask: *What are some ways that people in your community help to make it a better place?*

Summarize Have children turn to page 16 and guide them in summarizing the selection. (Answers should include important information from the story.)

🔍 Text Evidence

Have partners work together to answer questions on page 16. Remind children to use their Author's Purpose charts.

Author's Purpose (Answers will vary but should note that the author wanted to describe communities in the city and how city dwellers help each other.)

Vocabulary (The text reads, "An adult helps them cross the street." The picture shows a crossing guard escorting children across a street. These clues tell us that *cross* means "to go across.")

Write About Reading (Answers will vary but could mention that people can help out with gardens, raise money to help. Doormen help people who live in their buildings.)

Read "Magic Anansi"

Encourage children to read the paired selection "Magic Anansi" on pages 17–19. Have them summarize the selection and compare it to "City Communities." Have them work with a partner to answer the "Make Connections" questions on page 19.

Independent Reading

Have pairs of children reread "City Communities." Have them talk about what the family will do in their new community.

 ✓ *Quick Check* Can students identify Author's Purpose? If not, review and reteach using the instruction on page 154 and assign the Unit 3 Week 3 digital mini-lesson.

Can students respond to the selection using text evidence? If not, provide sentence frames to help them organize their ideas.

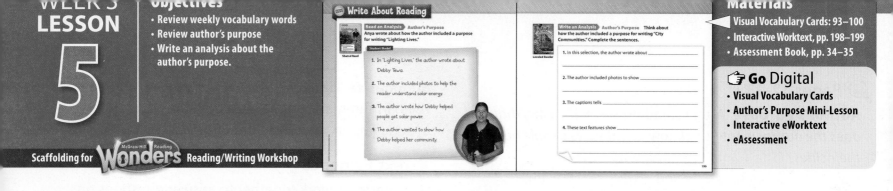

WEEK 3
LESSON 5

Objectives
• Review weekly vocabulary words
• Review author's purpose
• Write an analysis about the author's purpose.

Scaffolding for **Wonders** Reading/Writing Workshop

Materials
• Visual Vocabulary Cards: 93–100
• Interactive Worktext, pp. 198–199
• Assessment Book, pp. 34–35

☞ **Go** Digital
• Visual Vocabulary Cards
• Author's Purpose Mini-Lesson
• Interactive eWorktext
• eAssessment

REVIEW AND RETEACH

5–10 Minutes   RI.2.6   RI.2.8   L.2.4a   CCSS

Weekly Vocabulary

Display one **Visual Vocabulary Card** at a time and guide children to use the vocabulary word in a sentence. If children have difficulty creating a sentence, have them find the word in "Lighting Lives" or "City Communities" and use context clues to define the vocabulary word.

Comprehension: Author's Purpose

I Do Write and say: *Jack grew up near the beach. He studies the sea and sea life. He thinks protecting sea life is important. At the zoo, he teaches kids about the lives of dolphins.* Ask: *What are the clues about the author's purpose in this passage?* Circle: "He studies the sea and sea life." Circle: "He thinks protecting sea life is important." Ask: *Why does the author include these details?* Say: *I think the author is saying that Jack cares a lot about the sea and sea life and wants to protect it.*

We Do Display: *Nate and Liz love plants and trees. They decided to build a garden in Los Angeles. They raised money for a big garden with different kinds of plants and trees.* Ask: *Let's circle the clues about the author's purpose in this passage.* ("Nate and Liz love plants and trees. They decided to build a garden.") Ask: *Why does the author include these details?* (The author wants to show how Nate and Liz decided to build a garden.)

You Do Display: *Fireman John gives tours of his firehouse. He teaches children about being a fireman. He explains how to use the equipment. He enjoys being a fireman.* Guide partners to ask each other questions about clues to the author's purpose. Then have them tell the author's purpose.

WRITE ABOUT READING

25–35 Minutes   W.2.1   W.2.5   W.4.9   CCSS

Read an Analysis

• Guide children to look back at "Lighting Lives" in the **Interactive Worktext**. Have volunteers review the details about the author's purpose in the text they marked on page 191 and summarize the text. Repeat with pages 192–195. *Why did the author write the selection?*

• Read aloud the directions on page 198. Read aloud the student model. *This student's work is not a summary. It is an analysis, or description, of how the author used sequence in "Lightning Lives."*

• *When you write an analysis, you should include key details from the story that tell about the story. Read Anya's first sentence. Circle the details.* (the author wrote about Debby Tewa) *In what part of the story do you learn these details?* (the beginning)

• *Read the second sentence. Anya writes how text features help the reader understand the story. Draw a box around the details.* (photos to help the reader understand solar energy.) Guide children to find a photo that helps them understand the story and fill in the sentence frame: *This photo helps me understand the story because _____.*

• Guide children to point to the third sentence. This sentence gives more details about how Debby helped people. *What details does Anya include?* (The author wrote how Debby helped people get solar power.)

• Model analyzing how the author used details to write the story. Read the last sentence that Anya wrote. *Why is this sentence a good ending?* (Anya tells the author's purpose.)

Analytical Writing · Write an Analysis

Guided Writing Read the writing prompt on page 199 together. Guide children to review their Author's Purpose charts for "City Communities." Have children use their charts to complete the sentence starters. Children can also write an analysis using another selection previously read this week.

Peer Conference Guide children to read their analysis to a partner. Listeners should summarize the strongest clues that support the author's purpose in the beginning, middle, and ending sentences. They should discuss any parts that are unclear.

Teacher Conference Check children's writing for complete sentences and whether they included details from the selection. Review the ending sentence and ask: *What did the author use text features to show?* If necessary, guide children to revise their sentence by adding more details.

Level Up

▲ Approaching Leveled Reader

▲ Reading/Writing Workshop

▲ Apprentice Leveled Reader

▲ Interactive Worktext

IF children read the Apprentice Level Reader and the **Interactive Worktext** Shared Read fluently and answer the Respond to Reading questions

THEN read together the Approaching Level Reader main selection and the **Reading/Writing Workshop** Shared Read from *Reading Wonders*. Have children take notes as they read, using self-stick notes. Then ask and answer questions about their notes.

Writing Rubric

	4	3	2	1
Text Evidence	Includes three or more details from the text.	Includes two or more details from the text.	Includes only one detail from the text.	No text evidence is cited.
Writing Style	Writes in complete sentences. Uses correct spelling and grammar.	Uses complete sentences. Writing has spelling and grammar errors.	Few complete sentences. There are many spelling and grammar errors.	Writing is not accurate or in complete sentences.

ASSESSMENT

Weekly Assessment

Have children complete the Weekly Assessment using **Assessment** book pages 34–35.

▶ **Mid-Unit Assessment,** pages 88 – 95

▶ **Fluency Assessment,** pages 250 – 265

CCSS TESTED SKILLS

✔ COMPREHENSION	✔ VOCABULARY:
• Author's Purpose RI.2.6, RI.2.8	• Context Clues L.2.4
• Sequence RL.2.5	
• Author's Purpose RI.2.6, RI.2.8	

Using Assessment and Writing Scores

↻ RETEACH	IF ...	THEN ...
COMPREHENSION	Students answer 0–5 multiple-choice items correctly ...	... reteach tested skills using instruction on pages 364–375.
VOCABULARY	Students answer 0–2 multiple-choice items correctly ...	... reteach tested skills using instruction on page 364.
WRITING	Students score mostly 1–2 on weekly writing rubrics throughout the unit ...	... reteach writing using instruction on pages 376–377.

Fluency Assessment

Conduct assessments individually using the differentiated fluency passages in Assessment. Students' expected fluency goal for this Unit is 62–82 WCPM with an accuracy rate of 95% or higher.

Weeks 4 and 5

Monitor students progress on the following to inform how to adjust instruction for the remainder of the unit.

ADJUST INSTRUCTION	
ACCESS COMPLEX TEXT	If students need more support for accessing complex text, provide additional modeling of prompts in Lesson 2 of Week 4, pages 160–161, and Week 5, pages 170–171. After you model how to identify the text evidence, guide students to find text evidence in Lessons 3 and 4, in Week 4, pages 162–165, and Week 5, pages 172–175.
FLUENCY	For those students who need more support with Fluency, focus on the Fluency lessons in the Foundational Skills Kit.
WRITING	If students need more support incorporating text evidence in their writing, conduct the Write About Reading activities in Lesson 4 and 5 as group writing activities.
FOUNDATIONAL SKILLS	Review students' individualized progress in *Reading Wonders* Adaptive Learning to determine which foundational skills to incorporate into your lessons for the remainder of the unit.

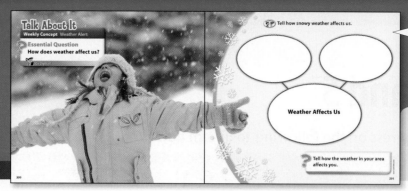

WEEK 4 LESSON 1

Objectives
- Develop oral language
- Build background about the weather
- Understand and use weekly vocabulary
- Read an expository text

Scaffolding for **Wonders** Reading/Writing Workshop

Materials
- Interactive Worktext, pp. 200–209
- Visual Vocabulary Cards: 101–108
- High-Frequency Word Cards

☞ **Go** Digital
- Interactive eWorktext
- Visual Vocabulary Cards

WEEKLY CONCEPT

5–10 Minutes   RI.2.1 RI.2.2 SL.2.1a   CCSS

Talk About It

Essential Question Read aloud the Essential Question on page 200 of the **Interactive Worktext:** *How does weather affect us?* Explain that weather can affect us in many ways. Say: *Depending on the weather, we may choose to go outside or stay inside. We also may choose to wear different kinds of clothing, based on the weather.*

- Discuss the photograph on page 200. Ask: *What is happening in this picture?* (A girl is catching snowflakes on her tongue.) *What is the weather?* (It is a snowy day.)

I Do Say: *I am going to look at the photo and think about how the weather affects this girl. I see she is wearing a winter coat and hat and gloves. This clothing keeps her warm on a snowy winter day. I will put this information on the web on page 201. I will write that we dress warmly on snowy days.*

We Do Say: *Let's think about other types of weather and how it affects us. Can someone tell us how rainy weather affects us?* (On rainy days, we wear boots and carry umbrellas.) Guide children to think of other ways rainy days can affect them, such as how on rainy days children play indoors rather than outdoors. Have children choose one way rain affects us to add to their web.

You Do Guide partner to work together to talk about how different types of weather and how it affects us. Children can include more severe weather, such as hurricanes or blizzards as well.

REVIEW VOCABULARY

10–15 Minutes   L.2.4c L.2.5a L.2.6 RF.2.3   CCSS

Review Weekly Vocabulary Words

- Use the **Visual Vocabulary Cards** to review the weekly vocabulary.

- Read together the directions on page 202 of the **Interactive Worktext.** Then complete the activity.

1 harsh Have volunteers suggest *harsh* sounds as you list them on the board. Have children use this sentence frame: _____ *is a* harsh *sound.* (Possible answers: an alarm, thunder, a screaming baby) Then have children think of *harsh* types of weather. (Possible answers: thunderstorm, tornado, hurricane)

2 warning Remind children that a *warning* is a notice of something dangerous or harmful that may happen. Tell children that sometimes a *warning* can come in the form of a sound. Ask children what *warning* sounds they have heard. Have children use this sentence frame: _____ *is a* warning *sound I have heard.* (Possible answer: fire alarm, car alarm)

3 event Write the word *event* on the board. Invite volunteers to suggest words that describe an *event.* (Possible answers: special, big, fun, important) Have children use one or more of these words as they tell about a school *event.* (Possible answers: a play, a music performance, a sports event)

4 prevent Write this sentence on the board: *Only you can* prevent *forest fires.* Have a volunteer suggest an synonym for *prevent.* (stop) Then ask: *How does someone* prevent *being cold in snowy weather?* (Possible answers: dress warmly, stay inside.)

5 **damage** Discuss different kinds of *damage* with children, such as to a book or a toy. Explain that *damage* can happen to both living (people, animals, trees) and nonliving things (bikes, houses). Ask: *What damage can happen to a car?* (Possible answers: It can get dented. The windows could get broken.)

6 **destroy** Show children an item and ask how the item could be *destroyed*. Ask them to name something fragile that a strong wind might *destroy* by completing the following sentence starter: *A strong wind might destroy _____.* (Possible answers: a flower, a kite)

7 **dangerous** Guide children to identify the root word, or smaller word, in *dangerous*. (danger) Model using the word *dangerous* in a sentence: *It is* dangerous *to use a saw without a parent's help.* Have children name something that is *dangerous* to do in the kitchen. (Possible answers: use the stove, microwave, or oven)

8 **weather** Help children write a sentence that describes the picture they drew. Have them use the following sentence starter: *My favorite kind of* weather *is _____.* (Possible answers: warm, sunny, cool)

High-Frequency Words

Have children look at page 203 in the **Interactive Worktext**. Help them read, spell, and write each high-frequency word. Guide partners to use each word in a sentence. Then read the story aloud with children. Guide partners to work together to reread the story and circle the high-frequency words. (from, these, down, many, together, place) Listen in and provide assistance reading the high-frequency words, as necessary.

ELL ENGLISH LANGUAGE LEARNERS

Display the **High-Frequency Word Cards** for: *from, many, down, these, place, together.* Write a sentence with each word on the board. Have children echo-read each sentence, and point out the high-frequency word. Then ask them to use the word in a new sentence.

READ COMPLEX TEXT

15–20 Minutes   RI.2.1   RI.2.2   SL.2.1b

Read "Tornado!"

- Have children turn to page 204 in the **Interactive Worktext** and read aloud the Essential Question. Point to the tornado in the picture and read the title aloud. Say: *What is this storm called?* (a tornado) Say: *Tornadoes are powerful storms. Let's read about how tornadoes form and how they affect people's lives.* Have children echo-read the title.

- Read the story together. Note that the weekly vocabulary words are highlighted in yellow. Expand Vocabulary words are highlighted in blue.

- As children read, have them use the "My Notes" section on page 204 to write questions they have. Children can also write words they don't understand or things they want to remember. Model how to use the "My Notes" section. *I wonder where tornadoes happen. I will write this question in the "My Notes" section to try to answer as I read.*

ELL ENGLISH LANGUAGE LEARNERS

As you read together, have children highlight parts of the text they have questions about. After reading, review the questions children have. Then help them locate the answers to their questions in the text.

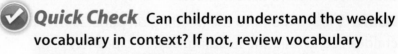

Quick Check Can children understand the weekly vocabulary in context? If not, review vocabulary using the **Visual Vocabulary Cards** before teaching Lesson 2.

Can children read high-frequency words in context? If not, review using the Read/Spell/Write routine and the High-Frequency Word Cards.

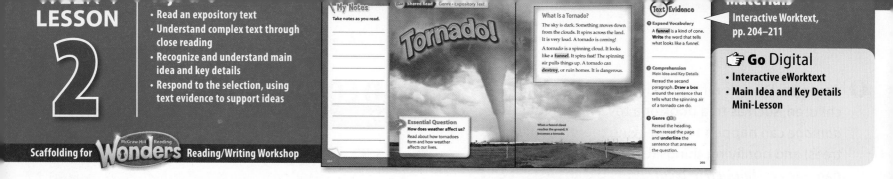

LESSON 2

- Read an expository text
- Understand complex text through close reading
- Recognize and understand main idea and key details
- Respond to the selection, using text evidence to support ideas

Scaffolding for **Wonders** Reading/Writing Workshop

REREAD COMPLEX TEXT

20-25 Minutes   RI.2.1   RI.2.2   L.2.6   **CCSS**

Close Reading: "Tornado!"

Reread "Tornado!" from **Interactive Worktext** pages 204–209 with children. As you read together, discuss important passages in the text. Guide children to respond to questions using evidence from the text.

Pages 204–205

Expand Vocabulary Reread the first two sentences of the second paragraph aloud. Guide children to locate the word *funnel* on the page. Write *funnel* on the board. Explain that a *funnel* is a kind of cone. Take a piece of construction paper and roll it into the shape of a cone. Turn it upside down and say: *This is a* funnel. *What looks like a* funnel, *according to the text?* (a tornado) Guide children to write the answer.

Main Idea and Key Details Say: *Now we know how a tornado looks. Let's find out more about what tornadoes are like.* Reread the second paragraph with children. Ask: *Which sentence tells you what the spinning air of a tornado can do?* (The spinning air can pull things up.) Model drawing a box around the sentence. Guide children to draw a box around the sentence.

Genre A C T Point to the heading on page 205. Have children echo read the heading. Say: *In expository text, headings tell what a section of text is about. I can see that this section of text will tell me what a tornado is. Which sentence tells what a tornado is?* (A tornado is a spinning cloud.) Guide children to underline the sentence.

Page 206

Expand Vocabulary Reread the first paragraph with children. Write the word *rough* on the board and explain that something *rough* shows power and force. Ask: *What does the text say* rough *storms have?* (high winds). Have children reread the third sentence. Guide children to see that thunderstorms are a kind of *rough* storm. Ask: *What else do* rough *storms have?* (thunder and lightning)

Main Idea and Key Details Reread aloud the last two sentences of the first paragraph with children. Say: *These two sentences tell us how a thunderstorm becomes a tornado. What makes a thunderstorm become a tornado?* Model finding text evidence to answer the question. Have children draw a box around the sentence that gives the answer. (The winds can spin to the ground.)

Main Idea and Key Details Reread the page heading aloud. Remind children that this section of text is explaining how a tornado forms. Have children reread the second paragraph. Ask: *How long does a tornado last? Find the key detail that tells you.* Guide children to draw a box around the key details that give the answer. (Most tornadoes do not stay on the ground for long.)

Page 207

Expand Vocabulary Have children chorally read the heading on page 207. Say: *Let's find out where most tornadoes happen.* Have children reread the paragraph. Help children locate the word *area*. Explain that *area* means *place*. Ask: *In what* area *do most tornadoes in the United States take place?* (Tornado Alley) Explain that Tornado Alley is in the middle of the United States.

Main Idea and Key Details Have children reread the page. Then ask: *Why do tornadoes form in Tornado Alley?* Guide children to draw a box around the words that tell. (Scientists think they form here because warm air mixes with cool air.)

Genre Point to the photo and caption on page 207. Explain that sometimes an author will include a photo to help the reader visualize what the author is writing about. The author will also sometimes provide captions to give more information about the text. Have children reread the caption and ask: *What can tornadoes destroy?* Guide children to underline the words that tell you. (trees and homes)

Page 208

Main Idea and Key Details Reread the heading and the first paragraph with children. Say: *The heading tells me that this page will explain how tornadoes affect people. What does the paragraph tell us weak tornadoes can do?* Guide children to draw a box around the sentence that tells them. (destroy signs)

Main Topic and Key Details Tell children to reread the second paragraph. Say: *Underline the sentences that tell you how people find out if a tornado is coming.* (They listen to the radio. They watch the news on television.)

Expand Vocabulary Have children reread the last two sentences. Explain that to *repair* something means to fix it. Ask: *What might people* repair *after a tornado?* Guide children to find text evidence on the page to support their answer. (They repair damage from tornadoes.)

Page 209

Genre Direct children to reread the sidebar on page 209. Ask: *What is the title of the chart?* (Ways to Stay Safe). Ask: *Where should you go during a tornado? Underline the sentence that tells you.* (Go to a room with no windows.) Guide children to underline the words in the sidebar.

Main Idea and Key Details Review with children all the answers that they drew boxes around on pages 205–209. Tell them to think about what these clues have in common. If children have difficulty, guide them to see that many of the clues deal with the harm a tornado can cause. Say: *Write the main idea of this selection.* (Possible answers: Tornadoes can cause a lot of harm. Tornadoes are very serious weather events.)

RESPOND TO READING

10–20 Minutes   RI.2.1   RI.2.2   SL.2.1a

Respond to "Tornado!"

Read aloud the questions on page 210 of the **Interactive Worktext** about "Tornado!" Then read aloud the "Discussion Starter" for each of the questions. Guide children to work with a partner to answer the questions orally using the "Discussion Starters." Have children find text evidence to support their answers. Ask children to write the page number(s) on which they found the text evidence for each question.

1. *What are tornadoes?* (Possible answers: I read that a tornado is a spinning cloud. Most tornadoes starts as thunderstorms. They are rough and have high winds. Text Evidence: pp. 205, 206)

2. *How can tornadoes cause damage?* (I read that weak tornadoes can destroy signs. Strong tornadoes can tear down homes. Text Evidence: p. 208)

3. *How can people stay safe during tornadoes?* (Possible answers: I read that people should listen to the radio and watch the news on television. Children should listen to directions from a parent or teacher; Text Evidence: pp. 208, 209)

After children discuss the questions on page 210, have them use the sentence starters to answer the question on page 211. Circulate and provide guidance.

 Quick Check **Do children understand vocabulary in context? If not, review and reteach using the instruction on page 166.**

Can children identify the main idea & key details? If not, review and reteach using the instruction on page 166 and assign the Unit 3 Week 4 digital mini-lesson.

Can children write a response to "Tornado!" If not, review the sentence starters and prompt children to respond orally. Help them write their responses.

Objectives
- Access prior knowledge
- Understand and use new vocabulary words
- Read high-frequency words
- Read expository text

Materials
- "Weather All Around" Apprentice Leveled Reader
- High-Frequency Word Cards

☞ **Go** Digital
- Apprentice Leveled Reader e-book
- Downloadable High-Frequency Word Cards

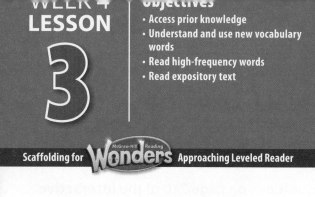

Scaffolding for **Wonders** Approaching Leveled Reader

McGraw-Hill Reading

Weather All Around
by Deborah November

PAIRED READ Colors in the Sky

...ther changes through ...year.

Each season has different weather. In many places, summer is hot and sunny. Fall is cool. Winter is cold. Spring is warm and rainy.

BEFORE READING

10–15 Minutes   SL.2.1   SL. 2.6   L.2.6   RF.2.3f   **CCSS**

Introduce "Weather All Around"

- Read the Essential Question on the title page of "Weather All Around" **Apprentice Leveled Reader:** *How does weather affect us?*

- Read the title of the main read. Point to the cover. *What kind of weather do you see in this picture?* (rain) *What is the girl holding?* (an umbrella) *Let's read to learn more about different kinds of weather.*

High-Frequency Words

Display the **High-Frequency Word Cards** for the words *cold, even, fall, how, people,* and *your.* Use the Read/Spell/Write routine to teach each word. Guide partners to use each word in a sentence. Provide assistance reading the high-frequency words, as necessary.

Expand Vocabulary

Before reading "Weather All Around," help children read the following words that they will encounter. Display each word below. Use the Define/Example/Ask routine. Tell children to look for the word later on as they read "Weather All Around."

1 **emergency** (page 9)

Define: something serious that comes without any warning and calls for fast action

Example: At school we learned what to do in case of an *emergency.*

Ask: What are some weather *emergencies* that you know about?

2 **flat** (page 6)

Define: smooth and even without hills or bumps

Example: My grandparents live where the land is *flat* and you can see for miles.

Ask: What kind of land would be the opposite of *flat*?

3 **hurricanes** (page 4)

Define: a storm with strong winds and heavy rain

Example: Many buildings were blown down by the strong winds of the *hurricane.*

Ask: What kind of weather makes up a *hurricane*?

4 **kit** (page 9)

Define: a collection of tools or equipment for a particular purpose

Example: We put some bottled water in our home emergency *kit.*

Ask: What are some things that belong in an emergency *kit*?

5 **storms** (page 4)

Define: a strong wind with heavy rain, hail, sleet, or snow

Example: The *storm* blew many leaves off our tree.

Ask: What are some things that happen in a *storm*?

DURING READING

20–30 Minutes   RI. 2.1   RI.2.6   L.2.4a

Shared Reading

Tell children you will now read "Weather All Around." Tell them to note the vocabulary and high-frequency words you just introduced as you read the story. Stop to model understanding of the story as you go.

Pages 2–3

High-Frequency Words Make sure children can read the high-frequency words *fall* and *cold*.

Comprehension Check Model beginning to read the story. Say: *The first thing I notice is that people are shown doing different activities outside. I know that weather is an important part of being outside. I see that different weather means very different activities. As I read, I'll be on the look-out for how different weather affects what we do.*

Vocabulary Read page 3. Ask: *What word is used to describe the fall?* (cool) *What word is used to describe winter?* (cold) Talk about the difference between the two.

Pages 4–5

High-Frequency Words Make sure children can read the high-frequency words *how* and *people*.

Comprehension Check *On page 4, I learn that a hurricane is a dangerous storm. The picture shows the storm swirling around a center. I wonder if that causes the strong winds. On page 5, I see that* people *putting boards over their windows to stop the wind from blowing things in. This is one way to get ready for a storm.*

Pages 6–7

High-Frequency Words Make sure children can read the high-frequency word *even*.

Expand Vocabulary After reading page 6, ask: *Why do you think that a place that is* flat *is also very windy?* (There is nothing in the way of the wind to slow it down.)

Pages 8–9

High-Frequency Words Make sure children can read the high-frequency word *your*.

Comprehension Check *I read on page 8 about how to stay safe during a blizzard. I notice that page 9 gives information about an emergency kit. I'll stop here to make sure I understand what I am reading. I can think about why it is important to have an emergency kit during a weather emergency like a blizzard. I can also think about what should be included in the kit.*

Pages 10–11

Vocabulary Read page 11. Focus on the word *tornado*. Ask: *What does the text tell you about a* tornado? (It is a big storm that spins.) *What can you tell about a* tornado *from looking at the picture?* (It is long and thin and gets wider at the top. It looks like it is moving fast.)

Pages 12–13

Comprehension Check *I read here that a desert is a place that is hot and dry. This picture shows me a desert and I can see that it is a place where not much can grow. I also read that few animals can live in such a hot, dry place. I think that a desert is a very different place from the kinds of places that get hurricanes, which are very wet.*

Pages 14–15

Comprehension Check *This picture shows a place where the weather is warm and sunny. I see that a father and girl are in the water. Before we were reading about storms and other bad weather. Now we are back to good weather. Both are important to know about.*

 Quick Check **Can children understand vocabulary in context? If not, review and reteach using the instruction on page 166 and assign the Unit 3 Week 4 digital mini-lesson.**

Can children read the high-frequency words in context? If not, review using the Read/Spell/Write routine and the High-Frequency Word Cards.

Objectives
- Understand complex text through close-reading
- Read expository text
- Recognize and understand main idea and key details
- Respond to the selection using text evidence to support ideas

Materials
- "Weather All Around" Apprentice Leveled Reader
- Graphic Organizer: Main Idea and Key Details

☞ **Go** Digital
- Apprentice Leveled Reader eBook
- Downloadable Graphic Organizer
- Main Idea and Key Details Mini-Lesson

Scaffolding for **Wonders** Approaching Leveled Reader

DURING READING

20–30 Minutes   RI.2.1 RI.2.5 RI.2.6 **CCSS**

Tell children they will now reread the selection, "Weather All Around." Review the vocabulary and high-frequency words that they will encounter as they read.

Close Reading

Pages 2–3

Main Idea and Key Details Remind children that the main idea of a text is what the text is mostly about. Explain to children that good readers look for key details. The key details help them figure out the main idea. Reread pages 2 and 3. Ask: *What do you learn about on these pages?* (Weather changes. Summer is hot. Fall is cool. Winter is cold. Spring is warm.) Model filling in the Main Idea and Key Details Chart.

Genre **ACT** Explain that expository text gives important facts about a topic. Point to the photographs and labels on page 3 and say: *Expository text includes text features such as photographs with labels. These features give readers more information about the topic.* Ask: *How do the pictures and labels help you better understand weather and the seasons?* (Each season is labeled, and the photos show things people do during each season.)

Connection of Ideas **ACT** Say: *Choose one season and tell how weather affects activities people do at that time.* (If people want to make a snowman in the winter, then the weather must be cold and snowy.)

Pages 4–5

Main Idea and Key Details Reread page 4. Ask: *What does the text tell you about the kind of weather some places have?* (The text states that some places have hurricanes.) Help children record key details in their Main Idea and Key Details charts.

Genre **ACT** Point to the picture on page 5, read the caption and the feature "What to Do in a Weather Emergency." Ask: *What does the list tell you about?* (Things to do to stay safe in bad weather like stay calm and go to a safe place.)

STOP AND CHECK Read the question in the Stop and Check box on page 5. (People should make sure they will be safe where they are and have the supplies they need.)

Pages 6–7

Main Idea and Key Details Reread pages 6 and 7. Ask: *What do you learn about wind from this page?* (Wind can make a big storm even bigger. Flat places are windy.) *What happens when wind blows in a flat area?* (Flat places can be very windy.) *What do we call a snowstorm with lots of wind?* (blizzard) Guide children as they include details in their Main Idea and Key Details charts.

Pages 8–9

Main Idea and Key Details Reread pages 8 and 9. Ask: *What are the key details on these pages about?* (how to prepare for a blizzard)

Genre **ACT** Tell children to look at the picture on page 9. Ask: *Why do you think this emergency kit includes a flashlight?* (Sometimes during storms the electricity goes out and a flashlight can be used to see in the dark.)

STOP AND CHECK Read the question in the Stop and Check box on page 9. (You should try to stay home.)

Pages 10–11

Main Idea and Key Details Reread pages 10 and 11. Ask: *What do we learn about different kinds of weather on page 10?* (A tornado is a storm that is big and spins.) Have children fill this in on their Main Idea and Key Details charts.

STOP AND CHECK Read the question in the Stop and Check box on page 11. (You can find out what the weather will be and then get ready for it.)

Pages 12–13

Main Idea and Key Details After rereading pages 12 and 13, ask: *What kind of weather does a desert have?* (A desert is hot and dry. It doesn't rain there for a long time.) Guide children as they include these details in their Main Idea and Key Details charts.

Genre (A C T) *How does the picture on these pages help you understand what a desert is like?* (The picture shows that the desert is so dry that it has cracked.)

STOP AND CHECK Read the question in the Stop and Check box on page 13. (A desert is hot and dry.)

Pages 14–15

Organization (A C T) Ask: *What kind of weather does this page tell about?* (sunny weather) *How is that different than the weather on the other pages?* (mostly they told about bad weather) *Why do you think the author chose this kind of weather for the last page?* (It ends the book on a more positive note.)

Main Idea and Key Details Reread the details on your Main Idea and Key Details Chart. Ask: *What are all of the details about in this book?* (many different kinds of weather) *What does this tell you about the main idea?* (that there are many kinds of weather that affects people in many ways) Guide children to fill this in on their Main Idea and Key Details charts.

AFTER READING

10–15 Minutes   RI.2.2   RI.2.6   RI.2.9   RF.2.4a   W.2.8   (CCSS)

Respond to Reading

Compare Texts Guide children in comparing the information in "Weather All Around" with the information in "Tornado." Help children think about ways that weather affects us. Then ask: *How does weather affect what you and your friends do?*

Summarize Have children turn to page 16 and guide them in summarizing the selection. (Answers should include important details and the main idea.)

Text Evidence

Have partners work together to answer questions on page 16. Remind children to use their Main Idea and Key Details charts.

Main Idea and Key Details (Answers will vary but should give details about blizzards, hurricanes, and tornadoes.)

Vocabulary (The text reads, "Other places are very hot and dry. A desert is like that." The picture shows a parched, cracked landscape with little or no vegetation. Both build the understanding that a desert is a place that is hot and dry.)

Write About Reading (Answers will vary but should list key items such as food, water, a radio, blankets, flashlights, and matches.)

Read "Colors in the Sky"

Encourage children to read the paired selection "Colors in the Sky" on pages 17–19. Have them summarize the selection and compare it to "Weather All Around." Have them work with a partner to answer the "Make Connections" questions on page 19.

Independent Reading

Have pairs of children reread "Weather All Around." Have them talk about ways that different kinds of weather can affect what people do.

 Quick Check Can students identify Main Idea and Key Details? If not, review and reteach using the instruction on page 166 and assign the Unit 3 Week 4 digital mini-lesson.

Can students respond to the selection using text evidence? If not, provide sentence frames to help them organize their ideas.

WEEK 4
LESSON
5

Objectives
• Review weekly vocabulary words
• Review main idea and key details
• Write an opinion about an author's use of main idea and key details

Scaffolding for **WONDERS** Reading/Writing Workshop

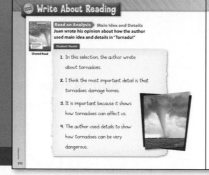

Materials
Visual Vocabulary Cards: 101–108
• Interactive Worktext, pp. 212–213
• Assessment Book, pp. 36–37

☞ **Go** Digital
• Visual Vocabulary Cards
• Main Idea and Key Details Mini-Lesson
• eAssessment

REVIEW AND RETEACH

5–10 Minutes   RI.2.1   RI.2.2   L.2.4a   CCSS

Weekly Vocabulary

Display one **Visual Vocabulary Card** at a time and guide children to use the vocabulary word in a sentence. If children have difficulty creating a sentence, have them find the word in "Tornado!" or "Weather All Around" and use context clues in the passage to define the vocabulary word.

Comprehension: Main Idea and Key Details

I Do   Write and say: *Corn is a yummy food. However, corn has many other uses. It can be made into fuel for cars. It can be used in the making of paper. Corn can even be used to make tires.* Say: *To find the main idea, we need to look for key details. I see that some sentences give details about corn.* Underline the third sentence and write *key detail.* Say: *This sentence gives a key detail about corn.* Underline the fourth and fifth sentence and write *key detail.* Ask: *I see that all three key details tell me about things that are made from corn. So, the main idea is: Many things can be made from corn.*

We Do   Display: *Earthquakes can be scary. They can cause buildings to collapse. This can cause fires. Earthquakes can also cause flooding.* Say: *What is one key detail?* (Earthquakes can cause buildings to collapse.) Ask: *What other key details can you find?* (Earthquakes can cause fires *and* cause flooding.)

You Do   Guide partners to discuss what the details or clues above have in common. Have partners work together to write the main idea of the passage.

WRITE ABOUT READING

25–35 Minutes   W.2.1   W.2.8   W.4.9   CCSS

Read an Analysis

• Guide children to look back at "Tornado!" in the **Interactive Worktext**. Have volunteers review the details about the main idea and key details in the text they marked on page 205 and summarize the text. Repeat with pages 206–209. *How did the author use main idea and key details?*

• Read aloud the directions on page 212. Read aloud the student model. *This student's work is not a summary. It is his opinion of how the author used main idea and key details in "Tornado!"*

• *When you write an opinion, you should include your thoughts about the key details from the story. Read Juan's first sentence. Circle the detail.* (The author wrote about tornadoes.) *In what part of the story do you learn this detail?* (the beginning)

• *Read the second sentence. Draw a box around the detail.* (tornadoes damage homes) *Guide children to choose the detail they think is most important by filling in the oral sentence frame: I think the most important detail is _____.*

• Guide children to point to the third sentence. *Why does Juan think this detail is important?* (it shows how tornadoes can affect us)

• Model analyzing how the author used details to write the story. Read the last sentence that Juan wrote. *Why is this sentence a good ending?* (Juan tells how the author used details.)

Write an Analysis

Analytical Writing

Guided Writing Read the writing prompt on page 213 together. Guide children to review their Main Idea and Key Details charts for "Weather All Around." Have children use their charts to complete the sentence starters. Children can also write their opinion using another selection previously read this week.

Peer Conference Guide children to read their opinions to a partner. Listeners should summarize the strongest details that support the beginning, middle and ending sentences. They should discuss any parts that are unclear.

Teacher Conference Check children's writing for complete sentences and whether they included details from the story. Review the ending sentence and ask: *Did the author use details to support the story?* If necessary, guide children to revise their sentence by adding more details.

Level Up

▲ Apprentice Leveled Reader

▲ Approaching Leveled Reader

▲ Interactive Worktext

▲ Reading/Writing Workshop

IF children read the Apprentice Level Reader and the **Interactive Worktext** Shared Read fluently and answer the Respond to Reading questions

THEN read together the Approaching Level Reader main selection and the **Reading/Writing Workshop** Shared Read from *Reading Wonders*. Have children take notes as they read, using self-stick notes. Then ask and answer questions about their notes.

Writing Rubric

	4	3	2	1
Text Evidence	Includes three or more details from the text.	Includes two or more details from the text.	Includes only one detail from the text.	No text evidence is cited.
Writing Style	Writes in complete sentences. Uses correct spelling and grammar.	Uses complete sentences. Writing has spelling and grammar errors.	Few complete sentences. There are many spelling and grammar errors.	Writing is not accurate or in complete sentences.

ASSESSMENT

Weekly Assessment

Have children complete the Weekly Assessment using **Assessment** book pages 36–37.

WEEK 5
LESSON
1

Objectives
• Develop oral language
• Build background about expressing yourself
• Understand and use weekly vocabulary
• Read an expository text

Materials
Interactive Worktext, pp. 214–221
• Visual Vocabulary Cards: 109–116
• High-Frequency Word Cards

☞ Go Digital
• Interactive eWorktext
• Visual Vocabulary Cards

Scaffolding for **Wonders** Reading/Writing Workshop

McGraw-Hill Reading

WEEKLY CONCEPT

5-10 Minutes   SL.2.1a   SL.2.4   CCSS

Talk About It

Essential Question Read aloud the Essential Question on page 214 of the **Interactive Worktext**: *How do you express yourself?* Explain that there are many different ways that people like to show their feelings and their thoughts. Say: *Some people like to draw or paint to express themselves. Some people like to play an instrument.*

• Discuss the photograph on page 214. Ask: *What is happening in this picture?* (There is a family dancing at home.) Have children describe what they see. (The mom is doing a turn. The dad and daughter are holding hands and stretching out their arms.)

I Do Say: *I am going to look at the photo and think about how this family is expressing themselves. They are expressing themselves by dancing. I will write on the web on page 215 how they are expressing themselves.*

We Do Say: *Let's think about other ways that people express themselves. I know that people also enjoy expressing themselves by drawing or painting.* Guide children to think of other ways people express themselves. Then have children choose one way to add to their web.

You Do Guide partners to work together to talk about how they express themselves. Have children use the words from the web to start their sentences: *I express myself by* _____.

REVIEW VOCABULARY

10–15 Minutes   L.2.5a   L.2.4c   L.2.6   RF.2.3f   CCSS

Review Weekly Vocabulary Words

• Use the **Visual Vocabulary Cards** to review the weekly vocabulary.

• Read together the directions on page 216 of the **Interactive Worktext**. Then complete the activity.

1 **understand** Say: *I understand English [and another language if applicable]. What language(s) do you understand?* Have children respond, using the following oral sentence starter: *I understand* _____. (Possible answers: English, Spanish, and so on.)

2 **movements** Write the word *movements* on the board. Have a volunteer identify the root word, or "smaller word," in *movements*. (move) Guide children to understand what the word *movements* means. Then have children use this oral sentence frame: _____ *and* _____ *are two* movements *a basketball player might make.* (Possible answers: dribbling, shooting, passing)

3 **cheered** Write the word *cheered* and underline the word *cheer*. Explain that the word *cheer* is the root word of the word *cheered*. Discuss with children when you might *cheer* for something. Say: *I cheered in the movie theater when the superhero saved the town.* Have children use the words *cheered* in a sentence. (Possible answers: at a sports game, at a parade)

4 **sounds** As the children listen, make a variety of *sounds*. Say: *A cough is a* sound. *A telephone ring is a* sound. The have children tell what *sounds* they can still hear while listening quietly, using this oral sentence starter: *The* sounds *I hear are* _____. (Possible answers: the clock ticking, other people breathing, noises in the hallway)

⑤ rhythm Tap on your desk. Have children repeat the *rhythm*. Do this a few times, using a variety of different *rhythms*. Have children describe the *rhythms*. Then have partners create their own *rhythm* and say to their partner: *Now repeat this* rhythm.

⑥ music Play a few kinds of *music* for children. Say: *Our class radio plays* music. Then have children use the following oral sentence frame: _____ *and* _____ *play* music. (Possible answers: a radio, a stereo, a TV)

⑦ concert Invite volunteers to describe *concerts* they have attended, both in and out of school. Then have children use this oral sentence frame: *A person might go to a* _____ *to see or hear a* concert. (Possible answers: theater, music hall)

⑧ instrument Invite volunteers to tell about an *instrument* they play. List all of the *instruments* mentioned on the board. Assist children as they draw their picture. Then have children tell about their drawing, using this oral sentence starter: *My favorite musical* instrument *is the* _____. (Possible answers: guitar, piano, drums)

High-Frequency Words

Have children look at page 217 in the **Interactive Worktext**. Help them read, spell, and write each high-frequency word. Guide partners to use each word in a sentence. Then read the story aloud with children. Guide partners to work together to reread the story and circle the high-frequency words. (four, because, show, their, says, give) Listen in and provide assistance reading the high-frequency words, as necessary.

ELL ENGLISH LANGUAGE LEARNERS

Display the **High-Frequency Word Cards** for: *show, their, says, because, give, four*. Write a sentence with each word on the board. Have children echo-read each sentence, and point out the high-frequency word. Then ask them to use the word in a new sentence.

READ COMPLEX TEXT

15–20 Minutes   RI.2.1 RI.2.2 SL.2.1b **CCSS**

Read "They've Got the Beat!"

- Have children turn to page 218 in the **Interactive Worktext** and read the Essential Question aloud. Echo-read the title with children. Point to the image of the chorus director on page 218 and ask: *What is the chorus director using to express himself?* (his hands and his voice) *Let's read about how the members of this chorus express themselves.*

- Read the article together. Note that the weekly vocabulary words are highlighted in yellow. Expand Vocabulary words are highlighted in blue.

- As children read, have them use the "My Notes" section on page 218 to write questions they have. Children can also write words they don't understand or things they want to remember. Model how to use the "My Notes" section. Say: *I see a picture of a girl on page 219. I wonder who she is and what she has to say about the chorus. I will write a question about her in the "My Notes" section.*

ELL ENGLISH LANGUAGE LEARNERS

As you read together, have children highlight parts of the text they have questions about. After reading, review the questions children have. Then help them locate the answers to their questions in the text.

 Quick Check Can children understand the weekly vocabulary words in context? If not, review vocabulary using the **Visual Vocabulary Cards** before teaching Lesson 2.

Can children read high-frequency words in context? If not, review using the Read/Spell/Write routine and the High-Frequency Word Cards.

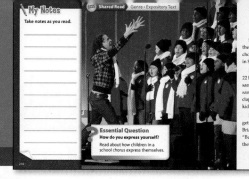

WEEK 5
LESSON 2

Objectives
• Read an expository text
• Understand complex text through close reading
• Recognize and understand main idea and key details
• Respond to the selection using text evidence to support ideas

Scaffolding for **Wonders** McGraw-Hill Reading/Writing Workshop

Materials
Interactive Worktext, pp. 218–223

☞ **Go Digital**
• Interactive eWorktext
• Main Idea and Key Details Mini-Lesson

REREAD COMPLEX TEXT

20–25 Minutes   RI.2.6   RI.2.8   L.2.4a   CCSS

Close Reading: "They've Got the Beat!"

Reread "They've Got the Beat!" from **Interactive Worktext** pages 218–221 with children. As you read together, discuss important passages in the text. Guide children to respond to questions using evidence from the text.

🔍 Pages 218–219

Main Idea and Key Details Remind children that the main idea is the most important point that an author makes about a topic. Say: *Key details support the main idea. As you read you should decide which details are key, or important, details. Then you can think about how these key details are connected. This will help you find the main idea.* Reread the second paragraph with children. Ask: *What are two events or places where the chorus sang?* Model drawing a box around the words that tell. (the White House and awards show) Guide children to draw a box around the answers.

Sentence Structure Ⓐ Ⓒ Ⓣ Point to the quotation marks in the third paragraph. Say: *Quotation marks show that someone is speaking. The words inside the quotation marks are what is being said. To find out who is speaking, look right before or right after the words in quotes.* Reread the third paragraph aloud. Ask: *Who is speaking in the third paragraph?* Model underlining the name. (Brianna Crispino) Have children underline the answer.

Expand Vocabulary Point to the word *recalls* in the third paragraph. Say: *When somebody recalls something, they remember it. What is it that Brianna Crispino recalls feeling when she sees joy on people's faces?* Guide children to underline their answers. (excited)

🔍 Page 220

Expand Vocabulary Reread the first three sentences with children. Point to the word *divided*. Say: Divided *means split up. What is* divided *into two groups?* Guide children to circle the answer. (the chorus) Ask: *What are the names of the two groups?* (the sopranos and the altos) *What does each group do?* (The sopranos sing high notes. The altos sing lower sounds.)

Main Idea and Key Details Reread the first paragraph with children. Remind children to look for key details in the text. Ask: *What does the chorus use to keep the rhythm?* (drums) *Why is it important for the singers to keep the rhythm?* Guide children to draw a box around the answer. (That way they sing well together.)

Sentence Structure Ⓐ Ⓒ Ⓣ Reread the last two sentences in the first paragraph with children. Point to the word *they*. Say: *The word* they *is a pronoun. To find the word that a pronoun refers to, you can look at the sentences just before or just after the sentence with the pronoun in it. What does the pronoun* they *refer to?* Guide children to underline the answer. (singers)

Genre Ⓐ Ⓒ Ⓣ Point to the bar graph at the bottom of page 220. Explain that this graph shows the different types of voices in an adult chorus. Explain that each type of voice is shown in a bar. Point to the top of the Sopranos bar and slide your finger over to the numbers on the side. Ask: *How many sopranos are there in this chorus?* (17) Continue by asking questions about the remaining bars.

Page 221

Expand Vocabulary Reread the first two sentences of the second paragraph with children. Point to the word *encourages*. Say: *When a person* encourages *something, he wants you to do it. What is it that Greg Breinberg* encourages *the chorus to use?* Instruct children to circle the answer. (movements)

Main Idea and Key Details Have children reread the page. Remind them to pay attention to key details in the text. Ask: *How much does the chorus practice each week?* (They practice three hours each week.) Instruct children to draw a box around the answer.

Main Idea and Key Details Remind children that the main idea of a text is the most important point the author is trying to make. The key details give clues to help figure out the main idea. Say: *Review your notes about key details and think about what these details have in common. What is the main idea of the selection?* Instruct children to write their answers. (Public School 22 has a talented chorus.)

RESPOND TO READING

15–20 Minutes | SL.2.1a RI.2.1 RI.2.2

Respond to "They've Got the Beat!"

Guide children to read aloud the questions about "They've Got the Beat!" on page 222 of the **Interactive Worktext**. Then read aloud the "Discussion Starter" for each of the questions. Have children work with a partner to answer the questions orally using the "Discussion Starters." Have children find text evidence to support their answers. Ask children to write the page number(s) on which they found the text evidence for the questions.

1. *Where do singers in the chorus express themselves?* (Possible answers: I read that the chorus sang at the White House. They also sang at an awards show. Text Evidence: p. 219)

2. *What do the singers in the chorus use when they sing?* (Possible answers: The singers use drums to keep the rhythm. They express themselves by moving their hands. This helps them show their feelings. Text Evidence: pp. 220, 221)

3. *Why do the singers work hard?* (Possible answers: Singing is a big job. The singers work hard because they want to give it their best. Text Evidence: p. 221)

After children discuss the questions on page 222, have them use the sentence starters to answer the question on page 223. Circulate and provide guidance.

 Quick Check Do children understand vocabulary in context? If not, review and reteach using the instruction on page 176.

Can children identify the main idea and key details? If not, review and reteach using the instruction on page 176 and assign the Unit 3 Week 5 digital mini-lesson.

Can children write a response to "They've Got the Beat!" If not, review the sentence starters and prompt children to respond orally. Help them write their responses.

WEEK 5
LESSON

3

Objectives
- Access prior knowledge
- Understand and use new vocabulary words
- Read high-frequency words
- Read an expository text

Scaffolding for **Wonders** Approaching Leveled Reader

Materials
"The Sounds of Trash" Apprentice Leveled Reader
- High-Frequency Word Cards

☞ **Go** Digital
- Apprentice Leveled Reader eBook
- Downloadable High-Frequency Word Cards

BEFORE READING

10–15 Minutes   SL.2.1a   SL.2.6   L.2.6   RF.2.3f   CCSS

Introduce "The Sounds of Trash"

- Read the Essential Question on the title page of "The Sounds of Trash" **Apprentice Leveled Reader:** *How do you express yourself?*

- Read the title of the main read. Turn to the title page. Ask: *What kind of instrument do you see here?* (guitar) *This guitar looks like it was made from trash. Let's read to learn more about how to make instruments out of things we don't need anymore.*

High-Frequency Words

Display the **High-Frequency Word Cards** for the words *how, make, or, put, they,* and *your.* Use the Read/Spell/Write routine to teach each word. Guide partners to use each word in a sentence. Provide assistance reading the high-frequency words, as necessary.

Expand Vocabulary

Before reading "The Sounds of Trash," help children read the following words that they will encounter. Display each word below. Use the Define/Example/Ask routine. Tell children to look for the word later on as they read "The Sounds of Trash."

 act (page 2)

Define: to play a part in a play or drama

Example: Next year, I will *act* in the school play.

Ask: What have you seen somebody *act* in?

2 **express** (page 3)

Define: to show how you feel

Example: I *express* myself by singing songs.

Ask: What is one way you *express* yourself?

3 **pluck** (page 7)

Define: to pull and let go quickly

Example: John will *pluck* the guitar strings to play the guitar.

Ask: What have you ever *plucked*?

4 **vibrate** (page 7)

Define: to move steadily, sometimes causing a sound

Example: A piano's strings *vibrate* when you play the keys.

Ask: What else can *vibrate*?

DURING READING

20–30 Minutes   RI.2.6   RI.2.7   L.2.4a   CCSS

Shared Reading

Tell children you will now read "The Sounds of Trash." Tell them to note the vocabulary and high-frequency words you just introduced as you read the story. Stop to model understanding of the story as you go.

Pages 2–3

High-Frequency Words Make sure children can read the high-frequency word *or.*

Comprehension Check Model beginning to read the story. Say: *The first thing I notice is that these kids are making art. I know that art is one way to express yourself. I also know from the title that this text will be about making sounds. I will continue reading to find out more about how I can express myself with sounds.*

Vocabulary Read page 2. Focus on the word *act*. Ask: *What does it mean to act?* (to play a part in a show) *Why is the author asking if you like to act? How is that the same as painting or dancing?* (They are ways of expressing yourself.)

Pages 4–5

High-Frequency Words Make sure children can read the high-frequency words *how, make,* and *they*.

Comprehension Check *On page 4, I see a picture of bottles in a recycling bin. The caption tells me I can make things with trash. I read that I can use bottles and tubes to express myself. I wonder how I can do that. I will read on to find out more about it.*

Comprehension Check *On page 5, I see a boy blowing into a bottle. The caption tells me that a bottle can be an instrument. This is an instrument you can make from trash!*

Pages 6–7

Comprehension Check *The heading reads "How to Make a Guitar." Then I see the materials I need and the steps I must follow. If I follow these steps, I can make my own guitar. I see that this is a book that tells how to really make things! You just need to get the materials and follow the steps.*

Vocabulary Point to the word *vibrate*. Say: *The strings on a guitar will* vibrate *when you play them. This means they move back and forth very fast and make a sound. That is the way that sound is made.*

Pages 8–9

High-Frequency Words Make sure children can read the high-frequency word *your*.

Comprehension Check *I read the heading on page 8. It reads "How to Make a Trombone." A trombone is a horn. Then I see a section called "What you need." The materials you need to make a trombone are 2 cardboard tubes, paper, scissors and tape. I can find these things very easily. On page 9, there is a picture of the trombone. This picture will help me follow the steps to make a trombone.*

Pages 10–11

Comprehension Check *On page 10, I read the instructions for how to make maracas. Maracas are instruments you shake. I read in the instructions that to make maracas you can put beans or rice in plastic bottles. On page 11, I see a picture. The picture shows a pile of beans going into a bottle. I think I will make my maracas by putting beans in a bottle.*

Pages 12–13

Comprehension Check *When I read page 12, I see instructions for making drums. This makes me excited because drums are my favorite instruments! On page 13, I read that I can hit the can with the pencils. I think its cool that I can make drumsticks out of pencils.*

Vocabulary Focus on the words *plastic* and *metal*. Invite children to name things that are plastic and things that are metal. Ask: *How is metal different from plastic?* (Possible answer: Metal is harder and colder and it is often shiny.) *How do you think the metal side of the drum will sound compared to the plastic side?* (Possible answer: The metal side might have more of a crashing sound, the plastic more of a thumping sound.)

Pages 14–15

High-Frequency Words Make sure children can read the high-frequency word *put*.

Comprehension Check *I read on page 14 what I can do now that I know how to make instruments. I read that I can play music with other kids and put on a concert. This is a great way to express myself. On page 15, I see a picture of kids playing music and expressing themselves. It looks like fun!*

 Quick Check **Can children understand vocabulary in context? If not, review and reteach using the instruction on page 176 and assign the Unit 3 Week 5 digital mini-lesson.**

Can children read the high-frequency words in context? If not, review using the Read/Spell/Write routine and the High-Frequency Word Cards.

WEEK 5 LESSON 4

Objectives
- Understand complex text through close-reading
- Read an expository text
- Recognize and understand main idea and key details
- Respond to the selection using text evidence to support ideas

Scaffolding for **Wonders** Approaching Leveled Reader

Materials
- "The Sounds of Trash" Apprentice Leveled Reader
- Graphic Organizer: Main Idea and Key Details

☞ **Go Digital**
- Apprentice Leveled Reader eBook
- Downloadable Graphic Organizer
- Main Idea and Key Details Mini-Lesson

DURING READING

20–30 Minutes   RI.2.1 RI.2.2. RI.2.5 RI. 2.7 **CCSS**

Tell children they will now reread the selection, "The Sounds of Trash." Review the vocabulary words that they will encounter as they read.

Close Reading

 **Pages 2–3**

Sentence Structure **ACT** Reread pages 2 and 3 with children. Point out all of the question marks. Ask: *What kinds of sentences are these?* (questions) Explain that asking questions is a good way to get the reader involved in the beginning of a book.

Main Idea and Key Details Remind children that the main idea is the most important point that an author makes about a topic. Key details support the main idea. Say: *As you read, think about the details and decide which are key or important. Then think about how these details are connected. This will help you find the main idea.* Point to the picture on page 3. Ask: *What are the children in the picture doing?* (singing) *What does the text say about singing and playing instruments?* (These are ways to express yourself.) Guide children to record the details on their Main Idea and Key Details charts.

Pages 4–5

Main Idea and Key Details Say: *In expository text, key details can sometimes be found in the photographs and captions. What does the caption tell you?* (You can make things with trash.) *Let's read on to find what we can make with trash.* Ask: *According to the text, what can you make with trash?* (instruments) Have children record this on their Main Idea and Key Details charts.

STOP AND CHECK Read the question n the Stop and Check box on page 5. (You can use them to make instruments that you can really play.)

Pages 6–7

Genre **ACT** Remind children that expository text may include text features. Point out that this book tells how to make things and that all the "how-to" features follow the same format. Point to the head on page 6. Ask: *What are we going to learn to do here?* (make a guitar) Point to the first subhead. Say: *What will this section tell you?* (the things you will need to make a guitar) Point to the last head. Ask: *What will this section tell you?* (what to do to make the guitar) Point out the numbers. Explain that these show the order in which you do each thing.

Sentence Structure **ACT** Reread the first two sentences on page 7 with children. Point to the word *they*. Say: *The text reads "they move, or vibrate." What moves or vibrates?* (the rubber bands)

STOP AND CHECK Read the question in the Stop and Check box on page 7. (the strings or rubber bands)

Pages 8–9

Prior Knowledge **ACT** Explain that a trombone is a horn. Pantomime playing a trombone and moving the slide. Point to the moving part of the trombone on page 9. Say: *The trombone is special because you can make it longer and shorter. This changes the sound.*

Main Idea and Key Details Reread pages 8 and 9 with children. Say: *What do we learn to make on page 8?* (trombone) *What does the text say we can do with these instruments?* (play music) Guide children to record the information in their Main Idea and Key Details charts.

STOP AND CHECK Read the question in the Stop and Check box on page 9. (Press your lips on the tube and hum. Move the tube up and down.)

Pages 10–11

Prior Knowledge Children may not be familiar with maracas. Say: *Maracas are instruments originally from Latin America. Some people call them "shakers" because you shake them to make a sound.* Reread pages 10 and 11 with children. Ask: *What is used to make maracas?* (a plastic bottle and dry beans)

Pages 12–13

Main Idea and Key Details Reread pages 12 and 13 with children. Ask: *What do we learn how to make on page 12 and 13?* (drums) *What items do we need to make these drums?* (coffee can with plastic lid, 2 pencils, 2 erasers) *What do you do with the pencils and erasers?* (Put the erasers on the pencil and use them as drumsticks.)

Pages 14–15

Main Idea and Key Details Review the details on your chart. Ask: *What do all of these details have in common?* (They tell how to make instruments.) Reread pages 14 and 15 with children. Ask: *What does the author tell you to do on page 14?* (Put on a concert and express yourself.) Point out that this combined with the details can help you to know the main idea. Guide children to state the main idea. (We can express ourselves through instruments that we can make.) Help children record this on their Main Idea and Key Details charts.

STOP AND CHECK Read the question in the Stop and Check box on page 14. (You shake the maracas and bang the drum to make a sound.)

AFTER READING

 10–15 Minutes   RI.2.2   RI.2.3   RI.2.9   RF.2.4b   W.2.8   **CCSS**

Respond to Reading

Compare Texts Guide children in comparing the events in "The Sounds of Trash" with "They've Got the Beat!" Help children think about different kinds of music. Then ask: *How do you like to express yourself?*

Summarize Have children turn to page 16 and guide them in summarizing the selection. (Answers should include key details and the main idea.)

Text Evidence

Have partners work together to answer questions on page 16. Remind children to use their Main Idea and Key Details charts.

Main Idea and Key Details (The main idea is that you can make instruments from recycled things to share your ideas and feelings through music [pages 3–5]. The text gives examples of instruments you can make [pages 6, 8, 10, 12].)

Vocabulary (The text reads, "Stretch the rubber bands around the box." For the rubber bands to fit around the box, the bands have to stretch. So *stretch* means "to pull to make longer.")

Write About Reading (Student answers will vary, but should include details about how to make an instrument.)

Read "Talking Underwater"

Encourage children to read the paired selection "Talking Underwater" on pages 17–19. Have them summarize the selection and compare it to "The Sounds of Trash." Have them work with a partner to answer the "Make Connections" questions on page 19.

Independent Reading

Have pairs of children reread "The Sounds of Trash." Have them retell the story making sure to include the main idea and key details.

✓ *Quick Check* Can students identify main idea and key details? If not, review and reteach using the instruction on page 176 and assign the Unit 3 Week 5 digital mini-lesson.

Can students respond to the selection using text evidence? If not, provide sentence frames to help them organize their ideas.

WRITE & ASSESS

WEEK 5 LESSON

5

Objectives
- Review weekly vocabulary words
- Review main idea and key details
- Write an analysis about an author's use of main idea and key details

Scaffolding for **Wonders** Reading/Writing Workshop

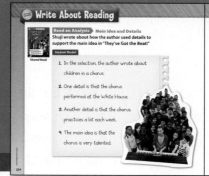

Materials
Visual Vocabulary Cards:
109–116
- Interactive Worktext, pp. 224–225
- Assessment Book, pp. 38–39

Go Digital
- Visual Vocabulary Cards
- Main Idea/Details Mini-Lesson
- Interactive eWorktext
- eAssessment

REVIEW AND RETEACH

5–10 Minutes   RI.2.1   RI.2.2   L.2.4a

Weekly Vocabulary

Display one **Visual Vocabulary Card** at a time and guide children to use the vocabulary word in a sentence. If children have difficulty creating a sentence, have them find the word in "They've Got the Beat!" or "The Sounds of Trash" and use context clues in the passage to define the vocabulary word.

Comprehension: Main Idea and Key Details

I Do   Write and say: *People all around the world raise goats. Most goats are raised for their milk. The milk is turned into cheese. Some goats are raised for their wool.* Say: *I will look for key details. I read that most goats are raised for their milk.* Underline the second sentence and write "key detail." *I also read that goats are also raised for their wool.* Underline the fourth sentence and write "key detail."

We Do   Work with children to determine the main idea. *What do these details have in common?* (They are all about the reasons that people raise goats.) *So, the main idea is: Goats are useful to people in many ways.*

You Do   Display: *Jon used to play guitar all the time. Then he switched to drums. After that he took singing lessons. Next, Jon wants to learn to play piano.* Say: *To find the main idea you must first find key details. Then you must look at how the details are connected.* Guide one partner to ask the other to identify key details and the other to identify the main idea. Have partners discuss what the key details had in common. (John enjoys studying music.)

WRITE ABOUT READING

25–35 Minutes   W.2.2   W.2.8   W.4.9

Read an Analysis

- Guide children to look back at "They've Got the Beat!" in the **Interactive Worktext**. Have volunteers review the details that support the main idea they marked on page 219. Repeat with pages 220–221. *How did the author use details to support the main idea?*

- Read aloud the directions on page 224. Read aloud the student model. *This student's work is not a summary. It is an analysis, or description, of how the author used details to support the main idea in "They've Got the Beat!"*

- *When you write an analysis, you should include details from the text. Read Shuji's first sentence. Circle the details.* (the author wrote about children in a chorus) *In what part of the story do you learn this detail?* (the beginning)

- *Read the second sentence. Circle the details.* (the chorus performed at the White House) *What part of the story does this come from?* (the beginning)

- *Guide children to point to the third sentence. Circle the details.* (the chorus practices a lot each week) *What part of the story does this come from?* (the end)

- Model analyzing how the author used details to support the main idea. Talk about what the details have in common. Then read the last sentence that Shuji wrote. *Draw a box around the main idea.* (the chorus is very talented)

Write an Analysis

Analytical Writing

Guided Writing Read the writing prompt on page 225 together. Guide children to review their Main Idea and Key Details charts for "The Sounds of Trash." Have children use their charts to complete the sentence starters. Children can also write an analysis using another selection previously read this week.

Peer Conference Guide children to read their analysis to a partner. Listeners should summarize the strongest details that support the main idea. They should discuss any parts that are unclear.

Teacher Conference Check children's writing for complete sentences and whether they included details from the story. Review the ending sentence and ask: *Did the author use details to support the story?* If necessary, guide children to revise their sentence by adding more details.

Level Up

▲ Approaching Leveled Reader

▲ Reading/Writing Workshop

▲ Apprentice Leveled Reader

▲ Interactive Worktext

IF children read the Apprentice Level Reader and the **Interactive Worktext** Shared Read fluently and answer the Respond to Reading questions

THEN read together the Approaching Level Reader main selection and the **Reading/Writing Workshop** Shared Read from *Reading Wonders*. Have children take notes as they read, using self-stick notes. Then ask and answer questions about their notes.

Writing Rubric

	4	3	2	1
Text Evidence	Includes three or more details from the text.	Includes two or more details from the text.	Includes only one detail from the text.	No text evidence is cited.
Writing Style	Writes in complete sentences. Uses correct spelling and grammar.	Uses complete sentences. Writing has spelling and grammar errors.	Few complete sentences. There are many spelling and grammar errors.	Writing is not accurate or in complete sentences.

ASSESSMENT

Weekly Assessment

Have children complete the Weekly Assessment using **Assessment** book pages 38–39.

WEEK 6

▶ **Unit Assessment,**
pages 140 – 148

▶ **Fluency Assessment,**
pages 250 – 265

▶ **Exit Test,**
pages 196 – 204

Unit 3 Assessment

CCSS **TESTED SKILLS**

✔ **COMPREHENSION**	✔ **VOCABULARY:**
• Author's Purpose RI.2.6, RI.2.8	• Context Clues L.2.4a
• Sequence RL.2.5	
• Author's Purpose RI.2.6, RI.2.8	
• Main Idea and Key Details RI.2.1, RI.2.2	
• Main Idea and Key Details RI.2.1, RI.2.2	

Using Assessment and Writing Scores

↻ **RETEACH**	**IF ...**	**THEN ...**
COMPREHENSION	Students answer 0–7 multiple-choice items correctly ...	... reteach tested skills using instruction on pages 364–375.
VOCABULARY	Students answer 0–3 multiple-choice items correctly ...	... reteach tested skills using instruction on page 364.
WRITING	Students score mostly 1–2 on weekly Write About Reading rubrics throughout the unit ...	... reteach writing using instruction on pages 376–377.

LEVEL UP	**IF ...**	**THEN ...**
COMPREHENSION	Students answer 8–10 multiple-choice items correctly ...	... have students read the *Weather All Around* Approaching Leveled Reader. Use the Level Up lesson on page on page 178.
WRITING	Students score mostly 3–4 on weekly Write About Reading rubrics throughout the unit ...	... use the Level Up Write About Reading lesson on page 179 to have students compare two selections from the unit.

Fluency Assessment

Conduct assessments individually using the differentiated fluency passages in **Assessment**. Students' expected fluency goal for this Unit is 62–82 WCPM with an accuracy rate of 95% or higher.

Exit Test

If a student answers 13–15 multiple choice items correctly on the Unit Assessment, administer the Unit 3 Exit Test at the end of Week 6.

Time to Exit

Exit Text

If...

Students answer 13–15 multiple choice items correctly...

Fluency Assessment

If...

Students achieve their Fluency Assessment goal for the unit...

Level Up Lessons

If...

Students are successful applying close reading skills with the Approaching Leveled Reader in Week 6...

If...

Students score mostly 4–5 on the Level Up Write About Reading assignment...

Foundational Skills Kit

If...

Students have mastered the Unit 3 benchmark skills in the Foundational Skills Kit and *Reading Wonders* Adaptive Learning...

Then...

... consider exiting the student from *Reading WonderWorks* materials into the Approaching Level of *Reading Wonders*.

Apprentice to Approaching Level

L.2.5 RI.2.10

▶ Read Approaching Leveled Reader

Approaching Leveled Reader

Apprentice Leveled Reader

Weather All Around

Before Reading

Preview Discuss what children remember about weather patterns and how weather affects us. Tell them they will be reading a more challenging version of "Weather All Around."

Vocabulary Use the routines on the **Visual Vocabulary Cards** to review the Weekly Vocabulary words. Use pages 164 to review the Expand Vocabulary words.

A C T During Reading

▶ **Genre** Review with children that expository text sometimes explains why or how something happens. Review these text features: captions and map. Point to the caption and photo on page 4 and ask: *What is the middle of a hurricane called?* (the eye) Next, direct children to look at the map on page 6 and ask: *How does this map help us know more about the Great Plains?* (It shows where the Great Plains are located.)

▶ **Sentence Structure** Review that when children come across a question in the text, they can keep reading to find the answer. Read page 4 aloud and point out the question at the end of the paragraph: Ask: *What do you think the author will tell us on the next page?* (how people can stay safe from a hurricane) Guide children to read page 5 and discuss the answer.

▶ **Purpose** Ask: *Is the purpose of this text is to inform or to entertain readers?* (inform) Remind children that to figure out the purpose of a text, they can ask, "*What does the author want me to know about a topic?*" Read page 8 aloud and ask: *Why might people stay home if a snowstorm is coming?* (to stay safe)

▶ Write About Reading

Interactive Worktext Shared Read

Apprentice Leveled Reader

After Reading

Ask children to complete the Respond to Reading on page 16 after they have finished reading. Provide support with the vocabulary strategy question, as needed.

Write About Reading

RI.3.9   W.4.9

Read an Analysis

- Distribute the Unit 3 Downloadable Model and Practice. Point out that the model compares two related texts that children have read in Unit 3, the **Interactive Worktext** Shared Read "Tornado!" and the **Apprentice Leveled Reader** "Weather All Around." Read the sentences aloud to children.

- Point out the key details in each sentence that come from the texts. Point out the signal words *too* and *both*. Explain to children that these words show readers that the sentences are comparing two different texts.

- Ask: *What details show that the two texts are alike?* (Both texts tell about how bad weather affects us. Both texts tell people to stay safe at home.) *How is "Weather All Around" different?* ("Weather All Around" tells about many kinds of weather, not just tornadoes.)

- Model analyzing how the student compared details. Read the last sentence. *Why is this a good comparison?* (The student gave evidence to show how the two texts were the same.)

Write an Analysis

Guided Writing Tell children that they will be comparing the **Interactive Worktext** Shared Read "Lighting Lives" and the **Apprentice Leveled Reader** "City Communities." Explain to children that they will compare how the authors describe different ways people help out their community.

- Guide children to compare the two texts as they complete the sentences on the Unit 3 Downloadable Model and Practice.

- Point out the signal words, such as *also, both*, and *different, to children and discuss how these words are used to compare the texts.*

- Alternatively, let children select two texts to compare.

Teacher Conference Check children's writing for complete sentences. Did they use key details to tell how the texts are the same and different? Did they use text evidence? Did they write in complete sentences?

Writing Rubric

	4	3	2	1
Text Evidence	Includes three or more details from the text.	Includes two or more details from the text.	Includes only one detail from the text.	No text evidence is cited.
Writing Style	Writes in complete sentences. Uses correct spelling and grammar.	Uses complete sentences. Writing has spelling and grammar errors.	Few complete sentences. There are many spelling and grammar errors.	Writing is not accurate or in complete sentences.

UNIT 4 PLANNER
Our Life, Our World

Week 1
Different Places

Week 2
Earth Changes

Week 3
Our Culture Makes Us Special

ESSENTIAL QUESTION
What makes different parts of the world different?

Build Background

Vocabulary
L.2.4a *eerie, growth, layers, lively, location, region, seasons, temperate*

Access Complex Text A C T
Organization

Comprehension
RI.2.9 Skill: Compare and Contrast
Respond to Reading

Write About Reading *Analytical Writing*
W.4.9 Inform/Explain: Genre

ESSENTIAL QUESTION
How does the Earth change?

Build Background

Vocabulary
L.2.4a *active, earth, explode, island, local, properties, solid, steep*

Access Complex Text A C T
Genre

Comprehension
RI.2.3 Skill: Cause and Effect
Respond to Reading

Write About Reading *Analytical Writing*
W.4.9 Inform/Explain: Cause and Effect

ESSENTIAL QUESTION
How are kids around the world different?

Build Background

Vocabulary
L.2.4a *common, costume, customs, favorite, parades, surrounded, travels, wonder*

Access Complex Text A C T
Connection of Ideas

Comprehension
RI.2.9 Skill: Compare and Contrast
Respond to Reading

Write About Reading *Analytical Writing*
W.4.9 Inform/Explain: Compare and Contrast

ASSESSMENT

✔ Quick Check
Vocabulary, Comprehension

✔ Weekly Assessment
Assessment Book, pp. 40–41

✔ Quick Check
Vocabulary, Comprehension

✔ Weekly Assessment
Assessment Book, pp. 42–43

✔ Quick Check
Vocabulary, Comprehension

✔ Weekly Assessment
Assessment Book, pp. 44–45

✔ MID-UNIT ASSESSMENT
Assessment Book, pp. 96–103

Fluency Assessment
Assessment Book, pp. 250–265

Use the Foundational Skills Kit for explicit instruction of phonics, structural analysis, fluency, and word recognition. Includes *Reading Wonders* Adaptive Learning.

Week 4
Folktales About Nature

ESSENTIAL QUESTION
How can we understand nature?

Build Background

Vocabulary
L.2.4a *ashamed, boast, dash, holler, plenty, similarities, victory, wisdom*

Access Complex Text
Genre

Comprehension
RL.2.2 Skill: Theme
Respond to Reading

Write About Reading
W.4.9 Inform/Explain: Theme

Week 5
Poems About Nature

ESSENTIAL QUESTION
What excites us about nature?

Build Background

Vocabulary
L.2.4a *drops, excite, outdoors, pale*

Poetry Words
alliteration, free verse, repetition, simile

Access Complex Text
Connection of Ideas

Comprehension
RL.2.2 Skill: Theme
Respond to Reading

Write About Reading
W.4.9 Opinion: Word Choice

Week 6
ASSESS

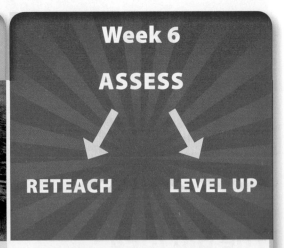

RETEACH   LEVEL UP

Reteach
Comprehension Skills
Vocabulary
Write About Reading

Level Up
Read Approaching Leveled Reader
Write About Reading: Compare Texts

A S S E S S M E N T

✓ Quick Check
Vocabulary, Comprehension
✓ Weekly Assessment
Assessment Book, pp. 46–47

✓ Quick Check
Vocabulary, Comprehension
✓ Weekly Assessment
Assessment Book, pp. 48–49

✓ Unit Assessment
Assessment Book, pp. 149–157
✓ Fluency Assessment
Assessment Book, pp. 250–265

EXIT TEST
Assessment Book, pp. 205–213

UNIT 4 OPENER,
pp. 226–227

The Big Idea

How do different environments make the world an interesting place?

Talk About It

Read aloud the Big Idea on page 226 of the **Interactive Worktext:** How do different environments make the world an interesting place? Ask children if they have ever been to a forest. Have volunteers describe the forest. If children have difficulty, model describing a forest. Ask children to tell what they find interesting about forests.

Discuss the photo on pages 226–227. Ask: *What do you see in the picture?* (A waterfall in a forest) *What else do you see?* (rocks, plants, a tree) *What do you find interesting about the picture?* (Answers will vary.)

Then say: Let's name some other environments that we have seen or visited. (jungle, desert, beach and so on.) *How is a beach different from a forest?* Have children discuss with their partners. Instruct children to come up with two ways they are different. Then have partners share their ideas with the group.

Then say: *Let's look back at our Big Idea. How do different environments make the world an interesting place?* Have children discuss with partners and then share their ideas with the group. Explain to children that they will be discussing the Big Idea throughout the unit. Each week they will talk, read and write about different environments.

Build Fluency

Each week, use the **Interactive Worktext** Shared Reads and **Apprentice Leveled Readers** for fluency instruction and practice. Keep in mind that reading rates vary with the type of text that children are reading as well as the purpose for reading. For example, comprehension of complex informational texts generally requires slower reading.

Explain/Model Use the Fluency lessons on pages 378–382 to explain the skill. Then model the skill by reading the first page of the week's Shared Read or Leveled Reader.

Practice/Apply Choose a page from the Shared Read or Leveled Reader. Have one group read the top half of the page one sentence at a time. Remind children to apply the skill. Have the second group echo-read the passage. Then have the groups switch roles for the second half of the page. Discuss how each group applied the skill.

> **Weekly Fluency Focus**
>
> **Week 1** Pronunciation
> **Week 2** Phrasing
> **Week 3** Expression
> **Week 4** Expression
> **Week 5** Phrasing

Foundational Skills Kit You can also use the **Lesson Cards** and **Practice** pages from the **Foundational Skills Kit** for targeted Fluency instruction and practice.

Access Complex Text

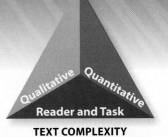

Qualitative | Quantitative

Reader and Task

TEXT COMPLEXITY

Interactive Worktext

	Week 1	Week 2	Week 3	Week 4	Week 5
	"Alaska: A Special Place"	"Into the Sea"	"Happy New Year!"	"Why the Sun and the Moon Live in the Sky"	"Snow Shape"
Quantitative	Lexile 430 TextEvaluator™ 17	Lexile 490 TextEvaluator™ 6	Lexile 420 TextEvaluator™ 10	Lexile NP TextEvaluator™ NP	Lexile NP TextEvaluator™ NP
Qualitative	• Organization • Vocabulary	• Genre • Vocabulary	• Connection of Ideas • Vocabulary	• Genre • Vocabulary	• Connection of Ideas • Vocabulary
Reader and Task	The Weekly Concept lessons will help determine the reader's knowledge and engagement in the weekly concept.				
	Weekly Concept: p. 186 Questions and tasks: pp. 188–189	Weekly Concept: p. 196 Questions and tasks: pp. 198–199	Weekly Concept: p. 206 Questions and tasks: pp. 208–209	Weekly Concept: p. 218 Questions and tasks: pp. 220–221	Weekly Concept: p. 228 Questions and tasks: pp. 230–231

Apprentice Leveled Reader

	Week 1	Week 2	Week 3	Week 4	Week 5
	"Rocky Mountain National Park"	"Earthquakes"	"Sharing Cultures"	"Why Turtles Live in Water"	"A Hike in the Woods"
Quantitative	Lexile 270 TextEvaluator™ 12	Lexile 290 TextEvaluator™ 6	Lexile 260 TextEvaluator™ 16	Lexile NP TextEvaluator™ NP	Lexile 240 TextEvaluator™ 6
Qualitative	• Organization • Prior Knowledge • Genre • Connection of Ideas • Vocabulary	• Genre • Connection of Ideas • Vocabulary	• Connection of Ideas • Organization • Genre • Vocabulary	• Genre • Connection of Ideas • Organization • Vocabulary	• Connection of Ideas • Vocabulary
Reader and Task	The Weekly Concept lessons will help determine the reader's knowledge and engagement in the weekly concept.				
	Weekly Concept: p. 186 Questions and tasks: pp. 190–193	Weekly Concept: p. 196 Questions and tasks: pp. 200–203	Weekly Concept: p. 206 Questions and tasks: pp. 210–213	Weekly Concept: p. 218 Questions and tasks: pp. 222–225	Weekly Concept: p. 228 Questions and tasks: pp. 232–235

See page 383 for details about Text Complexity measures.

WEEKLY LESSON 1

Objectives
• Develop oral language
• Build background about different places
• Understand and use weekly vocabulary
• Read expository text

Talk About It
Weekly Concept Different Places

Essential Question
What makes different parts of the world different?

Name the features of a desert.

Desert Region

Talk with a partner about the region where you live.

Materials
• Interactive Worktext, pp. 228–235
• Visual Vocabulary Cards: 117–124
• High-Frequency Word Cards

Go Digital
• Interactive eWorktext
• Visual Vocabulary Cards

Scaffolding for Wonders Reading/Writing Workshop

WEEKLY CONCEPT

5–10 Minutes   SL.2.1b   SL.2.4

Talk About It

Essential Question Read aloud the Essential Question on page 228 of the **Interactive Worktext:** *What makes different parts of the world different?* Say: *A region is any large area or territory.* Explain that there are many different regions in the world. Tell children that different regions look and feel very different from each other. Say: *Different regions have different climates, or temperatures, types of landforms and plants, trees and flowers.*

• Discuss the photograph on page 228. Ask: *What type of region do we see in this picture?* (a desert) Ask: *What do you know about a desert?* Have children discuss what they know about a desert.

I Do Say: *I am going to look at the photo and think about the features of a desert. I see that the ground is rocky and sandy.* Point to the rocky and sandy areas of the photograph. Say: *I will add this information to the web on page 229.*

We Do Say: *Let's think about other features of a desert. Look at the photograph and share your ideas with your partner.* Ask volunteers to share their ideas aloud. Then have children choose one feature of a desert to add to their web.

You Do Guide partners to work together to talk about the features of the desert. Have children use the words from the web to start their sentences: *A desert region has _____.* You may wish to continue the discussion of different regions around the world by having children describe the region where you live.

REVIEW VOCABULARY

10–15 Minutes   L.2.5a   L.2.6   RF.2.3

Review Weekly Vocabulary Words

• Use the **Visual Vocabulary Cards** to review the weekly vocabulary.

• Read together the directions on page 230 of the **Interactive Worktext**. Then complete the activity.

1 **layers** Have children brainstorm items that have *layers*. Tell children that people often wear *layers* of clothing. (shirt, sweater, coat) Encourage children to also think of food items that come in *layers*. Have children use this sentence frame: _____ *is a food that has* layers. (Possible answers: sandwich, lasagna, cake)

2 **region** Guide children to brainstorm different *regions*. Tell them that deserts, wetlands, forests, and mountains are all different kinds of *regions*. Have children use the following sentence frame: _____ *live in a mountain* region. (Possible answers: bears, goats, eagles)

3 **location** Discuss with children where certain buildings are located in your community. Ask: *What is the* location *our school? What is the* location *of the library?* Then assist children as they describe the *location* of their home.

4 **lively** Ask children to name some things that they do at parties. (Possible answers: eat, play games) Ask a volunteer to act out how a *lively* person might act at a party. Have children use this sentence starter: *A* lively *person might _____.* (Possible answers: dance, sing, laugh, tell jokes)

⑤ growth Ask children to name things that *grow*. (Possible answers: plants, animals, people) Then ask: *Do you grow? How do you measure your* growth? (Possible answers: with a scale, with a tape measure) Then help children complete the activity. (Possible answers: garden, field)

⑥ temperate Ask: *What word do we know that sounds very similar to the word* temperate? (temperature) Explain that a *temperate* climate is one that is not too hot and not too cold. Then help children complete the activity, using this sentence frame: *A person might wear _____ and _____ in a* temperate *climate.* (Possible answers: a long-sleeve shirt, pants)

⑦ eerie Provide an example of an *eerie* sound, such as a creaking door in an old building. Ask for a volunteer to tell another sound that could be *eerie*. Then ask a volunteer to suggest another word that will work in place of *eerie* in the sentence. (scary)

⑧ seasons Write the names of the four *seasons* on the board: *spring, summer, fall/autumn, winter*. Help children write a caption for their tree picture, using the following sentence starter: *My favorite* season *is _____.*

High-Frequency Words

Have children look at page 231 in the **Interactive Worktext**. Help them read, spell, and write each high-frequency word. Guide partners to use each word in a sentence. Then read the story aloud with children. Guide partners to work together to reread the story and circle the high-frequency words. (very, years, also, there, another, part) Listen in and provide assistance reading the high-frequency words, as necessary.

> **ELL ENGLISH LANGUAGE LEARNERS**
>
> Display the **High-Frequency Word Cards** for: *part, very, also, another, years, there*. Write a sentence with each word on the board. Have children echo-read each sentence, and point out the high-frequency word. Then ask them to use the word in a new sentence.

READ COMPLEX TEXT

15–20 Minutes   RI.2.3 RI.2.5 SL.2.1b **CCSS**

Read "Alaska: A Special Place"

- Have children turn to page 232 in the **Interactive Worktext** and read aloud the Essential Question. Point to the photograph. Say: *What are some features of Alaska?* (mountains) *Let's read to find out what makes Alaska different from other places.* Have children echo-read the title.

- Read the story together. Note that the weekly vocabulary words are highlighted in yellow. Expand Vocabulary words are highlighted in blue.

- As children read, have them use the "My Notes" section on page 232 to write questions they have. Children can also write words they don't understand or things they want to remember. Model how to use the "My Notes" section. *When I read the first paragraph on page 233, I find out that Alaska is a state with many regions. I will write a question about how one region in Alaska is different from another region in the "My Notes" section.*

> **ELL ENGLISH LANGUAGE LEARNERS**
>
> As you read together, have children highlight parts of the text they have questions about. After reading, review the questions children have. Then help them locate the answers to their questions in the text.

 Quick Check Can children understand the weekly vocabulary in context? If not, review vocabulary using the **Visual Vocabulary Cards** before teaching Lesson 2.

Can children read high-frequency words in context? If not, review using the Read/Spell/Write routine and the High-Frequency Word Cards.

WEEK 1 LESSON

2

Objectives
- Read expository text
- Understand complex text through close reading
- Recognize and understand how to compare and contrast
- Respond to the selection using text evidence to support ideas

Scaffolding for **Wonders** Reading/Writing Workshop

Materials
Interactive Worktext, pp. 232–237

👉 **Go** Digital
- Interactive eWorktext
- Compare and Contrast Mini-Lesson

REREAD COMPLEX TEXT

20–25 Minutes RI.2.3 RI.2.5 L.2.4a **CCSS**

Close Reading: "Alaska: A Special Place"

Reread "Alaska: A Special Place" with children from **Interactive Worktext** pages 232–235. As you read together, discuss important passages in the text. Guide children to respond to questions using evidence from the text.

 Pages 232–233

Prior Knowledge **A C T** Explain to children that expository selections often give information to readers about a topic. Say: *Sometimes authors include text features, such as a map or a diagram, to give readers more information.* Point to the map on page 233 and say: *Maps are drawings that show the surface features of an area. They often have a key that tells you what the symbols on the map stand for.* Then review the key for the map of Florida with children.

Expand Vocabulary Explain to children that a *feature* is a special part of a place or thing. Reread the second paragraph aloud. Say: *In the second paragraph, I read about a mountain in Alaska called Mt. McKinley. This must be a land feature.* Guide children to circle the word in the paragraph that tells the land *feature*. (mountain)

Organization **A C T** Point out the heading "Land Features" on page 233. Explain to children that authors can organize expository or informational text by including headings that tell what the text under the heading will be about it. Reread the third paragraph aloud and ask: *What land feature does this paragraph give facts and information about?* Guide children to write the word that tells. (glaciers)

Vocabulary **A C T** Explain to children that expository selections often have many new vocabulary words and concepts. If children have difficulty with the words *glaciers* or *volcanoes*, display pictures of them for reference.

Compare and Contrast Say: *When we* compare, *we tell how they are alike. When we* contrast, *we tell how things are different.* Have children look at the map. Say: *Two regions on this map are alike because they both have the same land feature. Which land feature can be found in two of the regions?* Guide children to draw a box around this land feature on the map. (pictures of mountains)

 Page 234

Expand Vocabulary Have children reread the first paragraph. Explain that *temperature* refers to the hotness or coldness of the air in an environment. Ask: *What is the* temperature *like in the Arctic region?* Guide children to circle the sentence that tells. (It is very cold.)

Prior Knowledge **A C T** Explain to children that the Arctic region is one of Earth's coldest regions. Alaska is the only state in the United States that has land in the Arctic region. Seven other countries also have land in the Arctic region.

Compare and Contrast Remind children that when we compare two things, we tell how they are alike, and when we contrast two things, we tell how they are different. Have them reread the second paragraph. Ask: *How is southern Alaska different from northern Alaska?* Guide children to draw a box around the sentence that tells. (It is warmer there.)

Organization Point out the photo of the walruses and the caption below it. Explain to children that captions can give more facts and information about the topic. Read the caption out loud. Have children reread the two headings on the page. Ask: *What heading do the photo and caption go with?* Guide children to underline the heading that tells. (Animals)

Page 235

Organization Point to the heading and remind children that they use headings in expository selections to help tell what the text below the heading will be about. Have children reread the first paragraph. Ask: *What sentence tells what the section "Daylight and Darkness" will be about?* Guide children to underline their answers. (The seasons are special here.)

Expand Vocabulary Have children reread the second paragraph. Explain that *darkness* means having little or no light. Ask: *What could you do in Alaska during 60 days of darkness?* Guide children to circle the words that tell. (play soccer after school in the dark)

Compare and Contrast Have children reread the page. Ask: *The author is telling about the seasons in Alaska. Which two seasons are being compared in this section of text?* Guide children to write their answers. (summer and winter)

RESPOND TO READING

10–20 Minutes   RI.2.3   RI.2.5   SL.2.1b

Respond to "Alaska: A Special Place"

Read aloud the questions about "Alaska: A Special Place" on page 236 of the **Interactive Worktext**. Then read aloud the "Discussion Starter" for each of the questions. Guide children to work with a partner to answer the questions orally using the "Discussion Starters." Have children find text evidence to support their answers. Ask children to write the page number(s) on which they found the text evidence for each question.

1. *What is special about Alaska's land features?* (Possible answers: Alaska has the tallest mountain in the states. Northern Alaska has glaciers. Text Evidence: p. 233)

2. *What is special about the temperature and animals in Alaska?* (Possible answers: I read that the northern region is very cold. The southern region is warmer. Some animals you may find in these regions are polar bears and black bears. Text Evidence: p. 234)

3. *What are the seasons like in Alaska?* (Possible answers: During the summer in Alaska, the sun does not set for many days. Winter in Alaska is different because the sun does not rise in some parts. Text Evidence: p. 235)

After children discuss the questions on page 236, have them use the sentence starters to answer the question on page 237. Circulate and provide guidance.

✓ *Quick Check* Do children understand vocabulary in context? If not, review and reteach using the instruction on page 194.

Can children identify compare and contrast? If not, review and reteach using the instruction on page 194 and assign the Unit 4 Week 1 digital mini-lesson.

Can children write a response to "Alaska: A Special Place"? If not, review the sentence starters and prompt children to respond orally. Help them write their responses.

Objectives

- Understand and use new vocabulary words
- Read an expository text
- Recognize and understand compare and contrast
- Understand complex text through close reading

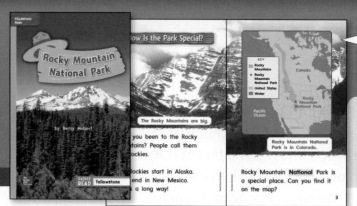

Materials

"Rocky Mountain National Park" Apprentice Leveled Reader: pp. 2–7

- Compare and Contrast Graphic Organizer

☞ **Go** Digital

- Apprentice Leveled Reader eBook
- Downloadable Graphic Organizer
- Compare and Contrast Mini-Lesson

Scaffolding for **Wonders** Approaching Leveled Reader

BEFORE READING

10–15 Minutes   SL.2.1a   SL.2.6   L.2.5a   L.2.6   **CCSS**

Introduce "Rocky Mountain National Park"

- Read the Essential Question on the title page of "Rocky Mountain National Park" **Apprentice Leveled Reader:** *What makes different parts of the world different? We will read about Rocky Mountain National Park. Rocky Mountain National Park is in Colorado.*

- Read the title aloud. Point to the pictures and diagrams. Ask: *Is this text fiction or nonfiction?* (nonfiction) *This nonfiction text gives facts and information about a real place, Rocky Mountain National Park. Let's read to find out what makes this park special.*

Expand Vocabulary

Display each word below. Say the words and have children repeat them. Then use the Define/Example/Ask routine to introduce each word.

1 **meadows** (page 6)

Define: fields of grassy land

Example: The *meadows* were full of flowers and golden grass.

Ask: Are there *meadows* where you live? What could you do in them?

2 **national** (page 3)

Define: having to do with a land united under one government

Example: Many people visit America's *national* parks.

Ask: What *national* holidays do we celebrate?

3 **zones** (page 4)

Define: areas with different features or uses

Example: The four *zones* at the picnic had different food and games.

Ask: If you were in charge of one picnic *zone* what would you have in it?

DURING READING

20–30 Minutes   RI.2.1   RI.2.2   RI.2.5   L.2.4a   L.2.5   **CCSS**

Close Reading

🔍 **Pages 2–3**

Prior Knowledge Ask: *What do you know about our country's national parks?* Explain that the United States has 58 national parks. These areas of land are protected by our national government. Everything in the park, including the plants and animals, are also protected. They cannot be hurt or taken away. Discuss what children might see if they went to a national park. Ask: *Can a person take plants from a national park?* (no)

Genre Explain that nonfiction often has text features to give more information. Point to the map. Say: *What does this map show us about the Rocky Mountains?* (The Rocky Mountains are very long.) Point to the map key. Say: *This feature is called a map key. It tells how to use the map.* Review the map key. Ask: *What does the map tell us that text does not?* (Answers will vary but may include where Rocky Mountain National Park is located and how long the mountain chain is.)

Main Topic and Key Details *Remind children that the main topic of a selection is what the selection is mostly about.* Ask: *What is this selection about?* (Rocky Mountain National Park) *What details have you learned so far?* (The Rocky Mountains start in Alaska and end in New Mexico.)

Pages 4–5

Compare and Contrast Say: *When we compare two or more things, we tell how they are alike. When we contrast two or more things, we tell how they are different. We can look for clue words such as,* like, just as, *and the same to compare and words such as* but, different, *and* unlike, *which contrast.* Read page 4 with children. Ask: *Which clue word signals that the three life zones are going to be contrasted?* (different) Ask: *How are the life zones different from each other?* (They have different plants and animals. They have different climates.) Model recording *Life Zones* in the middle section of their Compare and Contrast charts.

Genre **A C T** Point to the diagram on page 4. Say: *This diagram shows the three life zones. What does it tell us that the text doesn't?* (where each of the life zones in the park are) Ask: *Which life zone is the highest in the park?* (Alpine Tundra)

Vocabulary Explain that children can use the diagram to help understand the word *zone.* Ask: *In the diagram, what is different about the areas of land in each of the three zones?* (The zones are different colors. the zones are at different heights.) *Can two zones be in the same place?* (no) *This is a clue to the meaning of* zone.

Vocabulary On page 4 focus on the word *climate.* Say: *Climate is what the weather is like in a place over a long period of time.* Ask: *What is the climate like where you live?*

Organization **A C T** Point to the heading on page 5 and read it along with children. Say: *The author has organized the text using a compare and contrast text structure. Each section will give facts and information about one of the three life zones to show how it is different from the other two. We can use the headings to know which life zone the author will tell about next. We know from page 4 that the life zones have different animals, plants, and climates. We also know from the diagram that each zone is at a different level in the park.* Read page 5 with children. Ask: *Which life zone does this section of text tell about?* (the montane) Have children point to the text evidence in the second sentence.

STOP AND CHECK Read the question in the Stop and Check box on page 4. (Answer: three)

Pages 6–7

Compare and Contrast Say: *We'll compare and contrast the montane life zone with one of the other zones in Rocky Mountain National Park.* Help children add *Montane Life Zone* as the heading of the left section of their charts. *Let's read and look for information about the montane to add to our charts.* Read page 6 with children. Ask: *What information tells us how the montane zone's climate is different from the other two zones?* (The montane is the warmest zone.) Help children record *the warmest zone* in the left section of their charts.

Compare and Contrast Say: *Let's look for another detail that tells how the montane zone is different from the other two zones. What kinds of trees grow in the montane zone?* (aspen trees, tall pine trees) Have children point to the text evidence on the page, and help them record these details in their charts.

Genre **A C T** Explain to children that in nonfiction texts, captions will sometimes give information that is not found anywhere else in the text. Say: *We know from the text that squirrels eat seeds. Let's read the caption to see if we can find out more information about squirrels.* Read the caption with children. Ask: *What is one type of seed the caption tells us squirrels like to eat?* (pine nuts)

STOP AND CHECK Read the question in the Stop and Check box on page 7. (Possible answers: The montane is the warmest zone. It has tall pine trees and aspen trees. Flowers grow in meadows. Squirrels, elk, bobcats, and bluebirds live in this zone.)

Have partners review their Compare and Contrast charts for pages 2–7 and discuss what they have learned.

 Quick Check Do children understand weekly vocabulary in context? If not, review and reteach using the instruction on page 194.

Can children identify compare and contrast? If not, review and reteach using the instruction on page 194 and assign Unit 4 Week 1 digital mini-lesson.

Objectives
- Understand and use new vocabulary words
- Read an expository text
- Recognize and understand expository text
- Understand complex text through close reading

Scaffolding for **Wonders** Approaching Leveled Reader

Materials
- "Rocky Mountain National Park" Apprentice Leveled Reader: pp. 8–20
- Compare and Contrast Graphic Organizer

☞ **Go Digital**
- Apprentice Leveled Reader eBook
- Downloadable Graphic Organizer
- Compare and Contrast Mini-Lesson

BEFORE READING

5–10 Minutes   SL.2.1a   SL.2.6   L.2.5   L.2.6   CCSS

Expand Vocabulary

Display each word below. Say the words and have children repeat them. Then use the Define/Example/Ask routine to introduce each word.

1 bend (page 9)

Define: to use force to cause a thing to become curved

Example: We saw a strong wind *bend* the small tree.

Ask: What could you *bend* with your hands?

2 dens (page 13)

Define: places where wild animals rest or sleep

Example: Some animal *dens* are under the ground.

Ask: Would bears or birds live in dens?

3 forests (page 8)

Define: a large area with a lot of trees and bushes

Example: We saw many trees on a walk in the forest.

Ask: Would a forest have many trees or very *few*?

4 frozen (page 11)

Define: hardened by the cold

Example: The lake is *frozen* in winter.

Ask: Is something that is *frozen* hot or cold?

5 twisted (page 9)

Define: to turn or bend a thing to change its shape

Example: The grape vines *twisted* up the fence.

Ask: What is a *twisted* road like?

DURING READING

20–30 Minutes   RI.2.1   RI.2.2   RI.2.4   L.2.4b   L.2.6   CCSS

Close Reading

🔍 **Pages 8–9**

Vocabulary Write the word *subalpine* on the board and underline the prefix *sub-*. Say: *The* subalpine *life zone is located above the montane life zone in Rocky Mountain National Park.* Use your hands to mime one zone being above the other. Point the prefix *sub-*. *The prefix* sub- *means* under *or* below. *For example, a* submarine *is a boat that floats* under *the water.* Subzero *is below* freezing temperature. Ask: *What does the word* subalpine *mean?* (below the alpine)

Organization Ⓐ Ⓒ Ⓣ Remind children that the author has organized the text using a compare and contrast text structure. Ask: *What is the author contrasting in this selection?* (the different life zones in Rocky Mountain National Park) Point out the heading. Ask: *What life zone will the author give facts and information about in this section of text?* (the subalpine)

Genre Ⓐ Ⓒ Ⓣ Read the caption with children on page 9. Ask: *How long can trees in the subalpine zone live?* (hundreds of years)

🔍 **Page 10**

Connection of Ideas Ⓐ Ⓒ Ⓣ Ask: *Does it look warm or cold in this picture?* (cold) Read the caption with children. Ask: *What helps pine martens stay warm in the subarctic life zone?* (They have thick fur.)

STOP AND CHECK Read the question in the Stop and Check box on page 10. (Possible answer: The subalpine is the middle zone. It rains more here. There are dark forests. Mule deer, pine martens, and juncos live there)

Page 11

Vocabulary Point to the word *Tundra* in the heading. Explain to children that *tundra* is a large area of land in the arctic region that has no trees. Say: *Look at the photo. How does this photo help us understand what the word* tundra *means?* (It shows a large area with no trees.) *What words would you use to tell what the alpine tundra is like?* (Possible answers: rocky, snowy, cold)

Key Details Read the heading with children. Ask: *Which life zone is the topic of this section of text?* (the alpine tundra) Say: *We can find key details about a topic in the text, photos, and captions of an informational selection.* Read page 11 with children. Ask: *What is the ground like in this zone?* (It is always frozen.)

Pages 12–13

Compare and Contrast Help children review the information in their Compare and Contrast Graphic charts. Say. *Now we will look for details about the alpine tundra zone that tell how it is different from the montane.* Model adding the heading *Alpine Tundra Zone* to their charts. Ask: *How is the climate in this zone different from the warmer climate of the montane?* (It snows a lot.) *What kind of trees grow in this zone?* (There are no trees.)

Connection of Ideas **A C T** Explain that both trees and flowers are types of plants. Say: *We know that the ground is frozen in the alpine tundra zone. We also know there are no trees.* Ask: *Does frozen ground help trees grow in the alpine tundra zone?* (no) *Can plants grow in this zone?* (yes) *What type of plants can grow in the tundra?* (small, low plants and some flowers)

Pages 14–15

Organization **A C T** Read pages 14–15. Ask children which zone these pages tell about. (They don't tell about a zone, they tell about the whole park) Ask: *What other part of the book did not tell about a particular zone?* (the beginning)

STOP AND CHECK Read the question in the Stop and Check box on page 15. (It is the highest zone in the park. It snows a lot. The ground is always frozen. No trees grow there.)

AFTER READING

10–15 Minutes   RI.2.3   RI.2.4   RI.2.9   L.2.4b   L.2.6   CCSS

Respond to Reading

Compare Texts Ask children to compare features such as climate, mountains, plant life, and animal life in "Alaska: A Special Place" and "Rocky Mountain National Park." What makes these places special? What do you want to know about what makes different parts of the world different? Discuss with a partner.

Summarize Have children turn to page 16 and summarize the selection. Answers should include details that show how different park zones have different features.

Text Evidence

Have partners work together to answer questions on page 16. Remind children to use their Compare and Contrast Charts.

Compare and Contrast (Answers will vary but should explain that the zones are at different elevations have different climates and kinds of plants and animals.)

Vocabulary (the subalpine zone; center, in between.)

Write About Reading (Answers will vary but should point out that more plants grow in the warmer zones.)

Independent Reading

Encourage children to read the paired selection "Yellowstone" on pages 17–19. Have them summarize the selection and compare it to "Rocky Mountain National Park." Have them work with a partner to answer the "Make Connections" questions on page 19.

Quick Check Can children identify compare and contrast? If not, review and reteach using the instruction on page 194 and assign the Unit 4 Week 1 digital mini-lesson.

Can children respond to the selection using text evidence? If not, provide sentence frames to help them organize their ideas.

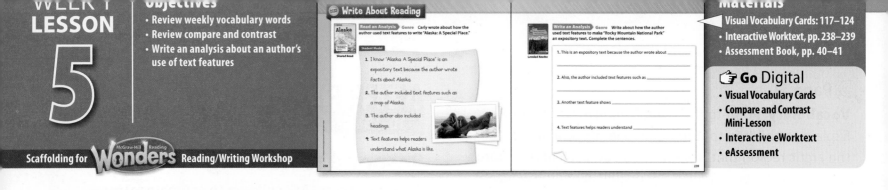

WEEKLY
LESSON

5

• Review weekly vocabulary words
• Review compare and contrast
• Write an analysis about an author's use of text features

Scaffolding for **Wonders** Reading/Writing Workshop

Materials
Visual Vocabulary Cards: 117–124
• Interactive Worktext, pp. 238–239
• Assessment Book, pp. 40–41

Go Digital
• Visual Vocabulary Cards
• Compare and Contrast Mini-Lesson
• Interactive eWorktext
• eAssessment

REVIEW AND RETEACH

5–10 Minutes   R.I.2.3   RI.2.5   L.2.4a

Weekly Vocabulary

Display one **Visual Vocabulary Card** at a time and guide children to use the vocabulary word in a sentence. If children have difficulty creating a sentence, have them find the word in "Alaska: A Special Place" or "A Special Sunset" and use context clues in the passage to define the vocabulary word.

Comprehension: Compare and Contrast

I Do Write and say: *Tennis and soccer are both fun sports. Tennis is played on a court, but soccer is played on a field. Tennis players use racquets to hit the ball, unlike soccer players, who kick the ball. Tennis matches have no time limit, but soccer matches do.* Ask: *What clue word shows how tennis and soccer are alike in the first sentence?* Circle "both" and say: *When we compare, we think about how things are alike. I know that clue words such as* similar, both, *and* also *can signal a comparison.*

We Do Say: *When we contrast, we think about how things are different.* Ask: *What clue word shows how tennis and soccer are different in the second sentence? The clue words* unlike *and* but *can help signal a contrast.* Guide children to circle "but" and write *contrast.*

You Do Display: *Rosa and Mike both like pizza. Rosa likes sausage pizza, but Mike likes plain. Guide one partner to ask a question about comparisons or contrasts in the text. Have the other partner find a clue word that helps to answer the question. Have partners switch and discuss their answers.*

WRITE ABOUT READING

25–35 Minutes   W.2.2   W.2.8   W.4.9

Read an Analysis

• Guide children to look back at "Alaska: A Special Place" in the **Interactive Worktext**. Have volunteers review the details they marked on page 233 and summarize the text. Repeat with pages 234–235. *How did the author make the selection expository text?*

• Read aloud the directions on page 238. Read aloud the student model. *This student's work is not a summary. It is an analysis, or description, of how the author made "Alaska: A Special Place" an expository text.*

• *When you write an analysis, you should include key details from the text that tell about the selection. Read Carly's first sentence.* Guide children to circle the topic of the selection. (Alaska) Ask: *What part of the selection does this detail appear?* (the beginning)

• *Read the second sentence. Draw a box around the details in Carly's writing.* (text features such as a map of Alaska)

• *Guide children to point to the third sentence. This sentence tells of another text feature the author included. Guide children to name the text feature.* (headings) Ask: *How does the author use headings to help you understand the topic?* (Headings help organize information.)

• *The third part is the concluding statement. A good concluding statement sums up the paragraph and gives the reader closure.* Have children underline the concluding statement. *Why is this a good ending?* (It says how the author uses text features to tell more about the topic.)

Analytical Writing **Write an Analysis**

Guided Writing Read the writing prompt on page 239 together. Have children review the text features used in "Rocky Mountain National Park." Tell them to use the sentence starters to help them figure out what information to write in each section. If children have difficulty, have them select a section and find a text feature. Ask: *How does the author use this text feature?*

Peer Conference Have children read their analysis to a partner. Listeners should summarize the strongest text evidence that supports the topic sentence and discuss any sentences that are unclear.

Teacher Conference Check children's writing for complete sentences and whether they included details from the selection. Review the last sentence and ask: *Does the author use details to support the story?* If necessary, have children revise their sentences by adding more details.

Level Up

▲ Approaching Leveled Reader

▲ Reading/Writing Workshop

▲ Apprentice Leveled Reader

▲ Interactive Worktext

IF children read the Apprentice Level Reader and the **Interactive Worktext** Shared Read fluently and answer the Respond to Reading questions

THEN read together the Approaching Level Reader main selection and the **Reading/Writing Workshop** Shared Read from *Reading Wonders*. Have children take notes as they read, using self-stick notes. Then ask and answer questions about their notes.

Writing Rubric

	4	3	2	1
Text Evidence	Includes three or more details from the text.	Includes two or more details from the text.	Includes only one detail from the text.	No text evidence is included.
Writing Style	Writes in complete sentences. Uses correct spelling and grammar.	Uses complete sentences. Writing has spelling and grammar errors.	Few complete sentences. There are many spelling and grammar errors.	Writing is not accurate or in complete sentences.

ASSESSMENT

Weekly Assessment

Have children complete the Weekly Assessment using **Assessment** book pages 40–41.

WEEK 2 LESSON 1

Objectives
- Develop oral language
- Build background about our changing earth
- Understand and use weekly vocabulary
- Read expository text

Materials
- Interactive Worktext, pp. 240–247
- Visual Vocabulary Cards: 125–132
- High-Frequency Word Cards

☞ **Go** Digital
- Interactive eWorktext
- Visual Vocabulary Cards

Scaffolding for **Wonders** Reading/Writing Workshop

WEEKLY CONCEPT

5–10 Minutes   RI.2.3   RI.2.5

Talk About It

Essential Question Read aloud the Essential Question on page 240 of the **Interactive Worktext:** *How does the Earth change?* Explain that the Earth is always changing. Say: *It can change quickly, such as when an earthquake happens. But it can also change slowly, such as when wind or rain washes away parts of Earth.*

- Discuss the photograph on page 241. Ask: *What is happening in the picture?* (There is water running through a rocky area.) Ask: *What else do you see in the picture?* (There is an arch made out of rock.)

I Do Say: *I am going to look at the photo and think about how the Earth in this picture is changing.* (The water is washing away the rocks, slowly over time.) Say: *I will write on the web on page 241 how the Earth is changing.*

We Do Say: *Let's think about other ways the Earth changes. Can someone think of a way the Earth changes at the beach?* Have a volunteer suggest one way the Earth changes at the beach. (The oceans washes away the sand.) Have partners discuss and add one way to their webs.

You Do Guide partners to work together to talk about how the Earth changes. Encourage them to think of ways the Earth changes both quickly and slowly. Have chldren use the words from the web to start their sentences: *The Earth changes when _____.*

REVIEW VOCABULARY

10–15 Minutes   L.2.5a   L.2.6   RF.2.3

Review Weekly Vocabulary Words

- Use the **Visual Vocabulary Cards** to review the weekly vocabulary.

- Read together the directions on page 242 of the **Interactive Worktext**. Then complete the activity.

1 **solid** Describe why your desk and the chalkboard are both *solid*. Then help children use the word *solid* in a sentence. Provide the following sentence starter as necessary: _____ *and* _____ *are* solid *things I put in my backpack.* (Possible answers: a book, a pencil)

2 **properties** Ask children to tell how ice and water are alike and how they are different. List the *properties* of each on the board. Then, help children complete the following sentence frame: _____ *and* _____ *are* properties *of ice.* (Possible answers: solid, cold)

3 **steep** Display the picture of a hill and describe why it is *steep*. Have children name something that they walked on that was *steep*. (Possible answers: mountain, stairs) Have them use this sentence frame: _____ *is/are* steep. Then have children demonstrate walking up a *steep* staircase.

4 **Earth** Write *Earth* and *earth* on the board. Ask a volunteer to suggest the difference between the two. Explain that when writing about our planet, most people usually spell *Earth* with a capital *E*. Then help children complete the activity in their books. (Possible answers: It would cover the earth in snow.)

5 **active** Review the meaning of the word *active* wth children. Tell children one way you like to be *active*. Then have them use the following sentence starter: *An* active *person* _____. (Possible answers: runs, plays) Have children answer the prompt. (running)

6 **local** Write the word *local* at the top of the board. Make two columns underneath: one labeled SAME, the other labeled OPPOSITE. Have volunteers suggest synonyms for the word *local* as you list them in the first column (near, close, nearby) and antonyms as you list them in the second column. (far, faraway)

7 **explode** Write the word *explode* on the board. Say: *When something* explodes, *it makes an explosion.* Ask: *How would you describe an explosion?* Then have children use the following sentence starter: *When* volcanoes explode, *they are* _____. (loud)

8 **island** Have volunteers name any *islands* they know. Explain that an *island* can be very big or very small. Point out some *islands* on a map. Assist children as they draw a picture of an *island*. Help children label their picture. Then give children this sentence starter: *The name of my* island *is* _____.

High-Frequency Words

Have children look at page 243 in the **Interactive Worktext**. Help them read, spell, and write each high-frequency word. Guide partners to use each word in a sentence. Then read the story aloud with children. Guide partners to work together to reread the story and circle the high-frequency words. (water, Some, carry, even, fall, wash) Listen in and provide assistance reading the high-frequency words, as necessary.

> **ELL ENGLISH LANGUAGE LEARNERS**
>
> Display the **High-Frequency Word Cards** for: *carry, fall, even, some, wash, water*. Write a sentence with each word on the board. Have children echo-read each sentence, and point out the high-frequency word. Then ask them to use the word in a new sentence.

READ COMPLEX TEXT
15–20 Minutes   RI.2.3   RI.2.5   SL.2.1b

Read "Into the Sea"

- Have children turn to page 244 in the **Interactive Worktext** and read aloud the Essential Question. Point to the picture. Say: *This sandcastle is being hit by waves. Let's read to find out how this sandcastle is connected to how the Earth changes.* Have children echo-read the title.

- Read the story together. Note that the weekly vocabulary words are highlighted in yellow. Expand Vocabulary words are highlighted in blue.

- As children read, have them use the "My Notes" section on page 244 to write questions they have. Children can also write words they don't understand or things they want to remember. Model how to use the "My Notes" section. *When I read the title, it makes me think about things going into the sea. I wonder what goes into the sea. I will write a question about this in the "My Notes" section.*

> **ELL ENGLISH LANGUAGE LEARNERS**
>
> As you read together, have children highlight parts of the text they have questions about. After reading, review the questions children have. Then help them locate the answers to their questions in the text.

 Quick Check Can children understand the weekly vocabulary in context? If not, review vocabulary using the **Visual Vocabulary Cards** before teaching Lesson 2.

Can children read high-frequency words in context? If not, review using the Read/Spell/Write routine and the High-Frequency Word Cards.

WEEK 2 LESSON 2

Objectives
- Read expository text
- Understand complex text through close reading
- Recognize and understand cause and effect
- Respond to the selection using text evidence to support ideas

Scaffolding for **Wonders** McGraw-Hill Reading **Reading/Writing Workshop**

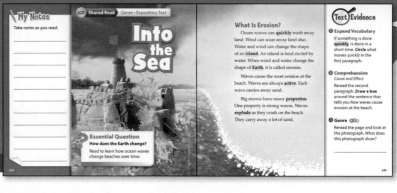

Materials
Interactive Worktext, pp. 244–249

☞ **Go** Digital
- Interactive Worktext
- Cause and Effect Mini-Lesson

REREAD COMPLEX TEXT

20–25 Minutes   RI.2.3 RI.2.4 RI.2.5 L.2.5a **CCSS**

Close Reading: "Into the Sea"

Reread "Into the Sea" with children from **Interactive Worktext** pages 244–247. As you read together, discuss important passages in the text. Guide children to respond to questions using evidence from the text.

Page 245

Expand Vocabulary Remind children that if something happens *quickly*, it happens in a short amount of time. Guide them to reread the first paragraph. Say: *I read that ocean waves can* quickly *wash away land.* Guide children to circle their answers. (ocean waves)

Cause and Effect Remind children that a *cause* is what makes something happen. An *effect* is what happens. Have children reread the second paragraph. Ask: *How do waves* cause *erosion at the beach?* Say: *I know that erosion is when water changes the shape of land. I read that the waves in the ocean carry the sand away. This must be how erosion at the beach happens.* Guide children to draw a box around their answer. (Each wave carries away sand.)

Genre ACT Guide children to think about what they know about expository text. Remind them that it gives important facts about a subject. Have children reread the page and look at the photograph. Ask: *What does the photograph show?* Guide children to write their answer. (Possible answers: erosion, or waves washing away the sand.)

Page 246

Cause and Effect Guide children to reread the heading and the first paragraph. Explain that this paragraph is all about the erosion of beaches. Ask: *What is the cause of buildings getting washed away?* Guide children to write their answer. (water or waves)

Genre ACT Point to the photographs at the top of the page. Explain that the two photographs show the same location at different points in time. The photo on the left shows the beach before erosion occurred. Have children look at the photo on the right and ask: *How has the beach changed?* (Possible answers: There is less sand. The tree is falling in the water because there is less sand to hold it up.)

Genre ACT Remind children that this expository text is about erosion, which is something that happens in real life. Have children reread the first paragraph. Ask: *How can erosion be dangerous?* Have them underline the sentence that tells. (Some buildings can even be washed away.)

Expand Vocabulary Explain to children that when things *smash* into one another, they hit very hard, or with great force. Have them reread the second paragraph. Ask: *What do waves* smash *into?* Have children circle the words that answer. (the bottom of the cliffs) Ask: *What happens when the water smashes into the cliffs?* (rock washes away) You may wish to draw a picture of a cliff and show how the rocks at the bottom get washed away, leaving no support for the rocks above it.

Page 247

Vocabulary Point out the term *sea walls* in bold print. Explain that authors sometimes use word in bold print when they are important to the understanding of the story. Guide children to look at the photo on page 247. Ask: *What do you see in the picture?* (a large wall of rocks) Explain that a large wall of rocks is a *sea wall.* Say: *Let's continue reading to see what the* sea wall *does.*

Genre Ⓐ Ⓒ Ⓣ Then have children reread the first paragraph. Ask: *What is a way that some communities are trying to stop the erosion of beaches?* Children should underline the text that tells the answer. (These communities have built sea walls to stop erosion.)

Cause and Effect Have children reread the second paragraph. Ask: *What is the* effect *of a sea wall?* Children should draw a box around the sentences that answer the question. (When waves hit the wall, they slow down. They can't pull sand away.)

Cause and Effect Have children reread the last paragraph. Ask: *What is the* effect *of the rule that buildings must be built far from the water?* Children should draw a box around the text that answers the question. (They won't wash away.)

RESPOND TO READING

10–20 Minutes

SL.2.1b   RI.2.3

Respond to "Into the Sea"

Read aloud the questions on page 248 of the **Interactive Worktext**. Guide children to read the question about "Into the Sea." Then read aloud the "Discussion Starter" for each of the questions. Guide children to work with a partner to answer the questions orally using the "Discussion Starters." Have children find text evidence to support their answers. Ask children to write the page number(s) on which they found the text evidence for each question.

1. *What is erosion?* (<u>Possible answers</u>: Erosion happens when wind and water change the shape of the land. Waves cause erosion by washing away the sand. <u>Text Evidence</u>: p. 245)

2. *How does erosion change the land?* (<u>Possible answers</u>: Erosion can change beaches by washing them away. Erosion can also wash away buildings and rocks. <u>Text Evidence</u>: pp. 245, 246)

3. *How can people stop erosion?* (<u>Possible answers</u>: Some people who live near beaches build sea walls. Sea walls stop erosion because they slow down waves. <u>Text Evidence</u>: p. 247)

After children discuss the questions on page 248, have them use the sentence starters to answer the question on page 249. Circulate and provide guidance.

 Quick Check Do children understand vocabulary in context? If not, review and reteach using the instruction on page 204.

Can children identify cause and effect? If not, review and reteach using the instruction on page 204 and assign the Unit 4 Week 2 digital mini-lesson.

Can children write a response to "Into the Sea"? If not, review the sentence starters and prompt children to respond orally. Help them write their answers.

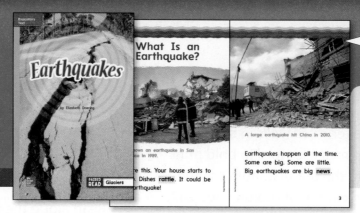

WEEK 2 LESSON

3

Objectives
- Understand and use new vocabulary words
- Read an expository text
- Recognize and understand cause and effect
- Understand complex text through close reading

Scaffolding for **WONDERS** Approaching Leveled Reader

Materials
- "Earthquakes" Apprentice Leveled Reader: pp. 2–7
- Cause and Effect Graphic Organizer

Go Digital
- Apprentice Leveled Reader eBook:
- Downloadable Graphic Organizer
- Cause and Effect Mini-Lesson

BEFORE READING

10–15 Minutes   SL.2.1a   SL.2.6   L.2.5a   L.2.6   **CCSS**

Introduce "Earthquakes"

- Read the Essential Question on the title page of "Earthquakes" **Apprentice Leveled Reader:** *How does the Earth change? We will read about earthquakes and how they affect Earth.*

- Read the title aloud. Point to the pictures and diagrams in the book. Ask: *Is this text fiction or nonfiction?* (nonfiction) *This nonfiction text gives information about earthquakes. Let's read to find out about earthquakes.*

Expand Vocabulary

Display each word below. Say the words and have children repeat them. Then use the Define/Example/Ask routine to introduce each word.

1 caused (page 7)

Define: made a thing happen

Example: Dropping the cup on the floor *caused* it to break.

Ask: What *caused* the ice to melt—warmer weather or colder weather?

2 news (page 3)

Define: the story of something that just happened

Example: We listen to the radio to hear *news* about the world.

Ask: What kind of event might be *news*?

3 rattle (page 2)

Define: to make hard, short, knocking sounds

Example: The wind made the windows *rattle*.

Ask: When do you hear things *rattle*?

DURING READING

20–25 Minutes   RI.2.1   RI.2.3   RI.2.4   RI.2.5   RI.2.6   **CCSS**

Close Reading

🔍 **Pages 2–3**

Cause and Effect Read page 2 with children. Say: *When something happens, that is the* effect. *The thing that makes it happen is the* cause. *The text says, "Your house starts to shake. Dishes rattle." These things are the* effect. *What is the* cause? *Let's finish the paragraph. It says it could be an earthquake. An earthquake is the* cause *of your house shaking and your dishes rattling. Let's look for causes and effects as we read.* Help children record this cause and effect on their Cause and Effect charts.

Prior Knowledge   Point out the photograph and caption on page 3 to children. Explain that one reason that this earthquake was so destructive was that many buildings were not well made. They were built cheaply and shoddily, so when an earthquake hit, they collapsed and hurt many more people than should have been hurt. Ask: *Why might it be important that people who know about earthquakes carefully look at buildings in the United States?* (to make sure that if an earthquake hits, it won't destroy the building) *Why would what the buildings are made from be important?* (If a building is not made of solid materials, it will fall down easily and hurt a lot of people.)

Genre AC T Remind children that expository texts give true facts about real things. Have them look at the photo on page 2. Ask: *What are these men doing?* (using a hose) *Why might they be using the hose?* (to put out a fire) *Often, there are text features, such as section headers, maps, graphs, or photos that guide the reader through the text.* Have children look at the header on page 2. Say: *This text is going to give us information about a topic. Look at the header at the top of the page. What information are we going to learn about in this section?* (We are going to learn what an earthquake is.)

Vocabulary Read the first sentence on page 2, "Picture this." Ask: *What is a picture?* (a drawing, photograph, or painting) *What does it mean to* picture *something?* (to imagine something or to make a picture of it in your head) *What is the first sentence asking you to do?* (to imagine being in an earthquake)

Pages 4–5

Genre AC T Look at the map and the caption on page 4 with children. Remind them that there are often text features that help you better understand an expository text. There are often captions with maps and other text features that tell you what they mean. Children can use them together with the text on the page to learn more about the subject of the selection. Say: *Look at the map. Read the caption. What does the star stand for?* (It is the center of the earthquake.) *How much did the people closest to the star feel the earthquake?* (They felt it the most.) *How much did the people near the largest circle feel the earthquake?* (They felt it the least.)

Cause and Effect Read page 5 with children and look at the photo of the effect of an earthquake in Japan. Point out that this man is standing in the middle of a road and that it would take a lot of force and energy to put cracks that large in concrete. Say: *The text says that the ground in Japan moved 8 feet. That is the* effect. *What is the* cause *that made it move?* (a big earthquake)

Pages 6–7

Connection of Ideas AC T Read page 6 with children. Examine the photo of the fault. Help students think about the text and the connection between faults and earthquakes. Say: *The text says that earthquakes often happen along fault lines. Do you think a place with many faults would have more earthquakes or fewer earthquakes than somewhere with few faults?* (more earthquakes)

Prior Knowledge AC T Read page 7 with children. Point out that the Mississippi River is not in an area of the United States that often has earthquakes. Also convey to children that it is a very large river that is able to absorb a lot without much effect. However, if a natural event is strong enough, even something as powerful as the Mississippi River can be affected. Say: *What effect did the big earthquakes that hit the Mississippi River have?* (huge waves) *What kind of damage might huge waves cause?* (flooding)

STOP AND CHECK Read the question in the Stop and Check box on page 7. (Possible answers: Earthquakes happen in many places. Strong earthquakes make the ground move. Earthquakes often happen along fault lines.)

Have partners review their Cause and Effect charts for pages 2–7 and discuss what they have learned.

 Quick Check **Do children understand weekly vocabulary in context?** If not, review and reteach using the instruction on page 204.

Can children identify cause and effect? If not, review and reteach using the instruction on page 204 and assign Unit 4 Week 2 digital mini-lesson.

WEEK 2 LESSON 4

Objectives
- Understand and use new vocabulary words
- Read an expository text
- Recognize and understand expository text
- Understand complex text through close reading

Scaffolding for **Wonders** Approaching Leveled Reader

Materials
- "Earthquakes" Apprentice Leveled Reader: pp. 8–20
- Cause and Effect Graphic Organizer

☞ **Go Digital**
- Apprentice Leveled Reader eBook
- Downloadable Graphic Organizer
- Cause and Effect Mini-Lesson

BEFORE READING

5–10 Minutes   SL.2.1a SL.2.6 L. 2.5 L.2.6 CCSS

Expand Vocabulary

Display each word below. Say the words and have students repeat them. Then use the Define/Example/Ask routine to introduce each word.

1 reach (page 10)

Define: get to

Example: A teacher's voice must be loud to *reach* the children in the back row.

Ask: How far would you need to go to *reach* the ocean?

2 shore (page 12)

Define: where water and land meet

Example: I stood on the *shore* and let the water wash over my feet.

Ask: What might you see at the *shore*?

3 surface (page 8)

Define: the outside of something

Example: The *surface* of a turtle's shell is hard.

Ask: What is the *surface* of a pinecone like?

4 waves (page 9)

Define: ripples from moving

Example: When the building fell down, we could feel the *waves* as the ground shook.

Ask: When do you feel *waves* of movement?

DURING READING

15–20 Minutes   RI.2.1 RI.2.3 RI.2.5 RI.2.6 CCSS

Close Reading

🔍 **Pages 8–9**

Genre Ⓐ Ⓒ Ⓣ Read page 8 with children. Remind them that an expository text often has text features that help them understand the subject of the text better. Help them to identify the text features that tells them what this section will be about. Ask: *What is this section about?* (what causes earthquakes) *How can you tell?* (the head) Then point to the diagram. Have them use the labels to point to Earth's crust, the land and the ocean. Ask: *How does this diagram help you understand the text?* (It shows the parts of Earth)

Cause and Effect Reread page 9 with children. Point out the map at the top of the page. Read the caption with children. Ask: *What does this map show?* (the plates that make up Earth's crust) *What is the* cause *of rocks inside the earth exploding?* (Earth's plates pushing and pulling) Have children record causes and effects on their Cause and Effect charts.

STOP AND CHECK Read the question in the Stop and Check box on page 9. (Possible answer: The rocks in Earth explode. This causes shock waves.)

🔍 **Pages 10–11**

Genre Ⓐ Ⓒ Ⓣ Read page 10 with children. Remind them about text features that are common in expository texts, such as section heads, diagrams, and illustrations. Ask: *What is this section about?* (It is about shock waves and how they create earthquakes.) *How do you know?* (the section head is "Shock Waves") *Where does a shock wave begin?* (underground) *What is the name for the point where shock waves begin?* (the focus)

Cause and Effect Have students read page 11. Point out the photo at the bottom of the page. *Can earthquakes happen underwater?* (yes) *What effect do earthquakes underwater have?* (They cause giant waves.)

Vocabulary Help children connect the usual meaning of the word *shock* with *shock waves. What does* shock *usually mean* (a changes that causes a surprise or upset) *How does this help you understand a shock wave?* (It is a wave that causes change and upset in Earth.)

STOP AND CHECK Read the question in the Stop and Check box on page 11. (<u>Possible answer</u>: They begin underground at the focus.)

Pages 12–13

Connection of Ideas **ACT** Ask: *What is a tsunami?* (a giant ocean wave) *Why might a tsunami be dangerous?* (They are very big and powerful. They could smash buildings or hurt people.)

Genre **ACT** Have children look at the photo and the text on page 13. Have children think about how the photo supports the text. Ask: *What does a tsunami look like when it is near land? Use the photo and the text to describe it.* (It looks like a giant wall of water. It is curled at the top.)

STOP AND CHECK Read the question in the Stop and Check box on page 13. (<u>Possible answer</u>: Tsunami waves are one effect. Earthquakes can also cause buildings to shake and fall.)

Pages 14–15

Connection of Ideas **ACT** Have children read page 14. Point out the photo and caption at the bottom of the page. Ask: *What does this machine do?* (it tells how strong an earthquake is) *Why do people want to learn more about earthquakes?* (If we know more, we can protect people when one happens. We can also make buildings safer.)

STOP AND CHECK Read the question in the Stop and Check box on page 15. (<u>Possible answer</u>: Most earthquakes are small.)

AFTER READING

10–15 Minutes   L.2.4a   L.2.6   RI.2.3   RI.2.5   W.2.8

Respond to Reading

Compare Texts Have children think about how earthquakes and erosion are connected. How are they both dangerous? How are people trying to keep safe from earthquakes and erosion? Ask: *How does each of these things make the earth change?*

Summarize Have students turn to page 16 and summarize the selection. Answers should include details that show the causes and effects of earthquakes.

Text Evidence

Have partners work together to answer questions on page 16. Remind them to use their Cause and Effect charts.

Cause and Effect (They can cause tsunamis.)

Vocabulary (The diagram shows the focus of an earthquake underground. These clues tell us that a *focus* is "the underground center of an earthquake.")

Write About Reading (Earth's crust is made of plates that move. When the plates slide by each other or pull away, this can cause rock deep underground to explode and send out shock waves. When the shock waves reach Earth's surface, this causes an earthquake.)

Independent Reading

Encourage students to read the paired selection "Glaciers" on pages 17–19. Have them summarize the selection and compare it to "Earthquakes." Have them work with a partner to answer the questions on page 19.

 Quick Check **Can students identify cause and effect? If not, review and reteach using the instruction on page 204 and assign the Unit 4 Week 2 digital mini-lesson.**

Can students respond to the selection using text evidence? If not, provide sentence frames to help them organize their ideas.

Integrate WRITE & ASSESS

Objectives
- Review weekly vocabulary words
- Review cause and effect
- Write an analysis about the author's use of cause and effect

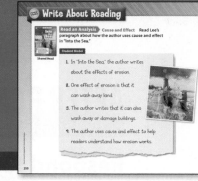

Materials
- Visual Vocabulary Cards: 125–132
- Interactive Worktext, pp. 250–251
- Assessment Book, pp. 42–43

☞ **Go Digital**
- Visual Vocabulary Cards
- Cause and Effect Mini-Lesson
- Interactive eWorktext
- eAssessment

Scaffolding for **Wonders** Reading/Writing Workshop

REVIEW AND RETEACH

5–10 Minutes   L.2.4a   RI.2.3   CCSS

Weekly Vocabulary

Display one **Visual Vocabulary Card** at a time and guide children to use the vocabulary word in a sentence. If children have difficulty creating a sentence, have them find the word in "Into the Sea" or "Earthquakes" and use context clues to define the vocabulary word.

Comprehension: Cause and Effect

I Do   Write and say: *The rain started when I went to bed. When I woke up, there were puddles in my street. I put on my boots and went to school.* Ask: *What is the cause of the puddles in the street?* Say: *Think about the first sentence. It started to rain. Rain makes puddles, so rain is the cause of the puddles. Puddles are the effect of rain.*

We Do   Display: *I went to the park with my dad. I let go of the balloon I was carrying. It floated away. I watched it get smaller and smaller as it got farther away.* Ask: *What is the effect of my letting go of the balloon?* (It floated away.) *How do you know?* (I know that if you let go of a balloon, it will float away. Letting go causes the balloon to float away.)

You Do   Display: *Mimi put on her nicest clothes. Her friend Lisa was having her birthday party today. Mimi wrapped a present for Lisa. Then her mom took her to the party. She had a great time. Lisa also had a good time and she loved the present.* Guide partners to work together to find matching causes and effects.

WRITE ABOUT READING

25–35 Minutes   W.2.2   W.2.8   W.4.9   CCSS

Read an Analysis

- Guide children to look back at "Into the Sea" in the **Interactive Worktext**. Have volunteers review the details about the author's use of cause and effect they marked on page 245 and summarize the text. Repeat with pages 246–247. *How did the author use cause and effect?*

- Read aloud the directions on page 250. Read aloud the student model. *This student's work is not a summary. It is an analysis, or description, of how the author used cause and effect in "Into the Sea."*

- *When you write an analysis, you should include key details from the text that tell about the selection. Read Lee's first sentence. What important detail is included in this sentence? Circle the details.* (Lee tells what the author wrote about.) *What part of the story do the details come from?* (the beginning)

- *Read the second sentence. Lee gives an example of an effect of erosion. Draw a box around the details you see in Lee's writing.* (It can wash away the land.) Ask children if there are other examples of effects that Lee could have included. (Erosion can wash away cliffs.)

- Guide children to point to the third sentence. *Lee gives another example of an effect of erosion. Draw a box around what the effect is.* (It can also wash away or damage buildings.)

- *Read the last sentence that Lee wrote.* Ask: *Why is this sentence a good ending?* (It tells how the author uses cause and effect to write the selection.)

✏️ *Analytical Writing* Write an Analysis

Guided Writing Read the writing prompt on page 251 together. Have children review their Cause and Effects charts for "Earthquakes." Have them use their charts to complete the sentence starters. If children have difficulty, have them select a chapter and find a cause and effect. Children can also write the analysis using another selection previously read this week.

Peer Conference Have children read their analysis to a partner. Listeners should summarize the details that supports the causes and effects and discuss any sentences that are unclear.

Teacher Conference Check children's writing for complete sentences and text evidence that supports their topic. Review the concluding statement. *Does this sentence tie all of the elements together?* If necessary, have children revise their sentences by adding more details.

Level Up

▲ Apprentice Leveled Reader

▲ Approaching Leveled Reader

▲ Interactive Worktext

▲ Reading/Writing Workshop

IF children read the `Apprentice Level` Reader and the **Interactive Worktext** Shared Read fluently and answer the Respond to Reading questions

THEN read together the `Approaching Level` Reader main selection and the **Reading/Writing Workshop** Shared Read from *Reading Wonders*. Have children take notes as they read, using self-stick notes. Then ask and answer questions about their notes.

Writing Rubric

	4	3	2	1
Text Evidence	Includes three or more details from the text.	Includes two or more details from the text.	Includes only one detail from the text.	No text evidence is included.
Writing Style	Writes in complete sentences. Uses correct spelling and grammar.	Uses complete sentences. Writing has spelling and grammar errors.	Few complete sentences. There are many spelling and grammar errors.	Writing is not accurate or in complete sentences.

ASSESSMENT

Weekly Assessment

Have children complete the Weekly Assessment using **Assessment** book pages 42–43.

Teach and Model

WORKTEXT

WEEK 3 LESSON 1

Objectives
- Develop oral language
- Build background about how our culture makes us special
- Understand and use weekly vocabulary
- Read realistic fiction

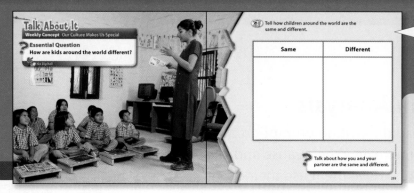

Materials
- Interactive Worktext, pp. 252–259
- Visual Vocabulary Cards: 133–140
- High-Frequency Word Cards

☞ **Go Digital**
- Interactive eWorktext
- Visual Vocabulary Cards

WEEKLY CONCEPT

5–10 Minutes   SL.2.1b SL.2.4 **CCSS**

Talk About It

Essential Question Read aloud the Essential Question on page 252 of the **Interactive Worktext:** *How are kids around the world different?* Explain that children around the world are different in many ways. They are also similar in ways. Say: *Children all around the world go to school. They all learn. But they do not all learn the exact same things. Children in United States learn how to read and write in English. Children in some other countries learn to read and write in different languages.*

Discuss the photograph on page 252. Ask: *What is happening in this picture?* (I see children in a classroom with a teacher.)

I Do Say: *I am going to look at the photo and think about how this classroom is different from our classroom.* (The children are sitting on the floor, rather than on chairs.) *I will write this difference on the chart on page 253.*

We Do Say: *If you look at our chart, you will see we have another column that says "Same." Let's think about ways the children in this classroom are the same as us. I notice that they have computers in the classroom. That is similar to our classroom.* Guide children to think of other similarities between the children in the photograph and themselves or their classroom. Then have children choose one way they are the same to add to the chart.

You Do Guide partners to work together to talk about other ways that the children in this picture are either the same or different from themselves or their classroom. Have children use words from the chart to

start their sentences: *These children are the same.as (or different from) us because _____.*

REVIEW VOCABULARY

10–15 Minutes   L.2.4a L.2.5a **CCSS**

Review Weekly Vocabulary Words

- Use the **Visual Vocabulary Cards** to review the weekly vocabulary.

- Read together the directions on page 254 of the **Interactive Worktext**. Then complete the activity.

1 **wonder** Describe something that you *wonder* about. Have a volunteer describe something that they *wonder* about. Give children this oral sentence starter: *I often* wonder *about _____.* Have volunteers share how they act when they wonder about something.

2 **customs** Give children an example of a *custom* that the school takes part in. Have children name other school customs. Then invite volunteers to name birthday customs they have seen or experienced. (Possible answers: having a birthday party, opening presents, blowing out candles on a cake)

3 **parade** Ask children if they have ever been to or seen a *parade*. Ask what the *parade* was for. Have children complete the following oral sentence frame: *One reason there might be a* parade *in my town is _____.* (Possible answers: a holiday, a team wins a championship)

4 **common** Ask children to explain what makes something *common*. If necessary, explain the opposite of *common: uncommon.* Give an example of an uncommon sport, such as curling. Ask children to name a *common* sport. Then have volunteers name *common* games. Have children say the following oral

sentence frame: *One* common *game I play is* _____.
(Possible answers: tag, kickball, hopscotch, jump rope)

5 **travels** Display pictures of land vehicles, such as cars and trains. Lead a discussion about how they *travel* across land and roads. Then have volunteers suggest things that *travel* across the sky. Have children fill in this sentence frame: *A* _____ travels *across the sky.* (Possible answers: plane, helicopter, blimp, shooting star)

6 **costume** Have a volunteer describe a *costume* they have worn in a play or show. Then have children use this sentence frame: *To a dress up party, I would like to wear a* _____ costume. (Possible answers: pirate, cowboy, cartoon character)

7 **favorite** Ask volunteers to name foods that people normally eat at lunch. Write them on the board. Have children complete the following sentence frame: *My* favorite *food to eat at lunch is* _____. (Possible answers: turkey sandwich, cookies, apple)

8 **surrounded** Assist children as they draw a picture of something they could be *surrounded* by in the city. Have children describe their picture, using this sentence starter: *In the city, I am* surrounded *by* _____. (Possible answers: buildings, people)

High-Frequency Words

Have children look at page 255 in the **Interactive Worktext.** Help them read, spell, and write each high-frequency word. Guide partners to use each word in a sentence. Then read the story aloud with children. Guide partners to work together to reread the story and circle the high-frequency words. (Both, old, You, before, full, down) Listen in and provide assistance reading the high-frequency words, as necessary.

> **ELL ENGLISH LANGUAGE LEARNERS**
>
> Display the **High-Frequency Word Cards** for: *down, you, old, both, full, before.* Write a sentence with each word on the board. Have children echo-read each sentence, and point out the high-frequency word. Then have them use the word in a new sentence.

READ COMPLEX TEXT

15–20 Minutes RL.2.3 RL.2.5 SL.2.1b

Read "Happy New Year!"

- Have children turn to page 256 in the **Interactive Worktext** and read aloud the Essential Question. Point to the picture. Say: *What are the people in the picture doing?* (watching fireworks) *Let's read to find out how kids around the world celebrate holidays differently.* Have children echo-read the title.

- Read the selection together. Note that the weekly vocabulary words are highlighted in yellow. Expand Vocabulary words are highlighted in blue.

- As children read, have them use the "My Notes" section on page 256 to write questions they have. Children can also write words they don't understand or things they want to remember. Model how to use the "My Notes" section. *When I read the first paragraph on page 257, I find out that the narrator celebrated the New Year in two different places. I wonder what the New Year holiday in China is like. I will write a question about this in the "My Notes" section.*

> **ELL ENGLISH LANGUAGE LEARNERS**
>
> As you read together, have children highlight parts of the text they have questions about. After reading, review the questions children have. Then help them locate the answers to their questions in the text.

 Quick Check Can children understand the weekly vocabulary in context? If not, review vocabulary using the **Visual Vocabulary Cards** before teaching Lesson 2.

Can children read high-frequency words in context? If not, review using the Read/Spell/Write routine and the High-Frequency Word Cards.

WEEK 3 LESSON 2

Objectives
- Read realistic fiction
- Understand complex text through close reading
- Recognize and understand compare and contrast
- Respond to the selection using text evidence to support ideas

Scaffolding for **Wonders** McGraw-Hill Reading/Writing Workshop

Materials
Interactive Worktext, pp. 256–261

☞ **Go Digital**
- Interactive eWorktext
- Compare and Contrast Mini-Lesson

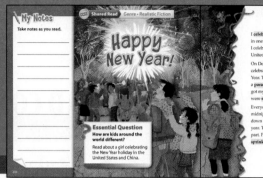

REREAD COMPLEX TEXT

20–25 Minutes   RL.2.3   RL.2.5   L.2.5a

Close Reading: "Happy New Year!"

Reread "Happy New Year!" from **Interactive Worktext** pages 256–259 with children. As you read together, discuss important passages in the text. Guide children to respond to questions using evidence from the text.

🔍 Pages 256–257

Expand Vocabulary Have children reread the first paragraph. Explain that people all over the world celebrate, or honor special days or events, with ceremonies or other activities. Say: *When I reread the first paragraph, I read that the girl* celebrated *the New Year in the United States and China.* Guide children to circle the holiday she *celebrated.* (the New Year)

Connection of Ideas **A C T** Say: *We read that the girl's city had a celebration to welcome the New Year.* Have children reread the page. Ask: *What did the girl mean when she said she was "surrounded by fun"?* Guide children to write the name of something fun. (a parade, a band, face painting)

Expand Vocabulary Have children reread the third paragraph. Explain that when something is *sprinkled,* it is spread around in drops or small pieces. Say: *When I read the last paragraph, I understand that people gathered in a park to celebrate the New Year. I read that fireworks* sprinkled *down from the sky.* Guide children to circle the answer. (fireworks)

🔍 Page 258

Vocabulary Explain to children that a simile uses the words *like* or *as* to compare two different things. Have children reread the first paragraph. Then ask: *When the author says "The plane is like a whale in the sky," what does the author mean?* (A whale is similar to a plane because they are both very large.)

Compare and Contrast Explain to children that they can compare and contrast the characters and events in a story. Say: *To compare, look for ways that two or more characters or events are alike. To contrast, look for two or more ways that things are different.* Reread the first paragraph aloud. Say: *Draw a box around the sentence that compares how long the New Year celebrations last in China and in the United States.* Guide children to draw a box around the sentence that tells. (It lasts for fifteen days, not just one night.)

Expand Vocabulary Have children reread the second paragraph. Say: *People want to know more about a person or a thing that is* interesting. *What does the girl think is* interesting? Guide children to circle the words that tell. (Chinese customs) Ask: *What custom is interesting to the girl?* (having dumplings for dinner to celebrate the New Year)

Compare and Contrast Say: *Let's look for ways that an event in China was the same as an event in the United States.* Read the second paragraph aloud. Ask: *Which New Year's event in China was the same as New Year's events in the United States?* Guide children to circle their answers. (parade/fireworks.)

Page 259

Connection of Ideas Read the first two paragraphs aloud. Say: *The narrator is explaining customs that take place during the Chinese New Year celebration. Now look at the picture.* Ask: *What event is shown the picture?* Guide children to draw a box around their answer in the text. (Chinese lion dance.)

Compare and Contrast Say: *When showing a comparison, an author may use clue words such as* both *and* also *to show how two or more characters and events are similar. When we read, we can look for these clue words to help signal how the characters and events are alike.* Read the third paragraph aloud. Ask: *How are the celebrations alike?* Guide children to draw a box around the sentence that tells. (They were both family celebrations to welcome the New Year!)

Expand Vocabulary Have children reread the third paragraph. Explain that the word *welcome* means to greet in a friendly way. Ask: *What does the girl welcome?* Guide children to write the answer. (the New Year)

RESPOND TO READING

10–20 Minutes   SL.2.1a   RL.2.3

Respond to "Happy New Year!"

Read aloud the questions about "Happy New Year!" on page 260 of the **Interactive Worktext**. Then read aloud the "Discussion Starter" for each of the questions. Guide children to work with a partner to answer the questions orally using the "Discussion Starters." Have children find text evidence to support their answers. Ask children to write the page number(s) on which they found the text evidence for each question.

1. *How is the New Year celebration in China different from the celebration in the United States?* (Possible answers: I read that the celebration in China lasts for 15 days. One custom in China is to eat dumplings. Text Evidence: pp. 258)

2. *How do children in China dress during the New Year celebration?* (Children in China wear red. This is because it brings good luck. Text Evidence: p. 258)

3. *What events take place during the Chinese New Year celebration?* (Possible answers: Chinese children watch a parade with firecrackers. On the last day they see a Lantern Festival. Text Evidence: pp. 258, 259)

After children discuss the questions on page 260, have them use the sentence starters to answer the question on page 261. Circulate and provide guidance.

 Quick Check Do children understand vocabulary in context? If not, review and reteach using the instruction on page 214.

Can children identify compare and contrast? If not, review and reteach using the instruction on page 214 and assign the Unit 4 Week 3 digital mini-lesson.

Can children write a response to "Happy New Year!" If not, review the sentence starters and prompt children to respond orally. Help them write their answers.

WEEK 3 LESSON 3

Objectives
- Understand and use new vocabulary words
- Read realistic fiction
- Recognize and understand compare and contrast
- Understand complex text through close reading

Materials
- "Sharing Cultures" Apprentice Leveled Reader: pp. 2–7
- Compare and Contrast Graphic Organizer

☞ **Go Digital**
- Apprentice Leveled Reader eBook
- Downloadable Graphic Organizer
- Compare and Contrast Mini-Lesson

Scaffolding for **Wonders** Approaching Leveled Reader

BEFORE READING

10–15 Minutes   SL.2.1a   SL.2.6   L.2.5a   L.2.6   (CCSS)

Introduce "Sharing Cultures"

- Read the Essential Question on the title page of "Sharing Cultures" **Apprentice Leveled Reader:** *How are kids around the world different?* Say: *We will read about customs from around the world. In this story, a teacher and her class will share customs that come from different countries.*

- Read the title aloud and point to the illustration. Ask: *What is the class doing?* (listening to their teacher) Ask: *Is this text fiction or nonfiction?* (fiction) *This story shows an illustration of the teacher wearing a sari. Let's read to find out what a sari is and why she is wearing it.*

Expand Vocabulary

Display each word below. Say the words and have children repeat them. Then use the Define/Example/Ask routine to introduce each word.

① suppose (page 7)

Define: to think something will happen

Example: *I suppose* if I could go anywhere, I would go to Africa.

Ask: *Suppose* it will rain, do you think it will rain or do you know for sure?

② wish (page 7)

Define: to hope for, to want

Example: I *wish* my best friend lived next door.

Ask: What would you *wish* for?

DURING READING

20–25 Minutes   RL. 2.1   RL.2.3   RL.2.5   RL.2.7   L.2.4a   (CCSS)

Close Reading

🔍 **Pages 2–3**

Prior Knowledge Ⓐ Ⓒ Ⓣ Remind children that *customs* are ways of acting or events that a group of people has done over and over again. *In this selection, we will read about customs from different countries around the world that people have brought with them when they came to the United States. Mrs. Gupta and her family are from the country of India. India is the seventh largest country in the world. It is located in Southeast Asia.* On a map, point out the location of India and the location of the United States. Ask: *Is India part of the United States?* (No, India is a country.) Keep the map out and point to each new location as you read the rest of the story.

Connection of Ideas Ⓐ Ⓒ Ⓣ Read pages 2 and 3 with children. Say: *We read that Mrs. Gupta's class is surprised by what she is wearing.* Point to the illustration on page 2 and ask: *What is Mrs. Gupta wearing?* (a sari) Ask: *Why might her class be surprised that she is wearing a sari?* (They have never seen her wear a sari before.) Ask: *Why is Mrs. Gupta wearing a sari?* (Wearing a sari is one custom she wants to share with her class.) Point out that she tells the class they will be learning about each other's customs. Ask: *What do you think might happen in the rest of the book?* (Children will share their customs.)

Vocabulary Ask: *What is the rice pancake called?* (dosa) *How do you know?* (Look at the label) Point out that many of the customs in this book are named in labels.

STOP AND CHECK Read the question in the Stop and Check box on page 3. (Many Indian women wear saris. Indians also eat rice cakes.)

Pages 4–5

Organization (A)(C)(T) Remind children that *events* are the main things that happen in a story. Say: *Authors may organize a story using sequence, or the order in which the events happen. Words such as* first, next, then, the next day *and* last *can help show a story's sequence.* Read page 4 with children. Ask: *In the first sentence, I see the words* the next day. *What does this tell you about how the children will share customs in class?* (The teacher shared a custom yesterday. The class starts sharing the day after.)

Connection of Ideas (A)(C)(T) Read the last paragraph on page 5. Have children point to Alex. Ask: *What is Alex feeling?* (He seems worried that he doesn't have anything cool to share.) Have children find Alex on pages 2 and 3. Say: *Alex seems to be an important character. Lets pay attention to see if he finds something to share.*

Compare and Contrast Explain to children that they can compare and contrast the characters and events in a story. Say: *To compare, look for ways that two or more characters or events are alike. To contrast, look for ways that two or more characters and events are different.* Read page 5 with children. Ask: *How are Mrs. Gupta and Darel alike?* (They each share a custom from their country.) *How are Mrs. Gupta and Darel different?* (Mrs. Gupta is the teacher. She shares customs from India. Darel is a student. He shares a custom from Australia.) Model filling out the Compare and Contrast Chart with children.

Pages 6–7

Genre (A)(C)(T) Remind children that fiction has made-up characters, settings, and events. Ask: *Are the characters in this story real or made up? How can you tell?* (They are made-up characters. They speak in dialogue and have made-up names.) Point out that sometimes fiction also contains real information like you might find in nonfiction. This can be confusing. *Ask: What in this story is real? What have you learned so far?* (The customs we are learning about are real. Women in India really do wear saris. People in Australia have big instruments called didgeridoos.) Have children look for more information about the real world.

Key Details Read page 6 with children. Remind them that key details in the words and pictures give a reader more information. Ask: *What custom from Japan is Akita sharing with the class?* (giving dolls at New Year) Point to the picture and say: *What does this picture show us?* (what the doll looks like) Read the label and ask: *What do you think a* daruma *is?* (the kind of doll Akita gives on New Year)

Compare and Contrast Read page 7 with children. Say: *We know that Akita is sharing a custom from Japan. This custom is to give dolls at New Year. New Year is a holiday. Think back. Do the customs that we read about from India and Australia happen at a special time or holiday?* (no) Help children add the country, holiday, and custom to their Compare and Contrast charts.

Connection of Ideas (A)(C)(T) Reread the last line on page 7. Ask: *Who is Alex?* (He is the boy on page 5 who was worried he wouldn't have something fun to share.) *How do you think Alex is feeling now?* (He is probably less worried now that he has an idea.)

STOP AND CHECK Read the question in the Stop and Check box on page 7. (In Australia, people play an instrument called a didgeridoo. In Japan people give dolls called daruma at New Year.)

Have partners review their Compare and Contrast charts for pages 2–7 and discuss what they have learned.

✅ *Quick Check* **Do children understand weekly vocabulary in context? If not, review and reteach using the instruction on page 214.**

Can children compare and contrast characters and events? If not, review and reteach using the instruction on page 214 and assign Unit 4 Week 3 digital mini-lesson.

Objectives
• Understand and use new vocabulary words
• Read realistic fiction
• Recognize and understand compare and contrast
• Understand complex text through close reading

Sharing Cultures
by Christopher Herrera
illustrated by Laura Jacobsen

Materials
• "Sharing Cultures" Apprentice Leveled Reader: pp. 8–20
• Compare and Contrast Graphic Organizer

☞ **Go** Digital
• Apprentice Leveled Reader eBook
• Downloadable Graphic Organizer
• Compare and Contrast Mini-Lesson

Scaffolding for **Wonders** Approaching Leveled Reader

BEFORE READING

5–10 Minutes   SL.2.1a SL.2.6 L.2.5a L.2.6 CCSS

Expand Vocabulary

Display each word below. Say the words and have children repeat them. Then use the Define/Example/Ask routine to introduce each word.

❶ brightly (page 10)

Define: in a way that gives a lot of light

Example: The fire burned *brightly* after we added more wood.

Ask: What shines *brightly* in the daytime sky?

❷ crowd (page 11)

Define: a lot of people gathered together

Example: Grace could not find her friend in the *crowd*.

Ask: Where might you see a large *crowd* of people?

❸ mermaid (page 12)

Define: a fantasy sea creature that has a woman's head and body and a fish's tail.

Example: The teacher read a story about a *mermaid* who lived in the sea.

Ask: What would someone in a *mermaid* costume wear?

❹ order (page 9)

Define: when things are in the right place

Example: Quinn put his toys in *order* after playing with them.

Ask: Do you put books in *order* by subject or author?

DURING READING

15–20 Minutes   RL.2.1 RL.2.5 RL.2.7 L.2.6 CCSS

Close Reading

🔍 **Pages 8–9**

Key Detail Ask: *What kind of custom does Awo share with the class?* (a game) *Let's look at the picture to find out more information about Awo's game. What does Awo's game look like?* (It has two sides. Each side has holes in it.) Read the label. *What do you think* Oware *is?* (Oware is the name of the game.)

Compare and Contrast Ask: *How is the custom Awo shares like Akita's custom.* (Both are types of games or toys.) *How are these customs different from Miss Gupta's?* (She shared things that you wear or eat, not what you can play with.) Have children add this to their Compare and Contrast charts.

🔍 **Page 10–11**

Connection of Ideas Ⓐ Ⓒ Ⓣ Read page 10 with children and point to the picture. Ask: *Where is this picture taking place?* (in Russia) *How is that different from the other pictures?* (they took place in the classroom) *Why is this picture different?* (Anton is telling about the sledding. He didn't bring in something to show.)

Compare and Contrast Remind children that when they look for contrasts, they look for the way things are not alike. Say: *Think back to the custom Awo shares with the class. How are the customs that Awo and Anton share with the class different?* (Awo shows the class a game from Ghana. Anton shows the class a dance from Russia.)

STOP AND CHECK Read the question in the Stop and Check box on page 11. (In Ghana, people play a game with a board and stones called Oware. In Russia, children go sledding and dancing.)

Pages 12–13

Sentence Structure A C T Read the page 13 with children. Explain that instead of repeating a character's name, writers sometimes use words such as *she* and *he* to make their writing smoother. Reread the page to children and say: *The author uses the word* she *instead of repeating which character's name?* (Benita)

Vocabulary Have children reread page 12. Point out the word *Carnival*. Explain that it is a holiday in Brazil. Ask: How have you heard the word *carnival* used? (a festival or celebration of some kind) Point out that while it does not mean an official holiday in our country, the words and meanings are connected.

Pages 14–15

Connection of Ideas A C T Ask: *When did Alex get his idea for what he would share?* (when Akita shared her New Years dolls) *What do you think gave him the idea then?* (his storyteller is also a doll)

Purpose A C T Remind children that authors can have many different reasons for writing a story. Often with fiction the reason is to tell a story about what characters do and how they learn and grow. Ask: *What do you think the characters learned in this story?* (to respect each other's customs) Point out that sometimes fiction stories are also meant to tell information. Ask: *What real information did you learn from reading this story?* (Answers will vary about different customs in the book.)

STOP AND CHECK Read the question in the Stop and Check box on page 15. (Akita and Alex both have a custom that uses a doll. Akita's custom comes from Japan, where people give dolls at New Year. Alex's storyteller doll is a Native American custom.)

AFTER READING

10–15 Minutes   RL.2.3   RL.2.5   RL.2.7   L.2.4a   W.2.8

Respond to Reading

Compare Texts Ask children to compare "Happy New Year!" and "Sharing Cultures." Ask: *How do the authors of the selections present information about customs from around the world?*

Summarize Have children turn to page 16 and summarize the selection. Summaries should compare and contrast details they have learned about people and customs from around the world.

Text Evidence

Have partners work together to answer questions on page 16. Remind children to use their Compare and Contrast charts.

Compare and Contrast (Answers will vary but should note that all of the customs tell something about the children's families and their cultures.)

Vocabulary (The text reads, "Stories are how we pass on our customs." *Pass* means "to share in this case.")

Write About Reading (Answers should include details of how two customs are the same and different.)

Independent Reading

Encourage children to read the paired selection "Music Around the World" on pages 17–19. Have them summarize the selection and compare it to "Sharing Cultures." Have them work with a partner to answer the "Make Connections" questions on page 19.

 Quick Check Do children know how to compare and contrast characters and events? If not, review and reteach using the instruction on page 214 and assign the Unit 4 Week 3 digital mini-lesson.

Can children respond to the selection using text evidence? If not, provide sentence frames to help them organize their ideas.

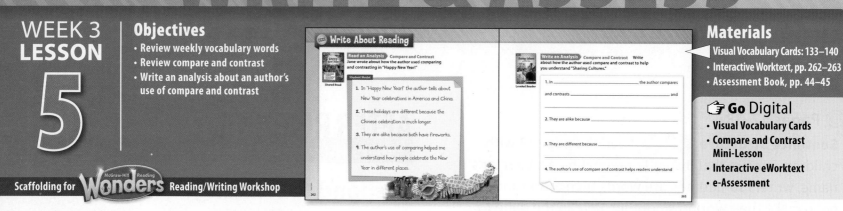

WEEK 3 LESSON 5

Objectives
- Review weekly vocabulary words
- Review compare and contrast
- Write an analysis about an author's use of compare and contrast

Materials
- Visual Vocabulary Cards: 133–140
- Interactive Worktext, pp. 262–263
- Assessment Book, pp. 44–45

Go Digital
- Visual Vocabulary Cards
- Compare and Contrast Mini-Lesson
- Interactive eWorktext
- e-Assessment

Scaffolding for **Wonders** Reading/Writing Workshop

REVIEW AND RETEACH

5–10 Minutes   RL.2.3   L.2.4a

Weekly Vocabulary

Display one **Visual Vocabulary Card** at a time and guide children to use the vocabulary word in a sentence. If children have difficulty creating a sentence, have them find the word in "Happy New Year!" or "Sharing Cultures" and use context clues to define the vocabulary word.

Comprehension: Compare and Contrast

I Do   Write and say: *Will and Fred both go to music camp. They play different instruments. Will plays guitar, but Fred plays piano. The boys have the same dream. They want to be in a band.* Say: *You can compare the characters and events in a story. To compare two things, think about how they are alike. What are two ways the boys are alike?* Circle: "Will and Fred both go to music camp." Circle: "The boys have the same dream." *The clue words* both *and* same *are signals that the writer is comparing what they both want to do.*

We Do   Say: *To contrast two things, think about how they are different.* Ask: *How are the the boys in the story different?* (They play different instruments.) *How can you tell?* (The clue word *different* is a signal word in the second sentence.) Have children look for another clue word that shows a constrast. (but)

You Do   Display: *Anna and Meg went on a trip. They stayed for a week. Anna wanted to swim, but Meg wanted to hike.* Guide one partner to tell if the characters and events are being compared or contrasted. Have them point out the clue words. Have partners switch and discuss their answers.

WRITE ABOUT READING

25–35 Minutes   W.2.3   W.2.8   W.4.9

Read an Analysis

- Guide children to look back at "Happy New Year!" in the **Interactive Worktext**. Have volunteers review the details about the author's use of compare and contrast they marked on page 257 and summarize the text. Repeat with pages 258–259. *How did the author use compare and contrast?*

- Read aloud the directions on page 262. Read aloud the student model. *This student's work is not a summary. It is an analysis, or description, of how the author used compare and contrast in "Happy New Year!"*

- *When you write an analysis, you should include key details from the text that tell about the story. Read Jane's first sentence. Circle the details.* (New Year celebrations in America and China) *What part of the story do details come from?* (the beginning)

- *Read the second sentence and third sentences. Ask: How do these comparisons help you understand the text?* (It helps me understand how people celebrate the New Year in different ways.) *What part of the story do details come from?* (the middle)

- Read the last sentence that Jane wrote. *Why is this sentence a good ending?* (It tells how the author used compare and contrast to help readers understand the text.)

✏️ Analytical Writing **Write an Analysis**

Guided Writing Read the writing prompt on page 263 together. Guide children to review their Compare and Contrasts charts for "Sharing Cultures." Have children use their charts to complete the sentence starters. Children can also write the analysis using another selection previously read this week.

Peer Conference Guide children to read their analysis to a partner. Listeners should summarize the details that support the beginning, middle, and ending sentences. They should discuss any sentences that are unclear.

Teacher Conference Check children's writing for complete sentences and whether they included details from the story. Review the last sentence and ask: *Did the author explain how comparing and contrasting helps readers understand the story?* If necessary, have the child revise their sentences by thinking about the author's use of compare and contrast.

Level Up

▲ Apprentice Leveled Reader

▲ Approaching Leveled Reader

▲ Interactive Worktext

▲ Reading/Writing Workshop

IF children read the Apprentice Level Reader and the **Interactive Worktext** Shared Read fluently and answer the Respond to Reading questions

THEN read together the Approaching Level Reader main selection and the **Reading/Writing Workshop** Shared Read from *Reading Wonders*. Have children take notes as they read, using self-stick notes. Then ask and answer questions about their notes.

Writing Rubric

	4	3	2	1
Text Evidence	Includes three or more details from the text	Includes two or more details from the text	Includes only one detail from the text	No text evidence is cited
Writing Style	Writes in complete sentences. Uses correct spelling and grammar	Uses complete sentences. Writing has spelling and grammar errors	Few complete sentences. There are many spelling and grammar errors	Writing is not accurate or in complete sentences

ASSESSMENT

Weekly Assessment

Have children complete the Weekly Assessment using **Assessment** book pages 44–45.

▶ **Mid-Unit Assessment,** pages 96 – 103

▶ **Fluency Assessment,** pages 250 – 265

CCSS TESTED SKILLS

✔ COMPREHENSION	✔ VOCABULARY:
• Compare and Contrast RI.2.3, RI.2.9	• Context Clues L.2.4
• Cause and Effect RI.2.3	
• Compare and Contrast RL.2.3, RL.2.9	

Using Assessment and Writing Scores

⟳ RETEACH	IF ...	THEN ...
COMPREHENSION	Students answer 0–5 multiple-choice items correctly ...	... reteach tested skills using instruction on pages 364–375.
VOCABULARY	Students answer 0–2 multiple-choice items correctly ...	... reteach tested skills using instruction on page 364.
WRITING	Students score mostly 1–2 on weekly writing rubrics throughout the unit ...	... reteach writing using instruction on pages 376–377.

Fluency Assessment

Conduct assessments individually using the differentiated fluency passages in Assessment. Students' expected fluency goal for this Unit is 62–82 WCPM with an accuracy rate of 95% or higher.

Weeks 4 and 5

Monitor students progress on the following to inform how to adjust instruction for the remainder of the unit.

ADJUST INSTRUCTION	
ACCESS COMPLEX TEXT	If students need more support for accessing complex text, provide additional modeling of prompts in Lesson 2 of Week 4, pages 220–221, and Week 5, pages 230–231. After you model how to identify the text evidence, guide students to find text evidence in Lessons 3 and 4, in Week 4, pages 222–225, and Week 5, pages 232–235.
FLUENCY	For those students who need more support with Fluency, focus on the Fluency lessons in the Foundational Skills Kit.
WRITING	If students need more support incorporating text evidence in their writing, conduct the Write About Reading activities in Lesson 4 and 5 as group writing activities.
FOUNDATIONAL SKILLS	Review students' individualized progress in *Reading Wonders* Adaptive Learning to determine which foundational skills to incorporate into your lessons for the remainder of the unit.

WEEK 4 LESSON 1

Objectives
- Develop oral language
- Build background about folktales about nature
- Understand and use weekly vocabulary
- Read a folktale/drama

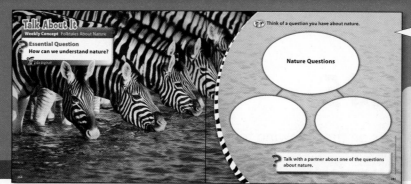

Materials
- Interactive Worktext, pp. 264–271
- Visual Vocabulary Cards: 141–148
- High-Frequency Word Cards

☞ **Go** Digital
- Interactive eWorktext
- Visual Vocabulary Cards

Scaffolding for **Wonders** McGraw-Hill Reading **Reading/Writing Workshop**

REVIEW VOCABULARY

5–10 Minutes   SL.2.1b   SL.2.4

Talk About It

Essential Question Read aloud the Essential Question on page 264 of the **Interactive Worktext:** *How can we understand nature?* Explain that for years people have been trying to explain nature through stories. Say: *People have written stories such as: How did the sun and moon get into the sky? How did the leopard get his spots? Why is the sky blue?* Explain that people wanted answers to these questions so they wrote folktales to explain nature.

- Discuss the photograph on page 264. Ask: *What do you see in the picture?* (A bunch of zebras drinking from a river.) *What do you notice about the zebras?* (Possible answers: They have black and white stripes. They all look alike.)

I Do Say: *I am going to look at the photo and think of a question I have about nature. When I look at the zebras, I wonder why they have stripes. I will write this question on the web on page 265.*

We Do Say: *Let's think about other questions we may have about zebras or other animals or plants in nature.* Guide children to think about a question about nature. Then have children choose one of these questions to add to their web.

You Do Guide partners to work together to talk about questions they have about nature. If they have difficulty, provide these topics to think about: wild animals, pets, trees, the daytime and nighttime skies, and so on. Have children use the words from the web to start their sentences: *My question about nature is _____.*

REVIEW VOCABULARY

10–15 Minutes   L.2.4a   L.2.5b   RF.2.3

Review Weekly Vocabulary Words

- Use the **Visual Vocabulary Cards** to review the weekly vocabulary.

- Read together the directions on page 266 of the **Interactive Worktext.** Then complete the activity.

1 **plenty** Point out that the cafeteria has *plenty* of food to serve everyone. Explain that when you have *plenty* of something, you have a lot of it. Then have children look around the classroom. Ask children: *What do we have* plenty *of _____?* Have children respond: *We have* plenty *of _____.* (Possible answers: pens, paper, chalk, desks)

2 **wisdom** Ask children to think about a time when people taught them things or shared their *wisdom.* Have them describe what each person did. Have children use this sentence frame: *_____ helped me with their* wisdom. (Possible answers: grandparent, teacher, parent) Have children explain what they learned from each person.

3 **similarities** Point out to children the *similarities* between a pad of paper and the board. Point out the *similarities* between your desk and the children's desks. Ask volunteers to point out the *similarities* between pens and markers. (Possible answers: Both are used to write. Both come in many colors.)

4 **victory** Share a *victory* you remember. Then give children this oral sentence starter: *I'd like to have a* victory *in _____.* (Possible answers: soccer, chess) Then have a volunteer demonstrate the way people act when they win a *victory* in a game.

⑤ holler Invite children to brainstorm a time that they had to *holler* to get someone's attention. Have children chorally read the sentence with you. Ask volunteers to name another word that will work in place of *holler* in the same sentence. (<u>Possible answers</u>: yell, shout)

⑥ ashamed Write the word *ashamed* on the board. Ask: *What's another word for* ashamed? (embarrassed) What word means the opposite of *ashamed*? (proud) Then have children use this oral sentence starter: *I'd be* ashamed *of* _____. (<u>Possible answers</u>: not telling the truth, breaking something that isn't yours)

⑦ boast Invite volunteers to suggest things that they are good at. For this partner activity, give children the following sentence starter: *I don't mean to* boast*, but I* _____. (<u>Possible answers</u>: can swim very fast, can do a cartwheel)

⑧ dash Guide children to brainstorm when they might have to *dash* somewhere. Then have children describe the picture they drew, using this oral sentence starter: *This is how I look when I* dash _____. (<u>Possible answers</u>: across the finish line, out of the rain)

High-Frequency Words

Have children look at page 267 in the **Interactive Worktext**. Help them read, spell, and write each high-frequency word. Guide partners to use each word in a sentence. Then read the story aloud with children. Guide partners to work together to reread the story and circle the high-frequency words. (start, on, me, make, No, come) Listen in and provide assistance reading the high-frequency words, as necessary.

> **ELL ENGLISH LANGUAGE LEARNERS**
>
> Display the **High-Frequency Word Cards** for: *no, on, me, come, make, start*. Write a sentence with each word on the board. Have children echo-read each sentence, and point out the high-frequency word. Then ask them to use the word in a sentence.

READ COMPLEX TEXT

15–20 Minutes   RL.2.2   RL.2.6   SL.2.1b CCSS

Read "Why the Sun and Moon Live in the Sky"

- Have children turn to page 268 in the **Interactive Worktext** and read the Essential Question aloud. Read the title with children. Say: *What will this story explain to us about nature?* (It will explain why the sun and the moon live in the sky.) Point to the picture on page 268. Ask: *Is this a nonfiction story about the real sun and moon?* (no) *This is a play based on a folktale, and Sun and Moon are characters. Let's read about how Sun and Moon ended up in the sky.*

- Read the story together. Note that the weekly vocabulary words are highlighted in yellow. Expand Vocabulary words are highlighted in blue.

- As children read, have them use the "My Notes" section on page 268 to write questions they have. Children can also write words they don't understand or things they want to remember. Model how to use the "My Notes" section. Say: *When I read the first few lines on page 269, I wonder what a* narrator *is. I will write a question about the* it *in the "My Notes" section.*

> **ELL ENGLISH LANGUAGE LEARNERS**
>
> As you read together, have children highlight parts of the text they have questions about. After reading, review the questions children have. Then help them locate the answers to their questions in the text.

 Quick Check Can children understand the weekly vocabulary words in context? If not, review vocabulary using the **Visual Vocabulary Cards** before teaching Lesson 2.

Can children read high-frequency words in context? If not, review using the Read/Spell/Write routine and the High-Frequency Word Cards.

WEEK 4
LESSON

2

Objectives
- Read a folktale/drama
- Understand complex text through close reading
- Recognize and understand theme
- Respond to the selection using text evidence to support ideas

Materials
Interactive Worktext,
pp. 268–273

👉 **Go** Digital
- Interactive eWorktext
- Theme Mini-Lesson

Scaffolding for **Wonders** Reading/Writing Workshop

REREAD COMPLEX TEXT

20–25 Minutes   RL.2.2   RL.2.6   L.2.4a   **CCSS**

Close Reading: "Why the Sun and Moon Live in the Sky"

Reread "Why the Sun and Moon Live in the Sky" from **Interactive Worktext** pages 268–271 with children. As you read together, discuss important passages in the text. Guide children to respond to questions using evidence from the text.

 Pages 268–269

Genre Ⓐ**C**Ⓣ   Point to the top of page 268 where the genre is displayed. Ask: *What is the genre of this selection?* (drama) *A drama is a play. A play is a story that is intended to be performed. An actor plays each character and the story is acted out on stage.* Now turn to page 269 and read the first paragraph aloud. Say: *Sometimes plays are based on other works. Some plays are based on books or even movies. What is this play based on?* (an African folktale) Guide children to underline the answer.

Prior Knowledge Ⓐ**C**Ⓣ   Read the list of characters on page 269. Children may not be familiar with what a narrator in a play is. Point to the word *Narrator*. Say: *The narrator is a character that does not take part in the action. Instead, the narrator tells the audience about the characters and events in the play.* Ask: *In the second paragraph, what does the narrator tell us about Sun, Moon, and Water?* (That they used to live on Earth.)

Expand Vocabulary Reread Sun's first line. Point out the word *visit* to children and write the word on the board. Say: *To* visit *means to go and see someone. Who will Sun visit?* (Water) Model circling the name of the character. Guide children to circle the name.

Theme Remind children that the theme of a story or play is the main message the author wants the reader to know. Say: *We can find the theme by thinking about what the characters do and say.* Reread Sun's lines. Ask: *Who is Sun talking about?* (Water) *How does Sun feel about Water?* (Water is a good friend) Guide children to write their answer. Say: *We can use this answer to help us find the theme at the end of the story.*

 Page 270

Genre Ⓐ**C**Ⓣ   Point out the sentences in parentheses at the top of the page. Explain to children that these are called *stage directions*. Say: *Stage directions tell what the characters in a play are doing.* Reread the stage directions with children. Ask: *What is the first thing that Sun does, according to the stage directions?* (Sun visits Water) Model underlining the first stage direction. Ask: *What is the second thing Sun does?* (Sun runs home.). Guide children to underline the second stage direction.

Theme Remind children that they should pay attention to what the characters do and say, in order to find the theme. Reread the narrator's lines with children. Ask: *What did Sun and Moon do for their friend Water?* Guide children to draw a box around the words that give them the answer. (Sun and Moon made their home larger.) *What does this tell you about Sun and Moon's friendship with Water?* (Sun and Moon care about Water a lot.)

Expand Vocabulary Point to the word *raised*. Chorally read the word with children. Say: *If you* raised *something, you moved it to a higher spot. What do Sun and Moon* raise? (the roof of their home) Guide children to circle the words that give them the answer. (They raised the roof higher.)

Page 271

Theme Have children reread the page. Remind children to look for things the characters do and say that give a clue to the theme. Ask: *What do Sun and Moon do for their friend Water?* (They fly into the sky to make room for Water.) Instruct children to draw a box around the words that tell them what Sun and Moon do. (Sun and Moon flew to the sky.)

Theme Tell children to go back and read their clues about the theme. Then have them think about what the clues have in common. Ask: *What does the author want you to understand about friendship?* Guide children to write their answer. (Possible answer: Friends sometimes do difficult things for each other.)

Genre Remind children that this play is a retelling of a folktale. Say: *A folktale is a story that is based on the customs or traditions of a group of people. Folktales are told orally and handed down from one generation to another.* Ask: *After reading the story, what do you think was the tradition of the people who originally told this story?* (Possible answer: They wanted to answer questions about nature.)

RESPOND TO READING

10–20 Minutes   **SL.2.1a RL.2.2 RL.2.6** (CCSS)

Respond to "Why the Sun and the Moon Live in the Sky"

Read aloud the questions on page 272 of the **Interactive Worktext**. Then read aloud the "Discussion Starter" for each of the questions. Guide children to work with a partner to answer the questions orally using the "Discussion Starters." Have children find text evidence to support their answers and write the page number(s) on which they found the text evidence for each question.

1. *What happens in the beginning of the play?* (Possible answers: Sun and Moon want to invite their friend Water to their house. Water doesn't visit because their house is too small. Text Evidence: p. 270)

2. *What do Sun and Moon do for their friend Water?* (Possible answers: Sun and Moon decide to make their house bigger. The raise the roof and add rooms. Text Evidence: p. 270)

3. *What happens when Water arrives?* (Possible answers: Water carries many fish, frogs and crabs. The water rises higher and higher. Sun and Moon fly to the sky. Text Evidence: p. 271)

After children discuss the questions on page 272, have them use the sentence starters to answer the question on page 273. Circulate and provide guidance.

 Quick Check Do children understand vocabulary in context? If not, review and reteach using the instruction on page 226.

Can children identify theme? If not, review and reteach using the instruction on page 226 and assign the Unit 4 Week 4 digital mini-lesson.

Can children write a response to "Why the Sun and Moon Live in the Sky"? If not, review the sentence starters and prompt children to respond orally. Help them write their sentences.

Objectives
- Understand and use new vocabulary words
- Read a folktale/drama
- Recognize and understand theme
- Understand complex text through close reading

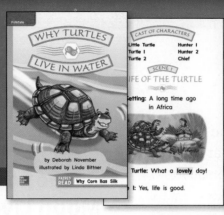

Materials
"Why Turtles Live in Water" Apprentice Leveled Reader: pp. 2–7
- Theme Graphic Organizer

☞ **Go Digital**
- Apprentice Leveled Reader eBook
- Downloadable Graphic Organizer
- Theme Mini-Lesson

Scaffolding for **Wonders** Approaching Leveled Reader

BEFORE READING

10–15 Minutes   SL.2.1a   SL.2.6   L.2.5   L.2.6   (ccss)

Introduce "Why Turtles Live in Water"

- Read the Essential Question on the title page of "Why Turtles Live in Water" **Apprentice Leveled Reader:** *How can we understand nature? We will read a drama about why turtles live in the water.*

- Read the title aloud. Point to the pictures and diagrams. Ask: *Who are the main characters in this story?* (turtles and monkeys) *This play tells the story of why turtles came to live in water.*

Expand Vocabulary

Display each word below. Say the words and have children repeat them. Then use the Define/Example/Ask routine to introduce each word.

1 **hunters** (page 4)

Define: people who look for wild animals to kill.

Example: The *hunters* waited for the rabbit to come out of its hole.

Ask: What do *hunters* do with the animals they get?

2 **hurry** (page 4)

Define: to go fast

Example: The boy will *hurry* and run to the bus stop.

Ask: What will you *hurry* to do today?

3 **lovely** (page 2)

Define: pretty or pleasing

Example: The beautiful sunset made the sky look *lovely*.

Ask: What have you seen that is *lovely*?

DURING READING

20–25 Minutes   RL.2.1   RL.2.2   RL.2.7   L.2.5   L.2.6   (ccss)

Close Reading

🔍 **Pages 2–3**

Genre Ask: *How does a play differ from a story?* (A play is meant to be acted out.) Review the features of a play. Point to the "Cast of Characters" heading at the top of page 2. Say: *This section lists the characters in the play. Another word for the characters is the* cast. *What characters are in the* cast *of this play?* (Little Turtle, Turtle 1, Turtle 2, Hunter 1, Hunter 2, and Chief)

Genre 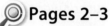 Continue to point out features of a play. Point to the "Scene 1" heading on page 2. Say: *Plays are divided into scenes. In each scene, a different part of the story will take place.* Ask: *What is the title of this scene?* (Life of the Turtle) Say: *The* setting *of a scene is where and when the scene takes place. Usually, each scene has a different setting.* Reread the page with children. Ask: *When does Scene 1 take place?* (a long time ago) Remind children that the names in bold tell who is speaking.

Vocabulary Read the lines at the bottom of page 2 with children. Ask: *What does Little Turtle think is lovely?* (the day) *What would a lovely day be like?* (probably sunny and warm) *How can you tell this is true from the pictures?* (The grass is green. It looks sunny.)

Key Details Read page 3 with children. Ask: *What do the turtles feel about their lives?* (They are very happy.) *How can you tell?* Point to the text evidence. (They say life is good, they play every day, and they have plenty to eat.)

STOP AND CHECK Read the question in the Stop and Check box on page 3. (They get to play in the grass and they always have plenty to eat.)

Pages 4–5

Vocabulary Read page 4 with children. Ask: *What are hunters?* (people who want to capture or kill animals) *Why are the turtles running from them?* (so they won't get captured)

Theme Remind children that the theme is the main message the author wants the reader to know. Say: *To find the theme, we will look at what the characters do and say. What does Turtle 2 tell Little Turtle to do on page 4?* (run *or* hurry) *Are turtles usually slow or fast?* (slow) *Will Little Turtle be able to get away from the hunters using his speed?* (no) If children have difficulty answering this last question, tell them to look at the picture on page 5 for clues. Guide children to record this information on their Theme charts.

Genre **ACT** Point to the top of page 5. Read the banner that says "Scene 2." Ask children what this means. (that the setting or action changes) Read the scene title, "Capture", together. Ask: *Where does this scene take place?* (a path in the jungle) *How can you tell?* (It comes after the word "setting," which means where something takes place.)

Vocabulary Point to the word *path*. Ask: *What is a path?* (a small road that has been cleared in the woods) *How can you tell what this word means by looking at the words and pictures.* (The picture shows a clearing, and the words say it is in the jungle.)

Genre **ACT** Remind children that although this story is in the form of a play, it is based on a folktale. Explain that folktales often have animals as the main characters. Tell children to look at the picture on page 5. Ask: *What kind of animals are the hunters in the story?* (monkeys)

Connection on Ideas **ACT** Ask: *Who was captured on this page?* (Little Turtle) *Why did he get captured and not his friends?* (He probably didn't run fast enough. They were ahead of him.)

STOP AND CHECK Read the question in the Stop and Check box on page 4. (Hunters are coming, and he's not safe.)

Pages 6–7

Theme Read page 6 with children. Remind children that they still need to look for clues about the theme by noticing what the characters say and do. Ask: *What does Little Turtle say about the hunters?* (They are fast.) *How does Little Turtle feel about being caught? Point to the text evidence.* (He is sad.) Guide children to record their answers on their Theme charts.

Connection of Ideas **ACT** Have children read page 7. Point to the illustration and say: *Authors include illustrations to help tell the story.* Point to the village at the end of the road in the illustration. Ask: *What do you see at the end of the road?* (a village, a group of houses or huts) *By including this picture, what does the author want the reader to think happens next?* (The hunters will take Little Turtle to the village.)

STOP AND CHECK Read the question in the Stop and Check box on page 7. (Two hunters from a village caught Little Turtle.)

Have partners review their Theme charts for pages 2–7 and discuss what they have learned.

Quick Check Do children understand weekly vocabulary in context? If not, review and reteach using the instruction on page 226.

Can children identify theme? If not, review and reteach using the instruction on page 226 and assign the Unit 4 Week 4 digital mini-lesson.

Objectives
- Understand and use new vocabulary words
- Read a folktale/drama
- Recognize and understand drama
- Understand complex text through close reading

Materials
- "Why Turtles Live in Water" Apprentice Leveled Reader: pp. 8–20
- Theme Graphic Organizer

☞ **Go Digital**
- Apprentice Leveled Reader eBook
- Downloadable Graphic Organizer
- Theme Mini-Lesson

Scaffolding for **Wonders** Approaching Leveled Reader

BEFORE READING

5–10 Minutes   SL.2.1a   SL.2.6   L 2.6   L.2.4   L.2.5a   CCSS

Expand Vocabulary

Display each word below. Say the words and have children repeat them. Then use the Define/Example/Ask routine to introduce each word.

① chief (page 9)

Define: the leader of a group

Example: The principal is the *chief* of the school.

Ask: Who is the *chief* of the classroom?

② drown (page 11)

Define: to die from being unable to breathe under water

Example: Divers breathe air from tanks when they are under water, so they do not *drown*.

Ask: What have you learned about swimming, so that you will not *drown*.

DURING READING

10–15 Minutes   RL.2.2   RL.2.3   RL.2.5   L.2.5   L.2.6   CCSS

Close Reading

🔍 **Pages 8–9**

Genre Reread page 8 with children. Point to the top of the page. Ask: *What is the name of scene 3?* (The Village) *What is the setting of this scene?* (the hunters' village) *What do you think might happen in the hunter's village?* (Answers will vary but should focus on the fate of the turtle.)

Vocabulary Read page 8 with children. Explain that a *village* is a place where people live. Ask: *What are some other names for places where people live?* (town, city, neighborhood, community) Explain that *villages* are usually small, whereas cities and towns are bigger.

Vocabulary Point to the word *chief* on page 9. Tell children that a *chief* is the leader of a group. Say: *Look at the illustration on page 9. What kind of animal is the* chief *of the village?* (a giraffe) *How does the giraffe look like a chief?* (He seems to be wearing special clothes like a chief might wear.)

🔍 **Pages 10–11**

Organization Read pages 10 and 11 with children. Explain to children that this part of the story is organized by problem and solution. Ask: *What is the problem the chief is asking about?* (how to cook Little Turtle *or* how to take off Little Turtle's shell) *What does the Chief offer as a solution?* (break Little Turtle's shell with sticks) Then ask: *What is Turtle's problem?* (He needs to get away so we won't be eaten.)

Theme Have children look at the illustration on pages 10–11. Ask: *Is Little Turtle bigger or smaller than the other animals who want to eat him?* (smaller) Say: *This will make it hard for Little Turtle to escape. What will Little Turtle have to do to escape?* (He will have to trick the others.) Guide children to see that Little Turtle will have to use intelligence to escape since he is so much smaller than the others. Have them add this clue to their Theme charts.

Vocabulary Read Little Turtle's line on page 11 with children. Point to the word *drown* and say: Drown *means to die from being unable to breathe under water. Why might Little Turtle tell the chief to throw him in the water and* drown *him?* (He says that because turtles can swim and Little Turtle can escape.)

Pages 12–13

Theme Reread Hunter 1's line on page 13 with children. Ask: *How did Little Turtle trick the others?* (Little Turtle told them he would drown in the water, but he knew he would not.)

STOP AND CHECK Read the question in the Stop and Check box on page 12. (The village animals want to cook and eat Little Turtle.)

Pages 14–15

Connection of Ideas Reread Little Turtle's line on page 14. Say: *Let's go back and read the title of the play.* Chorally read the title with children. Say: *The play tells us why turtles live in water. Think about what has happened in the story. Why do turtles live in water according to the story?* (so they will be safer from being caught and eaten)

Theme Have children review their Theme charts. Ask children to turn to a partner, discuss their notes, and try and come up with a theme to the story. Point out that Little Turtle had a big problem in this story. Ask: *How did he solve his problem?* (He used his brain and tricked the hunters.) *Why were the hunters surprised that Little Turtle got away?* (because he was so little and slow) *What is the theme of the selection?* (Even if we are smaller or weaker than others or feel helpless, we can think of ways to solve our problems.)

STOP AND CHECK Read the question in the Stop and Check box on page 15. (Little Turtle said, "Don't take out the cooking pots. I did not drown!")

AFTER READING

10–15 Minutes RL. 2.1 RL.2.2 W.2.8 L.2.4a L.2.6 (CCSS)

Respond to Reading

Compare Texts Ask children to compare "Why Turtles Live in Water" and "Why the Sun and Moon Live in the Sky." What does each story explain about nature? Are the stories realistic? Why or why not? Discuss with a partner.

Summarize Have children turn to page 16 and summarize the selection. Answers should include details show the theme.

Text Evidence

Have partners work together to answer questions on page 16. Remind children to use their Theme charts.

Theme (Even the small and weak can think of ways to solve their problems.)

Vocabulary (They were tricked because Little Turtle told them to throw him in the water to drown him but that was really a way for him to escape.)

Write About Reading (Answers will vary, but children should note that this folktale explains why turtles live in the water.)

Independent Reading

Encourage children to read the paired selection "Why Corn Has Silk" on pages 17–19. Have them summarize the selection and compare it to "Why Turtles Live in Water." Have them work with a partner to answer the "Make Connections" questions on page 19.

✓ *Quick Check* Can children identify the theme? If not, review and reteach using the instruction on page 226 and assign the Unit 4 Week 4 digital mini-lesson.

Can children respond to the selection using text evidence? If not, provide sentence frames to help them organize their ideas.

WRITE & ASSESS

Objectives
- Review weekly vocabulary words
- Review theme
- Write an analysis about an author's use of theme

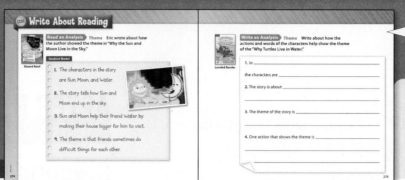

Materials
- Visual Vocabulary Cards: 141–148
- Interactive Worktext, pp. 274–275
- Assessment Book, pp. 46–47

☞ **Go** Digital
- Visual Vocabulary Cards
- Theme Mini-Lesson
- Interactive eWorktext
- eAssessment

Scaffolding for **Wonders** Reading/Writing Workshop

REVIEW AND RETEACH

5–10 Minutes   RL.2.2   RL.2.6   L.2.4a

Weekly Vocabulary

Display one **Visual Vocabulary Card** at a time and guide children to use the vocabulary word in a sentence. If children have difficulty creating a sentence, have them find the word in "Why the Sun and Moon Live in the Sky" or "Why Turtles Live in Water" and use context clues in the passage to define the vocabulary word.

Comprehension: Theme

I Do Write and say: *Jen had a best friend, Nisha. One day at school, Jen had her very favorite lunch. Jen was hungry and planned to eat it all. Nisha came to sit by Jen. Nisha looked sad. "I forgot my lunch," Nisha said. Jen looked at her own food. She really wanted to eat it all, but Nisha was her best friend. "Come share my lunch with me!" Jen said to Nisha.* Say: *Remember, to find the theme of a story, we need to think about what the characters do and say.* Say: *I read that Jen and Nisha are best friends. I think that is a clue to the theme.*

We Do Say: *I also read that Jen is very hungry. But I see that she gives half of her lunch to Nisha. What do these clues tell me about the theme? I see that all the clues have to do with the importance of friendship.* Ask: *What do you think the theme is?* (<u>Possible answer</u>: Nothing is more important than friendship.)

You Do Display: *Every day Jim's mom wakes him up so he will not be late for school. After school, his mom picks him up in the car. At home, his mom helps him with his homework. Then Jim's mom makes dinner.* Have partners look at the characters' actions and what they say to come up with the theme of the story.

WRITE ABOUT READING

25–35 Minutes   W.2.3   W.2.8   W.4.9

Read an Analysis

- Guide children to look back at "Why the Sun and Moon Live in the Sky" in the **Interactive Worktext**. Have volunteers review the details about the author's use of theme they marked on page 269 and summarize the text. Repeat with pages 270–271. *How did the actions and words of characters show the theme?*

- Read aloud the directions on page 274. Read aloud the student model. *This student's work is not a summary. It is an analysis, or description, of how the characters' words and actions show the theme in "Why the Sun and Moon Live in the Sky."*

- *When you write an analysis, you should include key details from the text. Circle the topic sentence. What important information is included in this sentence?* (Eric tells who the characters are in the story.)

- *In the middle of the student model, Eric explains what the story is about. Circle the important details.* (how Sun and Moon end up in the sky) *It also tells important clues to the theme. Underline the clue.* (Sun and Moon help their friend Water.)

- Model analyzing how the author used theme to write the story. Read the last sentence Eric wrote. *What does Eric say is the theme?* (Friends sometimes do difficult things for each other.)

Level Up

▲ Approaching Leveled Reader

▲ Reading/Writing Workshop

▲ Apprentice Leveled Reader

▲ Interactive Worktext

Analytical Writing — Write an Analysis

Guided Writing Read the writing prompt on page 275 together. Have children review their Theme charts for "Why Turtles Live in Water" and use the charts to complete their sentence starters. Children can also write the analysis using another selection previously read this week. If children have difficulty, help them find an example of a character's actions that gives a clue to the theme.

Peer Conference Guide children to read their analysis to a partner. Listeners should summarize the details that support the theme and discuss any parts that are unclear.

Teacher Conference Check children's writing for complete sentences and whether they included details from the story. Review the last sentence and ask: *Did the author use clues to support the theme?* If necessary, guide children to revise the revise their sentences by adding details.

IF children read the Apprentice Level Reader and the **Interactive Worktext** Shared Read fluently and answer the Respond to Reading questions

THEN read together the Approaching Level Reader main selection and the **Reading/Writing Workshop** Shared Read from *Reading Wonders*. Have children take notes as they read, using self-stick notes. Then ask and answer questions about their notes.

Writing Rubric

	4	3	2	1
Text Evidence	Includes three or more details from the text	Includes two or more details from the text	Includes only one detail from the text	No text evidence is cited.
Writing Style	Writes in complete sentences. Uses correct spelling and grammar.	Uses complete sentences. Writing has spelling and grammar errors.	Few complete sentences. There are many spelling and grammar errors.	Writing is not accurate or in complete sentences.

ASSESSMENT

Weekly Assessment

Have children complete the Weekly Assessment using **Assessment** book pages 46–47.

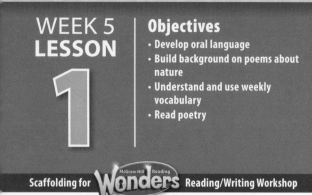

WEEK 5 LESSON 1

Objectives
- Develop oral language
- Build background on poems about nature
- Understand and use weekly vocabulary
- Read poetry

Scaffolding for **Wonders** McGraw-Hill Reading Reading/Writing Workshop

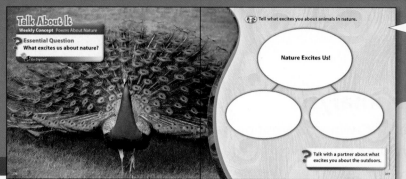

Materials
- Interactive Worktext, pp. 276–283
- Visual Vocabulary Cards: 149–152
- High-Frequency Word Cards

☞ **Go Digital**
- Interactive eWorktext
- Visual Vocabulary Cards

WEEKLY CONCEPT

5–10 Minutes   SL.2.1a SL.2.4 CCSS

Talk About It

Essential Question Read aloud the Essential Question on page 276 of the **Interactive Worktext:** *What excites us about nature?* Tell children that there are many things in nature that people find exciting. Say: *Some people find the seasons very exciting. They enjoy seeing the flowers in spring or the leaves change in fall.* Ask: *What do you find exciting about the seasons?* Encourage children to tell why they like a particular season.

- Discuss the photograph on page 276: Ask: *What is happening in this picture?* (A peacock has its blue and green feathers spread out wide.)

I Do Say: *I am going to look at the photo and think about how nature excites us. I see that the peacock has a huge plume of feathers spread out. It looks pretty amazing. I will write about a peacock's feathers on the web on page 277.*

We Do Say: *Let's think about other animals that are amazing.* Name an animal that you find amazing and share it with the class. Guide children to think of other animals that excite them and describe how these animals are amazing. Then have children choose one animal to add to their web.

You Do Guide partners to work together to talk about other aspects of nature that excites them, such as land features (mountains, waterfalls, glaciers, and so on) or the seasons. Have children use the words from the web to start their sentences: _____ *are exciting because* _____.

REVIEW VOCABULARY

10–15 Minutes   L.2.5a L.2.6 RF.2.3f CCSS

Review Weekly Vocabulary Words

- Use the **Visual Vocabulary Cards** to review the weekly vocabulary.

- Read together the directions on page 278 of the **Interactive Worktext**. Then complete the activity.

1 **outdoors** Write the word *outdoors*. Underline the words *out* and *doors*. Explain that *outdoors* is a compound word. Guide children to understand that if they know the meanings of the two smaller words in a compound word, they can figure out its meaning. Have volunteers tell what they like to do *outdoors*. Then have children name the word that means the opposite of *outdoors*. (indoors)

2 **pale** Hold up examples of objects that are dark blue and *pale* blue. Guide children to understand the meaning of *dark* and *pale*. Then have children think of something that is *pale* pink. Have them use this oral sentence frame: *Both* _____ *and* _____ *can be* pale *pink.* (Possible answers: flamingos, bubblegum, flowers, baby clothes, frosting on cupcakes, and so on)

3 **excite** Describe a time you were *excited* about something. Use gestures or movements to show how you felt. Have a volunteer share something that might *excite* them. Then have children use this oral sentence frame: _____ *would* excite *me on my birthday.* (Possible answers: presents, birthday cake, people singing "Happy Birthday")

4 **drops** Explain to children that liquids, when they spill, can fall in *drops*. Then help children draw their pictures of *drops* of water. Have children describe their pictures, using this sentence frame: Drops *of water look like* _____ *when they land on the ground.*

Review Weekly Poetry Words

- Read together the directions for the "Poetry Words" activity on page 279 of the **Interactive Worktext**. Read each poem aloud with children. Then complete the activity.

5 **repetition** Write the word *repetition*. Have a volunteer suggest a word that is like *repetition*. (repeat) Explain that *repetition* helps create a rhythm in the poem. Read the poem "Spring" aloud for children. Have children call out "Repetition!" whenever a phrase is repeated. Then help children underline an example of *repetition* in "Spring." ("I can," "It is the first day of spring!")

6 **simile** Write the following on the board: _____ *is like (a)* _____. _____ *is as* _____ *as a* _____. Tell children that whenever they see a line in a poem set up in either of these two ways, that line is a *simile*. Help children circle a *simile* in "Spring." Then have children use this oral sentence frame: _____ *is a* simile *in the poem*. (Possible answers: "the warm sun is like a hug"; "the green grass. It looks like a giant rug")

7 **free verse** Point out that all *free verse* poems have one thing in common: they do not have to rhyme. Also tell children that most *free verse* poems do not have a consistent rhythm. Then assist children as they circle two words at the end of two sentences in the poem "Summer" that do not rhyme. (Answers will vary.)

8 **alliteration** Help children learn how to use *alliteration*. Display words that all start with the same letter, such as *Bill bakes banana bread*. Have a volunteer underline the letter *b* in each word. Then help children draw a box around an example of *alliteration* in the poem "Summer." Have children use this oral sentence starter: *An example of* alliteration *from the poem is* _____. ("cool off with cold cups of ice cubes") Underline the letter *c* in the words *cook, cold, cups, cubes*.

READ COMPLEX TEXT

15–20 Minutes   RL.2.1   RL.2.2   SL.2.1b

Read "Snow Shape"; "Nature Walk"; "In the Sky"

- Have children turn to page 280 in the **Interactive Worktext** and read the Essential Question aloud. Have children echo-read the poems' titles with you. Point to the image on page 280 and ask: *What is the girl lying down in?* (snow) *Let's read some poems about snow and other things in nature.*

- Read the poems together.

- As children read, have them use the "My Notes" section on page 280 to write questions they have. Children can also write words they don't understand or things they want to remember. Model how to use the "My Notes" section. Say: *When I look at the picture on page 280, I see the girl is making a shape in the snow. I wonder if the poem will tell me why she does it. I will write a question about it in the "My Notes" section.*

ELL ENGLISH LANGUAGE LEARNERS

As you read together, have children highlight parts of the text they have questions about. After reading, review the questions children have. Then help them locate the answers to their questions in the text.

 Quick Check Can children understand the weekly vocabulary words in context? If not, review vocabulary using the **Visual Vocabulary Cards** before teaching Lesson 2.

WEEK 5
LESSON

2

Objectives
- Read poetry
- Understand complex text through close reading
- Recognize and understand theme
- Respond to the selection using text evidence to support ideas

Scaffolding for **Wonders** McGraw-Hill Reading Reading/Writing Workshop

Materials
Interactive Worktext, pp. 280–285

☞ **Go Digital**
- Interactive eWorktext
- Theme Mini-Lesson

REREAD COMPLEX TEXT

20–25 Minutes RL.2.2 RL.2.1 L.2.6 **CCSS**

Close Reading: "Snow Shape," "Nature Walk," and "In the Sky"

Reread "Snow Shape," "Nature Walk," and "In the Sky" from **Interactive Worktext** pages 280–283 with children. As you read together, discuss important passages in the text. Guide children to respond to questions using evidence from the text.

Pages 280–281

Free Verse Reread lines 1–2 with children. Explain to children that free verse is a type of poem. Say: *In free verse, the words do not need to rhyme.* Ask: *What are the last words in lines 1 and 2?* (sky and ground) *Do these words rhyme?* (no)

Alliteration Remind children that *alliteration* is the repetition of the same sound at the beginning of words. Say aloud an example of alliteration (e.g., *Big, bright, ball*) Reread lines 3 and 4 of "Snow Shape" aloud. Ask: *What three words in these lines begin with the same sound?* Guide children to circle the words. (so, soft, smooth)

Theme Remind children that the theme of a poem is the main message or lesson. Say: *This poem's theme is that snow is pretty and fun to play in.* Reread the poem with children. Say: *Find a detail that supports this theme.* Guide children to draw a box around the detail they find. (Answers will vary but should include one detail about how pretty snow looks or what the poet does while making her shape in it.) Have children continue to find supporting details.

Connection of Ideas A C T Reread the last 5 lines. Point at the picture and say: *The poet has made a four-foot shape in the snow.* Ask: *What is the shape of?* (the poet) *Does the poet tell us how she did it?* (yes) *How does she do it?* Guide children to underline the words that tell. (I slide my arms up and down. I move my legs in and out.)

Page 282

Simile Remind children that a *simile* is a comparison using the words *like* or *as*. Give the children an example of a simile (e.g., *your smile is as bright as the sun*) Reread lines 1–4 with children. Ask: *What does the poet compare leaves to in these lines?* Guide children to circle the words that give them the answer. (a blanket)

Connection of Ideas A C T Reread lines 5–8 with children. Ask: *What smells like clean cotton towels?* (the air) Explain to children that the pronoun *it* is used in place of the word *air* in line 8. Have children write the answer.

Theme Remind children that they can try to find what the author wants you to know, in order to find the theme. Reread lines 9–11. Ask: *What is the poem about?* (taking a walk in the fall) *How does the poet feel about taking a walk in the fall?* Guide children to draw a box around the sentence that tells. (It's a wonderful time!) Point out that this is the theme of the poem. Explain that sometimes the theme of a poem or story is stated in the text.

Page 283

Connection of Ideas A C T Point to the picture on page 283 and say: *Remember, you can find information in the pictures to help you understand a poem.* Reread the poem with children. Ask: *What is the poet looking at in the sky?* Guide children to write their answers. (a cloud)

Repetition Remind children that repetition is when a poet uses a word over and over again. Say: *Repetition can make give a poem a rhythm and make it more fun to read.* Have children reread lines 3–6 of the poem. Ask: *What word does the poet repeat to begin these lines of the poem?* (Look) What other words repeat in these lines? (I see a ...) Instruct children to circle the words.

Theme Remind children that the theme is what the author wants you to understand. Ask: *Where does the author say you can see all kinds of shapes?* (in a cloud) *What does the poet want you to understand about what will happen when you look at a cloud?* Instruct children to write their answer. (A cloud's shape changes.) For extra support, have children go back and draw a box around each sentence that is a clue to the theme.

RESPOND TO READING

10–20 Minutes   SL.2.1a   RL.2.1   RL.2.2   **CCSS**

Respond to "Snow Shape"

Guide children read the questions about "Snow Shape" on page 284 of the **Interactive Worktext**. Then read aloud the "Discussion Starter" for each of the questions. Guide children to work with a partner to answer the questions orally using the "Discussion Starters." Have children find text evidence to support their answers. Ask children to write the page number(s) on which they found the text evidence for each question.

1. *How does the narrator describe snow in the poem?* (Possible answers: I read that the color of the snow looks bright white. The poet also says it looks like it would feel soft and smooth. Text Evidence: p. 281)

2. *What does the narrator do in the snow?* (Possible answers: First, the narrator falls straight back into the snow. Then the narrator moves her arms and legs. Text Evidence: p. 281)

3. *Why is the narrator excited at the end of the poem?* (Possible answers: The narrator is excited to see a shape of herself. I know the narrator is excited because of the exclamation point. Text Evidence: p. 281)

After children discuss the questions on page 284, have them use the sentence starters to answer the question on page 285. Circulate and provide guidance.

 Quick Check Do children understand vocabulary in context? If not, review and reteach using the instruction on page 236.

Can children identify the theme? If not, review and reteach using the instruction on page 236 and assign the Unit 4 Week 5 digital mini-lesson.

Can children write a response to "Snow Shape"? If not, review the sentence starters and prompt children to respond orally. Help them write their responses.

Objectives
- Understand and use new vocabulary words
- Read fiction
- Recognize and understand theme
- Understand complex text through close reading

Materials
- "A Hike in the Woods" Apprentice Leveled Reader: pp. 2–9
- Theme Graphic Organizer

☞ **Go** Digital
- Apprentice Leveled Reader eBook
- Downloadable Graphic Organizer
- Theme Mini-Lesson

Scaffolding for **Wonders** Approaching Leveled Reader

BEFORE READING

10–15 Minutes   SL.2.1a   SL.2.6   L.2.5a   L.2.6   CCSS

Introduce "A Hike in the Woods"

- Read the Essential Question on the title page of "A Hike in the Woods" **Apprentice Leveled Reader:** *What excites us about nature? We will read a story about two boys who go hiking in the woods.*

- Read the title aloud. Point to the pictures and diagrams. Ask: *Who are the main characters in this story?* (two boys) *This story tells about a boy who loves the woods and wants to take his friend on a hike.*

Expand Vocabulary

Display each word below. Say the words and have students repeat them. Then use the Define/Example/Ask routine to introduce each word.

1 bare (page 3)

Define: not covered

Example: With just a T-shirt on, my arms are *bare.*

Ask: What do *bare* trees look like?

2 creek (page 7)

Define: a small river or stream

Example: We like to fish in the *creek.*

Ask: What is another word for *creek?*

3 woods (page 3)

Define: a large outdoor place with trees

Example: The deer live in the *woods.*

Ask: What could you see on a hike in the *woods?*

DURING READING

20–30 Minutes   RL.2.1   RL.2.2   RL.2.7   L.2.5   L.2.6   CCSS

Close Reading

🔍 **Pages 2–3**

Vocabulary Read the title aloud to children. Point to the word *hike.* Say: *A hike is a walk, usually somewhere in nature. When people take a* hike, *they usually walk a long distance outdoors. One reason for a hike is to look at plants and animals. Where are some places you would like to take a* hike? *What would you hope to see on your* hike? (Answers will vary, but should mention some of the plants and animals a person might see on a hike in nature.)

Sentence Structure A C T Read page 2 with children. Point to the quotation marks. Say: *Remember, these are quotation marks. They show that someone is speaking. The words inside the quotation marks show what the person is saying. To find who is speaking, look at the words right before or right after the quotation marks. Who is speaking on page 2?* (Lee) *Who is Lee waiting for?* (his friend Jeff)

Character, Setting and Events Remind children that the characters are the people in the story, the setting is where the story takes place, and the events are the things that happen in the story. Read page 3 with children. Ask: *Who are the main characters so far in the story?* (Lee and Jeff) *Where is Lee at the beginning of the story?* (at his house) *Where is Lee planning to take Jeff?* (into the woods)

🔍 Pages 4–5

Theme Remind children that the theme is the main message that the author wants the reader to get from reading the story. Say: *To find the theme, you must look for key details in the text. Then you can use key details as clues to figure out the main message, or theme.* Remind children that there can be more than one theme in a story. Ask: *What is Lee's opinion about the woods?* (He loves the woods in winter.) *What is one thing he loves about the woods in winter?* (The pale branches are pretty.) Guide children to record the information on their Theme charts.

Sentence Structure A C T Read page 5 with children. Point to the exclamation points on the page. Say: *These are exclamation points. The author uses them to show that someone is excited about something. Who is excited?* (Lee) *What is he so excited about?* (His friend Jeff has arrived.)

STOP AND CHECK Read the question in the Stop and Check box on page 5. (Lee wants to show Jeff the woods around his house.)

🔍 Pages 6–7

Characters, Setting, Events Remind children that the setting is where the story takes place. Say: *The setting can change during a story as the characters move from place to place. To find the setting, look for clues in the text.* Read page 6 with children. Ask: *What is the setting of the story on page 6?* (Lee's room) If children have difficulty, guide them to find the information in the first sentence.

Sentence Structure A C T Have children read the second sentence on page 6. Point to the question mark and say: *This is a question mark. When you see a question mark at the end of a sentence, it means a question is being asked. Who is asking the question in the second sentence?* (Jeff) *What does Jeff ask?* (What should we do?)

🔍 Pages 8–9

Theme Remind children that the theme is the main message the author wants the readers to know. Say: *Sometimes, there can be more than one theme in a story. Let's look for key details on this page to help us find a theme. Lee has just told Jeff that they will go for a hike in the woods. Read the first sentence.* After children read, ask: *What was Jeff's first reaction?* (He was very quiet.) *Let's find out why Jeff was so quiet. What does Jeff say about the woods at the end of the page* (He has never been in the woods.) *Does Jeff think he will have a good time?* (no) Guide children to record the information on their Theme charts.

Connection of Ideas A C T Say: *Illustrations can help us to understand what characters are thinking and how they are feeling. Look at the illustrations on pages 8 and 9. Look at Lee in both pictures how do you think he is feeling?* (happy and excited) *What does the illustration tell you about how Jeff is feeling?* (He looks worried or scared.) *Think about what you have read on page 8. Why do you think Jeff is worried?* (He has never been in the woods and doesn't think the hike will be fun.)

STOP AND CHECK Read the question in the Stop and Check box on page 9. (Jeff has never been in the woods and is not excited about going there.)

Have partners review their Theme Charts for pages 2–9 and discuss what they have learned.

✅ ***Quick Check*** Do students understand weekly vocabulary in context? If not, review and reteach using the instruction on page 236.

Can students identify theme? If not, review and reteach using the instruction on page 236 and assign Unit 4 Week 5 digital mini-lesson.

Objectives
• Understand and use new vocabulary words
• Read fiction
• Recognize and understand theme
• Understand complex text through close reading

Materials
"A Hike in the Woods" Apprentice Leveled Reader: pp. 10–20
• Theme Graphic Organizer

☞ **Go** Digital
• Apprentice Leveled Reader eBook
• Downloadable Graphic Organizer
• Theme Mini-Lesson

The boys looked for animals. Leaves crunched under their feet.

"Look!" Lee pointed at a rabbit. Jeff grinned.

BEFORE READING

5–10 Minutes   SL.2.1a   SL.2.6   L.2.4a   L.2.5a   L.2.6   CCSS

Expand Vocabulary

Display each word below. Say the words and have students repeat them. Then use the Define/Example/Ask routine to introduce each word.

1 **crunched**   (page 11)

Define: made a crackling noise

Example: The corn chip *crunched* in my mouth as I chewed it.

Ask: What is something that *crunched* when you chewed it?

2 **glide**   (page 13)

Define: to fly smoothly without a lot of effort

Example: The seagulls *glide* over the water, looking for fish.

Ask: What have you seen *glide*?

3 **grinned**   (page 11)

Define: smiled widely

Example: When mom brought out the ice cream, we all *grinned*.

Ask: Tell about a time when you *grinned*.

DURING READING

15–20 Minutes   RL.2.2   RL.2.3   RL.2.5   L.2.5   L.2.6   CCSS

Close Reading

🔍 **Pages 10–11**

Characters, Setting, Events 10. Say: *It looks like there is a new character in the story. Let's read the page to find out who it is.* Read page 10 with children. Ask: *Who is the new character in the story?* (Lee's dad) Ask: *What is the new setting?* (the woods)

Connection of Ideas **A** **C** **T** Read page 11 with children. Point to the illustration. Ask: *How does the illustration connect to the last sentence on the page?* (The illustration shows Jeff grinning and the text reads "Jeff grinned.") *How is this different from the way he was acting before?* (Before he was quiet and looked sad.) *What changed?* (He got excited about seeing a rabbit.)

Theme Remind children that the theme is the main message the author wants the reader to know, and that to find the theme they must look for key details in the text. Say: *We have read that Jeff is a little scared of the woods. What do the boys see on page 11?* (The boys see a rabbit.) *What does Jeff do?* (He grins.) *How does this show that Jeff may change his mind about the woods?* (Jeff smiles when he sees the rabbit, which may mean he is getting excited to be in the woods.) Guide children to record the information in their Theme charts.

🔍 **Pages 12–13**

Theme Say: *Let's look for more clues that Jeff may be changing his mind about the woods.* Read the first paragraph of page 12 with children. Ask: *What does Lee's dad give the boys when they get to the creek?* (hot chocolate) *What does Jeff say about it?* (He says its good.) *How does Jeff look now?* (He looks happy.)

STOP AND CHECK Read the question in the Stop and Check box on page 12. (At the creek, the boys drink hot chocolate and throw pebbles in the water.)

Prior Knowledge Ⓐ Ⓒ Ⓣ Point to the bird on page 13. Say: *This bird is called a heron. They live near water. They stand very still and look for fish. Then they move quickly to grab the fish! Herons are very tall birds, as tall as some of you.*

Vocabulary Read page 13. Ask: *What does the word* suddenly *mean?* (happens unexpectedly and quickly) *What do the boys next that helps you understand* suddenly? (jumped up)

🔍 Pages 14–15

Theme Say: *Let's look for more clues that will help us understand the theme, or main message, of the story.* Read the first line of page 15 with children. Ask: *How can you tell that Jeff is having a good time?* (He laughed.) Read the rest of page 15 with children. Ask: *Has Jeff changed his mind about the woods?* (yes) *How do you know?* (because he says the woods are great) *What do you think this says about the theme?* (That it can be a good idea to try something you don't think you will like.) Guide children to record the information on their Theme charts.

STOP AND CHECK Read the question in the Stop and Check box on page 15. (The boys jump when a heron suddenly flies out from some bushes.)

AFTER READING

10–15 Minutes   RL.2.3   RL.2.5   RL.2.9   L.2.4.a   W.2.8   (CCSS)

Respond to Reading

Compare Texts Ask students to compare "A Hike in the Woods" and the poems "Snow Shape," "Nature Walk," and "In the Sky." *What parts of nature do the story and poems talk about? Do they make you excited about nature? Why or why not?* Discuss with a partner.

Summarize Have students turn to page 16 and summarize the selection. (Answers should include details that relate to the theme.)

🔍 Text Evidence

Have partners work together to answer questions on page 16. Remind students to use their Theme charts.

Theme (Jeff's feelings change from being uninterested in the woods [page 8] to thinking they are "great.")

Vocabulary (The text reads, "The boys sat and threw pebbles into the creek. Drops of water splashed up." The picture shows Lee throwing a small stone. These clues tell us that *pebbles* are small stones.)

Write About Reading (The author's message is that trying something can change your mind about it. Jeff does not like the woods but then he gets to like them.)

Independent Reading

Encourage students to read the paired selection "The Woods" on pages 17–19. Remind them to look for examples of simile and alliteration. Have them summarize the selection and compare it to "A Hike in the Woods." Have them work with a partner to answer the "Make Connections" questions on page 19.

✓ *Quick Check* Can students identify theme? If not, review and reteach using the instruction on page 236 and assign the Unit 4 Week 5 digital mini-lesson.

Can students respond to the selection using text evidence? If not, provide sentence frames to help them organize their ideas.

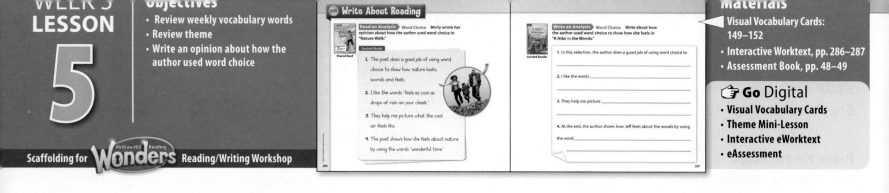

WEEK 5
LESSON

5

Objectives
• Review weekly vocabulary words
• Review theme
• Write an opinion about how the author used word choice

Scaffolding for **Wonders** Reading/Writing Workshop

Materials
• Visual Vocabulary Cards: 149–152
• Interactive Worktext, pp. 286–287
• Assessment Book, pp. 48–49

☞ **Go** Digital
• Visual Vocabulary Cards
• Theme Mini-Lesson
• Interactive eWorktext
• eAssessment

REVIEW AND RETEACH

5–10 Minutes   RL.2.1   RL.2.2 .L.2.4a

Weekly Vocabulary

Display one **Visual Vocabulary Card** at a time and guide children to use the vocabulary word in a sentence. If children have difficulty creating a sentence, have them find the word in "Snow Shape," "Nature Walk," "In the Sky," or "A Hike in the Woods" and use context clues to define the vocabulary word.

Comprehension: Theme

I Do Write and say: *Joy and her friends like to play sports and games together. They eat pizza and ice cream. When Joy is sad, her friends make her feel better.* Say: *I can use clues to figure out the theme. I read that Joy and her friends like to play and eat together.* Underline the first and second sentences and write, "clue." Say: *The last sentence tells me that when Joy is sad, her friends make her feel better.* Underline the last sentence and write "clue." Say: *When I think about these clues, I can come up with the theme: Joy and her friends have a good friendship.*

We Do Display: *In my hometown, the weather is nice. It is sunny most of the time. People are friendly. People say "hi" to each other on the street. People like to live in my hometown.* Say: *To find the theme, we must look for clues. What does the author say about the weather in his hometown?* (The weather is nice. It is sunny most of the time.) *What does the author say about the people?* (They are friendly. They say "hi" to each other.) Write the clues on the board.

You Do Ask: *What do these clues have in common?* Guide partners to work together to determine the theme. (The author's hometown is a nice place to live.)

WRITE ABOUT READING

25–35 Minutes   W.2.1   W.2.8   W.4.9

Read an Analysis

• Guide children to look back at "Nature Walk" in the **Interactive Worktext**. Have volunteers point out examples of word choice. *How did the author use word choice to show how she feels in this poem?*

• Read aloud the directions on page 286. Read aloud the student model. *This student's work is not a summary. It is an opinion of how the poet used word choice to shows how she feels in "Nature Walk."*

• *When you write an opinion, you tell your thoughts about the poem. In this student model, the student gave her opinion of how the author used word choice in the poem. Read Molly's first sentence. Circle the information from the poem.* (Molly writes that the poet does a good job of using word choice to describe how nature looks, sounds, and feels.) *What part of the poem does this come from?* (the beginning)

• *Read the second sentence. Draw a box around the words from the poem that Molly liked.* ("feels as cool as drops of rain on your cheek") *What part of the poem is she writing about?* (the middle)

• *Point to the third sentence. This sentence explains how the author's word choice helped Molly understand the poem. What information does Molly include?* (that the words help her picture what cool air feels like in the fall)

• Model analyzing how the poet used word choice. Read the last sentence that Molly wrote. *Why is this sentence a good ending?* (Molly writes that the poet used words to show how she feels about nature.)

![Analytical Writing] Write an Analysis

Guided Writing Read the writing prompt on page 287 together. Guide children to review the author's use of Word Choice for "A Hike in the Woods." Have children complete the sentence starters. Children can also write an analysis using another selection previously read this week.

Peer Conference Guide children to read their analysis to a partner. Listeners should summarize the strongest use of word choice in the beginning, middle, and end of the story. They should discuss any parts that are unclear.

Teacher Conference Check children's writing for complete sentences and whether they included details from the story. Review the ending sentence and ask: *Did the author use details about word choice to support the story?* If necessary, guide children to revise their sentence by adding more details.

Level Up

▲ Approaching Leveled Reader

▲ Reading/Writing Workshop

▲ Apprentice Leveled Reader

▲ Interactive Worktext

IF children read the `Apprentice Level` Reader and the **Interactive Worktext** Shared Read fluently and answer the Respond to Reading questions

THEN read together the `Approaching Level` Reader main selection and the **Reading/Writing Workshop** Shared Read from *Reading Wonders*. Have children take notes as they read, using self-stick notes. Then ask and answer questions about their notes.

Writing Rubric

	4	3	2	1
Text Evidence	Includes three or more details from the text.	Includes two or more details from the text.	Includes only one detail from the text.	No text evidence is cited.
Writing Style	Writes in complete sentences. Uses correct spelling and grammar.	Uses complete sentences. Writing has spelling and grammar errors.	Few complete sentences. There are many spelling and grammar errors.	Writing is not accurate or in complete sentences.

ASSESSMENT

Weekly Assessment

Have children complete the Weekly Assessment using **Assessment** book pages 48–49.

▶ **Unit Assessment,**
pages 149 – 157

▶ **Fluency Assessment,**
pages 250 – 265

▶ **Exit Test,**
pages 205 – 213

Unit 4 Assessment

CCSS TESTED SKILLS

✔ COMPREHENSION	✔ VOCABULARY:
• Compare and Contrast RI.2.3, RI.2.9	• Context Clues L.2.4a
• Cause and Effect RI.2.3	
• Compare and Contrast RL.2.3, RL.2.9	
• Theme RL.2.2	
• Theme RL.2.2	

Using Assessment and Writing Scores

🔄 RETEACH

RETEACH	IF ...	THEN ...
COMPREHENSION	Students answer 0–7 multiple-choice items correctly ...	... reteach tested skills using instruction on pages 364–375.
VOCABULARY	Students answer 0–3 multiple-choice items correctly ...	... reteach tested skills using instruction on page 364.
WRITING	Students score mostly 1–2 on weekly Write About Reading rubrics throughout the unit ...	... reteach writing using instruction on pages 376–377.

🔼 LEVEL UP

LEVEL UP	IF ...	THEN ...
COMPREHENSION	Students answer 8–10 multiple-choice items correctly ...	... have students read the *Rocky Mountain National Park* Approaching Leveled Reader. Use the Level Up lesson on page on page 238.
WRITING	Students score mostly 3–4 on weekly Write About Reading rubrics throughout the unit ...	... use the Level Up Write About Reading lesson on page 239 to have students compare two selections from the unit.

Fluency Assessment

Conduct assessments individually using the differentiated fluency passages in **Assessment**. Students' expected fluency goal for this Unit is 62–82 WCPM with an accuracy rate of 95% or higher.

Exit Test

If a student answers 13–15 multiple choice items correctly on the Unit Assessment, administer the Unit 4 Exit Test at the end of Week 6.

Time to Exit

Exit Text

If...

Students answer 13–15 multiple choice items correctly...

Fluency Assessment

If...

Students achieve their Fluency Assessment goal for the unit...

Level Up Lessons

If...

Students are successful applying close reading skills with the Approaching Leveled Reader in Week 6...

If...

Students score mostly 4–5 on the Level Up Write About Reading assignment...

Foundational Skills Kit

If...

Students have mastered the Unit 4 benchmark skills in the Foundational Skills Kit and *Reading Wonders* Adaptive Learning...

Then...

... consider exiting the student from *Reading WonderWorks* materials into the Approaching Level of *Reading Wonders*.

Read Approaching Leveled Reader

Approaching Leveled Reader

Apprentice Leveled Reader

Write About Reading

Interactive Worktext Shared Read

Apprentice Leveled Reader

Apprentice to Approaching Level

L.2.5   RI.2.10

Rocky Mountain National Park

Before Reading

Preview Discuss what children remember about the Rocky Mountains and what makes this part of the world different. Tell them they will be reading a more challenging version of "Rocky Mountain National Park."

Vocabulary Use the routines on the **Visual Vocabulary Cards** to review the Weekly Vocabulary words. Use pages 190 and 192 to review the Expand Vocabulary words.

A C T During Reading

▶ **Specific Vocabulary** Review with children the following science words that are new to this level: *krummholz trees* (page 9) and *ptarmigans* (page 13). Provide the meaning of each word. Point out specific names of species that the Approaching Leveled Reader to replace the generic terms used in the Apprentice Leveled Reader including *Abert's squirrel* (page 7) and *Engelmann spruce* (page 8). Tell children that these are the scientific names given to each plant or animal and they are named for the people who discovered them.

▶ **Purpose** Remind children that to identify an author's purpose, they can ask themselves, *"What does the author want me to know about a topic?"* Have children read page 4 and look at the diagram. Say: *The author tells us that Rocky Mountain National Park has three different life zones. What does the author want you to know about the difference between each zone?* (Each zone covers a different height. The zones have different plants and animals.)

▶ **Genre** Say: *Expository text includes text features such as chapter titles and maps.* Point to the chapter title on page 2. Say: *Chapter titles tell readers what each chapter will be about. If the chapter's title is a question, the chapter will answer the question. What is the title of chapter 1?* (How Is the Park Special?) *What will this chapter tell about?* (ways the park is special) Have children look at the map on page 3 and read the caption. Ask: *Is Rocky Mountain National Park a real place or a made-up place?* (real) *How do you know?* (The caption says it is located in Colorado.)

After Reading

Ask children to complete the Respond to Reading on page 16 after they have finished reading. Provide support with the vocabulary strategy question, as needed.

Write About Reading

RI.3.9   W.4.9   CCSS

Read an Analysis

- Distribute the Unit 4 Downloadable Model and Practice. Point out that the model compares two related texts that children have read in Unit 4, the **Interactive Worktext** Shared Read "Alaska: A Special Place" and the **Apprentice Leveled Reader** "Rocky Mountain National Park." Read the sentences aloud.

- Point out the key details in each sentence that come from the texts. Point out the signal word *both*. Explain to children that this word shows readers that the sentence is comparing two different texts.

- Ask: *What details show that the two texts are alike?* (Both texts tell about places on earth that are unique. Both texts tell about the land features and animals that live in each place. Both include maps that give more information about a place.) *How is "Rocky Mountain National Park" different?* ("Rocky Mountain National Park" tells about three different zones in one place, not about one place.)

- Model analyzing how the student supported her opinion. *How does this student support her opinion?* (She gave evidence to show how both texts tell about land features and animals in a place.)

Write an Analysis

Guided Writing Tell children that they will compare the **Interactive Worktext** Shared Read "Into the Sea" and the **Apprentice Leveled Reader** "Earthquakes." Explain that they will compare how the authors describe different ways the Earth can change.

- Guide children to compare the two texts as they complete the sentences on the Unit 4 Downloadable Model and Practice.

- Point out the signal words, such as *also, both*, and *different, to children and discuss how these words are used to compare the texts.*

- Alternatively, let children select two texts to compare.

Teacher Conference Check children's writing for complete sentences. Did they use key details to tell how the texts are the same and different? Did they use text evidence? Did they write in complete sentences? Did they use evidence to support their opinion?

Writing Rubric

	4	3	2	1
Text Evidence	Includes three or more details from the text.	Includes two or more details from the text.	Includes only one detail from the text.	No text evidence is cited.
Writing Style	Writes in complete sentences. Uses correct spelling and grammar.	Uses complete sentences. Writing has spelling and grammar errors.	Few complete sentences. There are many spelling and grammar errors.	Writing is not accurate or in complete sentences.

UNIT 5 PLANNER
Let's Make a Difference

Week 1 **Being a Good Citizen**	**Week 2** **Cooperation Works!**	**Week 3** **Our Heroes**

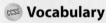 BALLOT BOX

Week 1 — Being a Good Citizen

ESSENTIAL QUESTION
What do good citizens do?

Build Background

CCSS Vocabulary
L.2.4a *champion, determined, issues, promises, responsibility, rights, volunteered, votes*

Access Complex Text
Connection of Ideas

CCSS Comprehension
RL.2.6 Skill: Point of View
Respond to Reading

CCSS Write About Reading *Analytical Writing*
W.4.9 Inform/Explain: Point of View

Week 2 — Cooperation Works!

ESSENTIAL QUESTION
How do people get along?

Build Background

CCSS Vocabulary
L.2.4a *amused, cooperate, describe, entertained, imagination, interact, patient, peaceful*

Access Complex Text
Sentence Structure

CCSS Comprehension
RL.2.6 Skill: Point of View
Respond to Reading

CCSS Write About Reading *Analytical Writing*
W.4.9 Inform/Explain: Point of View

Week 3 — Our Heroes

ESSENTIAL QUESTION
What do heroes do?

Build Background

CCSS Vocabulary
L.2.4a *agree, challenging, discover, heroes, interest, perform, study, succeed*

Access Complex Text
Genre

CCSS Comprehension
RI.2.6 Skill: Sequence
Respond to Reading

CCSS Write About Reading *Analytical Writing*
W.4.9 Opinion: Sequence

A S S E S S M E N T

✓ Quick Check
Vocabulary, Comprehension

✓ Weekly Assessment
Assessment Book, pp. 50–51

✓ Quick Check
Vocabulary, Comprehension

✓ Weekly Assessment
Assessment Book, pp. 52–53

✓ Quick Check
Vocabulary, Comprehension

✓ Weekly Assessment
Assessment Book, pp. 54–55

✓ MID-UNIT ASSESSMENT
Assessment Book, pp. 104–111

Fluency Assessment
Assessment Book, pp. 266–281

Use the Foundational Skills Kit for explicit instruction of phonics, structural analysis, fluency, and word recognition. Includes *Reading Wonders* Adaptive Learning.

Week 4
Preserving Our Earth

ESSENTIAL QUESTION
How can we protect the Earth?

Build Background

CCSS Vocabulary
L.2.4a *curious, distance, Earth resources, enormous, gently, proudly, rarely, supply*

Access Complex Text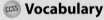
Sentence Structure

CCSS Comprehension
RL.2.5 Skill: Problem and Solution
Respond to Reading

CCSS Write About Reading *Analytical Writing*
W.4.9 Inform/Explain: Problem and Solution

Week 5
Rights and Rules

ESSENTIAL QUESTION
Why are rules important?

Build Background

CCSS Vocabulary
L.2.4a *exclaimed, finally, form, history, public, rules, united, writers*

Access Complex Text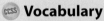
Purpose

CCSS Comprehension
RI.2.3 Skill: Cause and Effect
Respond to Reading

CCSS Write About Reading *Analytical Writing*
W.4.9 Inform/Explain: Cause and Effect

Week 6
ASSESS

RETEACH   LEVEL UP

Reteach
Comprehension Skills
Vocabulary
Write About Reading

Level Up
Read Approaching Leveled Reader
Write About Reading:
Compare Texts

A S S E S S M E N T

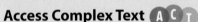 **Quick Check**
Vocabulary, Comprehension

 **Weekly Assessment**
Assessment Book, pp. 56–57

 Quick Check
Vocabulary, Comprehension

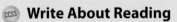 **Weekly Assessment**
Assessment Book, pp. 58–59

 Unit Assessment
Assessment Book, pp. 158–166

 Fluency Assessment
Assessment Book, pp. 266–281

EXIT TEST
Assessment Book, pp. 214–222

Unit **5**

Let's Make a Difference

The **Big Idea**
How can people make a difference?

UNIT 5 OPENER,
pp. 288–289

The Big Idea

How can people make a difference?

Talk About It

Read aloud the Big Idea on page 288 of the **Interactive Worktext:** *How can people make a difference?* Ask children to tell about a time when someone made a difference in their lives. Children may describe events such as a friend lending a helping hand, or a parent teaching them something.

Discuss the photo on pages 288–289. Ask: *What is happening in the picture?* (people are cleaning up a beach) *What else do you see?* (recycling bags, plastic bottles, children's vests) *How are these children making a difference?* (They are cleaning up the beach so people can enjoy their visits to the beach.)

Then say: Now let's think of ways people make a difference in our community. Have children name people in their community. Then have them work with their partners to think of those that have made a difference. Afterwards, have partners share their ideas with the group.

Then say: *Let's look back at our Big Idea. How do people make a difference?* Tell children that people can make a difference in large and small ways. Explain to children that they will be discussing the Big Idea throughout the unit. Each week they will talk, read and write about different people and how they made a difference in their communities.

Build Fluency

Each week, use the **Interactive Worktext** Shared Reads and **Apprentice Leveled Readers** for fluency instruction and practice. Keep in mind that reading rates vary with the type of text that children are reading as well as the purpose for reading. For example, comprehension of complex informational texts generally requires slower reading.

Explain/Model Use the Fluency lessons on pages 378–382 to explain the skill. Then model the skill by reading the first page of the week's Shared Read or Leveled Reader.

Practice/Apply Choose a page from the Shared Read or Leveled Reader. Have one group read the top half of the page one sentence at a time. Remind children to apply the skill. Have the second group echo-read the passage. Then have the groups switch roles for the second half of the page. Discuss how each group applied the skill.

Weekly Fluency Focus

Week 1 Intonation
Week 2 Expression
Week 3 Phrasing
Week 4 Intonation
Week 5 Pronunciation

Foundational Skills Kit You can also use the **Lesson Cards** and **Practice** pages from the **Foundational Skills Kit** for targeted Fluency instruction and practice.

Access Complex Text

A C T

Interactive Worktext

	Week 1	Week 2	Week 3	Week 4	Week 5
	"A Difficult Decision"	"Soccer Friends"	"César Chávez"	"The Art Project"	"Visiting the Past"
Quantitative	Lexile 360 TextEvaluator™ 16	Lexile 400 TextEvaluator™ 16	Lexile 460 TextEvaluator™ 6	Lexile 480 TextEvaluator™ 14	Lexile 500 TextEvaluator™ 16
Qualitative	• Connection of Ideas • Vocabulary	• Sentence Structure • Connection of Ideas • Vocabulary	• Genre • Connection of Ideas • Vocabulary	• Sentence Structure • Prior Knowledge • Vocabulary	• Purpose • Genre • Vocabulary
Reader and Task	The Weekly Concept lessons will help determine the reader's knowledge and engagement in the weekly concept.				
	Weekly Concept: p. 246 Questions and tasks: pp. 248–249	Weekly Concept: p. 256 Questions and tasks: pp. 258–259	Weekly Concept: p. 266 Questions and tasks: pp. 268–269	Weekly Concept: p. 278 Questions and tasks: pp. 280–281	Weekly Concept: p. 288 Questions and tasks: pp. 290–291

Apprentice Leveled Reader

	Week 1	Week 2	Week 3	Week 4	Week 5
	"Fixing the Playground"	"Rainy Day"	"Rudy Garcia-Tolson"	"Let's Carpool"	"Government Rules"
Quantitative	Lexile 250 TextEvaluator™ 8	Lexile 290 TextEvaluator™ 12	Lexile 290 TextEvaluator™ 6	Lexile 230 TextEvaluator™ 11	Lexile 370 TextEvaluator™ 6
Qualitative	• Connection of Ideas • Genre • Sentence Structure • Vocabulary	• Sentence Structure • Connection of Ideas • Vocabulary	• Genre • Connection of Ideas • Purpose • Vocabulary	• Sentence Structure • Prior Knowledge • Connection of Ideas • Vocabulary	• Purpose • Genre • Connection of Ideas • Vocabulary
Reader and Task	The Weekly Concept lessons will help determine the reader's knowledge and engagement in the weekly concept.				
	Weekly Concept: p. 246 Questions and tasks: pp. 250–253	Weekly Concept: p. 256 Questions and tasks: pp. 260–263	Weekly Concept: p. 266 Questions and tasks: pp. 270–273	Weekly Concept: p. 278 Questions and tasks: pp. 282–285	Weekly Concept: p. 288 Questions and tasks: pp. 292–295

See page 383 for details about Text Complexity measures.

WEEKLY LESSON 1

Objectives
• Develop oral language
• Build background about being a good citizen
• Understand and use weekly vocabulary
• Read realistic fiction

Scaffolding for **Wonders** McGraw-Hill Reading/Writing Workshop

WEEKLY CONCEPT

5–10 Minutes SL.2.1a SL.2.4

Talk About It

Essential Question Read aloud the Essential Question on page 290 of the **Interactive Worktext:** *What do good citizens do?* Explain that when you are a good citizen, you do things that are good for your community. Provide examples of citizens doing good deeds, such as volunteering to clean up a town park or cleaning up your sidewalk or street. Say: *Good citizens care for their community and neighbors.*

• Discuss the photograph on page 290. Ask: *What is happening in the picture?* (Children are standing in line to vote. They are putting their votes in a ballot box.)

I Do Say: *I am going to look at the photo and think about how this person is a good citizen. This person is a good citizen because they are exercising their right to vote. These children are choosing something or someone they think is the best. I will write on the web on page 291 how this person is being a good citizen.*

We Do Say: *Let's think about other ways a person can be a good citizen. One way a person can be a good citizen is by trying to return something that someone lost.* Ask: *Have you ever found something and brought it to the lost and found?* (Answers will vary.) Have children discuss ways of being a good citizen and then choose one way to add to their web.

You Do Guide partners to work together to talk about how to be a good citizen. Have children use the words from the web to start their sentences: *Good citizens _____.*

REVIEW VOCABULARY

10–15 Minutes L.2.5a L.2.6 RF.2.3f

Review Weekly Vocabulary Words

• Use the **Visual Vocabulary Cards** to review the weekly vocabulary.

• Read together the directions on page 292 of the **Interactive Worktext**. Then complete the activity.

1 **determined** Ask children to tell how they *determined* which book they read last. Then tell how you *determined* something. Say: *The teacher* determined *which day to take a class trip. What is another word for* determined? (Possible answers: decided, chose)

2 **champion** Ask children to tell about any games or contests they might have won. If children are having difficulty, remind them of any classroom games or contests they might have won. Then have children use this oral sentence starter: *I would like to be a* champion *of _____.* (Answers will vary.)

3 **responsibility** Ask children to think about what *responsibilities* they have at school, especially in your classroom. Have them describe their *responsibilities.* Use this oral sentence starter: *One* responsibility *I have at school is _____.* (Possible answers: erase the board, clean the bookshelf, clean up my materials)

4 **promises** Ask children to think about what, if any, *promises* they have made. Tell them that when some people make *promises,* they "shake on it." Have partners shake hands as they say, "I *promise.*" Then have partners share *promises* they have made to their friends or family members. (Answers will vary.)

5 **issues** Discuss with children fitness *issues*, including getting enough sleep and exercising. Guide children to think of who might come to the classroom to talk about such *issues*. Use the following oral sentence starter: *A _____ talks about fitness* issues. (Possible answers: physical education teacher, doctor)

6 **rights** Ask children to think about what *rights* they have. Use this sentence starter: *Children have the* right *to _____.* Then have children discuss the *rights* that adults have, but that children don't have. Use this frame: *_____ and _____ are two* rights *that adults have.* (Possible answers: the right to drive a car, the right to vote for president)

7 **votes** Tell children that the word *vote* can be used as both a noun and a verb. Say: *I will* vote *for you. You have my* vote. Then have children announce the results of their question with this sentence frame: *_____ got the most* votes. (Possible answers: apples, pears)

8 **volunteered** Ask children to talk about something they *volunteered* to do at school this year. Have children use this sentence starter to describe their picture: *This year, I* volunteered *to _____.* (Possible answers: paint a mural, clean up the classroom)

High-Frequency Words

Have children look at page 293 in the **Interactive Worktext**. Help them read, spell, and write each high-frequency word. Guide partners to use each word in a sentence. Then read the story aloud with children. Guide partners to work together to reread the story and circle the high-frequency words. (Try, Who, right, We, saw, So) Listen in and provide assistance reading the high-frequency words, as necessary.

ELL ENGLISH LANGUAGE LEARNERS

Display the High-Frequency Word Cards for: *who, so, we, saw, try, right*. Write a sentence with each word on the board. Have children echo-read each sentence, and point out the high-frequency word. Then ask them to sue the word in a new sentence.

READ COMPLEX TEXT

15–20 Minutes   RL.2.6   RL.2.3   SL.2.1b

Read "A Difficult Decision"

- Have children turn to page 294 in the **Interactive Worktext** and read the Essential Question aloud. Echo-read the title with children. Point to the image of the video game on page 295 and say: *It looks like someone left their game at the playground. What would a good citizen do if he or she found something that someone had lost?* (try to return it) *Let's read to find out what happens in the story.*

- Read the story together. Note that the weekly vocabulary words are highlighted in yellow. Expand Vocabulary words are highlighted in blue.

- As children read, have them use the "My Notes" section on page 294 to write questions they have. Children can also write words they don't understand or things they want to remember. Model how to use the "My Notes" section. Say: *When I read the first paragraph on page 295, I see the word* equipment. *I wonder what* equipment *is. I will write a question about the word* equipment *in the "My Notes" section.*

ELL ENGLISH LANGUAGE LEARNERS

As you read together, have children highlight parts of the text they have questions about. After reading, review the questions children have. Then help them locate the answers to their questions in the text.

✓ *Quick Check* Can children understand the weekly vocabulary words in context? If not, review vocabulary using the **Visual Vocabulary Cards** before teaching Lesson 2.

Can children read high-frequency words in context? If not, review using the Read/Spell/Write routine and the High-Frequency Word Cards.

WEEK 1
LESSON

2

Scaffolding for **Wonders** McGraw-Hill Reading Reading/Writing Workshop

Objectives
• Read realistic fiction
• Understand complex text through close reading
• Recognize and understand point of view
• Respond to the selection using text evidence to support ideas

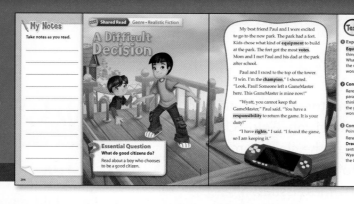

Materials
Interactive Worktext, pp. 294–299

☞ **Go** Digital
• Interactive eWorktext
• Point of View Mini-Lesson

REREAD COMPLEX TEXT

20–25 Minutes   RL.2.6   RL.2.3   L.2.4a   CCSS

Close Reading: "A Difficult Decision"

Reread "A Difficult Decision" from **Interactive Worktext** pages 294–297 with children. As you read together, discuss important passages in the text. Guide children to respond to questions using evidence from the text.

🔍 Pages 294–295

Expand Vocabulary Reread the first paragraph aloud. Point out the word *equipment*. Say: Equipment *is a set of things used for a purpose. In this story the author is writing about playground* equipment. *What kind of* equipment *got the most votes in the story?* (the fort) Model circling the word that answers the question and ask children to do the same.

Connection of Ideas Say: *Today's story is about what a boy named Wyatt should do with a game he finds at the park.* Reread the second and third paragraphs with children. Ask: *What does Paul think Wyatt should do with the game?* Model underlining the words that give the answer (return it), and guide children to do the same.

Point of View Remind children that a character's point of view is what he or she thinks about something. Say: *To find a characters point of view, we have to look for clues in what the character says and does.* Reread the last paragraph with children. Ask: *What is Wyatt's point of view about the GameMaster?* (He thinks he should keep it.) Guide children to draw a box around the sentence that shows Wyatt's point of view. ("I found the game, so I am keeping it.")

🔍 Page 296

Connection of Ideas A C T Reread the first paragraph with children. Ask: *Does Paul think Wyatt is a good citizen or a bad citizen at school?* (a good citizen) Ask: *What does Paul say Wyatt does at school?* (solve problems) Ask: *What sentence shows that Paul thinks Wyatt is a good citizen?* ("When there are issues like this as school, you help solve the problems there.") Guide children to underline this sentence.

Expand Vocabulary Reread the second paragraph with children. Help children to locate the word *offered*. Say: *If you offered something, you gave it.* Ask: *What does Paul offer to Wyatt in the second paragraph?* Guide children to write the word that tells them what Paul *offered.* (help or his thoughts)

Point of View Remind children that on the previous page, Wyatt felt that he should keep the GameMaster he found. Reread the third paragraph aloud. Ask: *Has Wyatt changed his mind?* (yes) *How has Wyatt's point of view changed?* (He thinks he should return the GameMaster.) Guide children to draw a box around the sentence that tells what Wyatt decided. (I couldn't keep the game because it wasn't mine.)

🔍 Page 297

Expand Vocabulary Have children reread the first paragraph. Help children locate the word *hopeless* on the page. Say: *The suffix* -less *means without so to be* hopeless *means to be without hope. Who is* hopeless *in the first paragraph?* (the boy who lost his game) Instruct children to write their answer. Ask: *Why is the boy* hopeless? (Possible answer: He lost his game.)

Point of View Say: *We can find out the boy's point of view by reading what he says*. Have children reread the last two sentences of the first paragraph. Ask: *What is the boy's point of view about losing the game?* (He was not careful.) Instruct children to draw a box around the text evidence that shows the boy's point of view.

Connection of Ideas **A C T** Say: *At the end of the story Wyatt makes a decision. Reread the last paragraph*. After children have finished rereading, ask: *What does Wyatt decide to always do to be a better citizen?* Guide children to underline the words that give the answer. (try to do the right thing)

Connection of Ideas **A C T** Point to the title of the story. Ask: What was the difficult decision in this selection? (whether to keep the GameMaster or return it to its owner) Ask: *Why did the author call it "Difficult"?* (Because the boy really liked the GameMaster and wanted to keep it.)

RESPOND TO READING

Respond to "A Difficult Decision"

Read aloud the questions about "A Difficult Decision" on page 298 of the **Interactive Worktext**. Guide children read the questions and "Discussion Starters." Guide partners to answer the questions orally using the "Discussion Starters." Have children find text evidence to support their answers. Ask children to write the page number(s) on which they found the text evidence for each question.

1. *In the beginning, why do Paul and Wyatt disagree?* (Possible answers: I read that Wyatt finds a GameMaster. Paul thinks that they should return it. Wyatt thinks that he should be able to keep it. Text Evidence: p. 295)

2. *Why does Wyatt change his mind?* (Possible answers: Paul tells Wyatt it is wrong to keep it. Wyatt realizes that he should return the game. Text Evidence: p. 296)

3. *How does the end of the story show that the boys are good citizens?* (Possible answers: Paul and Wyatt are good citizens because they return a lost object to its owner. Wyatt promises to try to do the right thing. Text Evidence: p. 297)

After children discuss the questions on page 298, have them use the sentence starters to answer the question on page 299. Circulate and provide guidance.

 Quick Check **Do children understand vocabulary in context? If not, review and reteach using the instruction on page 254.**

Can children identify point of view? If not, review and reteach using the instruction on page 254 and assign the Unit 5 Week 1 digital mini-lesson.

Can children write a response to "A Difficult Decision"? If not, review the sentence starters and prompt children to respond orally. Help them write their answers.

LESSON 3

- Understand and use new vocabulary words
- Read realistic fiction
- Recognize and understand point of view
- Understand complex text through close reading

"Fixing the Playground" Apprentice Leveled Reader: pp. 2–7
- Point of View Graphic Organizer

☞ **Go** Digital
- Apprentice Leveled Reader eBook
- Downloadable Graphic Organizer
- Point of View Mini-Lesson

BEFORE READING

10–15 Minutes   SL.2.1a   SL.2.6   L.2.5a   L.2.6   **CCSS**

Introduce "Fixing the Playground"

- Read the Essential Question on the title page of "Fixing the Playground" **Apprentice Leveled Reader:** *What do good citizens do? We will read a realistic fiction story about members of a family that act as good citizens.*

- Read the title aloud. Point to the pictures. Ask: *Who are the main characters in this story?* (a family) *This story tells of a family that works to fix up a neighborhood playground. Let's read to find out how citizens work together to make their neighborhood better.*

Expand Vocabulary

Display each word below. Say the words and have children repeat them. Then use the Define/Example/Ask routine to introduce each word.

1 **blame** (page 4)

  Define: to say or think that something is the cause of something bad.

  Example: We *blame* our parrots for waking us up too early by talking loudly.

  Ask: What could you *blame* for waking you up early?

2 **mayor** (page 6)

  Define: the leader of a town or city

  Example: The *mayor* has promised to build new roads in our town.

  Ask: Who is the *mayor* of your town?

3 **ruined** (page 4)

  Define: messed up or made bad

  Example: When the basement flooded, everything in it was *ruined*.

  Ask: What can be *ruined* by too much rain?

4 **suggested** (page 7)

  Define: gave an idea

  Example: When Dad asked what we should have for dinner, I *suggested* fish.

  Ask: What was the last thing you *suggested*?

DURING READING

20–30 Minutes   RL.2.1   RL.2.6   RL.2.7   L.2.6   **CCSS**

Close Reading

 Pages 2–3

Genre **A** **C** **T**   Say: *Remember, realistic fiction is a made-up story about people and events that could happen in real life.* Point to the family in the picture. Ask: *What do we see here?* (a family) *What is the family doing?* (taking a walk) Point to the houses in the background of the picture. Ask: *Where are they? What is the setting?* (They are in a neighborhood.) *Could all of these things (the family, taking a walk, the neighborhood) exist in real life?* (yes) *That is how we know this story is realistic fiction.*

Point of View   Say: *The character's point of view is how the character sees things and what the character thinks about the events in the story. To find a character's point of view, we need to look at what the character does and says. What is Josh's point of view about the playground?* (He is upset that the swings are broken.) *How do you know?* (Because he says he wants to swing, but he can't.) Guide children to record the information in their Point of View Graphic charts.

Connection of Ideas Point to the picture of the playground and say: *Think about the Essential Question. What do you think a good citizen would do about the broken playground?* (fix it up) *What do you predict the family will do in the story?* (Possible answer: They will try to fix up the playground.)

Pages 4–5

Point of View Read the page 4 with students. Ask: *Who are Max and his sister, Jordan, talking about?* (their little brother, Josh) *Look at what the characters say to find their point of view. What is Jordan's point of view about why Josh was fussing during the walk?* (He was upset because he just wanted to play.) Guide children to record the information in their Point of View charts.

Connection of Ideas Ask: *What does Max mean when he says he doesn't blame Josh?* (He doesn't blame him for ruining their walk.) *Why doesn't he blame Josh?* (The playground is a mess. He may think little kids need a place to play.)

Point of View Read page 5 with children. Ask: *What is Jordan's point of view about keeping the playground clean?* (She thinks people should clean it.) *Who does she think should fix the swings?* (the city) Guide children to record the information in their Point of View charts.

STOP AND CHECK Read the question in the Stop and Check box on page 5. (The swings are broken.)

Pages 6–7

Connection of Ideas Explain to children that sometimes the author will include illustrations to show what the characters are doing. Point to the picture and ask: *What is the family doing while they have a conversation?* (They are eating dinner.) *What was Mom doing in the illustration on the previous pages?* (cooking) *What do you think she was cooking?* (the dinner they are eating)

Point of View Have children read page 6. Ask: *What person does Josh think might be able to help with the playground?* (the mayor) *What is Jordan's point of view about calling the mayor?* (She thinks he is busy with other issues.) Guide children to record the information in their Point of View charts.

Connection of Ideas Ask: *What does Max ask on page 6?* (how to get the playground cleaned up) Read page 7 with children. Ask: *Who has an idea?* (Mom) *What is Mom's idea?* (to have the family clean the playground) If children have difficulty, review the meaning of the word *suggested*. Explain that when someone *suggested* something they gave an idea.

Vocabulary Focus on the word *office*. Ask: *What is an office?* (a place where someone works) Ask: *Why is Dad calling the Mayor's office?* (to find out if they will be allowed to fix the playground) Point out that the word *office* means "a place of work." But it can also mean the people who work there. The people in the mayors office can answer the questions.

Have partners review their Point of View for pages 2–7 and discuss what they have learned.

✓ **Quick Check** Do children understand weekly vocabulary in context? If not, review and reteach using the instruction on page 254.

Can children identify point of view? If not, review and reteach using the instruction on page 254 and assign the Unit 5 Week 1 digital mini-lesson.

4
- Read realistic fiction
- Recognize and understand point of view
- Understand complex text through close reading

Go Digital
- Apprentice Leveled Reader eBook:
- Downloadable Graphic Organizer
- Point of View Mini-Lesoon

Scaffolding for **Wonders** Approaching Leveled Reader

BEFORE READING

5–10 Minutes   SL.2.1a   SL.2.6   L.2.5a   L.2.6   CCSS

Expand Vocabulary

Display each word below. Say the words and have children repeat them. Then use the Define/Example/Ask routine to introduce each word.

1 **donate** (page 9)

Define: to give something to help others

Example: The school asked people to *donate* money for a new swimming pool.

Ask: What is something you could *donate* to someone who needs help?

2 **supplies** (page 8)

Define: things needed to do a job

Example: If you want to draw a picture, you will need *supplies*, such as pencils, paper, and crayons.

Ask: What kind of *supplies* do you need to build a house?

DURING READING

15–20 Minutes   RL.2.1   RL.2.6   RL.2.7   RF.2.4   L.2.4   CCSS

Close Reading

Pages 8–9

Connection of Ideas **A C T** Say: *Remember, the family has decided to fix up the playground.* Read the first paragraph on page 8 with children. Ask: *Who else will help the family?* (the city and other people) *How do you know?* (Dad says they will ask people to volunteer and the city will give them supplies.)

Point of View Read the second paragraph on page 8 with children. Point to the word *vote* and say: *When you* vote *for someone, you choose them over someone else. Who gets Jordan's* vote *in this paragraph?* (the mayor) *What does that tell us about Jordan's point of view about the mayor?* (She thinks the mayor is doing a good job. She likes the mayor possibly because he says they can fix the playground.) Guide children to record the information on their Point of View charts.

Sentence Structure **A C T** Read page 9. Point to the word *it* in the second sentence. Say: *To find what the word* it *refers to, we can look at the sentence that comes before it. What does the word* it *refer to?* (a sign)

Pages 10–11

Vocabulary Read page 10 with children. Point to the word *too* in the second and third sentences. Say: Too *is a multiple meaning word. It can either mean "very" or "also."* Read the second sentence out loud. Say: *Max does not want the sign to be* too *high. What is the meaning of the word* too *in this sentence?* (very) Read the third sentence aloud: Say: *Max wants the kids to be able to see the sign, too. What is the meaning of the word* too *in this sentence?* (also)

Point of View Read page 11 with children. Ask: *What is Bobby's point of view about the playground?* (He thinks kids need a safe place to play.)

STOP AND CHECK Read the question in the Stop and Check box on page 11. (The family's plan is to fix the playground by asking for helpers. They hope that people will bring tools.)

Pages 12–13

Sentence Structure A C T Read page 12 with children. Help children locate the exclamation point on page 12. Say: *This mark is called an exclamation point. Authors use exclamation points to show surprise or excitement. What is the author showing excitement about in this story?* (that so many people wanted to help clean up the playground)

Pages 14–15

Point of View Remind children that to find the point of view, they must look for clues in the text. Ask: *Who came out to help fix up the playground?* (the neighbors) Read page 14 aloud. Ask: *What is the neighbors' point of view about helping?* (They feel good about it.) Guide children to record the information on their Point of View charts.

STOP AND CHECK Read the question in the Stop and Check box on page 14. (Many volunteers from the neighborhood came to help.)

AFTER READING

10–15 Minutes   RL.2.3   RL.2.6   W.2.8   L.2.4a   L.2.6   CCSS

Respond to Reading

Compare Texts Ask children to compare "A Difficult Decision" and "Fixing the Playground." What do good citizens do in each story? What problems did each of the characters face? Would you do the same thing if you faced the same problems? Why or why not? Discuss with a partner.

Summarize Have children turn to page 16 and summarize the selection. (Answers should include details about the characters' points of views.)

Text Evidence

Have partners work together to answer questions on page 16. Remind children to use their Point of View charts.

Point of View (Josh became upset when his dad tells him that he can't play on the swings because they are broken.)

Vocabulary (The text says that Josh cries because he wants to swing. Dad tells him he can't swing. Then the text says he "kept fussing." *Fussing* means "to cry or complain.")

Write About Reading (Answers will vary but should explain that Josh's feelings have changed at the end of the story. He is happy because now he can use the swings. The picture on p. 15 shows him smiling and playing happily on the swings. We know this is different from how he felt at the beginning of the story when he was upset that he couldn't use the swings.)

Independent Reading

Encourage children to read the paired selection "Hero" on pages 17–19. Have them summarize the selection and compare it to "Fixing the Playground." Have them work with a partner to answer the questions on page 19.

 Quick Check Can children identify the point of view? If not, review and reteach using the instruction on page 254 and assign the Unit 5 Week 1 digital mini-lesson.

Can children respond to the selection using text evidence? If not, provide sentence frames to help them organize their ideas.

Objectives
• Review weekly vocabulary words
• Review point of view
• Write an analysis about an author's use of point of view

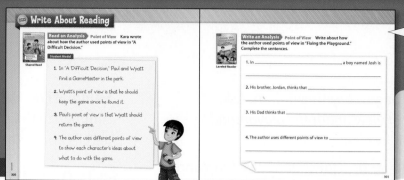

Materials
• Vocabulary Cards: 153–160
• Interactive Worktext, pp. 300–301
• Assessment Book, pp. 50–51

☞ **Go** Digital
• Visual Vocabulary Cards
• Point of View Mini-Lesson
• Interactive eWorktext
• eAssessment

Scaffolding for **Wonders** McGraw-Hill Reading Reading/Writing Workshop

---

REVIEW AND RETEACH

5–10 Minutes   RL.2.6   RL.2.3   L.2.4a   CCSS

Weekly Vocabulary

Display one **Visual Vocabulary Card** at a time and guide children to use the vocabulary word in a sentence. If children have difficulty creating a sentence, have them find the word in "A Difficult Decision" or "Fixing the Playground" and use context clues in the passage to define the vocabulary word.

Comprehension: Point of View

I Do Write and say: *Josie and her brother were playing. Their mother asked, "How about going to the movies?" "Yes!" said Josie, jumping with excitement.* Say: *Remember, you can determine a character's point of view by what the character says and does.* Underline the third sentence. Say: *I read that Josie says "Yes" and jumps with excitement. So, I know that Josie's point of view is that she wants to go see the movie.*

We Do Display and say: *Brian was building with his new blocks. His Dad said he needed to walk the dog with him. He didn't want to. "Can we wait 10 minutes? I'm almost done with my building," said Brian.* Say: *To find a character's point of view, we must look at what the character thinks and says. What does Brian do when is it time to walk the dog?* (He asks if it can wait ten minutes.) *What is Brian's point of view about going to walk the dog?* (He didn't want to.) *What is his father's point of view?* (He thinks the dog needs to be walked.)

You Do Display: *Tim woke up to find it was raining. "I don't like the rain," said Tim. "I wish I could go out and play basketball." "Aw, Tim," said his Mom. "The plants need the rain."* Have partners ask each other questions to identify Tim and his mom's points of view.

WRITE ABOUT READING

25–35 Minutes   W.2.3   W.2.8   W.4.9   CCSS

Read an Analysis

• Guide children to look back at "A Difficult Decision" in the **Interactive Worktext**. Have volunteers review the details about the author's use of point of view they marked on page 295 and summarize the text. Repeat with pages 296–297. *How did the author show the character's point of view in the selection?*

• Read aloud the directions on page 300. Read aloud the student model. *This student's work is not a summary. It is an analysis, or description, of how the author shows the character's point of view in "A Difficult Decision."*

• *When you write an analysis, you should include evidence from the selection that show how the author used point of view. Read Kara's first sentence. Circle the evidence.* (Paul and Wyatt find a GameMaster in the park.) *In what part of the story do you learn this?* (the beginning)

• *Read the second sentence. Draw a box around the evidence that shows a character's point of view.* (Wyatt's point of view is that he should keep the game since he found it.) *What part of the story is she writing about?* (the middle)

• *Guide children to point to the third sentence. This sentence gives evidence that shows another character's point of view. What detail did Kara include?* (Paul's point of view is that Wyatt should return the game.)

• *Model analyzing how the author showed the characters' points of view in the story. Read the last sentence that Kara wrote. Why is this sentence a good ending?* (Kara tells how the author used different points of view.)

Analytical Writing **Write an Analysis**

Guided Writing Read the writing prompt on page 301 together. Have children review their Point of View charts for "Fixing the Playground." Have children use their charts to complete the sentence starters. If children have difficulty, have them find an example of a character's words that show the point of view. Ask: *How does the author use this example to show the character's point of view?*

Peer Conference Have children read their analysis to a partner. Listeners should summarize the details that support the character's points of view. They should discuss any sentences that are unclear.

Teacher Conference Check children's writing for complete sentences and whether they included details from the story. Review the last sentence and ask: *Did the author use details to support the characters' points of view?* If necessary, guide children to revise their sentences by adding more details.

Level Up

▲ **Approaching Leveled Reader**

▲ **Reading/Writing Workshop**

▲ **Apprentice Leveled Reader**

▲ **Interactive Worktext**

IF children read the **Apprentice Level** Reader and the **Interactive Worktext** Shared Read fluently and answer the Respond to Reading questions

THEN read together the **Approaching Level** Reader main selection and the **Reading/Writing Workshop** Shared Read from *Reading Wonders*. Have children take notes as they read, using self-stick notes. Then ask and answer questions about their notes.

Writing Rubric

	4	3	2	1
Text Evidence	Includes three or more details from the text.	Includes two or more details from the text.	Includes only one detail from the text.	No text evidence is included.
Writing Style	Writes in complete sentences. Uses correct spelling and grammar.	Uses complete sentences. Writing has spelling and grammar errors.	Few complete sentences. There are many spelling and grammar errors.	Writing is not accurate or in complete sentences.

ASSESSMENT

Weekly Assessment

Have children complete the Weekly Assessment using **Assessment** book pages 50–51.

Teach and Model WORKTEXT

Objectives
- Develop oral language
- Build background about people cooperating
- Understand and use weekly vocabulary
- Read fiction

Materials
- Interactive Worktext, pp. 302–309
- Visual Vocabulary Cards: 161–168
- High-Frequency Word Cards

 Go Digital
- Interactive eWorktext
- Visual Vocabulary Cards

Scaffolding for **Wonders** Reading/Writing Workshop

WEEKLY CONCEPT

5–10 Minutes   SL.2.1b   SL.2.4

Talk About It

Essential Question Read aloud the Essential Question on page 302 of the **Interactive Worktext**: *How do people get along?* Explain that there are many times that people need to cooperate to get things done. Provide examples of people cooperating, such as in playing games or working on school or work projects together. Say: *People need to cooperate for many reasons. Let's find out how people can cooperate.*

- Discuss the photograph on page 302. Ask: *What is happening in the picture?* (Children are playing a game called tug-of-war. Children are pulling a rope.) Explain that this game uses a rope, and there are children at both ends of the rope. The goal is to pull the rope to your side.

> **I Do** Say: *I am going to look at the photo and think about how these children are cooperating. I see they are working together to pull the rope. I will write on the web on page 303 how they are working together.*

> **We Do** Say: Let's think about other ways these children are cooperating. Ask: *How do they know when to pull the rope? Talk with your partner about what it takes to cooperate in this game.* Then have children choose one way the children in the photo are cooperating and add it to their web.

> **You Do** Guide partners to work together to talk about how people cooperate in other situations. Have them think about something they have done that took cooperation. Have children use this sentence starter: When you cooperate, you _____. (Possible answers: listen to each other, help each other)

REVIEW VOCABULARY

10–15 Minutes   L.2.4a   L.2.6   RF.2.3f

Review Weekly Vocabulary Words

- Use the **Visual Vocabulary Cards** to review the weekly vocabulary.

- Read together the directions on page 304 of the **Interactive Worktext**. Then complete the activity.

1 describe Have children think about their favorite animal without saying it out loud. Then have them use three words to *describe* that animal to a partner. Have the partner use this sentence frame to guess the animal: *The animal being* described *is* _____. (Answers will vary.)

2 interact Have two children *interact* with one another as the rest of the class watches. Ask children to think about the different people that they *interact* with each day. Have them complete this sentence frame: *I* interact *with* _____ *on my way to school each day.* (Possible answers: bus driver, crossing guard)

3 cooperate Have volunteers describe what it means for two people to *cooperate*. Invite one pair to show how two people *cooperate* to keep a balloon up in the air for 15 seconds. Then have children suggest sports in which people need to *cooperate* as you list them on the board. Guide children to explain how they *cooperate*.

4 patient Ask children if they consider themselves a *patient* person. Ask them what makes a person *patient*. Have them act out how a *patient* person waits for a friend to arrive. Ask: *What is the opposite of* patient? (Possible answers: impatient, or not able to wait) Then have them act out how a person who is *impatient* acts.

5 amused Ask children to describe what people do when they are *amused*. (laugh, smile) Invite volunteers to suggest words that are related to the word *amused*. (amuse, amusement, amusing) If necessary, provide children with an example of a joke.

6 peaceful Write the word *peaceful*. Have children underline the root word *peace* and circle the suffix *-ful*. Explain to children that *-ful* means *full of* in this case. Have children complete the sentence frame: *A place that I think is* peaceful *is* _____. (Possible answers: study hall, bedroom, woods)

7 entertained Invite volunteers to suggest words that are related to the word *entertained*. (entertain, entertainment) Have children tell about the last time they were *entertained* by someone or something. Then have them describe the last time they themselves *entertained* someone. (Answers will vary.)

8 imagination Explain to children that anything is possible when they use their *imagination*. Tell them to close their eyes and *imagine* what the ocean floor looks like. Have them describe their picture using this sentence starter: *When I use my* imagination, *I see* _____.

High-Frequency Words

Have children look at page 305 in the **Interactive Worktext**. Help them read, spell, and write each high-frequency word. Guide partners to use each word in a sentence. Then read the story aloud with children. Guide partners to work together to reread the story and circle the high-frequency words. (laughed, get, fly, use, our, today) Listen in and provide assistance reading the high-frequency words, as necessary.

ELL ENGLISH LANGUAGE LEARNERS

Display the **High-Frequency Word Cards** for: *laughed, use, today, our, fly, get*. Write a sentence with each word on the board. Have children echo-read each sentence, and point out the high-frequency word. Then ask them to use the word in a new sentence.

READ COMPLEX TEXT

15–20 Minutes   RL.2.6 RL.2.3 SL.2.1b

Read "Soccer Friends"

- Have children turn to page 306 in the **Interactive Worktext** and read aloud the Essential Question. Point to the illustration. Say: *What are these girls doing?* (getting ready for soccer practice) *Let's read to find out how people get along when there is a problem.* Have children echo-read the title.

- Read the story together. Note that the weekly vocabulary words are highlighted in yellow. Expand Vocabulary words are highlighted in blue.

- As children read, have them use the "My Notes" section on page 306 to write questions they have. Children can also write words they don't understand or things they want to remember. Model how to use the "My Notes" section. *When I read the first three paragraphs on page 307, I find out Kelly is worried about a new girl on the soccer team who is a fast runner. I will write a question about why she is worried about this new girl in the "My Notes" section.*

ELL ENGLISH LANGUAGE LEARNERS

As you read together, have children highlight parts of the text they have questions about. After reading, review the questions children have. Then help them locate the answers to their questions in the text.

✓ *Quick Check* Can children understand the weekly vocabulary in context? If not, review vocabulary using the **Visual Vocabulary Cards** before teaching Lesson 2.

Can children read high-frequency words in context? If not, review using the Read/Spell/Write routine and the High-Frequency Word Cards.

WEEK 2
LESSON 2

Objectives
• Read fiction
• Understand complex text through close reading
• Recognize and understand point of view
• Respond to the selection using text evidence to support ideas

Materials
Interactive Worktext, pp. 306–311

☞ **Go** Digital
• Interactive eWorktext
• Point of View Mini-Lesson

Scaffolding for **Wonders** Reading/Writing Workshop

REREAD COMPLEX TEXT

20–25 Minutes   RL.2.6   RL.2.3   L.2.6   CCSS

Close Reading: "Soccer Friends"

Reread "Soccer Friends" from **Interactive Worktext** pages 306–309 with children. As you read together, discuss important passages in the text. Guide children to respond to questions using evidence from the text.

🔍 Pages 306–307

Sentence Structure Ⓐ Ⓒ Ⓣ Reread the second paragraph with children. Remind children that a paragraph sometimes has dialogue, or a character's exact words, in it. Remind children that quotation marks show the words a character speaks. Ask: *Who speaks in the second paragraph?* (Tara) *Who is Tara speaking to?* (Kelly) Guide children to underline the words that tell what Tara says to Kelly. (That is Selena. She is a fast runner.)

Expand Vocabulary Reread the third paragraph aloud. Point to the word *worried*. Say: *If you are* worried, *you feel nervous about something. Why is Kelly* worried? (She is worried that Selena will be faster than she is.) Guide children to write their answers. If children have difficulty, point out the second sentence in the paragraph. Guide children to see that Kelly is proud of being the fastest on the team, and she worries that Selena may replace her as the fastest.

Point of View Say: *To find the point of view, we must think about what the characters do and say*. Reread the third paragraph with children. Ask: *What is Kelly's point of view about racing against Selena?* (Kelly thinks she can beat Selena.) Model drawing a box around the sentence that tells Kelly's point of view. (I can beat her.)

🔍 Page 308

Sentence Structure Ⓐ Ⓒ Ⓣ Reread the second sentence with children. Say: *This sentence has two parts separated by the word* but. But *means "except" or "however." What does the first part of the sentence tell us?* (that Kelly ran as fast as she could) What does the second part of the sentence tell us? (that she could not beat Selena) Guide children to underline the words that tell what Kelly was not able to do. (she could not beat Selena)

Connection of Ideas Ⓐ Ⓒ Ⓣ Reread the second paragraph with children. Say: *Let's think about why Kelly was not amused*. Explain to children that if they don't understand something that happens in a story, they should go back and reread the text that came before. Ask: *Why was Kelly not amused?* (She wasn't amused because she was upset that she had just lost a race to Selena.)

Point of View Reread the third and fourth paragraph with children. Say: *Kelly is talking about her race with Selena. We can look at what she says to find her point of view. What is her point of view about losing the race?* Guide children to draw a box around the sentence that tells them Kelly's point of view. (It stinks to get beaten.)

Expand Vocabulary Have children echo-read the word *disappointed* in the last paragraph. Say: Disappointed *means feeling sad because you did not get what you wanted. Who is* disappointed *in the story?* (Kelly) *Why do you think she is disappointed?* (She didn't win the race.) Guide children to write Kelly's name.

Page 309

Expand Vocabulary Ask children to reread the first paragraph. Write the word *goalie* on the board. Say: *A goalie is a person who guards against goals in a soccer game. Who is the goalie in the first paragraph?* (Selena) *Underline the words that tell what Selena did when she was goalie.* (She quickly blocked a goal.)

Expand Vocabulary Point to the word *thumped* in the second paragraph. Say: *If something was thumped it was hit hard and made a dull sound. Circle the words that tell what Kelly thumped.* (the ball)

Point of View Remind children that at the beginning of the story, Kelly was worried about playing with Selena. Have children reread the fourth paragraph. Ask: *What is Kelly's point of view at the end of the story?* (She wants to work together with Selena.) *Draw a box around the words that tell you.* (I think our team can be great if we cooperate and work together.)

RESPOND TO READING

10–20 Minutes   SL.2.1a RL.2.6 RL.2.3 **CCSS**

Respond to "Soccer Friends"

Read aloud the questions about "Soccer Friends" on page 310 of the **Interactive Worktext**. Then read aloud the "Discussion Starter" for each of the questions. Have children work with a partner to answer the questions orally using the "Discussion Starters." Have children find text evidence to support their answers. Ask children to write the page number(s) on which they found the text evidence for each question.

1. *How does Kelly feel about Selena in the beginning of the story?* (Possible answers: Tara says that Selena is a fast runner. Kelly feels worried because she thought she was the fastest runner on the team. Text Evidence: p. 307)

2. *What happens at practice?* (Possible answers: Selena beats Kelly in a race. Kelly's mom tells Kelly that Selena may be good for the team. Text Evidence: p. 308)

3. *What happens at the end of the story?* (Possible answers: Kelly and Selena work together to help their team win. I read that Selena tells Kelly that she did a great job. Kelly decides to be Selena's friend. Text Evidence: p. 309)

After children discuss the questions on page 310, have them use the sentence starters to answer the question on page 311. Circulate and provide guidance.

 Quick Check Do children understand vocabulary in context? If not, review and reteach using the instruction on page 264.

Can children identify point of view? If not, review and reteach using the instruction on page 264 and assign the Unit 5 Week 2 digital mini-lesson.

Can children write a response to "Soccer Friends"? If not, review the sentence starters and prompt children to respond orally. Help them write their responses.

Objectives
- Understand and use new vocabulary words
- Read fiction
- Recognize and understand point of view
- Understand complex text through close reading

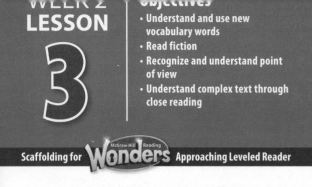

by Jerome Anderson
illustrated by Marcy Tippmann

Materials
- "Rainy Day" Apprentice Leveled Reader: pp. 2–9
- Point of View Graphic Organizer

☞ **Go** Digital
- Apprentice Leveled Reader eBook
- Downloadable Graphic Organizer
- Point of View Digital Mini-Lesson

Scaffolding for **Wonders** Approaching Leveled Reader

BEFORE READING

10–15 Minutes   SL.2.1a   SL.2.6   L.2.5a   L.2.6   CCSS

Introduce "Rainy Day"

- Read the Essential Question on the title page of "Rainy Day" **Apprentice Leveled Reader:** *How do people get along? We will read a fiction story about two girls who get along, even though their plans had to change.*

- Read the title aloud. Point to the pictures. Ask: *Who is the main character in this story?* (a young girl) *What is the weather like outside?* (It is raining.) *What do you like to do when it is raining out? Let's read to find out how a girl and her cousin find ways to have fun even though it is raining.*

Expand Vocabulary

Display each word below. Say the words and have children repeat them. Then use the Define/Example/Ask routine to introduce each word.

1 **awful** (page 8)

Define: very bad

Example: I was sick and felt *awful*.

Ask: What word means the opposite of *awful*?

2 **drummed** (page 3)

Define: something that made a beating or tapping sound

Example: The boy tapped and *drummed* his fingers on the counter.

Ask: If you *drummed* your fingers on your desk, what did you do?

3 **moaned** (page 2)

Define: to make a noise or say something that means you are not happy

Example: "I don't want to go to the dentist," Lars *moaned*.

Ask: What have you *moaned* about?

DURING READING

20–30 Minutes   RL.2.1   RL.2.6   L.2.4   L.2.6   L.4.5   CCSS

Close Reading

🔍 **Pages 2–3**

Point of View Explain to children that a character's point of view is what the character thinks about the events in the story. Read page 2 with children. Say: *To find the point of view, we can look at what a character says and does.* Point to the picture on page 2 and say: *Does Jenna look happy or sad in this picture?* (sad) *That gives a clue about her point of view. Now let's look at what she says. What is Jenna's point of view about the rain?* (She doesn't like the rain.) *What is Jenna's point of view about how the day will be?* (She thinks the day will not be fun.) Guide children to record the information in their Point of View charts.

Connection of Ideas Read page 3 with children. Remind children of the Essential Question about how people get along. Ask: *What does Jenna do in the second paragraph on page three?* (She shouts "And it's noisy!") *Is shouting a good way to get along with people?* (no)

Pages 4–5

Vocabulary Read page 4 with children. Say: *Sometimes we use expressions that have a different meaning than the real meaning of the words. For example, a person might say he has "run out of steam" if he is tired. These expressions form a word picture of how something looks, sounds, acts, or feels. They are called idioms. What is the idiom on this page?* (When Gran says that Jenna "woke up on the wrong side of the bed.") *To understand an idiom, you must look for clues in the story. What do we already know about Jenna's mood?* (She is in a bad mood.) *So what might it mean to "wake up on the wrong side of the bed"?* (to be in a bad mood)

Sentence Structure (A C T) Point out that Gran begins her sentence with the words "Sounds like. " Remind children that usually there would be a noun or pronoun at the beginning of such a sentence. Ask: *What is Gran talking about?* (how Jenna sounds) Explain that the sentence should begin with the word *It*. But this is dialogue and people don't always talk in complete sentences. Say: *This is how Gran might really talk.*

Key Details Remind children that pictures can help tell more about how a character feels. Read page 5 . Ask: *How do you think Gran feels about the rain?* (She likes it.) *How do you know?* (The picture shows her smiling and the text says that she is amused.)

STOP AND CHECK Read the question in the Stop and Check box on page 5. (Jenna is not happy about the rain. She thinks it is boring and noisy.)

Pages 6–7

Point of View Explain to children that different characters in a story can have different points of view. Read page 6 with children. Say: *Who comes to visit Jenna?* (her cousin Nikki) *Maybe Nikki has a different point of view about the rain. What does the picture tell you about Jenna's point of view.* (She looks happy.) *What do the words tell you?* (She has been waiting months to wear her rain boots.) Guide children to record the information in their Point of View charts.

Sentence Structure (A C T) Read page 7 with children. Ask: *Which words show that someone asked a question on this page?* (Nikki asked) *What question did Nikki ask?* (See the yellow ducks?) Point out that this sentence does not begin with a question word, but that you can tell its a question because of the question mark. The real sentence would be *"Can you see the yellow ducks?"* Explain that the author might have left these words off to sound more like a real girl is talking.

Pages 8–9

Key Details Read page 9 with children. Ask: *Who is speaking on page 9?* (Aunt Susan) *What does Aunt Susan think will happen with the rain?* (She thinks it might stop later.) *How do you know?* (She says maybe the sun will come out.)

Sentence Structure (A C T) Read the last sentence on page 9 aloud. Say: *Aunt Susan thinks the girls can stay entertained until "then." To find out what "then" refers to, look for clues in the same paragraph. What else does Aunt Susan say in this paragraph?* (Maybe the sun will come out later.) *What does "then" refer to in the second sentence?* (*Then* refers to later, when the sun comes out.)

Have partners review their Point of View charts for pages 2–9 and discuss what they have learned.

✔ *Quick Check* Do children understand weekly vocabulary in context? If not, review and reteach using the instruction on page 264.

Can children identify point of view? If not, review and reteach using the instruction on page 264 and assign the Unit 5 Week 2 digital mini-lesson.

Objectives
• Understand and use new vocabulary words
• Read fiction
• Recognize and understand point of view
• Understand complex text through close reading

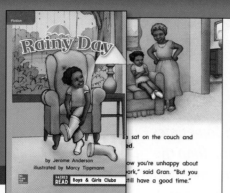

Materials
"Rainy Day" Apprentice Leveled Reader: pp. 10–20
• Point of View Graphic Organizer

☞ **Go** Digital
• Apprentice Leveled Reader eBook
• Downloadable Graphic Organizer
• Point of View Mini-Lesson

Scaffolding for **Wonders** Approaching Leveled Reader

BEFORE READING

5–10 Minutes   SL.2.1a SL.2.6 L.2.5a L.2.6   CCSS

Expand Vocabulary

Display each word below. Say the words and have children repeat them. Then use the Define/Example/Ask routine to introduce each word.

1 inside (page 12)

Define: in something, not outside or shown

Example: I opened my jacket to show the *inside* pocket has a bag of peanuts.

Ask: Why are *inside* swimming pools built?

2 pouted (page 10)

Define: showed not being happy, often by pushing your lips out and looking upset

Example: When his mom would not give him ice cream, Joe frowned and *pouted*.

Ask: What has made you *pout*? Show what a *pout* looks like.

DURING READING

15–20 Minutes   RL.2.1 RL.2.2 RL.2.6 RL.2.7 L.2.4a   CCSS

Close Reading

Pages 10–11

Vocabulary Point to the word *pouted* on page 10. Say: *Someone who* pouted *showed they were not happy.* Point to the picture of Jenna on page 10. Say: *This is what someone who is* pouting *looks like. What other words on the page give a clue to the meaning of* pouted? (I know you're unhappy about the park, Jenna.)

Sentence Structure Ⓐ Ⓒ Ⓣ Ask: *What does Nikki say to Jenna on page 11?* (I like the rain but I'm sorry you're sad.) Point out that this sentence has two parts. Ask: *What do we find out about how Nikki feels in the first half of the sentence?* (She likes the rain.) *What do we find out about how she feels in the second half of the sentence* (She is sorry Jenna is sad.) *What word connects the two parts of this sentence?* (but) Explain that the word *but* helps us to know that the character is having two feelings that may not go together that easily.

Point of View Say: *A character's point of view can change during the story. Jenna has been grumpy and upset in the story so far. What is a clue in the text that shows her point of view may be changing?* (The text says "Jenna knew Gran was right.") Point to the picture on the page. Ask: *What is another clue that Jenna is starting to feel better?* (In the picture, Jenna is smiling instead of frowning.)

STOP AND CHECK Read the question in the Stop and Check box on page 11. (Jenna pouts because she wanted to go to the park.)

Pages 12–13

Connection of Ideas Ⓐ Ⓒ Ⓣ Review the Essential Question with children. Say: *Sometimes we do things we do not like so that we can get along with others. We have read that Jenna does not like the rain. What does Jenna offer to do, so that she can get along with Nikki?* (She offers to go outside with Nikki.)

Connection of Ideas Ⓐ Ⓒ Ⓣ Read page 13 with children. Say: *Nikki knows that Jenna does not like the rain. What idea does she have that might make the rainy day fun for Jenna?* (to have an inside picnic)

Pages 14–15

Key Details Read page 14 with children. Ask: *How does Jenna feel about the new plan?* (She thinks it will be fun.)

Point of View Read page 15 with children. Remind children that sometimes a character's point of view can change during a story. Ask: *What was Jenna's point of view about the rainy day at the beginning of the story?* (She didn't like it.) *What is Jenna's point of view about the rainy day on page 15?* (She thinks it is not so bad.) Guide children to record the information in their Point of View charts.

STOP AND CHECK Read the question in the Stop and Check box on page 15. (The new plan is that the girls will go outside first, then they will make lunch and have an inside picnic.)

AFTER READING

10–15 Minutes   RL.2.1   RL.2.2   RL.2.6   W.2.8   L.2.4a   CCSS

Respond to Reading

Compare Texts Ask children to compare "Soccer Friends" and "Rainy Day." What problem do the main characters face in each story? How do the kids get along? Discuss with a partner.

Summarize Have children turn to page 16 and summarize the selection. (Answers should include details that shows the characters' points of view.)

Text Evidence

Have partners work together to answer questions on page 16. Remind children to use their Point of View charts.

Point of View (Jenna feels very upset about the rain at first. The text on p. 2 says that she finds it boring and worries that her day won't be fun. Then on p. 6, Nikki arrives. On p. 7 she says that she wants to try her boots out in puddles outside. She is happy that it's raining. Both of the girls are happy by the end of the story when they make a new plan.)

Vocabulary (The text on p. 2 reads, "Now the day won't be fun. Rain is so boring." We can guess that *boring* must be the opposite of fun from the context of the sentence.)

Write About Reading (Answers will vary but should explain that Jenna's point of view changes after her Gran and Nikki make her realize that she can still have a fun day even though it's raining. The text on p. 11 says that Jenna realized that Gran was right. Jenna agrees to go outside and then make lunch and have an inside picnic afterwards. By this time, Jenna is feeling happier.)

Independent Reading

Encourage children to read the paired selection "Boys & Girls Clubs" on pages 17–19. Have them summarize the selection and compare it to "Rainy Day." Have them work with a partner to answer the questions on page 19.

✓ *Quick Check* Can children identify the point of view? If not, review and reteach using the instruction on page 254 and assign the Unit 5 Week 2 digital mini-lesson.

Can children respond to the selection using text evidence? If not, provide sentence frames to help them organize their ideas.

REVIEW AND RETEACH

5–10 Minutes   RL.2.6 RL.2.3 L.2.4a CCSS

Weekly Vocabulary

Display one **Visual Vocabulary Card** at a time and guide children to use the vocabulary word in a sentence. If children have difficulty creating a sentence, have them find the word in "Soccer Friends" or "Rainy Day" and use context clues in the passage to define the vocabulary word.

Comprehension: Point of View

I Do   Write and say: *Nate pointed to some ants on the ground. "Ants are gross," Nate said. Joon said, "Ants are cool. They can carry 50 times more than their body weight." "Wow! Ants are cool," Nate said.* Say: *Point of view is what the characters think about events in a story.* Ask: *Which clue tells you Nate's point of view about ants at the beginning of the story?* Circle "Ants are gross." Write: *Nate's Point of View: He doesn't like ants.* Ask: *Which clue tells you Joon's point of view?* Circle: "Ants are cool." Write: *Joon's Point of View: She likes ants.*

We Do   Say: *A character's point of view can change during a story.* Ask: *Which clue tells you Nate's point of view at the end of the story?* Circle: *"Wow! Ants are cool."* Write: *Nate's point of view: He likes ants, now.*

You Do   Display: *"I don't like peas," Matt said. Lea said, "I like peas. They are sweet and tasty. Try a few." Matt ate them and said, "Peas are good. I like them."* Guide one partner to ask the other to identify clues and each character's point of view. Have partners switch and discuss their answers. Have them discuss how Matt's point of view changes in the story.

WRITE ABOUT READING

25–35 Minutes   W.2.3 W.2.8 W.4.9 CCSS

Read an Analysis

- Guide children to look back at "Soccer Friends" in the **Interactive Worktext**. Have volunteers review the details about the author's use of point of view they marked on page 307 and summarize the text. Repeat with pages 308–309. *How did the author show the character's point of view in the selection?*

- Read aloud the directions on page 312. Read aloud the student model. *This student's work is not a summary. It is an analysis, or description, of how the author showed the character's point of view in "Soccer Friends."*

- *When you write an analysis, you should tell evidence from the story that shows the character's point of view. Read Emil's first sentence. What details about a character's point of view does Emil include? Circle the evidence.* (Kelly's point of view is that it is not fun to get beaten in a race.) *In what part of the story do you learn this detail?* (in the middle)

- *Read the second sentence. Draw a box around the evidence from the story where you see another point of view.* (Kelly's mother's point of view is that it is good for the team to have Selena.) *What part of the story is he writing about?* (the middle)

- *Guide children to point to the third sentence. This sentence explains what happened at the end of the story. What details does Emil include?* (Kelly thinks that her team can be great if she and Selena cooperate.)

- *Model analyzing how the author showed characters' point of view. Read the last sentence that Emil wrote. Why is this sentence a good ending?* (Emil understands why the author showed different points of view.)

Write an Analysis

Analytical Writing

Guided Writing Read the writing prompt on page 313 together. Have children review their Point of View charts for "Rainy Day." Have children use these charts to complete the sentence starters. Children can also write the analysis using another selection previously read this week.

Peer Conference Guide children to read their analysis to a partner. Listeners should summarize the details that support the beginning, middle, and ending sentences. They should discuss any parts that are unclear.

Teacher Conference Check children's writing for complete sentences and and whether they included details from the story. Review the last sentence and ask: *Did the author use details to show points of view?* If necessary, guide children to revise their sentences by adding details from the story.

Level Up

▲ Approaching Leveled Reader

▲ Reading/Writing Workshop

▲ Apprentice Leveled Reader

▲ Interactive Worktext

IF children read the Apprentice Level Reader and the **Interactive Worktext** Shared Read fluently and answer the Respond to Reading questions

THEN read together the Approaching Level Reader main selection and the **Reading/Writing Workshop** Shared Read from *Reading Wonders*. Have children take notes as they read, using self-stick notes. Then ask and answer questions about their notes.

Writing Rubric

	4	3	2	1
Text Evidence	Includes three or more details from the text.	Includes two or more details from the text.	Includes only one detail from the text.	No text evidence is included.
Writing Style	Writes in complete sentences. Uses correct spelling and grammar.	Uses complete sentences. Writing has spelling and grammar errors.	Few complete sentences. There are many spelling and grammar errors.	Writing is not accurate or in complete sentences.

ASSESSMENT

Weekly Assessment

Have children complete the Weekly Assessment using **Assessment** book pages 52–53.

WEEK 3 LESSON 1

Objectives
- Develop oral language
- Build background about heroes
- Understand and use weekly vocabulary
- Read a biography

Materials
Interactive Worktext, pp. 314–321
- Visual Vocabulary Cards: 169–176
- High-Frequency Word Cards

☞ **Go** Digital
- Interactive eWorktext
- Visual Vocabulary Cards

Scaffolding for **Wonders** McGraw-Hill Reading Reading/Writing Workshop

WEEKLY CONCEPT

5–10 Minutes   SL.2.1a SL.2.4 CCSS

Talk About It

Essential Question Read aloud the Essential Question on page 314 of the **Interactive Worktext:** *What do heroes do?* Explain that a hero is someone who is looked up to by others because of his or her achievements and courage. Say: *A fireman is an example of a hero to many people. Firemen risk their lives to save other people's lives.*

- Discuss the photograph on page 314. Ask: *What is happening in the picture?* (A fireman is putting out a fire with a hose.) Have children identify what else they see in the picture. (firetruck in the background; fireman wearing a helmet, a protective jacket, and gloves)

I Do Say: *I am going to look at the photo and think about how this fireman is a hero. The fireman is risking his life to put out a fire and possibly save people's lives. I will write on the chart on page 315 how he is a hero.* Read aloud the headings for each column and write the information for each column as you read it aloud.

We Do Say: *Let's think about other heroes who we know or have heard of. Think about people who show courage and bravery in their lives.* Guide children to think of heroes they have either read about or know of. Have them explain why they think they are heroes. Then have children choose one person and add them to their charts.

You Do Guide partners to work together to talk about other heroes they know of. Have them use words from the chart to start their sentences: _____ *is a hero. What makes them a hero is* _____.

REVIEW VOCABULARY

10–15 minutes   L.2.4a L.2.6 RF.2.3 CCSS

Review Weekly Vocabulary Words

- Use the **Visual Vocabulary Cards** to review the weekly vocabulary.

- Read together the directions on page 316 of the **Interactive Worktext**. Then complete the activity.

1 **agree** Have partners list foods they like to eat. Then have them figure out which foods they both *agree* on. Have children use this sentence starter: *I agree with you about* _____. Using your head and face, nod to show children what it looks like when you *agree* with someone. Have children imitate your actions.

2 **interest** Guide children to brainstorm things that they like to do in their free time. Tell them that these hobbies show their *interests*. Have children ask their partner the following question: *Do you have an interest in* _____? (Answer will vary.)

3 **challenging** Write the word *challenging* on the board. Name something that is challenging for you. Have children think of other things that are *challenging* to them. Then make a list of words that mean the same as *challenging*. (Possible answers: difficult, hard)

4 **succeed** Guide children to brainstorm their favorite subject. Ask them to think about what they can do to *succeed* at it. Ask volunteers what someone should do to *succeed* at playing softball. (Possible answers: practice, ask a coach for help)

5 **heroes** Guide children to brainstorm people who they think are *heroes*. (Possible answers: mother, fire fighter) Have children use the following sentence starter: *These people are* heroes *because* _____. (Possible answers: they are brave, they help people)

6 **study** Guide children to name the school subjects they *study* as you list them on the board. Then use this sentence frame: *The first subject I* study *at school each day is* _____. (Possible answers: math, science)

7 **perform** Invite volunteers to suggest words that are related to the word *perform*. (performer, performance) Have children brainstorm groups of people who perform on stage. (singers, dancers, actors) Then use this sentence starter: *I want to* perform *a* _____ *on stage.* (song, dance, scene)

8 **discover** Invite children to brainstorm things they might see in the woods. (plants, animals, rocks) Then assist children as they draw a picture of something they might *discover* in the woods. Have children complete this sentence: *I might* discover *a* _____ *on a walk in the woods.* (Possible answers: deer, walking trail, hidden stream)

High-Frequency Words

Have children look at page 317 in the **Interactive Worktext**. Help them read, spell, and write each high-frequency word. Guide partners to use each word in a sentence. Then read the story aloud with children. Guide partners to work together to reread the story and circle the high-frequency words. (first, called, all, was, did, hurt) Listen in and provide assistance reading the high-frequency words, as necessary.

> **ELL ENGLISH LANGUAGE LEARNERS**
>
> Display the **High-Frequency Word Cards** for: *called, was, first, did, hurt, all*. Write a sentence with each word on the board. Have children echo-read each sentence, and point out the high-frequency word. Then ask them to use the word in a new sentence.

READ COMPLEX TEXT

15–20 Minutes   RI.2.3   RI.2.7   SL.2.1b   CCSS

Read "César Chávez"

- Have children turn to page 318 in the **Interactive Worktext** and read aloud the Essential Question. Point to the picture. Say: *This man's name is César Chávez. He is a hero.* Have children repeat: *hero. Let's read to find out what he did to become a hero.* Have children echo-read the title.

- Read the story together. Note that the weekly vocabulary words are highlighted in yellow. Expand Vocabulary words are highlighted in blue.

- As children read, have them use the "My Notes" section on page 318 to write questions they have. Children can also write words they don't understand or things they want to remember. Model how to use the "My Notes" section. *When I read the title, I wonder what I will learn about César Chávez. How is he a hero? I will look for answers as I read.*

> **ELL ENGLISH LANGUAGE LEARNERS**
>
> As you read together, have children highlight parts of the text they have questions about. After reading, review the questions children have. Then help them locate the answers to their questions in the text.

 Quick Check Can children understand the weekly vocabulary in context? If not, review vocabulary using the **Visual Vocabulary Cards** before teaching Lesson 2.

Can children read high-frequency words in context? If not, review using the Read/Spell/Write routine and the High-Frequency Word Cards.

WEEK 3 LESSON

2

Objectives
- Read a biography
- Understand complex text through close reading
- Recognize and understand sequence
- Respond to the selection using text evidence to support ideas

Scaffolding for **McGraw-Hill Reading Wonders** Reading/Writing Workshop

Materials
Interactive Worktext, pp. 318–323

👉 **Go Digital**
- Interactive eWorktext
- Sequence Mini-Lesson

REREAD COMPLEX TEXT

20–25 Minutes   RI.2.3   RI.2.7   L.2.4a   **CCSS**

Close Reading: "César Chávez"

Reread "César Chávez" with children from **Interactive Worktext** pages 318–321. As you read together, discuss important passages in the text. Guide children to respond to questions using evidence from the text.

 Page 319

Genre **A C T**   Remind children that a biography gives true facts about a real person; in this selection, César Chávez. Say: *Biographies often tell about a person's life in the order the events happen.* Have children reread the third paragraph. Ask: *What did César Chávez do when he was young?* Say: *I read that Cesar worked on his family's farm.* Guide children to underline their answer. (César worked on the family farm as a young boy.)

Sequence   Remind children that *sequence* is the order in which things happen. *Sequence* is especially important for biographies because you can see how events in a person's life build him or her into an adult. Have children reread the third and fourth paragraphs. Ask: *What happened after César worked on his family farm?* Guide children to write their answer. (César went to school.)

Expand Vocabulary   Have children reread the fourth paragraph. Tell them that if someone is *punished,* he or she is made to suffer for doing something wrong. Ask: *Why was César* punished *at school?* Have children circle their answers. (for speaking Spanish)

🔍 **Page 320**

Genre **A C T**   Remind children that an expository text often has text features, such as photos, graphs, and charts. These features can help explain the information they are reading about or give additional information. Have children look at the time line at the bottom of the page. Say: *A time line shows the most important events of a person's life in the order they happened.* Show how to read the time line from left to right. Have children read along with you. Ask: *In what year did César convince farm workers to strike?* Have them underline their answers. (1965)

Sequence   Guide children to reread the first two paragraphs. Ask: *Where did César's family go after the drought killed the plants on their farm?* Guide children to write their answer. (His family moved to California.) Ask: *Why did they go to California?* (to work on the farms there)

Expand Vocabulary   Explain to children that if you *complain* about something, you say that you are unhappy about it. Have them reread the last paragraph. Ask: *Why did the workers* complain? Have children circle the words that answer. (The work they had to do made their backs hurt and their fingers bleed.) Ask: *What happened when the workers* complained? (The farm owners fired them.)

Page 321

Sequence Have children reread the first two paragraphs. Ask: *What did César tell the workers to do after he learned they were not being treated fairly?* Children should draw a box around the text that answers the question. (César told the workers to stop working.) Ask: *What happened when the workers stopped working?* (The grapes began to rot, and the landowners lost money.)

Sequence Have children reread the second paragraph. Ask: *What did the landowners do after they talked to César?* Children should draw a box around the text that answers the question. (They promised better pay.)

Expand Vocabulary Explain to children that if you *improve* something, you make it better. Have them reread the last paragraph. Ask: *What did César Chávez work to* improve *during his life?* Have children circle the words that answer. (farm workers' lives) Ask: *Do you think César Chávez was a hero? Why or Why not?* (Answers will vary.)

Connection of Ideas A C T Have children look back at page 319. Explain that when César was punished unfairly at school, his mother taught him to find calm ways to solve problems. Ask: *How did this lesson help him later in life?* (He learned how to help improve farm workers' lives peacefully. He learned to win struggles without fighting.)

RESPOND TO READING

10–20 Minutes SL.2.1a RI.2.3 RI.2.7

Respond to "César Chávez"

Guide children to echo read the questions about "César Chávez" on page 322 of the **Interactive Worktext**. Then read aloud the "Discussion Starter" for each of the questions. Guide children to work with a partner to answer the questions using the "Discussion Starters." Have children find text evidence to support their answers. Ask children to write the page number(s) on which they found the text evidence for each question.

1. *What lessons did César learn as a child?* (Possible answers: César's parents taught him about hard work and respect. His mother taught him to find peaceful ways to solve problems. Text Evidence: p. 319)

2. *Why did César want to help migrant workers?* (Possible answers: Migrant workers had difficult lives because they worked hard for little money. César decided to take action because he knew migrant workers were not treated fairly. Text Evidence: pp. 320, 321)

3. *How did César help migrant workers?* (Possible answers: César's plan was for migrant workers to strike, or stop working. I read that this made the farm owners promise better pay. Text Evidence: p. 321)

After children discuss the questions on page 322, have them use the sentence starters to answer the question on page 323. Circulate and provide guidance.

 Quick Check Do children understand vocabulary in context? If not, review and reteach using the instruction on page 274.

Can children identify sequence? If not, review and reteach using the instruction on page 274 and assign the Unit 5 Week 3 digital mini-lesson.

Can children write a response to "César Chávez"? If not, review the sentence starters and prompt children to respond orally. Help them write their responses.

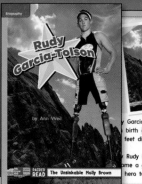

WEEK 3 LESSON 3

Objectives
- Understand and use new vocabulary words
- Read a biography
- Recognize and understand sequence
- Understand complex text through close reading

Materials
- "Rudy Garcia-Tolson" Apprentice Leveled Reader: pp. 2–9
- Sequence Graphic Organizer

☞ **Go** Digital
- Apprentice Leveled Reader eBook
- Downloadable Graphic Organizer
- Sequence Mini-Lesson

Scaffolding for **Wonders** Approaching Leveled Reader

BEFORE READING

10–15 Minutes   SL.2.1a SL.2.6 L.2.5a L.2.6 **CCSS**

Introduce "Rudy Garcia-Tolson"

- Read the Essential Question on the title page of "Rudy Garcia-Tolson" **Apprentice Leveled Reader:** *What do heroes do? We will read about what makes a person a hero and why people call him or her a hero.*

- Read the title aloud. Point to the photographs. Ask: *Is this text fiction or nonfiction?* (nonfiction) *This nonfiction text is called a biography. It gives true information about a person. Let's read to learn about Rudy Garcia-Tolson.*

Expand Vocabulary

Display each word below. Say the words and have children repeat them. Then use the Define/Example/Ask routine to introduce each word.

① athletes (page 9)

Define: people who play a sport

Example: My sisters are soccer *athletes* in high school.

Ask: In what sports are your friends *athletes*?

② defects (page 2)

Define: something wrong with a thing

Example: These cracks are *defects* in the sidewalk.

Ask: How could you fix a *defect* in a mug?

③ healthy (page 9)

Define: not sick, strong

Example: It took a week for me to be *healthy* after I got the flu.

Ask: What can you do to stay *healthy*?

④ medal (page 8)

Define: a reward for winning or doing well, usually a small piece of metal that tells what was done

Example: Athletes who do well in the Olympics get a *medal*.

Ask: What is something you could do that would earn you a *medal*?

DURING READING

20–30 Minutes   RI.2.3 RI.2.4 RI.2.5 RI.2.6 L.2.4a **CCSS**

Close Reading

🔍 **Pages 2–3**

Genre   Remind children that a biography gives true facts about a real person. Like other nonfiction, it may include text features that guide the reader through the text. Have children look at the cover of the book. Say: *This text is going to tell us information about a person. Who are we going to learn about?* (Rudy Garcia-Tolson) *How do you know?* (His name is the title of the book.) Guide children to look at the photograph at the top of page 2. Say: *Since we know that this story is going to be about Rudy Garcia-Tolson, who do you think this is a photo of?* (Rudy Garcia-Tolson) *What can you tell about him from the photograph?* (He seems to be wearing an athletic outfit, and he has man-made legs.)

Sequence Read pages 2 and 3 with children. Explain that often biographies begin with explaining why the person is important. Then they go back to explain how he or she got to be important. Say: *Biographies are often told in the sequence of someone's life. What did the doctors do first?* (They tried to fix Rudy's legs.) *Did that work?* (no) *What did they do next?* (They gave Rudy new legs.) *Let's pay attention to the sequence of events. It will help us better understand the most important information.* Help children record sequence details on their Sequence charts.

Pages 4–5

Genre **A C T** Remind children that biographies often have text features that help a reader better understand the life of the book's subject. Read page 2 with children. Say: *What did Rudy get when he was five years old?* (new legs) *How did they change his life?* (He could walk and run.) Point out the photo and caption. *Why does this book have a picture of a leg made of plastic and metal?* (The picture shows the kind of leg that Rudy got.) *Why is it important to see this leg?* (You can often better understand how something works if you can see it.)

STOP AND CHECK Read the question in the Stop and Check box on page 4. (Answers will vary but might include that Rudy was born with problems with his hands and feet, and when he was five, doctors gave him new legs.)

Sequence Read page 5 with children. Say: *Think about what we read on the last page. What happened after Rudy got new legs?* (He started to play sports.) Have children add this information to their Sequence charts.

Pages 6–7

Connection of Ideas **A C T** Read page 6 with children and look at the photo. Say: *The text says that Rudy did not need his new legs to swim. Why do you think this is true?* Point out the photo for children to refer to. (It looks like his new legs are only for the lower half of his legs. He wouldn't need them to swim because he uses the upper part of his legs to get the power to kick.)

Sequence Read page 7 with children. Say: *What sport did Rudy try after swimming?* (triathlon) *What is the sequence of events in a triathlon race?* (first, racers swim; then, they bike; last, they run) *When did Rudy finish his first triathlon?* (when he was ten years old) Help children record this event on their Sequence charts.

Pages 8–9

Key Details Read page 8 with children. Say: *When did Rudy first go to the Paralympic Games?* (2004) *Where did they take place?* (Greece) *What sport did Rudy compete in?* (swimming) *How did he do?* (He won a gold medal.) *How old was Rudy when this happened?* (16 years old)

STOP AND CHECK Read the question in the Stop and Check box on page 8. (Answers will vary but may include that Rudy swam in the Olympics and did triathlons.)

Connection of Ideas **A C T** Read page 9 with children. Say: *Why would doctors study Rudy to make better legs?* (They might try ideas out with Rudy. If an idea worked well for him, they could use that idea to make better legs for other people.) *Why would Rudy want to live at a training center?* (He can live with other athletes who are working toward the same goals.)

Vocabulary Focus on the word *train*. Say: The word *train has more than one meaning. What meanings can you think of?* (Possible answers: a railway train, practice to help you accomplish a goal) *How can you tell which meaning of* train *is correct here?* (The text is talking about Rudy trying to get in shape for the Paralympics, so it is the second meaning.)

Have partners review their Sequence charts for pages 2–9 and discuss what they have learned.

 Quick Check Do children understand weekly vocabulary in context? If not, review and reteach using the instruction on page 274.

Can children identify sequence? If not, review and reteach using the instruction on page 274 and assign the Unit 5 Week 3 digital mini-lesson.

WEEK 3
LESSON
4

• Understand and use new vocabulary words
• Read a biography
• Recognize and understand sequence
• Understand complex text through close reading

Materials

"Rudy Garcia-Tolson" Apprentice Leveled Reader: pp. 10–20
• Sequence Graphic Organizer

☞ Go Digital
• Apprentice Leveled Reader eBook
• Downloadable Graphic Organizer
• Sequence Mini-Lesson

Scaffolding for **Wonders** Approaching Leveled Reader

BEFORE READING

5–10 Minutes   SL.2.1a   SL.2.6   L.2.5a   L.2.6   CCSS

Expand Vocabulary

Display each word below. Say the words and have students repeat them. Then use the Define/Example/Ask routine to introduce each word.

1 **inspires** (page 12)

Define: gives someone the feeling that he or she can do something

Example: When you hear a story of someone brave, it *inspires* you to be brave.

Ask: What has someone you know done that *inspires* you?

2 **motto** (page 13)

Define: a short saying that reminds you of your beliefs

Example: Jo's *motto* is "Be kind to others."

Ask: What could be your *motto*?

DURING READING

15–20 Minutes   RI.2.1   RI.2.3   RI.2.5   RI.2.6   CCSS

Close Reading

Pages 10–11

Genre **A C T** Remind children that a biography is nonfiction that tells the true story of a real person. Review with them what they've learned about Rudy Garcia-Tolson. Then read page 10 with children. Say: *What was the name of the triathlon that Rudy entered?* (the Ironman) *Did Rudy finish the race?* (Yes, the text says he never gave up.)

Sequence Reread page 11 with children. Ask: *What happened in 2012?* (Rudy went to the Paralympic games in England.) *How did Rudy do?* (He won a silver medal.) Have children record important events on their Sequence charts.

STOP AND CHECK Read the question in the Stop and Check box on page 11. (He trains with other athletes and eats healthy food. He also helps doctors study ways to make better legs.)

Pages 12–13

Prior Knowledge Point out the header at the top of page 12. Explain that heroes can be many different kinds of people. There are people like César Chávez, who fought for the right of others to be treated fairly. There are people like firefighters who save people's lives. There are also people like Rudy, who have overcome some difficulty in their lives and who can tell others that they can overcome things that are hard in their lives.

Connection of Ideas **A C T** Read page 12 with children and point out the photo and its caption. Say: *The text says that Rudy is a hero. Why might he be a kind of hero to the boy in the picture?* (Possible answer: The boy might think he couldn't play baseball because he is in a wheelchair. But if he heard Rudy talk or knew about his story, then he could think he could also be an athlete.)

Sequence Have children read page 13. Say: *After he became a successful athlete, Rudy decided to do other things. What else does he do now?* (Rudy travels from city to city.) *Why does he do that?* (to tell about his life)

Vocabulary Read Rudy's motto. Focus on the word *weapon*. Point out that *weapon* means a tool used for fighting. The tool can be a quality we have. Ask: *How is bravery a weapon?* (It gives you the courage to fight.)

Pages 14–15

Genre Ⓐ Ⓒ Ⓣ Remind children that biographies often have text features that help them to better understand the story of someone's life. Point out pages 14 and 15 to children. Ask: *What is this text feature called?* (a time line) *What does it show?* (It shows important dates of a person's life.) *How is it helpful in a biography?* (You can quickly see all the things that the writer thinks are important in the person's life.)

Sequence Have children read pages 14 and 15. Ask: *What is the first important event on the time line?* (Rudy is born.) *What year was that?* (1988) *What happened after Rudy won a gold medal in Greece?* (He moved to the Olympic Training Center.) *What is the last event on the time line?* (He won a silver medal at the Paralympic Games in England.)

Purpose Ⓐ Ⓒ Ⓣ Focus on Rudy's motto. Ask: *What is Rudy's motto?* (A brave heart is a powerful weapon.) *How does that motto describe Ruby's life?* (Answers will vary but should focus on how he could fight his limitations with his bravery and accomplish a lot.) Ask: *How do you think knowing Rudy's story could help others?* (It might help people to test what they think are their limits to follow their dreams.)

STOP AND CHECK Read the question in the Stop and Check box on page 15. (Possible answer: Rudy inspires others by showing people they can work hard and succeed. He travels and tells people about his life. His motto is "A brave heart is a powerful weapon.")

AFTER READING

10–15 Minutes   RI.2.1 RI.2.3 RI.2.9 W.2.8 L.2.4b CCSS

Respond to Reading

Compare Texts Have children think about how Rudy Garcia-Tolson and Margaret Brown are connected. How can they both be considered heroes? What did they do in their lives that make them good examples of how to live a good life? Ask: *Why would people consider Rudy and Margaret Brown heroes? Do you think one is more of a hero than the other? Why? Discuss with a partner.*

Summarize Have students turn to page 16 and summarize the selection. (Answers should include details that show the sequence of events in Rudy Garcia-Tolson's life.)

Text Evidence

Have partners work together to answer questions on page 16. Have children focus include details about the sequence of events in Rudy's life.

Sequence Possible answers: At age 5, Rudy got "new legs" (p. 4). At age 10, he finished his first triathlon (p. 7). At age 16, he swam in the Paralympic Games in Greece and won a gold medal (p. 8).

Vocabulary A triathlon is an athletic event that includes three different sports: swimming, biking, and running. The word part "athlon" sounds like athlete.

Write About Reading Possible Answers: Rudy was born with birth defects (p. 2). At age 5, doctors gave him "new legs" (p. 4). Then he could play sports (p. 5). He swam in races and won (p. 6). At age 10, he finished a triathlon (p. 7). At age 16, he swam and won a gold medal in the Paralympic Games in Greece (p. 8). In 2012, he won a silver medal in the Games in England (p. 11).

Independent Reading

Encourage students to read the paired selection "The Unsinkable Molly Brown" on pages 17–19. Have them summarize the selection and compare it to "Rudy Garcia-Tolson." Have them work with a partner to answer the "Make Connections" questions on page 19.

 Quick Check Can students identify sequence? If not, review and reteach using the instruction on page 274 and assign the Unit 5 Week 3 digital mini-lesson.

Can students respond to the selection using text evidence? If not, provide sentence frames to help them organize their ideas.

WEEK 3
LESSON
5

Objectives
• Review weekly vocabulary words
• Review sequence
• Write an analysis about how the author used sequence

Scaffolding for Wonders Reading/Writing Workshop

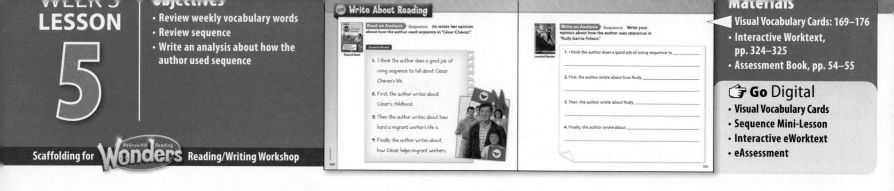

Materials
• Visual Vocabulary Cards: 169–176
• Interactive Worktext, pp. 324–325
• Assessment Book, pp. 54–55

⌨ Go Digital
• Visual Vocabulary Cards
• Sequence Mini-Lesson
• Interactive eWorktext
• eAssessment

REVIEW AND RETEACH

5–10 Minutes   L.2.4a   RI.2.3   RI.2.5   CCSS

Weekly Vocabulary

Display one **Visual Vocabulary Card** at a time and guide children to use the vocabulary word in a sentence. If children have difficulty creating a sentence, have them find the word in "César Chávez" or "Rudy Garcia-Tolson" and use context clues to define the vocabulary word.

Comprehension: Sequence

I Do Write and say: *I got out my crayons. I drew a picture of our cat for my mom. She hung it up on the refrigerator.* Ask: *What is the sequence of the events in this story?* Say: *Think about the order of the things that happened. First, I got my crayons. Then, I drew a picture. Finally, my mom hung it up. One thing happened after another. That is the sequence of events.*

We Do Display and say: *I helped my dad make pasta. First, we filled a pot with water. Then it boiled. We put the pasta in and it cooked.* Ask: *What was the first thing that happened in the sequence of events?* (We filled a pot with water.) *How do you know?* (It says so in the second sentence.) Ask: *What happened after they filled the pot?* (Then it boiled.) Continue asking questions.

You Do Display and say: *Leah was bored one afternoon. She asked her mom if she wanted to play with her. First, she and her mom played a card game. Then they made iced tea. Finally, they read a book together.* Guide partners to ask each other sequence questions, such as: *What happened first? What happened next? What happened last?*

WRITE ABOUT READING

25–35 Minutes   W.2.2   W.2.8   W.4.9   CCSS

Read an Analysis

• Guide children to look back at "César Chávez" in the **Interactive Worktext**. Have volunteers review the details about how the author used sequence they marked on page 319 and summarize the text. Repeat with pages 320–321. *How did the author's use of sequence help you understand the selection?*

• Read aloud the directions on page 324. Read aloud the student model. *This student's work is not a summary. It is an opinion of how the author used sequence in "César Chávez."*

• *When you write an opinion, you should include your view about evidence from the selection that show sequence. Read Jin's first sentence. What is Jin's opinion about the use of sequence in the selection?* (Jin thinks the author did a good job of using sequence to tell about Cesar Chavez's life.) *What part of the story does the evidence come from?* (the beginning)

• *Read the second sentence. Draw a box around the evidence from the story you see in Jin's writing.* (First the author writes about Cesar's childhood.) *What word tells you where in the selection this detail comes from?* (First)

• *Guide children to point to the third sentence. What evidence does Jin include?* (Then the author writes about how hard a migrant worker's life is.)

• Model analyzing how the author used sequence. Read the last sentence that Jin wrote. *What additional text evidence does the author use?* (Jin tells what the author wrote about at the end of the story using the word, *finally*.)

Analytical Writing Write an Analysis

Guided Writing Read the writing prompt on page 325 together. Have children review their Sequence charts for "Rudy Garcia-Tolson." Have children use their charts to complete the sentence starters. Children can also write the analysis using another selection previously read this week.

Peer Conference Guide children to read their analysis to a partner. Listeners should summarize the details that support the beginning, middle, and ending sentences. they should discuss any parts that are unclear.

Teacher Conference Check children's writing for complete sentences and whether they included details from the story. Review the last sentence and ask: *Did the author use details to support the story?* If necessary, guide children to revise their sentences by adding more details.

Level Up

▲ Approaching Leveled Reader

▲ Reading/Writing Workshop

▲ Apprentice Leveled Reader

▲ Interactive Worktext

IF children read the Apprentice Level Reader and the **Interactive Worktext** Shared Read fluently and answer the Respond to Reading questions

THEN read together the Approaching Level Reader main selection and the **Reading/Writing Workshop** Shared Read from *Reading Wonders*. Have children take notes as they read, using self-stick notes. Then ask and answer questions about their notes.

Writing Rubric

	4	3	2	1
Text Evidence	Includes three or more details from the text.	Includes two or more details from the text.	Includes only one detail from the text.	No text evidence is cited.
Writing Style	Writes in complete sentences. Uses correct spelling and grammar.	Uses complete sentences. Writing has spelling and grammar errors.	Few complete sentences. There are many spelling and grammar errors.	Writing is not accurate or in complete sentences.

ASSESSMENT

Weekly Assessment

Have children complete the Weekly Assessment using **Assessment** book pages 54–55.

CCSS TESTED SKILLS

✔ COMPREHENSION	✔ VOCABULARY:
• Point of View RL.2.6	• Context Clues L.2.4
• Point of View RL.2.6	
• Sequence RI.2.6, RI.2.8	

Using Assessment and Writing Scores

RETEACH	IF ...	THEN ...
COMPREHENSION	Students answer 0–5 multiple-choice items correctly ...	... reteach tested skills using instruction on pages 364–375.
VOCABULARY	Students answer 0–2 multiple-choice items correctly ...	... reteach tested skills using instruction on page 364.
WRITING	Students score mostly 1–2 on weekly writing rubrics throughout the unit ...	... reteach writing using instruction on pages 376–377.

Fluency Assessment

Conduct assessments individually using the differentiated fluency passages in Assessment. Students' expected fluency goal for this Unit is 79–99 WCPM with an accuracy rate of 95% or higher.

Weeks 4 and 5

Monitor students progress on the following to inform how to adjust instruction for the remainder of the unit.

ADJUST INSTRUCTION	
ACCESS COMPLEX TEXT	If students need more support for accessing complex text, provide additional modeling of prompts in Lesson 2 of Week 4, pages 280–281, and Week 5, pages 290–291. After you model how to identify the text evidence, guide students to find text evidence in Lessons 3 and 4, in Week 4, pages 282–285, and Week 5, pages 292–295.
FLUENCY	For those students who need more support with Fluency, focus on the Fluency lessons in the Foundational Skills Kit.
WRITING	If students need more support incorporating text evidence in their writing, conduct the Write About Reading activities in Lesson 4 and 5 as group writing activities.
FOUNDATIONAL SKILLS	Review students' individualized progress in *Reading Wonders* Adaptive Learning to determine which foundational skills to incorporate into your lessons for the remainder of the unit.

Objectives
• Develop oral language
• Build background about preserving our Earth
• Understand and use weekly vocabulary
• Read a fiction story

Talk About It
Weekly Concept Preserving Our Earth
Essential Question
How can we protect the Earth?

Name ways we can protect the Earth's resources.

Preserve the Earth

Talk with a partner about ways to protect the Earth's resources at school.

Materials
Interactive Worktext, pp. 326–333
• Visual Vocabulary Cards: 177–184
• High-Frequency Word Cards

☞ **Go** Digital
• Interactive eWorktext
• Visual Vocabulary Cards

Scaffolding for **Wonders** Reading/Writing Workshop

WEEKLY CONCEPT

5–10 Minutes   SL.2.1a   SL.2.4   CCSS

Talk About It

Essential Question Read aloud the Essential Question on page 326 of the **Interactive Worktext:** *How can we protect the Earth?* Explain that Earth has many resources, such as water, air, and land. Say: *We need to protect the Earth's resources so we have them when we need them.* Give an example, such as water. Explain that if we leave the faucet on while we are brushing our teeth, we are wasting water. Say: *If everyone wastes water, we will no longer have enough for everyone.*

Discuss the photograph on page 326. Ask: *What is happening in the picture?* (Three children are helping to plant a tree. They are using a shovel and gloves.)

I Do Say: *I am going to look at the photo and think about how these children are protecting the Earth. I know that trees give us oxygen to breathe and help clean the air. I will write on the web on page 327 how planting a tree can help protect the Earth.*

We Do Say: *Let's think about other ways we can protect the Earth's resources.* Ask: *How can we protect the land? How can we keep the land clean?* Guide children to think of ways to protect the land. Then have them choose one way to add to their webs.

You Do Guide partners to work together to talk about other ways to protect the Earth's resources: land, water, or air. Have children use the words from the web to start their sentences: *We can protect the Earth by _____.*

REVIEW VOCABULARY

10–15 Minutes   L.2.4c   L.2.5a   L.2.6   RF.2.3f   CCSS

Review Weekly Vocabulary Words

• Use the **Visual Vocabulary Cards** to review the weekly vocabulary.

• Read together the directions on page 328 of the **Interactive Worktext**. Then complete the activity.

1 **enormous** Invite volunteers to suggest things that are *enormous* as you list them on the board. (Possible answers: elephant, airplane) Then have children complete the following sentence frame: *The opposite of enormous is _____.* (tiny, small)

2 **curious** Ask children if they would be *curious* about what is behind a locked door. Then have them tell what *curious* means. (wanting to learn about something) Have volunteers name things they have been *curious* about. Have them explain why.

3 **proudly** Have children explain why a person might feel *proud.* (worked hard, accomplished something) If necessary, give an example of a time you did something *proudly.* Have children use this oral sentence starter: *A child would smile* proudly *if he or she _____.* (Possible answers: finished a puzzle, won a game)

4 **rarely** Model using the word *rarely* in a sentence: *I am so busy that I* rarely *go to the movies anymore.* Guide children to identify the root word, or "smaller word," in *rarely.* (rare) If necessary, explain what the word *rare* means. Have children use this oral sentence frame: *_____ happen* rarely. (Possible answers: parades, snowstorms)

⑤ distance Have children look around and name something they see in the *distance*. Invite them to use this sentence frame: *I can see a* _____ *in the* distance. (Answers will vary.)

⑥ supply Ask children to give an example of something they might keep a *supply* of in their desk. (Possible answers: school supplies, tissues) Then have them complete the following sentence frame: *My family keeps a* supply of _____ *in the house.* (Possible answers: food, paper towels, batteries)

⑦ gently Demonstrate knocking on your desk. First knock hard, then *gently*. Have children note the difference. Then help children describe things they should do *gently*. (Possible answers: pet a kitten, hold a baby)

⑧ Earth resources Have children name *Earth resources* that they know. Write them on the board. If necessary, give an example to start. Then assist children as they draw a picture of nature that includes two or more *Earth resources*. Help children label their picture, using the following sentence frame: _____ *and* _____ *are both* Earth resources. (Possible answers: water, trees)

High-Frequency Words

Have children look at page 329 in the **Interactive Worktext**. Help them read, spell, and write each high-frequency word. Guide partners to use each word in a sentence. Then read the story aloud with children. Guide partners to work together to reread the story and circle the high-frequency words. (has, read, far, what, into, off) Listen in and provide assistance reading the high-frequency words, as necessary.

> **ELL ENGLISH LANGUAGE LEARNERS**
>
> Display the **High-Frequency Word Cards** for: *has, far, off, read, into, what.* Write a sentence with each word on the board. Have children echo-read each sentence, and point out the high-frequency word. Then ask them to use the word in a new sentence.

READ COMPLEX TEXT

15–20 Minutes   RL.2.3   RL.2.5   SL.2.1b

Read "The Art Project"

- Have children turn to page 330 in the **Interactive Worktext** and read aloud the Essential Question. Point to the illustration. Say: *What are the teacher and her class talking about?* (a flyer announcing an art contest) *Let's read to find out how the class protects the Earth.* Have children echo-read the title.

- Read the story together. Note that the weekly vocabulary words are highlighted in yellow. Expand Vocabulary words are highlighted in blue.

- As children read, have them use the "My Notes" section on page 330 to write questions they have. Children can also write words they don't understand or things they want to remember. Model how to use the "My Notes" section. *When I read the first two paragraphs on page 331, I find out that the class wants to enter an art contest. I wonder what kind of art project they will make. I will write a question about this in the "My Notes" section.*

> **ELL ENGLISH LANGUAGE LEARNERS**
>
> As you read together, have children highlight parts of the text they have questions about. After reading, review the questions children have. Then help them locate the answers to their questions in the text.

 Quick Check Can children understand the weekly vocabulary in context? If not, review vocabulary using the **Visual Vocabulary Cards** before teaching Lesson 2.

Can children read high-frequency words in context? If not, review using the Read/Spell/Write routine and the High-Frequency Word Cards.

WEEK 4 LESSON 2

Objectives
- Read a fiction story
- Understand complex text through close reading
- Recognize and understand problem and solution
- Respond to the selection using text evidence to support ideas

Scaffolding for **WONDERS** Reading/Writing Workshop

Materials
Interactive Worktext, pp. 330–335

Go Digital
- Interactive eWorktext
- Problem and Solution Mini-Lesson

REREAD COMPLEX TEXT

20–25 Minutes   L.2.4a RL.2.3 RL.2.5   **CCSS**

Close Reading: "The Art Project"

Reread "The Art Project" from **Interactive Worktext** pages 330–333 with children. As you read together, discuss important passages in the text. Guide children to respond to questions using evidence from the text.

 Pages 330–331

Problem and Solution Say: *A plot is what happens in a story. A plot usually has a* problem. *A problem is something that needs to be changed, completed, or figured out. The problem is often at the beginning of the story. To find the problem in a story, you should ask yourself, "What do the characters want to do?"* Reread the second paragraph with children. Ask: *What problem does the class face at the beginning of the story?* Guide children to draw a box the sentence that tells. (Our supply of art materials is low.)

Expand Vocabulary Explain to children that when you *recycle*, you use something again. Have children reread that last paragraph. Ask: *What does Pablo want to* recycle? Guide children to write the word that tells. (paper)

Prior Knowledge **A C T** Explain to children that people in many communities across the United States recycle items such as paper, glass, metal cans, and plastic bottles to help save Earth's resources. This also cuts down on the amount of trash we create. Say: *Recycled paper is used to make more paper and egg cartons. Metal can be used to make bikes and plastic bottles can be used to make carpet or toys.* Ask: *Why do people recycle?* (to help save Earth's resources and cut down on the amount of trash we create)

Sentence Structure **A C T** Explain to children that that word *so* is used in sentence as a conjunction. Say: *A conjunction joins two parts of a sentence together.* Read aloud the last sentence on the page and circle the word *so*. Say: *The word* so *connects the first part of the sentence to the remaining part.* Ask: *How does the class react when Pablo speaks up?* (The class was surprised.)

 Page 332

Problem and Solution Ask: *What is the class's problem?* (They do not have enough art supplies.) Have children reread the first three paragraphs and ask: *What does Grace say the class could use for art materials?* Guide children to draw a box around the words that tell. (old string and wire hangers) Explain that Grace and Pablo are taking steps to solving the problem in the story.

Sentence Structure **A C T** Explain to children that stories often contain dialogue. Say: *Dialogue is the words that the characters speak.* Have children locate the quotation marks in the first paragraph. Say: *Quotation marks signal that a character is speaking. The words inside the quotation marks are dialogue.* Point out the words *Hal said* and say: *These words show which character is speaking.* Have children reread the fourth paragraph. Ask: *Which sentences in this paragraph tell what Pablo said?* Guide children to underline the sentences that tell. (We can fold the paper into cranes. Then we can attach the cranes to a frame. We can make a mobile.)

Expand Vocabulary Explain to children that when you *attach* something, you connect it to something else. Read the fourth paragraph aloud. Ask: *What will the class attach the cranes to?* Guide children to write the words that tell. (a frame)

Page 333

Expand Vocabulary Explain to children that if someone is *creative*, he or she can do something in a new way. Say: *You can be creative with things you no longer need and use them in a new way.* Read the last paragraph aloud. Ask: *Who is creative in this story?* Guide children to circle the words that tell. (the class)

Sentence Structure Remind children that when they read the word *said* before or after a character's name, they can use the character's name to signal who is speaking. Have children reread the last sentence. Ask: *Who is speaking in this sentence?* (Grace) Have children draw a box around the words that tell them who is speaking. (Grace said)

Problem and Solution Say: *At the beginning of the story we found the problem was that the class does not have enough art supplies. Did the characters solve the problem?* (yes) Have children review their notes and think back to the steps the class took to solve their problem. Ask: *What was the solution to the problem?* Guide children to write their answers. (They used recycled materials to make a mobile.)

RESPOND TO READING
10–20 Minutes   SL.2.1a   RL.2.3   RL.2.5

Respond to "The Art Project"

Read aloud the questions about "The Art Project" on page 334 of the **Interactive Worktext** with children. Then read aloud the "Discussion Starter" for each of the questions. Guide children to work with a partner to answer the questions using the "Discussion Starters." Have children find text evidence to support their answers. Ask children to write the page number(s) on which they found the text evidence for each question.

1. *What does the class want to do?* (Possible answers: I read that Mrs. Simon's class decides to enter an art contest. The problem is that they don't have enough materials. Text Evidence: p. 331)

2. *What kind of project does the class decide to make?* (Possible answers: Pablo says the class should use recycled paper. They also use old string and wire hangars. The class decides to make a mobile with paper cranes. Text Evidence: pp. 331, 332)

3. *How does the children's art project help protect the Earth?* (Possible answers: The class wins a prize. By using these materials, the class saves Earth's resources. Text Evidence: p. 333)

After children discuss the questions on page 334, have them use the sentence starters to answer the question on page 335. Circulate and provide guidance.

✓ *Quick Check* Do children understand vocabulary in context? If not, review and reteach using the instruction on page 286.

Can children identify problem and solution? If not, review and reteach using the instruction on page 286 and assign the Unit 5 Week 4 digital mini-lesson.

Can children write a response to "The Art Project"? If not, review the sentence starters and prompt children to respond orally. Help them write their responses.

WEEK 4 LESSON 3

Objectives
- Understand and use new vocabulary words
- Read fiction
- Recognize and understand problem and solution
- Understand complex text through close reading

Scaffolding for **Wonders** Approaching Leveled Reader

Materials
- "Let's Carpool" Apprentice Leveled Reader: pp. 2–6
- Problem and Solution Graphic Organizer

👉 **Go** Digital
- Apprentice Leveled Reader eBook
- Downloadable Graphic Organizer
- Problem and Solution Mini-Lesson

BEFORE READING

10–15 Minutes   SL.2.1a   SL.2.6   L.2.5a   L.2.6   **CCSS**

Introduce "Let's Carpool"

- Read the Essential Question on the title page of "Let's Carpool" **Apprentice Leveled Reader:** *How can we protect Earth? We will read about how carpooling can help protect Earth.*

- Read the title aloud. Point to the pictures. Ask: *Is this text fiction or nonfiction?* (fiction) Point to the pictures on page 2 and 3 and ask: *What is this family doing?* (The kids are getting ready for school. Their mother is in the car trying to get them to hurry.) *This story will tell how one family solves their problem of driving too much and also learns to protect Earth's resources.*

Expand Vocabulary

Display each word below. Say the words and have children repeat them. Then use the Define/Example/Ask routine to introduce each word.

1 replied (page 2)

Define: to have answered someone by speaking, writing, or with an action

Example: When Dan asked if it was snowing, I *replied* by nodding my head.

Ask: If you replied to a question, what did you do?

2 rush (page 3)

Define: a busy or hurried state

Example: There was a *rush* to get inside when the rain started.

Ask: If you are in a *rush* every morning, what could you do differently?

3 sighed (page 6)

Define: made a long, deep breathing sound because of sadness, tiredness, or relief

Example: Brad *sighed* with relief when he found his lost birthday card.

Ask: If you *sighed* after getting home from a long day, how did you feel?

DURING READING

20–30 Minutes   RL.2.1   RL.2.3   RL.2.6   L.2.4a   L.2.5a   **CCSS**

Close Reading

🔍 **Pages 2–3**

Prior Knowledge **ACT** Ask: *What do you know about carpooling? Have you ever shared a ride with someone? If you have ever made a plan where one child's parents take a group of children somewhere and another child's parents pick the group up to bring them home, then you have carpooled.* Explain that carpooling is a way of sharing rides. Many people like to carpool because it cuts down on the number of cars on the road. Carpooling also helps save gas and money. Say: *Many cities have special lanes on busy roads that are just for people who carpool. To be in this special lane, the car must have more than one person in it. These lanes help people get to where they are going faster because carpool lanes have fewer cars in them than the regular lanes have.* Ask: *How many people does it take to carpool?* (more than one) *Why do people like to carpool?* (Carpooling cuts down on the number of cars on the road. Carpooling also saves gas and money.)

Connection of Ideas **ACT** Read page 3 aloud, emphasizing the exclamation points and ask: *Why do you think Mom is excited and in a big rush every morning?* (Mom has to drive Emma, Kate, and Josh to school every morning. They are always late.)

Sentence Structure Ⓐ Ⓒ Ⓣ Review with children that fiction often contains dialogue, or the words characters speak to each other. Point out the quotation marks in the first paragraph and say: *The words the characters speak are set inside quotation marks. You can look for a character's name just before or right after the quotation marks to see which character is speaking.* Read the first paragraph aloud and ask: *Which character is speaking?* (Mrs. Carter) *How do you know?* (The words "Mrs. Carter said" are right after the quotation marks.) Point to the exclamation and explain that this mark shows that the speaker is excited. Read the second paragraph and ask: *Which character is speaking in this paragraph?* (Emma) *Is Emma excited?* (yes) *How do you know?* (There is an exclamation point at the end of what she says.) Read the last paragraph with children and ask: *Which character is speaking in this paragraph?* (Josh) Point out that the word *replied* is used instead of *said*, but it still means someone is speaking. It is a way of saying he answered or spoke back.

Pages 4–5

Problem and Solution Review with children that the events in a story often center on a problem and a solution. Say: *The problem is what characters want to do or want to change or needs to find out. The solution is the steps the characters take to solve the problem.* Explain that once children find the problem, they should note the steps the characters take to solve the problem. Ask: *What problems are the characters in this story having?* (They are late and rushing to get to school on time. Josh lost his backpack. Everybody is upset.) Model recording the information on a Problem and Solution Chart.

Connection of Ideas Ⓐ Ⓒ Ⓣ Read the last sentence on page 4 with children. Ask: *What do the capital letters and exclamation point show about their mother?* (She is still excited. She is in a hurry.)

Sentence Structure Ⓐ Ⓒ Ⓣ Read page 5 with children and ask: *Which words show that a character asked a question on this page?* (Mom asked)

Page 6

Vocabulary Read page 6 with children and ask them to look at the picture. Mimic *sighing* and have children repeat. Say: *The children are very busy with after-school activities. Do you think their mother sighed because she is tired of driving or because she feels good the children are so busy?* (Their mother *sighed* because she is tired of driving.)

STOP AND CHECK Read the question in the Stop and Check box on page 6. (The children are late for school.)

Have partners review their Problem and Solution charts for pages 2–6 and discuss what they have learned.

✓ *Quick Check* Do children understand weekly vocabulary in context? If not, review and reteach using the instruction on page 286.

Can children identify compare and contrast? If not, review and reteach using the instruction on page 286 and assign Unit 5 Week 4 digital mini-lesson.

WEEK 4 LESSON 4

Objectives
- Understand and use new vocabulary words
- Read fiction
- Recognize and understand problem and solution
- Understand complex text through close reading

Scaffolding for **WONDERS** Reading Approaching Leveled Reader

Materials
- "Let's Carpool" Apprentice Leveled Reader: pp. 7–20
- Problem and Solution Graphic Organizer

☞ **Go Digital**
- Apprentice Leveled Reader eBook
- Downloadable Graphic Organizer
- Problem and Solution Mini-Lesson

BEFORE READING

5–10 Minutes   SL.2.1a   SL.2.6   L.2.6   CCSS

Expand Vocabulary

Display each word below. Say the words and have children repeat them. Then use the Define/Example/Ask routine to introduce each word.

1 carpool (page 9)

Define: to share a ride with other people to work or school

Example: Lin and Pat *carpool* to school with their friend Pam.

Ask: Where is one place you could *carpool* to with other people?

2 practice (page 11)

Define: a place to learn or train to become better at something

Example: Jan worked on hitting the ball at softball *practice*.

Ask: What could you learn at soccer *practice*?

3 schedule (page 13)

Define: a list of times, events, or things to do

Example: Paul had to look at his *schedule* to see when he could meet Mary.

Ask: What is on your *schedule* for this Saturday?

DURING READING

15–20 Minutes   RL.2.1   RL.2.3   RL.2.5   L.2.4e   CCSS

Close Reading

🔍 **Page 7**

Problem and Solution Read page 7 with children and ask: *What problem does Mrs. Carter have?* (She is tired of driving.) Model recording this information on the Problem and Solution Chart

🔍 **Pages 8–9**

Author's Purpose Read page 8 with children and ask: *What does the author want you to know about what happens when people drive too much?* (It is bad for the air we breathe. It is bad for Earth and wastes gas.)

Problem and Solution Read page 9 with children. Say: *The problem in the story is that Mrs. Carter is tired of driving and that driving is bad for Earth. What step does Josh take to help solve the problem?* (Josh's idea is to carpool.) Help children add this information to their Problem and Solution charts.

🔍 **Pages 10–11**

Organization A C T Explain to children that stories are often organized in the order in which the events happen. Say: *So far, the events in this story all take place on the same day. The story starts in the morning. Then, Mrs. Carter picks the children up from their activities and drives them home.* Read page 10 with children and ask: *Which words show that the Carters went to visit the Laws on the same day Josh had his idea to carpool?* (That night)

Problem and Solution Ask: *What step did the family take to solve the problem of Mrs. Carter being tired of driving?* (They went to next door and asked another family to carpool to with them.) Help children add this information to their Problem and Solution charts.

Connection of Ideas Ask: *Why do you think the Laws loved the idea of carpooling with Josh and his family?* (Possible answer: Josh and Evan are on the same soccer team, so the Laws will also be driving less.)

Pages 12–13

Key Details Read page 12. Ask: *Which key detail shows that other neighbors were interested in sharing rides?* (Other neighbors wanted to carpool, too.)

STOP AND CHECK Read the question in the Stop and Check box on page 12. (Josh suggested that his family could carpool with neighbors.)

Problem and Solution Read page 13 with children. Ask: *What step did Mrs. Carter take to help solve the problem?* (Mrs. Carter made a schedule showing when each family would drive.) Help children add this information to their Problem and Solution charts.

Pages 14–15

STOP AND CHECK Read the question in the Stop and Check box on page 15. (The Carters thought Josh's carpool idea was great.)

Problem and Solution Remind children that a solution is the way a problem is solved. Say: *Think back to the problem and the steps the characters took to solve the problem. What was the solution to the family's problem?* (The family decided to carpool.) Help children add this information to their Problem and Solution charts.

AFTER READING

10–15 Minutes   RL.2.3   RL.2.5   RL.2.9   L.2.4a   W.2.1   CCSS

Respond to Reading

Compare Texts Guide children in comparing the way characters solve a problem in "The Art Project" with the way characters solve a problem in "Let's Carpool." Ask: *What are some ways people can solve a problem and help protect Earth?* Compare how the characters in both stories are able to improve their lives and help Earth at the same time.

Summarize Have children turn to page 16 and summarize the selection. (Answers should include details about the problem and that show the steps the characters took to solve their problem.)

Text Evidence

Have partners work together to answer questions on page 16. Remind children to use their Problem and Solution charts.

Problem and Solution (The problem is that Mrs. Carter has to drive a lot. This is not good for the air and uses a lot of gas. On p. 7, the text says that Mrs. Carter is "tired of driving." On p. 8, Josh says people drive too much, which is bad for the air and uses too much gas. On p. 9, Josh's solution is to carpool and drive to school with another family.)

Vocabulary (*Backpack* has the smaller words *back* and *pack*. It is a pack that you carry on your back.)

Write About Reading (Decide which problems carpooling could solve. With parents, speak to neighbors to find out where they drive and at what times. Then compare places and times people have in common and work out a schedule.)

Independent Reading

Encourage children to read the paired selection "The Clean Air Campaign" on pages 17–19. Have them summarize the selection and compare it to "Let's Carpool." Have them work with a partner to answer the "Make Connections" questions on page 19.

 Quick Check Can children identify problem and solution? If not, review and reteach using the instruction on page 286 and assign the Unit 5 Week 4 digital mini-lesson.

Can children respond to the selection using text evidence? If not, provide sentence frames to help them organize their ideas.

WEEK 4
LESSON
5

Objectives
• Review weekly vocabulary words
• Review problem and solution
• Write an analysis about an author's use of problem and solution

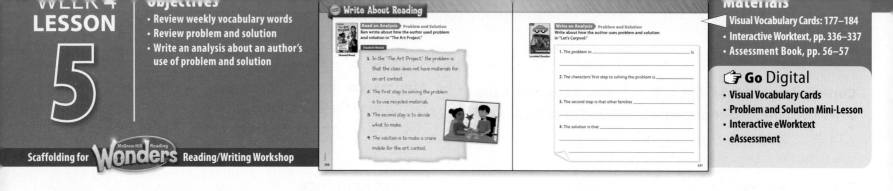

Materials
Visual Vocabulary Cards: 177–184
• Interactive Worktext, pp. 336–337
• Assessment Book, pp. 56–57

Go Digital
• Visual Vocabulary Cards
• Problem and Solution Mini-Lesson
• Interactive eWorktext
• eAssessment

Scaffolding for **Wonders** Reading/Writing Workshop

REVIEW AND RETEACH

5–10 Minutes   RL.2.3   RL.2.5   L.2.4a   CCSS

Weekly Vocabulary

Display one **Visual Vocabulary Card** at a time and guide children to use the vocabulary word in a sentence. If children have difficulty creating a sentence, have them find the word in "The Art Project" or "Let's Carpool" and use context clues in the passage to define the vocabulary word.

Comprehension: Problem and Solution

I Do Write and say: *Jen and Mike wanted to practice basketball. They found their ball. The ball was flat. It would not bounce. Jen found the pump. She pumped up the ball. Now the ball bounced perfectly.* Ask: *What problem do the characters face?* Circle: "The ball was flat. It would not bounce." Write: *Problem.* Say: *The problem is what the characters want to do, want to change, or need to find out. The solution is the way the problem is solved.*

We Do Ask: *What steps do the characters take to solve the problem?* Circle: "Jen found the pump. She pumped up the ball." Write: *Steps to Solution.* Say: *At the end of the story I can ask if the characters solved the problem and how they did it.* Have a volunteer circle the solution. (The ball bounced perfectly.)

You Do Display: *Maria's cat was lost. Maria put up flyers with her phone number and her cat's picture. A woman called Maria to say she found her cat. Maria got her cat back.* Have partners ask each other to identify the problem, steps to solve the problem, and the solution. Have partners discuss their answers.

WRITE ABOUT READING

25–35 Minutes   W.2.3   W.2.8   W.4.9   CCSS

Read an Analysis

• Guide children to look back at "The Art Project" in the **Interactive Worktext**. Have volunteers review the details about how the author used problem and solution they marked on page 331 and summarize the text. Repeat with pages 332–333. *How did the author use problem and solution in the selection?*

• Read aloud the directions on page 336. Read aloud the student model. *This student's work is not a summary. It is an analysis, or description, of how the author used problem and solution in "The Art Project."*

• *When you write an analysis, you should include text from the selection that show problem and solution. Read Ben's first sentence. Circle the evidence.* (The class does not have materials for an art project) *Does this detail show a problem or solution?* (a problem) *What part of the story does this evidence come from?* (the beginning)

• *Read Ben's second sentence. Draw a box around the evidence that shows a solution.* (The characters' first step to solving the problem is to use recycled materials.) *What part of the story is he writing about?* (the middle)

• Guide children to point to the third sentence. *This sentence gives more evidence about characters in the story. What evidence does Ben include?* (The second step is to come up with an idea for how to use the materials.)

• Model analyzing how the author used problem and solution. Read the last sentence that Ben wrote. Why is this sentence a good ending? (It tells how the characters solve the problem.)

Write an Analysis

Guided Writing Read the writing prompt on page 337 together. Guide children to review their Problem and Solution charts for "Let's Carpool." Have children use their charts to complete the sentence starters. Children can also write an analysis using another selection previously read this week.

Peer Conference Guide children to read their analysis to a partner. Listeners should summarize the details that support the beginning, middle, and ending sentences. They should discuss any parts that are unclear.

Teacher Conference Check children's writing for complete sentences and whether they included details from the story. Review the last sentence and ask: *Did the author use details to support the story?* If necessary, guide children to revise their sentences by adding more details.

Level Up

▲ Approaching Leveled Reader

▲ Reading/Writing Workshop

▲ Apprentice Leveled Reader

▲ Interactive Worktext

IF children read the Apprentice Level Reader and the **Interactive Worktext** Shared Read fluently and answer the Respond to Reading questions

THEN read together the Approaching Level Reader main selection and the **Reading/Writing Workshop** Shared Read from *Reading Wonders*. Have children take notes as they read, using self-stick notes. Then ask and answer questions about their notes.

Writing Rubric

	4	3	2	1
Text Evidence	Includes three or more details from the text.	Includes two or more details from the text.	Includes only one detail from the text.	No text evidence is included.
Writing Style	Writes in complete sentences. Uses correct spelling and grammar.	Uses complete sentences. Writing has spelling and grammar errors.	Few complete sentences. There are many spelling and grammar errors.	Writing is not accurate or in complete sentences.

ASSESSMENT

Weekly Assessment

Have children complete the Weekly Assessment using **Assessment** book pages 56–57.

WEEK 5 LESSON 1

Objectives
- Develop oral language
- Build background how rules are important
- Understand and use weekly vocabulary
- Read an expository text

Scaffolding for **Wonders** *McGraw-Hill Reading* Reading/Writing Workshop

Materials
- Interactive Worktext, pp. 338–345
- Visual Vocabulary Cards: 185–192
- High-Frequency Word Cards

☞ **Go** Digital
- Interactive eWorktext
- Visual Vocabulary Cards

WEEKLY CONCEPT

5-10 Minutes SL.2.1a SL.2.4

Talk About It

Essential Question Read aloud the Essential Question on page 338 of the **Interactive Worktext:** *Why are rules important?* Explain that rules are important for many reasons. Provide examples of rules in your school, such as raising your hand to speak. Say: *We raise our hands to speak so that each person can be heard. If everyone speaks at the same time, we can't hear each person's thoughts. This rule helps us communicate better.*

- Discuss the photograph on page 338. Ask: *What is happening in the picture?* (A family is going for a bike ride.) Have children tell what else they see in the picture. (The family is on a country road. They are wearing helmets. There are signs on the road.)

I Do Say: *I am going to look at the photo and think about what rules the family is abiding by. I see the family is wearing helmets. Wearing helmets is a rule that helps keep people safe. I will write this rule on my chart on page 339. I will also tell why this rule is important.*

We Do Say: *Let's think about other rules this family is following. I see they are wearing neon yellow vests. This allows cars to see them on the road. This keeps the bikers safe.* Guide children to think of other rules for the bikers to follow in the photograph. Have them discuss and then add their rules to their chart.

You Do Guide partners to work together to talk about other rules they know of either at school or in their town. Have children use the words from the chart to complete these sentence starters: *One rule is _____. It is important because _____.*

REVIEW VOCABULARY

10–15 Minutes L.2.5a L.2.6 RF.2.3

Review Weekly Vocabulary Words

- Use the **Visual Vocabulary Cards** to review the weekly vocabulary.

- Read together the directions on page 340 of the **Interactive Worktext.** Then complete the activity.

1 **exclaimed** Invite a volunteer to make a short *exclamation*, then have the other children tell what happened. For example, volunteer Tina *exclaims*, "It's Friday!" Have the other children say: *"It's Friday!" Tina* exclaimed. Then help children name another word for *exclaimed*. (Possible answers: shouted, yelled, cried)

2 **united** Write *United States* on the board. Guide children to understand why our country has this name. Say: *People can also be* united. Then have children use this oral sentence starter: *I united with other children when we _____.* (Possible answers: played a game, worked on a project together)

3 **history** Tell one quick story about the *history* of your town. Have children use this oral sentence frame: *I could go to _____ to learn about the* history *of our town.* (Possible answers: the library, city hall, a museum)

4 **form** Write the word *form* on the board. Say: *I form shapes out of paper when I make origami.* Ask children what else they can *form* with paper. (paper airplanes, a collage) Then invite children to *form* one big circle. As they are standing in line, have children chant: *We can* form *a circle!*

5 **finally** Model the word *finally* in a sentence: *After working on it all weekend, the kids* finally *finished the jigsaw puzzle.* Guide children to identify the root word, or "smaller word," in *finally*. (final) Then have children use this oral sentence starter: *After a long time, I finally _____!* (Answers will vary.)

6 **writers** Write the word *writers*. Have volunteers identify the root word. (write) Then have children use this oral sentence frame: Writers *might use _____ and _____ every* day to write. (<u>Possible answers</u>: a pen, paper, a computer, a typewriter)

7 **rules** Begin writing some of playground *rules* on the board—*we wait our turn, we listen to our teacher*, and so on. Then help children name things that might happen to someone who doesn't follow playground *rules*. (<u>Possible answers</u>: get hurt, get in trouble)

8 **public** Write the word *public*. Have a volunteer name a *public* place in the neighborhood. (park, library, town square) Assist children as they draw their pictures. Have children tell about their drawings, using this oral sentence frame: *_____ is a* public *place in my neighborhood.*

High-Frequency Words

Have children look at page 341 in the **Interactive Worktext**. Help them read, spell, and write each high-frequency word. Guide partners to use each word in a sentence. Then read the story aloud with children. Guide partners to work together to reread the story and circle the high-frequency words. (never, went, his, ten, that, such) Listen in and provide assistance reading the high-frequency words, as necessary.

ELL ENGLISH LANGUAGE LEARNERS

Display the High-Frequency Word Cards for: *ten, his, such, never, that, went.* Write a sentence with each word on the board. Have children echo-read each sentence, and point out the high-frequency word.

READ COMPLEX TEXT

15–20 Minutes   RI.2.3   RI.2.5   SL.2.1b

Read "Visiting the Past"

- Have children turn to page 342 in the **Interactive Worktext** and read aloud the Essential Question. Point to the picture. Say: *This family is going on a trip to Philadelphia. They will learn about some of the early rules people made for our country to follow. Rules keep people safe. Let's read to find out about different kinds of rules and how they are important.* Have children echo-read the title.

- Read the story together. Note that the weekly vocabulary words are highlighted in yellow. Expand Vocabulary words are highlighted in blue.

- As children read, have them use the "My Notes" section on page 342 to write questions they have. Children can also write words they don't understand or things they want to remember. Model how to use the "My Notes" section. *When I read the title, I wonder how rules are connected to visiting the past. What kind of rules did people follow in the past? I will write a question about rules in the "My Notes" section.*

ELL ENGLISH LANGUAGE LEARNERS

As you read together, have children highlight parts of the text they have questions about. After reading, review the questions children have. Then help them locate the answers to their questions in the text.

✓ *Quick Check* Can children understand the weekly vocabulary in context? If not, review vocabulary using the **Visual Vocabulary Cards** before teaching Lesson 2.

Can children read high-frequency words in context? If not, review using the Read/Spell/Write routine and the High-Frequency Word Cards.

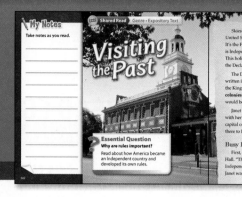

WEEK 5 LESSON 2

Objectives
- Read an expository text
- Understand complex text through close reading
- Recognize and understand cause and effect
- Respond to the selection using text evidence to support ideas

Materials
Interactive Worktext, pp. 342–347

Go Digital
- Interactive eWorktext
- Cause and Effect Mini-Lesson

Scaffolding for **Wonders** Reading/Writing Workshop

REREAD COMPLEX TEXT

20–25 Minutes   RI.2.3   RI.2.5   L.2.4a   CCSS

Close Reading: "Visiting the Past"

Reread "Visiting the Past" with children from **Interactive Worktext** pages 342–345. As you read together, discuss important passages in the text. Guide children to respond to questions using evidence from the text.

Page 343

Expand Vocabulary Have children reread the second paragraph. Explain to them that *colonies* are places that are under the control of a distant country. Ask: *What is the name of the country that controlled the* colonies? Guide children to circle their answers. (England)

Purpose **ACT** Remind children what they know about expository texts. Guide them to think about the fact that an expository text gives information and facts about a topic. Have children reread the page. Ask: *What is the* purpose *of the Declaration of Independence?* Guide children to underline the sentence in the text that tells the answer. (It told the King that the colonies were free from his rule. The colonies would be united to form a new country.)

Cause and Effect Remind children that the *cause* is what makes something happen, and the *effect* is what happens. Have children reread the third paragraph. Ask: *The* effect *was that the Chang family visited Philadelphia. What was the* cause *of their visit?* Guide children to draw a box around their answer. (to learn about their country's history)

Page 344

Expand Vocabulary Explain to children that if you *announce* something, you tell about it or make it known. Have them reread the second paragraph. Ask: *What is the first event that the Liberty Bell was used to* announce? Have children circle the words that answer. (the first public reading of the Declaration of Independence)

Cause and Effect Guide children to reread the second paragraph. Remind them to think about causes and effects as they read. Ask: *The* cause *is a President being elected. What is the* effect? Children should write their answer. (the Liberty Bell rang)

Page 345

Genre **ACT** Explain to children that expository texts often include text features, such as charts and graphs, that give more information about a topic. Point to the "Visit Philadelphia" chart at the top of page 345. Explain that this chart is in a travel book. Read the column headings aloud. Tell children that all of the places listed are famous places in Philadelphia. Read aloud the places and places descriptions. Then ask: *Who was Betsy Ross?* (She made the first American flag.)

Purpose **ACT** Remind children that the author's purpose for writing this selection seems to be to tell about how important Philadelphia was to America's history. Have children keep that in mind as they reread this page. Ask: *Why did the author include information about Ben Franklin?* Have them write their answers. (Possible answer: He lived in Philadelphia.)

Expand Vocabulary Explain to children that if you *frame* something, you create the outline for it or give it a shape. Have them reread the first paragraph. Ask: *What did Ben Franklin help* frame? Have children write the words that tell the answer. (the Constitution)

Cause and Effect Have children reread the page. Ask: *What was the effect of the Chang family's visit to Philadelphia?* Children should draw a box around the text that answers the question. ("I'll never forget this day!" Janet said.)

RESPOND TO READING

10–20 Minutes   SL.2.1a   RI.2.3   RI.2.5

Respond to "Visiting the Past"

Guide children to read the questions about "Visiting the Past" on page 346 of the **Interactive Worktext**. Then read aloud the "Discussion Starter" for each of the questions. Guide children to work with a partner to answer the questions orally using the "Discussion Starters." Have children find text evidence to support their answers and write the page number(s) on which they found the text evidence for each question.

1. *How did the colonies become independent?* (<u>Possible answers</u>: On July 4, 1776, the colonies became free from England. The statement the colonists sent was called the Declaration of Independence. <u>Text Evidence</u>: p. 343)

2. *Why was the Constitution written?* (<u>Possible answers</u>: The Constitution was written to create rules for our new country. Rules are important because they keep order in a country. <u>Text Evidence</u>: pp. 344, 345)

3. *What is one of the rules in the Constitution?* (<u>Possible answers</u>: One rule is that people could tell their own opinions. This rule was important because it gave people rights. <u>Text Evidence</u>: pp. 344, 345)

After children discuss the questions on page 346, have them use the sentence starters to answer the question on page 347. Circulate and provide guidance.

 Quick Check Do children understand vocabulary in context? If not, review and reteach using the instruction on page 296.

Can children identify cause and effect? If not, review and reteach using the instruction on page 296 and assign the Unit 5 Week 5 digital mini-lesson.

Can children write a response to "Visiting the Past"? If not, review the sentence starters and prompt children to respond orally. Help them write their responses.

WEEK 5 LESSON 3

Objectives
- Understand and use new vocabulary words
- Read an expository text
- Recognize and understand cause and effect
- Understand complex text through close reading

Scaffolding for **Wonders** McGraw-Hill Reading Approaching Leveled Reader

Materials
- "Government Rules" Apprentice Leveled Reader: pp. 2–9
- Sequence Graphic Organizer

☞ **Go** Digital
- Apprentice Leveled Reader eBook
- Downloadable Graphic Organizer
- Cause and Effect Mini-Lesson

BEFORE READING

10–15 Minutes   SL.2.1a   SL.2.6   L.2.5a   L.2.6   CCSS

Introduce "Government Rules"

- Read the Essential Question on the title page of "Government Rules" **Apprentice Leveled Reader:** *Why are rules important? We will read about what rules government has, how they affect government, and what is important about them.*

- Read the title aloud. Point to the photographs. Ask: *Is this text fiction or nonfiction?* (nonfiction) *This nonfiction text is called an expository text. It gives true information about something real. Let's read to learn about government rules.*

Expand Vocabulary

Display each word below. Say the words and have children repeat them. Then use the Define/Example/Ask routine to introduce each word.

1 medicines (page 9)

Define: something people use to treat sickness

Example: The doctor gave my dad *medicines* to make him better.

Ask: What *medicines* have you taken when you were not feeling well?

2 raw (page 7)

Define: not cooked

Example: The meat was *raw* before Mom put it on the grill.

Ask: What is something you can eat that is *raw*?

3 serve (page 6)

Define: to give something to someone, or do something for someone

Example: They will *serve* peas today in the lunchroom.

Ask: What kind of food would you *serve* for dinner?

DURING READING

20–30 Minutes   RI.2.3   RI.2.4   RI.2.5   RI.2.6   L.2.4a   CCSS

Close Reading

🔍 **Pages 2–3**

Purpose Ⓐ Ⓒ Ⓣ Point out that understanding the purpose of a text can help us understand what we are reading. Read the first sentence on page 2 with children. Ask: *What is the first sentence?* (Rules are important.) Ask: *What do you think the purpose of this book is?* (to tell about rules and why they are important) Say: *The purpose of this book is to teach about rules and why they are important. Let's look for different rules as we read and find out why they are important.*

Genre Ⓐ Ⓒ Ⓣ Remind children that expository texts give facts about a topic. The text features also can give additional information and help us understand what we are reading. Ask: *What is the name of this chapter?* (Rules Protect Us) *Let's look at the photo and read the caption. What does the photo show?* (people in the government meeting) *What does the caption say?* (The government makes rules carefully.)

Vocabulary Have children find the word *government* on page 2. Explain that the *government* is a group of people that make the laws and rules for a city, state, or country. Ask: *Who is a person you can think of that is in the government?* (Possible answers: mayor, president)

Cause and Effect Remind children that the *cause* is what makes something happen and the *effect* is what happens. Say: *Think about what we read on this page. What causes the government to have rules?* (To help keep us safe.) Have children include this on their Cause and Effect charts.

🔍 Pages 4–5

Purpose (ACT) Read pages 4 with children. Remind them that understanding the purpose helps us to understand what we are reading better. Say: *This book tells us why rules are important. Why do you think the author talks about national parks?* (There are rules that protect national parks.) *Why are the rules important?* (They make sure that people treat them well so that we can all enjoy the parks.)

STOP AND CHECK Read the question in the Stop and Check box on page 4. (Possible answers: There are over 400 parks. They are open to the public.)

Cause and Effect Read page 5 with children. Remind children that the *cause* is what makes something happen and the *effect* is what happens. Say: *Think about what we read on this page. What causes the government to have rules about food?* (Some food is not safe to eat.) *What happens when the government checks food?* (Food gets a stamp if it is safe.) Ask children what they think the effect of this is for people buying food. (They won't get unsafe food.) Have children include this on their Cause and Effect charts.

🔍 Pages 6–7

Connection of Ideas (ACT) Read page 6 with children and look at the photo. Say: *The photo caption says that eating well helps you learn. Why do you think that is true?* (Eating well keeps you healthy so you can go to school and focus on learning.)

Cause and Effect Read page 7 with children. Say: *A cause is what makes something happens. An effect is what happens. What is the effect if some foods are eaten raw?* (You can get sick.) Help children record this on their Cause and Effect charts.

STOP AND CHECK Read the question in the Stop and Check box on page 7. (Possible answer: The government's rules make sure that food is checked so it's safe to eat.)

🔍 Pages 8–9

Genre (ACT) Read page 8 with children. Remind them that text features such as charts and graphs provide more information about the subject of the text. Say: *Let's look at this chart. What is the title of the chart?* (How to Store Eggs Safely) *What kind of egg can be stored in the refrigerator the shortest amount of time—a raw egg or a hard-boiled egg?* (hard-boiled) *How long can you keep store-bought eggnog frozen?* (6 months)

Vocabulary Ask: *What are two meanings of the word* store? (a place to buy things, to keep things) *How can you tell which meaning of the word* store *is meant here?* (It is about how to store eggs safely. If I replace it the word *store* with the word *keep,* it makes sense. If I replace it with "place to buy things," it does not make sense.)

Cause and Effect Read page 9 with children. Say: *What happens after the government tests and approves a medicine?* (Stores can sell the medicine.)

STOP AND CHECK Read the question in the Stop and Check box on page 9. (Possible answers: Testing medicines makes sure they are safe for people to use.)

Have partners review their Cause and Effect charts for pages 2–9 and discuss what they have learned.

✅ *Quick Check* Do children understand weekly vocabulary in context? If not, review and reteach using the instruction on page 296.

Can children identify cause and effect? If not, review and reteach using the instruction on page 296 and assign Unit 5 Week 5 digital mini-lesson.

WEEK 5
LESSON
4

Objectives
- Understand and use new vocabulary words
- Read an expository text
- Recognize and understand cause and effect
- Understand complex text through close reading

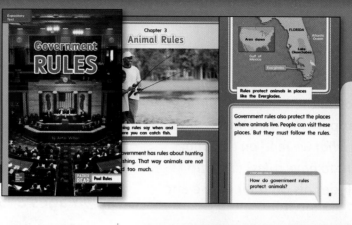

Materials
- "Government Rules" Apprentice Leveled Reader: pp. 10–19
- Cause and Effect Graphic Organizer

👉 **Go Digital**
- Apprentice Leveled Reader eBook
- Downloadable Graphic Organizer
- Cause and Effect Mini-Lesson

Scaffolding for **Wonders** Approaching Leveled Reader

BEFORE READING

5–10 Minutes   SL.2.1a   SL.2.6   L.2.5a   L.2.6

Expand Vocabulary

Display each word below. Say the words and have students repeat them. Then use the Define/Example/Ask routine to introduce each word.

❶ copy (page 12)

Define: to do the same thing as someone else

Example: It is not good to *copy* someone's ideas.

Ask: Why is it sometimes bad to *copy* something?

❷ inventors (page 13)

Define: people who think of new things and make them

Example: The *inventors* of the train wanted to find a way to get places faster.

Ask: How could an *inventor* come up with ideas?

DURING READING

10–15 Minutes   RI.2.1   RI.2.3   RI.2.5   RI.2.6

Close Reading

🔍 Pages 10–11

Cause and Effect Reread page 10 with children. Remind children of the connection between a *cause* and an *effect*. Ask: *What causes animals not to be hunted too much?* (The government has rules.) Ask children why that is a good thing. (Animals won't be killed and disappear.) Point out that that is an effect of the rules. Have children record this on their Cause and Effect charts.

Genre Ⓐ Ⓒ Ⓣ Reread page 11 with children. Remind them that they can use text features like maps and charts to learn more about the subject they are reading about. Ask: *What state does the map show?* (Florida) *What special part of Florida does the map point out?* (the Everglades) *Why?* (It is a place where rules protect animals from being hunted.)

STOP AND CHECK Read the question in the Stop and Check box on page 11. (Possible answer: Government rules make sure that animals are not hunted too much and that they have a place to live.)

🔍 Page 12–13

Purpose Ⓐ Ⓒ Ⓣ Point out the chapter title at the top of page 12 to children. Remind them that that they have been paying attention to all the different kinds of rules that the government makes. Read pages 12. Ask: *What is the purpose of this chapter?* (The government has many rules to protect people. They even make rules to protect people's ideas, which are different from food and animals and medicine.)

Connection of Ideas Read pages 13 with children and point out the photo and its caption. Say: *The text says that if the cereal name is trademarked, no one can copy this cereal name. Why is that important?* (Possible answer: It is important because then people can't buy something else by mistake and then be disappointed or hurt. That way people always know what they will get when they buy the cereal with that name.)

Page 14

Cause and Effect Have children read page 14. Ask: *What causes someone to need a patent?* (So someone else can't use his or her idea.) *Why is that important?* (People should be able to do what they chose to with their ideas. Other people won't be able to sell their ideas and make money off of them.) Have children add this to their Cause and Effect charts.

Purpose **A C T** Have children think about what they have learned reading this book. Lead them to think about the purpose of the text. Ask: *What do you think the purpose of this book is?* (Possible answer: The purpose is to tell how government rules protect many different parts of our lives. If we follow those rules, they make our lives safer and better.)

STOP AND CHECK Read the question in the Stop and Check box on page 14. (Having a patent makes sure that no one uses or sells an inventor's idea.)

AFTER READING
10–15 Minutes · · · · · L.2.6 · RI.2.3 · RI.2.9 · W. 2.8 · **CCSS**

Respond to Reading

Compare Texts Have children compare "Government Rules" to "Visiting the Past." Ask: *What did you learn about the government from the two texts? What did you learn about the importance of rules? Discuss with a partner.*

Summarize Have students turn to page 15 and summarize the selection. Answers should feature the cause and effect of government rules.

Text Evidence

Have partners work together to answer questions on page 15. Remind students to use their Cause and Effect charts.

Cause and Effect (Rules about how to cook foods properly keep people from getting sick [page 7].)

Vocabulary (a patent)

Write About Reading Answers will vary but should explain that rules are important because they keep people safe, preserve important places and animals, and protect writers' and inventors' ideas.

Independent Reading

Encourage students to read the paired selection "Pool Rules" on pages 16–18. Have them summarize the selection and compare it to "Government Rules." Have them work with a partner to answer the "Make Connections" questions on page 18.

 Quick Check Can students identify cause and effect? If not, review and reteach using the instruction on page 296 and assign the Unit 5 Week 5 digital mini-lesson.

Can students respond to the selection using text evidence? If not, provide sentence frames to help them organize their ideas.

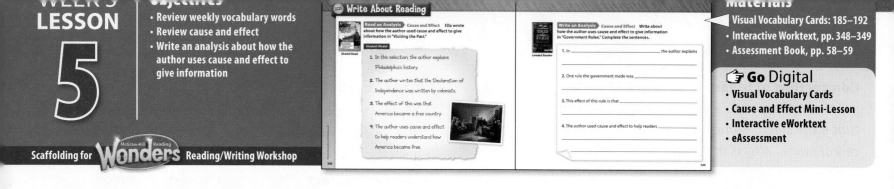

WEEK'S LESSON 5

Objectives
• Review weekly vocabulary words
• Review cause and effect
• Write an analysis about how the author uses cause and effect to give information

Materials
• Visual Vocabulary Cards: 185–192
• Interactive Worktext, pp. 348–349
• Assessment Book, pp. 58–59

☞ **Go** Digital
• Visual Vocabulary Cards
• Cause and Effect Mini-Lesson
• Interactive eWorktext
• eAssessment

Scaffolding for **Wonders** McGraw-Hill Reading Reading/Writing Workshop

REVIEW AND RETEACH

5–10 Minutes   L.2.4a   RI.2.3   RI.2.5   CCSS

Weekly Vocabulary

Display one **Visual Vocabulary Card** at a time and guide children to use the vocabulary word in a sentence. If children have difficulty creating a sentence, have them find the word in "Visiting the Past" or "Government Rules" and use context clues to define the vocabulary word.

Comprehension: Cause and Effect

I Do Write and say: *I left a pen in my pocket when it went through the washing machine, so it stained my jeans.* Say: *Remember that the* effect *is what happened and the* cause *is what made it happen. What is the effect? My jeans are stained. What made, or caused my jeans to get stained? I left a pen in the pocket and it went through the washing machine.*

We Do Display: *I walked home from school with my mom. The ice on the sidewalk was slippery. I fell down.* Ask: *What was the cause?* (The ice was slippery.) *What was the effect?* (I fell down.)

You Do Display the following two sets of sentences: *Tom took his dog to a dog park. There were lots of dogs playing in the park. Tom threw a stick. Tom's dog ran fast to get it.*

Rita was invited to her best friend Pam's birthday party. She wanted to give Rita a special present. She made her a beautiful necklace out of beads. Pam loved the present. Guide partners to work together to figure out the causes and effects of each pair.

WRITE ABOUT READING

25–35 Minutes   W.2.2   W.2.8   W.4.9   CCSS

Read an Analysis

• Guide children to look back at "Visiting the Past" in the **Interactive Worktext**. Have volunteers review the examples of cause and effect they marked on page 343. Repeat with pages 344–345. *How did the author use cause and effect to give information in the selection?*

• Read aloud the directions on page 348. Read aloud the student model. *This student's work is not a summary. It is an analysis, or description, of how the author used cause and effect to give information in "Visiting the Past."*

• *When you write an analysis, you should include key details from the text that tell how the author used cause and effect. Read Ella's first sentence. Circle the details.* (the author explains Philadelphia's history) *In what part of the story do you learn this detail?* (the beginning)

• *Read the second sentence. Draw a box around the part that show a cause or effect.* (the Declaration of Independence was written by colonists) *Does this detail show a cause or effect?* (cause) *What part of the story is she writing about?* (the middle)

• *Guide children to point to the third sentence. What information did Ella include?* (America became a free country) *Does this detail show cause or effect?* (effect)

• Model analyzing how the author used cause and effect. Read the last sentence that Ella wrote. *Why is this sentence a good ending?* (Ella writes how the author used cause and effect to help readers understand an event in history.)

Write an Analysis

Analytical Writing

Guided Writing Read the writing prompt on page 349 together. Guide children to review their Cause and Effect charts for "Government Rules." Have children use their charts to complete the sentence starters. Children can also write an analysis using another selection previously read this week.

Peer Conference Guide children to read their analysis to a partner. Listeners should summarize the strongest details that support the beginning, middle, and ending sentences. They should discuss any parts that are unclear.

Teacher Conference Check children's writing for complete sentences and whether they included details from the story. Review the ending sentence and ask: *Did the author use cause and effect to support the story?* If necessary, guide children to revise their sentence by adding more details.

Level Up

Apprentice Leveled Reader

▲ **Approaching Leveled Reader**

▲ **Interactive Worktext**

▲ **Reading/Writing Workshop**

IF children read the Apprentice Level Reader and the **Interactive Worktext** Shared Read fluently and answer the Respond to Reading questions

THEN read together the Approaching Level Reader main selection and the **Reading/Writing Workshop** Shared Read from *Reading Wonders*. Have children take notes as they read, using self-stick notes. Then ask and answer questions about their notes.

Writing Rubric

	4	3	2	1
Text Evidence	Includes three or more details from the text.	Includes two or more details from the text.	Includes only one detail from the text.	No text evidence is cited.
Writing Style	Writes in complete sentences. Uses correct spelling and grammar.	Uses complete sentences. Writing has spelling and grammar errors.	Few complete sentences. There are many spelling and grammar errors.	Writing is not accurate or in complete sentences.

ASSESSMENT

Weekly Assessment

Have children complete the Weekly Assessment using **Assessment** book pages 58–59.

Unit 5 Assessment

▶ **Unit Assessment,** pages 158 – 166

▶ **Fluency Assessment,** pages 266 – 281

▶ **Exit Test,** pages 214 – 222

CCSS TESTED SKILLS

✔ COMPREHENSION	✔ VOCABULARY:
• Point of View RL.2.6	• Context Clues L.2.4a
• Point of View RL.2.6	
• Sequence RI.2.6	
• Problem and Solution RL.2.3, RL.2.5	
• Cause and Effect RI.2.3	

Using Assessment and Writing Scores

RETEACH	IF ...	THEN ...
COMPREHENSION	Students answer 0–7 multiple-choice items correctly ...	... reteach tested skills using instruction on pages 364–375.
VOCABULARY	Students answer 0–3 multiple-choice items correctly ...	... reteach tested skills using instruction on page 364.
WRITING	Students score mostly 1–2 on weekly Write About Reading rubrics throughout the unit ...	... reteach writing using instruction on pages 376–377.

LEVEL UP	IF ...	THEN ...
COMPREHENSION	Students answer 8–10 multiple-choice items correctly ...	... have students read the *Rudy Garcia-Tolson* Approaching Leveled Reader. Use the Level Up lesson on page 300.
WRITING	Students score mostly 3–4 on weekly Write About Reading rubrics throughout the unit ...	... use the Level Up Write About Reading lesson on page 301 to have students compare two selections from the unit.

Fluency Assessment

Conduct assessments individually using the differentiated fluency passages in **Assessment**. Students' expected fluency goal for this Unit is 79–99 WCPM with an accuracy rate of 95% or higher.

Exit Test

If a student answers 13–15 multiple choice items correctly on the Unit Assessment, administer the Unit 5 Exit Test at the end of Week 6.

Time to Exit WonderWorks

Exit Text

If...

Students answer 13–15 multiple choice items correctly...

Fluency Assessment

If...

Students achieve their Fluency Assessment goal for the unit...

Level Up Lessons

If...

Students are successful applying close reading skills with the Approaching Leveled Reader in Week 6...

If...

Students score mostly 4–5 on the Level Up Write About Reading assignment...

Foundational Skills Kit

If...

Students have mastered the Unit 5 benchmark skills in the Foundational Skills Kit and *Reading Wonders* Adaptive Learning...

Then...

... consider exiting the student from *Reading WonderWorks* materials into the Approaching Level of *Reading Wonders*.

WEEK 6

► **Read Approaching Leveled Reader**

Approaching Leveled Reader

Apprentice Leveled Reader

► **Write About Reading**

Interactive Worktext Shared Read

Apprentice Leveled Reader

Apprentice to Approaching Level

L.2.5 RI.2.10

Rudy Garcia-Tolson

Before Reading

Preview Discuss what children remember about Rudy Garcia-Tolson and what heroes do. Tell them they will be reading a more challenging version of "Rudy Garcia-Tolson."

Vocabulary Use the routines on the **Visual Vocabulary Cards** to review the Weekly Vocabulary words. Use pages 270 and 272 to review the Expand Vocabulary words.

A C T During Reading

▶ **Organization** Remind children that one way an author can organize a text is by using sequence or telling the events in order. Remind children that they can look for sequence words such as *first, next, then, last,* and *now* to help them understand the sequence. Read page 6 with children and point out the second paragraph. Say: *The first paragraph tells about Rudy as a boy, but the second paragraph tells about him as a grown up.* Remind children to think about the sequence of the selection as they read.

▶ **Specific Vocabulary** Review the following content words that are new to this level: *practiced* (page 6), *healthful* (page 9), *goal* (page 9), *world record* (page 11). Provide the meaning of each word. Model how to use available context clues to determine each word's meaning, and use photos when possible to provide visual clues.

▶ **Genre** Say: *A biography is the true story of a real person's life. It is written by another person. A biography may include text features such a time line. A time line shows when important events in a person's life happened. Reading a time line can help you understand the sequence of events.* Point out the time line on pages 12–13 and say: *This time line shows that in 1988 Rudy was born on September 14. What important event happened in 1993?* (Rudy's legs were removed.) *Rudy won gold and bronze medals in the Paralympic Games in China. In what year did this happen?* (2008)

After Reading

Ask children to complete the Respond to Reading on page 16 after they have finished reading. Provide support with the vocabulary strategy question, as needed.

Write About Reading

RI.3.9   W.4.9   **CCSS**

Read an Analysis

- Distribute the Unit 5 Downloadable Model and Practice. Point out that the model compares two related texts that children have read in Unit 5, the **Interactive Worktext** Shared Read "César Chávez" and the **Apprentice Leveled Reader** "Rudy Garcia-Tolson." Read the sentences aloud to children.

- Point out the key details in each sentence that come from the texts. Point out the signal word *both*. Explain to children that this word shows readers that the sentence is comparing two different texts.

- Ask: *What details show that the two texts are alike?* (Both texts tell about people who are heroes to others. Both texts tell how each person did not let problems stop him from helping others.) *How is "Rudy Garcia-Tolson" different from Cesar Chavez?* ("Rudy Garcia-Tolson" tells about an athlete, not a farm worker.)

- Model analyzing how the student compared details. Read the last sentence. *Why is this a good comparison?* (The student gave evidence to show how the two heroes are similar.)

Write an Analysis

Guided Writing Tell children that they will compare the **Interactive Worktext** Shared Read "Visiting the Past" and the **Apprentice Leveled Reader** "Government Rules." Explain to children that they will compare how the authors describe different ways rules are important.

- Guide children to compare the two texts as they complete the sentences on the Unit 5 Downloadable Model and Practice.

- Point out the signal words, such as *also, both*, and *different, to children and discuss how these words are used to compare the texts.*

- Alternatively, let children select two texts to compare.

Teacher Conference Check children's writing for complete sentences. Did they use key details to tell how the texts are the same and different? Did they use text evidence? Did they write in complete sentences?

Writing Rubric

	4	3	2	1
Text Evidence	Includes three or more details from the text.	Includes two or more details from the text.	Includes only one detail from the text.	No text evidence is cited.
Writing Style	Writes in complete sentences. Uses correct spelling and grammar.	Uses complete sentences. Writing has spelling and grammar errors.	Few complete sentences. There are many spelling and grammar errors.	Writing is not accurate or in complete sentences.

UNIT 6 PLANNER
How on Earth?

Week 1 **Plant Myths and Facts**	**Week 2** **We Need Energy**	**Week 3** **Team Up To Explore**

ESSENTIAL QUESTION *What do myths help us understand?*	**ESSENTIAL QUESTION** *How do we use energy?*	**ESSENTIAL QUESTION** *Why is teamwork important?*
Build Background	**Build Background**	**Build Background**
CCSS Vocabulary L.2.4a *appeared, crops, develop, edge, golden, rustled, shining, stages*	**CCSS Vocabulary** L.2.4a *electricity, energy, flows, haul, power, silent, solar, underground*	**CCSS Vocabulary** L.2.4a *exploration, important, machines, prepare, repair, result, scientific, teamwork*
Access Complex Text Connection of Ideas	**Access Complex Text** Organization	**Access Complex Text** Sentence Structure
CCSS Comprehension RL.2.2 Skill: Theme Respond to Reading	**CCSS Comprehension** RI.2.8 Skill: Author's Purpose Respond to Reading	**CCSS Comprehension** RI.2.2 Skill: Main Idea and Key Details Respond to Reading
CCSS Write About Reading *Analytical Writing* W.4.9 Inform/Explain: Theme	**CCSS Write About Reading** *Analytical Writing* W.4.9 Inform/Explain: Author's Purpose	**CCSS Write About Reading** *Analytical Writing* W.4.9 Opinion: Main Idea and Details

A S S E S S M E N T

✅ *Quick Check* Vocabulary, Comprehension	✅ *Quick Check* Vocabulary, Comprehension	✅ *Quick Check* Vocabulary, Comprehension
✅ **Weekly Assessment** Assessment Book, pp. 60–61	✅ **Weekly Assessment** Assessment Book, pp. 62–63	✅ **Weekly Assessment** Assessment Book, pp. 64–65

✅ **MID-UNIT ASSESSMENT**
Assessment Book, pp. 112–119

Fluency Assessment
Assessment Book, pp. 266–281

Use the Foundational Skills Kit for explicit instruction of phonics, structural analysis, fluency, and word recognition. Includes *Reading Wonders* Adaptive Learning.

Week 4
Money Matters

ESSENTIAL QUESTION
How do we use money?

Build Background

CCSS Vocabulary
L.2.4a *invented, money, prices, purchase, record, system, value, worth*

Access Complex Text
Purpose

CCSS Comprehension
RI.2.3 Skill: Problem and Solution
Respond to Reading

CCSS Write About Reading
W.4.9 Inform/Explain: Genre

Week 5
The World of Ideas

ESSENTIAL QUESTION
Where can your imagination take you?

Build Background

CCSS Vocabulary
L.2.4a *create, dazzling, imagination, seconds*

Poetry Words
beats, message, metaphor, repeated lines

Access Complex Text
Connection of Ideas

CCSS Comprehension
RL.2.6 Skill: Point of View
Respond to Reading

CCSS Write About Reading
W.4.9 Opinion: Word Choice

Week 6
ASSESS

RETEACH   LEVEL UP

Reteach
Comprehension Skills
Vocabulary
Write About Reading

Level Up
Read Approaching Leveled Reader
Write About Reading:
Compare Texts

A S S E S S M E N T

✓ Quick Check
Vocabulary, Comprehension

✓ Weekly Assessment
Assessment Book, pp. 66–67

✓ Quick Check
Vocabulary, Comprehension

✓ Weekly Assessment
Assessment Book, pp. 68–69

✓ Unit Assessment
Assessment Book, pp. 167–175

✓ Fluency Assessment
Assessment Book, pp. 266–281

EXIT TEST
Assessment Book, pp. 223–231

ABOUT UNIT 6

UNIT 6 OPENER,
pp. 350–351

The Big Idea

What keeps our world working?

Talk About It

Read aloud the Big Idea on page 350 of the **Interactive Worktext:** *What keeps our world working?* Ask children to tell about a time they learned how something worked. Children may describe events such as when they learned how a toy or video game works, or how a tool is used, such as a bike pump.

Discuss the photo on pages 350–351. Ask: *What do you see in the picture?* (a city with skyscrapers and a bridge going over a river) *What else do you see?* (a train going over a bridge, a boat in the water) *How do the things in the picture help this city to keep working?* (Skyscrapers provide offices for workers; bridges allow people to get to their jobs; boats help bring goods to people.)

Then say: Now let's think about our community. *What helps our community keep working?* Have children work think of what helps their community keep working. Afterwards, have partners share their ideas. Help them see that curiosity has helped create all the things that keep their community going. Explain that people invented roads, bridges, buildings, schools and so on.

Then say: *Let's look back at our Big Idea. What keeps our world working?* Explain to children that they will be discussing the Big Idea throughout the unit. Each week they will talk, read and write about different things that keep our world moving forward.

Build Fluency

Each week, use the **Interactive Worktext** Shared Reads and **Apprentice Leveled Readers** for fluency instruction and practice. Keep in mind that reading rates vary with the type of text that children are reading as well as the purpose for reading. For example, comprehension of complex informational texts generally requires slower reading.

Explain/Model Use the Fluency lessons on pages 378–382 to explain the skill. Then model the skill by reading the first page of the week's Shared Read or Leveled Reader.

Practice/Apply Choose a page from the Shared Read or Leveled Reader. Have one group read the top half of the page one sentence at a time. Remind children to apply the skill. Have the second group echo-read the passage. Then have the groups switch roles for the second half of the page. Discuss how each group applied the skill.

> **Weekly Fluency Focus**
>
> **Week 1** Expression
> **Week 2** Intonation
> **Week 3** Pronunciation
> **Week 4** Intonation
> **Week 5** Expression

Foundational Skills Kit You can also use the **Lesson Cards** and **Practice** pages from the **Foundational Skills Kit** for targeted Fluency instruction and practice.

 **Access Complex Text**

Qualitative — Quantitative

Reader and Task

TEXT COMPLEXITY

Interactive Worktext

	Week 1	Week 2	Week 3	Week 4	Week 5
	"Why Fir Tree Keeps His Leaves"	"Pedal Power"	"Dive Teams"	"The Life of a Dollar Bill"	"A Box of Crayons"
Quantitative	Lexile 440 TextEvaluator™ 6	Lexile 570 TextEvaluator™ 19	Lexile 550 TextEvaluator™ 18	Lexile 550 TextEvaluator™ 6	Lexile NP TextEvaluator™ NP
Qualitative	• Connection of Ideas • Genre • Vocabulary	• Organization • Genre • Vocabulary	• Sentence Structure • Vocabulary	• Purpose • Genre • Connection of Ideas • Vocabulary	• Connection of Ideas • Genre • Vocabulary
Reader and Task	The Weekly Concept lessons will help determine the reader's knowledge and engagement in the weekly concept.				
	Weekly Concept: p. 306 Questions and tasks: pp. 308–309	Weekly Concept: p. 316 Questions and tasks: pp. 318–319	Weekly Concept: p. 326 Questions and tasks: pp. 328–329	Weekly Concept: p. 338 Questions and tasks: pp. 340–341	Weekly Concept: p. 348 Questions and tasks: pp. 350–351

Apprentice Leveled Reader

	Week 1	Week 2	Week 3	Week 4	Week 5
	"The Apples of Idun"	"Wind Power"	"Digging for Sue"	"How to Be a Smart Shopper"	"Matt's Journey"
Quantitative	Lexile 300 TextEvaluator™ 6	Lexile 390 TextEvaluator™ 6	Lexile 390 TextEvaluator™ 6	Lexile 370 TextEvaluator™ 6	Lexile 350 TextEvaluator™ 10
Qualitative	• Connection of Ideas • Genre • Vocabulary	• Organization • Prior Knowledge • Genre • Vocabulary	• Sentence Structure • Genre • Connection of Ideas • Prior Knowledge • Vocabulary	• Purpose • Genre • Connection of Ideas • Vocabulary	• Connection of Ideas • Genre • Vocabulary
Reader and Task	The Weekly Concept lessons will help determine the reader's knowledge and engagement in the weekly concept.				
	Weekly Concept: p. 306 Questions and tasks: pp. 310–313	Weekly Concept: p. 316 Questions and tasks: pp. 320–323	Weekly Concept: p. 326 Questions and tasks: pp. 330–333	Weekly Concept: p. 338 Questions and tasks: pp. 242–245	Weekly Concept: p. 348 Questions and tasks: pp. 352–355

See page 383 for details about Text Complexity measures.

LESSON

1

- Develop oral language
- Build background about myths
- Understand and use weekly vocabulary
- Read a myth

Scaffolding for **WONDERS** Reading/Writing Workshop

Talk About It
Weekly Concept Plant Myths and Facts

Essential Question
What do myths help us understand about plants?

Plant Myths

Create your own myth about a flower or plant.

▶ Interactive Worktext, pp. 352–359
- Visual Vocabulary Cards: 193–200
- High-Frequency Word Cards

☞ **Go** Digital
- Interactive eWorktext
- Visual Vocabulary Cards

WEEKLY CONCEPT

5–10 Minutes   SL.2.1a   SL.2.4

Talk About It

Essential Question Read aloud the Essential Question on page 352 of the **Interactive Worktext:** *What do myths help us understand about plants?* Explain that a myth is a story that tells why something is the way it is. Tell children that some myths were created to help people understand how plants develop. Ask: *Did you ever wonder why a certain plant or flower is the way it is? Many people over time have had these same questions. Some people created myths, or stories, to answer these questions.*

Discuss the photograph on page 352. Ask: *What is happening in the picture?* (A girl is blowing the seeds off of a dandelion flower.) Say: *When a dandelion flower gets old and dies, it's petals turn to fluff.*

I Do Say: *When I look at this photo, I think about a myth. Does anyone know the myth about dandelion flowers? The myth says that when a dandelion dies, you will get a wish if you blow away its seeds with one breath. I will write this myth on the web on page 353.*

We Do Say: *Let's think about other myths we know and what they tell us about plants.* Ask: *Does anyone know the myth about a four-leaf clover?* (Finding a four-leaf clover is lucky. Since most clovers have three leaves, it is rare to find a four-leaf clover.) Have children add this myth to their web.

You Do Guide partners to work together to think about a new plant myth. Have them think about plants, flowers, or trees and come up with a myth about why they are the way they are. Have children use the words from the web to start their sentences: *Our plant myth is _____.*

REVIEW VOCABULARY

10–15 Minutes   L.2.5a   L.2.6   RF.2.3f

Review Weekly Vocabulary Words

- Use the **Visual Vocabulary Cards** to review the weekly vocabulary.

- Read together the directions on page 354 of the **Interactive Worktext**. Then complete the activity.

1 **shining** Tell children on sunny days, you can see the shining sun. Have children look around the classroom for other things that can be described as *shining*. Use the following oral sentence frame: *I see a shining _____.* (Possible answers: light, lamp) Then guide children to circle their answer in their books. (dime)

2 **golden** Write the word *golden* on the board. Have a volunteer underline the root word *gold*. Ask children what they think the word *golden* means. Guide children to understand that something that is *golden* looks like gold. Then use this oral sentence frame: *_____ is/are golden.* (Possible answers: sunlight, apples, leaves in fall, raisins)

3 **rustled** Explain that in the fall, when the leaves blew in the wind, they make a soft sound. Say: *The leaves rustled as they rubbed together.* Give each child a piece of scrap paper. Have children rub the papers together to make a *rustling* sound. Say: *The paper rustled.* Have children repeat the action and the sentence.

4 **edge** Point to the *edge* of a book. Place the book on a table and then roll a pencil off the *edge* of the book and say: *The pencil rolled off the edge of the book.* Have children think of other things in the classroom that also have *edges*. Use the following oral sentence frame: *A _____ has an edge.* (Possible answers: paper, desk, cabinet, door, bookshelf)

5 stages Ask a volunteer to tell another meaning for the word *stages*. (performance spaces) Then guide children to name the different *stages* in a person's life. (Possible answers: baby, child, teenager, adult) Finally, have children suggest synonyms for the word *stages*. (Possible answers: parts, periods)

6 develop Draw a picture of a kitten on the left side of the board and a picture of a cat on the right side. Write the word *develop* in between the two pictures. Say: *A kitten will* develop *into a cat.* Then draw a picture of a puppy and say: *A puppy will* develop *into a _____.* (dog) Draw a picture of a dog.

7 appeared Write the word *appeared* on the board. Make a list of words that mean the same as *appeared*. (Possible answers: arrived, came into view) Have children read the sentence aloud. Then guide children to identify a word that means the opposite of *appeared*. (disappeared)

8 crops Invite volunteers to name *crops* as you list them on the board. Give an example to start, if necessary. Have children use this sentence frame: _____ *and* _____ *are* crops *that farmers grow.* (Possible answers: corn, soybeans, cotton) Then assist children as they draw a picture of a *crop* of pumpkins.

High-Frequency Words

Have children look at page 355 in the **Interactive Worktext**. Help them read, spell, and write each high-frequency word. Guide partners to use each word in a sentence. Then read the story aloud with children. Guide partners to work together to reread the story and circle the high-frequency words. (warm, green, Yes, cold, why, any) Listen in and provide assistance reading the high-frequency words, as necessary.

ELL ENGLISH LANGUAGE LEARNERS

Display High-Frequency Word Cards *any, cold, green, warm, why, yes.* Write a sentence with each word. Have children echo-read each sentence, and point out the high-frequency word.

READ COMPLEX TEXT
15–20 Minutes   SL.2.1b   RL.2.1   RL.2.2

Read "Why Fir Tree Keeps His Leaves"

- Have children turn to page 356 in the **Interactive Worktext** and read the Essential Question aloud. Echo-read the title with children. Point to the image of the fir tree on page 356 and say: *This is an illustration of the character Fir Tree from the story. How is Fir Tree different from the other trees in the picture?* (His leaves are green. His top is pointed.) *Let's read a myth that tells why fir trees keep their leaves.*

- Read the story together. Note that the weekly vocabulary words are highlighted in yellow. Expand Vocabulary words are highlighted in blue.

- As children read, have them use the "My Notes" section on page 356 to write questions they have. Children can also write words they don't understand or things they want to remember. Model how to use the "My Notes" section. Say: *When I read page 357, I see the word* patient. *I wonder what* patient *means. I will write a question about the word* patient *in the "My Notes" section.*

ELL ENGLISH LANGUAGE LEARNERS

As you read together, have children highlight parts of the text they have questions about. After reading, review the questions children have. Then help them locate the answers to their questions in the text.

 Quick Check Can children understand the weekly vocabulary words in context? If not, review vocabulary using the **Visual Vocabulary Cards** before teaching Lesson 2.

Can children read high-frequency words in context? If not, review using the Read/Spell/Write routine and the High-Frequency Word Cards.

WEEK 1
LESSON 2

Objectives
- Read a myth
- Understand complex text through close reading
- Recognize and understand theme
- Respond to the selection using text evidence to support ideas

Scaffolding for **Wonders** Reading/Writing Workshop

Materials
Interactive Worktext, pp. 356–361

☞ **Go** Digital
- Interactive eWorktext
- Theme Mini-Lesson

REREAD COMPLEX TEXT

20–25 Minutes   RL.2.1   RL.2.2   L.2.5a   L.2.6   CCSS

Close Reading: "Why Fir Tree Keeps His Leaves"

Reread "Why Fir Tree Keeps His Leaves" from **Interactive Worktext** pages 356–359 with children. As you read together, discuss important passages in the text. Guide children to respond to questions using evidence from the text.

🔍 Page 356–357

Genre **ACT** Say: *This story is a myth. Myths are made-up stories. Myths explain why things are the way they are. They often answer a question and have an important lesson or message that the author wants readers to understand. Look at the title on page 356.* Have children echo-read the title. Ask: *What question will this myth answer?* (Why does a fir tree keep its leaves?) Reread the first page with children and ask: *What is one way you can tell this is a made-up story?* (Fir Tree is a talking tree. Trees cannot speak in real life.)

Connection of Ideas **ACT** Review the week's Essential Question. Explain that although myths have elements that do not seem real, they do try to explain things that exist in the real world. Reread the third paragraph aloud. Ask: *What does this myth tell you about fir trees' leaves in the fall?* Guide children to underline the sentence that tells. (Fir Tree's leaves stayed green.)

Expand Vocabulary Explain to children that when you are *patient,* you wait calmly. Model waiting *patiently* and then have children do the same at their desks. Reread the last paragraph aloud and ask: *Who does Mother Nature tell to be* patient? Guide children to circle the words that tell. (Fir Tree)

Theme Say: *The theme of a story is the main message the author wants to tell the reader. The theme is usually not directly stated by the author. With many stories, the reader must figure out the theme. To find the theme, you must think about what the characters say and do.* Reread the last two paragraphs with children. Ask: *Why doesn't Fir Tree like his leaves?* Guide children to write their answers. (He wants his leaves to change colors.)

🔍 Page 358

Connection of Ideas **ACT** Say: *Let's see what else this myth can teach us about nature.* Reread the first paragraph aloud and have children look at the picture. Ask: *What season is it at this point in the story?* (winter) *How do you know?* (It looks cold outside. It is snowing.) *How did Maple, Oak, and Elm change?* Guide children to write their answers. (These trees lost their leaves.)

Theme Have children reread the first paragraph. Say: *Let's look for more clues about the theme. We know that Fir Tree does not want to be different from the other trees. What is different about Fir Tree?* Guide children to draw a box around the sentence that tells. (Fir Tree's green leaves remained.)

Expand Vocabulary Explain to children that if a person *protested,* he or she complained. Reread the second paragraph aloud and ask: *Who is it that Fir Tree* protested *to?* Guide children to circle the name of the character. (Mother Nature) Ask: *Why did Fir Tree protest?* (He didn't want to be different.)

Page 359

Expand Vocabulary Explain to children that if you *approached* someone or something, you went up to it. Have children reread the second paragraph. Ask: *Who* approached *Fir Tree?* (Squirrel) *What question did Squirrel ask when she* approached *Fir Tree?* Guide children to circle the text that tells. (May I build a nest in your branches?)

Theme Have children reread the last paragraph. Say: *Usually there will be important clues to the theme at the end of a story. Pay attention to how a character thinks and feels. How does Fir Tree feel about his leaves at the end of the story?* Guide children to draw a box around the sentence that shows how Fir Tree feels. (He is proud of his green leaves.)

Theme Tell children to look back at their notes about the theme. Say: *At first, Fir Tree does not like his leaves. Why?* (He wants to be the same as the other trees.) *In the winter, Fir Tree complains that he is different. What happens to his leaves to make him different from the others?* (He keeps his leaves while the other trees lose theirs.) *At the end of the story Fir Tree is able to give a warm home to Squirrel because he still has his leaves. How does this make Fir Tree feel?* (He feels proud of his green leaves.) *Using these clues and any notes you have taken, what is the theme of the selection?* Guide children to write their answer. (It is okay to be different.)

RESPOND TO READING

10–20 Minutes SL.2.1a RL.2.1 RL.2.2

Respond to "Why Fir Tree Keeps His Leaves"

Guide children to read aloud the questions about "Why Fir Tree Keeps His Leaves" on page 360 of the **Interactive Worktext**. Read aloud the "Discussion Starter" for each question. Guide children to work with a partner to answer the questions orally using the "Discussion Starters." Have children find text evidence to support their answers. Ask children to write the page number(s) on which they found the text evidence.

1. *How is Fir Tree different from other trees?* (<u>Possible answers</u>: I read that Fir Tree is different because his leaves don't change colors. His leaves stay the same all year. <u>Text Evidence</u>: p. 357)

2. *What happens to the trees in the winter?* (<u>Possible answers</u>: In the winter, the other trees lose their leaves. Fir Tree keeps his leaves. <u>Text Evidence</u>: p. 358)

3. *What is the purpose of Fir Tree's leaves?* (<u>Possible answers</u>: Fir Tree learns the purpose of his leaves when a squirrel asks to build a nest in his branches. The Fir Tree's leaves give shelter to animals in the winter. <u>Text Evidence</u>: p. 359)

After children discuss the questions on page 360, have them use the sentence starters to answer the question on page 361. Circulate and provide guidance.

 Quick Check Do children understand vocabulary in context? If not, review and reteach using the instruction on page 314.

Can children identify theme? If not, review and reteach using the instruction on page 314 and assign the Unit 6 Week 1 digital mini-lesson.

Can children write a response to "Why Fir Tree Keeps His Leaves"? If not, review the sentence starters and prompt children to respond orally. Help them write their responses.

WEEK 1
LESSON

3

Objectives
• Understand and use new vocabulary words
• Read a myth
• Recognize and understand theme
• Understand complex text through close reading

Scaffolding for **Wonders** Approaching Leveled Reader

Materials
• "The Apples of Idun" Apprentice Leveled Reader: pp. 2–10
• Theme Graphic Organizer

☞ **Go** Digital
• Apprentice Leveled Reader
• Downloadable Graphic Organizer
• Theme Mini-Lesson

BEFORE READING

10–15 Minutes   SL.2.1a   SL.2.6 L   L.2.5a   L.2.6   CCSS

Introduce "The Apples of Idun"

• Read the Essential Question on the title page of "The Apples of Idun" **Apprentice Leveled Reader:** *What do myths help us understand? We will read a myth about the god Loki, who learns a lesson about tricking others.*

• Read the title aloud. Point to the pictures. Ask: *What kind of story is this?* (a myth) *Myths are old stories that oten teach us lessons about life. Let's read about the god Loki, the goddess Idun, and some special apples. While we read we can look for the lesson these characters learn.*

Expand Vocabulary

Display each word below. Say the words and have children repeat them. Then use the Define/Example/Ask routine to introduce each word.

1 **begged** (page 7)

Define: to ask for something very strongly

Example: I *begged* my parents to let me go to the party.

Ask: What is another word for *begged*?

2 **compare** (page 10)

Define: to point out what is the same between two or more things

Example: We *compared* the apples and found that they were both big and red.

Ask: How would you *compare* an orange to a lemon?

3 **gods** (page 2)

Define: beings that have special powers

Example: The Greek *god* Apollo can heal any living thing.

Ask: Are *gods* real people or made-up characters that can do special things?

4 **swooped** (page 5)

Define: came down from above

Example: The seagull *swooped* down and grabbed the bread from my hand.

Ask: Why might a bird *swoop* down from the sky?

DURING READING

20–30 Minutes   RL.2.1   RL.2.2   RL.2.3   RL.2.5   RL.2.7   CCSS

Close Reading

🔍 Pages 2–3

Genre Ⓐ Ⓒ Ⓣ   Read pages 2–3 with children. Remind them that "The Apples of Idun" is a myth. Explain that many cultures in the world tell stories about gods and goddesses. Review the definition of *gods* with children. Explain that cultures all over the world have myths peopled with gods and goddesses. These stories have been told for thousands years. Point out that this story comes from Norse culture. If available show the area of the world on a map. Say: *Loki and Odin are Norse gods. Odin is sometimes called "Allfather" because he is the father of many gods. Loki can make fire and turn into animals. Loki is called a "trickster" because he sometimes tricks others.*

Connection of Ideas Ⓐ Ⓒ Ⓣ   Ask: *Why do Loki and Odin think that a trick is being played on them?* (The meat they were trying to cook over a fire would not cook.)

Pages 4–5

Genre **A C T** Read page 4 with children. Say: *Sometimes, animals that appear in myths can talk. They can also do things that animals in real life cannot do. What is the talking animal on this page?* (an eagle) Reread the second paragraph on page 4 aloud. Ask: *What else does this eagle say it can do that a real eagle could not do?* (The eagle says it will cook the meat.)

Vocabulary Read the first three sentences on page 5 with children. Point to the word *swooped*. Say: *Sometimes we can look at the illustrations to give us clues to the meaning of a word.* Point to the illustration on page 5. Tell children to look at then picture. Then with your finger, trace the painted blue line in the illustration that shows the eagle swooping downward. Ask: *What does* swooped *mean?* (flew down from the sky)

Pages 6–7

Theme Say: *The theme of a story is the main message the author wants the reader to understand. Often it is a message about how we should or should not act in life. The theme is usually not stated directly. The reader must figure it out. To find the theme, you must think about what the characters say and do.* Go back to page 4 and review the last two paragraphs on that page with children. Ask: *What is the agreement between the eagle and the two gods, Loki and Odin?* (The eagle will cook the meat, and the gods will share it with the eagle.) Go to page 5 and review the paragraph with children. Ask: *What does Loki do when the eagle swoops in and grabs the meat?* (He hits the eagle with a stick.) Read page 6 with children. Point to the illustration and say: *What happens to Loki after trying to trick the eagle?* (The eagle grabs the stick and carries Loki into the sky.) Guide children to record the information in their Theme charts.

STOP AND CHECK Read the question in the Stop and Check box on page 6. (The eagle is a storm giant in disguise.)

Connection of Ideas **A C T** Have children echo-read the title of the chapter 2 at the top of page 7. Ask: *What do you think this chapter will be about?* (the apples of Idun) Read page 7 with children. Say: *What does the eagle want Loki to get for him?* (the apples of Idun) *Why do you think the eagle wants the apples of Idun?* (The apples are special.) Explain that the apples must be special because the title of the story is "The Apples of Idun" and that the eagle, who is really a storm giant, would probably not want regular apples.

Pages 8–9

Vocabulary Read page 8 with children. Help children locate the word *goddess*. Say: *A* goddess *is a female god.* Review the definition of *gods* with children. *Who is the goddess in this story?* (Idun) *What does Idun do?* (She grows golden apples that keep the gods young.)

Sentence Structure **A C T** Reread the second paragraph on page 8. Point to the word *he* in the second sentence and say: *The word* he *is a pronoun that refers to a character's name. To find the character, we can look at what comes before. What character does* he *refer to?* (Loki) *How do you know?* (I see the words "Loki was tired and hurt," before the word *he*.)

STOP AND CHECK Read the question in the Stop and Check box on page 8. (Idun's apples keep the gods young.)

Pages 10

STOP AND CHECK Read the question in the Stop and Check box on page 10. (Loki says that he saw apples just like hers.)

Have partners review their notes on theme for pages 2–10 and discuss what they have learned.

✓ *Quick Check* Do children understand weekly vocabulary in context? If not, review and reteach using the instruction on page 314.

Can children identify theme? If not, review and reteach using the instruction on page 314 and assign the Unit 6 Week 1 digital mini-lesson.

WEEKLY
LESSON
4

• Understand and use new vocabulary words
• Read a myth
• Recognize and understand theme
• Understand complex text through close reading

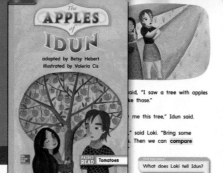

Materials

• "The Apples of Idun" Apprentice Leveled Reader: pp. 11-20
• Theme Graphic Organizer

☞ Go Digital

• Apprentice Leveled Reader eBook
• Downloadable Graphic Organizer
• Theme Mini Lesson

Scaffolding for **WONDERS** Approaching Leveled Reader

BEFORE READING

5–10 Minutes   SL.2.1a   SL.2.6   L. 2.5a   L. 2.6   CCSS

Expand Vocabulary

Display each word below. Say the words and have children repeat them. Then use the Define/Example/Ask routine to introduce each word.

1 mistake (page 15)

Define: something that is wrong

Example: It is a *mistake* for you to not do your school work.

Ask: What is one *mistake* you have made?

2 moments (page 11)

Define: small periods of time

Example: Most earthquakes last for only a few *moments*.

Ask: What is another word for *moments*?

3 searched (page 12)

Define: If you *searched* for something, you looked for it.

Example: We *searched* for hours for the missing backpack.

Ask: What have you *searched* for in your house?

DURING READING

15–20 Minutes   RL.2.1   RL.2.2   RL.2.3   RL.2.7   L.2.4   CCSS

Close Reading

Page 11

Vocabulary Read page 11 with children. Help children locate the word *snatched* on the page. Say: *We read that the eagle storm giant* snatched *Idun. Look at the illustration. What does* snatched *mean?* (took or grabbed)

Theme Say: *Remember, the theme is the main message the author wants the reader to understand. To find the theme, you must look at what the characters do and say.* Remind children that Loki has gone to see Idun because he has promised to get her apples for the eagle storm giant. Read page 10 with children. Say: *Why does Loki tell Idun to bring some of the golden apples?* (so they can compare them to the apples on another tree) *Remember we read that Loki is a trickster. He tricks others. Why do you think he really wanted her to bring her apples?* (so that the storm giant could take them from her) *Does the trick work?* (yes) Point to the illustration on page 11. Ask: *How does Loki feel about tricking Idun?* (It looks like he feels bad about it.) Guide children to record the information about Loki tricking Idun on their Theme charts.

Pages 12–13

Connection of Ideas **A C T** Read page 12 with children. Say: *It says here that the gods began to grow old. Why are they growing old?* (They do not have Idun's apples to keep them young.) *Whose fault is it that the gods are growing old?* (Loki's) *Why?* (He tricked Idun and the eagle storm giant took her and her apples away.)

STOP AND CHECK Read the question in the Stop and Check box on page 12. (After a few days without Idun's apples, the gods began to grow old.)

Genre ACT Read page 13 with children. Remind children that gods in myths have special powers. Ask: *What is one of Loki's special powers?* (He can change into a falcon.)

Pages 14–15

Connection of Ideas ACT Go back to the title of chapter 3 on page 11. Echo read the title of chapter 3 with children. Read page 14 with children. Ask: *Why do you think the title of this chapter is "The Chase"?* (The eagle storm giant will chase Loki.)

Theme Remind children that to find the theme they must look at what the characters do and say. And then think about what this means. Read page 15 with children. Ask: *How did Loki fix his mistake?* (He brought Idun back. She fed the gods, and they grew young again.) Guide children to record the information in their Theme charts.

Theme Tell children to review the information they have recorded in their Theme charts. Say: *What happens when Loki tricks the eagle in the beginning of the story?* (The eagle carries him into the sky and won't let go.) *Does this make Loki happy?* (no) *What happens when Loki tricks Idun in chapter 3?* (Idun gets taken away, and the gods grow old.) *How does Loki feel about this?* (He feels bad that he tricked Idun.) *What is one theme of the story?* (We should not trick others.) *What does Loki do at the end of the story?* (He fixes his mistake.) *What is another theme of the story?* (We can fix our mistakes.)

STOP AND CHECK Read the question in the Stop and Check box on page 15. (Loki turned into a falcon, flew to the storm giant's home, and found Idun and her apples. He turned them into nuts and flew off with them in Idun's basket.)

AFTER READING

10–15 Minutes   RL.2.1   RL.2.2   W.2.8   L.2.4   L.2.6

Respond to Reading

Compare Texts Ask children to compare "Why Fir Tree Keeps His Leaves" and "The Apples of Idun." What does each myth help us to understand? What is similar about the two stories? What is different? Discuss with a partner.

Summarize Have children turn to page 16 and summarize the selection. Answers should include details about the theme of both selections.

Text Evidence

Have partners work together to answer questions on page 16. Remind children to use their Theme charts.

Theme (The message is not to play tricks on others but that you can also fix your mistakes.)

Vocabulary (The illustration shows a bird. The text reads "Loki turned into a falcon. He flew to the storm giant's house." These clues tell us that a *falcon* is a bird.)

Write About Reading (Answers will vary but should include facts from the story such as how Loki got angry at the eagle and tried to hit him, how the eagle took Loki and made him promise to bring him Idun and the apples, how Loki tricked Idun into leaving the city, and how Loki made things right in the end.)

Independent Reading

Encourage children to read the paired selection "Tomatoes" on pages 17–19. Have them summarize the selection and compare it to "The Apples of Idun." Have them work with a partner to answer the questions on page 19.

 Quick Check Can children identify the theme? If not, review and reteach using the instruction on page 314 and assign the Unit 6 Week 1 digital mini-lesson.

Can children respond to the selection using text evidence? If not, provide sentence frames to help them organize their ideas.

WEEK 1
LESSON
5

Objectives
- Review weekly vocabulary words
- Review theme
- Write an analysis about an author's use of clues to tell the theme

Scaffolding for **Wonders** Reading/Writing Workshop

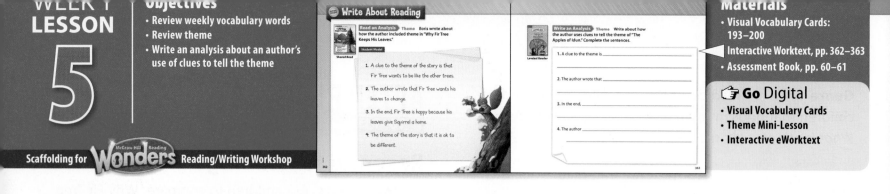

Materials
- Visual Vocabulary Cards: 193–200
- Interactive Worktext, pp. 362–363
- Assessment Book, pp. 60–61

☞ **Go Digital**
- Visual Vocabulary Cards
- Theme Mini-Lesson
- Interactive eWorktext

REVIEW AND RETEACH

5–10 Minutes   L.2.4a   RL.2.1   RL.2.2

Weekly Vocabulary

Display one **Visual Vocabulary Card** at a time and guide children to use the vocabulary word in a sentence. If children have difficulty creating a sentence, have them find the word in "Why Fir Tree Keeps His Leaves" or "The Apples of Idun" and use context clues in the passage to define the vocabulary word.

Comprehension: Theme

I Do Write and say: *Lila wanted a new bike, but it cost a lot of money. Lila offered to help people in the neighborhood with chores in return for a little money. Soon, Lila had enough money to buy the bike. "Wow!" said Lila, "It was worth all the hard work!"* Say: *Remember, to find the theme, we need to think about what the characters do and say. The first sentence tells me that Lila wants a new bike. Then I see that Lila decides to work for the money. Soon, Lila gets the bike and thinks it is worth all the hard work.* Underline last sentence. Say: *So, the theme of this story is "Hard work is worth it in the end."*

We Do Display: *Heather was nervous about her soccer game. "You'll do great," her friend Lisa said. "You just have to believe in yourself." This made Heather feel better. She decided to do her best. Heather's team won. She had a great game.* Say: *How does Heather feel about the soccer game?* (She was nervous.) *What does Heather's friend tell her?* (Her friend says Heather has to believe in herself.) *How does that make Heather feel?* (It made her feel better.) *How does Heather do in the game?* (She had a great game.)

You Do Guide partners to identify what these things have in common. Have partners work together to come up with the theme. (You have to believe in yourself.)

WRITE ABOUT READING

25–35 Minutes   W.2.3   W.2.8   W.4.9

Read an Analysis

- Guide children to look back at "Why Fir Tree Keeps His Leaves" in the **Interactive Worktext**. Have volunteers review how the author included the theme that they marked on page 357. Repeat with pages 358–359. *How did the author show the theme in the selection?*

- Read aloud the directions on page 362. Read aloud the student model. *This student's work is not a summary. It is an analysis of how the author shows the theme in "Why Fir Tree Keeps His Leaves."*

- *When you write an analysis, you should include clues from the text that give clues to the theme. Read Boris's first sentence. Circle the details.* (Fir Tree wants to be like other trees.) *In what part of the story do you learn this detail?* (the beginning)

- *Read the second sentence. Draw a box around another clue to the theme of Boris's story.* (Fir tree wants to lose leaves like the other trees.) *What part of the story is he writing about?* (the middle)

- Guide children to point to the third sentence. This sentence gives another clue to the theme of the story. *What details does Boris include?* (Fir Tree is happy because his leaves give Squirrel a home.)

- Read the last sentence that Boris wrote. *Why is this sentence a good ending?* (Boris tells the theme of the story.)

Analytical Writing ## Write an Analysis

Guided Writing Read the writing prompt on page 363 together. Guide children to review their Theme charts for "The Apples of Idun." Have children use their charts to complete the sentence starters. Children can also write an analysis using another selection previously read this week.

Peer Conference Guide children to read their analysis to a partner. Listeners should summarize the strongest clues that support the theme. They should discuss any parts that are unclear.

Teacher Conference Check children's writing for complete sentences and whether they included details from the story. Review the ending sentence and ask: *Did the author use details to support the theme?* If necessary, guide children to revise their sentence by adding more details.

Level Up

▲ Approaching Leveled Reader

▲ Reading/Writing Workshop

▲ Apprentice Leveled Reader

▲ Interactive Worktext

IF children read the Apprentice Level Reader and the **Interactive Worktext** Shared Read fluently and answer the Respond to Reading questions

THEN read together the Approaching Level Reader main selection and the **Reading/Writing Workshop** Shared Read from *Reading Wonders*. Have children take notes as they read, using self-stick notes. Then ask and answer questions about their notes.

Writing Rubric

	4	3	2	1
Text Evidence	Includes three or more details from the text.	Includes two or more details from the text.	Includes only one detail from the text.	No text evidence is cited.
Writing Style	Writes in complete sentences. Uses correct spelling and grammar.	Uses complete sentences. Writing has spelling and grammar errors.	Few complete sentences. There are many spelling and grammar errors.	Writing is not accurate or in complete sentences.

ASSESSMENT

Weekly Assessment

Have children complete the Weekly Assessment using **Assessment** book pages 60–61.

Objectives
- Develop oral language
- Build background on how we use energy
- Understand and use weekly vocabulary
- Read expository text

Materials
◀ Interactive Worktext, pp. 364–371
- Visual Vocabulary Cards: 201–208
- High-Frequency Word Cards

☞ **Go Digital**
- Interactive eWorktext
- Visual Vocabulary Cards

Scaffolding for **McGraw-Hill Reading Wonders** Reading/Writing Workshop

WEEKLY CONCEPT

5-10 Minutes   SL.2.1a   SL.2.4

Talk About It

Essential Question Read aloud the Essential Question on page 364 of the **Interactive Worktext:** *How do we use energy?* Explain that energy comes from many sources. Say: *Electricity is a form of energy that people use every day. Electricity can come from solar power, wind power, and other sources. One way people use electricity is to cook food on stoves and in ovens. We plug stoves in to an electrical outlet to get energy.*

- Discuss the photograph on page 364. Ask: *What is happening in this picture?* (A boy and a girl are using a kitchen mixer to prepare some food.)

▋**I Do** Say: *I am going to look at the photo and think about how these children are using energy. Their mixer uses electricity to combine the ingredients in the bowl. I will write on the web on page 365 how they are using energy.*

▋**We Do** Say: *Let's think about other ways we use energy at home. We also use energy to power our lights. Most lights and lamps use electricity.* Guide children to think of other ways they use electricity or energy at home. Then have children choose one way they use energy to add to their web.

▋**You Do** Guide partners to work together to talk about other ways they use energy. Encourage them to think of other places, such as school, where they use energy. Have children use the words from the web to start their sentences: *We use energy to _____.*

REVIEW VOCABULARY

10–15 Minutes   L.2.4d   L.2.5a   L.2.6   RF.2.3

Review Weekly Vocabulary Words

- Use the **Visual Vocabulary Cards** to review the weekly vocabulary.

- Read together the directions on page 366 of the **Interactive Worktext**. Then complete the activity.

❶ electricity Tell children that things that "run" on *electricity* need to be plugged into an outlet. Walk around the classroom with children, pausing at each outlet to see what's plugged in. Use this opportunity to stress that plugs and outlets can be dangerous. Have children list everything that needs *electricity*. Use this sentence frame: *A _____ needs* electricity *to work*. (Possible answers: clock, computer)

❷ haul Act out for children what it looks like when someone *hauls* something heavy by pulling it along the floor. Have children imitate your actions as they pretend to *haul* a heavy box across the classroom floor. Then help children write a synonym for the word *haul*. (Possible answer: carry)

❸ silent Ask children to brainstorm activities that are hard to do in a noisy classroom. Then have children use this oral sentence starter: *I need the classroom to be* silent *when I'm _____*. (Possible answers: taking a test, reading)

❹ power Display pictures of different types of batteries. Explain that many objects are *powered* by batteries. Ask children to think of items that use batteries and use the following sentence frame: *A _____ runs on battery* power. (Possible answers: watch, flashlight, cell phone, camera, tablet computer, smoke alarm)

5 flows Show children a picture of water *flowing* out of a pitcher. Go through the items listed in the activity one by one and ask: *Does toast* flow *out of a pitcher into a glass?* Have children respond: *No, toast* <u>cannot</u> flow. (milk, juice)

6 energy Explain that certain appliances use a lot of *energy.* Say: *A computer uses a lot of* energy. Have them list household items by using this sentence frame: *A _____ uses a lot of* energy. (<u>Possible answers</u>: refrigerator, air conditioner)

7 underground Write the word *underground.* Explain that if they know the meanings of the two smaller words in a compound word, they can figure out its meaning. Underline the words *under* and *ground.* Then have children use this oral sentence frame: *_____ grow* underground. (roots)

8 solar Ask children how they would go about inventing a machine that runs on sunlight, or *solar* power. Talk about a problem such a machine might solve. Have children draw their *solar* machines and tell what their machine does, using this sentence starter: *My* solar *machine _____.* (Answers will vary.)

High-Frequency Words

Have children look at page 367 in the **Interactive Worktext.** Help them read, spell, and write each high-frequency word. Guide partners to use each word in a sentence. Then read the story aloud with children. Guide partners to work together to reread the story and circle the high-frequency words. (by, or, Here, your, used, long) Listen in and provide assistance reading the high-frequency words, as necessary.

> **ELL ENGLISH LANGUAGE LEARNERS**
>
> Display the **High-Frequency Word Cards** for: *or, by, your, here, long, used.* Write a sentence with each word on the board. Have children echo-read each sentence, and point out the high-frequency word.

READ COMPLEX TEXT

15–20 Minutes   SL.2.1b   RI.2.6   RI.2.8   **CCSS**

Read "Pedal Power"

- Have children turn to page 368 in the **Interactive Worktext** and read the Essential Question aloud. Echo-read the title with children. Point to the photo of the family bicycling on page 368 and ask: *What are these people doing?* (riding bicycles) *Let's read an expository text about how people can make bicycle-powered energy.*

- Read the story together. Note that the weekly vocabulary words are highlighted in yellow. Expand Vocabulary words are highlighted in blue.

- As children read, have them use the "My Notes" section on page 368 to write questions they have. Children can also write words they don't understand or things they want to remember. Model how to use the "My Notes" section. Say: *When I read the first sentence on page 369, I learn that* energy *is the ability to do work. I want to remember this so I will write it in the "My Notes" section.*

> **ELL ENGLISH LANGUAGE LEARNERS**
>
> As you read together, have children highlight parts of the text they have questions about. After reading, review the questions children have. Then help them locate the answers to their questions in the text.

✔ *Quick Check* Can children understand the weekly vocabulary words in context? If not, review vocabulary using the **Visual Vocabulary Cards** before teaching Lesson 2.

Can children read high-frequency words in context? If not, review using the Read/Spell/Write routine and the High-Frequency Word Cards.

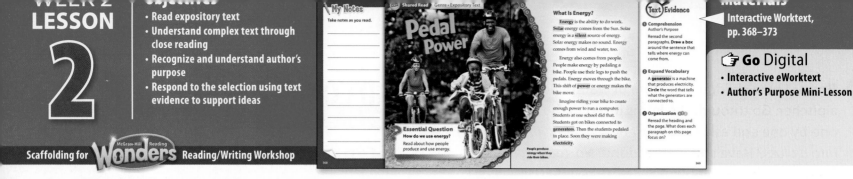

WEEK 2
LESSON 2

- Read expository text
- Understand complex text through close reading
- Recognize and understand author's purpose
- Respond to the selection using text evidence to support ideas

Scaffolding for **WONDERS** Reading/Writing Workshop

Materials

Interactive Worktext, pp. 368–373

☞ **Go** Digital
- Interactive eWorktext
- Author's Purpose Mini-Lesson

REREAD COMPLEX TEXT

20–25 Minutes   L.2.4a   RI.2.6   RI.2.8   RI.2.5   RI.2.6   **CCSS**

Close Reading: "Pedal Power"

Reread "Pedal Power" with children from **Interactive Worktext** pages 368–371. As you read together, discuss important passages in the text. Guide children to respond to questions using evidence from the text.

🔍 Pages 368–369

Author's Purpose Review that an author's purpose is the main reason an author writes a text. Say: *An author writes a nonfiction text to answer, describe, or explain information about a topic. To help find an author's purpose for writing a selection, find clues in the text and ask yourself, "What does the author want me to know?"* Reread the second paragraph aloud and ask: *Where can energy come from?* Guide children to draw a box around the sentence that tells. (Energy also comes from people.)

Expand Vocabulary Explain to children that *generators* are machines that produce electricity. Say: *The* generators *in this selection get their energy from people.* Generators *can also get their energy from gasoline.* Generators *can be used to supply people with electricity when the power goes out during an emergency.* Reread the last paragraph aloud and ask: *What are the* generators *in this paragraph connected to?* Guide children to circle the word that tells them. (bikes)

Organization Ⓐ Ⓒ Ⓣ Point to the heading at the top of the page and read it aloud. Explain to children that authors of expository, or informational text, often include a heading to tell readers what the text below the heading will be about. Have children reread the page. Ask: *What is the focus of each paragraph on this page?* Guide children to write their answer. (energy)

🔍 Page 370

Author's Purpose Remind children that authors of nonfiction texts often write to give information on a topic or explain how something works. Reread the first paragraph aloud. Ask: *What is the author explaining in this paragraph?* Guide children to draw a box around the words that tell. (bike-energy)

Genre Ⓐ Ⓒ Ⓣ *Expository texts may have text features such as subheadings, photographs and captions, or diagrams with labels.* Ask: *What text features do you see on this page?* (a subheading and a diagram with labels) Point to the diagram and ask: *What does this diagram show?* (a bicycle generator) *Which parts of the bicycle generator are labeled?* (generator, battery, stand, rear wheel, and pedal)

Expand Vocabulary Explain to children that a *battery* is tool that can make and store electricity. Ask: *What are some of the things you use that get their power from a battery?* (Answers will vary but may include toys, games, a remote control, and portable music players.) Reread the second paragraph aloud and guide children to circle the *battery* in the diagram.

Organization Ⓐ Ⓒ Ⓣ Point to the heading at the top of the page and read it aloud. Ask: *What is this section of text about?* (how bike-energy works) Explain to children that this section is also about how we can store bike energy in a battery by riding bicycles. Have children underline the two ways that energy from the battery can be used. (used right away, used later)

Page 371

Expand Vocabulary Explain to children that to *produce* is to make or create something. Say: *For example, the sun produces heat and light. Some cows and goats produce milk.* Reread the first paragraph aloud and ask: *When people ride bikes in gyms, what do they* produce? Guide children to circle the word that tells. (energy)

Author's Purpose Review with children that bicycles can be used to create energy. Say: *This energy can be used immediately or stored in a battery for later use.* Ask: *What machine can be powered by a bicycle?* Guide children to draw a box around the text that tells. (fans)

Author's Purpose Have children think about what they have learned in this selection and what the author wanted them to know about pedal power and bicycle energy. Have them reread their clues on pages 368–371 and ask: *Using the clues about what the author wants you to know, why do you think the author wrote this selection?* (to give information about bicycle-powered energy)

RESPOND TO READING

15–20 Minutes   SL.2.1a   RI.2.6   RI.2.8

Respond to "Pedal Power"

Read aloud the questions on page 372 of the **Interactive Worktext.** Guide children read the questions about "Pedal Power." Then read aloud the "Discussion Starter" for each of the questions. Guide children to work with a partner to answer the questions orally using the "Discussion Starters." Have children find text evidence to support their answers and write the page number(s) on which they found the text evidence for each question.

1. *How can you make energy with a bike?* (Possible answers: I read that you can make energy when you pedal a bike. The bike's rear wheel spins a generator to make electricity. Text Evidence: pp. 369, 370)

2. *When can the energy be used?* (Possible answers: Electricity can be used right now. Electricity can also be stored in a battery. Text Evidence: p. 370)

3. *What kinds of things can bike energy power?* (Possible answers: Energy from bicycles can power laptops. Energy from bicycles works best for small machines. Text Evidence: pp. 370, 371)

After children discuss the questions, have them use the sentence starters to answer the question on page 373. Circulate and provide guidance.

 Quick Check Do children understand vocabulary in context? If not, review and reteach using the instruction on page 324.

Can children identify the author's purpose? If not, review and reteach using the instruction on page 324 and assign the Unit 6 Week 2 digital mini-lesson.

Can children write a response to "Pedal Power"? If not, review the sentence starters and prompt children to respond orally. Help them write their responses.

Objectives
- Understand and use new vocabulary words
- Read an expository text
- Recognize and understand author's purpose
- Understand complex text through close reading

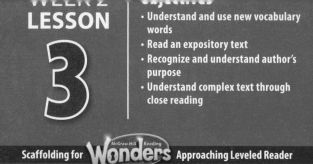

Materials
- "Wind Power" Apprentice Leveled Reader: pp. 2–9
- Author's Purpose Graphic Organizer

👉 **Go Digital**
- Apprentice Leveled Reader eBook
- Downloadable Graphic Organizer
- Author's Purpose Mini-Lesson

Scaffolding for **Wonders** Approaching Leveled Reader

BEFORE READING

10–15 Minutes   SL.2.1a   SL.2.6   L.2.5a   L.2.6

Introduce "Wind Power"

- Read the Essential Question on the title page of "Wind Power" **Apprentice Leveled Reader:** *How do we use energy? We will read an expository text about the energy we can make from wind.*

- Read the title aloud. Preview the pictures. Ask: *Do you think this text is fiction or nonfiction?* (nonfiction) *What helps you know that this is a nonfiction selection?* (The photos show windmills. There is a diagram on one of the pages.) *This type of nonfiction text is called expository text. Expository text gives facts and information about a topic. Let's read about how wind can be turned into power that people can use.*

Expand Vocabulary

Display each word below. Say the words and have children repeat them. Then use the Define/Example/Ask routine to introduce each word.

1 grind (page 6)

Define: to turn something into small pieces by crushing it

Example: We *grind* the pepper into powder and put it in the soup.

Ask: What is another word for *grind*?

2 pump (page 4)

Define: to force to move in a direction

Example: The tire was flat, so I will *pump* air into it.

Ask: If you *pump* air into a ball, are you pushing air into the ball or pulling air out?

DURING READING

20–30 Minutes   RI.2.1   RI.2.3   RI.2.5   RI.2.6   RI.2.7

Close Reading

🔍 **Pages 2–3**

Genre Ⓐ Ⓒ Ⓣ Read page 2 with children. Say: *Expository text gives facts and information about a topic. How can you tell this is an expository text?* (The author is giving facts and information about wind.)

Genre Ⓐ Ⓒ Ⓣ Point to the picture on page 2. Say: *Expository text may include text features, like this photograph. What is the picture of?* (a sailboat) Point to the caption. Say: *In expository text, a photograph might have a caption, like this. The caption can help you understand why the author included the picture in the text.* Read the caption with children. Ask: *Why did the author include this photograph?* (to show the reader how wind can power a boat)

STOP AND CHECK Read the question in the Stop and Check box on page 3. (The sun's energy warms the air, which rises. Cooler air moves in to take its place. This moving air is wind.)

🔍 **Pages 4–5**

Prior Knowledge Ⓐ Ⓒ Ⓣ Children may be unfamiliar with windmills and how they work. Point to the picture of the windmill. Say: *This is a windmill.* Point to the arms of the windmill and say: *When the wind blows, the arms of the windmill spin. This movement makes energy, which can be used to do other jobs.* Read page 4 with children. Ask: *What is one thing that windmills can do?* (pump water)

Key Details Read page 5 with children. Ask: *Why do some places need water pumped to the surface?* (Some places are very dry.) Read the caption on page 5 with children. Ask: *What kind of place can use the water that windmills pump to the surface?* (farms) *How do you think the farms use water?* (to help grow crops.)

Vocabulary Focus on the word *surface*. Say: *Windmills pump water up to the* surface. *I can understand the word* surface *by looking at the words and sentences around it. I look at the phrases "pump water up" and at the fact that the water was "underground." This helps me to know that* surface *means the top or outside layer. That is where the water is going.*

Author's Purpose Remind children that an author's purpose is the main reason an author writes a text. An author might write to give information about a topic. An author might also try to convince readers to feel a certain way about a topic. Say: *To find the author's purpose, you must find clues in the text and ask yourself, "What does the author want me to know?" Think about what you have read so far. What does the author want you to know about wind and wind power?* (The author wants me to know how wind is made and how wind power can be used.) Guide children to record the information in their Author's Purpose charts.

STOP AND CHECK Read the question in the Stop and Check box on page 5. (pump water to the surface)

Pages 6–7

Organization ACT Read the heading with children. Ask: *What is this section about?* (The History of Windmills) Ask: *What did we learn about before?* (how wind can make power and how wind is made) Explain that this book is organized into sections that tell about different aspects of wind power. First, they learned about the wind and how it can be used for power. Now, they are learning about wind power long ago.

Prior Knowledge ACT Read pages 5 and 6 with children. Children may not be familiar with the places mentioned on these pages. Help children locate the China, the Middle East ,and the Netherlands on map.

Compare and Contrast Remind children that when we compare two things, we tell how they are alike. Explain that when we contrast two things, we tell how they are different. Read the second paragraph on page 7 with children. Say: *Compare the windmills on this page with the windmills on page 5. What do both of types of windmills help people to do?* (They help people farm.) *Now contrast the windmills on page 7 with the windmills on page 5. How are they being used differently?* (The windmills on page 7 are being used to pump water away from the land. The windmills on page 5 are being used to pump water up to the surface.)

STOP AND CHECK Read the question in the Stop and Check box on page 7. (People used windmills to pump water out of the low-lying land so they could farm it.)

Pages 8–9

Key Details Read page 8 with children. Say: *Remember, key details are the most important facts in a selection. They give more information about a topic. What is wind power used to make today?* (electricity) *In expository text, you can also find key details in the captions. According to the caption on page 8, what things can wind power send electricity to?* (machines)

Genre ACT Say: *Expository text uses text features like headings. Headings tell the reader what the next section will be about.* Read page 9 with children. Ask: *What is the heading on page 9?* (Wind Turbines) *What is a wind turbine?* (a kind of engine) *What does a wind turbine do?* (A wind turbine makes electricity.)

Have partners review their notes on theme for pages 2–9 and discuss what they have learned.

✓ *Quick Check* Do children understand weekly vocabulary in context? If not, review and reteach using the instruction on page 324.

Can children identify the author's purpose? If not, review and reteach using the instruction on page 324 and assign the Unit 6 Week 2 digital mini-lesson.

WEEK 2
LESSON

4

Objectives
• Understand and use new vocabulary words
• Read expository text
• Recognize and understand author's purpose
• Understand complex text through close reading

Materials
• "Wind Power" Apprentice Leveled Reader: pp. 10–19
• Author's Purpose Graphic Organizer

☞ **Go** Digital
• Apprentice Leveled Reader eBook Downloadable Graphic Organizer
• Author's PurposeMini-Lesson

Scaffolding for **Wonders** Approaching Leveled Reader

BEFORE READING

5–10 Minutes SL.2.1a SL.2.6 L.2.5a L.2.6 L.2.4a

Expand Vocabulary

Display each word below. Say the words and have children repeat them. Then use the Define/Example/Ask routine to introduce each word.

❶ linked (page 10)

Define: joined together

Example: We *linked* our arms when we crossed the street together.

Ask: What are two things that can be *linked*?

❷ source (page 14)

Define: a place, person, or thing where something comes from

Example: The lake is the *source* of our water.

Ask: From what *source* do you get your drinking water?

❸ stretch (page 11)

Define: to reach, or to cover a distance

Example: The Rocky Mountains *stretch* from the southwestern United States all the way up into Canada.

Ask: If you *stretch* your body, do you stand up straight or curl into a ball?

DURING READING

15–20 Minute RI.2.1 RI.2.3 RI.2.6 RI.2.7 L.2.4a

Close Reading

🔍 **Pages 10–11**

Vocabulary Read page 10 with children. Point to the term "wind farm." *To find the meaning of* wind farm, *we can look for clues in the text and pictures. What does a wind farm have?* (many turbines) *What do the turbines do?* (They make electricity.) Point to the picture and ask: *What is this a picture of? Read the caption for clues.* (a wind farm) *Using the clues, what is the definition of a* wind farm? (a big field with turbines that make electricity)

Connection of Ideas **A C T** Read page 11 with children. Say: *Look at the pictures of turbines on this page. What thing from earlier in the selection do turbines look like?* (windmills) *How are windmills and turbines similar?* (They both use wind to make power.)

Author's Purpose Remind children that authors decide what information to include in a book and that there is a reason why they chose this information. Ask: *What does a wind turbine do?* (It makes electricity or power.) *Why is that important information to know about wind?* (Power is necessary to our lives and hard to make or get.) Add this information to their Author's Purpose charts.

Organization **A C T** Ask: *What are we learning about now?* (wind farms) Point out that before we learned about how people used the wind to make electricity long ago. Now we are learning about how we use the wind to make electricity today. Explain that in this way the book is organized by what came first.

STOP AND CHECK Read the question in the Stop and Check box on page 11. (People build wind farms to make a lot of electricity.)

Pages 12–13

Connection of Ideas Ask: *What are two problems with wind farms that the author mentions in the text?* (They are noisy. They can hurt birds and bats.) Point to the picture and say: *The author has included a picture to help the reader understand the text better. Look at the picture and read the caption. How do you think wind farms can hurt birds and bats?* (When birds and bats fly through wind farms, they might get hit by the wind turbines.)

Page 14

Author's Purpose Remind students that an author's purpose is the main reason an author writes a text. Explain that an author might have strong beliefs about a topic and write to convince the reader to feel the same way. Say: *To find the author's purpose, you must find clues in the text and ask yourself, "What does the author want me to know?"* Read page 14 with children. Ask: *What are the two kinds of energy sources the author writes about on this page?* (wind power and oil) Ask: *Which does the author think is better?* (The author thinks wind power is better.) *What are the author's reasons?* (Wind is cleaner, it costs less, and we will never run out of it.) Guide children to record their answers in their Author's Purpose charts.

Connection of Ideas Point to the photo of the smoke stack and read the caption. Say: *The text on this page tells how wind power is clean. Does this photo show wind power* (no) *What does it show?* (smoke coming from another form of power) *Why is this a good photo for this page?* (It shows how other forms of power can be dirty.)

Author's Purpose Tell children to review the information in their Author's Purpose charts. Say: *The author can have more than one purpose for writing a text. Review the information in your Author's Purpose graphic organizers. What is one reason the author wrote this selection?* (to give facts and information about wind and wind power) *What is another reason?* (to convince the reader that wind power is better than oil)

STOP AND CHECK Read the question in the Stop and Check box on page 14. (Wind farms can be noisy and make the ground shake.)

AFTER READING

10–15 Minutes   RI.2.3   RI.2.6   W.2.8   L.2.4a   L.2.6

Respond to Reading

Compare Texts Ask children to compare "Pedal Power" and "Wind Power." What does each text teach us about how we use energy? What is similar about the two stories? What is different? Discuss with a partner.

Summarize Have children turn to page 15 and summarize the selection. (Answers should include details about the author's purpose.)

Text Evidence

Have partners work together to answer questions on page 15. Remind children to use their Author's Purpose graphic organizer.

Author's Purpose (The author wrote this text to provide information about wind and wind power and to help people understand why using wind power is a good idea.)

Vocabulary (The text reads, "People want to improve wind farms. New turbines are quieter. People are making them safer, too." The examples in the text show that people want to make wind farms better.)

Write About Reading (Answers will vary but should explain that the author says that wind power is clean, it costs less than oil, it is plentiful, and it won't run out.)

Independent Reading

Encourage children to read the paired selection "A Solar House" on pages 16–18. Have them summarize the selection and compare it to "Wind Power." Have them work with a partner to answer the questions on page 18.

✓ *Quick Check* Can children identify the author's purpose? If not, review and reteach using the instruction on page 324 and assign the Unit 6 Week 2 digital mini-lesson.

Can children respond to the selection using text evidence? If not, provide sentence frames to help them organize their ideas.

WEEK 2 LESSON 5

Objectives
- Review weekly vocabulary words
- Review author's purpose
- Write an analysis about how the author used clues and text features to tell the purpose

Scaffolding for **Wonders** Reading/Writing Workshop

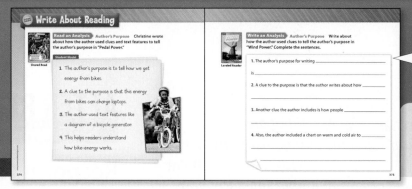

Materials
- Visual Vocabulary Cards: 201–208
- Interactive Worktext, pp. 374–375
- Assessment Book, pp. 62–63

☞ **Go** Digital
- Visual Vocabulary Cards
- Author's Purpose Mini-Lesson

REVIEW AND RETEACH

5–10 Minutes   RI.2.6 RI.2.8 L.2.6

Weekly Vocabulary

Display one **Visual Vocabulary Card** at a time and guide children to use the vocabulary word in a sentence. If children have difficulty creating a sentence, have them find the word in "Pedal Power" or "Wind Power" and use context clues in the passage to define the word.

Comprehension: Author's Purpose

I Do Write and say: *A dam is a structure that is built across a river. It traps the water and uses the water for many things. Dams can be a source of drinking water. Water from dams can be used for crops. It can even be used to make energy for electricity.* Say: *What does the author want me to know? In the first sentence the author wants me to know what a dam is. I also read details about dams and what they can do. From these clues I can tell the author's purpose is to inform the reader about ways water from dams is used.*

We Do Display: *Solar energy is energy that comes from the sun. It is a clean source of energy. It does not use up Earth's resources or harm the environment. Solar energy can be used to heat homes, power small electronic machines, and even for cooking.* Say: *Let's look for clues to find the author's purpose. What does the author think about solar energy?* (Solar energy does not harm the environment.) *How is solar energy used?* (It is used to heat homes, cook food, and power small machines.)

You Do Say: *What is the author's purpose for writing this selection?* Guide partners to see what the clues have in common. Have them identify the author's purpose. (to explain what solar energy is and how it is used)

WRITE ABOUT READING

25–30 Minutes   W.2.2 W.2.8 W.4.9

Read an Analysis

- Guide children to look back at "Pedal Power" in the **Interactive Worktext**. Have volunteers review the details about the author's purpose they marked on page 369. Repeat with pages 370–371. *How did the author use clues to tell the purpose of the selection?*

- Read aloud the directions on page 374. Read aloud the student model. *This student's writing is not a summary. It is an analysis of how the author uses clues and text features to tell the purpose in "Pedal Power."*

- *When you write an analysis, you should include details from the selection that show the author's purpose. Read Christine's first sentence. Circle the details.* (The author's purpose is to tell how we get energy from bikes.)

- *Read the second sentence. Christine writes about another clue to the author's purpose. Draw a box around the clues from the story about the author's purpose.* (bikes can be attached to generators to make electricity) *What part of the story is she writing about?* (the middle)

- Guide children to point to the third sentence. This sentence tells about the text features that support the author's purpose. *What text feature does Christine include?* (a diagram of a bicycle generator)

- Model analyzing how the author used clues and text features to show the author's purpose. Read the last sentence that Christine wrote. *Why is this a good ending?* (Christine tells how clues and text features help readers understand how bike-energy works.)

Level Up

Approaching Leveled Reader

Apprentice Leveled Reader

Interactive Worktext

Reading/Writing Workshop

IF children read the Apprentice Level Reader and the **Interactive Worktext** Shared Read fluently and answer the Respond to Reading questions

THEN read together the Approaching Level Reader main selection and the **Reading/Writing Workshop** Shared Read from *Reading Wonders*. Have children take notes as they read, using self-stick notes. Then ask and answer questions about their notes.

Analytical Writing Write an Analysis

Guided Writing Read the writing prompt on page 375 together. Guide children to review their Author's Purpose charts for "Wind Power." Have children use their charts to complete the sentence starters. Children can also write an analysis using another selection previously read this week.

Peer Conference Guide children to read their analysis to a partner. Listeners should summarize the strongest details that support the beginning, middle, and ending sentences. They should discuss any parts that are unclear.

Teacher Conference Check children's writing for complete sentences and whether they included details from the story. Review the ending sentence and ask: *Did the author use details to explain the author's purpose?* If necessary, guide children to revise their sentence by adding more details.

Writing Rubric

	4	3	2	1
Text Evidence	Includes three or more details from the text.	Includes two or more details from the text.	Includes only one detail from the text.	No text evidence is cited.
Writing Style	Writes in complete sentences. Uses correct spelling and grammar.	Uses complete sentences. Writing has spelling and grammar errors.	Few complete sentences. There are many spelling and grammar errors.	Writing is not accurate or in complete sentences.

ASSESSMENT

Weekly Assessment

Have children complete the Weekly Assessment using **Assessment** book pages 62–63.

• Interactive eWorktext
• Visual Vocabulary Cards

Tell about a time you were on a team.

WEEKLY CONCEPT

5-10 Minutes   SL.2.1a   SL.2.4   CCSS

Talk About It

Essential Question Read aloud the Essential Question on page 376 of the **Interactive Worktext:** *Why is teamwork important?* Explain that teamwork is important in many ways. When exploring a new place, teamwork is important for many reasons. Having teammates can help keep you safe. It can also help you do things that you couldn't do on your own.

• Discuss the photograph on page 377. Ask: *What is happening in the picture?* (A team of people is climbing a snowy mountain. They have a lot of equipment.)

I Do   Say: *I am going to look at the photo and think about how teamwork is important. I see that the people are tied together with ropes. I think this is to keep them safe. If one person falls, the rope prevents the person from sliding down the mountain. I will write "Teamwork can keep people safe" on the web on page 377.*

We Do   Say: *Let's think about other reasons that teamwork is important. In mountain climbing, if you travel with a team, you can travel farther. This is because you and your teammates can each carry some of the materials you need. There is a lot of gear that you need with mountain climbing.* Guide children to think of other ways teamwork is important. Then have children add one way to the web.

You Do   Guide partners to work together to talk about other ways that teamwork is important. Children can think about teams of explorers or other teams. Have children use the words from the web to start their sentences: *Teamwork is important because _____.*

REVIEW VOCABULARY

10–15 minutes   L.2.5a   L.2.4d   RF.2.3f   CCSS

Review Weekly Vocabulary Words

• Use the **Visual Vocabulary Cards** to review the weekly vocabulary.

• Read together the directions on page 378 of the **Interactive Worktext.** Then complete the activity.

1 **teamwork** Write the word *teamwork* and explain that *teamwork* is a compound word. Guide children to understand that if they know the meanings of the two smaller words in a compound word, they can figure out its meaning. Have children use this oral sentence starter: *My partner and I use* teamwork *when we _____.* (Answers will vary.)

2 **prepare** Ask children to tell about parties they might have been to either at home or at school. Have children use this oral sentence frame: *I need to _____ to* prepare *for a party.* (Possible answers: clean the house, put up decorations, set out food)

3 **machines** Point out various *machines* in the classroom. Say: *A computer is a* machine. Then have children complete this oral sentence frame: *_____ and _____ are* machines *people use to cook.* Then guide them to think of *machines* that can be used to clean a house. (Possible answers: vacuum cleaner, dishwasher, carpet cleaning machine)

4 **repair** Point out that sometimes things break and need *repair.* Ask: *If the pipes under the kitchen sink were leaking, who would you call to* repair *it?* (a plumber) Guide children to read the sentence and think of another word for *repair.* (fix)

Unit 6

5 **important** Discuss with children the importance of safety when crossing the street. Have children use this oral sentence starter: *When I cross the street, it is* important *to* _____. Guide children to write their answers. (Possible answers: wait for the light/walk sign, look both ways)

6 **scientific** Write the word *scientific* on the board. Ask: *Does any part of this word remind you of a subject you study at school?* (science) Guide children to understand what the word *scientific* means.

7 **result** Tell children you will tell about something that happened and then say the *result*. Say: *I didn't study for today's test. As a* result, *I failed the test.* Then guide children to tell what might happen as a *result* of practicing the piano. (Possible answer: you play the piano better)

8 **exploration** Invite children to name things in a desert. Write them on the board. Then assist children as they draw a picture of something they might see on an *exploration* of the desert. Finally, have children describe their pictures, using this sentence frame: *I might see* _____ *on an* exploration *of the desert.* (Possible answers: a snake, a cactus, sand)

High-Frequency Words

Have children look at page 379 in the **Interactive Worktext**. Help them read, spell, and write each high-frequency word. Guide partners to use each word in a sentence. Then read the story aloud with children. Guide partners to work together to reread the story and circle the high-frequency words. (jump, back, going, don't, always, done) Listen in and provide assistance reading the high-frequency words, as necessary.

> **ELL ENGLISH LANGUAGE LEARNERS**
>
> Display the **High-Frequency Word Cards** for: *done, back, jump, don't, going, always.* Write a sentence with each word on the board. Have children echo-read each sentence, and point out the high-frequency word.

READ COMPLEX TEXT
15–20 Minutes   RI.2.2   RI.2.6   RI.2.8   SL.2.1b

Read "Dive Teams"

- Have children turn to page 380 in the **Interactive Worktext** and read aloud the Essential Question. Point to the picture. Say: *This diver is working together with a team. Teamwork makes your job easier and lets you get more things done.* Have children repeat: *teamwork. Let's read to find out about the work the team does together.* Have children echo-read the title.

- Read the story together. Note that the weekly vocabulary words are highlighted in yellow. Expand Vocabulary words are highlighted in blue.

- As children read, have them use the "My Notes" section on page 380 to write questions they have. Children can also write words they don't understand or things they want to remember. Model how to use the "My Notes" section. *When I read the title, I wonder what dive teams do. I will write my question down and take notes that will help answer it as I read.*

> **ELL ENGLISH LANGUAGE LEARNERS**
>
> As you read together, have children highlight parts of the text they have questions about. After reading, review the questions children have. Then help them locate the answers to their questions in the text.

 Quick Check Can children understand the weekly vocabulary in context? If not, review vocabulary using the **Visual Vocabulary Cards** before teaching Lesson 2.

Can children read high-frequency words in context? If not, review using the Read/Spell/Write routine and the High-Frequency Word Cards.

LESSON 1   **327**

WEEK'S
LESSON

2

Objectives
• Read an expository text
• Understand complex text through close reading
• Recognize and understand main idea and key details
• Respond to the selection using text evidence to support ideas

Scaffolding for **WONDERS** Reading/Writing Workshop

Materials
Interactive Worktext, pp. 380–385

☞ **Go** Digital
• Interactive eWorktext
• Main Idea and Key Details Mini-Lesson

REREAD COMPLEX TEXT

20–25 Minutes   RI.2.2   RI.2.6   RI.2.8   L.2.5a   **CCSS**

Close Reading: "Dive Teams"

Reread "Dive Teams" with children from **Interactive Worktext** pages 380–383. As you read together, discuss important passages in the text. Guide children to respond to questions using evidence from the text.

 Page 381

Sentence Structure **ACT** Remind children that long sentences often contain a lot of information. They should read them carefully and remember what they now about how sentences are put together to be able to get as much information as they can. Read the first paragraph aloud and ask: *What are two reasons that people may want to explore the ocean?* Point to the second sentence in the first paragraph. Guide children to underline their answer. (to see how animals live, to search for ships)

Expand Vocabulary Have children reread the second paragraph. Tell them that if someone is an *expert* at something, he or she knows a lot about it. Ask: *What is Gloria an* expert *at?* Have children write their answers. (diving)

Main Idea and Key Details Remind children that the *main idea and key details* work together to give you a better idea of what a text is about. If you identify the key details, even if the main idea is not stated, you can use what you know from the details to find the main idea. Have children reread the third paragraph. Ask: *What job does Gloria have on the dive team?* Guide children to draw a box around their answer. (Gloria decides to photograph what the team discovers.)

Page 382

Main Idea and Key Details Have children reread the first paragraph with you. Explain to children that the information in this paragraph is about teamwork. Then ask: *Why is teamwork important?* Guide children to draw a box around the sentence that tells. (Team members divide up the tasks to get the job done.)

Expand Vocabulary Explain to children that if you *divide* something, you break it into smaller parts. Have them reread the first paragraph. Ask: *What did the team members* divide? Guide children to write the word that tells. (tasks) Discuss how to divide up tasks, if children having difficulty understanding what this means.

Sentence Structure **ACT** Remind children that an expository text often has long sentences that contain important information. Read the third paragraph aloud. Ask: *Why does the captain stay on the boat?* Guide children to underline the words that tell. (His job is to communicate with the divers.)

Genre **ACT** Point to the map at the top of page 382. Explain that expository texts sometimes include a map. Say: *A map is a drawing that show the features of a place. A map often contains symbols that show the features of a place, such as cities or sites. These symbols are explained in a key.* Point to the key on the map and have children locate the home base. Explain that the home base is where the dive team sets up their base before doing a dive. Then have them find the home base on the map and tell what city it is in. (Tallahassee)

Page 383

Expand Vocabulary Explain to children that if you *spot* something, you see or notice it. Model *spotting* something in the classroom, such as the clock on the wall. Read the first paragraphs aloud. Ask: *What is it that the team member* spots*?* Guide children to circle the answer. (the ship)

Main Idea and Key Details Have children reread the second paragraph. Ask: *What does the team do with the results?* Guide children to draw a box around the sentence that tells. (The team now has important results to share.)

Main Idea and Key Details Review with children that the main idea is the most important point the author makes about a topic. Have children think about the key details that they have read in this selection. Ask: *What do you think is the main idea of this selection?* Guide children to write their response. (Possible answer: Teamwork is important for a diving team.)

RESPOND TO READING

15–20 Minutes   SL.2.1a   RI.2.2   RI.2.6   RI.2.8

Respond to "Dive Teams"

Guide children to read the questions about "Dive Teams" on page 384 of the **Interactive Worktext.** Then read aloud the "Discussion Starter" for each of the questions. Guide children to work with a partner to answer the questions orally using the "Discussion Starters." Have children find text evidence to support their answers. Ask children to write the page number(s) on which they found the text evidence for each question.

1. *What is a dive team?* (Possible answers: I read that a dive team is a group that explores the ocean. A dive team has people who work at different jobs. Text Evidence: p. 381)

2. *How do people on a dive team work together?* (Possible answers: The team divides up the tasks. Before a dive, each team member prepares for their jobs. Text Evidence: p. 382)

3. *Why is it important for people on the team to work together?* (Possible answers: This helps the team get the job done. At the end, the dive team has important results to share. Text Evidence: p. 383)

After children discuss the questions on page 384, have them use the sentence starters to answer the question on page 385. Circulate and provide guidance.

 Quick Check **Do children understand vocabulary in context? If not, review and reteach using the instruction on page 334.**

Can children identify the main idea and key details? If not, review and reteach using the instruction on page 334 and assign the Unit 6 Week 3 digital mini-lesson.

Can children write a response to "Dive Teams"? If not, review the sentence starters and prompt children to respond orally. Help them write their responses.

Objectives
- Understand and use new vocabulary words
- Read an expository text
- Recognize and understand main idea and key details
- Understand complex text through close reading

Materials
- *"Digging for Sue"* Apprentice Leveled Reader: pp. 2–7
- Main Idea and Key Details Graphic Organizer

Go Digital
- Apprentice Leveled Reader eBook
- Downloadable Graphic Organizer
- Main Idea and Key Details Mini-Lesson

Scaffolding for **Wonders** Approaching Leveled Reader

BEFORE READING

10–15 Minutes   SL.2.1a   SL.2.6   L.2.6   CCSS

Introduce "Digging for Sue"

- Read the Essential Question on the title page of "Digging for Sue" **Apprentice Leveled Reader:** *Why is teamwork important? We will read about how working in a team is a way to get things done better than one person can do alone.*

- Read the title aloud. Point to the photographs. Ask: *Is this text fiction or nonfiction?* (nonfiction) *This nonfiction text is called an expository text. It gives true information about something real. Let's read to find out about the fossils of a dinosaur.*

Expand Vocabulary

Display each word below. Say the words and have children repeat them. Then use the Define/Example/Ask routine to introduce each word.

1 cliff (page 3)

Define: rocks that are often very high up and steep

Example: We are not supposed to play near the *cliff* because we may fall off.

Ask: Where could you see a *cliff*?

2 fossils (page 2)

Define: the remains of an animal or plant from long ago

Example: The scientist dug up the *fossils* of a plant that is no longer around.

Ask: Where could you go to see *fossils*?

3 guessed (page 3)

Define: gave an answer without being sure

Example: She *guessed* at the number of leaves on the tree.

Ask: How could you *guess* the number of marbles that are in a jar?

DURING READING

20–30 Minutes   RI.2.1   RI.2.2   RI.2.5   L.4a   CCSS

Close Reading

Pages 2–3

Genre A C T Remind children that an expository text gives true facts about real things. There are usually text features that help the reader know that topic. Say: *Look at the cover. What is the title?* (Digging for Sue) *What do you think this book is going to be about?* (dinosaur bones) Then have children look at page 2. Point out the header at the top of the page. Say: *What kind of dinosaur bones are we going to read about?* (T. rex) *How do you know?* (The heading is "The Mighty T. rex.") *Look at the illustration. What kind of dinosaur do you think it is?* (a T. rex)

Main Idea and Key Details Read pages 2 and 3 with children. Review that the main idea is the most important point the author makes about a topic. Explain that if they pay attention to the details throughout the text they can find out about the main idea. Ask: *Why were Sue Hendrickson and her team in South Dakota?* (They were looking for fossils.) *What did Sue see on the ground?* (some small bones) *What did she think about them?* (She guessed that they were T. rex bones.) *Let's pay attention to key details as we read. It will help us better understand the main idea.* Help children record key details on their Main Idea and Key Details charts.

Sentence Structure A C T Point to the last sentence on page 2, "They helped us know more about these unfriendly giants." Remind children that they can find out what the word *they* refers to by looking at the previous sentence. Ask: *What does* they *refer to?* (the fossils)

STOP AND CHECK Read the question in the Stop and Check box on page 3. (Answers will vary but might include: We know from scientific studies of T. rex fossils.)

Pages 4–5

Genre **A C T** Look at the photo and the header on page 4. Say: *Read the header at the top of the page. What is this chapter called?* (The Dig) *What is the person in the photograph doing?* (digging up fossils) *What do you think this chapter is going to be about?* (digging up the T. rex fossil that Sue found)

Connection of Ideas **A C T** Read the text on page 4 with children. Say: *The text says that Sue's team used hand tools because machines might hurt the bones.* Have children think about the machines that they know that dig up earth and rocks. Ask: *How might machines hurt the bones?* (If the machines are big and powerful, they might not be gentle enough to get small bones out of the earth. They could break the very old, delicate bones before people got a chance to study them.)

Vocabulary Read the first two sentences on page 5. Ask: *What does the word* skull *mean? How does the first sentence help you understand it?* (It says that the team found many bones, so the skull is probably a kind of bone.) Then point to picture and read the caption. Ask: *How do the picture and caption help you to understand the word* skull *better?* (The picture looks like a head of a dinosaur, and the caption tells about the teeth. I think the skull is the bone part of the head.)

Main Idea and Key Details Read page 5 with children. Say: *How large was the skull of the T. rex?* (five feet long) *Why do you think that the team named the T. rex Sue?* (She was the one who found the bones.) Point out the picture on the page to children. Ask: *Did the T. rex have sharp or dull teeth?* (sharp) *Why do you think that the T. rex had sharp teeth?* (to eat other dinosaurs)

Pages 6–7

Connection of Ideas **A C T** Read page 6 with children and look at the photo. Say: *The text says that some of the dinosaur's bones had not moved for many years, but that some had moved or were missing. Why might there be some missing or moved bones?* (Answers will vary but may include that other animals could have moved them after the dinosaur died and that people may also have moved them.)

Main Idea and Key Details Read page 7 with children. Say: *What were some ways that Sue's team protected the bones they dug up?* (They left some rock around the bones. They also put plaster on the bones.) *Why would they need to be protected?* (The bones would be moved and they could get bumped or dropped on the way.) *Where did the bones end up?* (the Field Museum in Chicago) Help children record this event in their Main Idea and Key Details charts.

STOP AND CHECK Read the question in the Stop and Check box on page 8. (Answers will vary but might include that, first, they dug down to the bones with picks and shovels, then, they dug away the rock surrounding the bones but left some rock so the bones would not break, and, last, they covered the bones with plaster to protect them.)

Have partners review their Main Idea and Key Details charts for pages 2–7 and discuss what they have learned.

✓ Quick Check Quick Check Do children understand weekly vocabulary in context? If not, review and reteach using the instruction on page 334.

Can children identify main idea and key details? If not, review and reteach using the instruction on page 334 and assign Unit 6 Week 3 digital mini-lesson.

WEEK 3 LESSON

4

Objectives
- Understand and use new vocabulary words
- Read expository text
- Recognize and understand main idea and key details
- Understand complex text through close reading

Scaffolding for **Wonders** **Approaching Leveled Reader**

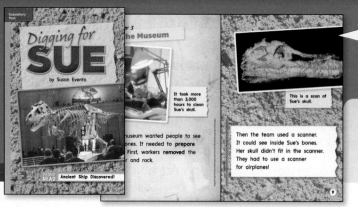

Materials
- "Digging for Sue" Apprentice Leveled Reader: pp. 8–19
- Main Idea and Key Details Graphic Organizer

☞ **Go** Digital
- Apprentice Leveled Reader eBook
- Downloadable Graphic Organizer
- Main Idea and Key Details Mini-Lesson

BEFORE READING

5–10 Minutes   SL.2.1a SL.2.6 L.2.6

Expand Vocabulary

Display each word below. Say the words and have students repeat them. Then use the Define/Example/Ask routine to introduce each word.

① models (page 10)

Define: copies of a thing

Example: We made *models* of our hands in clay.

Ask: Why would it be helpful to make *models* of dinosaur bones?

② removed (page 8)

Define: took away

Example: We *removed* the snow from the sidewalk with a shovel.

Ask: What is something you have *removed* that was simple to do?

③ skeleton (page 11)

Define: the bones in a body

Example: Doctors used an X-ray machine to look at my *skeleton*.

Ask: Why is your *skeleton* important?

DURING READING

15–20 Minutes   RI.2.1 RI.2.3 RI.2.5

Close Reading

🔍 **Pages 8–9**

Genre Ⓐ Ⓒ Ⓣ Read page 8 with children and point out the photo and its caption. Ask: *What does the caption tell us this is a picture of?* (a person cleaning Sue's skull) *How long did it take to clean the skull?* (more than 3,000 hours) Then point out the text on the page.

Connection of Ideas Ⓐ Ⓒ Ⓣ Remind children about what they read previously. Say: *The text says that the first thing that the workers did was to remove the plaster and rock. Why was there plaster and rock with the bones?* (The workers left plaster and rock on the bones to protect them as they traveled to the museum.)

Man Idea and Key Details Read page 9 with children. Remind them to look for details to help them understand the main idea. Ask: *What did the team do on this page?* (They used a scanner to see inside Sue's bones). *How did they have to scan the skull?* (They had to use a scanner for airplanes.) Add these details to the Main Idea and Key Details charts.

🔍 **Pages 10–11**

Genre Ⓐ Ⓒ Ⓣ Read pages 10–11 with children. Point out that the text on page 10 states that it was hard to put Sue back together. Ask: *What were some things that the team had to do to put Sue back together?* (They fixed cracks with glue; they repaired bones with a kind of clay; they made models of missing bones.)

STOP AND CHECK Read the question in the Stop and Check box on page 11. (The casts were used to make a model of Sue's skeleton.)

🔍 Pages 12–13

Genre Ⓐ Ⓒ Ⓣ Read page 12 with children. Point out the photo with the caption. Say: *The photo caption says that the skull is very heavy. What does the text say that the team did so they could attach the skull to the rest of the skeleton?* (They made a model of the skull made of plastic.) *How would that be helpful?* (It was much lighter than the real skull.)

Prior Knowledge Ⓐ Ⓒ Ⓣ As children read page 13, explain and demonstrate the size of the T. rex skeleton. Walk off 41 feet in the classroom. Explain that a ton is 2,000 pounds.

🔍 Page 14

Sentence Structure Ⓐ Ⓒ Ⓣ Read page 14 with children. Point to the first sentence in the second paragraph. Ask children to read until they reach the comma. Remind them that a comma means to pause. Ask: *What does the first part of this sentence tell us?* (As a result of finding new bones, or because we found new bones) Say: *The second part of the sentence should tell us what happened because we found new bones. What does it say happened?* (We learn more about dinosaurs.)

Main Idea and Key Details Have children review the selection. Then have them reread and compare the key details that they have added to their chart throughout the course of their reading. Ask: *If you look at the key details that you have added to the Main Idea and Key Details Chart, what do you think the main idea of this expository text is?* (Possible answer: The main idea is that a team of people worked very hard and spent many hours to learn about Sue the T. rex. There is a lot you can learn from fossils.)

STOP AND CHECK Read the question in the Stop and Check box on page 14. (Possible answer: They learned that she was about 41 feet long, weighed more than 7 tons, and died at about age 28. Scans also showed that some T. rex bones are placed like a bird's bones. This might mean that birds are related to dinosaurs.)

AFTER READING

10–15 Minutes   L.2.4a   L.2.6   RI.2.3   RI.2.9

Respond to Reading

Compare Texts Have children think about the connections between the team in "Digging for Sue" and the team in "Dive Teams." How was their work the same? How was it different? Ask: *Which team would you like to work on? What job would you like to do on that team?*

Summarize Have children turn to page 16 and summarize the selection. (Answers should include details from the Main Idea and Key Details Chart.)

🔍 Text Evidence

Have partners work together to answer questions on page 15. Remind children to use their Main Idea and Key Details charts.

Main Idea and Key Details (T. rex was a huge dinosaur. Important T. rex fossils were discovered in 1990 that helped us learn about them.)

Vocabulary (From the text we can guess that a cast helps you make a copy of something else. A cast is "a mold used to shape an object.")

Write About Reading (That there is a lot to learn from studying fossils.)

Independent Reading

Encourage students to read the paired selection "Ancient Ship Discovered!" on pages 16–18. Have them summarize the selection and compare it to "Digging for Sue." Have them work with a partner to answer the questions on page 18.

✓ *Quick Check* Can students identify main idea and key details? If not, review and reteach using the instruction on page 334 and assign the Unit 6 Week 3 digital mini-lesson.

Can students respond to the selection using text evidence? If not, provide sentence frames to help them organize their ideas.

WEEK 3
LESSON

5

• Review weekly vocabulary words
• Review main idea and key details
• Write an analysis about how the author used key details to support the main idea

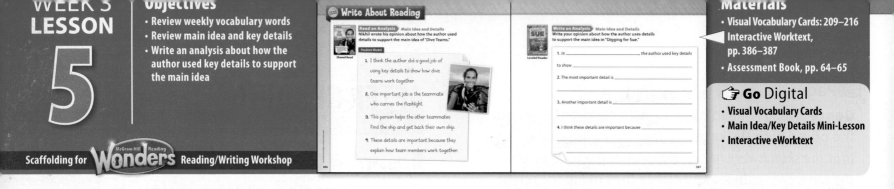

Materials
• Visual Vocabulary Cards: 209–216
• Interactive Worktext, pp. 386–387
• Assessment Book, pp. 64–65

☞ **Go** Digital
• Visual Vocabulary Cards
• Main Idea/Key Details Mini-Lesson
• Interactive eWorktext

Scaffolding for **Wonders** Reading/Writing Workshop

REVIEW AND RETEACH

5–10 Minutes   RI.2.2 RI.2.6 RI.2.8 L.2.4a

Weekly Vocabulary

Display one **Visual Vocabulary Card** at a time and guide children to use the vocabulary word in a sentence. If children have difficulty creating a sentence, have them find the word in "Dive Teams" or "Digging for Sue" and use context clues to define the vocabulary word.

Comprehension: Main Idea and Key Details

I Do Write and say: *I dance when my mom puts on music. I want my dad to listen to music on the radio in the car. I listen to music on my headphones in my room while I am alone.* Ask: *What is the main idea of these sentences?* Say: *Think about the key details that you know: I dance when there is music; I want to listen to music in the car; I listen to music when I'm by myself. If you put together these details, you can see that the main idea is "I like music."*

We Do Display and say: *Trees give us shade when it is hot outside. They keep soil from washing away in the rain. They provide food for animals and people.* Ask: *What is the main idea of these sentences, based on these key details?* (Trees are important and helpful.) *How do you know?* (All of these sentences tell ways that trees are important and helpful.)

You Do Display and say: *Did you ever think about joining a swim team? You will learn a lot about swimming. You will make a lot of friends. Your coach will help you improve. You will have fun swim competitions.* Guide partners to work together to figure out what each main idea is that is supported by the details.

WRITE ABOUT READING

25–35 Minutes   W.2.2 W.2.8 W.4.9

Read an Analysis

• Guide children to look back at "Pedal Power" in the **Interactive Worktext**. Have volunteers review the details used to support the main idea they marked on page 381. Repeat with pages 382–383. *How did the author use details to support the main idea in the selection?*

• Read aloud the directions on page 386. Read aloud the student model. *This student's work is not a summary. It is an analysis that tells a student's opinion about how the author used details to support the main idea in "Dive Teams."*

• *Read Nikhil's first sentence. Circle the details.* (the author did a good job of using key details to show how dive teams work together) *How can you tell that this sentence is an opinion?* (the words "I think") *What part of the story do the details come from?* (the beginning)

• *Read the second sentence. Nikhil writes what he thinks is an important detail in the selection. Draw a box around the details that best support the main idea.* (One member of the team carries a flashlight during dives.) *What part of the story is he writing about?* (the middle)

• Guide children to point to the third sentence. This sentence gives more details that Nikhil thinks are important. *What details does Nikhil include?* (helps their teammates find sunken ships)

• Read the last sentence that Nikhil wrote. *Why is this sentence a good ending?* (Nikhil tells why the details he wrote about show how team members work together.)

✏️ *Analytical Writing* Write an Analysis

Guided Writing Read the writing prompt on page 387 together. Guide children to review their Main Idea and Details charts for "Digging for Sue." Have children use their charts to complete the sentence starters. Children can also write an opinion using another selection previously read this week.

Peer Conference Guide children to read their opinon to a partner. Listeners should summarize the strongest details that support the beginning, middle, and ending sentences. They should discuss any parts that are unclear.

Teacher Conference Check children's writing for complete sentences and whether they included details from the selection. Review the ending sentence and ask: *Did the author use details to support their opinion?* If necessary, guide children to revise their sentence by adding more details.

Level Up

▲ Apprentice Leveled Reader

▲ Approaching Leveled Reader

▲ Interactive Worktext

▲ Reading/Writing Workshop

IF children read the Apprentice Level Reader and the **Interactive Worktext** Shared Read fluently and answer the Respond to Reading questions

THEN read together the Approaching Level Reader main selection and the **Reading/Writing Workshop** Shared Read from *Reading Wonders*. Have children take notes as they read, using self-stick notes. Then ask and answer questions about their notes.

Writing Rubric

	4	3	2	1
Text Evidence	Includes three or more details from the text.	Includes two or more details from the text.	Includes only one detail from the text.	No text evidence is cited.
Writing Style	Writes in complete sentences. Uses correct spelling and grammar.	Uses complete sentences. Writing has spelling and grammar errors.	Few complete sentences. There are many spelling and grammar errors.	Writing is not accurate or in complete sentences.

ASSESSMENT

Weekly Assessment

Have children complete the Weekly Assessment using **Assessment** book pages 64–65.

▶ **Mid-Unit Assessment,** pages 112 – 119

▶ **Fluency Assessment,** pages 266 – 281

CCSS **TESTED SKILLS**

✔ COMPREHENSION	✔ VOCABULARY:
• Theme **RL.2.2**	• Context Clues **L.2.4**
• Author's Purpose **RI.2.6, RI.2.8**	
• Main Idea and Key Details **RI.2.1, RI.2.2**	

Using Assessment and Writing Scores

↻ RETEACH	IF ...	THEN ...
COMPREHENSION	Students answer 0–5 multiple-choice items correctly ...	... reteach tested skills using instruction on pages 364–375.
VOCABULARY	Students answer 0–2 multiple-choice items correctly ...	... reteach tested skills using instruction on page 364.
WRITING	Students score mostly 1–2 on weekly writing rubrics throughout the unit ...	... reteach writing using instruction on pages 376–377.

Fluency Assessment

Conduct assessments individually using the differentiated fluency passages in Assessment. Students' expected fluency goal for this Unit is 79–99 WCPM with an accuracy rate of 95% or higher.

Weeks 4 and 5

Monitor students progress on the following to inform how to adjust instruction for the remainder of the unit.

ADJUST INSTRUCTION	
ACCESS COMPLEX TEXT	If students need more support for accessing complex text, provide additional modeling of prompts in Lesson 2 of Week 4, pages 340–341, and Week 5, pages 350–351. After you model how to identify the text evidence, guide students to find text evidence in Lessons 3 and 4, in Week 4, pages 342–345, and Week 5, pages 352–355.
FLUENCY	For those students who need more support with Fluency, focus on the Fluency lessons in the Foundational Skills Kit.
WRITING	If students need more support incorporating text evidence in their writing, conduct the Write About Reading activities in Lesson 4 and 5 as group writing activities.
FOUNDATIONAL SKILLS	Review students' individualized progress in *Reading Wonders* Adaptive Learning to determine which foundational skills to incorporate into your lessons for the remainder of the unit.

WEEK 4
LESSON

1

• Develop oral language
• Build background about money
• Understand and use weekly vocabulary
• Read an expository text

Materials
Interactive Worktext, pp. 388–395
• Visual Vocabulary Cards: 217–224
• High-Frequency Word Cards

☞ Go Digital
• Interactive eWorktext
• Visual Vocabulary Cards

Scaffolding for **Wonders** Reading/Writing Workshop

WEEKLY CONCEPT

5–10 Minutes   SL.2.1a SL.2.4   CCSS

Talk About It

Essential Question Read aloud the Essential Question on page 388 of the **Interactive Worktext:** *How do we use money?* Explain that we use money in many ways. Say: *Money is used to buy things, or goods, such as food and clothing. It is also used to buy services, such as baby-sitting or cleaning. People also save money and some give money to charity. Let's think about how we use money.*

• Discuss the photograph on page 388. Ask: *What is happening in the picture?* (Two children are buying granola bars.) Have children look carefully at the picture to tell what else they see in the picture. (One boy has a dollar bill and is giving it to a store clerk.)

I Do Say: *I am going to look at the photo and think about how we use money.* (These children are using money to buy the granola bars.) *I will write how we use money on the chart on page 389. I see there are two headings on the chart. The word "Goods" means things that are sold. I will write "Food" under the Goods heading, since food is a good.*

We Do Say: *Let's think about a service people can buy with their money. Our school has a food delivery service that brings food to the cafeteria. The school pays money for someone to deliver the food.* Guide children to think of other services the school might use. Then have children choose one service and add it to their chart.

You Do Guide partners to work together to think of goods and services their families spend money on. Have children use the words from the chart to start their sentences: *My family buys goods, such as _____. A service my family uses is _____.*

REVIEW VOCABULARY

10–15 Minutes   L.2.5a L.2.6 RF.2.3   CCSS

Review Weekly Vocabulary Words

• Use the **Visual Vocabulary Cards** to review the weekly vocabulary.

• Read together the directions on page 390 of the **Interactive Worktext.** Then complete the activity.

❶ **invented** Write the word *invent* on the left side of the board. Have volunteers name synonyms as you list them under the word *invent*. (Possible answers: make, create) Then write the word *invented* on the right side of the board. Ask volunteers to tell the past tense of each of the synonyms listed as you list them under *invented*. (Possible answers: made, created)

❷ **system** Ask children to think about what *systems* are used in the classroom. Tell them about a *system* you use to keep the books organized. Have partners tell each other about what *systems* they have for doing things, including keeping their clothes organized. (Answer will vary.)

❸ **record** Show children the book or notepad you use to keep a record of childrens' names, assignments, and so on. Say: *I keep a record of this information.* Invite volunteers to tell where they keep *records* of things. Have children use this sentence starter: *I keep a record of new words _____.* (Possible answer: in a notebook)

❹ **money** Draw a cent sign (¢) on the board and ask children to identify it. Then ask for a volunteer to come up to the board and draw a dollar sign ($). Tell children that these two signs are used when we write about *money*. Guide children to tell what kind of *money* is used in the United States. (Possible answers: U.S. dollars; dollars and cents; bills and coins)

5 **value** Hold a nickel in one hand and five pennies in the other. Say: *The value of a nickel is five cents.* Have children repeat. Then hold a dime in one hand. Have children use this oral sentence frame: *The value of a dime is _____.* (ten cents)

6 **prices** Invite children to talk about experiences they've had inside various stores. Ask: *When you go to a store, how do you know how much something costs?* Children can use the following sentence starter: *I can find the prices of things in a store _____.* (Possible answers: on price tags, on stickers, on the wall)

7 **purchase** Review the meaning of the word *purchase.* Then ask a child to use this oral sentence starter: *I purchase _____.* Then have the rest of the group guess where the purchase is being made: *[Child's name] goes to a _____ to purchase _____.* Guide children to think of where people purchase a book. Use: *I purchase a book at a _____.* (bookstore)

8 **worth** Name something that is *worth* a lot of money. Write them on the board. Then have children use the following oral sentence frame to describe their picture: *A _____ is worth a lot of money.* (Possible answers: car, airplane, boat, diamond ring)

High-Frequency Words

Have children look at page 391 in the **Interactive Worktext**. Help them read, spell, and write each high-frequency word. Guide partners to use each word in a sentence. Then read the story aloud with children. Guide partners to work together to reread the story and circle the high-frequency words. (buy, her, number, again, where, when) Listen in and provide assistance reading the high-frequency words, as necessary.

ELL ENGLISH LANGUAGE LEARNERS

Display the **High-Frequency Word Cards** for: *again, buy, her, number, when, where.* Write a sentence with each word on the board. Have children echo-read each sentence, and point out the high-frequency word.

READ COMPLEX TEXT

15–20 Minutes   RL.2.3   RL.2.5   SL.2.1b

Read "The Life of a Dollar Bill"

- Have children turn to page 392 in the **Interactive Worktext** and read aloud the Essential Question. Point to the photo on the page. Say: *Why do you think the boy in this photo is excited?* (He is holding a bunch of one-dollar bills.) *Let's read to find out about the different places a dollar bill is made and where it can travel during its lifetime.* Have children echo-read the title.

- Read the story together. Note that the weekly vocabulary words are highlighted in yellow. Expand Vocabulary words are highlighted in blue.

- As children read, have them use the "My Notes" section on page 392 to write questions they have. Children can also write words they don't understand or things they want to remember. Model how to use the "My Notes" section. *When I read the first paragraph on page 393, I find out that dollar bills are printed on a machine that can print many bills at the same time. I will write a question in the "My Notes" section about why the government needs to print so many bills at once.*

ELL ENGLISH LANGUAGE LEARNERS

As you read together, have children highlight parts of the text they have questions about. After reading, review the questions children have. Then help them locate the answers to their questions in the text.

✓ **Quick Check** Can children understand the weekly vocabulary in context? If not, review vocabulary using the **Visual Vocabulary Cards** before teaching Lesson 2.

Can children read high-frequency words in context? If not, review using the Read/Spell/Write routine and the High-Frequency Word Cards.

WEEK 4 LESSON 2

Objectives
- Read expository text
- Understand complex text through close reading
- Recognize and understand problem and solution
- Respond to the selection using text evidence to support ideas

Materials
Interactive Worktext, pp. 392–397

☞ **Go** Digital
- Interactive eWorktext
- Problem and Solution Mini-Lesson

Scaffolding for McGraw-Hill Reading **WONDERS** Reading/Writing Workshop

REREAD COMPLEX TEXT

15–20 Minutes   L.2.4a   RI.2.3   RI.2.5   RI.2.7   **CCSS**

Close Reading: "The Life of a Dollar Bill"

Reread "The Life of a Dollar Bill" with children from **Interactive Worktext** pages 392–395. As you read together, discuss important passages in the text. Guide children to respond to questions using evidence from the text.

Pages 392–393

Purpose **A C T**   Say: *The purpose of a text is the author's reason for writing it. The author may want to answer, explain, or describe something. To help understand an author's purpose, it helps to ask "What does the author want me to know about a topic?"* Read the second paragraph aloud and ask: *What does the author want you to do in this selection?* Guide children to underline the words that tell. (follow a dollar bill)

Expand Vocabulary Explain to children that an *allowance* is money given to someone each week. Say: *Sometimes children get an allowance for doing certain jobs around the house like helping with the dishes or taking out the garbage.* Ask: *Who gives the boy his allowance?* Guide children to write their answers. (his mom)

Problem and Solution Say: *You can think about a problem and how it is solved to help make text connections. The solution may be on the same page as the problem, or it may be found further along in the selection. There may be more than one problem and solution in a text.* Read the last paragraph aloud. Ask: *What problem does the boy face when he finds a book to buy?* Guide children to draw a box around the sentence that tells. (He is not sure it is worth it.)

Page 394

Expand Vocabulary Explain to children that if something is *usable*, it is able to be used again. Demonstrate the word's meaning by pointing to different objects in the room, such as a desk, and ask: *Is this desk usable?* (Possible answers: Either yes or no, it is broken.) Have children reread the first paragraph and ask: *What is the man not sure is usable?* Guide children to circle the words that tell. (the dollar bill)

Problem and Solution Have children reread the last paragraph. Say: *The problem is that the man is not sure his dollar bill is usable.* Have children reread the last paragraph. Ask: *What steps does the man take to solve this problem?* Guide children to draw a box around the sentence that tells. (He takes it to his local bank and trades it for a new one.)

Purpose **A C T**   Remind children that they can look for clues to the author's purpose as they read. Have children ask themselves: *"What does the author want me to know?"* Read the page aloud. Ask: *What is the purpose of this section of text?* Guide children to write their answers. (to show how a dollar bill travels and gets worn)

Genre **A C T**   Review with children that expository texts often use text features such as headings, photos, and graphs to help give readers more information about a topic. Point to the bar graph and say: *This bar graph gives information about how long paper money lasts in the United States. The information at the bottom of the graph tells the different amounts each bill is worth. The information going up the side of the graph, tells time in years and half years. To read the graph, go to the top of each bill and look at the years to see how long the bill lasts.* Ask: *Which bill lasts the longest?* (a $50 bill) *About how long does it last?* (about 4½ years) *What bills needs to be replaced before the other bills?* ($5 and $10 bill)

Connection of Ideas Ask: *Why do you think the author put this graph in the selection?* (Because the selection is about dollar bills and includes information about a dollar bill gettings worn out.)

🔍 Page 395

Expand Vocabulary Explain that when something is *shredded*, it is cut up into small pieces. Say: *Dollar bills are shredded when they are old and torn and no longer usable.* Have children reread the first paragraph and ask: *Who decides if a dollar bill is shredded?* Guide children to circle the word that tells. (workers)

Problem and Solution Remind children that when they come across a problem in a text, they should read to look for details that tell how the problem is solved. Have children reread the second paragraph. Say: *The government has a problem when it shreds an old dollar bill. It has one less dollar that people need. What steps does the government take to solve this problem?* Guide children to draw a box around the sentence that tells. (The government prints a new dollar bill to replace the old one.)

Purpose Have children think back to information the author has presented in this selection. Say: *The headings tell us that first the dollar bill is printed. Next, the dollar bill travels, and, finally, the old dollar bill is replaced with a new one. Along the way we read that many different people use this dollar bill.* Have children reread the last paragraph and ask: *What does the selection tell us about dollar bills?* Guide children to underline the sentence that tells. (Each one has a busy life.)

RESPOND TO READING

Respond to "The Life of a Dollar Bill"

Guide children to read the questions about "The Life of a Dollar Bill" on page 396 of the **Interactive Worktext.** Then read aloud the "Discussion Starter" for each of the questions. Guide children to work with a partner to answer the questions orally using the "Discussion Starters." Have children find text evidence to support their answers. Ask children to write the page number(s) on which they found the text evidence for each question.

1. *How does a new dollar bill get into people's hands?* (<u>Possible answers</u>: I read that first the dollar bill is printed. Then it is sent to a big bank and then to a local bank. Then a family visits the bank and a boy gets the dollar bill for his allowance. <u>Text Evidence</u>: p. 393)

2. *How is a dollar bill used?* (<u>Possible answers</u>: The boy uses the dollar to buy a book. Then a girl saves it in a piggy bank. The bill gets worn. <u>Text Evidence</u>: p. 394)

3. *What happens when the dollar bill gets old?* (<u>Possible answers</u>: If the dollar bill can't be used again, it is cut into small pieces. Then the government prints a new bill to replace the old one. <u>Text Evidence</u>: p. 395)

After children discuss the questions on page 396, have them use the sentence starters to answer the question on page 397. Circulate and provide guidance.

✓ *Quick Check* Do children understand vocabulary in context? If not, review and reteach using the instruction on page 346.

Can children identify problem and solution? If not, review and reteach using the instruction on page 346 and assign the Unit 6 Week 4 digital mini-lesson.

Can children write a response to "The Life of a Dollar Bill"? If not, review the sentence starters and prompt children to respond orally. Help them write their responses.

Objectives

- Understand and use new vocabulary words
- Read an expository text
- Recognize and understand problem and solution
- Understand complex text through close reading

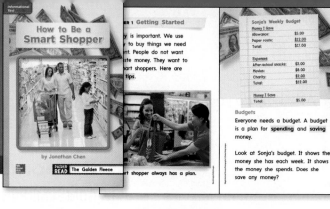

Materials

"How to Be a Smart Shopper" **Apprentice Leveled Reader:** pp. 2–7

- Problem and Solution Graphic Organizer

☞ **Go Digital**

- Apprentice Leveled Reader eBook
- Downloadable Graphic Organizer
- Problem and Solution Mini-Lesson:

BEFORE READING

10–15 Minutes   SL.2.1a   SL.2.6   L. 2.5a   L.2.6   CCSS

Introduce "How to Be a Smart Shopper"

- Read the Essential Question on the title page of "How to Be a Smart Shopper" **Apprentice Leveled Reader:** *How do we use money? We will read about different things we can do to become smart shoppers and get the most value for our money.*

- Read the title aloud. Point to the pictures. Ask: *Is this text fiction or nonfiction?* (nonfiction) Point to the chart on page 3 and ask: *Why do you think it is a good idea to write down how much money you have and how much money you spend each week?* (It can help you make sure you don't spend more money than you have. It can also show how much money you can save each week.) *This selection will give facts and information about how people can be smart shoppers and get the most out of their money. Let's read to find out things we can do to use our money in smarter ways when we shop.*

Expand Vocabulary

Display each word below. Say the words and have children repeat them. Then use the Define/Example/Ask routine to introduce each word.

1 saving (page 3)

Define: putting money away to use in the future

Example: Lexi is *saving* money to buy a new bike next summer.

Ask: What would you *save* money to buy?

2 spending (page 3)

Define: paying money for an item such as a shirt, or a service, such as a haircut

Example: Each week, Jason was *spending* all of his money on toy cars.

Ask: Why is *spending* more money than you have a problem?

3 tips (page 2)

Define: useful pieces of information

Example: The chef gave us helpful *tips* for making soups and salads.

Ask: If someone gives you safety *tips,* is that person telling information or asking questions?

DURING READING

20–30 Minutes   RI.2.1   RI.2.2   RI.2.4   RI.2.5   RI.2.6   CCSS

Close Reading

🔍 **Pages 2–3**

Purpose Point out that sometimes we can tell an author's purpose by the title. Read the title. Ask: *What does the title tell you that the book is going to do?* (teach you how to be a smart shopper) Turn to the page 2 and read it with children. Say: *On this page the author is telling us what the topic of t his book is about. He wants us to know that people want to be smart shoppers because they do not want to waste money.* Ask: *Why is money important?* (We use money to buy things we need or want.) *What is the author going to do in this selection?* (The author is going to give us tips about how to be smart shoppers.)

Problem and Solution Review with children that expository texts can tell about a problems and how to solve them. Say: *The author of this selection will give information about how smart shopping can solve the problem of wasting money.* Model adding "People waste money" to the Problem and Solution Chart. Say: *As we read, we'll look for ways to be smart shoppers and how to not waste money.*

Genre ACT Say: *In nonfiction, text features can give information not be found anywhere else in the text.* Read the chart with children and ask: *What does this chart show?* (Sonja's weekly budget) *How much money does Sonja have to spend?* ($17.00) *How do you know?* (It says so on the chart.) *How much money does Sonja spend?* ($12.00) *Can we find this information anywhere else on the page?* (no)

Problem and Solution Read page 3 with children and ask: *What does the text say that we need to have to solve the problem of wasting money?* (a budget) Model adding "Make a Budget," to the Problem and Solution Chart.

Pages 4–5

Vocabulary Read page 4. Focus on the phrase "comparison shop." Say: *In line 3, the author suggests we "comparison shop." What does it mean to compare?* (to see how things are alike) *How does the next sentence help you to understand what* comparison shop *means?* (It says you should go to different stores and check prices.)

Purpose ACT Read pages 4 and 5 with children and say: *This author gives two tips that can help people save money in this section of text. What two tips to save money does the author want you to know about?* (You can comparison shop at different stores and purchase things on the Internet to help save money.)

Connection of Ideas ACT Point to the photo on page 5 and reread the caption with children. Ask: *How does shopping on the computer help people save gas money?* (If people shop on the computer, they save money because they do not have to buy gas to drive to stores.)

STOP AND CHECK Read the question in the Stop and Check box on page 5. (so you don't waste money)

Pages 6–7

Genre ACT Review with children that readers can use chapter headings in expository selections to tell what information the author will give in the text that follows the heading. Read the chapter 2 heading aloud with children and ask: *What information do you think the author will tell about in this chapter?* (The author will give people tips on ways to save money at the supermarket.)

Problem and Solution Ask: *What problem is the author trying to solve in this selection?* (The author wants people to learn how to not waste money.) Read page 6 with children and ask: *What step does the author suggest to help people not waste money at the supermarket?* (The author thinks people should make a list when they go to the supermarket.) Model recording "Make a shopping list" on the Problem and Solution Chart.

Key Details Explain that the author thinks shopping lists are good to have when you shop at a supermarket. Ask: *How can making a shopping list help you save time and money at the supermarket?* (You'll save money because you will buy only the things you need. You'll save time because you will not be looking for extra things to buy.)

Connection of Ideas ACT Read page 7 with children and then read the caption below the picture. Ask: *When you see an item on sale at a supermarket, why should you make sure it is something you need to buy?* (Buying something you do not need does not save money, it wastes money.)

Have partners review their Problem and Solution charts for pages 2–7 and discuss what they have learned.

 Quick Check Do children understand weekly vocabulary in context? If not, review and reteach using the instruction on page 346.

Can children identify problem and solution? If not, review and reteach using the instruction on page 346 and assign Unit 6 Week 4 digital mini-lesson.

WEEK 4

LESSON

4

Objectives

• Understand and use new vocabulary words
• Read an expository text
• Recognize and understand problem and solution
• Understand complex text through close reading

Materials

• "How to Be a Smart Shopper" Apprentice Leveled Reader: pp. 8–19
• Problem and Solution Graphic Organizer

☞ **Go** Digital
• Apprentice Leveled Reader eBook
• Downloadable Graphic Organizer
• Problem and Solution Mini-Lesson

Scaffolding for **Wonders** Approaching Leveled Reader

BEFORE READING

5–10 Minutes   SL.2.1a   SL.2.6   L.2.5a   L.2.6   CCSS

Expand Vocabulary

Display each word below. Say the words and have children repeat them. Then use the Define/Example/Ask routine to introduce each word.

① product (page 8)

Define: anything that is made or created, such as yogurt or bread

Example: Many people tried the new *product* when the store gave it away for free.

Ask: What is one *product* your family buys at the supermarket?

② research (page 12)

Define: to carefully study a topic and learn facts about it

Example: Nora is going to the library to *research* robots for a report.

Ask: How could you *research* a favorite animal?

DURING READING

15–20 Minutes   RI.2.1   RI.2.2   RI.2.3   RI.2.5   RI.2.7   CCSS

Close Reading

🔍 Pages 8–9

Key Details Read page 8 with children and ask: *How can coupons help you save money?* (Coupons let you subtract money from the price of a product.) *Where is one place you can find coupons?* (the newspaper)

Purpose **A C T** Read page 9 with children. Say: *The author says that smart shoppers check their receipts to make sure the prices are correct. Why do you think the author wants you to know this information?* (The author knows that a receipt might show a price different from the price you were supposed to pay.)

Genre **A C T** Have children look at the photo of the receipt and say: *We read that a receipt is a record of what you bought. How does this photo help you know more about a receipt?* (The receipt shows the list of products that you bought. Next to each product is the product's price.)

STOP AND CHECK Read the question in the Stop and Check box on page 9. (A shopping list can save time and money. You won't buy things you don't need.)

🔍 Pages 10–11

Problem and Solution Read pages 10 and 11 with children and ask: *What can you do if two people both want something expensive, such as a bike, but there is only enough money to buy one bike?* (You can buy one bike for two people to share.) Help children add this information to their Problem and Solution charts.

STOP AND CHECK Read the question in the Stop and Check box on page 11. (Sharing is a good solution because it's fun to play together, and it saves money.)

Pages 12–13

Problem and Solution Read page 12 and 13 with children and ask: *What problem do Molly and her family face when they want to visit an amusement park?* (They do not know how much it would cost.) *How do Molly and her family solve the problem and not waste money?* (They do research to find out how much each thing will cost.) Help children add this information to their Problem and Solution charts.

Key Details Ask: *How much money will a visit to the amusement park cost per person?* ($20) *How much will it cost for the whole family?* ($60) *How much money does the family have in its budget for the trip?* ($70) *Does the family have enough money?* (Yes, the family has $70 in their budget, but the trip only costs $60.)

Page 14

Problem and Solution Read page 14 with children and ask them to think back about the steps they have written down in their Problem and Solution charts to help solve the problem of wasting money. Ask: *How can you solve the problem of wasting money and make sure you get the most out of your money?* (Be a smart shopper.) Help children add this to complete their Problem and Solution charts.

Purpose **ACT** Read the caption with children and have them look at the picture. Say: *The author says that being a smart shopper can be fun. Why do you think the author includes this information?* (The author wants readers to know that if they are smart shoppers and do not waste money, they will have more money in their budgets to do things that are fun.) *The author also says that being a smart shopper takes some work. What does the author mean by this statement?* (The things that smart shoppers do, such as making a budget, writing a shopping list, and planning a trip all take time and effort.)

STOP AND CHECK Read the question in the Stop and Check box on page 14. (It lets the family know how much their trip will cost and helps them see if they have enough money in their budget.)

AFTER READING

Respond to Reading

Compare Texts Guide children in comparing the way people solve a problem in "The Life of a Dollar Bill" with the way people solve a problem in "How to Be a Smart Shopper." Ask: *What are some ways people can solve a problem when they use money?*

Summarize Have children turn to page 15 and summarize the selection. (Answers should include details about how smart shoppers solve problems.)

Text Evidence

Have partners work together to answer questions on page 15. Remind children to use their Problem and Solution charts.

Problem and Solution (Possible answers include make a budget, comparison shop, purchase online, look for sales, use coupons, and share with others.)

Vocabulary (It means that the supermarket is selling something for less than it usually costs.)

Write About Reading (Comparison shopping is when a person checks the prices of something at different stores. It can help a person get the best price.)

Independent Reading

Encourage children to read the paired selection "The Golden Fleece" on pages 16–18. Have them summarize the selection and compare it to "How to Be a Smart Shopper." Have them work with a partner to answer the questions on page 18.

 Quick Check Can children identify problem and solution? If not, review and reteach using the instruction on page 346 and assign the Unit 6 Week 4 digital mini-lesson.

Can children respond to the selection using text evidence? If not, provide sentence frames to help them organize their ideas.

WEEK 4
LESSON
5

Objectives
- Review weekly vocabulary words
- Review problem and solution
- Write an analysis about an author's use of key details to make a selection expository

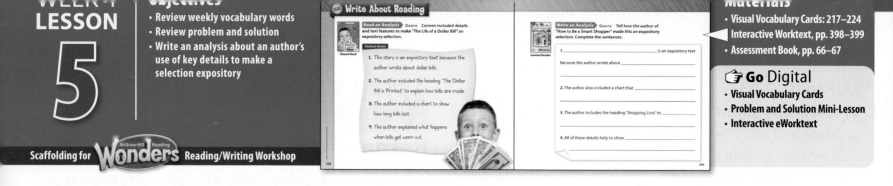

Scaffolding for **Wonders** Reading/Writing Workshop

REVIEW AND RETEACH

5–10 Minutes   RI.2.1   RI.2.3   L.2.4a   CCSS

Weekly Vocabulary

Display one **Visual Vocabulary Card** at a time and guide children to use the vocabulary word in a sentence. If children have difficulty creating a sentence, have them find the word in "The Life of a Dollar Bill" or "How to Be a Smart Shopper" and use context clues in the passage to define the vocabulary word.

Comprehension: Problem/Solution

I Do   Write and say: *Some people have trouble getting up in the morning. One way to help is to go to bed at the same time every night. You can also set an alarm clock and put it on the other side of the room.* Ask: *What problem does the author write about?* Circle: "Some people have trouble getting up in the morning." Write: "*Problem.*" Ask: *What is one step the author thinks could help solve this problem?* Circle: "go to bed at the same time every night." Write: "*Step to Solution.*" Say: *I can look for steps to solve the problem. At the end of the selection I can ask how the problem is solved.*

We Do   Display: *Too many old tires end up in garbage dumps. One company reuses these tires. Machines cut the tires into tiny pieces. The company sells the pieces to use in building roads and playgrounds. This is good for Earth and cuts down on waste.* Ask: *What problem does the author write about?* (Too many tires end up in garbage dumps.)

You Do   Guide partners to identify the steps to solve the problem above and the solution. Have partners use text evidence. (One company sells the tires to another company that reuses them.)

WRITE ABOUT READING

25–35 Minutes   W.2.2   W.2.8   W.4.9   CCSS

Read an Analysis

- Guide children to look back at "The Life of a Dollar Bill" in the **Interactive Worktext**. Have volunteers review page 393 to determine what makes this selection an expository text. Repeat with pages 394–395. *How did the author make the selection an expository text?*

- Read aloud the directions on page 398. Read aloud the student model. *This student's writing is not a summary. It is an analysis, or description, of how the author used details and text features to make "The Life of a Dollar Bill" an expository text.*

- *When you write an analysis, you should include key details from the text that tell why this is an expository selection. Read Carmen's first sentence. Circle the details.* (the author wrote about dollar bills) *In what part of the story do you learn this detail?* (the beginning)

- *Read the second sentence. Draw a box around a key detail that shows the genre of the selection.* (The author included the heading "The Dollar Bill is Printed" to explain how bills are made.) *What part of the story is she writing about?* (the middle)

- Guide children to point to the third sentence. This sentence gives examples of text features that show the selection is an expository text. *What text feature does Carmen include?* (a chart to show how long bills last)

- Read the last sentence that Carmen wrote. *What else does Carmen include in her analysis?* (Carmen writes what happens when a dollar bill gets worn out.)

✎ *Analytical Writing* Write an Analysis

Guided Writing Read the writing prompt on page 399 together. Guide children to review the selection "How to Be a Smart Shopper." Have children think about how the author used details and text features to write this expository text. Children can also write an analysis using another selection previously read this week.

Peer Conference Guide children to read their analysis to a partner. Listeners should summarize the strongest details and text features that support the beginning, middle, and ending sentences. They should discuss any parts that are unclear.

Teacher Conference Check children's writing for complete sentences and whether they included details from the story. Review the ending sentence and ask: *Did the author use details and text features to support the story?* If necessary, guide children to revise their sentence by adding more details.

Level Up

Apprentice Leveled Reader

▲ **Approaching Leveled Reader**

▲ **Interactive Worktext**

▲ **Reading/Writing Workshop**

IF children read the Apprentice Level Reader and the **Interactive Worktext** Shared Read fluently and answer the Respond to Reading questions

THEN read together the Approaching Level Reader main selection and the **Reading/Writing Workshop** Shared Read from *Reading Wonders*. Have children take notes as they read, using self-stick notes. Then ask and answer questions about their notes.

Writing Rubric

	4	3	2	1
Text Evidence	Includes three or more details from the text.	Includes two or more details from the text.	Includes only one detail from the text.	No text evidence is cited.
Writing Style	Writes in complete sentences. Uses correct spelling and grammar.	Uses complete sentences. Writing has spelling and grammar errors.	Few complete sentences. There are many spelling and grammar errors.	Writing is not accurate or in complete sentences.

ASSESSMENT

Weekly Assessment

Have children complete the Weekly Assessment using **Assessment** book pages 66–67.

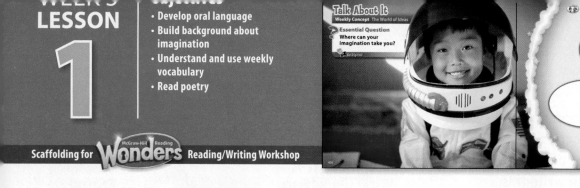

WEEK'S
LESSON

1

- Develop oral language
- Build background about imagination
- Understand and use weekly vocabulary
- Read poetry

Scaffolding for **Wonders** Reading/Writing Workshop
McGraw-Hill Reading

Materials
- **Interactive Worktext,** pp. 400–407
- **Visual Vocabulary Cards:** 225–228
- **High-Frequency Word Cards**

☞ **Go** Digital
- **Interactive eWorktext**
- **Visual Vocabulary Cards**

WEEKLY CONCEPT

5–10 Minutes   SL.2.1a   SL.2.4

Talk About It

Essential Question Read aloud the Essential Question on page 400 of the **Interactive Worktext:** *Where can your imagination take you?* Explain that your imagination can take you anywhere. Say: *You can imagine you are in a faraway or imaginary place. You can also imagine that you are doing extraordinary things or have become something amazing.*

- Discuss the photograph on page 400. Ask: *What is happening in the picture?* (A boy is wearing a space suit and helmet.)

▶ **I Do** Say: *I am going to look at the photo and think about what this boy is imagining. It looks to me as if he is imagining that he is an astronaut in space. He looks happy to be dressed up as an astronaut. I will write this on the web on page 401.*

▶ **We Do** Say: *Let's think about other things a person could imagine.* Ask: *What have you imagined yourself becoming when you grow up?* (Answers will vary.) Guide children to imagine what they'd like to be or do when they grow up. Then have children choose one answer to add to their web.

▶ **You Do** Guide partners to work together to talk about how they use their imaginations. Ask: *Do you use your imagination when you draw or create art? Do you imagine you can do something amazing?* Have children use words from the web to start their sentences: *I imagine I can _____.*

REVIEW VOCABULARY

10–15 Minutes   L.2.5a   L.2.6   RF.2.3

Review Weekly Vocabulary Words

- Use the **Visual Vocabulary Cards** to review the weekly vocabulary.

- Read together the directions on page 402 of the **Interactive Worktext**. Then complete the activity.

1 **seconds** Write the word *second* on the board. Below, list the word's different meanings as volunteers suggest them. (first, second, third; a second helping; one second of time) Ask: *How many* seconds *are in a minute?* (60) After children tell how long it takes them to eat lunch (minutes), have them use this oral sentence starter: *It takes only a few* seconds *for me to _____.* (Answers will vary.)

2 **create** Lead a discussion about the different things children have *created* in class this school year. Then have children name something they'd like to make in class, using this oral sentence frame: *I would like to* create *_____ this year.* (Answers will vary.) Then help children name another word for *create*. (Possible answers: make, invent)

3 **imagination** Name something you have *imagined.* Then have children think of a time they used their *imagination.* Have children use the following oral sentence starter: *When I used my* imagination, *I imagined _____.* (Answers will vary.)

4 **dazzling** Write the word *dazzling* on the board. Have volunteers suggest synonyms. (sparkling, flashy, shiny) Then assist children as they draw their picture. Have children describe their picture, using the word *dazzling* in their description.

Review Weekly Poetry Words

- Read together the directions for the Poetry Words activity on page 403 of the **Interactive Worktext**. Read the poem aloud with children. Then complete the activity.

5 **message** Write the word *message* on the board. Explain that the *message* is what the poet or author wants you to know after reading the poem or text. Have children tell what they think the *message*, of "Visiting Planets" is by using the following oral sentence starter: *The* message *in the poem is* _____. (Possible answer: using your imagination is fun)

6 **beats** Write the word *beats* on the board. Guide children to count out the *beats* in a poem by tapping the edge of their desks. Have children tap along with you as you count out the three *beats* in "the <u>cat</u> sat <u>on</u> the <u>mat</u>." Ask: *Can you hear how the* beats *make up the rhythm?* Continue tapping and counting with the first line of "Visiting Planets": "I <u>closed</u> my <u>eyes</u>." Have children use this oral sentence frame: *There are* _____ beats *in the first line of this poem.* (two)

7 **repeated lines** Write the term *repeated lines* on the board. Explain that poets use *repeated lines* in a poem for emphasis. Read aloud the poem, inviting the children to join in on the *repeated lines.* ("I closed my eyes.")

8 **metaphor** Write the terms *simile* and *metaphor* on the board. Under *simile*, write: "My dad is like a rock" and "My dad is as steady as a rock." Under *metaphor*, write: "My dad is a rock." Say a few similes and *metaphors,* and have children identify them by saying "simile" or "metaphor." Then discuss what the metaphor means. (Possible answer: My dad is steady or always there for me.) Assist children as they underline a *metaphor* in the poem. ("I was a rocket car"; "I was a bird")

READ COMPLEX TEXT

15–20 Minutes   RL.2.4   RL.2.6   SL.2.1b

Read "A Box of Crayons"; "What Story is This?"; "The Ticket"

- Have children turn to page 404 in the **Interactive Worktext** and read aloud the Essential Question. Say: *We're going to read some poems that have to do with imagination.* Have children repeat: *imagination. Let's read more about how we can use our imagination.* Have children echo-read the title.

- Read the story together.

- As children read, have them use the "My Notes" section on page 404 to write questions they have. Children can also write words they don't understand or things they want to remember. Model how to use the "My Notes" section. *When I read the title, I wonder what my imagination has to do with crayons. I will write a question in the "My Notes" section that will help answer my question as I read.*

> **ELL** ENGLISH LANGUAGE LEARNERS
>
> As you read together, have children highlight parts of the text they have questions about. After reading, review the questions children have. Then help them locate the answers to their questions in the text.

 Quick Check Can children understand the weekly vocabulary in context? If not, review vocabulary using the **Visual Vocabulary Cards** before teaching Lesson 2.

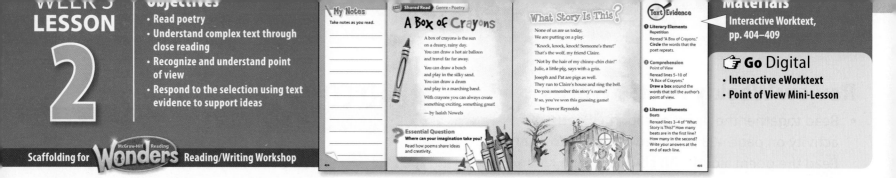

WEEK 5
LESSON

2

Objectives
• Read poetry
• Understand complex text through close reading
• Recognize and understand point of view
• Respond to the selection using text evidence to support ideas

Scaffolding for WONDERS Reading/Writing Workshop

REREAD COMPLEX TEXT

20-25 Minutes   RL.2.4   RL.2.6   L.2.4a   CCSS

Close Reading: "A Box of Crayons"; "What Story Is This?"; "The Ticket"

Reread "A Box of Crayons," "What Story Is This?" and "The Ticket" with children from **Interactive Worktext** pages 404–407. As you read together, discuss important passages in the text. Guide children to respond to questions using evidence from the text.

Page 405

Genre ACT Explain to children that the poems they will be reading today are rhyming poems. After reading each poem, have children identify the rhyming words in each stanza. You may also wish to have them review rhythm by having children clap the beats in each line.

Repetition Have children reread the "A Box of Crayons." Remind children that when a word or a line is repeated in a poem, it is of special interest to the writer, and they should pay close attention to it. Ask: *What words does the poet repeat?* Have children circle their answers. (You can draw)

Point of View Explain that the *point of view* is the way that the writer looks at or thinks about what he or she is writing about. Often, by reading the words of a poem, you can decide what the writer thinks about something, even if he or she doesn't say it. Have children reread lines 5–10 of "A Box of Crayons." Ask: *What words tell you the author's point of view about a box of crayons?* Guide children to draw a box around their answer. (you can always create something exciting, something great)

Beats Have children reread the third and fourth lines of "What Story is This?" Remind them that the *beats* in a line are the accented syllables that make the line's rhythm. Ask: *How many beats are in line 3? How many in line 4?* Have children write their answers. (line 3: four beats; line 4: four beats) If children have difficulty, underline the accented words and syllables as follows: "Knock, knock, knock! Someone's there!" "That's the wolf, my friend Claire.

Page 406

Connection of Ideas ACT Have children reread the first four lines. Remind them that these poems are about using their imagination. A ticket could be real. Ask: *What tells you that the ticket the poet is talking about is not real?* Have them underline their answers. (oceans deep, dazzling stars, lion's lair)

Beats Reread lines 7–8 with rhythm and have children echo read the lines. Then have children clap the rhythm as they reread the lines. Ask: *How many beats are in each line?* Have children count the beats as they reread the lines and write their answers. (line 7: three beats; line 8: three beats) If children have difficulty, have underline the accented beats as follows: I even rode a camel/ Through the desert, burning hot.

Point of View Guide children to reread the page. Remind children to think about what the speaker says and does to figure out his point of view. Ask: *What is the poet's point of view about the ticket in the poem?* Children should write their answer. (She thinks it is special.)

Page 407

Metaphor Remind children that a *metaphor* is a comparison between two unlike things that doesn't use the words *like* or *as*. Have them reread the second stanza on the page. Ask: *What is the metaphor in these lines?* Have children draw a box around the words that answer. (I'm a rocket)

Connection of Ideas Have children reread the last stanza. Ask: *What word tells you what the "special ticket" is that the poet uses to visit the places in the poem?* Have them underline their answer. (imagination)

Message Explain to children that the *message* of a poem is the overall understanding that the poet wants the reader to have after reading the poem. Have children reread the poem. Ask: *What is the* message *that the poet is trying to tell in this poem?* Have children write their answers. (Possible answer: If you use your imagination, you can go anywhere.)

RESPOND TO READING

10–20 Minutes   SL.2.1a   RL.2.6   W.4.9

Respond to "The Ticket"

Guide children to read the questions about "The Ticket" on page 408 of the **Interactive Worktext**. Then read aloud the "Discussion Starter" for each of the questions. Guide children to work with a partner to answer the questions orally using the "Discussion Starters." Have children find text evidence to support their answers. Ask children to write the page number(s) on which they found the text evidence for each question.

1. *What are some places the narrator uses the ticket to visit?* (Possible answers: I read that the ticket can take the narrator anywhere. The narrator goes to the stars. He also goes to a volcano. Text Evidence: p. 406)

2. *What does the narrator do on the trips he takes with his ticket?* (Possible answers: In the North Pole, the narrator builds an igloo. When he meets a great inventor, he helps him create a robot. Text Evidence: pp. 406–407)

3. *What does the ticket stand for?* (Possible answers: The ticket stands for the narrator's imagination. If you use your imagination, you can go places to. Text Evidence: p. 407)

After children discuss the questions on page 408, have them use the sentence starters to answer the question on page 409. Circulate and provide guidance.

✓ *Quick Check* **Do children understand vocabulary in context? If not, review and reteach using the instruction on page 356.**

Can children identify point of view? If not, review and reteach using the instruction on page 356 and assign the Unit 6 Week 5 digital mini-lesson.

Can children write a response to "The Ticket"? If not, review the sentence starters and prompt children to respond orally. Help them write their responses.

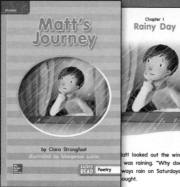

WEEK 5 LESSON 3

Objectives
- Understand and use new vocabulary words
- Read a fictional narrative
- Recognize and understand point of view
- Understand complex text through close reading

Materials
- "Matt's Journey" Apprentice Leveled Reader: pp. 2–8
- Point of View Graphic Organizer

☞ **Go Digital**
- Apprentice Leveled Reader eBook
- Downloadable Graphic Organizer
- Point of View Mini-Lesson

Scaffolding for **Wonders** Approaching Leveled Reader

BEFORE READING

10–15 Minutes   SL.2.1a SL.2.6 L.2.5a L.2.6 CCSS

Introduce "Matt's Journey"

- Read the Essential Question on the title page of "Matt's Journey" **Apprentice Leveled Reader:** *Where can your imagination take you? We will read about how a boy's imagination can take him places he could never go in his real life.*

- Read the title aloud. Point to the illustrations. Ask: *Is this text fiction or nonfiction?* (fiction) *This fiction text is called realistic fiction. It tells a story about things that could happen in real life, but the story and characters are fictional.*

Expand Vocabulary

Display each word below. Say the words and have students repeat them. Then use the Define/Example/Ask routine to introduce each word.

1 daydream (page 8)

Define: nice thoughts about things you would like to have happen

Example: I sat under the tree and had a *daydream* about being a king.

Ask: What have you ever had a *daydream* about?

2 join (page 7)

Define: to take part with others

Example: I would like to *join* the juggling club so that I can juggle with others.

Ask: What would you like to *join* others in doing?

3 steady (page 6)

Define: repeating over and over again a regular way

Example: The marching band's footsteps were *steady*.

Ask: What do you need to do using *steady* hands?

4 swayed (page 6)

Define: moved side to side slowly

Example: The trees *swayed* in the wind.

Ask: What have you *swayed* to?

DURING READING

20–30 Minutes   RL.2.1 RL.2.6 RL.2.7 L.2.4d CCSS

Close Reading

🔍 **Pages 2–3**

Genre Ⓐ Ⓒ Ⓣ Remind children that realistic fiction has characters, settings, and events that could exist in real life. Read page 2 with children. Say: *The picture is of a boy looking out the window while it rains. Do you think this is something that could happen in real life?* (yes) *Why?* (Possible answer: have done that, so I know it is real) Point out that as you read the book, you will pay attention to whether things could really happen.

Point of View Explain that a character's words and thoughts can tell us about his or her point of view—how he or she thinks about the events. Say: *Read what Matt thinks on the first page. Do you think that he is happy or sad that it is raining?* (sad) *Why do you think that?* (He wonders why it always rains on Saturday. He doesn't seem happy that it is raining.) *Right now, Matt's point of view is that the rain disappoints him. Let's see whether his point of view changes as the story goes on.* Guide students to keep track of important details regarding point of view on their Point of View charts.

Pages 4–5

Connection of Ideas (ACT) Read the text on pages 4 and 5 with children. Point out that Matt is watching the rain fall outside his window. He sees "shapes moving outside." Ask: *What does Max think the shapes look like?* (people or animals) *Do you think that they are going to be real?* (no) *Where do you think they are coming from?* (Matt's imagination) *Why do you think that?* (The text says Matt let his imagination take over.)

Vocabulary Point out the word *blurry* in the first line. Ask: *What doe the word* blurry *mean?* (not clear) *How does the picture help you understand the word* blurry? (It's hard to tell what is outside the window because its not clear.) *Why is is so* blurry? (The rain makes it hard to see.)

STOP AND CHECK Read the question in the Stop and Check box on page 4. (Matt thinks he sees people and animals moving outside.)

Vocabulary Read page 5 with children. Point out the word *rainforest*. Ask: *What two words are in* rainforest? (rain and forest) *How does this help them to understand what a* rainforest *is?* (It is a forest where it rains a lot.) Explain that a *rainforest* is a thick forest where it is warm all year round. It also gets a lot of rain every year. Many different kinds of plants and animals live in the *rainforest*. It might also be called a jungle.

Point of View Read page 5 with children. Guide children to look at the illustration. Ask: *What does Matt see the people in the rainforest doing?* (They are dancing.) *What are they wearing?* (large animal masks) *What does Matt think of the masks?* (He thinks they are cool. He wants one.)

Pages 6–7

Connection of Ideas (ACT) Read page 6 with children. Point out that the text says that "the rain fell in a steady beat." Say: *Then the masked people called to Matt: "Come dance with us!" Why might the rain's beat make Matt think of dancing?* (If something has a steady beat, it can make you want to dance.)

Point of View Read page 7 with children. Say: *How did Matt feel about the dancers?* (He wanted to join them.) *Was he able to join them?* (yes) *How did he join them?* (He closed his eyes and he was in the rainforest.) *Was he really in the rainforest?* (no) *How could he dance in the rainforest?* (He used his imagination.)

Page 8

Genre (ACT) Read page 8 with children. Point out that the text says "Mom's voice broke through his daydream." Say: *Is this something that might happen in real life?* (yes) *Why do think that?* (It might happen to a real kid.) Children may be confused about whether the Matt's imaginative journeys make the story a fantasy. Help them understand that it is a realistic story about a boy who has an active imagination. *So far, has anything happened that could not happen in real life?* (No, the dancing and the rainforest and other fantasy features are all in Matt's imagination.)

STOP AND CHECK Read the question in the Stop and Check box on page 8. (Matt imagines joining the rainforest dancers, wearing a mask, and dancing to the drumbeat.)

Have partners review their Point of View charts for pages 2–8 and discuss what they have learned.

✓ **Quick Check** Do children understand weekly vocabulary in context? If not, review and reteach using the instruction on page 356.

Can children identify point of view? If not, review and reteach using the instruction on page 356 and assign Unit 6 Week 5 digital mini-lesson.

WEEK 5 LESSON 4

Objectives
- Understand and use new vocabulary words
- Read a fictional narrative
- Recognize and understand point of view
- Understand complex text through close reading

Scaffolding for **Wonders** Approaching Leveled Reader

Materials
"Matt's Journey" Apprentice Leveled Reader: pp. 9–20
- Point of View Graphic Organizer

☞ **Go** Digital
- Apprentice Leveled Reader eBook
- Downloadable Graphic Organizer
- Point of View Mini-Lesson

BEFORE READING

5–10 Minutes   SL.2.1a SL.2.6 L.2.5a L.2.6

Expand Vocabulary

Display each word below. Say the words and have students repeat them. Then use the Define/Example/Ask routine to introduce each word.

1 faded (page 10)

Define: went away slowly

Example: Night *faded* into day as the sun came up.

Ask: If the sun's light *faded*, was the light very bright or not very bright?

2 scene (page 10)

Define: a place where something happens

Example: The parking lot was the *scene* of a crime.

Ask: Describe the *scene* in your classroom.

3 startled (page 12)

Define: felt a sudden shock or surprise

Example: I was *startled* when my brother sneaked up behind me and touched my arm.

Ask: Describe a time when you were *startled*.

DURING READING

15–20 Minutes   RL.2.1 RL.2.6 RL.2.7

Close Reading

🔍 **Page 9**

Point of View Read page 9 with children. Point out Matt's thoughts in the last paragraph. Say: *How do you think Matt feels about the sun's heat?* (He is excited about it.) *Why do you think that?* (He uses exclamation points when he is looking out the window. That means he is excited.) *What do you think Matt will do next?* (He will imagine himself in the desert.)

🔍 **Pages 10–11**

Connection of Ideas Reread page 10 with children. Point out that the setting has changed from Matt's kitchen to a desert. Ask: *Do you think that Matt is really in a desert?* (no) *What is happening?* (Matt is imagining himself in the desert.) *What is a clue that Matt is only imagining being in the desert?* (The camel can talk to him. That can't really happen.)

Point of View Reread page 11 with children. Remind them that they can figure out how a character feels, or his or her point of view, by taking note of what he or she does or says. Say: *The text says that "Matt was riding across the desert." How does Matt feel about riding a camel across the desert?* (He likes it.) *How can you tell?* (Right below, the text says "'This is fun!' thought Matt." So he must like the idea of riding a camel.)

🔍 **Pages 12–13**

Connection of Ideas Read page 12 with children. Say: *The text says that Matt's mom's voice "startled him." Why would his mom's voice startle him?* (He was daydreaming, or in his imagination again. So he might have forgotten that his mom was there.)

STOP AND CHECK Read the question in the Stop and Check box on page 12. (Matt imagines that the dog is a camel.)

Connection of Ideas (A C T) Read page 13 with children. Say: *Why might Matt's mouth feel "as dry as a desert"?* (He was imagining himself in a desert, so that might make him feel thirsty.)

Pages 14–15

Connection of Ideas (A C T) *What does Mom do when Matt tells her what he did that morning?* (She laughs and say she needs to feed his imagination.)

Point of View Have children review the selection. Then have them reread and compare the clues they gathered about Matt's points of view on their charts. Ask: *If you look at the clues that you have added to the Point of View Chart, what do you think Matt's point of view about his Saturday is?* (Possible answer: I think that Matt enjoys using his imagination to go places he can't go in his real life. The text on page 15 says that "Matt grinned." People grin when they are happy about something. Matt liked spending the morning in his imagination.)

STOP AND CHECK Read the question in the Stop and Check box on page 15. (Matt is hungry because he has been busy in his imagined adventures in the rainforest and the desert.)

AFTER READING

10–15 Minutes   RL.2.1   RL.2.4   RL.2.6   RL.2.7   W.2.8   **CCSS**

Respond to Reading

Compare Texts Have children think about the connections between the way that Matt uses his imagination and how the narrators of the poems use their imagination to think about what they see in different ways. What is similar in what they imagine and what is different? Ask: *Would you like to stay inside and imagine traveling with Matt or would you like to walk outside in the leaves or listen to music and let it transport you into your imagination? Why? Discuss with a partner.*

Summarize Have students turn to page 16 and summarize the story. (Answers should include details about the main character's point of view.)

Text Evidence

Have partners work together to answer questions on page 16. Remind students to use their Point of View charts.

Point of View At first Matt does not like the rain (page 2). He thinks, "Why does it always rain on Saturdays?" Then he uses his imagination to pretend he is somewhere else on page 4. After a while, the rain stops, but Matt continues to enjoy daydreaming.

Vocabulary (*Gobbled* means eat quickly.)

Write About Reading Answers will vary but might start with Matt being upset about the rain. Then Matt follows his imagination and his point of view changes. He has adventures. He feels he is dancing in the rainforest and that he is riding a camel in the desert.

Independent Reading

Encourage students to read the paired selection poems "Autumn Leaves" and "The Orchestra" on pages 17–19. Encourage them to look for examples of metaphor and to count the beats in the lines. Have them summarize the selections and compare them to "Matt's Journey." Have them work with a partner to answer the "Make Connections" questions on page 19.

 Quick Check Can students identify point of view? If not, review and reteach using the instruction on page 356 and assign the Unit 6 Week 5 digital mini-lesson.

Can students respond to the selection using text evidence? If not, provide sentence frames to help them organize their ideas.

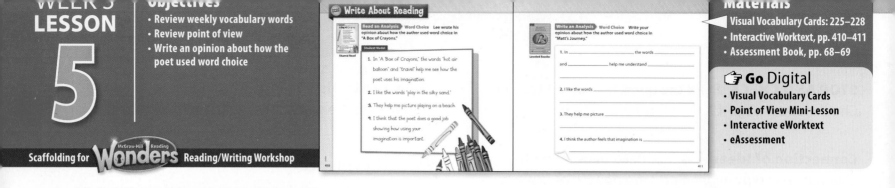

WEEK 5
LESSON
5

Objectives
• Review weekly vocabulary words
• Review point of view
• Write an opinion about how the poet used word choice

Scaffolding for **Wonders** Reading/Writing Workshop
McGraw-Hill Reading

Materials
Visual Vocabulary Cards: 225–228
• Interactive Worktext, pp. 410–411
• Assessment Book, pp. 68–69

👉 **Go** Digital
• Visual Vocabulary Cards
• Point of View Mini-Lesson
• Interactive eWorktext
• eAssessment

REVIEW AND RETEACH

5–10 Minutes RL.2.4 RL.2.6

Weekly Vocabulary

Display one **Visual Vocabulary Card** at a time and guide children to use the vocabulary word in a sentence. If children have difficulty creating a sentence, have them find the word in "A Box of Crayons," "What Story is This?" "The Ticket," or "Matt's Journey" and use context clues to define the vocabulary word.

Comprehension: Point of View

I Do   Write and say: *When it snows, I run outside. I throw snowballs. I like making snowmen. I love sledding down big hills.* Ask: *What is my* point of view *about winter?* Say: *Think about what I told you: I run outside; I throw snowballs, I like making snowmen, I love sledding down hills. If you put together these clues, you can see my* point of view *about winter is: I think it is great!*

We Do   Display: *When it rains out, it's very hard to get out of bed. I want to stay home. I don't get to play with my friends at the park.* Ask: *What is my* point of view *about rainy days?* (you don't like them very much) *How do you know?* (You said on rainy days you don't want to get out of bed. You want to stay home and you don't get to play with your friends. So your point of view must be that you don't like rainy days.)

You Do   Display: *The Yellow Lightning soccer team has a winning record. It has not yet lost a game this season! They have a great defense. They pass the ball well. They always have fun playing together.* Guide partners to work together to figure out what the author's point of view is. Encourage children to state the clues that helped them understand the author's point of view.

WRITE ABOUT READING

25–35 Minutes W.2.1 W.2.8 W.4.9

Read an Analysis

• Guide children to look back at "A Box of Crayons" in the **Interactive Worktext**. Have children think about the poet's word choices. *Did the poet use strong words? Did the word choices make the poems interesting? What is your opinion about how the poet used word choice?*

• Read aloud the directions on page 410. Read aloud the student model. *This student's work is not a summary. It is an opinion of how the poet used word choice in "A Box of Crayons."*

• *When you write an opinion, you tell your thoughts about the poem. In this student model, the student gave his opinion of how the author used word choice in the poem. Read Lee's first sentence. Circle the important information that he included in this sentence?* (hot air balloon, travel)

• *Read the second sentence. Lee shared other words that he liked from the poem. Draw a box around the words from the poem.* (play in the silky sand) *What is Lee's opinion of these words?* (He liked them.)

• *Guide children to point to the third sentence. In this sentence, Lee tells why he likes this choice of words. What does Lee include?* (The words help him picture playing on a beach.)

• Model giving an opinion on how well the poet used word choice. Read the last sentence that Lee wrote. *Why is this sentence a good ending?* (Lee writes that he thinks the poet does a good job showing that using your imagination is important.)

Write an Analysis

Analytical Writing

Guided Writing Read the writing prompt on page 411 together. Guide children to review the author's word choices in "Matt's Journey." Have children complete the sentence starters to write their opinions. Children can also write an opinion using another selection previously read this week.

Peer Conference Guide children to read their analysis to a partner. Listeners should summarize the use of word choices that support the beginning, middle and ending sentences. They should discuss any parts that are unclear.

Teacher Conference Check children's writing for complete sentences and whether they included details from the story. Review the ending sentence and ask: *Did the author give his or her opinion about how the author used word choice in the story?* If necessary, guide children to revise their sentence by adding more details.

Level Up

▲ Approaching Leveled Reader

▲ Reading/Writing Workshop

▲ Apprentice Leveled Reader

▲ Interactive Worktext

IF children read the **Apprentice Level** Reader and the **Interactive Worktext** Shared Read fluently and answer the Respond to Reading questions

THEN read together the **Approaching Level** Reader main selection and the **Reading/Writing Workshop** Shared Read from *Reading Wonders*. Have children take notes as they read, using self-stick notes. Then ask and answer questions about their notes.

Writing Rubric

	4	3	2	1
Text Evidence	Includes three or more details from the text.	Includes two or more details from the text.	Includes only one detail from the text.	No text evidence is cited.
Writing Style	Writes in complete sentences. Uses correct spelling and grammar.	Uses complete sentences. Writing has spelling and grammar errors.	Few complete sentences. There are many spelling and grammar errors.	Writing is not accurate or in complete sentences.

ASSESSMENT

Weekly Assessment

Have children complete the Weekly Assessment using **Assessment** book pages 68–69.

Unit Assessment

▶ **Unit Assessment,**
pages 167 – 176

▶ **Fluency Assessment,**
pages 266 – 281

▶ **Exit Test,**
pages 223 – 232

✔ COMPREHENSION	✔ VOCABULARY:
• Theme RL.2.2	• Context Clues L.2.4a
• Author's Purpose RI.2.6, RI.2.8	
• Main Idea and Key Details RI.2.1, RI.2.2	
• Problem and Solution RI.2.3	
• Point of View RL.2.6	

Using Assessment and Writing Scores

↻ RETEACH	IF ...	THEN ...
COMPREHENSION	Students answer 0–7 multiple-choice items correctly ...	... reteach tested skills using instruction on pages 364–375.
VOCABULARY	Students answer 0–3 multiple-choice items correctly ...	... reteach tested skills using instruction on page 364.
WRITING	Students score mostly 1–2 on weekly Write About Reading rubrics throughout the unit ...	... reteach writing using instruction on pages 376–377.

⬆ LEVEL UP	IF ...	THEN ...
COMPREHENSION	Students answer 8–10 multiple-choice items correctly ...	... have students read the "How to Be a Smart Shopper" Approaching Leveled Reader. Use the Level Up lesson on pager on page 358.
WRITING	Students score mostly 3–4 on weekly Write About Reading rubrics throughout the unit ...	... use the Level Up Write About Reading lesson on page 359 to have students compare two selections from the unit.

Fluency Assessment

Conduct assessments individually using the differentiated fluency passages in **Assessment**. Students' expected fluency goal for this Unit is 79–99 WCPM with an accuracy rate of 95% or higher.

Exit Test

If a student answers 13–15 multiple choice items correctly on the Unit Assessment, administer the Unit 6 Exit Test at the end of Week 6.

Time to Exit WonderWorks

Exit Text

If...
Students answer 13–15 multiple choice items correctly...

Fluency Assessment

If...
Students achieve their Fluency Assessment goal for the unit...

Level Up Lessons

If...
Students are successful applying close reading skills with the Approaching Leveled Reader in Week 6...

If...
Students score mostly 4–5 on the Level Up Write About Reading assignment...

Foundational Skills Kit

If...
Students have mastered the Unit 6 benchmark skills in the Foundational Skills Kit and *Reading Wonders* Adaptive Learning...

Then...
... consider exiting the student from *Reading WonderWorks* materials into the Approaching Level of *Reading Wonders*.

WEEK 6

▶ **Read Approaching Leveled Reader**

Approaching Leveled Reader

Apprentice Leveled Reader

▶ **Write About Reading**

Interactive Worktext Shared Read

Apprentice Leveled Reader

Apprentice to Approaching Level

L.2.5   RI.2.10

How to Be a Smart Shopper

Before Reading

Preview Discuss what children remember about "How to Be a Smart Shopper" and the different ways we use money. Explain they will now read a more challenging version of the book.

Vocabulary Use the routines on the **Visual Vocabulary Cards** to review the Weekly Vocabulary words. Use pages 342 and 344 to review the Expand Vocabulary words.

A C T During Reading

▶ **Genre** Review that informational texts often contain charts and graphs that give additional information to help readers understand a topic. Have children look at the graphic on page 3 showing a child's budget. Say: *This budget shows how much money a student has in a week and how much the student spends. How much money did the student save from a birthday?* ($15.00) *How much did the student spend on after-school snacks?* ($2.00) Continue guiding instruction with the graph on page 13, if necessary.

▶ **Prior Knowledge** Discuss where their families shop for food and who does the shopping. Ask them about making lists, using coupons, buying in bulk, and looking for sales or other good deals. Have them share their own shopping experiences. As well, ask them to tell about what they use their own money for and how they earn or otherwise acquire it.

▶ **Organization** Remind children that authors often organize informational texts using specific text structures such as cause and effect, compare and contrast, or problem and solution. Remind children that "How to Be a Smart Shopper" is organized by telling about a problem and then describing a solution to the problem. As children read Chapter 3, ask them to identify the main problem of the section (wanting something that costs too much) and the solutions the author gives to solve the problem (sharing, making a budget and planning ahead).

After Reading

Ask children to complete the Respond to Reading on page 16 after they have finished reading. Provide support with the vocabulary strategy question, as needed.

Write About Reading

RI.3.9   W.4.9

Read an Analysis

- Distribute the Unit 6 Downloadable Model and Practice. Point out that the model compares two related texts that children have read in Unit 6, the **Interactive Worktext** Shared Read "The Life of a Dollar Bill" and the **Apprentice Leveled Reader** "How to Be a Smart Shopper." Read the sentences aloud.

- Point out the key details in each sentence that come from the texts. Point out the signal word *both*. Explain to children that this word shows readers that the sentence is comparing two different texts.

- Point out the key details in each sentence that come from the texts. Point out the signal word *both*. Explain to children that this word shows readers that the sentence is comparing two different texts.

- Ask: *What details show that the two texts are alike?* (Both texts tell about ways people use money. Both include a graph that tells more about the topic. Both texts tell about the steps people take to solve a problem.) *How is* How to Be a Smart Shopper *different?* ("How to Be a Smart Shopper" tells about ways people can save money, not about where money travels.)

- Model analyzing how the student supported her opinion. *How does this student support her opinion?* (The student told how a graph in "The Life of a Dollar Bill" was more informative than the graph in "How to Be a Smart Shopper.")

Write an Analysis

Guided Writing Tell children that they will compare the **Interactive Worktext** Shared Read "Dive Teams" and the **Apprentice Leveled Reader** "Digging for Sue." Explain that they will compare how the authors describe ways that teamwork is important.

- Guide children to compare the two texts as they complete the sentences on the Unit 6 Downloadable Model and Practice.

- Point out the signal words, such as *also, both*, and *different, to children and discuss how these words are used to compare the texts.*

- Alternatively, let children select two texts to compare.

Teacher Conference Check children's writing for complete sentences. Did they use key details to tell how the texts are the same and different? Did they use text evidence? Did they write in complete sentences? Did they use evidence to support their opinion?

Writing Rubric

	4	3	2	1
Text Evidence	Includes three or more details from the text.	Includes two or more details from the text.	Includes only one detail from the text.	No text evidence is cited.
Writing Style	Writes in complete sentences. Uses correct spelling and grammar.	Uses complete sentences. Writing has spelling and grammar errors.	Few complete sentences. There are many spelling and grammar errors.	Writing is not accurate or in complete sentences.

Additional Resources

Reteach

Model Lessons

English Language Learner Strategies

Program Information

Vocabulary words. Focus on any words that children found difficult. Display the card and have children read the word. Show the image. Explain the word's meaning and have them repeat the meaning and use the word in a sentence. Provide sentence starters as needed. For example, say: *Something that is simple to do is _____ .* For more practice, have children use the Partner Talk activities on the Visual Vocabulary Cards.

- Have children write the words on a sheet of paper or index card. Say the meaning of a word. Have children hold up the card and say the word. Then have them repeat the meaning and use the word in a sentence orally.

- Have children write a sentence using each word. Then ask them to draw a picture to illustrate their sentence.

- For any vocabulary words that children continue to find troublesome, reinforce the meanings using the **Define/Example/Ask** routine. Describe the routine in detail to children.

    Define Tell children the meaning of the word using child-friendly language, or words they already know. For example, say: *The word* enormous *means "very big."* Try restating the definition or using it differently from the way it was first presented.

the school.

Ask Use a question to help children connect the word to known words and use the word in speaking. For example, ask: *What have you seen that is* enormous? *What words mean the same, or nearly the same, as* enormous? *What words mean the opposite of* enormous? Through questions, you can observe if children understand a word's meaning. If they don't, try using a series of Yes/No questions such as these: *Would an ant that is 10 feet tall be enormous? Is 20 feet an enormous distance for you to walk?*

- Always have children pronounce the words multiple times. Ask them to discuss meanings with a partner, which will give them opportunities to use the words in speaking and listening.

- If children confuse words that look or sound the same, such as *carnival* and *carnivore*, write the words on the board, one above the other. Say each word slowly. Have children repeat it. Then help children compare the spellings. Ask: *What's the same in both words? What's different?*

AUTHOR'S PURPOSE

RI.2.6 RI.2.8

Informational

Unit and Week	Pages
Unit 3 Week 1	132–139
Unit 3 Week 3	152–159
Unit 6 Week 2	328–335

I Do Write and say: *A snowplow is a truck that pushes snow. Snowplows move snow off the street. They are used after big snowstorms. They do very important work. Driving in snow can be very dangerous. They get the snow off the road so people can drive to work.*

Say: *Remember, the author's purpose is the main reason an author writes a text. An author might write to tell information, to explain a topic, or to describe something. To find the author's purpose for writing a selection, I can look for clues in the text and ask myself, "What does the author want me to know?" In the first sentence, I read that a snowplow is a truck that pushes snow. The author wants me to know what a snowplow is.* Underline the first sentence and write "what a snowplow is." Say: *The rest of the selection gives me details about snowplows and what they can do.* Draw an arrow pointing to the rest of the passage and write, "information about snowplows." *When I look at these clues, I can tell the author's purpose is to inform the reader about snowplows and why they are important.*

We Do Display: *Florida is a great place to live. There are beaches everywhere. The weather is almost always warm. There are lots of theme parks. There are also water parks. There are many things to do there. I know you would love it!* Ask: *What is the purpose of these sentences?* (to explain why Florida is a great place to live) *How can you tell?* (The writer states an opinion and then gives reasons for holding that opinion.)

You Do Display: *Fish make great pets. They are so much fun to watch. They swim and dart around their tanks. There are many different types of fish you can choose from. They come in many different colors and patterns. Fish are pretty when they swim. Also, it is easy to care for a fish.* Guide partners to work together to decide on the purpose of the text.

For more practice, have children use the digital minilesson or use an Interactive Worktext Shared Read or Apprentice Leveled Reader from one of the weeks in the chart above.

CAUSE AND EFFECT

| | RL.2.3 |

Informational

Unit and Week	Pages
Unit 4 Week 2	204–211
Unit 5 Week 5	298–305

I Do Write and say: *Ben's muscles are very sore today. That's because he played soccer all day yesterday!* Say: *Remember that the* effect *is what happened and the* cause *is what made it happen. The first sentence tells me what happened. That is the* effect. Underline the first sentence and write "effect." Say: *To find the cause I will ask myself "Why were Ben's muscles sore?" I read in the second sentence that Ben's muscles are sore because he played soccer all day.* Circle the second sentence and write "cause." *Say: The signal word "because" gave me a clue that the author is telling me about a cause.*

We Do Display: *Lee ate too much ice cream. So, now he feels sick.* Ask: *How does Lee feel?* (He feels sick.) *Is this a cause or an effect?* (effect) *What signal word tells you it is an effect?* (So) *Why does Lee feel sick?* (because he ate too much ice cream) *Is this a cause or an effect?* (cause)

You Do Display: Sara put her fishing pole in the water. *Then she caught a big fish. Bill sat in the boat reading a book. He did not catch any fish.* Guide partners to work together to decide on the causes and effects in the text. Have children identify the signal words.

For more practice, have children use the digital minilesson or use an Interactive Worktext Shared Read or Apprentice Leveled Reader from one of the weeks in the chart above.

CHARACTER, SETTING, EVENTS

| | RL.2.3   RL.2.7 |

Literature

Unit and Week	Pages
Unit 1 Week 2	18–25
Unit 1 Week 3	28–35

I Do Write and say: *Gary had a dog, named Nora. They were walking in the woods. It was a quiet afternoon. Nora found an old tennis ball. Gary threw the ball for Nora. Nora chased after it. They had a fun time together.*

Say: *To find the characters in the story I will ask myself, "Who are the people and animals in the story?"* Underline "Gary" and "Nora," and write "characters." Say: *Gary and Nora are the characters. To find the setting I will ask myself, "Where and when does the story take place?"* Underline the second and third sentences and write "setting." Say: *These sentences tell me that the setting is in the woods in the afternoon. To find the events, I will ask myself, "What are the things that happen in the story?"* Underline sentences two, four, five, and six. Write "events." Say: *These sentences tell me the events, or what happened in the story.*

We Do Display: *Tucker and Lily went to the market. There were lots of people there. Lily ate a banana. Tucker bought a gift for his Mom.* Ask: *Who are the characters in the story?* (Tucker and Lily) *What is the setting?* (the market) *What are the events?* (Lily ate a banana and Tucker bought a gift for his Mom.) *How do you know these are the events?* (because these are the things that happen in the story)

You Do Display: *Gram and John were at the beach. They played in the sand all morning. Gram built a sand castle. John looked for shells. They went for a swim in the afternoon.* Guide partners to work together to identify the characters, setting, and events.

For more practice, have children use the digital minilesson or use an Interactive Worktext Shared Read or Apprentice Leveled Reader from one of the weeks in this chart.

COMPARE AND CONTRAST

RL.2.3 **CCSS**

Literature

Unit and Week	Pages
Unit 4 Week 3	214–221

I Do Write and say: *Ted and Lea have the same goal. They both want to be doctors. They want to be different kinds, though. Lea wants to be a foot doctor. Ted wants to be a doctor for animals.*

Say: *You can compare and contrast characters and events in a story. To compare two things, think about how they are alike. To contrast two things, think about how they are different.* Circle "same" in the first sentence. Say: *The signal word same tells me that the author is showing how two things are alike. How are Ted and Lea alike in this story?* Underline the second sentence. Say: *I read here that Lea and Ted both want to be doctors. What is different about Ted and Lea?* Circle the "different" in the third sentence. Say: Different *is a signal word. It tells me the author is contrasting two things. What is different about Ted and Leah?* Underline "a foot doctor" in the fourth sentence and "a doctor for animals." Say: *I read here that Lea wants to be a foot doctor, but Ted wants to be a doctor for animals. That is how they are different.*

We Do Display: *Sandy and Jeff are friends. They are the same age. They both live on Kane Street but they were born in different towns. Also, Jeff is tall and Sandy is short.* Say: *Let's compare the two characters. How are Sandy and Jeff alike?* (They are the same age. The live on the same street.) *How do you know?* (The signal words "same" and "both" tell me these are ways they are alike.) *Let's contrast the two characters. How are they different?* (They are from different towns.) *What is the signal word that gives you a clue?* (different)

You Do Display: *Hal and Grace are in the same class at school. Hal likes math best. Grace loves to read stories. But they both love music. At lunch, they both like to eat turkey sandwiches. After school, they both play basketball.* Guide partners to work together to decide how the characters are alike and how they are different. Have children identify any signal words.

For more practice, have children use the digital minilesson or use an Interactive Worktext Shared Read or Apprentice Leveled Reader from the week in the chart above.

COMPARE AND CONTRAST

RI.2.3 RI.2.9

Informational

Unit and Week	Pages
Unit 4 Week 1	194–201

I Do Display and read aloud: *Dolphins and blue whales both live in the ocean. Both need air to breath. They look very different though. Blue whales are the biggest ocean animals. Dolphins are much smaller.* Say: *When you compare, you tell how things are alike. When you contrast, you tell how things are different. Readers can think about how an author compares and contrasts two things to understand how they are connected.* Circle "both" in the first sentence. Say: Both *is a signal word. It tells me the author is showing how two things are alike. How are dolphins and blue whales alike?* Underline "live in the ocean." *I also read in the second sentence that both need air to breath. How are dolphins and blue whales different?* Circle "different" in the third sentence. Say: *The signal word* different *tells me that blue whales and dolphins are different in how they look.*

We Do Display and say: *Pugs and boxers are both types of dogs. Pugs and boxers are different sizes. Pugs are small, but boxers are big.* Say: *Let's compare pugs and boxers. How are pugs and boxers alike?* (They are both types of dogs.) *How do you know?* (The signal word "both" tells me) *Let's contrast pugs and boxers. How are they different?* (They are different sizes.) *What signal word that gives you a clue?* (different)

You Do Display: *Live oaks and redwoods are pretty trees. They are both found in America. Live oaks and redwoods are different in some ways. Live oaks are found in the southeast, but redwoods are found in the northwest. Redwoods are much taller than live oaks.* Guide partners to work together to decide how the redwoods and live oaks are alike and how they are different. Have children identify any signal words.

For more practice, have children use the digital minilesson or use an Interactive Worktext Shared Read or Apprentice Leveled Reader from the week in the chart above.

KEY DETAILS

RI.2.1

Informational

Unit and Week	Pages
Unit 1 Week 1	8–15
Unit 1 Week 4	40–47
Unit 1 Week 5	50–57

I Do Write and say: *Dolphins are neat animals. Dolphins are friendly to humans. Dolphins make sounds and whistle to communicate. They are also smart and playful. That is why so many people love dolphins.*

Say: *Key details are the most important details of a selection. Usually, key details are facts. They explain more about the topic. The topic here is dolphins. To find the key details, I will ask myself, "Does this detail give me more information about dolphins?"* Underline the second sentence. Write "key detail." Say: *This sentence tells me that dolphins are friendly to humans. This is a key detail because it tells me more about the topic.* Underline "sounds" and "whistle" in the third sentence. Write "key details." Underline "smart" and "playful" in the fourth sentence. Write "key details." Say: *The fourth sentence tells me that dolphins are smart and playful. These are two more key details about dolphins.*

We Do Display: *A salmon is a fish. They are born in a stream. When they grow, they swim to the sea. They stay in the sea for years. Then they swim back to the stream. They lay their eggs there and die.* Ask: *Where are salmon born?* (in a stream) *Where do salmon go when they grow?* (to the sea) *Where do they go to lay their eggs?* (back to the stream) *Are these key details?* (yes) *How do you know?* (because they give more information about the topic)

You Do Display: *A seal is an animal that lives in the sea. They also spend time on land. Seals are mammals. They feed milk to their babies. Seals are very curious. They sometimes follow boats to see what is happening on the boat. Seals can be found all over the world.* Guide partners to work together to identify the key details.

For more practice, have children use the digital minilesson or use an Interactive Worktext Shared Read or Apprentice Leveled Reader from one of the weeks in the chart above.

KEY DETAILS

RL.2.1

Literature

Unit and Week	Pages
Unit 1 Week 1	8–15

I Do Write and say: *Austin and Ian are brothers. They go with their parents to visit their Grandma for her birthday. Austin brings her a card he made. Ian gives Grandma a drawing he made at school.*

Say: *Key details are the most important details of a selection.* Ask: *Why do Austin and Ian go to visit their Grandma? I can look for key details to learn the answer.* Circle "for her birthday" in the second sentence and write *key detail.* Say: *This part of the sentence tells me why they visit their Grandma. It is a key detail.* Then circle "Austin brings her a card" and "Ian gives Grandma a drawing" and write *key details.* Say: *These are two more key details because tell me important information about Grandma's birthday.*

We Do Display: *Freddy the frog was sitting in his pond. It was a sunny day. His friend Sam the salamander swam over to him. Sam asked him if he wanted to play hide and seek. Freddy said yes! Then he swam down to the bottom of the pond to hide.* Ask: *What key detail tells you who Sam is?* (his friend) *Where are Freddy and Sam?* (in a pond) *What does Sam want to do?* (play hide and seek) *Are these key details?* (yes) *How do you know?* (because they tell important information about what's happening in the story)

You Do Display: *Jennifer rode her bicycle with her Dad. They rode to the town fair. When they got there, they were very excited. They couldn't decide whether to have a lemonade or go on a ride first.* Guide partners to work together to ask each other questions to identify the key details.

For more practice, have children use the digital minilesson or use an Interactive Worktext Shared Read or Apprentice Leveled Reader from the week listed in the chart above.

MAIN IDEA AND KEY DETAILS

RI.2.1   RI.2.2   CCSS

Informational

Unit and Week	Pages
Unit 3 Week 4	164–171
Unit 3 Week 5	174–181
Unit 6 Week 3	338–345

I Do   Write and say: *Did you know that robots are all around us? There are robots that clean people's floors. Doctors use robots to heal people. Some people do not have an arm or a leg. They use robot arms to help them live.*

Say: *Remember, the main idea is the most important point an author makes about a topic. To find the main idea, I need to look for key details. I see that some of these sentences give details about robots.* Underline the second sentence and write "key detail." Say: *This sentence gives a key detail about robots. I will look for more key details about robots.* Underline the third and fifth sentences and write "key details." Say: *To find the main idea I will ask myself, "What do these details have in common?" I see that all three details tell me about the ways robots make our lives easier. So, the main idea is:* Robots do many things to make our lives easier.

We Do   Display: *Bees help our crops to grow. They also make honey. We use the honey to make our food taste sweet. We also use the wax bees make. We use it for lip balm, candles, and many other things.* Say: *Let's look at the key details in the sentences to find the main idea. What is one key detail?* (Bees help our crops to grow.) *What other key details can you find?* (We use bees' honey to make our food sweet; we use bees' wax for many things) *What do all the details have in common?* (They all tell how bees are useful to humans.) *What is the main idea of the passage?* (Bees are useful to humans in many ways.)

You Do   Display: *Days of heavy rain can cause dangerous floods. A flood can also happen when snow melts or water rises in a river and goes over the bank. Floods can ruin buildings. When flood water fills the streets, disease can spread. People can become stuck at home for days. Floods can even cause fires.* Guide partners to work together to identify the main idea and which details support the main idea.

For more practice, have children use the digital minilesson or use an Interactive Worktext Shared Read or Apprentice Leveled Reader from one of the weeks in the chart above.

MAIN TOPIC AND KEY DETAILS

RI.2.1　RI.2.2　 CCSS

Informational

Unit and Week	Pages
Unit 2 Week 3	90–97
Unit 2 Week 4	102–109

I Do Display and read aloud: *The birds live in a nest. The nest is high up in the tree. It is made of grass and sticks. The nest holds the birds' eggs. It keeps them safe.* Ask: *What is this paragraph about? I can look for a main topic.* Circle the words *birds* and *nest* in the first sentence. Say: *I notice the text is mostly about the birds' nest. The nest must be the main topic of the paragraph.* Underline sentences 2–5. Say: *These sentences give me important information about the birds' nest. That tells me that these are the key details.*

We Do Display and say: *Baking cookies is fun. You mix the ingredients in a bowl. You bake them in the oven. The cookies come out warm and tasty.* Ask: *What are these sentences mainly about?* (baking cookies) *How do you know?* (When I reread the sentences, they all tell something about baking cookies.) *Which key details tell how to make the cookies?* (You mix the ingredients in a bowl.; You bake them in the oven.) *How do you know these are key details?* (because they give important information about the main topic)

You Do Display: *Ana's new shoes are great. She can run fast in them. She can jump over puddles in them. Ana's new shoes feel good on her feet.* Have partners read the sentences out loud to each other. Then guide one partner to tell the main topic and the other to identify key details. Have partners switch and discuss their answers.

For more practice, have children use the digital minilesson or use an Interactive Worktext Shared Read or Apprentice Leveled Reader from one of the weeks in the chart above.

PLOT

RL.2.5　 CCSS

Literature

Unit and Week	Pages
Unit 2 Week 1	70–77

I Do Display and read aloud: *Jen and Frank are outside. Jen sees a dark cloud. She tells Frank it might rain. Frank stays outside. Jen goes in the house. It rains. Frank gets wet.* Say: *Remember, the plot is the key events that happen in the story. To find the plot, I can think about the key events in the beginning, middle, and end of the story.* Ask: *What does Jen do at the beginning of the story?* Circle "She tells Frank it might rain." Say: *At the beginning of the story Jen sees a dark could and tells Frank it might rain.* Ask: *What do Jen and Frank do in the middle of the story?* Circle the fourth and fifth sentences. Say: *I read that Frank stays outside and Jen goes in the house. How does the story end?* Circle the last sentence. Say: *The story ends with Frank getting wet.*

We Do Display and say: *Hiro got in the boat. He rowed the bow around the island. Then he stopped on the beach. Hiro took a swim. Then Hiro rowed his boat home.* Ask: *What did Hiro do after he stopped on the beach?* (He took a swim and rowed home.) *How do you know?* (I read it in the last two sentences.)

You Do Display: *Hanna and Burt want to fly their kite. They have to add a tail to the kite. Burt holds the string. Hanna ties the ribbon. Finally, the kite is ready to fly.* Guide one partner to ask a question and the other to answer it. Have partners focus on the events that happen in the beginning, middle and end of the story.

For more practice, have children use the digital minilesson or use an Interactive Worktext Shared Read or Apprentice Leveled Reader from the week listed in the chart above.

POINT OF VIEW

RL.2.6

Literature

Unit and Week	Pages
Unit 5 Week 1	256–263
Unit 5 Week 2	266–273
Unit 6 Week 5	360–367

I Do Write and say: *Joe is sitting alone. "Do you want to play checkers with me?" a girl asks. "Sure!" Joe says, smiling at his new friend.* Say: *Remember, you can figure out a character's point of view by what the character says and does.* Underline the third sentence. Say: *I read that Joe says "Sure" and smiles at his new friend. So, I know that Joe's point of view is that he wants to play checkers.*

We Do Display and say: *Eve is playing soccer with her team. Her coach says he needs her to come out of the match. She doesn't want to. "Can I play for five more minutes?" Eve asks. "I think I can score a goal."* Say: *To find a character's point of view, we must look at what the character thinks and says. What does Eve do when her coach asks her to stop playing?* (She asks if she can play for five more minutes.) *What is Eve's point of view about coming out of the match?* (She doesn't want to.) *What is her coach's point of view?* (He thinks Eve should come out of the match.)

You Do Display: *Jan is eating lunch. She puts her fork down. "I don't like fish," Jan says. "I want to have pizza for lunch." "Oh, Jan," her dad says. "Fish is good for you."* Have partners ask each other questions to identify Jan and her dad's points of view.

For more practice, have children use the digital minilesson or use an Interactive Worktext Shared Read or Apprentice Leveled Reader from one of the weeks in the chart above.

PROBLEM AND SOLUTION

RI.2.3

Informational

Unit and Week	Pages
Unit 6 Week 4	350–357

I Do Write and say: *Sometimes your bike tire can go flat. You can a patch kit at the store. You can fix the hole in the tire with a patch. Then you can put air in the tire. Now you can ride your bike!* Say: *One way an author can present information is by writing about a problem and a solution. You can think about the problem and how it is solved to make connections in the text. What is the problem in the text?* Underline the first sentence. Write "problem." Say: *The problem your bike has a flat tire. What are the steps taken to try to solve the problem?* Circle the third and fourth sentences. Write "steps to solve the problem. *What is the solution? The solution is to fix the hole and put air in the tire.*

We Do Display: *People have to pay for electricity. Some people want to save money on this. One way to help is to turn out the lights when they leave a room. They can watch less TV. They can wear a sweater indoors during the winter. Now they are using less electricity and will save money.* Ask: *What is the problem?* (Some people save money on electricity.) *What is one step people can take to solve this problem?* (They can turn out the lights when they leave a room.) *Have children identify the other steps to solving the problem.* (Watch less TV; wear a sweater indoors during the winter.) *What is the solution to the problem?* (Find ways to use less electricity and save money.)

You Do Display: *If you sprain your ankle, it can be painful. First, you should sit down. Put your ankle up on a pillow. You can also put ice on the ankle. These things can stop the swelling. Your ankle will not hurt as much.* Guide partners to work together to identify the problem, steps to solving the problem, and the solution.

For more practice, have children use the digital minilesson or use an Interactive Worktext Shared Read or Apprentice Leveled Reader from the week listed in the chart above.

PROBLEM AND SOLUTION

RL.2.3 RL.2.5

Literature

Unit and Week	Pages
Unit 2 Week 2	80–87
Unit 5 Week 4	288–295

I Do Write and say: *Sue and Abe want to buy a new board game. They don't have enough money to pay for the game. Sue and Abe ask Grandma to help them earn the money. Grandma lets Sue and Abe rake her leaves to earn the money.* Ask: *What problem do Sue and Abe have?* Circle "They don't have enough money to pay for the game." Ask: *What step do Sue and Abe take to solve their problem?* Circle "Sue and Abe ask Grandma to help them earn the money." Say: *How does Grandma help Sue and Abe solve their problem?* Circle "Grandma lets Sue and Abe rake her leaves to earn the money."

We Do Display and say: *Dev finds a backpack in the lunch room. The backpack belongs to someone else. Dev thinks about what she should do. Dev decides to bring the backpack to the Lost and Found.* Ask: *What problem does Dev face in this story?* (The backpack belongs to someone else.) *How does Dev solve this problem?* (Dev brings the backpack to the Lost and Found.)

You Do Display: *Kat is at the movies with her dad. She finds a seat where she can see the screen. A tall man sits in front of Kat. Now Kat cannot see the screen. Her dad tells Kat he will switch seats with her. Kat agrees to switch seats.* Guide one partner to ask a question about the problem or solution and the other partner to respond with details that answers it.

For more practice, have children use the digital minilesson or use an Interactive Worktext Shared Read or Apprentice Leveled Reader from one of the weeks in the chart above.

Unit and Week	Pages
Unit 3 Week 2	142–149

Unit and Week	Pages
Unit 5 Week 3	276–283

I Do Display and read aloud: *Karl wants to make lemonade. First, he squeezes the lemons and saves the juice. Next, he adds sugar. Then, Karl mixes them with water. At last, Karl has tasty lemonade.* Say: *The sequence is the order of the key events in a story. I know that words such as* first, next, then, *and* last *can help tell the order of what happens in a story.* Ask: *What happens first in the story?* Circle "he squeezes the lemons and saves the juice," and write *first. The word* first *tells me that this is the first thing to happen.* Ask: *What even happens next?* Circle "Next, he adds sugar," and write *next.* Continue with the remaining events.

We Do Display and say: *First Ben wakes up. Next, he brushes his teeth. Then, he goes downstairs for breakfast. Finally, he makes a bowl of cereal.* Ask: *What is the first event that happens?* (Ben wakes up.) *What clue word helps tell what the order of this event in the story?* (First) *What clue word tells what happens at the end of story?* (Finally)

You Do Display: *Cara jumped into the snow. First she rolled around in the snow. Next she threw handfuls of snow into the wind. Then, she made big snow balls. Last she shook off the snow from her coat.* Guide one partner to ask the other to identify the story's sequence of events. Have partners discuss the clue words to the sequence of events.

For more practice, have children use the digital minilesson or use an Interactive Worktext Shared Read or Apprentice Leveled Reader from the week listed in the chart above.

I Do Display and read aloud: *Anna made a vinegar volcano. First, she put a cup on newspaper. Next, she poured vinegar in the cup. Then, she added some baking soda. The last thing that happened was bubbles began to fizz up. It worked!* Say: *Sequence is the order in which events happen. Readers can think about a sequence of events to understand how events are connected. Words such as* first, then, next, *and* last *can help show when events happened.* Ask: *What did Anna do first?* Circle "she put a cup on newspaper," and underline *First.* Ask: *What event happens next?* Circle "she poured vinegar in the cup," and underline *Next.* Continue with the remaining events.

We Do Display and say: *First, Lee marked the space for his garden. Then he dug up the land. Next, he planted the seeds. The last thing Lee did was water the seeds.* Ask: *What is the first thing Lee did?* (marked the space for a garden) *What sequence word helps you understand this?* (First) *What sequence word tells what Lee does at the end of the selection?* (last)

You Do Display: *Rosa wanted to see if oil and water would mix. First, she put some water and cooking oil in a bottle. Then, she screwed on the lid and shook the bottle. Next she sat the bottle down and waited. At last the oil floated to the top. Oil and water do not mix!* Guide one partner to ask the other to identify the selection's sequence of events. Have partners discuss the sequence words that helped show how the events are connected.

For more practice, have children use the digital minilesson or use an Interactive Worktext Shared Read or Apprentice Leveled Reader from the week listed in the chart above.

THEME

RL.2.2 CCSS

Literature

Unit and Week	Pages
Unit 4 Week 4	226–233
Unit 4 Week 5	236–243
Unit 6 Week 1	318–325

For more practice, have children use the digital minilesson or use an Interactive Worktext Shared Read or Apprentice Leveled Reader from one of the weeks in the chart above.

I Do Display and read aloud: *Dre has a lot to do, but Nan asked Dre to come to her play. Dre ran home to eat dinner. He cleaned the dishes. He did his homework. Dre did not want to miss his friend's play. Dre hurried and made it on time. At then end, he clapped and clapped.* Say: *I can use the key details to figure out the theme. I read that Dre has many things to do, but he tries hard to see Nan's play.* Underline the first sentence and write, "key details." Say: *The last sentences tell me that Dre cares about his friend Nan.* Underline the last two sentences and write, "key details." Say: *When I think about these details, I can come up with the theme: Dre cares about his friend Nan.*

We Do Display and say: *Bree's little brother left for school in a hurry. He forgot to water his plant. Bree knew that the plant was special to his brother. Bree watered the plant for him. Bree wanted to do a nice thing. Bree's little brother came home and thanked Bree.* Say: *To find the theme, we must look for the key details. What does Bree do for her brother?* (water his plant) *Why does Bree do this for her brother?* (Bree wanted to be nice.)

You Do Display: *Lex likes to play with his soccer ball outside. Lex was kicking it in his yard. But he quickly got bored. He wished he had a friend to play with. Then he saw Sara sitting alone. Lex asked Sara to kick the ball with him. They had fun playing soccer together.* Have partners look at the characters' actions and what they say and do to come up with the theme of the story.

INFORM/EXPLAIN

W.2.2   W.2.5   W.4.9   CCSS

Unit and Week	Pages
U1W1	14–15
U1W2	24–25
U1W3	34–35
U1W5	56–57
U2W1	74–75
U2W2	84–85
U2W3	94–95
U2W5	116–117
U3W1	134–135
U3W2	144–145
U3W3	154–155
U3W5	176–177
U4W1	194–195
U4W2	204–205
U4W3	214–215
U4W4	226–227
U5W1	254–255
U5W2	264–265
U5W4	286–287
U5W5	296–297
U6W1	314–415
U6W2	324–325
U6W4	346–347

Review an Analysis

- Have children turn to a student model of an analysis that informs and explains in the **Interactive Worktext**. Read aloud the student model while children follow along.

- Explain to children that in this analysis the student informs and explains how an author developed the text. Point to the first sentence and identify the key details from the text. Then work with children to identify the key details in the remaining sentences. Point out how the details support the topic.

- Read aloud the last sentence. Have children turn to a partner and answer the questions: *What does this student explain about the text?*

Revise an Analysis

Revise Writing Work with children to select a writing product that they completed in Weeks 1–5 that would benefit from revision. Review with children the writing you selected and the related **Interactive Worktext** lesson. Discuss the writing selection and the checklist of items that the selection should include.

Guide children to check that their writing includes details from the selection. Have children identify whether or not the details support the topic. Remind children to include details from the beginning, middle and end of the selection.

Guide children to determine how best to revise their writing. Work with them to add or improve the elements that they found were missing or in need of work. Have children revise the writing based on their review.

Teacher Conference Compare children' revision to their original writing. Check children' writing for complete sentences. Did they cite text evidence to support their topic?

OPINION

W.2.1 W.2.5 W.4.9 CCSS

Unit and Week	Pages
U1W4	46–47
U2W4	106–107
U3W4	166–167
U4W5	236–237
U5W3	274–275
U6W3	334–335
U6W5	356–357

Review an Analysis

- Have children turn to a student model of an analysis that shares an opinion in the **Interactive Worktext**. Read aloud the student model while children follow along.

- Explain to children that in this analysis the student gives an opinion about the text. Point out opinion words, such as *I think, I like,* and *good/bad.* Have children point out facts, details, quotations, and other text evidence that support the student's opinion.

Revise an Analysis

Revise Writing Work with children to select a writing product that they completed in Weeks 1–5 that would benefit from revision. Review with children the writing you selected and the related **Interactive Worktext** lesson. Discuss the writing selection and the checklist of items that the selection should include.

Guide children to check that their writing begins with a topic sentence and that it includes the title of the selection. Have children identify whether or not the writing includes details from the text that support their opinion. Remind children to include details from the text.

Guide children to determine how best to revise their writing. Work with them to add or improve the elements that they found were missing or in need of work. Have children revise the writing based on their review.

Teacher Conference Compare children' revision to their original writing. Check children' writing for complete sentences. Did they include an opinion? Did they cite text evidence to support their opinion?

Writing Rubric

	4	3	2	1
Text Evidence	Includes three or more details from the text.	Includes two or more details from the text.	Includes only one detail from the text.	No text evidence was included.
Writing Style	Writes in complete sentences. Uses correct spelling and grammar.	Uses complete sentences. Writing has spelling and grammar errors.	Few complete sentences. There are many spelling and grammar errors.	Writing is not accurate or in complete sentences.

Intonation

RF.2.4a,
RF.2.4b

Objective **Read statements, questions, and exclamations in connected text**

I Do Explain that good readers change their voices to show what sentences mean. Tell children that they should read different types of sentences differently. Write these sentences on the board.

> *We go to the park. Where is the park? We love the park!* Read them in a flat monotone.

Then model reading each sentence with proper intonation. Explain how you decided to read each sentence differently. Model circling the punctuation in each sentence. Remind children that a sentence that ends with a period is read in a steady way. In a sentence that ends in a question mark, you raise your voice at the end. A sentence that ends with an exclamation point is read with strong feeling or excitement.

We Do Distribute the reading passage on **Practice**, page 30, from the [Foundational Skills Kit Phonics Practice Book or any other passage from the Practice Book]. As a group, circle and name the punctuation mark at the end of each sentence. Have the children tell how each sentence should be read. Provide corrective feedback.

Read aloud the passage and create a summary with the group. Point out how reading different types of sentences with proper expression helps readers understand the passage. Read aloud the passage again.

Use the Echo Read Routine on Fluency Card 5 [in the Foundational Skills Kit] and have children echo read the passage. Have children lead while you respond. Ask children to say how they read each phrase or sentence before you repeat it. Prompt them with this question each time it is your turn: How should I change my voice when I read this sentence?

Corrective Feedback Have partners practice reading the passage aloud to each other, focusing on reading sentences with correct intonation.

Have partners discuss the comprehension questions at the end of the passage. Then discuss the questions as a group.

Corrective Feedback Provide corrective feedback for errors in intonation, as well as errors in pronunciation. Point out the child's error and model reading the sentence or word correctly. Then have the child read the sentence or word again.

RF.2.4a,
RF.2.4b

Expression

Objective **Understand how to read dialogue with expression**

I Do Explain to children that a conversation that is written down is called *dialogue.* Say: When dialogue is read aloud, good readers use their voices to sound like the character who is speaking. They express the same feeling as the character. Ask children to listen as you pretend to be helping someone in a store:

> *"Can I help you? The greeting cards are against the wall. Let me know if you need anything else."*

Explain that if the words you just said were written down, they would be called dialogue. Tell children that there are special ways of writing dialogue so readers know who said which part of the conversation and how they sounded when they said those words. Write the sentences below. Model reading each sentence aloud.

> *"Sarah, did you practice for the soccer game?" John asked.*

> *"Yes, I practiced kicking all day long!" Sarah said.*

Circle all the quotation marks. Quotation marks show where someone's exact words begin and end. Reread just the spoken words.

Underline words that aren't enclosed in quotation marks. These words tell who is speaking. They may also tell how the speaker says the words.

Circle the punctuation marks inside the quotation marks. These marks help you know whether to ask a question, make a statement, or show strong feeling. Reread the spoken words, using your voice to indicate sentence changes.

We Do Distribute the passage on **Practice**, page 66. Guide children in circling the dialogue. Then have them underline the words that tells who is speaking. Next, have children echo read the passage with you.

You Do Have children partner-read the passage, reviewing the circled dialogue and underlined words. Remind children to read the dialogue as if they are the characters in the story. Have them alternate reading the other sentences.

Corrective Feedback Provide corrective feedback about reading dialogue. Point out the child's error and model reading the sentence correctly. Have the child read the sentence again.

Phrasing

RF.2.4a, RF.2.4b

Objective Demonstrate how to pause at commas and at the end of sentences, using the appropriate expression and intonation

Explain to children that good readers pause at the end of a sentence as they read aloud. The punctuation marks at the end of sentences tell readers how to change their voice for different kinds of sentences.

Write a **period (.)** on the board: A period tells readers to pause at the end of a sentence. Display these sentences: *The goat kicked the can. Then it began to talk.*

Model reading the sentences aloud, pausing at the end of each sentence. Point to each period as you pause.

Write a **question mark (?)** on the board. A question mark tells readers to raise their voice at the end of the question and then pause. Change the periods to question marks on the sentences you just wrote. Then model reading each sentence aloud, raising your voice and then pausing. Point to each question mark as you do so. *The goat kicked the can? Then it began to talk?*

Write an **exclamation point (!)** on the board. An exclamation point tells readers to read the sentence with strong feeling and then pause. Change the question marks to exclamation points on the sentences you wrote. Then model reading each sentence aloud, showing strong feeling and then pausing. Point to each exclamation mark. *The goat kicked the can! Then it began to talk!*

Write a **comma (,)** on the board. A comma tells readers to pause for a short amount of time. A comma can separate two parts of a sentence or items in a list. It is also used in dialogue. Display these sentences. *My cat has a gray coat, but she has white paws. I ate a peach, a pear, and an apple. "Thanks," said Mom.* Circle the comma in each sentence. Model reading the sentences aloud, pausing at and pointing to the commas.

We Do Distribute **Practice**, page 72. Guide children in circling the punctuation mark at the end of each sentence and to underline any commas. Then model reading one sentence at a time as children echo read after you. Repeat lines as needed. Then read the passage chorally with children.

You Do Have children practice partner reading the passage. Have them take turns reading the passage aloud, pausing at the end of each sentence. Remind them to use the appropriate expression and intonation for a period, an exclamation point, or a question mark.

Corrective Feedback Provide corrective feedback for correct intonation of punctuation marks. Point out the student's error and model reading the sentence correctly. Have the children repeat the sentence.

Rate

**RF.2.4a,
RF.2.4b**

Objective Identify and demonstrate when to slow down reading

I Do Explain to children that good readers slow down their pace of reading when the content is difficult. Explain that it is easier to think carefully about what you read when you read more slowly. Point out that it is helpful to slow down when reading nonfiction books or articles about science or social studies. When you slow down, you can pay attention to difficult vocabulary and complicated ideas.

Explain that a good reader must decide how and when to slow down reading.

- Is the text nonfiction? Is it about a social studies or science topic?
- Does the text have long words or unfamiliar vocabulary?
- Does the text have new ideas that you want to understand?

Read the following passage aloud. Guide children in recognizing that this is a nonfiction passage with technical words. Read it slowly and clearly. Think aloud as you encounter technical vocabulary by saying: I wonder what that means. I'm going to keep reading to find out.

> *A shooting star is a meteor. A meteor is a space rock. If the meteor lands on Earth, it is called a meteorite. The bright streak of a shooting star is hot glowing air. It is made from the heat of a meteor as it speeds through Earth's atmosphere.*

We Do Distribute **Practice**, page 63. Tell children that this is a nonfiction passage, so they should look for unfamiliar words. Model read the passage aloud at a slow pace. Help children understand that reading slowly will help them remember facts. Then do a choral reading with children.

You Do Have children partner-read the passage. Ask them to take turns reading the passage aloud. Have children discuss the comprehension questions. Then discuss the questions as a group.

Corrective Feedback Provide corrective feedback on slowing down to understand new words and text. Point out the child's error and model reading the sentence correctly. Have the child repeat the sentence.

Accuracy

RF.2.4a, RF.2.4b

Objective **Pronounce words with accuracy and fluency**

I Do Explain to children that when reading aloud, good readers pronounce each word clearly and correctly so their readers will not be confused.

Tell student to listen for a mistake as you say this sentence: *My mother said, "I am making (mumble, mumble).* Say: The way I read this sentence was confusing because you couldn't hear all the words.

Tell children to listen as you read this sentence: *The wee-ther is cold today.* Say: The way I read this sentence was confusing because I didn't pronounce all the words correctly. Point to the word *weather*. I should have pronounced that word /WETHer/, not /WEETHer/. Then you would have understood me.

Write the sentence below and model reading it two or three times, each time with clearer and more correct pronunciation of the words *wind* and *sky*. Then ask children to read the sentence, pronouncing each word clearly and correctly.

> *The wind blew the kite across the sky.*

We Do Distribute the passage on **Practice**, page 129 (or any other passage in the Practice Book). Model reading the passage aloud. Point out how you are reading every word clearly and correctly.

Then use the Echo Read Routine on Fluency Card 1. Read one sentence at a time and have children echo read it. Remind them to pronounce words clearly and correctly. Provide corrective feedback.

You Do Have partners echo read the passage aloud to each other. Tell children to let their partners know if they did not understand a word that was read.

Have partners discuss the comprehension questions at the end of the passage. Then discuss the questions as a group.

Corrective Feedback Provide corrective feedback for errors in pronunciation. Point out the child's error and model reading the sentence correctly. Have the child read the sentences again.

Text Complexity

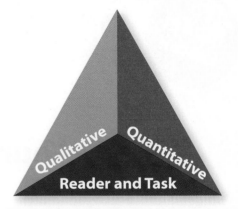

Qualitative   Quantitative

Reader and Task

Quantitative Measures

Two tools have been used to determine the quantitative dimension of text complexity for texts in *Reading WonderWorks*.

- **Lexile**

- (ETS) *Text Evaluator*™ measures more explicit feature of text
  - —Connection of Ideas
  - —Vocabulary
  - —Sentence Structure
  - —Organization

Reading WonderWorks provides complex texts for Grade 2 intervention students at their level and accelerates students into the Grades 2–3 text complexity band (as defined by the Common Core State Standards) by the end of the year. This allows them to exit the *Reading Wonders* Approaching group by the end of Grade 2.

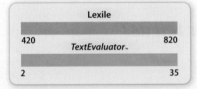

Text Complexity Range for Grades 2–3

Lexile	
420	820

TextEvaluator™	
2	35

Qualitative Measures

Specific aspects of the qualitative dimensions of text complexity are identified. Scaffolded instruction is provided to help students access these features of the text.

- Structure
  - —**Organization**
  - —**Genre**
- Language Conventionality and Clarity
  - —**Vocabulary**
  - —**Sentence Structure**
- Knowledge Demands
  - —**Prior Knowledge**
- Levels of Meaning/Purpose
  - —**Purpose**
  - —**Connection of Ideas**

Reader and Tasks

Readers' engagement and knowledge of the concept will influence the complexity of a text. In addition, the questions and tasks applied to a text will affect the complexity.

Model Lesson

Use Your Own Text

Get Ready

Choose your own text

- Use this lesson with a text of your choice.
- Assign reading of the text. You may wish to do this by section or chapters.
- Chunk the text into shorter important passages for rereading.
- Present an Essential Question.

Read the Text   *What does the author tell us?*

Assign the Reading

Ask children to read the assigned sections of the text independently. For sections that are more difficult for children, you may wish to read the text aloud or ask children to read with a partner.

Take Notes

As children read, ask them to take notes on difficult parts of the text. Model how to take notes on

- identifying details or parts that are unclear
- words they do not know
- information they feel is important
- ways in which information or events are connected
- the genre of the text

You may wish to have children complete a graphic organizer, chosen from within the unit, to take notes on important information as they read. The graphic organizer can help them summarize the text.

Help children access the complex features of the text. Scaffold instruction on the following features as necessary:

- Purpose
- Genre
- Vocabulary
- Sentence Structure

- Connection of Ideas
- Organization
- Prior Knowledge

Reread the Text *What does the text mean?*

Ask Text-Dependent Questions/Generate Questions

 Ask children to reread the shorter passages from the text, focusing on how the author provides information or develops the characters, setting, and plot. Focus questions on the following:

Literature Selections	**Informational Text**
Character, Setting, and Plot Development	Main Idea and Supporting Key Details
Word Choice	Word Choice
Genre	Text Structure
Point of View	Text Features
	Genre

Have children discuss questions they generated. As each child shares a question, ask all children to go back into the text to find text evidence to answer the question. Encourage children to

- point out the exact place within the text they found the evidence
- reread and paraphrase the section of the text that they think supports their answer
- discuss how well the cited evidence answers the question
- identify when an answer to a question cannot be found in the text

Write About the Text *Think about what the author wrote.*

Essential Question

Have children respond in writing to the Essential Question, considering the complete text. Children can work with a partner and use their notes and graphic organizers to locate evidence that can be used to answer the question.

Making the Most o
Collaborative Conversations

The Common Core State Standards state that students must have ample opportunities to take part in a variety of rich, structured conversations—as part of a whole class, in small groups, and with a partner.

Students should practice using the prompt and response frames below for collaborative conversations with partners until the frames become routine.

Core Skills	Prompt Frames	Response Frames
Elaborate and Ask Questions to Request Clarification	Can you tell me more about it? Can you give some details on…? Can you be more specific? What do you mean by…? How/Why is that important?	I think it means that… In other words… It's important because… It's similar to when…
Support Ideas with Text Evidence	What do you think of the idea that…? Can we add to this idea? Do you agree? What are other ideas /points of view? What else do we need to think about? How does that connect to the idea…?	The text says that… An example from another text is… According to… Some evidence that supports that is…
Build On and/or Challenge Partner's Idea	What do we know so far? To recap, I think that… I'm not sure that was clear. How can we relate what I said to the topic/question?	I would add that… I want to follow up on your idea… Another way to look at it is… What you said made me think of….
Paraphrase	What have we discussed so far? How can we summarize what we talked about? What can we agree upon? What are the main points or ideas we can share? What relevant details support the main points or ideas? What key ideas can we take away?	So, you are saying that… Let me see if I understand you… Do you mean that…? In other words… It sounds like you are saying that…
Determine the Main Idea and Supporting Details	What have we discussed so far? How can we summarize what we talked about? What can we agree upon? What are the main points or ideas we can share? What relevant details support the main points or ideas? What key ideas can we take away?	We can say that… The main idea seems to be… As a result of this conversation, we think that we should… The evidence suggests that…

Understanding English Language Learner Levels

The **English language learners** in your classroom have a variety of backgrounds. Each student has differences in ethnic background, first language, socioeconomic status, quality of prior schooling, and levels of language proficiency. In addition, English language learners bring diverse sets of academic knowledge and cultural perspectives that should be respected and leveraged to enrich learning.

Many English language learners bring oral language proficiency, literacy knowledge, and skills in their first languages that can be used to facilitate language and literacy development in English. It is important to note that students may be at different levels in each language domain (listening, speaking, reading, and writing). Systematic, explicit, and appropriately-scaffolded instruction help English language learners attain English proficiency and meet the high expectations defined in the Common Core State Standards.

Beginning

This level of language proficiency is often referred to as the "silent" stage, in which students' receptive skills are engaged. It is important that teachers and peers respect a language learner's initial silence or allow the student to respond in his or her native language. It is often difficult for teachers to identify the level of cognitive development at this stage, due to the limited proficiency in the second language.

Beginning students require significant language support in their early stages of language development. As they gain experience with English, support may become moderate or light for familiar tasks and topics.

The Beginning Student...

- recognizes English phonemes that correspond to phonemes produced in primary language;
- initially demonstrates more receptive than productive English skills;
- communicates basic needs and information in social and academic settings using gestures, learned words or phrases, and/or short sentences;
- follows one- or two-step oral directions;
- answers *wh-* questions (who, what, when, where, why, which);
- comprehends words, phrases, and basic information about familiar topics as presented through stories and conversations
- identifies concepts about print and text features;
- reads short grade-appropriate text with familiar vocabulary and simple sentences, supported by graphics or pictures;
- draws pictures and writes labels;
- expresses ideas using visuals and short responses;
- uses familiar vocabulary related to everyday and academic topics.

Intermediate

Students at this level begin to tailor their English language skills to meet communication and learning demands with increasing accuracy. They possess knowledge of vocabulary and grammatical structures that allow them to more fully participate in classroom activities and discussions. They are generally more comfortable producing both spoken and written language.

Intermediate students require moderate support for cognitively demanding activities and light support for familiar tasks and topics.

The Intermediate Student...

- pronounces most English phonemes correctly while reading aloud;
- communicates more complex personal needs, ideas, and opinions using increasingly complex vocabulary and sentences;
- follows multi-step oral directions;
- initiates and participates in collaborative conversations about social and academic topics, with support as needed;
- asks questions, retells stories or events, and comprehends basic content-area concepts;
- comprehends information on familiar and unfamiliar topics with contextual clues;
- reads increasingly complex grade-level text supported by graphics, pictures, and context clues;
- increases correct usage of written and oral language conventions;
- uses vocabulary learned, including academic language, to provide information and extended responses in contextualized oral and written prompts.

Advanced

Students at this level possess vocabulary and grammar structures that approach those of an English-proficient speaker. Advanced students demonstrate consistent general comprehension of grade-level content. They engage in complex social and academic activities.

While the English language proficiency of these students is advanced, some language support for accessing content is still necessary.

The Advanced Student...

- applies knowledge of common English morphemes in oral and silent reading;
- communicates complex feelings, needs, ideas, and opinions using increasingly complex vocabulary and sentences;
- understands more nonliteral social and academic language about concrete and abstract topics;
- initiates and sustains collaborative conversations about grade-level academic and social topics;
- reads and comprehends a wide range of complex literature and informational texts at grade level;
- writes using more standard forms of English on various academic topics;
- communicates orally and in writing with fewer grammatical errors;
- tailors language, orally and in writing, to specific purposes and audiences.

Facilitating Language Growth

Beginning

Student's Behaviors	Teacher's Behaviors	Questioning Techniques
• Points to or provides other nonverbal responses • Actively listens and responds to one- or two-step oral directions, especially commands • Initially, understands more than he or she can produce • Begins speaking in one- or two-word utterances, expanding to short phrases and simple sentences • Reads short grade-appropriate text with scaffolds • Draws pictures and writes labels	• Gestures • Focuses on conveying meanings and vocabulary development • Does not force students to speak right away (allows silent period) • Shows visuals and real objects • Writes words for students to see • Pairs students with more proficient learners • Provides speaking and writing frames and models • Asks *yes/no* and *either/or* questions	• Point to the _____. • Find the _____. • Put the _____ next to the _____. • Do you have the _____? • Is this the _____? • Who wants the _____? • Yes/no (Did you like the story?) • Either/or (Is this fiction or nonfiction?) • Short response *wh-* questions (Why did the dog hide?)

Intermediate

Student's Behaviors	Teacher's Behaviors	Questioning Techniques
• Produces increasingly complex sentences • Listens with greater understanding • Asks questions and retells stories or events • Reads increasingly complex grade-level text with scaffolds • Produces short written responses, including academic language	• Asks higher-order questions with one-word answers • Models correct responses • Ensures supportive, low-anxiety environment • Does not overtly call attention to grammar errors • Asks short *wh-* questions • Asks open-ended questions that stimulate language production	• General questions that encourage lists of words (What words describe the main character?) • Tell me about _____. • Talk about _____. • Describe _____. • How do you know? • Why? Why not?

Advanced

Student's Behaviors	Teacher's Behaviors	Questioning Techniques
• Participates in complex reading and writing activities • Demonstrates increased levels of accuracy and is able to produce language with varied grammatical structures and academic language • May need support in abstract, cognitively demanding subjects	• Fosters conceptual development and expanded literacy through content • Continues to make lessons comprehensible and interactive • Teaches critical thinking skills • Continues to be alert to individual differences in language and culture	• What is this selection about? • What does this character think? How do you know? • Compare/contrast _____. How are these similar/different? • Why do you think that_____? Yes, tell me more about _____. • Do you agree with the author's point of view? Why/why not?

ELL Collaborative Conversations

Strategies for English Language Learners

One of the most effective ways in which to increase the oral language proficiency of your English language learners is to give students many opportunities to do a lot of talking in the classroom. Providing the opportunities and welcoming all levels of participation will motivate students to take part in the class discussions. You can employ a few basic teaching strategies that will encourage the participation of all language proficiency levels of English language learners in whole class and small group discussions.

☑ Wait/Different Responses

- Be sure to give students enough time to answer the question.

- Let students know that they can respond in different ways depending on their levels of proficiency. Students can

    - answer in their native language;

    - ask a more proficient ELL speaker to repeat the answer in English;

    - answer with nonverbal cues (pointing to related objects, drawing, or acting out).

> **Teacher:** Where is Charlotte?
>
> **ELL Response:** (Student points to the web in the corner of the barn.)
>
> **Teacher:** Yes. Charlotte is sitting in her web. Let's all point to Charlotte.

☑ Repeat

- Give positive confirmation to the answers that each English language learner offers. If the response is correct, repeat what the student has said in a clear voice and at a slower pace. This validation will motivate other ELLs to participate.

> **Teacher:** How would you describe the faces of the bobcats?
>
> **ELL Response:** They look scared.
>
> **Teacher:** That's right, Silvia. They are scared. Everyone show me your scared face.

☑ Revise for Form

- Repeating an answer allows you to model the proper form for a response. You can model how to answer in full sentences and use academic language.

- When you repeat the answer, correct any grammar or pronunciation errors.

> **Teacher:** Who are the main characters in the story *Zathura*?
>
> **ELL Response:** Danny and Walter is.
>
> **Teacher:** Yes. Danny and Walter <u>are</u> the main characters. Remember to use the verb <u>are</u> when you are telling about more than one person. Let's repeat the sentence.
>
> **All:** Danny and Walter <u>are</u> the main characters.

☑ Clarify for Meaning

- Repeating an answer offers an opportunity to clarify the meaning of a response.

> **Teacher:** Where did the golden feather come from?
>
> **ELL Response:** The bird.
>
> **Teacher:** That's right. The golden feather came from the Firebird.

☑ Elaborate

- If students give a one-word answer or a nonverbal cue, elaborate on the answer to encourage multiple exchanges and model fluent speaking and grammatical patterns.

- Provide more examples or repeat the answer using proper academic language.

> **Teacher:** Why is the girls' mother standing with her hands on her hips?
>
> **ELL Response:** She is mad.
>
> **Teacher:** Can you tell me more? Why is she mad?
>
> **ELL Response:** Because the girls are late.
>
> **Teacher:** Ok. What do you think the girls will do?
>
> **ELL Response:** They will promise not to be late again.
>
> **Teacher:** Anyone else have an idea?

☑ Ask Questions about Key Details

- Prompt students to give a more comprehensive response by asking additional questions or guiding them to get to an answer.

> **Teacher:** Listen as I read the caption under the photograph. What information does the caption tell us?
>
> **ELL Response:** It tells about the butterfly.
>
> **Teacher:** What did you find out about the butterfly?
>
> **ELL Response:** It drinks nectar.
>
> **Teacher:** Yes. The butterfly drinks nectar from the flower.

Making the Most of Collaborative Conversations

Use all the speaking and listening opportunities in your classroom to observe students' oral language proficiency.

- Response to oral presentations
- Responding to text aloud
- Following directions
- Small group work
- Informal, social peer discussions
- One-on-one conferences

Scope & Sequence

	K	1	2	3	4	5	6
READING PROCESS							
Concepts About Print/Print Awareness							
Understand directionality (top to bottom; tracking print from left to right; return sweep, page by page)	✔						
Locate printed word on page	✔						
Develop print awareness (concept of letter, word, sentence)	✔						
Identify separate sounds in a spoken sentence	✔						
Understand that written words are represented in written language by a specific sequence of letters	✔						
Distinguish between letters, words, and sentences	✔						
Identify and distinguish paragraphs							
Match print to speech (one-to-one correspondence)							
Name uppercase and lowercase letters	✔						
Phonological Awareness							
Recognize and understand alliteration							
Segment sentences into correct number of words							
Identify, blend, segment syllables in words		✔					
Recognize and generate rhyming words	✔	✔					
Identify, blend, segment onset and rime	✔	✔					
Phonemic Awareness							
Count phonemes	✔	✔					
Isolate initial, medial, and final sounds	✔	✔					
Blend spoken phonemes to form words	✔	✔					
Segment spoken words into phonemes	✔	✔					
Distinguish between long- and short-vowel sounds	✔	✔					
Manipulate phonemes (addition, deletion, substitution)	✔	✔					
Phonics and Decoding /Word Recognition							
Understand the alphabetic principle	✔	✔					
Sound/letter correspondence	✔	✔	✔	✔			
Blend sounds into words, including VC, CVC, CVCe, CVVC words	✔	✔	✔	✔	✔	✔	✔
Blend common word families	✔	✔	✔	✔			
Initial consonant blends		✔	✔	✔	✔	✔	✔
Final consonant blends		✔	✔	✔	✔	✔	✔
Initial and medial short vowels	✔	✔	✔	✔	✔	✔	✔

KEY

✔ = Assessed Skill

Tinted panels show skills, strategies, and other teaching opportunities.

	K	1	2	3	4	5	6
Decode one-syllable words in isolation and in context	✔	✔	✔	✔	✔	✔	✔
Decode multisyllabic words in isolation and in context using common syllabication patterns		✔	✔	✔	✔	✔	✔
Monitor accuracy of decoding							
Identify and read common high-frequency words, irregularly spelled words	✔	✔	✔	✔	✔	✔	✔
Identify and read compound words, contractions		✔	✔	✔	✔	✔	✔
Use knowledge of spelling patterns to identify syllables		✔	✔	✔	✔	✔	✔
Regular plurals		✔	✔	✔	✔	✔	✔
Long vowels (silent *e*, vowel teams)	✔	✔	✔	✔	✔	✔	✔
Vowel digraphs (variant vowels)		✔	✔	✔	✔	✔	✔
r-Controlled vowels		✔	✔	✔	✔	✔	✔
Hard/soft consonants		✔	✔	✔	✔	✔	✔
Initial consonant digraphs		✔	✔	✔	✔	✔	✔
Medial and final consonant digraphs		✔	✔	✔	✔	✔	✔
Vowel diphthongs		✔	✔	✔	✔	✔	✔
Identify and distinguish phonemes (initial, medial, final)	✔	✔	✔				
Silent letters		✔	✔	✔	✔	✔	✔
Schwa words				✔	✔	✔	✔
Inflectional endings		✔	✔	✔	✔	✔	✔
Triple-consonant clusters		✔	✔	✔	✔	✔	✔
Unfamiliar and complex word families				✔	✔	✔	✔
Structural Analysis/Word Analysis							
Common spelling patterns (word families)			✔	✔	✔	✔	✔
Common syllable patterns			✔	✔	✔	✔	✔
Inflectional endings			✔	✔	✔	✔	✔
Contractions			✔	✔	✔	✔	✔
Compound words			✔	✔	✔	✔	✔
Prefixes and suffixes			✔	✔	✔	✔	✔
Root or base words			✔	✔	✔	✔	✔
Comparatives and superlatives			✔	✔	✔	✔	✔
Greek and Latin roots			✔	✔	✔	✔	✔
Fluency							
Apply letter/sound knowledge to decode phonetically regular words accurately	✔	✔	✔	✔	✔	✔	✔
Recognize high-frequency and familiar words	✔	✔	✔	✔	✔	✔	✔
Read regularly on independent and instructional levels							
Read orally with fluency from familiar texts (choral, echo, partner)							
Use appropriate rate, expression, intonation, and phrasing		✔	✔	✔	✔	✔	✔
Read with automaticity (accurately and effortlessly)		✔	✔	✔	✔	✔	✔
Use punctuation cues in reading		✔	✔	✔	✔	✔	✔
Adjust reading rate to purpose, text difficulty, form, and style							

	K	1	2	3	4	5	6
Repeated readings							
Timed readings		✔	✔	✔	✔	✔	✔
Read with purpose and understanding		✔	✔	✔	✔	✔	✔
Read orally with accuracy		✔	✔	✔	✔	✔	✔
Use context to confirm or self-correct word recognition		✔	✔	✔	✔	✔	✔

READING LITERATURE

Comprehension Strategies and Skills

	K	1	2	3	4	5	6
Read literature from a broad range of genres, cultures, and periods			✔	✔	✔	✔	✔
Access complex text			✔	✔	✔	✔	✔
Build background							
Preview and predict							
Establish and adjust purpose for reading							
Evaluate citing evidence from the text							
Ask and answer questions			✔	✔	✔	✔	✔
Inferences and conclusions, citing evidence from the text			✔	✔	✔	✔	✔
Monitor/adjust comprehension including reread, reading rate, paraphrase							
Recount/Retell							
Summarize			✔	✔	✔	✔	✔
Story structure (beginning, middle, end)			✔	✔	✔	✔	✔
Make connections between and across texts				✔	✔	✔	✔
Point of view			✔	✔	✔	✔	✔
Author's purpose							
Cause and effect			✔	✔	✔	✔	✔
Compare and contrast (including character, setting, plot, topics)			✔	✔	✔	✔	✔
Classify and categorize			✔				
Literature vs informational text			✔				
Illustrations, using			✔	✔			
Theme, central message, moral, lesson			✔	✔	✔	✔	✔
Problem and solution (problem/resolution)			✔	✔	✔	✔	✔
Sequence of events			✔	✔	✔	✔	✔

Literary Elements

	K	1	2	3	4	5	6
Character			✔	✔	✔	✔	✔
Plot development/Events			✔	✔	✔	✔	✔
Setting			✔	✔	✔	✔	✔
Stanza				✔	✔	✔	✔
Alliteration						✔	✔
Assonance						✔	✔
Dialogue							
Foreshadowing						✔	✔
Flashback						✔	✔

	K	1	2	3	4	5	6
Descriptive and figurative language			✔	✔	✔	✔	✔
Imagery					✔	✔	✔
Meter					✔	✔	✔
Onomatopoeia							
Repetition			✔	✔	✔	✔	✔
Rhyme/rhyme schemes			✔	✔	✔	✔	✔
Rhythm			✔				
Sensory language							
Symbolism							

Write About Reading/Literary Response Discussions

	K	1	2	3	4	5	6
Reflect and respond to text citing text evidence			✔	✔	✔	✔	✔
Connect literary texts to other curriculum areas							
Identify cultural and historical elements of text							
Evaluate author's techniques, craft							
Analytical writing							
Interpret text ideas through writing, discussion, media, research							
Book report or review							
Locate, use, explain information from text features			✔	✔	✔	✔	✔
Organize information to show understanding of main idea through charts, mapping							
Cite text evidence			✔	✔	✔	✔	✔
Author's purpose/ Illustrator's purpose							

READING INFORMATIONAL TEXT

Comprehension Strategies and Skills

	K	1	2	3	4	5	6
Read informational text from a broad range of topics and cultures			✔	✔	✔	✔	✔
Access complex text			✔	✔	✔	✔	✔
Build background							
Preview and predict			✔				
Establish and adjust purpose for reading							
Evaluate citing evidence from the text							
Ask and answer questions			✔	✔	✔	✔	✔
Inferences and conclusions, citing evidence from the text			✔	✔	✔	✔	✔
Monitor and adjust comprehension including reread, adjust reading rate, paraphrase							
Recount/Retell							
Summarize			✔	✔	✔	✔	✔
Text structure			✔	✔	✔	✔	✔
Identify text features			✔	✔	✔	✔	✔
Make connections between and across texts			✔	✔	✔	✔	✔
Author's point of view					✔	✔	✔	✔

	K	1	2	3	4	5	6
Author's purpose			✔				
Cause and effect			✔	✔	✔	✔	✔
Compare and contrast			✔	✔	✔	✔	✔
Classify and categorize			✔				
Illustrations and photographs, using			✔	✔	✔	✔	✔
Instructions/directions (written and oral)			✔	✔	✔	✔	✔
Main idea and key details			✔	✔	✔	✔	✔
Persuasion, reasons and evidence to support points/persuasive techniques						✔	✔
Predictions, making/confirming							
Problem and solution			✔	✔	✔	✔	✔
Sequence, chronological order of events, time order, steps in a process			✔	✔	✔	✔	✔
Writing About Reading/Expository Critique Discussions							
Reflect and respond to text citing text evidence		✔	✔	✔	✔	✔	✔
Analytical writing							
Interpret text ideas through writing, discussion, media, research							
Locate, use, explain information from text features			✔	✔	✔	✔	✔
Organize information to show understanding of main idea through charts, mapping							
Cite text evidence			✔	✔	✔	✔	✔
Author's purpose/Illustrator's purpose							
Text Features							
Recognize and identify text and organizational features of nonfiction texts			✔	✔	✔	✔	✔
Captions and labels, headings, subheadings, endnotes, key words, bold print			✔	✔	✔	✔	✔
Graphics, including photographs, illustrations, maps, charts, diagrams, graphs, time lines			✔	✔	✔	✔	✔

WRITING

	K	1	2	3	4	5	6
Writer's Craft							
Relevant supporting evidence			✔	✔	✔	✔	✔
Strong opening, strong conclusion			✔	✔	✔	✔	✔
Beginning, middle, end; sequence			✔	✔	✔	✔	✔
Precise words, strong words, vary words							
Transition words				✔	✔	✔	✔
Select focus and organization			✔	✔	✔	✔	✔
Points and counterpoints/Opposing claims and counterarguments							
Use reference materials (online and print dictionary, thesaurus, encyclopedia)							
Writing Applications							
Writing about text			✔	✔	✔	✔	✔
Analytical writing			✔	✔	✔	✔	✔
Penmanship/Handwriting							
Write legibly in manuscript using correct formation, directionality, and spacing							

	K	1	2	3	4	5	6

SPEAKING AND LISTENING

Speaking

	K	1	2	3	4	5	6
Participate in classroom activities and discussions							
Build on others' talk in conversation, adding new ideas							
Come to discussion prepared							
Paraphrase portions of text read alone or information presented							
Stay on topic when speaking							
Use language appropriate to situation, purpose, and audience							
Use verbal communication in effective ways and improve expression in conventional language							
Retell a story, presentation, or spoken message by summarizing							
Use complete, coherent sentences							
Deliver presentations (narrative, summaries, research, persuasive); add visuals							
Speak audibly (accuracy, expression, volume, pitch, rate, phrasing, modulation, enunciation)							

Listening

	K	1	2	3	4	5	6
Determine the purpose for listening							
Give oral directions							
Develop oral language and concepts							
Listen openly, responsively, attentively, and critically							
Listen to identify the points a speaker makes							
Listen responsively to oral presentations (determine main idea and key details)							
Ask and answer relevant questions (for clarification to follow-up on ideas)							
Identify reasons and evidence presented by speaker							
Recall and interpret speakers' verbal/nonverbal messages, purposes, perspectives							

LANGUAGE

Vocabulary Acquisition and Use

	K	1	2	3	4	5	6
Develop oral vocabulary and choose words for effect							
Use academic language			✔	✔	✔	✔	✔
Identify persons, places, things, actions			✔	✔			
Determine or clarify the meaning of unknown words			✔	✔	✔	✔	✔
Synonyms, antonyms, and opposites			✔	✔	✔	✔	✔
Use context clues such as word, sentence, paragraph, definition, example, restatement, description, comparison, cause and effect			✔	✔	✔	✔	✔
Use word identification strategies			✔	✔	✔	✔	✔
Unfamiliar words			✔	✔	✔	✔	✔
Multiple-meaning words			✔	✔	✔	✔	✔
Compound words			✔	✔	✔	✔	✔
Words ending in -er and -est			✔	✔	✔	✔	✔

	K	1	2	3	4	5	6
Root words (base words)			✔	✔	✔	✔	✔
Prefixes and suffixes			✔	✔	✔	✔	✔
Greek and Latin affixes and roots			✔	✔	✔	✔	✔
Inflectional endings			✔	✔	✔	✔	✔
Use print and online reference sources for word meaning (dictionary, glossaries)			✔	✔	✔	✔	✔
Homographs				✔	✔	✔	✔
Homophones			✔	✔	✔	✔	✔
Contractions			✔	✔	✔	✔	✔
Figurative language such as metaphors, similes, personification			✔	✔	✔	✔	✔
Idioms, adages, proverbs, literal and nonliteral language			✔	✔	✔	✔	✔
Listen to, read, discuss familiar and unfamiliar challenging text							
Identify real-life connections between words and their use							
Use acquired words and phrases to convey precise ideas							
Use vocabulary to express spatial and temporal relationships							
Identify shades of meaning in related words							
Morphology				✔	✔	✔	✔

Conventions of Standard English/Grammar, Mechanics, and Usage

	K	1	2	3	4	5	6
Sentence concepts: statements, questions, exclamations, commands							
Pronouns							
Contractions							
Conjunctions							
Commas							
Question words							
Quotation marks							
Prepositions							

Spelling

	K	1	2	3	4	5	6
Write irregular, high-frequency words	✔	✔	✔	✔	✔	✔	✔
ABC order	✔	✔					
Write letters	✔	✔					
Words with short vowels	✔	✔	✔	✔	✔	✔	✔
Words with long vowels	✔	✔	✔	✔	✔	✔	✔
Words with digraphs, blends, consonant clusters, double consonants			✔	✔	✔	✔	✔
Words with vowel digraphs and ambiguous vowels			✔	✔	✔	✔	✔
Words with diphthongs			✔	✔	✔	✔	✔
Words with r-controlled vowels			✔	✔	✔	✔	✔
Use conventional spelling			✔	✔	✔	✔	✔
Words with silent letters			✔	✔	✔	✔	✔
Words with hard and soft letters			✔	✔	✔	✔	✔
Inflectional endings including plural, past tense, drop final e and double consonant when adding -ed and -ing, changing y to i			✔	✔	✔	✔	✔

	K	1	2	3	4	5	6
Compound words			✔	✔	✔	✔	✔
Homonyms/homophones			✔	✔	✔	✔	✔
Prefixes and suffixes			✔	✔	✔	✔	✔
Root and base words				✔	✔	✔	✔
Syllables: patterns, rules, closed, open				✔	✔	✔	✔
Words with Greek and Latin roots						✔	✔
Words with spelling patterns, word families		✔	✔	✔	✔	✔	✔

RESEARCH AND INQUIRY

Study Skills

	K	1	2	3	4	5	6
Directions: read, write, give, follow (includes technical directions)			✔	✔	✔	✔	✔
Evaluate directions for sequence and completeness							
Use parts of a book to locate information							
Interpret information from graphic aids			✔	✔	✔	✔	✔
Use graphic organizers to organize information and comprehend text			✔	✔	✔	✔	✔

Research Process

	K	1	2	3	4	5	6
Generate and revise topics and questions for research							
Narrow focus of research, set research goals							
Find and locate information using print and digital resources			✔	✔	✔	✔	✔
Record information systematically (note-taking, outlining, using technology)							
Evaluate reliability, credibility, usefulness of sources and information							
Use primary sources to obtain information							
Organize, synthesize, evaluate, and draw conclusions from information							
Participate in and present shared research							

Technology

	K	1	2	3	4	5	6
Use computer, Internet, and other technology resources to access information							

College and Career Readiness Anchor Standards for READING

The K–5 standards on the following pages define what students should understand and be able to do by the end of each grade. They correspond to the College and Career Readiness (CCR) anchor standards below by number. The CCR and grade-specific standards are necessary complements—the former providing broad standards, the latter providing additional specificity—that together define the skills and understandings that all students must demonstrate.

Key Ideas and Details

1. Read closely to determine what the text says explicitly and to make logical inferences from it; cite specific textual evidence when writing or speaking to support conclusions drawn from the text.

2. Determine central ideas or themes of a text and analyze their development; summarize the key supporting details and ideas.

3. Analyze how and why individuals, events, and ideas develop and interact over the course of a text.

Craft and Structure

4. Interpret words and phrases as they are used in a text, including determining technical, connotative, and figurative meanings, and analyze how specific word choices shape meaning or tone.

5. Analyze the structure of texts, including how specific sentences, paragraphs, and larger portions of the text (e.g., a section, chapter, scene, or stanza) relate to each other and the whole.

6. Assess how point of view or purpose shapes the content and style of a text.

Integration of Knowledge and Ideas

7. Integrate and evaluate content presented in diverse media and formats, including visually and quantitatively, as well as in words.*

8. Delineate and evaluate the argument and specific claims in a text, including the validity of the reasoning as well as the relevance and sufficiency of the evidence.

9. Analyze how two or more texts address similar themes or topics in order to build knowledge or to compare the approaches the authors take.

Range of Reading and Level of Text Complexity

10. Read and comprehend complex literary and informational texts independently and proficiently.

 **Common Core State Standards**

English Language Arts

Grade 2

Each standard is coded in the following manner:

Strand	Grade Level	Standard
RL	2	1

Reading Standards for Literature

Key Ideas and Details

RL.2.1	Ask and answer such questions as *who, what, where, when, why*, and *how* to demonstrate understanding of key details in a text.
RL.2.2	Recount stories, including fables and folktales from diverse cultures, and determine their central message, lesson, or moral.
RL.2.3	Describe how characters in a story respond to major events and challenges.

Craft and Structure

RL.2.4	Describe how words and phrases (e.g., regular beats, alliteration, rhymes, repeated lines) supply rhythm and meaning in a story, poem, or song.
RL.2.5	Describe the overall structure of a story, including describing how the beginning introduces the story and the ending concludes the action.
RL.2.6	Acknowledge differences in the points of view of characters, including by speaking in a different voice for each character when reading dialogue aloud.

Integration of Knowledge and Ideas

RL.2.7	Use information gained from the illustrations and words in a print or digital text to demonstrate understanding of its characters, setting, or plot.
RL.2.9	Compare and contrast two or more versions of the same story (e.g., Cinderella stories) by different authors or from different cultures.

Range of Reading and Level of Text Complexity

RL.2.10	By the end of the year, read and comprehend literature, including stories and poetry, in the grades 2–3 text complexity band proficiently, with scaffolding as needed at the high end of the range.

Reading Standards for Informational Text

Key Ideas and Details

RI.2.1	Ask and answer such questions as *who, what, where, when, why,* and *how* to demonstrate understanding of key details in a text.
RI.2.2	Identify the main topic of a multiparagraph text as well as the focus of specific paragraphs within the text.
RI.2.3	Describe the connection between a series of historical events, scientific ideas or concepts, or steps in technical procedures in a text.

Craft and Structure

RI.2.4	Determine the meaning of words and phrases in a text relevant to a *grade 2 topic or subject area.*
RI.2.5	Know and use various text features (e.g., captions, bold print, subheadings, glossaries, indexes, electronic menus, icons) to locate key facts or information in a text efficiently.
RI.2.6	Identify the main purpose of a text, including what the author wants to answer, explain, or describe.

Integration of Knowledge and Ideas

RI.2.7	Explain how specific images (e.g., a diagram showing how a machine works) contribute to and clarify a text.
RI.2.8	Describe how reasons support specific points the author makes in a text.
RI.2.9	Compare and contrast the most important points presented by two texts on the same topic.

Range of Reading and Level of Text Complexity

RI.2.10	By the end of year, read and comprehend informational texts, including history/social studies, science, and technical texts, in the grades 2–3 text complexity band proficiently, with scaffolding as needed at the high end of the range.

Reading Standards: Foundational Skills

Phonics and Word Recognition

RF.2.3	Know and apply grade-level phonics and word analysis skills in decoding words.
RF.2.3a	Distinguish long and short vowels when reading regularly spelled one-syllable words.
RF.2.3b	Know spelling-sound correspondences for additional common vowel teams.
RF.2.3c	Decode regularly spelled two-syllable words with long vowels.
RF.2.3d	Decode words with common prefixes and suffixes.
RF.2.3e	Identify words with inconsistent but common spelling-sound correspondences.
RF.2.3f	Recognize and read grade-appropriate irregularly spelled words.

Fluency

RF.2.4	Read with sufficient accuracy and fluency to support comprehension.
RF.2.4a	Read on-level text with purpose and understanding.
RF.2.4b	Read on-level text orally with accuracy, appropriate rate, and expression on successive readings.
RF.2.4c	Use context to confirm or self-correct word.

College and Career Readiness Anchor Standards for WRITING

The K–5 standards on the following pages define what students should understand and be able to do by the end of each grade. They correspond to the College and Career Readiness (CCR) anchor standards below by number. The CCR and grade-specific standards are necessary complements—the former providing broad standards, the latter providing additional specificity—that together define the skills and understandings that all students must demonstrate.

Text Types and Purposes

1. Write arguments to support claims in an analysis of substantive topics or texts, using valid reasoning and relevant and sufficient evidence.

2. Write informative/explanatory texts to examine and convey complex ideas and information clearly and accurately through the effective selection, organization, and analysis of content.

3. Write narratives to develop real or imagined experiences or events using effective technique, well-chosen details, and well-structured event sequences.

Production and Distribution of Writing

4. Produce clear and coherent writing in which the development, organization, and style are appropriate to task, purpose, and audience.

5. Develop and strengthen writing as needed by planning, revising, editing, rewriting, or trying a new approach.

6. Use technology, including the Internet, to produce and publish writing and to interact and collaborate with others.

Research to Build and Present Knowledge

7. Conduct short as well as more sustained research projects based on focused questions, demonstrating understanding of the subject under investigation.

8. Gather relevant information from multiple print and digital sources, assess the credibility and accuracy of each source, and integrate the information while avoiding plagiarism.

9. Draw evidence from literary or informational texts to support analysis, reflection, and research.

Range of Writing

10. Write routinely over extended time frames (time for research, reflection, and revision) and shorter time frames (a single sitting or a day or two) for a range of tasks, purposes, and audiences.

English Language Arts

Grade 2

Each standard is coded in the following manner:

Strand	Grade Level	Standard
W	2	1

Writing Standards

Text Types and Purposes

W.2.1	Write opinion pieces in which they introduce the topic or book they are writing about, state an opinion, supply reasons that support the opinion, use linking words (e.g., *because, and, also*) to connect opinion and reasons, and provide a concluding statement or section.
W.2.2	Write informative/explanatory texts in which they introduce a topic, use facts and definitions to develop points, and provide a concluding statement or section.
W.2.3	Write narratives in which they recount a well-elaborated event or short sequence of events, include details to describe actions, thoughts, and feelings, use temporal words to signal event order, and provide a sense of closure.

Production and Distribution of Writing

W.2.5	With guidance and support from adults and peers, focus on a topic and strengthen writing as needed by revising and editing.
W.2.6	With guidance and support from adults, use a variety of digital tools to produce and publish writing, including in collaboration with peers.

Research to Build and Present Knowledge

W.2.7	Participate in shared research and writing projects (e.g., read a number of books on a single topic to produce a report; record science observations).
W.2.8	Recall information from experiences or gather information from provided sources to answer a question.

College and Career Readiness Anchor Standards for SPEAKING AND LISTENING

The K–5 standards on the following pages define what students should understand and be able to do by the end of each grade. They correspond to the College and Career Readiness (CCR) anchor standards below by number. The CCR and grade-specific standards are necessary complements—the former providing broad standards, the latter providing additional specificity—that together define the skills and understandings that all students must demonstrate.

Comprehension and Collaboration

1. Prepare for and participate effectively in a range of conversations and collaborations with diverse partners, building on others' ideas and expressing their own clearly and persuasively.

2. Integrate and evaluate information presented in diverse media and formats, including visually, quantitatively, and orally.

3. Evaluate a speaker's point of view, reasoning, and use of evidence and rhetoric.

Presentation of Knowledge and Ideas

4. Present information, findings, and supporting evidence such that listeners can follow the line of reasoning and the organization, development, and style are appropriate to task, purpose, and audience.

5. Make strategic use of digital media and visual displays of data to express information and enhance understanding of presentations.

6. Adapt speech to a variety of contexts and communicative tasks, demonstrating command of formal English when indicated or appropriate.

 **Common Core State Standards**

English Language Arts

Grade 2

Each standard is coded in the following manner:

Strand	Grade Level	Standard
SL	2	1

Speaking and Listening Standards

Comprehension and Collaboration

SL.2.1	Participate in collaborative conversations with diverse partners *about grade 2 topics and texts* with peers and adults in small and larger groups.
SL.2.1a	Follow agreed-upon rules for discussions (e.g., gaining the floor in respectful ways, listening to others with care, speaking one at a time about the topics and texts under discussion).
SL.2.1b	Build on others' talk in conversations by linking their comments to the remarks of others.
SL.2.1c	Ask for clarification and further explanation as needed about the topics and texts under discussion.
SL.2.2	Recount or describe key ideas or details from a text read aloud or information presented orally or through other media.
SL.2.3	Ask and answer questions about what a speaker says in order to clarify comprehension, gather additional information, or deepen understanding of a topic or issue.

Presentation of Knowledge and Ideas

SL.2.4	Tell a story or recount an experience with appropriate facts and relevant, descriptive details, speaking audibly in coherent sentences.
SL.2.5	Create audio recordings of stories or poems; add drawings or other visual displays to stories or recounts of experiences when appropriate to clarify ideas, thoughts, and feelings.
SL.2.6	Produce complete sentences when appropriate to task and situation in order to provide requested detail or clarification.

College and Career Readiness Anchor Standards for
LANGUAGE

The K–5 standards on the following pages define what students should understand and be able to do by the end of each grade. They correspond to the College and Career Readiness (CCR) anchor standards below by number. The CCR and grade-specific standards are necessary complements—the former providing broad standards, the latter providing additional specificity—that together define the skills and understandings that all students must demonstrate.

Conventions of Standard English

1. Demonstrate command of the conventions of standard English grammar and usage when writing or speaking.

2. Demonstrate command of the conventions of standard English capitalization, punctuation, and spelling when writing.

Knowledge of Language

3. Apply knowledge of language to understand how language functions in different contexts, to make effective choices for meaning or style, and to comprehend more fully when reading or listening.

Vocabulary Acquisition and Use

4. Determine or clarify the meaning of unknown and multiple-meaning words and phrases by using context clues, analyzing meaningful word parts, and consulting general and specialized reference materials, as appropriate.

5. Demonstrate understanding of figurative language, word relationships, and nuances in word meanings.

6. Acquire and use accurately a range of general academic and domain-specific words and phrases sufficient for reading, writing, speaking, and listening at the college and career readiness level; demonstrate independence in gathering vocabulary knowledge when encountering an unknown term important to comprehension or expression.

Common Core State Standards

English Language Arts

Grade 2

Each standard is coded in the following manner:

Strand	Grade Level	Standard
L	2	1

Language Standards

Conventions of Standard English

L.2.1	Demonstrate command of the conventions of standard English grammar and usage when writing or speaking.
L.2.1a	Use collective nouns (e.g., *group*).
L.2.1b	Form and use frequently occurring irregular plural nouns (e.g., *feet, children, teeth, mice, fish*).
L.2.1c	Use reflexive pronouns (e.g., *myself, ourselves*).
L.2.1d	Form and use the past tense of frequently occurring irregular verbs (e.g., *sat, hid, told*).
L.2.1e	Use adjectives and adverbs, and choose between them depending on what is to be modified.
L.2.1f	Produce, expand, and rearrange complete simple and compound sentences (e.g., *The boy watched the movie; The little boy watched the movie; The action movie was watched by the little boy*).
L.2.2	Demonstrate command of the conventions of standard English capitalization, punctuation, and spelling when writing.
L.2.2a	Capitalize holidays, product names, and geographic names.
L.2.2b	Use commas in greetings and closings of letters.
L.2.2c	Use an apostrophe to form contractions and frequently occurring possessives.
L.2.2d	Generalize learned spelling patterns when writing words (e.g., cage ⟶ badge; boy ⟶ boil).

Language Standards

L.2.2e	Consult reference materials, including beginning dictionaries, as needed to check and correct spellings.

Knowledge of Language

L.2.3	Use knowledge of language and its conventions when writing, speaking, reading, or listening.
L.2.3a	Compare formal and informal uses of English.

Vocabulary Acquisition and Use

L.2.4	Determine or clarify the meaning of unknown and multiple-meaning words and phrases based on grade 2 reading and content, choosing flexibly from an array of strategies.
L.2.4a	Use sentence-level context as a clue to the meaning of a word or phrase.
L.2.4b	Determine the meaning of the new word formed when a known prefix is added to a known word (e.g., *happy/unhappy, tell/retell*).
L.2.4c	Use a known root word as a clue to the meaning of an unknown word with the same root (e.g., *addition, additional*).
L.2.4d	Use knowledge of the meaning of individual words to predict the meaning of compound words (e.g., *birdhouse, lighthouse, housefly; bookshelf, notebook, bookmark*).
L.2.4e	Use glossaries and beginning dictionaries, both print and digital, to determine or clarify the meaning of words and phrases.
L.2.5	Demonstrate understanding of word relationships and nuances in word meanings.
L.2.5a	Identify real-life connections between words and their use (e.g., describe foods that are *spicy* or *juicy*).
L.2.5b	Distinguish shades of meaning among closely related verbs (e.g., *toss, throw, hurl*) and closely related adjectives (e.g., *thin, slender, skinny, scrawny*).
L.2.6	Use words and phrases acquired through conversations, reading and being read to, and responding to texts, including using adjectives and adverbs to describe (e.g., *When other kids are happy that makes me happy*).

Index

A

C

Captions, 1: 40–41, 50, 58 **2:** 101, 118, **3:** 128, 149, 161, 164, 173, 174, 178, **4:** 187, 189, 191, 192–193, 200–201, 202–203, 238, **5:** 271, 272, 292–293, 295, **6:** 318, 320–321, 322–323, 331, 332–333, 343, 345

Cause and effect. *See* Comprehension

Character, setting, events. *See* Comprehension.

Charts. *See* Graphic Organizers; Text features.

Chronological order. *See* Comprehension skills: sequence.

Close reading, 1: 8–9, 10–11, 12–13, 18–19, 20–21, 22–23, 28–29, 30–31, 32–33, 40–41, 42–43, 44–45, 50–51, 52–53, 54–55, **2:** 68–69, 70–71, 72–73, 78–79, 80–81, 82–83, 88–89, 90–91, 92–93, 100–101, 102–103, 104–105, 110–111, 112–113, 114–115, **3:** 128–129, 130–131, 132–133, 138–139, 140–141, 142–143, 148–149, 150–151, 152–153, 160–161, 162–163, 164–165, 170–171, 172–173, 174–175, **4:** 188–189, 190–191, 192–193, 198–199, 200–201, 202–203, 208–209, 210–211, 212–213, 220–221, 222–223, 224–225, 230–231, 232–233, 234–235, **5:** 248–249, 250–251, 252–253, 258–259, 260–261, 262–263, 268–269, 270–271, 272–273, 280–281, 282–283, 284–285, 290–291, 292–293, 294–295, **6:** 308–309, 310–311, 312–313, 318–319, 320–321, 322–323, 328–329, 330–331, 332–333, 340–341, 342–343, 344–345, 350–351, 352–353, 354–355

Collaborative conversations, 386, 390-391. *See also* Respond to Reading.

Common Core State Standards, 400-413

Compare and contrast. *See* Comprehension.

Comprehension

author's purpose, **3:** 122, 128–129, 132–133, 134–135, 139, 148–149, 152–153, 154–155, **5:** 284, **6:** 302, 318–319, 321, 322–323, 324–325. *See also* **Access complex text: purpose.**

cause and effect, **4:** 182, 198–199, 202–203, 204–205, **5:** 243, 290–291, 292–293, 294–295, 296–297

character, setting, events, **1:** 2, 18–19, 22–23, 24, 28–29, 32–33, 34–35

compare and contrast, **4:** 182, 188–189, 190–191, 192–193, 194, 208–209, 210–211, 212–213, 214–215, **6:** 321

details. *See* Comprehension: key details; main idea and key details, main topic and key details.

key details, **1:** 2–3, 8–9, 12–13, 14–15, 40–41, 44–45, 46–47, 50–51, 54–55, 56–57, **2:** 110–111, 114–115, 116, **3:** 142, **4:** 193, 211, 222, **5:** 261, 263, 271, 285, **6:** 321, 343, 344–345. *See also* **Comprehension skills: main idea and key details; main topic and key details.**

main idea and key details, **3:** 123, 160–161, 164–165, 166–167, 170–171, 174–175, 176–177, **6:** 302, 328–329, 330–331, 332–333, 334

main topic and key details, **2:** 62–63, 88–89, 92–93, 94–95, 100–101, 104–105, 106–107, **3:** 161, **4:** 190

plot, **2:** 62, 68–69, 72–73, 74–75

point of view, **5:** 242, 248–249, 250–251, 252–253, 254–255, 258–259, 260–261, 262–263, 264–265, **6:** 303, 350, 352–353, 354

problem and solution, **1:** 36, 60, **2:** 62, 78–79, 82–83, 84–85, 96, 120, **3:** 156, 180, **4:** 216, 224, 240, **5:** 243, 276, 280–281, 282–283, 284–285, 286–287, **6:** 300, 303, 336, 340–341, 343, 344–345, 346, 358, 360

sequence, **3:** 138–139, 142-143, 144–145, 180, **5:** 268–269, 271, 272–273, 274–275, 298, 300

setting. *See* Comprehension: character, setting, events.

summarize, **1:** 13, 15, 23, 25, 33, 34–35, 45, 46–47, 55, 57, **2:** 73, 74–75, 83, 84–85, 93, 94–95, 105, 106–107, 115, 117, **3:** 133, 134–135, 143, 144–145, 153, 154–155, 165, 166–167, 175, 177, **4:** 193, 194–195, 203, 204–205, 213, 214–215, 225, 226–227, 235, 237, **5:** 253, 254–255, 263, 264–265, 273, 274–275, 285, 286–287, **6:** 303, 305, 313, 315, 323, 325, 333, 335, 345, 347, 355, 357

theme, **4:** 183, 220–221, 224–225, 226–227, 230–231, 233, 234–235, 236, **6:** 302, 308–309, 311, 312–313, 314–315, 321

Connection of Ideas. *See* Access complex text.

Context clues. *See* Comprehension: context clues; Vocabulary strategies: context clues.

D

Details. *See* Comprehension: key details; main idea and key details, main topic and key details.

Diagrams, 2: 101, 106, **3:** 128–129, 134, **4:** 188, 190–191, 200, 202–203, 222, 232, 238, **6:** 318, 320, 324. *See also* Graphic Organizers: diagrams; Text features.

Dialogue, 4: 211, **5:** 258, 261, 280, 283

Drama. *See* Genre.

E

English Language Learners

comprehension, **1:** 7, 17, 27, 39, 49, **2:** 67, 77, 87, 99, 109, **3:** 127, 137, 147, 159, 169, **4:** 187, 197, 207, 219, 229, **5:** 247, 257, 267, 279, 289, **6:** 307, 317, 327, 339, 349

vocabulary, **1:** 7, 17, 27, 39, 49, **2:** 67, 77, 87, 99, **3:** 127, 137, 147, 159, 169, **4:** 187, 197, 207, 219, **5:** 247, 257, 267, 279, 289, **6:** 307, 317, 327, 339

Essential Question, 1: 2–3, 6–7, 9, 10, 16–17, 19, 20, 26–27, 29, 30, 38–39, 41, 42, 48–49, 51, 52, **2:** 62–63, 66–67, 69, 70, 76–77, 79, 80, 86–87, 89, 90, 98–99, 101, 102, 108–109, 111, 110, 112, **3:** 122–123, 126–127, 129, 130, 136–137, 139, 140, 146–147, 149, 150, 158–159, 161, 162, 168–169, 171, 172, **4:** 182–183, 186–187, 189, 190, 196–197, 199, 200, 206–207, 209, 210, 218–219, 221, 222, 228–229, 231, 232, **5:** 242–243, 246–247, 249, 250–251, 256–257, 259, 260, 262, 266–267, 269, 270, 278–279, 281, 282, 288–289, 291, 292, **6:** 302–303, 306–307, 308, 309, 310, 316–317, 319, 320, 326–327, 329, 330, 338–339, 341, 342, 348–349, 351, 352

Expand vocabulary. *See* Vocabulary.

Expository text. *See* Genre.

F

Fable. *See* Genre.

Fantasy. *See* Genre.

Fiction. *See* Genre.

Figurative language. *See* Literary Elements, Poetry: literary elements and features of; Writer's Craft; Writing traits: word choice.

Fluency

accuracy, 382

expression, **1:** 4, **2:** 64, **3:** 124, **4:** 184, **5:** 244, **6:** 304, 379

intonation, **1:** 4, **3:** 124, **5:** 244, **6:** 304, 378

phrasing, **1:** 4, **2:** 64, **3:** 124, **4:** 184, **5:** 244, 380

pronunciation, **2:** 64, **3:** 124, **4:** 184, **5:** 244, **6:** 304

rate, 381

Folktale. *See* Genre.

Forms of Poetry. *See* Poetry.

Free verse poems. *See* Poetry.

G

Genre. *See also* Access complex text.

biography, **5:** 266–267, 268–269, 270–271, 272–273, 298

drama, **3:** 172–173, 218–219, 220–221, 222–223, 224–225

expository text, **1:** 48–49, 50–51, 52–53, 54–55, **2:** 90–91, 92–93, 98–99, 100–101, 102–103, 104–105, **3:** 126–127, 128–129, 130–131, 132–133, 158–159, 160–161, 162–163, 164–165, 168–169, 170–171, 172–173, 174–175, 178, **4:** 186–187, 188–189, 190–191, 192–193, 194–195, 196–197, 198–199, 200–201, 202–203, 238, **5:** 268, 288–289, 290–291, 292–293, 294–295, **6:** 316–317, 318–319, 320–321, 322–323, 326–327, 328–329, 330–331, 332–333, 338–339, 340–341, 342–343, 344–345, 346–347

fable, **2:** 76–77, 78–79, 80–81, 82–83

fantasy, **1:** 6–7, 8–9, 10–11, 12–13, **6:** 353

fiction, **1:** 26–27, 28–29, 30–31, 32–33, **2:** 112–113, 114–115, **3:** 136–137, 138–139, 140–141, 142–143, **4:** 232–233, 234–235, **5:** 256–257, 258–259, 260–261, 262–263, 278–279, 280–281, 282–283, 284–285

folktale, **4:** 183, 218–219, 220–221, 222–223, 224–225

informational text, **1:** 48–49, 50–51, 52–53, 54–55, **2:** 90–91, 92–93, 98–99, 100–101, 102–103, 104–105, **3:** 126–127, 128–129, 130–131, 132–133, 158–159, 160–161, 162–163, 164–165, 168–169, 170–171, 172–173, 174–175, 178, **4:** 186–187, 188–189, 190–191, 192–193, 194–195, 196–197, 198–199, 200–201, 202–203, 238, **5:** 268, 288–289, 290–291, 292–293, 294–295, **6:** 316–317, 318–319, 320–321, 322–323, 326–327, 328–329, 330–331, 332–333, 338–339, 340–341, 342–343, 344–345, 346–347

magazine article, **1:** 78-81, **3:** 218-221, **5:** 342-345

myths, **6:** 302, 306–307, 308–309, 310–311, 312–313

narrative nonfiction, **1:** 38–39, 40–41, **2:** 86–87, 88–89, 118, **3:** 146–147, 148–149, 150–151, 152–153

play. *See* Genre: drama.

poetry, **2:** 63, 108–109, 110–111, 183, **3:** 228–229, 230–231, **6:** 303, 348–349, 350–351

realistic fiction, **1:** 16–17, 18–19, 22–23, 24–25, 66–67, 68–69, 70–71, 72–73, 74, **4:** 206–207, 208–209, 210–211, 212–213, **5:** 246–247, 248–249, 250–251, 252–253, 352

Graphic aids. *See* Graphic Organizers; Illustrations/photographs.

Graphic Organizers

charts

Author's Purpose, **3:** 132–133, 135, 152–153, 155, **6:** 321–322, 323

Beginning, Middle, End, *See* Plot

Cause and Effect, **4:** 200–201, 202–203, 205, **5:** 292–293, 294–295, 297

Character, Setting, Events, **1:** 22–23, 25, 32–33, 35

Compare and Contrast, **4:** 16, 98, 136, 190–191, 192–193, 206, 210–211, 212–213, 215

Key Details, **1:** 12–13, 15, 44–45, 47, 54–55, 57, **2:** 114–115

Main Idea and Key Details, **2:** 92–93, 104–105, 164–165, 167, 174–175, 177, **6:** 330–331, 332–333, 335

Main Topic and Key Details, **2:** 92–93, 95, 104–105, 107

Point of View, **5:** 250–251, 252–253, 260–261, 262–263, 265, **6:** 352–353, 354–355

Plot, **2:** 72–73

Problem and Solution, **2:** 82–83, 85, **5:** 282–283, 284–285, 287, **6:** 342–343, 344–345

Sequence, **3:** 142–143, 145

Theme, **4:** 222–223, 224–225, 227, 232–233, 234–235, **6:** 310–311, 312–313, 315

webs, **1:** 6, 26, 38, 48, **2:** 66, 76, 86, 108, **3:** 126, 146, 158, 168, **4:** 186, 196, 218, 228, **5:** 246, 256, 278, **6:** 306, 316, 326, 348

Graphs, **3:** 170, **6:** 340, 341, 358–359

H

Headings. *See* Text Features.

Higher-level thinking. *See* Comprehension skills.

I

Illustrations/photographs, using, **1:** 4, 6, 8, 16, 26, 29, 38, 40–41, 43, 44, 48–49, 50, 54–55, 58, **2:** 64, 66–67, 76, 86, 88–89, 92, 98, 103, 104–105, 108, 110, 114, 118, **3:** 122, 124, 126, 128–129, 136, 144–145, 146, 152, 154, 158, 161, 164, 168, 174, 178, **4:** 184, 186,–187, 189, 193, 196, 198–199, 200–201, 202–203, 206, 210, 218, 223, 224, 228, 233, 234, 238, **5:** 244, 246, 251, 256–257, 266, 268, 270–271, 272, 278–279, 288, 292–293, 295, 298, **6:** 304, 306–307, 311, 312–313, 316–317, 318, 320, 323, 326, 328, 330–331, 332–333, 338–339, 340, 343, 344, 348, 352, 353

Independent reading. *See* Reading independently.

Informational text. *See* Genre.

K

Key details. *See* Comprehension.
Key details chart. *See* Graphic Organizers: charts.

L

Lesson plans, suggested weekly, 1: 2–3, **2:** 62–63, **3:** 122–123, **4:** 182–183, **5:** 242–243, **6:** 302–303. *See also* Unit Planners.
Level Up, 1: 15, 25, 35, 47, 57, 58, 61; **2:** 75, 85, 95, 107, 117, 118, 121; **3:** 135, 145, 155, 167, 177, 178, 181; **4:** 195, 205, 215, 227, 237, 238, 241; **5:** 255, 265, 275, 287, 297, 298, 301; **6:** 315, 325, 335, 347, 357, 358, 361
Leveled Reader Lessons. *See* Apprentice Leveled Reader.
Listening. *See* Oral Language, Talk About It.
Literary Elements,
   alliteration, **4:** 229–230, 235
   beats, **6:** 349–350, 355
   message, **6:** 303, 349, 351
   metaphor, **6:** 349, 351, 355
   repetition, **4:** 229, 231; **6:** 349–350
   repeated lines, **6:** 303, 349, 350
   rhyme, **2:** 110–111, 115, **6:** 350
   rhythm, **2:** 109–111, 115
   simile, **4:** 229–230, 235
   word choice, **2:** 109, 111, 115–116
   See also Poetry: literary elements and features of.

M

Magazine article. *See* Genre.
Main idea. *See* Comprehension.
Main Idea and Key Details chart. *See* Graphic Organizers: charts.
Main Topic and Key Details chart. *See* Graphic Organizers: charts.
Maps. *See* Text features.
Message. *See* Literary Elements.

Metaphor. *See* Literary Elements; Poetry: literary elements and features of.
Myths. *See* Genre.

N

Narrative nonfiction. *See* Genre.
Narrator, 1: 32–33, **2:** 109, 110–111, **3:** 138, **4:** 207, 209, 219, 220, 231, **6:** 351, 355
Nonfiction. *See* Genre: Informational text; Writing: informative.
Note-taking, 1: 7, 17, 27, 39, 49, **2:** 67, 77, 87, 99, 109, **3:** 127, 137, 147, 159, 169, **4:** 187, 197, 207, 219, 229, **5:** 247, 257, 267, 279, 289, **6:** 307, 317, 327, 339, 349

O

Oral language, Talk About It, 1: 4, 6, 16, 26, 38, 48, **2:** 64, 66, 76, 86, 98, 108, **3:** 124, 126, 136, 146, 158, 168, **4:** 184, 186, 196, 206, 218, 228, **5:** 244, 246, 266, 278, 288, **6:** 304, 306, 316, 326, 338, 348
Organization. *See* Access complex text.

P

Play. *See* Genre: drama.
Plot. *See* Comprehension.
Poetry
   forms of
      free verse, **4:** 183, 229, 230
      rhyming, **2:** 110, **6:** 350
   literary elements and features of
      alliteration **4:** 183, 229, 230, 235
      beats, **2:** 109, 110, **6:** 303, 349, 350, 355
      message, **6:** 303, 349, 351
      metaphor, **6:** 303, 349, 351, 355
      repeated lines, **6:** 303, 349, 350
      repetition, **4:** 183, 229, 231, 350
      rhyme/rhyme schemes, **2:** 63, 109, 110, 115, **4:** 229, 230

   rhythm, **2:** 63, 109, 110, 115, **3:** 123, 169, **4:** 229, 231, **6:** 349, 350
   simile, **4:** 183, 208, 229, 230, 235, **6:** 349
   stanzas, **6:** 350–351
   word choice, **2:** 63, 109, 111, 116, **4:** 236, **6:** 356
   weekly words, **2:** 63, 109, **4:** 183, 229, **6:** 303, 349
   See also Genre: poetry.
Point of view. *See* Comprehension.
Point of View chart. *See* Graphic Organizers: charts.
Prior Knowledge. *See* Access complex text.
Problem and solution. *See* Comprehension.
Problem and Solution chart. *See* Graphic Organizers: charts.
Pronunciation. *See* Fluency.
Purpose. *See* Access complex text.

R

Reading independently, 1: 13, 23, 33, 45, 55, **2:** 73, 83, 93, 105, 115, **3:** 133, 143, 153, 165, 175, **4:** 193, 203, 213, 225, 235, **5:** 253, 263, 273, 285, 295, **6:** 313,323, 333, 345, 355
Realistic fiction. *See* Genre.
Repeated lines. *See* Literary Elements.
Repetition. *See* Literary Elements.
Respond to Reading, 1: 9, 13, 19, 23, 29, 33, 41, 45, 51, 55, **2:** 69, 73, 79, 83, 89, 93, 101, 105, 111, 115, **3:** 129, 133, 139, 143, 149, 153, 161, 165, 171, 175, **4:** 189, 193, 199, 203, 209, 213, 221, 225, 231, 235, **5:** 249, 253, 259, 263, 269, 273, 281, 285, 291, 295, **6:** 309, 313, 319, 323, 329, 333, 341, 345, 351, 355
Reteach, 364-375
Rhyme. *See* Literary Elements.
Rhyming poems. *See* Poetry: forms of poetry: rhyming.
Rhythm. *See* Literary Elements: rhythm.
Rubrics, writing, 1: 15, 25, 35, 47, 57, 59, **2:** 75, 85, 95, 107, 117, 119, **3:** 135, 145, 155, 167, 177, 179, **4:** 195, 205, 215, 227, 237, 239, **5:** 255, 265, 275, 287, 297, 299, **6:** 315, 325, 335, 347, 357, 359

S

Scoring rubrics. *See* Assessment.

Sentence Structure. *See* Access complex text.

Sequence of events. *See* Comprehension skills.

Sequence chart. *See* Graphic Organizers: charts.

Setting. *See* Comprehension skills: character, setting, events.

Shared Read Lessons, 1: 8–9, 18–19, 28–29, 40–41, 50–51, **2:** 68–69, 78–79, 88–89, 100–101, 110–111, **3:** 128–129, 138–139, 148–149, 160–161, 170–171, **4:** 188–189, 198–199, 208–209, 220–221, 230–231, **5:** 248–249, 258–259, 268–269, 280–281, 290–291, **6:** 308–309, 318–319, 328–329, 340–341, 350–351

Similes. *See* Literary Elements.

Speaking skills and strategies. *See* Oral Language, Talk About It.

Scope and Sequence, 392-399

Stanzas. *See* Poetry: literary devices and features of: stanzas.

Summarize. *See* Comprehension.

T

Talk About It. *See* Oral Language.

Text complexity. 383-385. *See also* Access complex text.

Text Evidence, 1: 8–9, 12–13, 15, 18–19, 22–23, 25, 28–29, 32–33, 35, 37, 40–41, 44–45, 47, 50–51, 54–55, 57, 59, **2:** 68–69, 72–73, 75, 78–79, 82–83, 85, 88–89, 62–93, 95, 97, 100–101, 104–105, 107, 110–111, 114–115, 117, 119, **3:** 128–129, 132–133, 135, 138–139, 142–143, 145, 148–149, 152–153, 155, 157, 160–161, 164–165, 167, 170–171, 174–175, 177, 178–179, **4:** 188–189, 191, 193, 195, 198–199, 203, 205, 208–209, 213, 215, 217, 220–221, 222–223, 225, 227, 230–231, 235, 237, 239, **5:** 248–249, 253, 254–255, 258–259, 263, 264–265, 268–269, 273, 274–275, 277, 280–281, 285, 286–287, 290–291, 295, 297, 299, **6:** 308–309, 313, 315, 318–319, 323, 325, 328–329, 333, 335, 337, 340–341, 345, 346–347, 350–351, 355, 357, 359

Text features

captions, 1: 40–41, 50, 58, **2:** 101, 118, **3:** 128, 149, 161, 164, 173–174, 178, **4:** 187, 189, 191, 192–193, 200–201, 202–203, 238, **5:** 271, 272, 292, 293, 295, **6:** 318, 320–321, 322–323, 331, 332–333, 343, 345

charts, 1: 50–51, 56, **2:** 89, **3:** 161, **5:** 268, 290, 293, 294, **6:** 342–343, 346, 358

diagrams, 2: 101, 106, **3:** 128–129, 134, **4:** 188, 190–191, 200, 202–203, 222, 232, 238, **6:** 318, 320, 324

graphs, 3: 170, **6:** 340–341, 358–359

headings, 1: 51, **2:** 88, 100, **3:** 128–129, 160–161, 173, **4:** 188–189, 191, 192–193, 194, 198, 222, **5:** 290, **6:** 318, 321, 330, 340–341, 343, 346

illustrations, 1: 8, 29, 50, **2:** 67, 76, 89, 114, **3:** 122, 144–145, **4:** 202, 210, 223, 224, 233, 234, **5:** 251, 257, 279, **6:** 307, 311, 312–313, 330, 352, 353

labels, 2: 92–93, 101, 103, 104–105, **3:** 128, 164, **4:** 202, 210–211, 212, **6:** 318

maps, 2: 118, **3:** 178, **4:** 188, 194, 201, 202, 238–239, **5:** 294, **6:** 328

multiple, 1: 50–51, **2:** 88–89, 92–93, 100–101, 104–105, **3:** 128–129, 160–161, 164–165, 174, **4:** 188–189, 190–191, 201, 202–203, **5:** 268, 270–271, 272–273, 292–293, 294, **6:** 318, 320–321, 322–323, 330–331, 332–333, 340–341, 342–343, 344–345

photographs, 1: 40–41, 43, 44, 49, 50, 54–55, 58, **2:** 88, 92, 103, 104–105, 110, 118, **3:** 128–129, 152, 154, 161, 164, 174, 178, **4:** 187, 189, 193, 198–199, 200–201, 203, 238, **5:** 268, 270–271, 272, 292–293, 295, 298, **6:** 317, 318, 320, 323, 330–331, 332–333, 339, 340, 343, 344

sidebar, 3: 161, 178

time lines, 5: 268, 273, 298

Theme. *See* Comprehension.

Theme chart. *See* Graphic Organizers: charts: Theme.

Time lines. *See* Text features.

U

Unit Planners, 1: 2–3, **2:** 62–63, **3:** 122–123, **4:** 182–183, **5:** 242–243, **6:** 302–303

V

Visual elements. *See* Text features.

Vocabulary

assess and reteach, 1: 9, 11, 14, 19, 21, 24, 29, 31, 34, 41, 43, 46, 51, 53, 56, **2:** 69, 71, 74, 79, 81, 84, 89, 91, 94, 101, 103, 106, 111, 113, 116, **3:** 129, 131, 134, 139, 141, 144, 149, 151, 154, 161, 163, 166, 171, 173, 176, **4:** 189, 191, 194, 199, 201, 204, 209, 211, 214, 221, 223, 206, 231, 233, 236, **5:** 249, 251, 254, 259, 261, 264, 269, 271, 274, 281, 283, 286, 291, 293, 296, **6:** 309, 311, 314, 319, 321, 324, 329, 331, 334, 341, 343, 346, 351, 353, 356

context clues, 1: 14, 24, 29, 34, 36, 43, 46, 55, 56, 58, 60, **2:** 71, 74, 83, 84, 91, 94, 96, 106, 116, 120, **3:** 133, 134, 143, 144, 153, 154, 156, 166, 176, 180, **4:** 191, 194, 203, 204, 214, 216, 226, 235, 236, 238, 240, **5:** 254, 261, 262, 264, 274, 276, 286, 296, 298, 300, **6:** 311, 313, 314, 322, 324, 334, 336, 346, 356, 360

define/example/ask routine, 1: 10, 20, 30, 42, 52, **2:** 70, 80, 90, 102, 112, **3:** 130, 140, 150, 162, 172, **4:** 190, 192, 200, 202, 210, 212, 222, 224, 232, 234, **5:** 250, 252, 260, 262, 270, 272, 282, 284, 292, 294, **6:** 310, 312, 320, 322, 330, 332, 342, 344, 352, 354

expand vocabulary, 1: 7, 8–9, 10, 17, 18–19, 20–21, 27, 28–29, 30, 40–41, 42, 49, 50–51, 52, 58, **2:** 67, 68–69, 70, 77, 78–79, 80, 87, 88–89, 90, 99, 100–101, 102, 112, 118, **3:** 127, 128, 130–131, 137, 138–139, 140–141, 147, 148–149, 150–151, 159, 160–161, 162–163, 169, 170–171, 172, 178, **4:** 187, 188–189, 190, 192, 197, 198, 200, 202, 207, 208–209, 210, 212, 219, 220, 222, 224, 232, 234, 238, **5:** 247, 250, 252, 257, 258–259, 260, 262, 267, 268–269, 270, 272, 279, 280–281, 282, 284, 289–290, 292, 294, 298, **6:** 307, 308–309, 310, 312, 317, 318–319, 320, 322, 327, 328–329, 330, 332, 339, 340–341, 342, 344, 352, 354, 358

high-frequency words, 1: 7, 10–11, 12, 17, 20–21, 22, 7, 30–31, 32, 39, 42–43, 44, 49, 52–53, 54, **2:** 67, 70–71, 72, 77, 80–81, 82, 87, 90–91, 92, 99, 102–103, 104, 109, 112–113, **3:** 127, 130–131, 132, 137, 140–141, 142, 147, 150–151, 152, 159, 162–163, 164, 169, 172–173, **4:** 187, 197, 207, 219, 229, **5:** 247, 257, 267, 279, 289, **6:** 307, 317, 327, 339, 349

W

Writing